Masterplots

2,010 Plot Stories & Essay Reviews
from the World's Fine Literature

Revised Edition

Including the Four Series
and Further Critical Evaluations

Edited by
FRANK N. MAGILL

Story Editor
DAYTON KOHLER

Volume Five
HAD - JOU
2443 - 3058

SALEM PRESS
Englewood Cliffs, New Jersey 07632

LIBRARY OF CONGRESS CATALOG CARD NUMBER 76-5606

REVISED EDITION
First Printing

PRINTED IN THE UNITED STATES OF AMERICA

LIST OF TITLES IN VOLUME FIVE

li

LIST OF TITLES IN VOLUME FIVE

lii

LIST OF TITLES IN VOLUME FIVE

LIST OF TITLES IN VOLUME FIVE

LIST OF TITLES IN VOLUME FIVE

HADRIAN'S MEMOIRS

Type of work: Novel
Author: Marguerite Yourcenar (1903-   )
Time: 76-138
Locale: Hispania Baetica, now modern Spain, Syria, Gaul, Germany, Britain, Greece, Mauretania, Palestine, Arabia, Egypt, and Rome
First published: 1951

Principal characters:
HADRIAN, Emperor of the Roman Empire and narrator
ULPIUS TRAJANUS, his uncle, later Emperor Trajan
ANTINOÜS, a handsome Bithynian youth, Hadrian's favorite
SIMON BAR KOKBA, leader of the Jewish revolt
MARCUS AURELIUS, Hadrian's adopted grandson and successor

Hadrian's Memoirs is a work of sound scholarship and unusual imaginative reconstruction. Not the least of the appeals which this novel holds for the modern reader is the light it throws on two of the great problems of our own time—the nature of man and the uses of power. Here these matters are presented as they shaped themselves in the experience of one man. The fact that this man was also a ruler of absolute power is only incidental to the total picture presented. Hadrian was also like the modern man in the contradictions and complexities of his character, and the novel is as much a study of ethical motivations as it is the story of a life. Some readers, in fact, may be baffled by the slight attention paid to purely biographical detail. For this reason it should be kept in mind that the novel is intended to be both a memoir and an apologia. Supposed to have been written in his last days when Hadrian, resigned to the prospect of death, felt himself exhausted by the responsibilities of his office, these memoirs take the form of a long letter addressed to his adopted grandson, the seventeen-year-old Marcus Aurelius. Under the circumstances it is only natural that the work should be philosophical in tone and much concerned with ideas of history, death, and immortality.

The public events of Hadrian's life can be briefly summarized. He was born in A.D. 76 in Hispania Baetica, in what is now modern Spain. His family was provincial, and though it had important connections in the greater Roman world there was no prospect that the boy would ever wear the imperial purple. About the year 86 he was placed under the guardianship of his uncle, Ulpius Trajanus, the general who later became the Emperor Trajan. It was Hadrian who, according to this account, carried to Trajan the news that he had been proclaimed by the legions. As the nephew of the emperor, he served in many of the campaigns on the outskirts of the Empire. Whether Trajan ever did adopt him formally as his heir remains somewhat clouded. Trajan's wife supported his cause, however, and a will was produced after Trajan's death. Hadrian, who had been in command of the Roman armies in Syria, succeeded his uncle in 117.

His first acts were to renounce Trajan's costly program of conquest and to consolidate the imperial powers at home. Abandoning completely the attempt to subjugate the Parthians, he made the Euphrates the eastern border of the Empire. His policy of stern but just Roman peace extended also to the wild Germanic tribes. In 119 he began his progress through Gaul, Germany, Spain, Britain, Greece, Mauretania, Syria, Palestine, Arabia, and Egypt. In Britain he ordered construction of the wall that bears his name, intended to keep the savage Picts north of the Solway. Returning to Rome in 131, and saddened by the death of his beloved Antinoüs, he issued a year later the *Edictum perpetuum* on which Justinian subsequently based his *Corpus juris.* In the same year the Jews, led by Simon Bar Kokba, revolted in protest against the establishment of a permanent Roman colony at Jerusalem and the dedication of a temple to Jupiter Capitolinus on the site of the Hebrew Temple. This revolt Hadrian put down with the utmost severity, and with the defeat of Simon Bar Kokba in 135 the eighteen hundred years of the Jewish dispersion began. On the whole, however, Hadrian was a wise and humane ruler who reduced taxes, alleviated the hardships of the slave class, and completed tremendous building programs in Athens and Rome. A patron of the arts, he was also a poet of some distinction whose best-known work is the appealing lyric beginning, "Animula, vagula, blandlua. . . ." He died at his villa at Baiae in 138.

Most of these incidents figure in the background of Mme. Yourcenar's novel, but usually it is not the event which is most important for her purpose but its significance to Hadrian's way of thinking and feeling. It is in the delicate handling of this material and the shift from outward circumstance to inward meaning that the novelist's achievement becomes apparent. It must also be kept in mind that she is dealing with a non-Christian milieu. To show Hadrian and his age from the modern viewpoint would strike a false note at the start; consequently, for purposes of morality as well as of art, she allows Hadrian to explain himself. The result is a study which is probably as close as any modern writer can ever get in presenting the pagan mind in a period before the concepts of a gap between body and soul, between the physical universe and eternal reality, became historical fact.

This aspect of the novel is more clearly revealed in the account of Hadrian's relations with Antinoüs, the handsome Bithynian youth who became his favorite. When the emperor's beloved was drowned in the Nile—the suggestion is that he committed suicide—during a trip to Egypt in 130, Hadrian was for a time inconsolable. Later he established a cult to deify the young man, built cities in his honor, and commissioned the statues which in many art museums today are still regarded as the symbols of immortal youthful beauty. There is no question of modern morality in the relationship existing between emperor and favorite, only a pagan delight in the beauty of the human form. Hadrian's attitude, though we would nowadays call it abnormal, reflects more than the perversions many of his contemporaries practiced because they were fashionable. In his view all pleasures enjoyed with art seemed chaste.

Another instance of Mme. Yourcenar's skillful handling is to be found in the story of Simon Bar Kokba's revolt. There was no idea of religious domination in Hadrian's decision to dedicate a shrine to Jupiter Capitolinus on the site of the Hebrew Temple; there was room in the Roman pantheon for the gods of all peoples, and the Romans were as willing to accept Jehovah within their religious framework as they had received, often through returning veterans, the gods of Egypt and other outposts of the Empire. Hadrian's act was really intended to symbolize the solidarity of the state, the principle of empire and the stabilizing influence of a culture and a civilization. But the Jews, although able to accept the idea of Roman citizenship and law, could not accept Jupiter as the symbol of unity because he stood for a different faith. It may be that Hadrian's moment of recoil when he was presented with Simon Bar Kokba's severed head marks the actual beginning of modern history, for the Jewish revolt signified the concept of passionate rejection which we find in all protests against systematized authority, whether in religion, in politics, or in science.

These are only two of the incidents which provide dying Hadrian with material for philosophical speculation. The approach of death, which first leads him to recall events and personalities of the past and to savor in recollection the sensations of experience, becomes in the end an attempt at self-understanding, an effort to penetrate his contradictions of sensualism and rationalism, of discipline and license, of philosophical detachment and emotional involvement, in order to see clearly the nature of man as reflected in himself. His speculations were directed toward a single and worthy end: to confront death with open eyes.

Mme. Yourcenar plays fair with her readers. In an appended Author's Note she lists her sources, tells where and why she has taken minor liberties with chronology or characters, and explains certain interpretations justified by the vagueness of actual history. Her own honesty and clarity of motive argue much for her portrait of a man and an age presented in this contemplative, intuitive, and beautifully styled historical novel. This is a work of fiction in which all details are relevant and everything is in proportion. A spirit of Roman gravity and serenity is apparent on every page.

HAJJI BABA OF ISPAHAN

Type of work: Novel
Author: James Morier (1780-1849)
Type of plot: Picaresque romance
Time of plot: Early nineteenth century
Locale: Persia
First published: 1824

Principal characters:
HAJJI BABA, a rogue
OSMAN AGHA, a Turkish merchant
ZEENAB, a slave girl

Critique:

The Adventures of Hajji Baba of Ispahan is a combination of travel book and rogue story, and it does for Persia very much what Le Sage's *Gil Blas* did for Spain. Persia, even in this day of broad travel, has never been widely viewed by Americans. Moreover, the Persia of the time of Napoleon Bonaparte was a Persia that has now disappeared. Customs and manners are as much a part of Morier's entertaining narrative as the picaresque humor of Hajji Baba's adventures and the satire of the rogue's shrewd comments on human nature.

The Story:

Hajji Baba was the son of a successful barber of Ispahan. By the time he was sixteen he had learned the barber's trade, as well as a store of bazaar tales and quotations from the Persian poets. With these he entertained the customers who came to his father's shop, among them a wealthy Turkish merchant named Osman Agha, who was on his way to Meshed to buy goatskins of Bokhara. So taken was this merchant with Hajji Baba that he begged the young man to accompany him on the journey. With his father's blessing and a case of razors, Hajji Baba set out with his new patron.

Before the caravan had been many days on its way it was attacked by a band of Turcoman robbers. Osman Agha had prudently sewed fifty gold ducats in the skullcap under his turban, but when the caravan was captured he was stripped of his finery and the skullcap was tossed in a corner of the robber chief's tent. The robbers spared Hajji Baba's life when they learned he was a skilled barber, and he became a favorite of the wife of the chief. One day he persuaded the foolish woman to let him borrow Osman Agha's cap. He ripped the gold pieces from the lining and hid them, against the time when he might escape from his captors. Osman Agha had been sold to some camel herders.

Hajji Baba traveled with the robbers on their raids throughout the region. One of these raids was on Ispahan itself, from which the robbers carried away a rich booty. But at the division of the spoils, Hajji Baba got only promises and praise.

One day the robbers encountered the armed escort of a Persian prince. When the others fled, Hajji Baba gladly allowed himself to be taken prisoner by the prince's men. They mistook him for a Turcoman, however, and cruelly mistreated him, stripping him of his clothes and his hidden gold. When he complained to the prince, the nobleman sent for the guilty ones, took the money from them, and then kept the gold himself.

Hajji Baba went with the prince and his train to Meshed, where he became a water vendor, carrying a leather bag filled with dirty water which he sold to pilgrims with assurances that it was holy water blessed by the prophet. With money so earned, he bought some tobacco which he blended with dung and then peddled through the streets of the holy city. His best customer, Dervish Sefer, introduced him to other dervishes. They applauded Hajji Baba's shrewdness and enterprise and invited him to become one of their number. But one day a complaint was lodged against him on account of the bad tobacco he sold, and the authorities beat his bare feet until he lost consciousness. Having in the meantime saved a small amount of money, he decided to leave Meshed, which seemed to him an ill-omened city.

He set out on his way to Teheran. On the road a courier overtook him and asked him to read some letters the messenger was carrying. One was a letter from a famous court poet, commending the bearer to officials high at court. Hajji Baba waited until the courier was fast asleep, took the messenger's horse, and rode away to deliver the courier's letters. Through these stolen credentials he was able to obtain a position of confidence with the court physician.

Hajji Baba remained with the physician, even though his post brought him no pay. He soon found favor with Zeenab, the physician's slave, and sought her company whenever he could do so without danger of being caught. Then the shah himself visited the physician's establishment and received Zeenab as a gift. Hajji Baba was disconsolate, but he was soon made happy by a new appointment, this time to the post of sub-lieutenant to the chief executioner of the shah. Again he received no pay, for he was supposed to get his money as other members of the shah's entourage did, by extortion. It was soon discovered that Zeenab was in a condition which could only be regarded as an insult to the shah's personal honor, and Hajji Baba was summoned to execute the girl. Soon afterward suspicion fell on him for his own part in the affair, and he fled to the holy city of Koom.

In Koom he pretended to be a priest. The shah made a pilgrimage to the city, and during his visit the chief priest presented Hajji Baba's petition to the ruler. Hajji Baba explained that he had acted in all innocence because he had no idea of the high honor to be conferred upon Zeenab. The shah reluctantly pardoned Hajji Baba and allowed him to return to Ispahan.

He arrived to discover that his father had died and that his fortune had disappeared. Hajji Baba sold his father's shop and used the money to set himself up as a learned scribe. Before long he found service with Mollah Nadan, a celebrated priest, who planned to organize an illegal but profitable marriage market. Hajji Baba was supposed to find husbands for women the mollah would provide. When Hajji Baba visited the three women for whom he was supposed to find husbands, he discovered them all to be ugly old hags, one the wife of his former master, the physician, who had recently died. Later, Hajji Baba discovered his first master, Osman Agha, who had finally escaped from the Turcomans and regained some of his fortune. Hajji Baba tricked Agha into marrying one of the three women.

Mollah Nadan undertook to gain favor by punishing some Armenians during a drought, but he incurred the shah's wrath and he and Hajji Baba were driven from the city. Mollah Nadan's property was confiscated. Hajji Baba stole back into the city to see if any of the mollah's property could be saved, but the house had been stripped. He went to visit the baths, and there he discovered Mollah Bashi, who had been taken with a cramp and had drowned. Hajji Baba was afraid that he would be accused of murder, as Mollah Bashi had helped to bring about Mollah Nadan's ruin. But the slave attendant failed to recognize Hajji Baba in the darkness and Hajji Baba escaped, dressed in the mollah's robes. On the horse of the chief executioner he set out to collect money owed to Mollah Bashi. In the clothes of the mollah and riding a fine horse, he cut a dashing figure until he met Mollah Nadan and was persuaded to change robes with him. Mollah Nadan was arrested and charged with the death of Mollah Bashi. Hajji Baba, who had kept the money he had collected, decided to become a merchant.

He encountered the caravan of the

widow of Mollah Bashi. She was taking her husband's body to Kerbelai for holy burial. When the leader of the caravan revealed that Hajji Baba was suspected of the murder, he began to fear for his life. But about that time a band of marauders attacked the caravan, and in the confusion Hajji Baba escaped. In Bagdad he reëncountered his old master, Osman Agha, and with him proceeded to invest the money he had available. He bought pipe sticks and planned to sell them at a profit in Constantinople.

There a wealthy widow sought him out and he decided to marry her, first, however, intimating that he was as wealthy as she. He married her and began to live on her income. But his old bazaar friends, jealous of his good luck, betrayed him to his wife's relatives. Thrown out as an imposter, he was obliged to seek the help of the Persian ambassador. The ambassador advised him not to seek revenge upon his former wife's relatives, as they would surely murder him in his bed. Instead, he found use for Hajji Baba in an intrigue developing among representatives of England and France. Hajji Baba was employed as a spy to find out what the foreign emissaries sought in the shah's court.

Here at last Hajji Baba found favor. He discovered that his life among cutthroats and rogues had admirably fitted him for dealing diplomatically with the representatives of foreign countries, and he was finally made the shah's representative in his own city of Ispahan. He returned there with considerable wealth and vast dignity, to lord it over those who had once thought his station in life far below their own.

Further Critical Evaluation of the Work:

Morier's romance is both an Oriental tale and a picaresque narrative. For its treatment of exotic customs and manners, the novel resembles such eighteenth century romances as Samuel Johnson's *The History of Rasselas, Prince of Abyssinia* (1759) and William Beckford's less philosophical *Vathek, an Arabian Tale* (1786). As a picaresque narrative, *Hajji Baba of Ispahan* resembles the episodic novels of Defoe and Smollett. Like most novels concerning a rogue-hero, Morier's book satirizes the foibles not only of the characters in the story, but also those of humankind. Hajji Baba is an amiable opportunist and schemer, experienced in the worldly arts of guile and deception, but not the sole rascal in the book. On the contrary, Hajji learns his impudent tricks from others, and although he is an apt pupil, he is simply more successful—not more wicked—than most people. As one of his teachers, the Dervish Sefer explains: "We look upon mankind as fair game—we live upon their weakness and credulity"; from such counsel, Hajji discovers how to expropriate, for the sake of his own ease, riches from the weak and stupid. In a world of scoundrels and fools, he is seen as amoral rather than immoral; the reader sympathizes with his desire, in the contest of life, to be the world's knave instead of its victim.

During the course of his roguish adventures, Hajji ranges through almost all the social levels and professions of Persian (and, indeed, Middle-Eastern) life. At various times he is a barber, a merchant, a robber, a slave, a "seller of smoke," a *saka* (water carrier), a *lûti* (privileged buffoon), a dervish, a physician's apprentice, a sublieutenant for the Chief Executioner, a scribe to a man of law, an ambassador to foreign powers, and finally, the Shah's deputy. He travels throughout the Middle East, from Cairo to Aleppo and Damascus; from Mecca and Medina to Lahore and Cashmere. Mostly, however, he travels through the cities and villages of early nineteenth century Persia, learning to understand the passions and weaknesses of his fellow men. In none of the ranks of society does he encounter true comradeship, civility, or altruism. At one point, after he escapes from the Turcoman robbers and throws himself at the mercy of his countryman, a Persian prince, he is robbed and threatened with further punishment by his protector. A simple muleteer chides Hajji for lamenting his losses. After all, what could he expect from a prince? "When once he or any man in power gets possession of a thing," the muleteer reasons, "do you think that he will ever restore it?"

In spite of Morier's broad-ranging satire, which sometimes approaches cynicism, his prevailing tone is comic rather than censorious. Hajji is, above all, an affable rogue, high-spirited and inventive, most resilient when he appears to be defeated. Through his resourceful imagination, he overcomes most of the obstacles in his way. Yet he is never wholly successful and triumphant, as are some other picaresque heroes in fiction. Morier is too much the realist to allow his adventurer the fullest enjoyment of his romantic dreams. Hajji's true love, Zeenab, is kept from him, first by the crafty physician Mizra Ahmak, and later by the Shah himself. Worse, as one of the royal executioners, poor Hajji is forced to witness her terrible death.

He suffers other misfortunes. When he is under the tutelage of the Turcoman bandits, he is forced to rob his own father; and years later, he arrives at his ancestral home just in time to watch the old man expire. After his father dies, Hajji and his mother quarrel and part on unfriendly terms. His marriage to the rich widow Shekerleb is dissolved by her kinsmen, when they discover that Hajji is not so rich as he had pretended to be. And he is not only humiliated but beaten on several occasions, once by order of the *Mohtesib* (inspector), who has our hero thrashed on the soles of his feet until he loses consciousness from the pain. Thus Morier avoids the romantic stereotype of the swaggering outlaw—the corsair, the highwayman, the outcast—popularized by Scott, Byron, Shelley, and others. Instead, his rogue-hero is a fellow mortal, perhaps less scrupulous than most of us, but unquestionably human in his weaknesses. In *Hajji Baba of Ispahan in England* (1828) Morier continues the tale of Hajji's adventures, this time as an envoy from Persia to the barbarians of the West.

HAKLUYT'S VOYAGES

Type of work: Travel narratives
Author: Richard Hakluyt (c. 1553-1616)
Type of plot: Adventure and exploration
Time of plot: c. 517 to 1600
Locale: The known world
First published: 1589

Critique:

This work is an anthology of the explorations and travels of British adventurers down to the author's own time. The accounts are bold and vigorous, usually giving only the main events of the journeys, many of them written by the men who made the voyages. Published by Hakluyt in refutation of a French accusation that the English were insular and spiritless, the book is of value in several lights. It gives faithful accounts of many sixteenth-century exploratory journeys; it is an index to the temper of Elizabethan England; and it reflects the enthusiasm for travel literature which was so prevalent at the time of the original publication.

The Stories:

The first group of voyages give thirty-eight accounts of travel and exploration made by Britons up to the end of the sixteenth century. The first stories go back to the medieval ages, for the narrative which begins the work is that of a probably mythical voyage by King Arthur of Britain to Iceland and the most northern parts of Europe in 517.

The first ten narratives deal with voyages made before 1066, the year of the Norman Conquest. They include such journeys as the conquest of the isles of Man and Anglesey by Edwin, King of Northumberland, in 624, the trips of Octher into Norway and Denmark in 890 and 891, the voyage of Wolstan into Danish waters in the tenth century, the voyage of King Edgar, with four thousand ships, about the island of Britain, and the journey of Edmund Ironside from England to Hungary in 1017.

The other voyages described are those taken after the Norman Conquest. The first of these is an account of a marvelous journey made by a company of English noblemen to escort the daughter of King Harold to Russia, to marry the Duke of Russia in 1067. The next account is of the surprising journey of an unknown Englishman who traveled as far into Asia as Tartaria in the first half of the thirteenth century.

One notable voyage describes the adventures of Nicolaus de Linna, a Franciscan friar, to the northern parts of Scandinavia. The twenty-second voyage was that of Anthony Jenkinson who traveled to Russia from England in order to return Osep Napea, the first ambassador from Muscovia to Queen Mary of England, to his own country in 1557.

Surprisingly, almost half of the journeys described in this first collection are those made to Russia by way of the Arctic Ocean, around northern Scandinavia. It is not ordinarily realized that there was any traffic at all between England and Russia at that time, because of the difficulty of both water and land transportation between the two countries.

The final narrative of the first group tells of the greatest event of Elizabethan England, the meeting of the British fleet with the great Armada which Philip II of Spain had sent to subdue England and win for Spain the supremacy of the seas.

The second group of voyages describe trips taken to the region of the Straits of Gibraltar and the countries surrounding the Mediterranean Sea. Eleven of these accounts describe trips made before the Norman Conquest in 1066 and fifty-two describe trips made after that date. The earliest story is that of Helena, the wife of a Roman emperor and a daughter of Coelus, one of the early kings of Britain. Helena, famous as the mother of Constantine the Great, who made Christianity the official religion of Rome, traveled to Jerusalem in 337 because of her interest in the early Christian church. She built several churches there and brought back to Europe a collection of holy relics. One of the relics was a nail reputed to be from the True Cross. It was incorporated some time later into the so-called Iron Crown of Lombardy.

Another voyage which took place before the Norman Conquest was that of a man named Erigena, who was sent by Alfred, King of the West Saxons, to Greece. Alfred was one of the most cultured of British kings in pre-medieval times and very much interested in the classic civilizations. His emissary, Erigena, went as far as Athens in 885, a long voyage for those ancient times.

Several of the post-Conquest voyages were trips made by Englishmen to help in the recovery of Jerusalem from the Saracens during the Crusades. Among the best known are those of Richard the First, often called the Lion-Hearted, and of Prince Edward, son of Henry III, who went to Syria in the last half of the thirteenth century.

Another story is a narrative of the voyage of the English ship, *Susan,* which took William Hareborne to Turkey in 1582. Hareborne was the first ambassador sent by a British monarch to the ruler of Turkey, who was at that time Murad Khan.

Another interesting voyage was that of Ralph Fitch, a London merchant. Between the years 1583 and 1591 he traveled to Syria, to Ormuz, to Goa in the East Indies, to Cambia, to the River Ganges, to Bengala, to Chonderi, to Siam, and thence back to his homeland. It was rare for people to travel, even in the spice trade, as far as did merchant

Fitch during the sixteenth century.

A third group of voyages are accounts connected with the exploration and discovery of America. The first account is of a voyage supposedly made to the West Indies in 1170 by Madoc, the son of Owen Guined, a prince of North Wales. It is also recorded that in February of 1488 Columbus offered his services to Henry VII of England and petitioned that monarch to sponsor a voyage to the westward seas for the purpose of discovering a new route to the East Indies. Bartholomew, brother of Columbus, repeated the request a year later, but was refused a second time by the English king.

Several voyages described are those made to America for the purpose of discovering a Northwest Passage to the Orient. The early voyage of Cabot is among them, as well as the voyages of Martin Frobisher and John Davis. Frobisher made three voyages in search of the Northwest Passage, in the three successive years between 1576 and 1578. John Davis also made three fruitless efforts to find the passage in the years from 1585 to 1587. All of these were an important part of the colonial effort in Hakluyt's own time.

Several exploratory trips to Newfoundland and the Gulf of the St. Lawrence River are also related, the earliest the voyage of Sir Humfrey Gilbert to Newfoundland. The ship *Grace* of Bristol, England, also made a trip up the Gulf of St. Lawrence, as far as Assumption Island. There are also accounts of trips made by explorers of other European nations in the New World, such as the journeys made in Canada as far as Hudson's Bay by Jacques Cartier in 1534 and 1535.

There are full accounts of all the voyages made to Virginia in the sixteenth century and the two unsuccessful attempts by Sir Walter Raleigh to found a colony there in 1585 and in 1587.

Another group of stories tell of both English and Spanish explorations of the Gulf of California. The voyage of Francis Drake is given, particularly that part of his around-the-world trip during which he sailed up the western coast of America to a point forty-three degrees north of the equator and landed to take possession of what he called Nova Albion, in the name of his monarch, Queen Elizabeth, thus giving the British a claim to that part of the New World.

Also described is a voyage taken under orders of the viceroy of New Spain by Francis Gualle. Gualle crossed the Pacific Ocean to the Philippine Islands, where he visited Manila. From there he went to Macao in the East Indies and to Japan, and returned from the Orient to Acapulco, Mexico, in the 1580's.

Another group of stories contain short accounts of trips by Englishmen to various parts of Spanish America. Among these were trips to Mexico City as early as 1555, barely a quarter of a century after it had been conquered by Cortez, as well as to the Antilles Islands in the West Indies, to Guiana, to the coast of Portuguese Brazil, to the delta of the Rio Plata, and to the Straits of Magellan.

Every schoolboy knows the stories of the first two voyages made to the Straits of Magellan and thence around the world, first by Magellan — the trip completed by surviving remnants of the expedition — and then by Sir Francis Drake. The third man to sail through the Straits and then to proceed around the world is one of the forgotten men of history. Hakluyt gave the credit for this trip to Thomas Cavendish, an Englishman who circled the globe in the years 1586 to 1588.

Further Critical Evaluation of the Work:

Richard Hakluyt, regarded as the first professor of modern geography at Oxford, made a point of getting to know the "chiefest Captains at sea, the greatest merchants, and the best Mariners of our nation." The result was *Hakluyt's Voyages,* an invaluable source book to students of the Age of Discovery and the place of England in it. As a boy, he watched the ships come to port from distant journeys, and early lessons in geography fired him with an eagerness to know more; studies at Oxford and a five-year period in Paris further set his resolution to collect the scattered records of English maritime discovery. Perhaps he began the work as a piece of propaganda, but it soon became more than that. The second edition grew to three volumes issued over as many years. He also translated narratives by Spanish explorers, but *Hakluyt's Voyages* remains his memorial, a true "prose epic" of the English people and nation. The massive work is more than a documentary history of exploration, for in it, alongside tales of adventure, are mingled historical and economic papers intended to establish British sovereignty at sea. The purpose of the huge undertaking was to encourage overseas settlement and foreign trade. (It was asserted that the income of the East India Company was greatly increased through *Hakluyt's Voyages.*)

To the modern reader, *Hakluyt's Voyages* is alive with Elizabethan spirit of adventure, and reflects the suddenly expanding world of the Tudors. The book contains, indeed, the raw material from which an English *Odyssey* might have been made. Although the work is basically an anthology, the stamp of Hakluyt's personality is over the entire book; his idealism, his admiration for brave men and noble deeds, and his ambitions for his nation are everywhere evident.

As much as anything else, *Hakluyt's Voyages* should be read as economic history; some of the pieces included might be considered real estate promoters' descriptions of lands to be developed. Merchants found the book invaluable, and the queen and her ministers saw it as a worthy psychological push toward the readiness of the nation to embrace an empire. The accounts of the voyages are told with a simplicity and directness far more effective than self-conscious artistry or literary pretensions; the tales are the matter-of-fact reporting of men of action. Among the most interesting accounts are those of Sir Walter Raleigh's unsuccessful attempts to found a colony in Virginia and the seeking of the fabled Northwest Passage to the Orient, but perhaps the most fascinating is the legendary voyage of Sir Francis Drake up the Western coast of America.

THE HAMLET

Type of work: Novel
Author: William Faulkner (1897-1962)
Type of plot: Psychological realism
Time of plot: Late nineteenth century
Locale: Mississippi
First published: 1940

Principal characters:
WILL VARNER, chief property owner in Frenchman's Bend
JODY, his son
EULA, his daughter
V. K. RATLIFF, a sewing machine salesman
AB SNOPES, a newcomer to Frenchman's Bend
FLEM SNOPES, his son
ISAAC SNOPES, an idiot relative
MINK SNOPES, another relative
LABOVE, schoolteacher at Frenchman's Bend
HENRY ARMSTID, a farmer

Critique:

Although more like a collection of long short stories than an integrated novel, this book displays Faulkner's genius in presenting the ironic humor in the folk legends of Mississippi. Yet Faulkner makes these tall tales, in spite of their definite locale, seem characteristic of almost any section of rural America. Some of the incidents are strung out over too many pages, but the author's skillful style carries them along successfully. He withholds the climax, the final irony of each episode, until the tale is fully exploited. In Flem Snopes, Faulkner has created one of his major characters—a man who is stubborn, arrogant, and ruthless in his drive for property and power.

The Story:

In his later years Will Varner, owner of the Old Frenchman place and almost everything else in Frenchman's Bend, began to turn many of his affairs over to his thirty-year-old son Jody. One day, while Jody sat in the Varner store, he met Ab Snopes, a newcomer to town, and Ab arranged to rent one of the farms owned by the Varners. Jody then found out from Ratliff, a salesman, that Ab had been suspected of burning barns on other farms where he had been a tenant. Jody and his father concluded that Ab's unsavory reputation would do them no harm. Jody became afraid, however, that Ab might burn some of the Varner property; as a sort of bribe, he hired Ab's son, Flem, to clerk in the store.

From Ratliff came the explanation of why Ab was soured on the world. Ab's principal grievance grew out of a horse-trading deal he once made with Pat Stamper, an almost legendary trader. Ab drove a mule and an old horse to Jefferson and, before showing them to Stamper, he skillfully doctored up the old nag. Stamper swapped Ab a team of mules that looked fine, but when Ab tried to drive them out of Jefferson the mules collapsed. To get back his own mule Ab spent the money his wife had given him to buy a milk separator. Stamper also forced him to purchase a dark, fat horse that looked healthy but rather peculiar. On the way home Ab ran into a thunderstorm and the horse changed from dark to light and from fat to lean. It was Ab's old horse, which Stamper had painted and then fattened up with a bicycle pump.

Will Varner's daughter, Eula, was a plump, sensuous girl who matured early. The new schoolteacher, Labove, fell in love with her the first day she came to the schoolhouse. An ambitious young man, Labove rode back and forth between Frenchman's Bend and the University, where he studied law and played on the football team. One day he attempted to seduce Eula after school had been dismissed; he failed and later was horrified to discover that Eula did not even mention the attempt to Jody. Labove left Frenchman's Bend forever.

As she grew older Eula had many suitors, the principal one being Hoake McCarron, who literally fought off the competition. When the Varners found out that Eula was pregnant, McCarron and two other suitors left for Texas. Flem Snopes then stepped in, married Eula, and went off on a long honeymoon.

The Snopes clan which had gathered in the wake of Ab and Flem began to have troubles within the family. The idiot boy, Isaac, was neglected and mistreated; when he fell in love with a cow, his behavior became a town scandal. Mink Snopes, another relative, was charged with murdering Jack Houston, who had impounded Mink's wandering cattle. Flem stayed away from town throughout this trouble. When Mink was brought to trial, Flem, who might have helped him, ignored the whole case. Mink was sent to jail for life.

Flem came back from his honeymoon accompanied by Buck Hipps, a Texan, and a string of wild, spotted horses. The Texan arranged to auction off these horses to farmers who had gathered from miles around. To start things off, the Texan gave one horse to Eck Snopes, provided that Eck would make the first bid on the next one. At this point Henry Armstid and his wife drove up. Henry, in spite of his wife's protests, bought a horse for five dollars. By dark all but three of the horses had been sold, and Henry was anxious to claim his purchase. He and his wife were almost killed in trying to rope their pony. Hipps wanted to return the Armstids' money. He gave the five dollars to Henry's wife, but Henry took the bill from her and gave it to Flem Snopes. Hipps told

Mrs. Armstid that Flem would return it to her the next day.

When the other purchasers tried to rope their horses, the spotted devils ran through an open gate and escaped into the countryside. Henry Armstid broke his leg and almost died. Eck Snopes chased the horse that had been given him and ran it into a boarding-house. The horse escaped from the house and ran down the road. At a bridge it piled into a wagon driven by Vernon Tull and occupied by Tull's wife and family. The mules pulling the wagon became excited and Tull was jerked out of the wagon onto his face.

The Tulls sued Eck Snopes for the damages done to Vernon and to their wagon; the Armstids sued Flem for damages to Henry and for the recovery of their five dollars. The justice of the peace was forced to rule in favor of the defendants. Flem could not be established as the owner of the horses, and Eck was not the legal owner of a horse that had been given to him.

One day Henry Armstid told Ratliff that Flem was digging every night in the garden of the Old Frenchman place, which Flem had acquired from Will Varner. Ever since the Civil War there had been rumors that the builder of the house had buried money and jewels in the garden. Henry and Ratliff took a man named Bookwright into their confidence and, with the aid of another man who could use a divining rod, they slipped into the garden after Flem had quit digging. After locating the position of buried metal, they began digging, and each unearthed a bag of silver coins. They decided to pool their resources and buy the land in a hurry. Ratliff agreed to pay Flem an exorbitant price. At night they kept on shoveling, but they unearthed no more treasure. Ratliff finally realized that no bag could remain intact in the ground for thirty years. When he and Bookwright examined the silver coins, they found the money had been minted after the Civil War.

But Armstid, now totally out of his mind, refused to believe there was no treasure. He kept on digging, day and night. People from all over the county came to watch his frantic shoveling. Passing by on his way to Jefferson, Flem Snopes paused only a moment to watch Henry; then with a flip of the reins he drove his horses on.

Further Critical Evaluation of the Work:

In *The Hamlet,* Faulkner explores the triumph of those amoral qualities which collectively have come to be called "Snopesism." Though never at its center, Flem Snopes, who epitomizes the worst qualities characteristic of the society arising to fill the power vacuum created by the decline of the great ante-bellum Southern families, dominates the book as an almost diabolically evil presence. V. K. Ratliff, the unifying narrative voice and moral center against whose intelligence and humanity Flem's greed, rapacity, and inhumanity are measured, represents the most stable moral force in the novel.

Through his sympathetic portrayal of such diverse characters as Ike Snopes, idiot lover of a cow, and the murderer Mink Snopes, Faulkner suggests that it is Flem alone who represents the evil associated with the Snopses. Flem, who breaks no law, is simply without human feeling of any sort, and hence guilty of the greatest sin. This fact is dramatized repeatedly as we see various characters become victims of their own or other's passions, while Flem, passionless himself, uses these human weaknesses to his own advantage. Flem's marriage of convenience to Eula Varner is perhaps the most overt example of this theme. To other men, Eula, an almost irresistible sexual force, symbolizes life and fecundity. Flem alone is untouched by her sexuality, and he marries her only for the advantage she brings him.

Ratliff's deep sense of humanity and his moral strength make him Flem's most worthy adversary, and he does indeed defeat Snopes in their first encounter. Within the scheme of the book, however, Flem must triumph over all. Thus, he is finally able to tempt Ratliff into speculating on the Old Frenchman's Place so he too can be cheated. At that point, evil is ascendant and Flem Snopes has at last conquered the world of Frenchman's Bend.

HAMLET, PRINCE OF DENMARK

Type of work: Drama
Author: William Shakespeare (1564-1616)
Type of plot: Romantic tragedy
Time of plot: c. 1200
Locale: Elsinore, Denmark
First presented: 1602

Principal characters:
HAMLET, Prince of Denmark
THE GHOST, Hamlet's father, former King of Denmark
CLAUDIUS, the present king
GERTRUDE, Hamlet's mother
POLONIUS, a courtier
OPHELIA, his daughter
LAERTES, his son
HORATIO, Hamlet's friend

Critique:

Whether *Hamlet* is considered as literature, as philosophy, or simply as a play, its great merit is generally admitted; but to explain in a few words the reasons for its excellence would be an impossible task. The poetry of the play is superb; its philosophy, although not altogether original with Shakespeare, is expressed with matchless artistry. The universality of its appeal rests in large measure on the character of Hamlet himself. Called upon to avenge his father's murder, he was compelled to face problems of duty, morality, and ethics, which have been the concern of men throughout the ages. In Hamlet himself are mirrored the hopes and fears, the feelings of frustration and despair, of all mankind.

The Story:

Three times the ghost of Denmark's dead king had stalked the battlements of Elsinore Castle. On the fourth night Horatio, Hamlet's friend, brought the young prince to see the specter of his father, two months dead. Since his father's untimely death, Hamlet had been grief-stricken and in an exceedingly melancholy frame of mind. The mysterious circumstances surrounding the death of his father had perplexed him; then too, his mother had married Claudius, the dead king's brother, much too hurriedly to suit Hamlet's sense of decency.

That night Hamlet saw his father's ghost and listened in horror to what it had to say. He learned that his father had not died from the sting of a serpent, as had been supposed, but that he had been murdered by his own brother, Claudius, the present king. The ghost added that Claudius was guilty not only of murder but also of incest and adultery. But the spirit cautioned Hamlet to spare Queen Gertrude, his mother, so that heaven could punish her.

The ghost's disclosures should have left no doubt in Hamlet's mind that Claudius must be killed. But the introspective prince was not quite sure that the ghost was his father's spirit, for he feared it might have been a devil sent to torment him. Debating with himself the problem of whether or not to carry out the spirit's commands, Hamlet swore his friends, including Horatio, to secrecy concerning the appearance of the ghost, and in addition told them not to consider him mad if from then on he were to act queerly.

Meanwhile Claudius was facing not only the possibility of war with Norway, but also, and much worse, his own conscience, which had been much troubled since his hasty marriage to Gertrude. In addition, he did not like the melancholia of the prince, who, he knew, resented the king's hasty marriage. Claudius feared that Hamlet would take his throne away from him. The prince's strange behavior and wild talk made the king think that perhaps Hamlet was mad, but he was not sure. To learn the cause of Hamlet's actions—madness or ambition—Claudius commissioned two of Hamlet's friends, Rosencrantz and Guildenstern, to spy on the prince. But Hamlet saw through their clumsy efforts and confused them with his answers to their questions.

Polonius, the garrulous old chamberlain, believed that Hamlet's behavior resulted from lovesickness for his daughter, Ophelia. Hamlet, meanwhile, had become increasingly melancholy. Rosencrantz and Guildenstern, as well as Polonius, were constantly spying on him. Even Ophelia, he thought, had turned against him. The thought of deliberate murder was revolting to him, and he was constantly plagued by uncertainty as to whether the ghost were good or bad. When a troupe of actors visited Elsinore, Hamlet saw in them a chance to discover whether Claudius were guilty. He planned to have the players enact before the king and the court a scene like that which, according to the ghost, took place the day the old king died. By watching Claudius during the performance, Hamlet hoped to discover for himself signs of Claudius' guilt.

His plan worked. Claudius became so unnerved during the performance that he walked out before the end of the scene. Convinced by the king's actions that the ghost was right, Hamlet had no reason to delay in carrying out the wishes of his dead father. Even so, Hamlet failed to take advantage of his first real chance after the play to kill Claudius. He came upon the king in an attitude of prayer, and could have stabbed him in the back. Hamlet did not strike because he believed that the king would die in grace at his devotions.

The queen summoned Hamlet to her chamber to reprimand him for his insolence to Claudius. Hamlet, remembering what the ghost had told him, spoke to her so violently that she screamed for help. A noise behind a curtain followed her cries, and Hamlet, suspecting that Claudius was eavesdropping, plunged his sword through the curtain, killing old Polonius. Fearing an attack on his own life, the king hastily ordered Hamlet to England in company with Rosencrantz and Guildenstern, who carried a warrant for Hamlet's death. But the prince discovered the orders and altered them so that the bearers should be killed on their arrival in England. Hamlet then returned to Denmark.

Much had happened in that unhappy land during Hamlet's absence. Because Ophelia had been rejected by her former lover, she went mad and later drowned. Laertes, Polonius' hot-tempered son, returned from France and collected a band of malcontents to avenge the death of his father. He thought that Claudius had killed Polonius, but the king told him that Hamlet was the murderer and even persuaded Laertes to take part in a plot to murder the prince.

Claudius arranged for a duel between Hamlet and Laertes. To allay suspicion of foul play, the king placed bets on Hamlet, who was an expert swordsman. At the same time, he had poison placed on the tip of Laertes' weapon and put a cup of poison within Hamlet's reach in the event that the prince became thirsty during the duel. Unfortunately, Gertrude, who knew nothing of the king's treachery, drank from the poisoned cup and died. During the contest, Hamlet was mortally wounded with the poisoned rapier, but the two contestants exchanged foils in a scuffle, and Laertes himself received a fatal wound. Before he died, Laertes was filled with remorse and told Hamlet that Claudius was responsible for the poisoned sword. Hesitating no longer, Hamlet seized his opportunity to act, and fatally stabbed the king. Then the prince himself died. But the ghost was avenged.

Further Critical Evaluation of the Work:

Hamlet has remained the most perplexing, as well as the most popular, of

Shakespeare's major tragedies. Performed frequently, the play has tantalized critics with what has become known as the Hamlet mystery. The mystery resides in Hamlet's complex behavior, most notably his indecision and his reluctance to act. Freudian critics have located his motivation in the psychodynamic triad of the father-mother-son relationship. According to this view, Hamlet is disturbed and eventually deranged by his Oedipal jealousy of the uncle who has done what, we are to believe, all sons long to do themselves. Other critics have taken the more conventional tack of identifying Hamlet's tragic flaw as a lack of courage or moral resolution. In this view, Hamlet's indecision is a sign of moral ambivalence which he overcomes too late.

The trouble with both of these views is that they presuppose a precise discovery of Hamlet's motivation. However, Renaissance drama is not generally a drama of motivation either by psychological set or moral predetermination. Rather, the tendency is to present characters, with well delineated moral and ethical dispositions, who are faced with dilemmas. It is the outcome of these conflicts, the consequences, which normally hold center stage. What we watch in *Hamlet* is an agonizing confrontation between the will of a good and intelligent man and the uncongenial role which circumstance calls upon him to play.

The disagreeable role is a familiar one in Renaissance drama—the revenger. The early description of Hamlet, bereft by the death of his father and the hasty marriage of his mother, makes him a prime candidate to assume such a role. One need not conclude that his despondency is Oedipal in order to sympathize with the extremity of his grief. His father, whom he deeply loved and admired, is recently deceased and he himself seems to have been finessed out of his birthright. Shakespeare, in his unfortunate ignorance of Freud, emphasized Hamlet's shock at Gertrude's disrespect to the memory of his father rather than love of mother as the prime source of his distress. The very situation breeds suspicion, which is reinforced by the ghastly visitation by the elder Hamlet's ghost and the ghost's disquieting revelation. The ingredients are all there for bloody revenge.

However, if Hamlet were simply to proceed to act out the role that has been thrust upon him, the play would be just another sanguinary potboiler without the moral and theological complexity which provides its special fascination. Hamlet has, after all, been a student of theology at Wittenberg. Hamlet's knowledge complicates the situation. First of all, he is aware of the fundamental immorality of the liaison between Gertrude and Claudius. Hamlet's accusation of incest is not an adolescent excess but an accurate theological description of a marriage between a widow and her dead husband's brother.

Hamlet's theological accomplishments do more than exacerbate his feelings. For the ordinary revenger, the commission from the ghost of the murdered father would be more than enough to start the bloodletting. But Hamlet is aware of the unreliability of otherworldly apparitions, and consequently he is reluctant to heed its injunction to perform an action which is objectively evil. In addition, the fear that his father was murdered in a state of sin and is condemned to hell not only increases Hamlet's sense of injustice but also, paradoxically, casts further doubt on the reliability of the ghost's exhortation. Is the ghost, Hamlet wonders, merely an infernal spirit goading him to sin?

Thus, Hamlet's indecision is not an indication of weakness, but the result of his complex understanding of the moral dilemma with which he is faced. He is unwilling to act unjustly, yet he is afraid that he is failing to exact a deserved retribution. He debates the murky issue and becomes unsure himself whether his behavior is caused by moral scruple or cowardice. He is in sharp contrast with the cynicism of Claudius and the verbose moral platitudes of Polonius. The play is in sharp contrast with the moral simplicity of the ordinary revenge tragedy. Hamlet's intelligence has transformed a stock situation into a unique internal conflict.

He believes that he must have greater certitude of Claudius' guilt if he is to take action. The device of the play within a play provides greater assurance that Claudius is suffering from a guilty conscience, but it simultaneously sharpens Hamlet's anguish. Having seen a recreation of his father's death and Claudius' response, Hamlet is able to summon the determination to act. However, he once again hesitates when he sees Claudius in prayer because he believes that the king is repenting and, if murdered at that moment, will go directly to heaven. Here Hamlet's inaction is not the result of cowardice nor even of a perception of moral ambiguity. Rather, after all of his agonizing, Hamlet once decided on revenge is so thoroughly committed that his passion cannot be satiated except by destroying his uncle body and soul. It is ironic that Claudius has been unable to repent and that Hamlet is thwarted this time by the combination of his theological insight with the extreme ferocity of his vengeful intention.

That Hamlet loses his mental stability is clear in his behavior towards Ophelia and in his subsequent meanderings. Circumstance has enforced a role whose enormity has overwhelmed the fine emotional and intellectual balance of a sensitive well-educated young man. Gradually he regains control of himself and is armed with a cold determination to do what he decides is the just thing. Yet, even then, it is only in the carnage of the concluding scenes that Hamlet finally carries out his intention. Having concluded that "the readiness is all," he strikes his uncle only after he has discovered Claudius' final scheme to kill him and Laertes, but by then he is mortally wounded.

The arrival of Fortinbras, who has been lurking in the background throughout the play, superficially seems to indicate that a new, more direct and courageous order will prevail in the place of the evil of Claudius and the weakness of Hamlet. But Fortinbras' superiority is only apparent. He brings stasis and stability back to a disordered kingdom, but he does not have the self-consciousness and moral sensitivity which destroy and redeem Hamlet.

Gerald Else has interpreted Aristotle's notion of *katharsis* to be not a purging of the emotions but a purging of a role of the moral horror, the pity and fear, ordinarily associated with it. If that is so, then Hamlet, by the conflict of his ethical will with his role, has purged the revenger of his horrific bloodthirstiness and turned the stock figure into a self-conscious hero in moral conflict.

Edward E. Foster

HAMPSHIRE DAYS

Type of work: Nature study
Author: William Henry Hudson (1841-1922)
First published: 1903

Despite the poverty and ill health from which W. H. Hudson suffered much of his life, the dominant mood of *Hampshire Days* is the quiet joy found in the creatures, plants, and seasons of nature. This mood may have been furthered by the Civil List pension granted the author in 1901, the year before he finished the work. He tells us that he returned to New Forest in December, 1902, to complete this book, which chronicles his activities and discoveries in Hampshire from 1900 to 1902. His purpose was to write of this "delectable spot in the best bird months of April, May, and June," but fortunately his vision included more than these months and a far wider variety of subjects, including Hampshire people, towns, and buildings, than this statement indicates.

Because Hudson was an important naturalist, one would expect much of the book to be devoted to the flora and fauna of Hampshire and its centuries-old forests, like Harewood, Wolmer and, especially, the somewhat misleadingly named New Forest. Hudson reveals his love of this particular forest on many pages and on one occasion speaks of it as containing the most beautiful forest landscape in all England. Its name derives from its being placed under forest laws by William the Conqueror in 1079. Of its present-day 130-square-mile area, thirty square miles are privately owned and forty-five of the remaining hundred are Crown woodlands, largely of oak and pine. Hudson lived in a former manor house in the forest while gathering material for his book. He was obviously concerned about the future of the forest, endangered by the abuse of the New Forest. This abuse was the unregulated raiding of the forest of its heath, game animals, rare species of birds, and plants. Hudson believed that only by government ownership of these

lands and by careful regulation could New Forest be restored to its former glory.

Hudson's interest in plant life is further revealed by his discussion of yew trees, particularly the Selborne yew, whose age he believed to exceed greatly the thousand years usually credited to a large churchyard yew, and the Farrington yew, both of which he numbers among his Hampshire favorites. He postulates that the practice of burying people beneath yews (with the consequent removal of a barrowful of roots for each grave) inflicts injury on the yew, and he concludes that the great size of the Selborne yew may result from the fact that only one grave was dug near it. As a naturalist, Hudson properly preferred wild nature to cultivated or garden nature, and he had little use for collectors of plants or animals if they killed in order to collect. He seems to have had little use for cut flowers; a picked rose, he says, lacks luster and means no more to the soul than a flower made from wax or paper. But roses growing wild convince one that there is no more beautiful sight in all the world.

The bulk of the book concerns such small creatures as birds, small mammals, and snakes. Hudson did not intend to present any very startling discoveries, but to reveal what he had learned about these animals of Hampshire: their mating habits, peculiarities of behavior, and some of the tales told of them. He discusses the mating game of several animals, as, for instance, the unusual behavior of the female *viridissima* (a variety of grasshopper) who, hypnotically drawn to the singing of the males, selects the one she wants and waits "to be taken in marriage." In the case of the white spider, however, the male is both irresistibly drawn to the somewhat larger, white female and at the same time made fearful by her poisonous fangs. Consequently, first he advances eagerly, only to be made wary, and then retreats.

Hudson had the naturalist's desire to test the truth of accepted nature tales, as his meticulous account of the cuckoo in the robin's nest shows. In order to verify the newly hatched cuckoo's supposed strength, he watched the developments in a nest containing, originally, three robin's eggs and one cuckoo egg. In time two of the robin eggs were ejected, one definitely by the cuckoo, as Hudson saw, but the cuckoo went even further. As Hudson watched, the preternaturally strong fledgling pushed a baby robin from the nest. In all his discussions of animal behavior he reveals the qualities shown here: the care in observation, the desire to test accepted ideas, and the obvious relish he took in reporting his findings.

Despite Hudson's obvious concern for plants and animals, his book also deals with man and his works. In fact, he devotes some chapters to these topics and only rarely is man totally absent from his discussions. He is careful to acknowledge his debt both to such earlier naturalists as Gilbert White and Moses Harris and to men of his own day who provided him with facts and stories. Of the chapters devoted to man, one deals with the Selborne atmosphere and discusses the appearance of the people, the scenery, and other aspects of the town. Another, devoted to the Hampshire people divides the inhabitants of this region into four types: the blond, which greatly outnumbers all others; the Saxon, also lighthaired with blue eyes, but heavier; those slight and narrow-headed, with brown skins, crow-black hair, and dark eyes; and those of average height, with oval faces and dark eyes and hair.

Hudson's concern for man and his ways is also seen in his interest in old folks and their stories of the past. In one instance, an old woman was able to explain how the lone grave beneath the great yew at Selborne came there; in another, an old woman told of the dashing career of her father, a horn-blower for the "Selborne mob" that attacked a poorhouse in a time of poverty. Such tales of the past were much to Hudson's liking; he gives them prominent places in this book.

Hampshire Days is the work of a manysided man: both Hudson the naturalist and Hudson the student of human nature are clearly visible. The personality that informs the work is that of a keenminded inquirer, capable of delighting himself in study but also capable of feeling compassion for both men and animals. Even though he seems to dislike the intrusions of man into nature's haunts, he has kind words for some of the young people he meets during his outings. And even though he delivers a lecture in Chapter One about the undesirability of such interference with nature as saving one of the robins ejected from its nest by the cuckoo, and the necessity of the death of great numbers of young birds each year, Hudson himself is guilty of such "interference." When a young blackbird shows itself incapable of getting food, Hudson intervenes. His explanation is that although he may dislike playing at providence among nature's creatures, he cannot free himself of pity.

A HANDFUL OF DUST

Type of work: Novel
Author: Evelyn Waugh (1903-1966)
Type of plot: Social satire
Time of plot: Twentieth century
Locale: England
First published: 1934

Principal characters:
TONY LAST, owner of Hetton Abbey
BRENDA LAST, his wife
JOHN, their son
MRS. BEAVER, an interior decorator
JOHN BEAVER, her son
JOCK GRANT-MENZIES, Tony's friend
DR. MESSINGER, an explorer
TODD, a half-caste trader who loved Dickens

Critique:

This novel, which portrays the decline of the English landed aristocracy, is full of foolish people who find their lives to be no more than "a handful of dust." The contrasts between the Gothic magnificence of Hetton Abbey, the lives of Brenda and Tony, and the aspirations of the successors to Tony's property, are effective instruments for bringing out the meaning of the story. The author writes finished dialogue; the narrative moves smoothly from beginning to end.

The Story:

John Beaver lived in London with his mother, an interior decorator. Beaver was a worthless young man of twenty-five who moved in the social circles of his mother's wealthy customers. He was not well liked, but he was often invited to parties and weekends to fill a space made vacant at the last moment.

One weekend Beaver was invited to Hetton Abbey by its young owner, Tony Last. Tony lived in the old Gothic abbey with his wife, Brenda, and his young son, John. It was Tony's dream that some day he would restore his mansion to its former feudal glory. Brenda was bored with her husband's attachment to the past, however; she found relief in her weekly trips to London.

Beaver's stay at Hetton Abbey was rather dull, but Brenda liked him and did her best to entertain him. On her next trip to London she saw him again and asked him to take her to a party. At first Beaver seemed reluctant; then he agreed to escort her.

Beaver and Brenda left the party early, creating some idle gossip. In a way, the gossipers were correct, for Brenda had definitely decided to have an affair with Beaver. She returned home to the unsuspecting Tony and told him that she was bored with life in the country. She said that she wanted to take some courses in economics at the university in London. Tony, feeling sorry for her, allowed her to rent a one-room flat in a building owned by Mrs. Beaver. Brenda moved to London and returned to Hetton Abbey only on weekends.

One day, when Tony went to London on impulse, he found that his wife already had engagements. He was forced to spend the evening getting drunk with his bachelor friend, Jock Grant-Menzies.

Tony's escapade bothered his conscience so much that when Brenda returned for the weekend she was able to persuade him to let Mrs. Beaver redecorate in modern style one of the rooms of the old house.

Brenda's conscience bothered her also. She tried to interest Tony in a girl she brought down for a weekend, but it was no use. He only wanted to have his wife back home. However, he still trusted her and suspected nothing of her intrigue in London.

Things might have gone on that way indefinitely if young John Last had not been killed by a horse while he was fox hunting. Tony sent Jock up to London to break the news to Brenda. At first Brenda thought that Jock was speaking of John Beaver's death, for he was out of town. When she learned the truth, she was relieved, realizing for the first time how much she cared for Beaver.

With young John dead, she felt that nothing held her to Tony any longer. She wrote, telling him everything, and asked for a divorce. Stunned, Tony could not believe that Brenda had been false to him. At last he consented to spend a weekend at Brighton with another woman to give her grounds for divorce.

Brenda's family was against the divorce and attempted to prevent it. Then, when they saw that the divorce would go through, they tried to force Tony to give Brenda more alimony than he had planned. He refused, for he could raise more money only by selling Hetton Abbey. The proposal angered him so much that he changed his mind about the divorce. He would not set Brenda free.

Tony, wishing to get away from familiar faces, accompanied an explorer, Dr. Messinger, on an expedition to find a lost city in the South American jungles. During the voyage across the Atlantic Tony had a short affair with a young French girl from Trinidad. But when she learned that he was married she would have nothing more to do with him.

Once the explorers had left civilization behind them, Tony found himself thinking of what was going on in London. He did not enjoy jungle life at all; insect bites, vermin, and vampire bats made sleep almost impossible.

When Negro boatmen had taken Tony and Dr. Messinger far up the Demarara River, they left the explorers in the hands of Indian guides. Then the expedition struck out into unmapped territory.

Meanwhile, back in London, Brenda no longer found Beaver an ardent lover. He had counted strongly on getting a considerable amount of money when he married Brenda; now Brenda could get neither the money nor a divorce.

Brenda began to grow desperate for money. She asked Mrs. Beaver for a job, but Mrs. Beaver thought that it would not look well for her to employ Brenda. A short time later Beaver decided to accompany his mother on a trip to California.

At last Tony and Dr. Messinger came to a river they believed must flow into the Amazon, and they ordered the Indians to build canoes. The Indians obeyed, but they refused to venture down the river. There was nothing for the white men to do but to continue the journey without guides. Soon after they set out Tony came down with fever. Dr. Messinger left him on shore and went on alone to find help, but the explorer drowned when his boat capsized. Tony in his delirium struggled through the jungle and came by chance to the hut of a trader named Todd, who nursed him back to health but kept him a prisoner. Tony was forced to read the novels of Dickens aloud to his captor. When some Englishmen came in search of Tony, the trader made them believe his captive had died of fever. Tony faced lifelong captivity to be spent reading over and over Dickens' novels to the illiterate half-caste, for no white man could travel in the jungle without native help.

Beaver left for California. Brenda knew that their affair was over. No news came from Tony in South America. Without his permission, Brenda could not draw upon the family funds.

Then Tony was officially declared dead, and Hetton Abbey became the property of another branch of the Last family. The new owner of Hetton Abbey bred silver fox. Although he had even fewer servants than his predecessor and had shut off most of the house, he still dreamed that some day Hetton Abbey would again be as glorious as it was in the days of Cousin Tony.

He erected a memorial to Tony at Hetton Abbey, but Brenda was unable to attend its dedication. She was engaged elsewhere with her new husband, Jock Grant-Menzies.

Further Critical Evaluation of the Work:

Drawn from T. S. Eliot's *The Waste Land,* the title of Waugh's novel suggests its theme and his attitude toward post-World War I civilization. In its last stages English society is "dust," spiritually dead. Without belief or purpose, its members wander from one relationship to another, seeking energy and vitality. The atmosphere is of hectic, but empty activity.

The only still point in this whirlwind is provided by Hetton Abbey. Associated with the Middle Ages, a time of Christian belief and social order, Tony Last's estate is a symbol of values which informs not only this novel but all of Waugh's satires. Indeed, if *A Handful of Dust* has a hero at all, it is the Gothic abbey. For despite the destructiveness of its owners and visitors, it alone survives—and, in fact, gives promise of growth at the end.

Tony Last, of course, is an unsuitable lord of this richly traditional home. If he is presented as sympathetic, he is also dramatized as morally effete, specifically in regard to his profligate wife, Brenda. Besides, he is an anachronism, unable to adapt to the new age. Just as he cannot bring himself to renovate Hetton, he cannot live in the twentieth century. The absurd end which Waugh designs for him—reading Dickens aloud to a madman for the rest of his life—is an apt, if cruel justice.

Tony's successors at Hetton, the Richard Lasts, are of different mettle. Energetic, resourceful, and more importantly, a growing family, the Lasts seek to restore the abbey to economic independence. So if in part Waugh derives his inspiration from Eliot's apocalyptic poem, the final chapter of the novel is one of hope, both in the revival of Hetton and also in the values it symbolizes: order, family, and continuity.

HANDLEY CROSS

Type of work: Novel
Author: Robert Smith Surtees (1803-1864)
Type of plot: Humorous satire
Time of plot: Nineteenth century
Locale: England
First published: 1843; enlarged 1854

Principal characters:
JOHN JORROCKS, a wealthy grocer
MRS. JORROCKS, his wife
BELINDA, his niece
PIGG, his huntsman
CAPTAIN DOLEFUL, a master of ceremonies

Critique:

Handley Cross is a fairly typical example of nineteenth-century English sporting tales. The novel contains little plot and little attempt at dramatic motivation, but to an enthusiastic fox hunter Handley Cross is fascinating because of its gusty hunting tales and the single-minded devotion of its characters to the sport. Jorrocks, appearing in a number of Surtees' works, is dear to devotees of the hard-riding, hard-drinking sporting set.

The Story:

For years Michael Hardy had been the leader of the hunt in Sheepwash Vale. While he did not pay quite all the expenses of the sport, his personality and vigor kept fox hunting popular in the district. Michael was one of the old school; his hounds were unkenneled and boarded here and there, and the horses were mostly pickups. At his death it seemed that fox hunting could no longer be accounted an attraction in the county.

There were some other difficulties. The village of Handley Cross was rapidly growing. Having discovered by chance the curative values of the local spring, a reprobate physician named Swizzle had set up as a spa doctor, and in a few years Handley Cross became a fashionable watering place. Swizzle was a perfect doctor for many people. He invariably prescribed game pie and rare beef for his patients, and advised two quarts of port wine at dinner. He became a familiar sight in the village, as he buttonholed his patients on the street and inspected their coated tongues and gouty joints. With this new fame as a health resort hotels and souvenir stands sprang up to bring life to the sleepy village.

But there is no good proposition without competition. Another shady practitioner, a sanctimonious doctor named Mello, moved in. He bought land with a small spring on it, poured epsom salts in the water every night, and set up a rival establishment. In no time the town was divided into Melloites and Swizzleites. The important change, however, was in the social life of Handley Cross.

Captain Doleful, a lean, hypocritical half-pay captain, appointed himself master of ceremonies for the town. With the help of august Mrs. Barnington, the social arbiter of the fashionable set, balls and teas soon became popular and social eminence became the goal of the visiting gentry.

In a resort so fashionable it was unthinkable not to have a hunt club. Captain Doleful and some other worthies attempted to carry on after Michael Hardy died, but their efforts were unsuccessful. For one thing, the leaders of the hunt rode in gigs, conveyances unthinkable in Hardy's day. In addition, the townspeople were too poor or too parsimonious to hire a whipper-in and a huntsman. Worst of all, subscribers to the hunt were often slow in paying; soon there were not enough funds to pay for damage done to crops and fences.

The fashionables decided that the only solution was a real master of the hunt, one not too elegant for a small spa but rich enough to pay the difference between subscriptions and expenses. A committee headed by Captain Doleful and the secretary Fleeceall decided to invite John Jorrocks, whose fame had spread far, to become master of the hunt. Accordingly a letter was sent, and the negotiations were soon brought to a conclusion, for Jorrocks was an easy victim.

After a life devoted to selling tea and other groceries, Jorrocks was a wealthy man. He had turned to hunting as a hobby, and in spite of his Cockney accent and ample girth, he was soon accepted in the field. Although he had the bad habit of selling cases of groceries to his fellow huntsmen, in Surrey Jorrocks soon became a fixture among the sporting set. Now, he was to be master in his own right. Captain Doleful secured a lodge for him, and the date was set for his arrival in Handley Cross.

On the appointed day, the four-piece band turned out and the whole town assembled at the station. Several of the villagers carried banners bearing the legend "Jorrocks Forever." When the train pulled in, Captain Doleful looked through the first-class section but found no Jorrocks. The second-class carriages produced no Jorrocks. Finally, on a flat car at the end of the train, he found Jorrocks and his family snugly sitting in their own coach with the horses already hitched. Loud were the cheers as the new hunt master drove through the streets of Handley Cross.

Jorrocks was soon installed in his new lodging with Mrs. Jorrocks and Belinda, his pretty niece. Belinda added greatly to Jorrock's popularity.

The new hunt master looked over his kennels and the few broken-down hacks in the stable. Besides building up both the pack and the stud, he had to have a real huntsman. He finally hired Pigg, chiefly because his skinny shanks and avowed delicate appetite outweighed his speech of such broad Scots that few could understand what he said. Jorrocks was quickly disillusioned about his new huntsman. When Pigg ate his first meal in the kitchen, there was a great uproar. Hurrying in, Jorrocks found Pigg greedily eating the whole supper joint and holding the other servants at bay. And Pigg could drink more ale and brandy than Jorrocks himself.

Many were the fine hunts that winter. Because Pigg was skillful and Jorrocks persistent, the collection of brushes grew fast. One night Jorrocks was far from home, separated from his trusty Pigg and the pack, and caught in a downpour of rain. He turned into the first gate he saw and knocked. An efficient groom took his horse and two flunkies politely conducted the dripping Jorrocks to his room. On the bed were dry clothes, in the small tub was hot water, and on the table was a bottle of brandy. Jorrocks peeled off his clothes and settled into the tub. He had just started on his third glass of brandy when some one knocked. Jorrocks ignored the noise for a while but the knocker was insistent.

At last a determined voice from the hall demanded his clothes. Jorrocks quickly got out of the tub, put on the clothes which did not fit, and took a firm, possessive grip on the brandy bottle. Then he shouted forcefully that he would keep the clothes.

When Jorrocks came down to dinner, he was surprised to be told that he was in Ongar Castle. His unwilling host was the Earl of Bramber, whose servants had mistaken Jorrocks for an invited guest and by mistake had put him in the room of a captain. Jorrocks looked at the angry captain, who was wearing an outfit of his host. Only Jorrocks' Cockney impudence could have brazened out such a situation.

At last the company sat down to dinner. As usual, Jorrocks drank too much, and while giving a rousing toast to fox hunting he fell fast asleep on the floor. He awoke immersed in water. Calling lustily for help, he struck out for the shore. When a flunky brought a candle, he saw that he had been put to bed in the bathhouse and that while walking in his sleep he had fallen into the small pool. But Jorrocks was irrepressible; in the morning he parted from the earl on good terms.

After a hard-riding winter, spring finally spoiled the hunting and the Jorrocks family left for London. Pigg stayed in Handley Cross to dispose of the dogs and horses. Captain Doleful bought Jorrocks' own mount for twenty-five pounds. When the horse became sick and died soon afterward, parsimonious Doleful sued Jorrocks for the purchase price. The court decided in favor of Jorrocks, holding that no one can warrant a horse to stay sound in wind and limb.

Jorrocks' business associates looked on his hunting capers as a tinge of madness. That fall Jorrocks was heard to exclaim in delight at the sight of a frostbitten dahlia; it would soon be fox hunting time. But at last Jorrocks was committed by a lunacy commission for falling victim to the fox hunting madness. In vain Jorrocks sputtered and protested; his vehemence only added to the charge against him. Poor, fat Jorrocks spent some time in an asylum before an understanding chancellor freed him. Luckily he regained his freedom before the hunting season was too far gone.

Further Critical Evaluation of the Work:

For some twenty years, Robert Smith Surtees regaled the huntsmen of Britain with his amusing tales of the grocer Jorrocks and his undying passion for all things having to do with the chase. Abused and ridiculed for his extreme love of the hunt, he is never totally absurd: there is too much intensity, sincerity, and humanity in the man's love of sport for him to be destroyed by his enemies and detractors. Although a cockney in manners and speech, a mere grocer by trade, he achieves a lovable nobility all his own.

In his encouraging address to Benjamin, one of his huntsmen or glorified stable boys, Jorrocks reveals the highminded values of character and true wordliness he associates with expertise in things of the hunt: There is no saying what "keenness combined with sagacity and cleanliness may accomplish." Benjamin is flattered into believing that he has all the "ingredients of a great man," and "hopportunity only is wantin' to dewelope them."

The hunt is everything to Jorrocks; it is the measure of all he holds dear. Everything else in life, including his grocery business and home, takes second place to the call of the hounds. Even when he is sorting his clothes, the primary consideration is what can be preserved for use in the hunt and what must be discarded because it no longer can be adapted to the hunt. He is so obsessed with his passion that he cannot, without some anxiety, entrust anything connected with hunting to others. When his celebrated horse is being auctioned, he constantly interrupts the auctioneer with praise of the animal's speed and leaping ability. Eventually, Jorrocks' passion becomes a form of madness, but Surtees insists, in a shower of good honor, on vindicating Jorrocks. As exaggerated as it is, his love of the hunt is too sincere *and* authentic to cause his downfall. He must be free to hunt again.

HANDY ANDY

Type of work: Novel
Author: Samuel Lover (1797-1868)
Type of plot: Comic romance
Time of plot: Nineteenth century
Locale: Ireland
First published: 1842

Principal characters:
ANDY ROONEY, a young Irish boy
SQUIRE EDWARD EGAN, his employer
MURTOUGH MURPHY, an attorney
SQUIRE GUSTAVUS O'GRADY, a rival landlord
EDWARD O'CONNOR, a gentleman and poet

Critique:

Written as a series of anecdotes published in twelve monthly installments, *Handy Andy* is not a cohesive novel insofar as plot is concerned. It is, on the other hand, excellent in character portrayal and atmosphere. The quality likely to hold the modern reader is its droll wit. Rich in Irish folkways, peppered with clever Irish tales, enhanced by Irish songs, *Handy Andy* is more than a series of tales revolving around a political issue, a stupid lout of a boy, and a lovable hero. Accused of flattering his countrymen, Lover replied that as an Irishman he was compelled to present his land as he saw it.

The Story:

Andy Rooney was, from the day he was born, a mischievous troublemaker. When he was old enough to work, his mother took him to Squire Egan of Merryvale Hall, who hired him as a stableboy. His literal mind and naïve ways frequently caused his superiors much agitation.

One day Squire Egan sent Andy to the post-office to get a letter. Thinking the postage unduly high, Andy stole two other letters in order to get his money's worth. The squire's letter was from Murtough Murphy, an attorney, and it concerned a forthcoming election for a county seat held by Sir Timothy Trimmer, who was expected to die before long. Murphy warned Egan that although he could be certain of most of the votes in the election, Squire O'Grady of Neck-or-Nothing Hall was likely to support the Hon. Sackville Scatterbrain, another candidate. It happened that one of the purloined letters was addressed to Gustavus O'Grady. Peering through the envelope, Egan made out some unflattering words about himself. In anger he threw the letter into the fire. To cover up his error he burned the other letter also and then told Andy that he destroyed them to protect such a foolish gossoon from detection.

Andy could never get anything straight. When Squire Egan sent him on an errand to get a document from Murtough Murphy and Mrs. Egan sent him to the apothecary shop, Andy left Murphy's paper on the counter of the store and took up, instead, O'Grady's packet of medicine. The apothecary then unknowingly gave O'Grady the document from Murphy. On receiving O'Grady's medicine, Squire Egan was insulted and challenged Murphy to a duel. O'Grady, insulted at the contents of Murphy's legal document, challenged M'Garry, the apothecary. The matter was soon straightened out; Handy Andy fared the worst.

Edward O'Connor was a gallant cavalier. Well-educated and gifted as a poet, he was a favorite among the men of the community. He was in love with Fanny Dawson but had not declared himself as yet. A misunderstanding between Fanny's father and Edward had resulted in the young man's banishment from the Dawson house. After the quarrel Major Dawson maintained an intense dislike for the poet. Although she brooded over the absence of her lover, Fanny was forced to obey her father's wishes.

While walking one night, Andy, after stumbling over a man stretched out in the middle of the road, hailed a passing jaunting car. The driver, learning that the drunken man was his brother, stayed behind to care for him and asked Andy to drive his carriage. The passenger, Mr. Furlong, said he was on his way to visit the squire. Assuming that he meant Squire Egan, Andy took Furlong to Merryvale Hall. But Furlong had wanted to see O'Grady on election business. Egan, continuing to deceive the visitor, sent for Murphy, and the two men contrived to pump as much information from Furlong as they could.

When the truth was revealed, Furlong set out for Neck-or-Nothing Hall. There he met with more mischief. O'Grady was in a terrible mood, for he had discovered that the letter announcing Furlong's arrival had gone astray. The climax came when O'Grady's daughter Augusta happened into Furlong's room while he was dressing. A moment later O'Grady's knock at the door sent her hiding under the bed to avoid discovery. O'Grady caught her, however, and insisted that Furlong marry her.

The Hon. Sackville Scatterbrain arrived in time for the nomination speeches, a lively affair with a great deal of shouting and much merriment. On election day Egan supporters succeeded in irritating O'Grady, who had no sense of humor and plenty of temper. Thinking the crowd too boisterous, O'Grady aroused the people by sending for the militia. When he ordered the militia to fire into the angry mob, Edward O'Connor rode into the crowd to disperse it and prevent the militia from firing. Impressed by his bravery, the militia captain refused to fire. O'Grady then challenged O'Connor to a duel. O'Connor wounded O'Grady. When the Hon. Sackville Scatterbrain won the election, Squire Egan began a suit to dispute its result.

Larry Hogan, one of O'Grady's employees, had learned about the purloining of O'Grady's letter, which Squire Egan had burned, and he hoped to put his knowledge to use by intimidating the squire. One night Andy happened to overhear Larry, who was very drunk, talking about his scheme. Confused, Andy went to Father Phil, his confessor, for advice. It so happened that the priest was attending to the nuptials of Matty Dwyer and James Casey. At the wedding feast Casey failed to appear. Fearing that his daughter would be disgraced, Jack Dwyer asked if any of the guests present would marry Matty. Andy boldly offered himself and the marriage was performed. After the couple had been left alone in their new cottage James Casey arrived, accompanied by a hedge-priest who performed a second ceremony. Andy, protesting, was dragged outside and tied to a tree.

O'Grady died from the ill effects of the wound O'Connor had given him. Because the dead man had been deep in debt and unpopular in the community, his body was in danger of being confiscated. To prevent such an action, the family made two coffins; one, the true coffin, was to be buried secretly at night. O'Connor, stumbling upon the scene of the clandestine burial, was struck with remorse at his own deed, but young Gustavus O'Grady forgave his father's slayer, who in return pledged himself to lifelong friendship with Gustavus.

When a beggar warned Mrs. Rooney that someone was plotting to carry off her niece Oonah, Andy disguised himself as the young girl. Kidnaped, he was taken to Shan More's cave, where Andy's wild entreaties so aroused the pity of Shan More's sister Bridget that she took the distressed captive to bed with her. Discovering her error in the morning, Bridget lamented her lost honor, which Andy righted by marrying her. Too late Andy discovered that he really loved Oonah and that he had married a woman of bad reputation.

It was learned that Lord Scatterbrain, disguised as a servant named Rooney, had married Andy's mother, only to desert her before Andy's birth. After the death of the old nobleman—the Hon. Sackville Scatterbrain, his nephew, did not dispute the succession—Andy became his heir, with a seat in the House of Lords. Off to London he went to learn fine manners and to enjoy his new estate. Shan More and Bridget followed to demand a settlement for the deserted wife. To escape the vulgar and persistent pair, Andy gladly gave Bridget some money.

Major Dawson met with an accident which resulted in his death. With the major gone, all obstacles between Fanny Dawson and Edward O'Connor were re-moved, and O'Connor was finally able to enter the Dawson house and to marry his Fanny.

Shan More made an attempt upon Andy's life. When the attempt failed Andy went to Shan's den, where he found a wounded man, an escaped convict, who proved to be Bridget's true husband. Rid of his wife, Andy was free to marry Oonah.

Further Critical Evaluation of the Work:

Musician, painter, songwriter, novelist, playwright, and performer, Samuel Lover was above all an entertainer, and it is as entertainment that *Handy Andy* has endured for nearly a century and a half. Farcical, full of dialect humor and slapstick comedy, the book stops at nothing in its efforts to provoke good humor and laughter.

One of the chief sources of amusement is Andy's ever-present ignorance. A poor, uneducated lad, Andy means well but invariably gets into trouble. To the unsophisticated readers of Lover's day, Andy's antics touched a familiar chord, as well as being funny in a very basic way. More than anything else, Lover possessed a horror of dullness, and perhaps this accounts for the frenetic pace of *Handy Andy*. Certainly, the little tales are full of action and nonsense. The humor is vigorous and rough-and-ready, but never malicious or cruel. Some of the humor directly attacks prejudices of and toward the Irish; one of the most amusing sequences deals with the potato, the Irish fondness for it and reliance upon it for nourishment and the English scorn towards it. A great deal of humor is made of the local elections, the canvassing for votes, and the competition between the parties. But whatever the issue involved, the characters tend to be portrayed in an affectionate and kindly light, and any humor at their expense is gentle rather than scornful or harsh. There is nothing satirical about this book. Lover has no intention of reforming anything with his humorous sketches.

Lover seldom attempted subtlety in his humor; the accounts of Sackville Scatterbrain on eelction day or of Andy's being kidnaped while disguised as a young girl are as broad as they are lively. The plot, such as it is, dealing with Andy's marriage, is contrived, and the surprise ending, revealing Bridget's actual husband, is hardly plausible, yet none of this matters, for it all is told with such humor that the reader willingly suspends disbelief. Although the novel is weak, Handy Andy himself nearly ranks with Pickwick and Micawber as a comic hero.

HANGMAN'S HOUSE

Type of work: Novel
Author: Donn Byrne (Brian Oswald Donn-Byrne, 1889-1928)
Type of plot: Regional romance
Time of plot: Early twentieth century
Locale: Ireland
First published: 1925

Principal characters:
JAMES O'BRIEN, Lord Glenmalure, Jimmy the Hangman
CONNAUGHT, his daughter
DERMOT McDERMOT, a neighbor
THE CITIZEN, Dinny Hogan the Irreconcilable's son
JOHN D'ARCY, Dermot's cousin, Connaught's husband

Critique:

In *Hangman's House*, Donn Byrne intended to write an Irish novel for Irishmen, people for whom their own country was a passion. An intense love for Irish landscape, horse-racing, coursing, Gaelic balladry, hunting, and the writer's freedom-loving countrymen is evident throughout the book. When the novel appeared, critics may have preferred his *Messer Marco Polo* or *The Wind Bloweth*, but revised judgment is likely to put *Hangman's House* above the latter. The book was written in Dublin in 1922 and 1923, while the country was still being harried by the armed resistance of Republican irreconcilables. The state of Ireland at that time is presented in Byrne's characterization of the Citizen, a splendid man who had direct control over those who wanted to fight for freedom. The novel has been dramatized for the stage and for motion pictures.

The Story:

Dermot McDermot lived in the most pleasant homestead in the County of Dublin. He was a serious, slight man of twenty-five, taking after his Quaker mother more than his Irish soldier father except in his intense love of Ireland and everything Irish.

Dermot's nearest neighbors were James O'Brien, Lord Glenmalure, and his daughter Connaught. They lived in a rather forbidding-looking house that the country people insisted on calling Jimmy the Hangman's House. James O'Brien had been a violent rebel in his youth, but he had found it to his advantage to make his peace with the English. Becoming Lord Chief Justice of Ireland, he was responsible for the hanging of many Fenians.

When Glenmalure was stricken on the bench, he was forced to retire. His condition becoming worse, he called in doctors from Dublin and then England. One told him that he would live a month, certainly no more than five weeks. Then he secretly sent off a letter to John D'Arcy, Dermot's cousin, son of an old friend called Tricky Mick. Dermot thought D'Arcy a twister; Connaught's father said he had merely made a youngster's mistake. Glenmalure knew John D'Arcy was devious but ambitious, and that he might make his way in politics with Connaught's money and Hangman Jimmy's backing. In the weeks remaining to him, Glenmalure made contacts for D'Arcy and then married him to Connaught. Glenmalure knew Dermot wanted to marry Connaught but would not leave his homestead; he thought Connaught, strong-willed as she was, could guide D'Arcy to a place in the world where she might even get a title.

Glenmalure had been a rebel of the

old days, but there were still plenty of young men ready for a war for freedom if the word were given. Those who directed the movement decided there must be no war. They sent back to Ireland the Citizen, a commander of cavalry in the French army, but also the son of old Dinny Hogan the Irreconcilable, who had fled from Ireland and gone to live in France after the last uprising. The Citizen was to spend a year in Ireland, to make sure the young men would keep in line.

He had another reason for going to Ireland. John D'Arcy had married and then deserted his sister Maeve. Her shame caused her death and her son's, and their deaths brought on Dinny Hogan's. Dinny's son was out for revenge.

Glenmalure died the night of Connaught's wedding. She and D'Arcy returned from their honeymoon immediately.

Dermot saw them at the Tara Hunt, one of the best in the country. The Citizen also turned up at the hunt and approached D'Arcy to ask if he had been in Paris in '95. D'Arcy, after swearing that he had never been in Paris, went to the police to expose the Citizen. Connaught could not understand why D'Arcy had lied about being in Paris; she was furious when she heard that he had informed on a hunted man.

Dermot knew D'Arcy feared the Citizen but could not understand why. He also heard that things were not going well at Glenmalure, that Connaught kept a woman relative with her constantly, while D'Arcy spent his time gambling with people who would never have dared enter the house during Glenmalure's lifetime. D'Arcy's backers in politics had reneged after Glenmalure died, and D'Arcy was at loose ends.

On St. Stephen's Day the first steeplechase of the year was held at the Hannastown races. Connaught's Bard of Armagh was entered. Dermot heard that long odds were being placed on him, though the horse should have been considered the best in the field. One of the bookmakers told him that D'Arcy had placed a large bet against the Bard, but that there were many small bets on him that would spell disaster to the poor people if the Bard did not run. On the day of the race Connaught's jockey did not show up. Dermot rode the Bard and won. He and Connaught found D'Arcy sobbing afterward because he had lost heavily. Then Dermot knew his cousin was a weakling. That night D'Arcy killed the Bard.

Connaught left home and even the gamblers refused to play with a man who had killed a horse. Connaught, meanwhile, was miserable in England. Dermot looked for D'Arcy to straighten him out, to offer him money to go away if that seemed best. D'Arcy told him that he had married Maeve. Thinking D'Arcy had been married to Maeve when he married Connaught, Dermot thrashed him and would probably have killed him if an innkeeper had not interfered. Dermot gave D'Arcy money and told him to leave the country.

Connaught came home a short time later to a house of bitterness and gloom. After she and Dermot finally admitted they loved each other, Dermot sought out the Citizen to see if they might not work out some way to keep the shame of D'Arcy's conduct from staining Connaught and yet dissolve that marriage so that he and Connaught could be married. The Citizen told Dermot that Maeve had actually died before D'Arcy married Connaught, though D'Arcy could not have known it at that time. Dermot's hands were tied.

D'Arcy, hearing that Maeve was dead, came back to Glenmalure, and Connaught sought refuge with Dermot and his mother. D'Arcy, finding her there, accused Connaught and Dermot of being lovers. When they admitted their feelings, he threatened to hale them into court, but Dermot's mother prevented him. Connaught went again to England. Knowing that Connaught would do nothing to him, D'Arcy began to sell off all the possessions in the house. Dermot made arrangements in Dublin to be informed whenever those things came on the market and he bought up all of them. One night Dermot decided to pick some of Connaught's own roses and send them to her. As he went toward the house Glenmalure looked empty and forbidding. At the gate he met the Citizen, bent on killing D'Arcy. Dermot, not wishing the Citizen to be soiled with the murder of a twister like D'Arcy, tried to persuade him to go away. But the Citizen was determined. Dermot was afraid to let him go in alone.

Inside they found D'Arcy dressed for travel. The house had been stripped and there was a smell of oil in it. Instead of killing D'Arcy outright, the Citizen allowed himself to be persuaded to a duel with pistols. D'Arcy shot before the signal had been given and wounded the Citizen. Then he smashed a lamp on the floor and dashed upstairs. The lamp started a sheet of fire that swept through the house as Dermot and the Citizen fought their way outside. D'Arcy caught his foot while jumping from a window and was dead when he hit the ground.

Dermot's mother went to Connaught for a while. Dermot had the walls of Glenmalure torn down and a neat cottage built in its place. The Citizen, recovered from his wound, went back to his regiment. Then Connaught came home.

Further Critical Evaluation of the Work:

Ireland and the strangely heroic Irish race are the subject of *Hangman's House,* perhaps Donn Byrne's most noted novel. Certain medieval prophets had accurately predicted that Ireland would be tyrannized by England for "a week of centuries" (seven centuries); and that week ended during the 1920's, the decade in which Donn Byrne's novel is set. The end of tyranny is the story's background theme. Despite the cluster of characters, ranging from the Citizen, to Lord Glenmalure, to Dermot McDermot, the dominant presence in the novel is Ireland's finally realized struggle for freedom. Thus the real protagonist of *Hangman's House* is Irish history, with its centuries of oppression.

Nevertheless, Donn Byrne is not hateful or propagandistic; the few British personalities in the novel are presented as decent men doing their duty, while Catholics are not painted as saints or Protestants as cohorts of the Anti-Christ. The one touch of overt Irish flag-waving occurs when a fairly amiable British officer seeks to bribe an Irish child into singing British rather than Irish ditties, but is calmly rejected. Otherwise, the novel's characters move through their lives as their ancestors have done for centuries, living under an oppressive pall that never vanquishes them. The Citizen is the strongest symbolic personality of the story, and Connaught a victim figure that is almost representative of Ireland itself. A curious void exists in the rather mild treatment of Lord Glenmalure, "The Hangman," who wreaks vengeance on many Fenians and who coerces Connaught into marriage with a spineless traitor for the most spurious of economic reasons. The selfishness and violence of Glenmalure—whose base actions are outwardly respectable and dignified —are treated more as a commentary on weak human beings than as a portrait of a willfully evil individual. The author's sensitivity for tints and color, as well as ability to use words musically, are evident in the story.

HARD TIMES

Type of work: Novel
Author: Charles Dickens (1812-1870)
Type of plot: Social criticism
Time of plot: Mid-nineteenth century
Locale: England
First published: 1854

Principal characters:
  THOMAS GRADGRIND, a schoolmaster and a believer in "facts"
  LOUISA GRADGRIND, his oldest daughter
  TOM GRADGRIND, Louisa's brother
  MR. BOUNDERBY, Louisa's husband, a manufacturer and banker
  SISSY JUPE, a waif befriended by the Gradgrinds
  MRS. SPARSIT, Bounderby's housekeeper
  STEPHEN BLACKPOOL, Bounderby's employee
  JAMES HARTHOUSE, a political aspirant

Critique:

This novel was Dicken's first story of outright social protest. Earlier works had contained sections of social criticism, but this was the first motivated entirely by the writer's feelings about contemporary British culture. The novel, appropriately dedicated to Thomas Carlyle, another critic of nineteenth-century British society, was based upon personal observations of life in Manchester, one of England's great manufacturing towns and the original for Dickens' Coketown. The story is loaded with the bitter sincerity of Dickens' dislike for the industrial conditions he found in his homeland. Unfortunately for the value of the novel as a social document, Dickens overdrew his portraits of the industrialists responsible for conditions he abhorred; his industrialists became sheer grotesques and monsters.

The Story:

Thomas Gradgrind, proprietor of an experimental private school in Coketown, insisted that the children under him learn facts and only facts. He felt that the world had no place for fancy or imagination. His own five children were models of a factual education. Never having been permitted to learn anything of the humanities, they were ignorant of literature and any conception of human beings as individuals. Even fairy tales and nursery rhymes had been excluded from their education.

One day, as he walked from the school to his home, Gradgrind was immensely displeased and hurt to find his two oldest children, Louisa and Tom, trying to peek through the canvas walls of a circus tent. Nor did it ease his mind to discover that the two youngsters were not at all sorry for acting against the principles under which they had been reared and educated. Later Gradgrind and his industrialist friend, Mr. Josiah Bounderby, discussed possible means by which the children might have been misled from the study of facts. They concluded that another pupil, Sissy Jupe, whose father was a clown in the circus, had influenced the young Gradgrinds.

Having decided to remove Sissy Jupe from the school, they set out immediately to tell the girl's father. When they arrived at the inn where the Jupes were staying, they found that the clown-father had deserted his daughter. Gradgrind, moved by sentiment, decided to keep the girl in his home and let her be educated at his school, all against the advice of Bounderby, who thought Sissy Jupe would be only a bad influence on the Gradgrind children.

Years passed, and Louisa and young Tom grew up. Gradgrind knew that Bounderby had long wished to marry Louisa. She, educated away from sentiment, agreed to marry Bounderby, who was thirty years her elder. Tom, an employee in Bounderby's bank, was very glad to have his sister marry Bounderby; he wanted a friend to help him if he got into trouble there. In fact, he advised his sister to marry Bounderby for that reason, and she, loving her brother, agreed to help him by marrying the wealthy banker.

Bounderby himself was very happy to have Louisa as his wife. After his marriage he placed his elderly housekeeper in rooms at the bank. Mrs. Sparsit, disliking Louisa, was determined to keep an eye on her for her employer's sake. After the marriage all seemed peaceful at the bank, at the Gradgrind home, and at the Bounderby residence.

In the meantime Gradgrind had been elected to Parliament from his district. He sent out from London an aspiring young politician, James Harthouse, who was to gather facts about the industrial city of Coketown, facts which were to be used in a survey of economic and social life in Britain. In order to facilitate the young man's labors, Gradgrind had given him a letter of introduction to Bounderby, who immediately told Harthouse the story of his career from street ragamuffin to industrialist and banker. Harthouse thought Bounderby a fool, but he was greatly interested in pretty Louisa.

Through his friendship with Bounderby, Harthouse met Tom Gradgrind, who lived with the Bounderbys. Harthouse took advantage of Tom's love for drink to learn more about Louisa. Hearing that she had been subjected to a dehumanizing education, and feeling that she would be easy prey for seduction because of her loveless marriage to the pompous Boundarby, Harthouse decided to test Louisa's virtue.

Before long Harthouse gained favor in her eyes. Neither realized, however, that Mrs. Sparsit, jealous and resenting her removal from the comfortable Bounderby house, spied on them constantly.

Everyone was amazed to learn one day that the Bounderby bank had been robbed. Chief suspect was Stephen Blackpool, an employee whom Bounderby had mistreated. Blackpool, who had been seen loitering in front of the bank, had disappeared on the night of the robbery. Suspicion also fell on a Mrs. Pegler, an old woman known to have been in Blackpool's company.

A search for Blackpool and Mrs. Pegler proved fruitless. Bounderby seemed content to wait; he said that the culprits would turn up sooner or later.

The affair between Louisa and Harthouse reached a climax when Louisa agreed to elope with the young man. Her better judgment, however, caused her to return to her father instead of running away with her lover. Gradgrind, horrified to see what his education had done to Louisa's character, tried to make amends for her. The situation was complicated by Mrs. Sparsit. She had learned of the proposed elopement and had told Bounderby. He angrily insisted that Louisa return to his home. Gradgrind, realizing that his daughter had never loved Bounderby, insisted that she be allowed to make her own choice. Harthouse, giving up all hope of winning Louisa, disappeared.

Mrs. Sparsit returned to act as Bounderby's housekeeper during Louisa's absence and tried to reinstate herself in Bounderby's confidence by tracing down Mrs. Pegler. To her chagrin, Mrs. Pegler turned out to be Bounderby's mother. Bounderby was furious, for his mother disproved his boasts about being a self-made man. Meanwhile Louisa and Sissy Jupe accidentally found Blackpool, who had fallen into a mine shaft while returning to Coketown to prove his innocence of the robbery. After his rescue he told that Tom Gradgrind was the real culprit. When the young man disappeared, his sister and father, with the help of Sissy Jupe, found him and placed him, disguised, in a circus until arrangements could be made for spiriting him out of the country.

Before he could escape, however, Bounderby's agents found Tom and arrested him. With the aid of the circus roustabouts he was rescued and put on a steamer which carried him away from the police and Bounderby's vengeance.

Mrs. Sparsit, who had caused Bounderby all kinds of embarrassment by producing Mrs. Pegler, was discharged from his patronage, much to her chagrin. Bounderby himself died unhappily in a fit a few years later. The Gradgrinds, all of them victims of an education of facts, continued to live unhappily, unable to see the human side of life.

Further Critical Evaluation of the Work:

Dickens began as an entertainer (*Pickwick Papers*) but gradually evolved into a moralist and social critic of major significance. In his early works there are heroes and villains; in his later, victims and victimizers. The distinction is important because it measures his development from a writer of fiction to an artist with a tragic vision.

Hard Times is a milestone in Dickens' art: caricature and allegorical names are used here in a form of Swiftian satire so bitter in its contempt and social rage that we almost forget that the same devices are used to create lovable human beings in his other works. Mr. Gradgrind is offensive in a very serious way. His reduction of everything to "facts" constitutes a *gradual grinding* away of the humanity of his pupils and his own children. Louisa marries to obtain advantages for her brother—in itself a noble act; but her blind willingness to set aside personal feelings and needs only makes her more vulnerable to Harthouse's attempts at seduction. It is finally Louisa's responsibility, from the depths of her own denied feelings, to educate Gradgrind to his deficiencies as a father and teacher.

Although Dickens' satirical dismissal of rationalistic Utilitarianism (the doctrine that the greatest good for the greatest number must be the goal of a statistically rigorous and "fact" conscious social reform) is brilliantly effective in the classroom scenes, he does not entirely convince us that Utilitarian education is directly responsible for the dehumanization of England. Dickens wanted to shock the middle-class reformers with the coldness of their ideas, but he himself was curiously limited in his own humanism. Humanitarian that he was, he did not entirely respect the humanity of the very working classes he championed. The portrait of Slackbridge, the trade union organizer, reveals Dickens' contempt of labor as a political force.

Throughout his life Dickens distrusted the people's ability to govern themselves; he always looked to the manufacturers and the aristocracy, the governing classes, to correct or avoid the evils of the society they held in trust. *Hard Times* is a blow at the ideas Dickens felt were preventing the leading classes from meeting their social responsibilities.

HARMONIUM

Type of work: Poetry
Author: Wallace Stevens (1879-1955)
First published: 1923

In the case of Wallace Stevens the proper understanding of his early poems as a new dimension of poetic reality was for the most part an exercise in hindsight. This is not the same thing as saying that at any time in his career he lacked the attention of serious criticism or a body of appreciative, well-wishing readers, only that he was sometimes admired for the wrong reasons.

Harmonium was published in 1923, at a time when the French Symbolists—Baudelaire, Mallarmé, Verlaine, Rimbaud, Laforgue—were being assimilated as influences and models, and the Imagist movement had not yet run its course. Because Stevens exhibited the tangential imagery, elisions, and regard for symbolic order of the first group and the concentrated exactness of the second, most readers found little in his poetry to link it with the native tradition. Instead, they seized upon the exotic and ornate qualities of his verse as if these were its final effect rather than a means to an end. Stevens appeared to be, at first reading, a poet whose purity of vision and absolute integrity insulated him from the material concerns of his society. Eliot in England and Joyce in Paris occupied just such positions of isolation and authority. Closer home, the author of "Le Monocle de Mon Oncle," "The Comedian as the Letter C," and "Peter Quince at the Clavier" seemed to provide a similar image of the dedicated artist.

But Stevens, as it later developed, was neither a master of décor for decoration's sake—the literary dandy and Whistler in words, as some called him—nor the alienated poet such as the period demanded. An aesthetic-moral writer of the highest order, he had already in *Harmonium* charted those areas of experience and precept which were to comprise the whole body of his work: the re-creation of the physical world in bold and brilliant imagery, the relation of imagination to reality, the nature and function of art, the poet's place in modern society, problems of structure and style. Stevens was not a poet of growth but of clarification, and his later books merely ordered and refined his vision and techniques. Unlike most poets, who achieve only a temporary balance between temperament and environment, he created a total world for his imagination and his belief in the nourishing power of art. Perhaps the greatest service he provided was to show by example the possible in poetry if man is to find a source of imaginative faith in an age of disbelief or to establish once more a sustaining relationship with the world about him. *Harmonium* "makes a constant sacrament of praise" to poetry—the imaginative ordering of experience—as the supreme fiction.

The unmistakable signature of these poems is the richness of their diction, the use of words not common to English poetry, at least in these plain-speaking times, a parade of brightly colored images and startling turns of phrase. Such words as fubbed, coquelicot, barque, phosphor, gobbet, fiscs, clavier, pannicles, girandoles, rapey, carked, diaphanes, unburgherly, minuscule, ructive, shebang, cantilene, pipping, curlicues, and funest reveal the poet's delight in the unusual and the rare. But as R. P. Blackmur pointed out long ago, Stevens' poetic vocabulary was not chosen for affected elegance, coyness, or calculated obscurity. These words give an air of rightness and inevitability within the contexts that frame them; it is not the word itself but its relationship to other words in the poem that gives to Stevens' poetry its striking qualities of style. It is the same with his images, the strategic effectiveness of "barbaric glass," "poems of plums," "venereal soil," "golden quirks and Paphian caricatures," "rosy chocolate and gilt umbrellas," "oozing cantankerous gum," "women of primrose and purl," "the emperor of ice cream," in conveying a luxuriance of sense impressions. This diction of odd angles of vision and strange surfaces gives the impression of language revitalized as if it were the invention of the poet himself. It becomes a part of what Stevens once called "the essential gaudiness of poetry," and it is capable of a variety of effects, as the following examples show.

The mules that angels ride come slowly down
The blazing passes from beyond the sun.
　　　　　("Le Monocle de Mon Oncle")

or:

Chieftain Iffucan of Azcan in caftan
Of tan with henna hackles, halt!
　　　　　("Bantams in Pine-Woods")

or:

　　　　　　　. . . and not to think
Of any misery in the sound of the wind,
In the sound of the leaves,

Which is the sound of the land
Full of the same wind
That is blowing in the same bare place

For the listener, who listens in the snow,
And, nothing himself, beholds
Nothing that is not there and the nothing that is.
　　　　　("The Snow Man")

Stevens' diction and imagery are not so much the verbalization of a mode of thought but in themselves a way of thinking. His poetry belongs to the order of solipsism, that philosophical theory which holds that the self is the only object of verifiable knowledge and that all things are re-created in the image of man in the act of perceiving the world. In his best poems this is the effect toward which Stevens' floating images tend, so that from the world of his verse one emerges with altered perspective. There is in it a different way of seeing, a rearrangement of the familiar pattern of experience by which poetry is no longer a way of looking at life but a form of life. Thus his images point to a passionate drive toward material comfort and rich living, as opposed to spiritual sterility in a world of waste and excess. In *Harmonium* the poles of his world become "our bawdiness unpurged by epitaph" and "the strict austerity of one vast, subjugating, final tone." He is aware of tradition corrupted and a world fallen into disorder, a realization of man dispossessed of unity between himself and his universe, of nature violated, of old faiths gone. Out of his knowledge he writes these lines on a Prufrock theme:

In the high west there burns a furious star.
It is for fiery boys that star was set
And for sweet-smelling virgins close to them.
The measure of the intensity of love
Is measure, also, of the verve of earth.
For me, the firefly's quick, electric stroke
Ticks tediously the time of one more year.
And you? Remember how the crickets came
Out of their mother grass, like little kin,
In the pale nights, when your first imagery
Found inklings of your bond to all that dust.

For a secular poet like Stevens, poetry was to become the "supreme fiction" and the imagination "the one reality in this imagined world," a way of imposing order on the chaos of experience. This is the theme of "Anecdote of the Jar," one of the simplest but most meaningful of the poems in *Harmonium*:

I placed a jar in Tennessee,
And round it was, upon a hill.

It made the slovenly wilderness
Surround that hill.

Here is the desire to impose order on the wildness of nature and, indirectly, of the world. It is not the image of the jar that is of first importance in the poem, but the act of placing the jar on such an eminence that it commands the landscape, so that

It took dominion everywhere.
The jar was gray and bare.
It did not give of bird or bush,
Like nothing else in Tennessee.

Stevens puts Keats' Grecian urn to other uses than those of contemplation or revelation.

This "rage for order" is worked out in more elaborate detail in "The Comedian as the Letter C." A fable in six parts, the poem is Stevens' most ambitious work before "Notes Toward a Supreme Fiction" on the relation of imagination to reality and the poet's place and function in society. It is characteristic of his self-satire that he should picture the poet as a picaresque mountebank trying to reconcile imagination to actuality. In Part I, "The World without Imagination," Crispin the subjectivist sets sail upon the sea of life, to discover that the romantic imagination which has given him eminence within his own limited milieu is a world preoccupied with things and therefore lacking in imagination. Romanticism being equated with egotism, Crispin in the second section, "Concerning the Thunderstorms of Yucatan," decides that the only reality lies in the senses. His love for the exotic ends when he is brought to a realization of the overwhelming and destructive powers of nature. The third division, "Approaching Carolina," follows Crispin through a realm of the imagination, symbolized by moonlight that is the antithesis of the sun, which lights up reality. Turning from the moon as a mere reflection of reality, Crispin in Part IV, "The Idea of a Colony," enters a new phase of art based on the community and regional ties. Disillusioned, he turns in Part V, "A Nice Shady Home,"

to domesticity, and like Candide he digs in his own garden; he will become a philosopher. Part VI, "A Daughter with Curls," deals with the final wisdom Crispin found in his return to earth:

Crispin concocted doctrine from the rout.
The world, a turnip once so readily plucked,
Sacked up and carried overseas, daubed out
Of its ancient purple, pruned to the fertile main,
And sown again by the stiffest realist,
Came reproduced in purple, family font,
The same insoluble lump.

Art, Stevens implies, cannot be made this or that, or be pursued like a chimera; it exists, separate and complete, in its own substance and shape.

There are times when Stevens' search for some standard of ultimate reality and the forms that it may take in poetry leads him away from concrete particularities into the realm of abstract speculation. If he appears at times more concerned with meaning than with being, the reader may also recognize in his work the power of a contemplative writer who insists upon the need of discipline in life as in art. As a modern, he sees the gap between the potential and the actual; consequently he must try to uncover causes, to create a way of seeing that his readers may share.

Stevens himself achieves the supreme, fictive mood of contemplation and understanding in "Sunday Morning," his best poem and one of the great poems of the century. Here in the spectacle of a woman eating her late breakfast on a Sunday morning we have a picture of modern boredom and uncertainty. The woman sits in external sunlight but also in the moral darkness of an age that has lost faith in the spiritual nature of man: "Why should she give her bounty to the dead?" The poet's answer is that happiness lies in the perception of nature, which in its recurrent changes and seasons creates an immortality in which man may share.

> We live in an old chaos of the sun,
> Or old dependency of day and night,
> Or island solitude, unsponsored, free,
> Of that wide water, inescapable.
> Deer walk upon our mountains, and
>   the quail
> Whistle about us their spontaneous
>   cries;
> Sweet berries ripen in the wilderness;
> And, in the isolation of the sky,

> At evening, casual flocks of pigeons
>   make
> Ambiguous undulations as they sink,
> Downward to darkness, on extended
>   wings.

Harmonium reveals a poet of moral and humane temper. Stevens' poems, disciplined and perfectly articulated, reflect a limited but significant picture of the modern sensibility.

HARP OF A THOUSAND STRINGS

Type of work: Novel
Author: H. L. Davis (1896-1960)
Type of plot: Historical-philosophical romance
Time of plot: Late eighteenth and early nineteenth centuries
Locale: The American prairie country, Tripoli, and Paris
First published: 1947

Principal characters:
MELANCTHON CRAWFORD,
COMMODORE ROBINETTE, and
APEYAHOLA, called Indian Jory, founders of a prairie town
JEAN-LAMBERT TALLIEN, a French revolutionist
THÉRÈSE DE FONTENAY, whom he loved
RENÉ DE BERCY, her fiancé
ANNE-JOSEPH THÉROIGNE, in love with de Bercy
MONSIEUR DE CHIMAY, a wealthy aristocrat and merchant

Critique:

Harp of a Thousand Strings is a novel linking the personalities and events of the French Revolution to the development of the American West. Behind this story of the naming of a prairie town lies the author's theory that the incidents of history are never final, that although they may change form or significance they continue to move like a slow ground-swell from country to country among people who have been affected by history's erosions and accretions. History itself is the thousand-stringed harp of the title, an instrument capable of endless vibrations and echoes. In order to present his theme of the reverberations of history, the writer made his novel contrapuntal in design. The American frontier, the Barbary wars, and the French Revolution are introduced briefly for thematic effect, later to be alternated and recombined. The pattern is one of triads. The three settings, America, Tripoli, and France; the three Americans, each corresponding to one of the drives in Tallien's career; the three choices Tallien must make and their consequences—all are essential to the craftsmanship and design of this unusual and rewarding historical novel.

The Story:

Old Melancthon Crawford had been one of the founders of a prairie town in the Osage country. In his last years his eccentricities became so marked that relatives had him sent back to his birthplace, a Pennsylvania village he had always hated, where they could keep an eye on him and the disposal of his property. After his departure on the eastbound stage Commodore Robinette and Apeyahola, a Creek Indian whom the settlers called Jory, climbed to the prairie swell where Crawford's trading post had stood. Talking about the past, they thought back to a decisive night the three had in common, a night when Tripoli was being bombarded by American naval guns during the war with Barbary pirates.

Under cover of the bombardment the three Americans, prisoners escaped from the pasha's dungeons, had taken refuge in a warehouse belonging to Thurlow and Sons, Boston merchants. Young Crawford was all for carrying away some loot he found in a storeroom, but Apeyahola and Robinette, the wounded sailor, were against the idea. During the argument Monsieur Tallien entered the warehouse. One-time Citizen President of the French National Convention, now an obscure consular official under Napoleon, he was there to keep an appointment with a Paris associate of Thurlow and

Sons. To pass the time while waiting, he told the tale of his rise and eventual ruin because of his love for the notorious Thérèse de Fontenay. Crawford, Robinette, and the Indian made a strange audience. Tallien told his story, however, because he saw each young American marked by one phase of his own career: vengeance, ambition, love.

Jean-Lambert Tallien, protégé of the old Marquis de Bercy, was intended for a career in law. During a visit to the de Bercy estate he watched Anne-Joseph Théroigne being carried forcibly away because she had attracted the interest of René, the young marquis, soon to marry the lovely Countess Thérèse de Fontenay. While Tallien stood watching the disappearing cart that carried Anne-Joseph, René rode up with the countess and haughtily ordered the student to open a gate. At Tallien's refusal the young nobleman raised his whip. Tallien struck the marquis' horse. The animal threw his rider and dragged him, unconscious and bleeding, by one stirrup.

Tallien hid in the woods while angry villagers hunted him with guns and pitchforks. Father Jarnatt, the parish priest, saved the fugitive and sent him off to Paris to seek his fortune in journalism. These things happened in the year the Bastille fell.

In Paris, Tallien again met Anne-Joseph Théroigne, by that time a rough-tongued, rabble-rousing virago, the friend of Robespierre and members of the Jacobin Club. It was she who helped Tallien to establish *L'Ami des Citoyens*, the revolutionary newspaper with which he placarded Paris. Because of her he led the assault on the Tuileries during the August riots. Later he became a deputy to the National Convention and a commissioner to the provinces. Anne-Joseph helped his rise in public favor because she expected to find him useful. Still loving René de Bercy, she had secretly aided his escape to England. Through Tallien she hoped eventually to locate Thérèse de Fontenay, whom she hated.

A man and a woman muffled in native costume entered the warehouse. The man was Monsieur de Chimay, who had come ashore from a French ship to arrange some trade business with Tallien. The woman was not introduced. Since they could not leave the warehouse before the bombardment ended, Tallien continued his story.

One day he heard his name called from a cartload of prisoners. In the wagon was Thérèse de Fontenay, whom he had never forgotten. Hoping to protect her from Anne-Joseph's fury, he denounced the virago for her help to de Bercy and thrust her into an angry mob that stripped and beat her. The woman, never recovering from that brutal treatment, lived mad for many years.

Thérèse was imprisoned in the Carmes. Through spies Tallien tried to take measures for her safety. At last, to save her life, he overthrew Robespierre and ended the Reign of Terror. Telling his story, he made it all sound simple; the others had to guess at the bribes, the promised reprisals, all the scheming of those three anxious days while he held prisoners the influential citizens of Paris and executed the *coup d'état* of Thermidor. Although he knew that Thérèse was involved in a plot for an émigré invasion, he married her later that year.

But choices made for her sake led to other choices that he neither expected nor wanted. Jealous of Captain Belleval, an officer attentive to Thérèse while she was in prison, he arranged to have the captain betrayed to the rebels of the Vendée. When the émigrés finally landed at Quiberon, all were captured. At the same time the peasant who had betrayed Belleval was taken prisoner. In his effort to save the peasant's life Tallien quarreled with General Hoche over the disposition of the other prisoners, and in the end he was forced to declare them enemies of the state and order their execution. Among those who perished was René de Bercy, who chose death with honor rather than accept Tallien's offer of escape to England.

When Tallien returned to Paris and told Thérèse, haltingly, what had happened, she said only that she knew at last what a life was worth. Months later Monsieur de Chimay arrived from London with some of de Bercy's keepsakes. De Chimay was in trade, an associate of the powerful Thurlow firm and a friend of Ouvrard, the influential banker who had become Thérèse's lover. Thérèse saw in the two men a power she could use to undermine that of her husband.

The shelling had ended; Tallien became silent. When he and de Chimay withdrew to transact their business, the woman gave the three Americans a case containing two pistols and a knife, each decorated with the crest of a hand holding a flower. For a moment she drew aside her veil and they saw the face of Thérèse de Fontenay. The Americans went out toward the harbor, each marked by a symbol of Tallien's defeat, but carrying with them also a memory of Thérèse's beauty.

Years later Robinette and Apeyahola, ragged and gaunt, were traveling overland from the Mississippi. Wanted by the authorities, the commodore because of an affair of gallantry in Spanish territory and for taking part in the Gutiérrez insurrection, Apeyahola for a murder in Georgia, they found carved on a tree the design of a hand holding a flower. That crest marked their trail to Crawford's trading post in the Indian country. There they stayed, philanderer, murderer, and thief. When the time came for them to name the village growing up around the old trading post, each remembered the woman they had seen briefly by candlelight in a dingy warehouse. So, out of the turmoil and blood of the French Revolution, Thérèse de Fontenay gave her name to a new town on the American prairie.

Further Critical Evaluation of the Work:

Harp of a Thousand Strings is not an easy novel to read. Characters are introduced abruptly, there are random digressions that seem to have little to do with the main narrative, and the writing makes no concessions to casual readers. Davis is not afraid to use coincidence in his plot as freely as Dickens did, occasionally straining the reader's credulity. But the novel has many merits, including the prose which is of a schooled intelligence, contemplative and elegant, and, subtle delineation of character. The reader comes to enjoy the play of the author's mind over the intricate—almost labyrinthine—situations and the equally scrupulous assessment of human motivation.

The style changes with the narrative. When Davis describes the three founding fathers in their dotage, he uses the garrulous, inventive ramblings of a frontier tale. As the scene shifts to France, the language takes on an epigrammatic, paradoxical elegance. He does not dwell on the tangible, surface impressions of the past found in most historical novels, but rather creates a dreamlike past, filled with shadow and light. Goyaesque images pervade the book, grotesque, shadowy scenes of hideous people engaged in vile acts. Yet the book is often very funny. This juxtaposition of wit and anger gives the novel a unique resonance and power.

Davis casts a wry eye at men such as Robespierre and Fouché and the hero of the novel, Tallien. The implication is that all men are mortal, are played on by history as much as they play upon history. The story shows how personal motives—and not always of the highest order—can influence the actions which make history. Many of the characters look back over their lives with anger and regret. Jory and the Commodore both gaze back on frustrated hopes and years of humiliation and bitterness, but the Commodore tells his friend that after a certain point one no longer should compare one's life to one's early expectations and hopes. Survival should be sufficient.

Like his contemporaries A. B. Guthrie Jr. and Walter Van Tilburg Clark, H. L. Davis was a literary pioneer of the American West, rediscovering and reinterpreting the past with the eyes of an artist and poet. Davis' novels are loosely plotted, almost picaresque, his style is quiet although at times complicated. What sets his work above the usual is his mood, what some critics have called "the magic qualities of place and emotion." He is a man who writes with the knowledge of the energies that make history and can present this awareness in tales which are lyrical, tragic, and sometimes comic.

Although an exact contemporary of the so-called Lost Generation which included Hemingway, Fitzgerald, and Dos Passos, Davis had little in common with them. He began fiction writing late and was never prolific. Almost twelve years elapsed between his first prize-winning novel, *Honey in the Horn,* and his next, *Harp of a Thousand Strings.* He always was a man and writer who followed his own vision, belonging to no coterie or school. First and foremost, he was a craftsman.

This craftsmanship is particularly evident in the complicated structure of *Harp of a Thousand Strings.* The story is framed by the rugged grandeur and squalor of the American frontier. The tale moves the reader from the American West to Tripoli to the France of the Revolution, back to Tripoli in the time of Napoleon, and then back to the American frontier. The reader seems to view the story through a series of refracting lenses. By the time he has finished the book, it has taken on the character of a legend: larger than life, abstract, and ripe with moral significance.

The theme of money and the craving for it runs through the novel beside the theme of lust for power. With the additional motifs of vengeance and thwarted love, these themes give the novel a bitter view of mankind. Only when he writes about nature does Davis attempt to paint a pretty picture. Men and man-created objects, whether cities or smaller creations, are treated harshly.

The author frequently makes comments about women. None of the female characters in the novel are very likable or admirable. Of the two principal women, one is passionately destructive, the other is cold and calculating. Both are self-centered. But this last is a trait shared by the male characters, as well. With the possible exception of Father Jarnatt, the characters are all self-seeking, concerned primarily with their own survival. Few of them are presented as vivid, living beings.

Only Anne-Joseph Théroigne emerges as a physical, dynamic human force, lingering in the imagination long after the book is finished. The best realized scenes are those of Anne-Joseph haranguing Parisian mobs during the Terror. Her animal vitality and vulgarity give the novel a needed push, and the book suffers when she drops from the scene.

But Davis is obviously not interested in that physical, dynamic side of characterization. His gift is for the analytical consideration of motives and emotions. The reader may not be able to visualize a character, but the reasoning processes of that character are quite clearly presented. The reader understands why the characters in the novel double-cross one another, even if he does not always care.

Harp of a Thousand Strings is an impressive achievement, a highly cerebral novel, which, although it does not greatly move the reader emotionally, provides rewarding moments of contemplation, and fascinating views of contrasting worlds. An intellectual maze, a collection of Chinese boxes, one inside the other, the novel draws the reader ever in, farther and farther, gradually demonstrating that the cycles we call history are all tightly fitted together. It is a book worth the effort of reading.

Bruce D. Reeves

THE HARP-WEAVER AND OTHER POEMS

Type of work: Poetry
Author: Edna St. Vincent Millay (1892-1950)
First published: 1922

Ten years before she was awarded a Pulitzer prize for *The Harp-Weaver and Other Poems,* Edna St. Vincent Millay's first and best-known poem, "Renascence," appeared in *The Lyric Year,* an anthology of one hundred poems by as many poets. The Vassar undergraduate, Vincent Millay, as her family and friends then called her, scored a signal victory in her contribution to the anthology, the freer form and the liberal spirit of her work standing out against the stilted Victorian verse and sentimentality found in most of the selections.

"All I could see from where I stood," the first line of "Renascence," begins a poem as regular in meter, rhythm, and rhyme as those by her romantic predecessors. But the new hedonism and the sharp, almost brittle metaphors based on both land- and seascapes create a quite different effect. The pain of omniscience, the poet's burden, is the theme. The imagery is dazzling in its exalted movement to a sensuous climax in which life is celebrated through all the senses.

"Renascence" was a promise of things to come, for the personal lyric was Miss Millay's forte. Her sonnets and her ballads, held in such beautiful balance in *The Harp-Weaver,* are always exact in craftsmanship, capturing at times the innocence of childhood and the sadness of lost ecstasy.

The title poem, "The Ballad of The Harp-Weaver," appearing at the end of the second section, brings into an almost medieval form saddened innocence and lyric tragedy. Written mostly in the traditional four-line ballad stanza with alternating rhymes, the poem varies subtly in meter and end-stopping to include occasional stanzas with a fifth line and shifting rhyme schemes. These last lines create the panic, the pain, and finally the exaltation of deep feeling. The narrative tells in the first person the story of a young boy of the slums living with his widowed mother who can do nothing to make a living and has nothing to sell except "a harp with a woman's head nobody will buy." In a fifth line, "she begins to cry" for the starving boy. This was in the late fall; by the winter all the furniture had been burned and the boy can do no more than watch his school companions go by, for he has no clothes to wear. He is disturbed by his mother's attempts to comfort him, to dandle him on her knee while "a-rock-rock-rocking," and to sing to him "in such a daft way." The counterpoint of the harp with a woman's head and "a wind with a wolf's head" suggests the lingering pain after the first panic. The final exaltation, however, is remarkable. A mystical event occurs: the mother weaves clothes for the Christ child, just the size of her own boy, and perishes at the harp, "her hands in the harp strings frozen dead." This odd juxtaposition of the Madonna and the Magi themes with the dance of death demonstrates Miss Millay's versatility and expertness with language.

Part V of the volume, "Sonnets from an Ungrafted Tree," creates its effect by quite opposite methods. This sequence concerns a woman who prosaically watches her unloved husband die and then tries to pick up the empty pieces of her own unloving life He had befriended her in school. when she would have accepted anyone, by flashing a mirror in her eyes; after his death she has a flash of awareness that he had loved her deeply, though he was in no way remarkable in living or in loving. Whatever heat was in this strange body which slept and ate beside her is now gone, the whole unclassified. The impact of this fact makes of these 238 lines a taut though expressionistic drama in which the unreality of the death is emotionally heightened by the very real, familiar objects which express the widow's desolation.

These macabre themes do not go unrelieved in Miss Millay's book. The opening lyric is the keynote to the first part, and "My Heart, Being Hungry" connects this volume with the earlier "Renascence." The lean heart feeds on "beauty where beauty never stood," and "sweet where no sweet lies," symbolized by the smell of rain on tansy. She continues the theme of the bitter-sweet, light-dark, the opposites of nature which make of the humblest experience something like pain, a pain of sensitive awareness of the tears of things. Always, however, there is pure aesthetic pleasure gained from deep-felt realizations, of

> A rock-maple showing red,
> Burrs beneath a tree

even in deepest grief, she says in "The Wood Road." In spite of the world's negations, the positive things endure. "The Goose-Girl" summarizes this belief:

> Spring rides no horses down the hill,
> But comes on foot, a goose-girl still.
> And all the loveliest things there be
> Come simply, so, it seems to me.
> If ever I said, in grief or pride,
> I tired of honest things, I lied;
> And should be cursed forevermore
> With love in laces, like a whore
> And neighbors cold, and friends unsteady,
> And Spring on horseback, like a lady!

In the second section Miss Millay divides her poems between the goose-girl and the lady, the first poem, "Departure," reflecting both. The adolescent girl, busy with her sewing, is pensive, even in despair over half-felt longings:

> It's little I care what path I take,
> And where it leads it's little I care:
> But out of this house, lest my heart break,
> I must go, and off somewhere.

She indulges in the pleasant emotion of self-pity, of her dead body found in a ditch somewhere, an adolescent drama which is interrupted by her mother's friendly query, "Is something the matter, dear?" An old legend retold in "The Pond" presents a suicide who picked a lily before she drowned, a grasp even in death after the beautiful.

The extremely short third section contains all these motifs and some strange new ones. "Never May the Fruit Be Plucked" extends the imagery of "My Heart, Being Hungry" to suggest that "He that would eat of love must eat it where it hangs," and that nothing tangible can be taken away forever. "The Concert" extends the internal monologue of the sewing girl, this time a new departure from rather than toward life and love. "Hyacinth," however, is something new and wonderfully strange:

> I am in love with him to whom a hyacinth is dearer
> Then I shall ever be dear.
> On nights when the field-mice are abroad he cannot sleep:
> He hears their narrow teeth at the bulbs of his hyacinths.
> But the gnawing at my heart he does not hear.

This gnawing at the heart is at least a real emotion, while in "Spring Song" a modern nothingness has replaced the reawakening season. The refrains suggest that modern life has driven out spring with its "Come, move on!" and "No parking here!" The poem ends:

> Anyhow, it's nothing to me.
> I can remember, and so can you.
> (Though we'd better watch out for you-know-who,
> When we sit around remembering Spring).
> We shall hardly notice in a year or two.
> You can get accustomed to anything.

Part IV, the most conventional, is made up of twenty-two unrelated sonnets. These are rather academic in theme and tone, containing as they do echoes of

Elizabeth Barrett Browning and John Keats. The first and last illustrate this point, though there are many sonnets in between which point to Miss Millay's individuality. In the first she prophetically reveals the sadness of life after the loss of a beloved. In the last she celebrates the glimpse of sheer beauty that was Euclid's in the "blinding hour" when he had his vision

Of light anatomized. Euclid alone

Has looked on beauty bare. Fortunate they
Who, though once only and then but far away,
Have heard her massive sandal set on stone.

The Harp-Weaver presents a poet with vision unclouded by the didacticism which mars some of her later work, for these poems vibrate with an inner fervor that needs no relationship to the political or social scene.

HAVELOK THE DANE

Type of work: Poem
Author: Unknown
Type of plot: Adventure romance
Time of plot: Tenth century
Locale: England and Denmark
First transcribed: c. 1350

Principal characters:
HAVELOK, a prince
GODARD, his guardian
GOLDEBORU, a princess
GODRICH, her guardian
GRIM, a fisherman

Critique:

Medieval romances in general follow a pattern, and *Havelok* is no exception. The hero is noble, brave, and pure; the heroine is noble, beautiful, and pure. There is a convenient supernatural element which helps along the plot. Virtue is rewarded and villainy is punished. *Havelok,* in spite of its adherence to the formula, is one of the more interesting of the romances to read, for it is reasonably concise and coherent. Its spirit of adventure hardly ever flags, and the plot is complicated enough to produce some feeling of suspense.

The Story:

Athelwold was a good king. No one dared offer him a bribe, and throughout all England people were at peace. He was a particular guardian to widows, children, and innocent maidens. A messenger might go peacefully from town to town with a hundred pounds of gold in a sack. Athelwold's only heir was a young daughter, still a baby.

When Athelwold knew that his death was upon him, he prayed for guidance and then summoned his earls and barons to his side. There was loud lamenting at the approaching end of their honored king. But Athelwold's chief concern was for his daughter's care. It was decided that Godrich, Earl of Cornwall, would be the most trustworthy to bring up the princess. Godrich swore a great oath to safeguard the infant Goldeboru and to hold her lands in trust until she could reign.

But Godrich watched the growing girl with envious eyes. She was fair to look upon, and Godrich could not bear to think of the day when she would be his sovereign. Acting then the part of a traitor, he took her secretly from Winchester to Dover and placed her in a remote castle. To guard the entrance he set his most trusted thanes with orders to let no one in to see the princess.

In Denmark, King Birkabeyn lay near death. He had reigned long and wisely, but he was leaving his son Havelok and his two little daughters without protection. He thought of his faithful friend, Godard, a rich man who was the most respected noble in the kingdom. Godard swore a great oath to guard the children well and to see that Havelok came into his inheritance when he became a man. After being shriven, Birkabeyn died content.

Godard was also a false-hearted traitor. On the seashore he cruelly slit the throats of the two tiny girls and then seized Havelok. The boy, terrified at what he had been forced to witness, begged for mercy. Instead of killing Havelok straightway, Godard called for Grim, a fisherman, and commanded him to bind the prince and cast him into the sea with an anchor around his neck. Anxious to please his lord, Grim seized the boy and bound him tightly. Then he took him home to wait for night.

As Havelok dozed on the rude bed in the fisherman's hut, a great light shone from his mouth. Grim's wife was frightened and called her husband. Grim, awed, freed Havelok from his bonds. Bundling his wife, his five children, and Havelok aboard his fishing boat, he set sail for England. The group went up the Humber to land in a likely cove. Since then the place has been called Grimsby.

For twelve years Havelok grew rapidly. He was an active boy and a prodigious eater. Luckily, Grim was a good fisherman, and he could trade his catches at the market in Lincoln. Corn and meat could be bought there, and ropes for the nets. Havelok, who helped Grim in all his labors was especially good at peddling fish.

A great famine came upon the north of England. The crops withered and the fish fled English shores. Day after day Grim's family became poorer. Havelok, touched by the suffering of his foster family, resolved to seek his fortune in Lincoln. Although he could ill spare it, Grim cut a cloak from new sailcloth for Havelok and wished him well. The prince set out for town with his new cloak, but he had neither shoes nor hose.

In the town Havelok starved for three days. No one would hire him and he could find no food. At length he heard a cry for porters. Looking quickly around, he saw the earl's cook with a catch of fish to carry. In his eagerness Havelok knocked down eight or nine other porters to get to the cook first. Strong as a bull, the youth carried the fish to the castle. The next day the cook cried again for a porter, and this time Havelok carried a huge load of meat.

In the castleyard the cook greatly admired the strong fellow. He gave Havelok bread and meat, as much as he could hold, and engaged him as a steady helper. Eating regularly and working hard, Havelok became widely known for his strength. On a certain feast day the retainers held a stone-putting contest. A group of men brought in a stone so huge one man could barely lift it. Havelok easily heaved it many yards.

Godrich, hearing of Havelok's fame, decided to use the youth in his scheme to gain control of the kingdom. Thinking him only a churl, Godrich had Goldeboru brought from Dover and ordered Havelok to marry her. Both young people objected, but Godrich had his way.

Havelok took his sorrowing bride back to Grim's cottage. That night the groom slept soundly but the bride stayed wakeful from shame at being mated to a churl. All at once a light issued from Havelok's mouth and a voice told Goldeboru of her husband's birth and destiny. Awaking Havelok, she advised him to go at once to Denmark to claim his throne.

In the morning Havelok persuaded the three Grim brothers to go with him on the trip to Denmark. Arriving in that land, the impoverished group met Ubbe, a noble who bought a ring from Havelok. Ubbe, greatly taken with Havelok and his beautiful bride, offered them a cottage for the night. The couple accepted gratefully, and soon were asleep after their long voyage.

In the night a band of robbers tried to break in after overpowering the guard set by Ubbe. When Havelok awoke, he set about him valiantly. He seized the door bar and slew robbers right and left. This feat won him more admiration. Ubbe assigned the young couple to a rich bower for the rest of the night. When Ubbe stole in for a look at his guests, he was astonished to see a light streaming from Havelok's mouth and a cross marked on his shoulder. By these signs he knew that Havelok was Birkabeyn's son and heir to the Danish throne.

Calling all the barons of Denmark together, Ubbe dubbed Havelok a knight and proclaimed him king. The assembled nobles passed judgment on Godard, the traitor, who was brought before Havelok, flayed, and hanged on a gallows with a great nail through his feet.

Now master of Denmark, Havelok sailed with a strong force to England to seize that kingdom from Godrich. The battle was joined near Lincoln. Although Godrich fought valiantly and wounded Ubbe, he was finally captured by the wrathful Danes. The false Earl of Cornwall, bound hand and foot, was brought before Havelok for judgment. Godrich was put upon an ass and taken into Lincoln, where his crime was proclaimed.

Then he was taken to a nearby green and burned to death.

Havelok married one of Grim's daughters to the cook who had befriended him and made the man Earl of Cornwall.

Grim's other daughter was married to the Earl of Chester. As for Havelok and Goldeboru, they lived together long and ruled wisely. Their union was blessed with fifteen children.

Further Critical Evaluation of the Work:

Unlike many medieval romances, whose locale is some legendary land completely unanchored to the real world, *Havelok the Dane* seems to take place in a geographical area, marked by association to Lincolnshire and the town of Grimsby. A town seal with the names "Grym," "Habloc," and "Goldeburgh," the story's three main protagonists, still exists. Although other attempts to tie down its historical validity have failed, *Havelok the Dane* may well be based upon popular local events.

Its author, although anonymous, seems to have been a conscientious middle-class writer concerned with down-to-earth matters such as justice, the value of hard work, and a man's being true to himself. The author's description of King Athelwold stresses, before prowess in battle, the ruler's integrity, fairness and concern for the weak. Athelwold, like Havelok, relates to the poor and underprivileged.

In contrast, the villains Godard and Godrich seem darker and totally consumed with evil. There is nothing to relieve their wickedness except Godard's relenting enough not to kill Havelok outright; instead, he commands the fisherman Grim to throw him into the sea after having tied an anchor around his neck.

The Latin subtitle of *Havelok the Dane* which states "Here begins the life of Havelok once king of England and Denmark" shows that the author, if not his audience, realized their half-Danish heritage. Though we have nothing to prove this, perhaps the tale arose out of some actual political situation.

Notwithstanding its geographical place-names and subtitle, however, the story is a typical wish fulfillment depicting the disguised, mistreated hero of royal birth who finds his true status, regains his kingdom, and gets the princess. *Havelok the Dane* has a double plot of this nature because Goldeboru, the maiden, also undergoes mistreatment and must regain her royal status before they marry and become King and Queen of Denmark and England.

The author has composed no knightly romance with trappings of rich armor and vestments; Havelok is a middle-class folk hero who fights with a door bar, takes part in a stone-heaving contest, spends most of his time as a steady cook's helper, and, when victorious, dispenses land and women as rewards.

Havelok the Dane is a very English medieval romance, tied to the land and common folk, and told with the rugged gusto of *Beowulf*.

A HAZARD OF NEW FORTUNES

Type of work: Novel
Author: William Dean Howells (1837-1920)
Type of plot: Novel of manners
Time of plot: The 1880's
Locale: New York City
First published: 1890

Principal characters:
BASIL MARCH, editor of a literary magazine
MR. FULKERSON, sponsor for the magazine
CONRAD DRYFOOS, publisher of the magazine
MR. DRYFOOS, Conrad's father, a newly rich millionaire
HENRY LINDAU, a socialist

Critique:

Although the structure of this novel is unwieldy and complex, many lovers of Howells' fiction consider it their favorite, perhaps because of the author's deft characterization of a number of varied personalities, more than one usually finds in a Howells novel. Howells, like Basil March in the novel, moved to New York City after a residence of many years in New England, and this novel is the result of that move and the new experiences it brought to Howells, both as a person and as a novelist. In *A Hazard of New Fortunes,* perhaps more than anywhere else in Howells' fiction, the author's own dissatisfaction with America and his interest in social improvement are to be found. In the preface to a later edition of the book, Howells expressed the belief that he had written it when he was at the apex of his powers as a novelist.

The Story:

In his youth Basil March had wished for a literary career. Family responsibilities turned him, however, to the insurance business, a field in which he proved to himself and his employers that he was but mediocre. After eighteen years with his firm, his employers decided to replace him and put him into a somewhat meaningless position. Rather than be so embarrassed, March resigned. Fortunately for him and his family's future, Mr. Fulkerson, a promoter of syndicated newspaper material, who had met the Marches years before, proposed that March take over the editorship of a new literary magazine that he was promoting. March at first demurred at Fulkerson's proposal, but the promoter, certain that March had the necessary taste and tact to be successful, finally persuaded him to take the position.

Mrs. March and their children had always lived in Boston, and so when the prospect of moving to New York City appeared, even though it meant a career for the husband and father, they needed considerable persuasion. At last Mrs. March was convinced that the removal to the larger city was imperative. She and her husband went to New York to find a flat in which they could make themselves comfortable. After many days of searching, Mrs. March returned to Boston, leaving her husband to make a decision about the editorship. He did so a short time later.

March's problems in connection with a staff did not prove as difficult as he had imagined. Fulkerson, the promoter, had engaged an artist, Angus Beaton, to serve as art director, procured a cover sketch for the first issue, and made all the financial arrangements with the magazine's backer, Mr. Dryfoos, who had recently made a fortune for himself through the control of natural gas holdings. Mr. Dryfoos, who was trying to win his son away from a career as a minister, had undertaken to finance the magazine in order to give his son Conrad a chance to enter business as the ostensible publisher of the periodical. Foreign articles and reviews were to be handled by an old German socialist, Henry Lindau, who had been March's tutor and whom the younger man had met accidentally in New York.

Despite March's fear and lack of confidence, the new magazine, *Every Other Week,* was a success from the very first issue; both the illustrations and the material caught the public fancy. On the periphery of the activities concerning the magazine, however, there were many complications. The Dryfoos family, who had been simple farm folk, wanted to be taken into society; at least the two daughters wanted to enter society. In addition, Christine, the older daughter, fell in love with the art editor, who was not in love with her. Fulkerson, the promoter, had also fallen in love. He was busy paying court to a southern girl who boarded at the same house he did, and the girl's father, a Virginia colonel, was after Fulkerson to have the magazine print at least a portion of his great work extolling the merits of slavery.

Because the magazine had been a success, Fulkerson suggested that for publicity purposes they should give a dinner party for members of the staff and the press. Mr. Dryfoos, who was asked to pay the bill for the proposed affair, vetoed the idea, but he agreed to have a small dinner party at his home for several of the men connected with the magazine. Among the guests was Henry Lindau, who had struck the millionaire's fancy because he had lost a hand fighting in the Civil War. Dryfoos did not realize that Mr. Lindau, who was doing the foreign language work for the magazine, was a socialist. At the dinner party the personalities and the principles of the men clashed openly. The next day the millionaire told Basil March bluntly that the old man was to be fired. March wished to stick by the old German socialist, but Mr. Lindau forced the issue by refusing to do any more work for the capitalistic owner of the magazine.

Another crisis occurred a short time later when Mr. Dryfoos and his son, who hated being a businessman rather than a minister, had an open clash of wills. The situation became so acute that the father, calling one day when his son was alone in the office, struck the young man in the face. Outside the office, the father also had trouble with his daughter, Christine, for he had forbidden his house to the art editor of the magazine, with whom she was in love.

At that time there was a streetcar strike in New York City. Young Conrad Dryfoos was very much in sympathy with the strikers, many of whom he knew as a result of his church work among the poor and sick of the city. At the instigation of a young woman whom he loved, he went out upon the streets to try to bring peace among the rioting strikers and the police. He saw Mr. Lindau, the aged, one-armed socialist, being beaten by a policeman; when he ran to interfere, he was struck by a stray bullet and was killed.

Mr. Dryfoos was heartbroken at the loss of his son, particularly because he felt that he had mistreated the young man. When he learned that his son had died trying to save Mr. Lindau from the policeman's club, he decided to accept the old man as a friend and to take care of him for the rest of his life. The decision came too late, however, for the old man died as a result of the beating he had received. In a last effort to show his change of heart, Mr. Dryfoos had Mr. Lindau's funeral conducted in his own home.

Still wishing to try to make his family happy, Mr. Dryfoos then swallowed his pride and went to see Angus Beaton, the artist. Confessing that he was sorry to have caused the young people unhappiness, he invited Beaton to resume his calls on Christine. The young man eventually pocketed his pride and called, but in spite of her love for him Christine rejected his suit forcibly and scratched his face.

A few days later, Mr. Dryfoos resolved to take his wife and daughters to Europe. Before he left, he went to the offices of the magazine, where everyone had been wondering what the fate of the publication would be and whether Conrad Dryfoos' death had destroyed his father's interest in the periodical. Mr. Dryfoos magnanimously consented to sell the periodical to Fulkerson and March at a low figure and with very low interest on the money they needed in order to purchase it. Both March and Fulkerson were extremely happy about the turn of events. March saw his future secure at last, and he also saw that he would have a free hand in shaping the editorial policy. Fulkerson was happy because he too foresaw a prosperous future. As the result of his expectations, he was able to marry and settle down.

Some months afterward they learned that the Dryfoos family had been taken up promptly by at least a portion of Parisian society. Christine Dryfoos had even become engaged to a penniless but proud French nobleman.

Further Critical Evaluation of the Work:

The plot of *A Hazard of New Fortunes* is strikingly autobiographical; the various events reflect Howells' hazarding of his own fortunes in leaving his literary domain in Boston for New York City and the editor's chair at *Harper's Magazine.* It was an astute move, for the literary center of America seemed to follow him.

The protagonists of this novel are also autobiographical. Featured in Howells' first novel, *Their Wedding Journey* (1872), which parallels the Howells' own honeymoon, Basil and Isabel March are also central to several of Howells' works of the 1890's. In *A Hazard of New Fortunes* they mature noticeably and develop a sense of the complicity of all men in one another's affairs. But learning this lesson took Howells himself beyond the comfortable surface of American life and exposed him to social and economic problems that aroused his concern but with which he was temperamentally unable to deal. Mr. Dryfoos' attempt to make amends after the death of his son reads like the end of *A Christmas Carol.* However, the labor unrest that indirectly caused Conrad's death calls for more than the redemption of a Scrooge. Naturalists such as Dreiser and Norris were to provide the fiction that would bring such social forces into focus.

Howells after *A Hazard of New Fortunes* is, therefore, a changed man. While he struggled with a new range of experience, the school of literary realism he had developed and propounded as editor and novelist proved inadequate for dealing with the more grim aspects of real life in America. Howells' succeeding novels reveal a new pensiveness, tentativeness, and diminished self-assurance. While no abrupt transition can be noted, experimentation with new literary forms in the utopian Altrurian romances, psychological symbolism in *The Shadow of a Dream,* manipulation of point of view in *The Landlord at Lion's Head,* all point to a diminishing confidence in the capacity of literary realism, and in Howells himself, to render into fiction the increasingly complex reality of American life.

HEADLONG HALL

Type of work: Novel
Author: Thomas Love Peacock (1785-1866)
Type of plot: Comedy of manners
Time of plot: Early nineteenth century
Locale: Wales
First published: 1816

Principal characters:
SQUIRE HEADLONG, the host
MR. FOSTER, the optimist
MR. ESCOT, the pessimist
MR. JENKISON, champion of the status quo

Critique:

Headlong Hall is a novel of talk, a satire on the pseudo-philosophers of the nineteenth century. There is virtually no plot and no character development. In fact, the characters seem to be merely abstract personages uttering pat phrases assigned to them by the author. But beneath the surface there is always keen awareness of the ridiculous in human behavior, dramatically presented by a writer who was intellectually wise enough to be tolerant of society's weaknesses.

The Story:

Squire Harry Headlong differed from the usual Welsh squire in that he, by some means or other, had become interested in books, in addition to the common interests of hunting, racing, and drinking. He had journeyed to Oxford and then to London in order to find the philosophers and men of refined tastes introduced to him in the world of literature. Having rounded up a group of intellectuals, he invited them to Headlong Hall for the Christmas holidays.

Three of the men formed the nucleus of his house party. The first was Mr. Foster, an optimist. To him everything was working toward a state of perfection, and each advancement in technology, in government, or in sociology was all for the good. He believed that man would ultimately achieve perfection as a result of his progress. Mr. Escot, on the other hand, saw nothing but deterioration in the world. The advances which Mr. Foster saw as improvement, Escot saw

as evidences of corruption and evil which would soon reduce the whole human race to wretchedness and slavery. The third man of the trio was Mr. Jenkison, who took a position exactly in the middle. He believed that the amount of improvement and deterioration balanced each other perfectly and that good and evil would remain forever in status quo.

These pholisophers, with a large company of other dilettantes, descended upon Headlong Hall. Among the lesser guests was a landscape gardener who made it his sole duty to persuade the squire to have his estate changed from a wild tangle of trees and shrubs into a shaved and polished bed of green grass. Mr. Foster thought the grounds could be improved; Mr. Escot thought any change would be for the worse, and Mr. Jenkison thought the scenery perfect as it was.

There were ladies present, both young and old, but they did not join in the philosophical discussions. Many of the talks occurred after the ladies had left the dinner table and as the wine was being liberally poured, for Squire Headlong was aware that the mellowness produced by good burgundy was an incentive to conversation. The discussions took various turns, all of them dominated by the diametrically opposed views of Foster and Escot and soothed by the healing words of Jenkison. Escot harped constantly upon the happiness and moral virtue possessed by the savages of the past, virtue which lessened with each encroachment of civilization. As the savage began to build villages and cities and to develop luxuries, he began also to suffer disease, poverty, oppression, and loss of morality. With this thesis Foster could not agree. He pointed to the achievements of civilization in fields other than those of a materialistic nature. Shakespeare and Milton, for example, could not have achieved their genius in the primitive life Escot applauded. Escot, refusing to concede an inch, pointed to Milton's suffering, stating also that even if one man did profit from the so-called advancements, fifty men regressed because of them. Mr. Jenkison agreed that the subject left something to be said on either side.

Between these learned discussions the gentlemen spent their time in attempts to fascinate the ladies. Escot had once been the suitor of one of the guests, but he had offended her father during an intellectual discussion and had fallen out of favor. He attempted now to regain his former place in her affection by humoring the father. During these periods of respite, the guests also entertained one another with singing and recitations, the selections being those they themselves had composed.

The squire, planning a magnificent ball, invited the whole neighborhood to be his guests. At the ball the wine flowed freely, so that even Foster and Escot forgot some of their differences. Escot, although he disapproved of any but aboriginal dances, danced often with the lady of his choice. Foster, of course,

thought the modern dance the utmost in refinement and an expression of the improved morality of man. Jenkison could see points both for and against the custom. During the evening Squire Headlong was reminded by a maiden relative that should he not marry soon there would be no one to carry on the name that had been honored for many centuries. As his name implied, the squire was not one to toy with an idea once it had entered his mind. Fixing on the lady of his choice in a matter of minutes, he proposed and was accepted. Then he arranged three other matches in an equally short time. Foster and Escot were aided in choosing brides and in getting permission from the father of Escot's beloved. Foster's bride, related to the squire, presented no obstacle. Seizing on another man, the squire told him of the plan and promptly chose a bride for that hapless individual.

Within a matter of days the weddings took place. Then the guests dispersed, after promising to gather again in August. Foster and Escot tried to the last to convince each other and the rest that only one philosophy was the true one, but Mr. Jenkison was not to fall into either of their traps. He would join them again in August, still convinced that there was merit in both their arguments. Neither was right or wrong, but each balanced the other, leaving the world in its usual status quo.

Further Critical Evaluation of the Work:

Headlong Hall, Peacock's first novel, has been characterized as apprentice work because his later exercises in the genre are even more successful. However, there is no awkwardness or hesitancy in this pioneer work; the later novels differ from it only in offering a richer variety of conversation and slightly more complex plots.

Plot is the least requisite element in a Peacock novel, and the author is inclined to mock even the minimal necessities of story-telling that he acknowledges. Chapter XIV of *Headlong Hall,* in which four marriages are clapped up in as many pages, is a reduction to absurdity of the propensity of popular novelists in his day to pair off their *dramatis personae* in the concluding chapters.

Characterization is not much more important to Peacock. What he provides instead is a group of quirky mouthpieces for different points of view, combined with caricatures, seldom malicious, of his associates. Aspects of his friend Shelley are caricatured in at least three of the novels (Foster is the Shelleyan figure in this one), and Shelley was highly amused by each portrayal. Peacock's wit, though sharp, is seldom wounding, and it touches virtually everywhere with a fine impartiality. He was delighted to learn of his readers' difficulty in ascertaining which, if any, of the opinions so entertainingly advanced in his novels he shared.

Opinions, or more precisely, the absurdity and pretentiousness with which people advance them and the gap between their propositions and their behavior, are the real subject of all the novels. Literary historians, noting the customary setting for Peacock's gatherings of indefatigable talkers, have called him the father of the "country house novel." His progeny have been numerous and often brilliant, including such dazzling performances as Douglas' *South Wind* and Huxley's *Crome Yellow,* but none has surpassed its progenitor in wit and geniality.

THE HEART IS A LONELY HUNTER

Type of work: Novel
Author: Carson McCullers (1917-1967)
Type of plot: Psychological realism
Time of plot: The 1930's
Locale: A Georgia mill town
First published: 1940

Principal characters:
MR. SINGER, a mute
MICK KELLY, an adolescent girl
BIFF BRANNON, a café proprietor
JAKE BLOUNT, a frustrated, idealistic workingman
DR. COPELAND, a Negro physician

Critique:

To read *The Heart Is a Lonely Hunter* as a novel of social criticism is to misinterpret the subtle yet precise art of Carson McCullers. Her true theme in this remarkable first novel is that sense of moral isolation, expressed in terms of loneliness and longing, which is both the social evil of the modern world and the inescapable condition of man. Four different but related stories illuminate Mrs. McCullers' theme through the experiences of Mick Kelly, Biff Brannon, Jake Blount, and Dr. Copeland. These people are drawn to Mr. Singer, the mute, because his physical infirmity seems to set him apart in the same way that their own sense of separation from the social community makes their lives incomplete. Mrs. McCullers was one of the most distinguished among our recent novelists, a writer whose fiction has both substance and significance.

The Story:

In a small town in the South there were two mutes, one a grossly fat Greek, the other a tall, immaculate man named Mr. Singer. They had no friends, and they lived together for ten years. After a lingering sickness the Greek became a changed man. When he began to be obscene in public, the cousin for whom he worked sent him to the state insane asylum. After that Mr. Singer was desolate.

He took all his meals at the New York Café owned by Biff Brannon. Biff was a stolid man with a weakness for cripples and sick people. When Jake Blount, a squat man with long, powerful arms, came to town, he went on a week-long drunk at Biff's expense. Biff had to find out what bothered Jake. Finding Mr. Singer eating at the café, Jake decided that he was the only person who could understand the message he was trying to give. One night Mr. Singer took Jake home with him. It was not until after he had slept that Jake realized Mr. Singer was a mute. He still felt, however, that the mute could understand him.

Mr. Singer had taken a room at the Kellys' boarding-house, where the daughter Mick, just entering her teens, was a gangly girl, always dressed in shorts, a shirt, and tennis shoes. She loved music and would go anywhere to hear it. Some nights she went to a big house in town where she could hear symphonic music through the open windows while she crouched in the shrubbery. At home no one realized what she wanted, until Mr. Singer moved there and let her talk to him when she was lonely.

Mick decided, after entering Vocational School, that she had to have some friends. Planning a dance, she invited only high school students. The house was decorated with tinsel. Mick borrowed an evening dress and high-heeled shoes from one of her sisters.

On the night of the party a throng of children arrived and separated into noisy groups. When Mick handed out the prom cards, the boys went to one side of the room, the girls to the other. Silence descended. No one knew how to start things. A boy finally asked Mick to prom with him. Outside the house all the neighborhood children had gathered. While Mick and Harry walked around the block, the neighborhood children joined the party. By the time Mick got back, the decorations were torn, the refreshments gone, and the invited and the uninvited guests mixed up so badly that the party was bedlam. Everyone congregated on the street to run races and jump ditches, the partygoers forgetful of their nearly-grown-up state. Mick finally called off the party after she had been knocked breathless on a jump she could have made easily in her tennis shoes.

Portia worked for the Kellys. Her father was Dr. Copeland, the only colored doctor in town. He was an idealistic man who had always worked hard to raise the standards of the Negro people. One dark night Mr. Singer had stepped up and helped him light a cigarette in the rain. It was the first time a white man had ever offered him help or smiled at him. When he told Portia about a deaf-mute boy patient of his, she assured him that Mr. Singer would help him.

Jake, who had found a job with a flying-jenny show, tried to rouse the workers. He spent each Sunday with Mr. Singer, explaining that he had first wanted to be an evangelist until he had been made aware of the inequality in the world. He had unintentionally insulted Dr. Copeland twice, but he was one of the first to talk about doing something for Willie, Dr. Copeland's son.

Willie had been sentenced to hard labor for knifing a man. At the prison camp he and two others tried to run away. They were put in a cold shack for three days with their bare feet hoisted up by a looped rope. Willie lost both feet from gangrene. Dr. Copeland, trying to see the judge about the case, was severely beaten up by a white crowd around the court house and put in jail. Mr. Singer and Portia obtained his release on bail, and Jake went with Mr. Singer to Dr. Copeland's house. There he argued the ethics of the case with the doctor all night, Jake too hysterical to be logical, the doctor too sick.

There was a peacefulness in Mr. Singer's face that attracted Mick. She followed him whenever she could. He bought a radio which he kept in his room for her to listen to. Those were hours of deep enjoyment for her. She felt that she had music in her that she would have to learn to write down.

She fascinated Biff. After his wife died, he watched Mick begin to grow up, but he seldom spoke to her. He was equally quiet with Mr. Singer when he visited at the Kelly boarding-house. Mr. Singer considered Mick pitiful, Jake crazy, Dr. Copeland noble, and Biff thoughtful; but they were always welcome to his room.

On his vacation Mr. Singer went to see his Greek friend. He took beautiful presents along with him, but the Greek was petulant over anything but food. Only there did Mr. Singer take his hands out of his pockets; then he wore himself out trying to tell the Greek with his hands everything he had seen and thought since the Greek went away. Although the Greek showed no interest, Mr. Singer tried even harder to entertain him. When he left, the Greek was still impassive.

Mr. Singer's board was the only steady money the Kellys could depend on. When one sister got sick, the loss of her salary threw the whole family in a quandary. Mick heard that a job was opening at the five-and-ten-cent store. The family in conclave decided she was too young to work. The fact that for the first time they were talking about her welfare prompted her to apply for the job. She got it, but each night she was too tired for anything but sleep.

It was again time for Mr. Singer to go to see his Greek friend. Laden down with presents, he made the long trip. When he reached the asylum office, the clerk told him the Greek was dead. Stricken, he found his way back to the town, left his luggage at the station, went to his room, and put a bullet through his chest.

Mr. Singer's death left his four friends confused. Dr. Copeland, still sick, brooded over it.

Jake Blount joined in a free-for-all at the flying-jenny grounds and, after hearing that the police were looking for him, left town.

Mick did not sleep well for weeks after the funeral. All that she had left was Mr. Singer's radio. She felt cheated because there was no time, no money, no feeling anymore for music, but she could never decide who had cheated her.

And Biff, who had watched Mr. Singer with Jake and Mick, was still puzzling over the relationships he had studied. He wondered whether, in the struggle of humanity, love might be the answer.

Further Critical Evaluation of the Work:

All of Carson McCuller's writing turns on the plight of the loving and the lonely, and it is this view of moral and spiritual isolation as the inescapable condition of man that makes *The Heart Is a Lonely Hunter* so impressive as a first novel. Although the book shows certain limitations resulting from the author's youth and inexperience, it nevertheless remains a remarkable work for a twenty-two-year-old to write. To read it as a novel of social criticism is to misunderstand the author's subtle art. One character is a fiery white radical and another is a fanatic black Marxist, but their political views are subordinate to the dominant theme of the novel: the loneliness of the individual and the frustrated struggle to communicate with others. Singer, the ironically named mute, is the focal figure in the story. It is to him that the other main characters turn when they wish to unburden themselves, to pour out their views, their ideas, their emotions.

It is ironic that Singer should be the one toward whom the others turn to release the tension and some of the confusion within them, since Singer hears nothing and is really the loneliest person in the story after the removal of his insane mute friend Antonapoulos to the asylum. With the death of Antonapoulos, Singer has no one to turn to and he shoots himself, while the others, who have given him nothing, continue their own self-centered lives.

Love and hatred struggle for mastery in McCuller's characters. Jake Blount, itinerant carnival worker, seethes with anger at the injustices which the common man endures in a capitalistic society that permits the rich to prey upon the poor. Dr. Copeland rages also against the inequities of capitalism, but he concentrates his hatred upon the whites who have for so long oppressed his race. Dr. Copeland's intemperance of thought and feeling brings him into conflict both with his family and with Blount, whose own intemperance makes a successful dialogue between himself and Copeland impossible despite their common anger at the political and economic system in which they live.

Mick Kelly is experiencing the pains of adolescence, suffering from self-consciousness, beset by the confusions which accompany her developing sexuality, indulging in dreams of the future—a future that will be frustrated forever by the economic situation of her family, and finally embittered by the realization that her Woolworth's job means doom to her hopes.

Biff Brannon, who keeps his café open at night as a haven for lonely people, seeks an understanding of those who come in not only to eat and drink but to talk. They are objects for his study, but they also help him to forget the loneliness he feels when they have gone. He is the last person one sees in the novel—alone, frightened, and awaiting the sun of a new day that will bring customers through the café door.

HEART OF DARKNESS

Type of work: Short story
Author: Joseph Conrad (Józef Teodor Konrad Korzeniowski, 1857-1924)
Type of plot: Symbolic romance
Time of plot: Late nineteenth century
Locale: The Belgian Congo
First published: 1902

Principal characters:
MARLOW, the narrator
MR. KURTZ, manager of the Inner Station, Belgian Congo
THE DISTRICT MANAGER
A RUSSIAN TRAVELER
KURTZ'S FIANCÉE

Critique:

In one sense, *Heart of Darkness* is a compelling adventure tale of a journey into the blackest heart of the Belgian Congo. The story presents attacks by the natives, descriptions of the jungle and the river, and characterizations of white men who, sometimes with ideals and sometimes simply for profit, invade the jungles to bring out ivory. But the journey into the heart of the Congo is also a symbolic journey into the blackness central to the heart and soul of man, a journey deep into primeval passion, superstition, and lust. Those who, like the district manager, undertake this journey simply to rob the natives of ivory, without any awareness of the importance of the central darkness, can survive. Similarly, Marlow, who is only an observer, never centrally involved, can survive to tell the tale. But those who, like Mr. Kurtz, are aware of the darkness, who hope with conscious intelligence and a humane concern for all mankind to bring light into the darkness, are doomed, are themselves swallowed up by the darkness and evil they had hoped to penetrate. Conrad manages to make his point, a realization of the evil at the center of human experience, without ever breaking the closely knit pattern of his narrative or losing the compelling atmospheric and psychological force of the tale. The wealth of natural symbols, the clear development of character, and the sheer fascination of the story make this a short story that has been frequently praised and frequently read ever since its publication in 1902. *Heart of Darkness* is, in both style and insight, a masterful short story.

The Story:

A group of men were sitting on the deck of the cruising yawl, *The Nellie,* anchored one calm evening in the Thames estuary. One of the seamen, Marlow, began reflecting that the Thames area had been, at the time of the invading Romans, one of the dark and barbarous areas of the earth. Dwelling on this theme, he then began to tell a story of the blackest, most barbarous area of the earth that he had experienced.

Through his aunt's connections, Marlow had once secured a billet as commander of a river steamer for one of the trading companies with interests in the Belgian Congo. When he went to Belgium to learn more about the job, he found that few of the officials of the company expected him to return alive. In Brussels he also heard of the distinguished Mr. Kurtz, the powerful and intelligent man who was educating the natives and at the same time sending back record shipments of ivory. The mysterious figure of Mr. Kurtz fascinated Marlow. In spite of the ominous hints that he gathered from various company officials, he became more and more curious about what awaited him in the Congo. During his journey, as he passed along the African coast, he reflected that the wilderness and the unknown seemed to seep right out to the sea. Many of the trading posts and stations the ship passed were dilapidated and looked barbaric. Finally, Marlow arrived at the seat of the government at the mouth of the river. Again, he heard of the great distinction and power of Mr. Kurtz who had, because of his plans to enlighten the natives and his success in gaining their confidence, an enormous reputation. Marlow also saw natives working in the hot sun until they collapsed and died. Marlow had to wait for ten impatient days at the government site because his work would not begin until he reached the district manager's station, two hundred miles up the river. At last the expedition left for the district station.

Marlow arrived at the district station to find that the river steamer had sunk a few days earlier. He met the district manager, a man whose only ability seemed to be the ability to survive. The district manager, unconcerned with the fate of the natives, was interested only in getting out of the country; he felt that Mr. Kurtz's new methods were ruining the whole district. The district manager reported also that he had not heard from Kurtz for quite some time, but had received disquieting rumors about his being ill.

Although he was handicapped by a lack of rivets, Marlow spent months supervising repairs to the antiquated river steamer. He also overheard a conversation which revealed that the district manager was Kurtz's implacable enemy, who hoped that the climate would do away with his rival.

The steamer was finally ready for use, and Marlow, along with the district manager, sailed to visit Kurtz at the inner station far up the river. The journey was difficult and perilous; the water was shallow; there were frequent fogs. Just as they arrived within a few miles of Kurtz's station, natives attacked the vessel

with spears and arrows. Marlow's helmsman, a faithful native, was killed by a long spear when he leaned from his window to fire at the savages. Marlow finally blew the steamboat whistle and the sound frightened the natives away. The district manager was sure that Kurtz had lost control over the blacks. When they docked, they met an enthusiastic Russian traveler who told them that Kurtz was gravely ill.

While the district manager visited Kurtz, the Russian told Marlow that the sick man had become corrupted by the very natives he had hoped to enlighten. He still had power over the natives, but instead of his changing them, they had debased him into an atavistic savage. Kurtz attended native rituals, had killed frequently in order to get ivory, and had hung heads as decorations outside his hut. Later Marlow met Kurtz and found that the man had, indeed, been corrupted by the evil at the center of experience. Marlow learned, from the Russian, that Kurtz had ordered the natives to attack the steamer, thinking that, if they did so, the white men would run away and leave Kurtz to die among his fellow savages in the wilderness. Talking to Marlow, Kurtz showed his awareness of how uncivilized he had become, how his plans to educate the natives had been reversed. He gave Marlow a packet of letters for his fiancée in Belgium and the manuscript of an article, written sometime earlier, in which he urged efforts to educate the natives.

The district manager and Marlow took Kurtz, now on a stretcher, to the river steamer to take him back home. The district manager contended that the area was now ruined for collecting ivory. Kurtz, full of despair and the realization that devouring evil was at the heart of everything, died while the steamer was temporarily stopped for repairs.

Marlow returned to civilization and, about a year later, went to Belgium to see Kurtz's fiancée. She still thought of Kurtz as the splendid and powerful man who had gone to Africa with a mission, and she still believed in his goodness and power. When she asked Marlow what Kurtz's last words had been, Marlow lied and told her that Kurtz had asked for her at the end. In reality, Kurtz, who had seen all experience, had in his final words testified to the horror of it all. This horror was not something, Marlow felt, that civilized ladies could, or should, understand.

Further Critical Evaluation of the Work:

Christened Teodor Jósef Konrad Nalecz Korzeniowski by his Polish parents, Joseph Conrad was able to write from firsthand knowledge of the sea and sailing. Early in his life he left the cold climate of Poland to travel to the warmer regions of the Mediterranean where he became a sailor. He began reading extensively and chose the sea as a vehicle for the ideas that were forming in his psyche. He traveled a great deal: to the West Indies, Latin America, Africa. Eventually he settled in England and perfected (through the elaborate process of translating from Polish into French into English) a remarkably subtle yet powerful literary style.

Criticism of Conrad's work in general and *Heart of Darkness* in particular has been both extensive and varied. Many critics concern themselves with Conrad's style; others focus on the biographical aspects of his fiction; some see the works as social commentaries; some are students of Conrad's explorations into human psychology; many are interested in the brooding, shadowy symbolism and philosophy that hovers over all the works. It is easy to see, therefore, that Conrad is a distinctively complex literary genius. E. M. Forster censured him as a vague and elusive writer who never quite clearly discloses the philosophy that lies behind his tales. Such a censure ignores Conrad's notion about the way some fiction can be handled. Partly as Conrad's mouthpiece, the narrator of *Heart of Darkness* states in the first few pages of the novel:

> The yarns of seamen have a direct simplicity, the whole meaning of which lies within the shell of a cracked nut. But Marlow was not typical (if his propensity to spin yarns be excepted), and to him the meaning of an episode was not inside like a kernel but outside, enveloping the tale which brought it out only as a glow brings out a haze, in the likeness of one of those misty halos that sometimes are made visible by the spectral illumination of moonshine.

The mention of the narrator brings up one of the most complex and intriguing features of *Heart of Darkness*: its carefully executed and elaborately conceived point of view. For one can detect (if careful in his reading) that the novel is in truth two narratives, inexorably woven together by Conrad's masterful craftsmanship. The outer frame of the story—the immediate setting—involves the unnamed narrator who is apparently the only one on the *Nellie* who is profoundly affected by Marlowe's tale, the inner story which is the bulk of the entire novella. Marlow narrates, and the others listen passively. The narrator's closing words show his feeling at the conclusion of Marlow's recounting of the events in the Congo:

> Marlow ceased, and sat apart, indistinct and silent, in the pose of a meditating Buddha. Nobody moved for a time. "We have lost the first of the ebb," said the Director suddenly. I raised my head. The offing was barred by a black bank of clouds, and the tranquil waterway leading to the uttermost ends of the earth flowed sombre under an overcast sky—seemed to lead into the heart of an immense darkness.

Since Marlow's narrative is a tale devoted primarily to a journey to the mysterious dark continent (the literal heart of darkness, Africa), a superficial view of the tale is simply that it is essentially an elaborate story involving confrontation with exotic natives, treacherous dangers of the jungle, brutal savagery, and even cannibalism. But such a view ignores larger meanings with which the work is implicitly concerned: namely, social and cultural implications; psychological workings of the cultivated European left to the uncivilized wilderness; and the richly colored fabric of symbolism that emerges slowly but inevitably from beneath the surface.

Heart of Darkness can also be examined for its social and cultural commentaries. It is fairly obvious that a perverted version of the "White Man's Burden" was the philosophy adopted by the ivory hunters at the Inner Station. Kurtz's "Exterminate the brutes!" shows the way a white man can exploit the helpless savage. The futile shelling from the gunboat into the jungle is also vividly portrayed as a useless, brutal, and absurd act perpetrated against a weaker, more uncivilized culture than the one that nurtured Kurtz.

Here the psychological phenomena of Marlow's tale emerge. Kurtz, a man relieved of all social and civilized restraints, goes mad after committing himself to the total pursuit of evil and depravity. And his observation "The horror! the horror!" suggests his final realization of the consequences of his life. Marlow realizes this too and is allowed (because he forces restraint upon himself) to draw back his foot from the precipice of madness. The experience leaves Marlow sober, disturbed, meditative, and obsessed with relating his story in much the same way Coleridge's Ancient Mariner must also relate his story.

On a symbolic level the story is rich; a book could easily be written on this facet of the novel. An arbitrary mention of some of the major symbols must suffice here: the Congo River that reminded Marlow early in his youth of a snake as it uncoiled its length into the darknes of Africa and furnished him with an uncontrollable "fascination of the abomination"; the symbolic journey into man's own heart of darkness revealing blindingly the evil of man's own nature and his capacity for evil; the irony of the quest when the truth is revealed not in terms of light but in terms of darkness (the truth brings not light but rather total darkness). The entire symbolic character of the work is capsuled at the end of Marlow's tale when he is forced to lie to Kurtz's intended spouse in order to preserve her illusion; the truth appears to Marlow as an inescapable darkness and the novel ends with the narrator's own observation of darkness.

Heart of Darkness is one of literature's most sombre fictions. It explores the fundamental questions about man's nature: his capacity for evil; the necessity for restraint; the effect of physical darkness and isolation on a civilized soul; and the necessity of relinquishing pride for one's own spiritual salvation. E. M. Forster's censure of Conrad may be correct in many ways, but it refuses to admit that through such philosophical ruminations Conrad has allowed generations of readers to ponder humanity's own heart of darkness.

Wayne E. Haskin

THE HEART OF MIDLOTHIAN

Type of work: Novel
Author: Sir Walter Scott (1771-1832)
Type of plot: Historical romance
Time of plot: Early eighteenth century
Locale: Scotland
First published: 1818

Principal characters:
DAVID DEANS, a dairyman
JEANIE DEANS, his daughter
EFFIE DEANS, another daughter
REUBEN BUTLER, Jeanie's betrothed
GEORDIE ROBERTSON, Effie's betrayer, in reality George Staunton
MEG MURDOCKSON, an evil woman
THE DUKE OF ARGYLE, Jeanie's benefactor

Critique:

The story of Jeanie Deans and her great effort to save her sister's life is supposedly based on fact. Fact or fiction, it is an exciting story, told as only Sir Walter Scott could tell it. *The Heart of Midlothian* is filled with suspense, mystery, and romance, and there is a happy ending. Many consider this Scott's greatest novel.

The Story:

The first knowledge Jeanie Deans had that her sister Effie was in trouble came just a few moments before officers of justice arrived at the cottage to arrest Effie for child murder. They told Jeanie and her father, David Deans, that Effie had borne a male child illegitimately and had killed him or caused him to be killed soon after he was born. Effie admitted the birth of the child but refused to name her seducer. She denied that she had killed her baby, saying that she had fallen into a stupor and had recovered to find that the midwife who attended her had disposed of the child in some fashion unknown to Effie. In the face of the evidence, however, she was convicted of child murder and sentenced to be hanged. Jeanie might have saved her sister, for it was the law that if a prospective mother had told anyone of her condition she would not be responsible for her baby's death. But Jeanie would not lie, even to save her sister's life. Since there was no one to whom Effie had told her terrible secret, there was no defense for her, and she was placed in the Tolbooth prison to await execution.

Another prisoner in the Tolbooth was Captain John Porteous, who was awaiting execution for firing into the crowd attending the hanging of Andrew Wilson, a smuggler. Wilson's accomplice, Geordie Robertson, had escaped, and the officers feared that Robertson might try to rescue Wilson. For that reason, Porteous and a company of soldiers had been sent to the scene of the execution to guard against a possible rescue. Because Porteous had fired into the crowd without provocation, killing several people, he was to be hanged. But when his execution was stayed for a few weeks, a mob headed by Robertson, disguised as a woman, broke into the prison, seized Porteous, and hanged him. For that deed Robertson became a hunted man.

Meanwhile Jeanie Deans, who had refused to lie to save her sister, had not forsaken Effie. When she visited Effie in prison, she learned that Robertson was the father of her child. He had left her in the care of old Meg Murdockson, considered by many to be a witch, and it must have been Meg who had killed or sold the baby. Meg's daughter Madge had long before been seduced by Robertson and had lost her mind for love of him, and Meg had sworn revenge on any other woman Robertson might love. But proving the old woman's guilt or Effie's innocence was not possible, for Robertson had disappeared, and Meg swore that she had seen Effie coming back from the river after drowning the baby.

Jeanie, determined to save her sister, decided to walk to London to seek a pardon from the king and queen. She told her plans to Reuben Butler, a minister to whom she had long been betrothed. Reuben had not been able to marry her, for he had no position other than that of an assistant schoolmaster and his salary was too small to support a wife. Although he objected to Jeanie's plan, he was able to aid her when he saw that she could not be swayed from her purpose. Reuben's grandfather had once aided an ancestor of the present Duke of Argyle, and Reuben gave Jeanie a letter asking the duke's help in presenting Jeanie to the king and queen.

The journey to London was a long and dangerous one. Once Jeanie was captured by Meg Murdockson, who tried to kill her so that she could not save Effie. But Jeanie escaped from the old woman and sought refuge in the home of the Rev. Mr. Staunton. There she met the minister's son, George Staunton, and learned from him that he was Geordie Robertson, the betrayer of her sister. He admitted his responsibility to Effie, telling Jeanie that he had planned and executed the Porteous incident in order to rescue Effie from the prison. But she had refused to leave with him. He had tried many other schemes to save her, including an attempt to force from Meg the confession that she had taken the baby, but everything had failed. He told Jeanie that he had been on his way to give himself up in exchange for Effie's release when he fell from his horse and was injured. He told Jeanie to bargain with the Duke of Argyle, and as a last resort to offer to lead the authorities to Robertson in exchange for Effie's pardon.

George promised not to leave his father's house until Effie was free.

Jeanie at last reached London and presented herself to the Duke of Argyle with Reuben's letter. The duke, impressed with Jeanie's sincerity and simplicity, arranged for an audience with the queen. She too believed Jeanie's story of Effie's misfortune, and through her efforts the king pardoned Effie, with the stipulation that she leave Scotland for fourteen years. Jeanie secured the pardon without revealing George Staunton's secret.

The duke was so impressed with Jeanie's goodness and honesty that he made her father the master of an experimental farm on one of his estates in Scotland, and he made Reuben the minister of the church. Jeanie's heart was overflowing with joy until she learned that Effie had eloped with her lover just three nights after her release from prison. No one knew where they were, as the outlaw's life was in constant danger because of his part in the Porteous hanging.

Reuben and Jeanie were married and were blessed with three fine children. They prospered in their new life, and Jeanie's only sorrow was her sister's marriage to George Staunton. She kept Effie's secret, however, telling no one that George was actually Robertson. After several years, George and Effie returned to London, George having inherited a title from his uncle, and as Sir George and Lady Staunton they were received in court society. Effie wrote secretly to Jeanie and sent her large sums of money which Jeanie put away without telling her husband about them. Even to him she could not reveal Effie's secret.

By chance Jeanie found a paper containing the last confession of Meg Murdockson, who had been hanged as a witch. In it Meg confessed that she had stolen Effie's baby and had given him to an outlaw. Jeanie sent this information to Effie, in London, and before long Effie, as Lady Staunton, paid Jeanie a visit. Effie had used a pretext of ill health to go to Scotland while her husband, acting on the information in Meg's letter, tried to trace the whereabouts of their son. Although it was dangerous for George to be in Scotland, where he might be recognized as Geordie Robertson, he followed every clue given in Meg's confession. In Edinburgh he met Reuben Butler, who was there on business, and secured an invitation to accompany Reuben back to the manse. Reuben, not knowing George's real identity, was happy to receive the Duke of Argyle's friend. Reuben, at that time, did not know that Effie was also a guest in his home.

As Reuben and George walked toward the manse, they passed through a thicket where they were attacked by outlaws. One, a young fellow, ran his sword through George and killed him. It was not until Reuben had heard the whole story of the Stauntons from Jeanie that he searched George's pockets and found there information which proved beyond doubt that the young outlaw who had killed George was his own son, stolen many years before. Because Effie was grief-stricken by George's death, Jeanie and Reuben thought it useless to add to her sorrow by revealing the identity of his assailant. Reuben later traced the boy to America, where the young man continued his life of crime until he was captured and probably killed by Indians.

Effie stayed with Reuben and Jeanie for more than a year. Then she went back to London and the brilliant society she had known there. No one but Jeanie and Reuben ever knew the secret of Effie and George. After ten years, Effie retired to a convent on the continent, where she spent her remaining years grieving for her husband and the son she had never known.

Reuben and Jeanie Butler, who had been so unavoidably involved in sordidness and crime, lived out their lives happily and carried their secret with them to the grave.

Further Critical Evaluation of the Work:

Many critics have considered this novel Scott's best; but, although *The Heart of Midlothian* has received much praise, the reasons for its success are different from those of most of the Waverley series. The novel does not have the usual Gothic props of ruined abbeys, spectres, prophesizing old hags, or lonely windswept castles. Only one scene, where Jeanie Deans meets George Staunton at moonrise in Nicol Muschat's Cairn, is typical of wild, picturesque settings so frequent in Scott's fiction.

The plot is based upon authentic historical events; the Porteous Riot of 1736 in Edinburgh's famous Old Tolbooth prison, or as it was commonly called "the heart of Midlothian," sets the action on its course. But the story is not actually one of social history involving questions of justice. Nor is it a study of Scottish Presbyterianism. Long debates on both these issues take up major portions of the work, but Scott comes to no clear conclusions. These issues do not provide the unifying force that holds the story together.

A strong moral theme is the binding element, for most of the main protagonists are caught in dilemmas of conscience. Jeanie Deans must decide between telling a lie to save her sister Effie's life or speaking the truth and thereby condemning her to execution. Effie herself has the choice of attempting to live virtuously as she was taught or being faithful to her dissipated, criminal lover. Their father, stern David Deans, must decide whether to adhere to his Presbyterian principles or come to terms with the human condition and forgive Effie. George Staunton, alias Robertson, is forced either to follow his wild inclinations and stay with his desperate associates or to reform and assume responsibilities of position and inheritance. He must also confront his obligation to marry Effie, whom he has wronged. These varied dilemmas of conscience constitute the texture of the novel.

The heroine is the one strong character in the novel, but she differs strikingly from the usual Waverley heroine, who is tall, beautiful, exceedingly well bred, romantic and, of course, wealthy. Jeanie Deans is the unusual: a peasant heroine, plain in appearance, not trained in social deportment, and lacking a romantic, Gothic background to aid her. Perhaps the moral seriousness of *The Heart of Midlothian* plus the fact that Scott drew his heroine from the lower classes not only make the novel popular but also give it a coherence and unity unusual in his fiction.

In most of Scott's novels minor characters, who are largely drawn from Scottish rural life and humble occupations, are more real than upper-class figures. When dealing with them Scott has a more energetic and colorful style. Critics often remark that the strength of his work lies in such characters as Caleb Balderstone of *The Bride of Lammermoor,* Edie Ochiltree and Maggie Mucklebackit of *The Antiquary,* Callum Beg and Widow Flockhart of *Waverly.* Scott reproduces their speech faithfully and with obvious relish.

But in *The Heart of Midlothian,* although he still opposes the upper-class culture—with that of the lower and exploits resulting tensions, he elevates a dairyman's daughter to the status of heroine. And, in spite of the unyielding virtue of her character and the contrived situation in which she becomes involved, he not only makes her believable, but also enlists the somewhat skeptical, hesitant reader on her side. She has common sense, and the rough, matter-of-fact elements in her daily life leave no doubt that she will conquer all adverse forces to triumph in Effie's cause. The law of retribution is at work here as in Scott's other novels, but Providence has a fresh, indefatigable agent in Jeanie. It is interesting that she was Scott's own favorite heroine.

Believable, too, are several scenes in *The Heart of Midlothian,* particularly the Porteous Riot which opens the novel. Scott handles realistically the mob's capture of Tolbooth prison and the lynching of Captain Porteous. Another well constructed scene, and one which is moving, if sentimental, is that of Effie's trial. In such sections Scott tightens his control of character interaction and effects economy of language.

However, the entire account of Jeanie's journey to London to obtain from Queen Caroline Effie's pardon slows down the novel and fails to hold the reader's interest. And the last section of the work—almost an epilogue—though required by Scott's publisher, does not seem to be required by the story itself. Jeanie and Reuben with their children and old David Deans live out a mellowed existence in picturesque Roseneath; their rural domesticity is only enlivened by the reunion of Jeanie and her sister (now Lady Staunton) and George's murder by his and Effie's unrecognized son.

If some portions of the novel seem protracted and rather unexciting, still the whole is well-knit and more logical than much of Scott's fiction. Because Scott considered the function of the novel to furnish "solace from the toils of ordinary life by an excursion into the regions of imagination," he ordinarily was indifferent to technique; instead, he concentrated on subject matter. He stressed factual accuracy but felt that too much care in composition might destroy what he termed "abundant spontaneity." Following his own dicta, he wrote rapidly with disregard for planning and revision. He improvised with careless haste and his novels often suffer from poor style and construction. Critics have repeatedly faulted his work for improper motivation and lack of organic unity.

However, one does not get the impression from reading *The Heart of Midlothian* that the author wrote at his usual breakneck speed, casually assembling scenes and characters together without forethought. Motivation is more properly furnished, characterization consistent, and, as mentioned, the dilemmas of conscience are carried through logically. Scott has dispensed in this novel with excess supernatural escapades and the often flamboyant trappings of decadent nobility. He concentrates on the sincerity and integrity of his lower-class protagonists to effect a democratic realism new in the historical English novel, a genre he himself had invented.

Muriel B. Ingham

THE HEART OF THE MATTER

Type of work: Novel
Author: Graham Greene (1904-   )
Type of plot: Psychological realism
Time of plot: World War II
Locale: British West Africa
First published: 1948

> Principal characters:
> MAJOR SCOBIE, police chief in one of the colony's districts
> MRS. SCOBIE, his wife
> MRS. ROLT, shipwreck victim, Scobie's mistress
> WILSON, a counter-intelligence agent
> YUSEF, a Syrian merchant

Critique:

The fears and hopes, friendships and petty rivalries, loves and hates of Europeans immured in a colony on the African coast afforded Graham Greene, who actually worked in such a place during World War II, the material for this novel. The book continues the study of British people under the influence of our times begun in Greene's earlier work. Major Scobie, like Arthur Rowe in *The Ministry of Fear,* is a relatively friendless man—a type that seems to have fascination for the author. Like Rowe, in the earlier novel, Major Scobie is placed in a position where he can choose between life or death: the high point in both novels is that at which the choice is made. Beyond the immediate story, however, there are larger implications. *The Heart of the Matter,* written by one of the leading Catholic novelists of the day, is actually a religious story, a fable of the conflict between good and evil. It is a drama of the human soul in mid-passage toward Heaven or Hell.

The Story:

For fifteen years Major Scobie, chief of police in a British West African district had built up a reputation for honesty. Then he learned that in spite of his labors he was to be passed over for the district commissionership in favor of a younger man. Those fifteen long years now seemed to him to have been too long and filled with too much work. Worse than his own disappointment was the disappointment of his wife. Mrs. Scobie needed the encouragement that a rise in official position would have given her, to compensate for the loss of her only child some years before and her unpopularity among the official family of the district.

A love for literature, especially poetry, had set Mrs. Scobie apart from the other officials and their wives. Once the difference was discerned, the other Britishers distrusted and disliked her. They even pitied the man whom she had married. Nor were the Scobies much happier than people imagined them to be. Mrs. Scobie hated the life she led, and her husband disliked having to make her face it realistically. Both drank. When she found he was not to be made district commissioner, she insisted that he send her to the Cape Colony for a holiday, even though German submarines were torpedoing many vessels at the time.

Scobie had not the money to pay expenses of the trip. For a previous excursion of hers from the colony he had already given up part of his life insurance. After trying unsuccessfully to borrow the money from the banks, he went to Yusef, a Syrian merchant, who agreed to lend him the money at four percent interest. Scobie knew that any dealings he had with Yusef would place him under a cloud, for the official British family knew

---

only too well that many of the Syrian's doings were illegal, including the shipment of industrial diamonds to the Nazis. Pressed by his wife's apparent need to escape the boredom of the rainy season in the coast colony, Scobie finally took the chance that he could keep clear of Yusef's entanglements, even though he knew that the Syrian hated him for the reputation of integrity he had built up during the past fifteen years.

To add to Scobie's difficulties, he learned that Wilson, a man supposedly sent out on a clerkship with a trading company, was actually an undercover agent working for the government on the problem of diamond smuggling. First of all, Scobie had no official information about Wilson's true activities; secondly, Wilson had fallen in love with Scobie's wife; and, thirdly, Mrs. Scobie had bloodied Wilson's nose for him and permitted her husband to see her admirer crying. Any one of the counts would have made Scobie uneasy; all three in combination made him painfully aware that Wilson could only hate him, as Wilson actually did.

Shortly after his wife's departure, a series of events began to break down Major Scobie's trust in his own honesty and the reputation he had built up for himself. When a Portuguese liner was searched on its arrival in port, Scobie found a suspicious letter in the captain's cabin. Instead of turning in the letter, he burned it—after the captain had assured him that the letter was only a personal message to his daughter in Germany. A few weeks later Yusef began to be very friendly toward Scobie. Gossip reported that Scobie had met and talked with the Syrian on several occasions, in addition to having borrowed money from the suspected smuggler.

One day word came that the French had rescued the crew and passengers of a torpedoed British vessel. Scobie was with the party who met the rescued people at the border between the French and British colonies. Among the victims was a young bride of only a few months whose husband had been killed in the war. While she recuperated from her exposure

in a lifeboat and then waited for a ship to return her to England, she and Scobie fell in love. For a time they were extremely careful of their conduct, until one day Mrs. Rolt, the rescued woman, belittled Scobie because of his caution. Scobie, to prove his daring as well as his love, sent her a letter which was intercepted by Yusef's agents. In payment for return of the letter Scobie was forced to help Yusef smuggle some gems from the colony. Wilson, Scobie's enemy, suspected the smuggling done by Scobie, but he could prove nothing.

Mrs. Rolt pleaded with Scobie to show his love by divorcing his wife and marrying her. Scobie, a Roman Catholic, tried to convince her that his faith and his conscience could not permit his doing so. To complicate matters further, Mrs. Scobie cabled that she was already aboard ship on her way back home from Capetown. Scobie did not know which way to turn. On her return Mrs. Scobie nagged him to take communion with her. Scobie, unable to receive absolution because he refused to promise to give up adultery, took the sacrament of communion anyway, rather than admit to his wife what had happened. He realized that according to his faith he was damning his soul.

The worry over his sins, his uneasiness about his job, the problem of Yusef, a murder that Yusef had had committed for him, and the nagging of both his wife and Mrs. Rolt—all these made Scobie's mind a turmoil. He did not know which way to turn, for the Church, haven for many, was forbidden to him because of his sins and his temperament.

In searching for a way out of his predicament Scobie remembered what he had been told by a doctor shortly after an official investigation of a suicide. The doctor had told Scobie that the best way to commit suicide was to feign angina and then take an overdose of evipan, a drug prescribed for angina cases. Carefully, Scobie made plans to take his life in that way because he wanted his wife to have his insurance money for her support after she returned to England. After studying the symptoms of angina, Scobie went to a doctor, who diagnosed Scobie's trouble from the symptoms he related. Scobie knew that his pretended heart condition would soon be common knowledge in the colony.

Ironically, Scobie was told that he had been reconsidered for the commissionership of the colony but that he could not be given the post because of his illness. To Scobie, the news made little difference, for he had already made up his mind to commit suicide.

To make his death appear convincing, he filled his diary with entries tracing the progress of his heart condition. One evening he took his overdose of evipan, his only solution to difficulties which had become more than he could bear. He died, and only one or two people even suspected the truth. One of these was Mrs. Scobie, who complained to the priest after he had refused to give Scobie absolution. The priest, knowing of Scobie's virtues as well as his sins, cried out to her that no one could call Scobie wicked or damned, for no one knew God's mercy.

Further Critical Evaluation of the Work:

The Heart of the Matter is an intelligent, perceptive, and humane *tour de force* on the spiritual capacities and moral dilemmas of Henry Scobie, husband, chief of police, and Catholic. Each of these roles contributes something to the complications of Scobie's situation. It must be admitted, however, that the novel, for all of its sensitivity and insight, is not a work of fiction of the first rank—perhaps just because it is a *tour de force*. Greene, while accepting a stern Roman Catholic framework, challenges us to find fault with a man who goes beyond dishonesty and infidelity to sacrilege and suicide. As Scobie degenerates, Greene dares us, despite the evidence, to cast the first stone by involving our sympathies and appealing to a higher law of mercy which is beyond man's capacity to understand or forgive.

The hothouse setting, in a British colony on the West African coast in the early 1940's, is interesting in its own right. It affords opportunity for commentary on the uncertainties of the period and the limitations of the colonial mentality. Yet, the setting is not the heart of the matter. Scobie's problems as a human being are always the central focus of the novel and they spring from the confluence of his circumstances, his roles, and his character. To the web of colonial life Scobie is a perpetual outsider. Too self-contained, too reflective, too honest with himself and others, he is not able to assume the roles and act out the rituals which will bring him local success. Circumstances contribute to the evolution of the central conflict, but the maritime warfare and diamond smuggling are, for Scobie, rather occasions for sin than sin itself. They provide a context in which Scobie's character agonizes and falters as he takes on his major roles. In each of these roles, his character shines through and it may be his ultimate transcendence that his strength of character maintains a stable core as its periphery comes into conflict with corrupting circumstances.

Scobie's first role is as husband to a wife who, to Scobie's credit, is far more irritating to us than to him. It is through Scobie's patience and understanding that we achieve any degree of sympathy for the human burden his wife bears.

In the related role of father of a deceased daughter we see more of Scobie's, and his wife's, suffering. However, he understands her while she lacks the sensitivity, despite her love for poetry, to reciprocate. Paradoxically, Scobie's honesty about his own limitations and compassion for the plight of others leads to a kind of hubris, which manifests itself first in his attempts to make his wife happy. It is this same desire to fix up the world, to provide totally for another's security and happiness, that embroils him in his later relationship with the vulnerable Mrs. Rolt and occasions his infidelity.

In his role as chief of police, Scobie has the sort of reputation for impeccable honesty and fairness which, combined with a lack of ambition, is likely to stimulate the suspicion, gossip, and animosity of his small-minded peers. It is one of the novel's many fine ironies that Scobie's honesty is compromised by the compassion he feels for his wife's plight, for it is his, perhaps excessive and blameworthy, even selfish, desire to free her that leads him to borrow money and put himself in the hands of Yusef. Indeed, it may ultimately be a desire to free himself, but it also lays him open to the less publicly dangerous but morally serious dishonesty with Mrs. Rolt. His desire, whether it is to please his wife or free himself, leads to a compromise of his office. His desire to provide insulation against suffering, whether it is compassionate or selfish, leads to a compromise of his marriage.

Scobie does not wish anything but to be at peace, and he hopes that if he can fix everything for his wife, and thereby free himself of her, he can find peace. Subsequently, Scobie's compassion for Mrs. Rolt turns into a love that brings his desire to repair other lives to an impasse when he wins Mrs. Rolt and his wife decides to return. In the chain of consequences and of flawed moral decisions, his attempt to comfort Mrs. Rolt by a reckless declaration of love further leads to complicity in murder. Scobie's actions are, thus far, morally imperfect but entangled in mixed emotions and motives. It is in his role as Catholic that he commits the ultimate transgressions against God and the divine power of forgiveness.

Violation of public trust and infidelity can be pardoned or extenuated, but Scobie, as Catholic, proceeds to the institutionally "unforgiveable" sins. His love for Mrs. Rolt makes valid confession impossible because his selfishness and compassion make it impossible for him to promise to give her up. His concern for his wife forces him to receive Communion, without absolution, so that he will not betray himself to her and thus wound her. In so doing, he does violence to Christ in the Eucharist. Although well aware that Christ, for love of man, makes himself vulnerable to abuse by his availability in the sacrament, Scobie allows his human motives to lead him to desecrate that trust by receiving Christ while in a state of sin. Having sacrificed Christ to selfishness and human compassion, Scobie is left totally desolate, and, unable to live with these conflicts, he commits the sin which theoretically puts him beyond God's mercy—suicide.

Nevertheless, we do not condemn Scobie. It is not that he is an automaton, a victim of circumstance. To excuse him on those grounds would trivialize the theology of the novel: "to understand all is to forgive all." Rather, we clearly recognize his progressive sins, but are led by Greene to participate in the mystery of divine mercy by extending compassion without selfishness. The compassion that contributed to Scobie's corruption may also be, raised to the divine level, his only hope of salvation.

Edward E. Foster

HEARTBREAK HOUSE

Type of work: Drama
Author: Bernard Shaw (1856-1950)
Time: 1913
Locale: Sussex, England
First presented: 1920

Principal characters:
CAPTAIN SHOTOVER, an English eccentric and visionary
LADY ARIADNE UTTERWORD, and
MRS. HESIONE HUSHABYE, his daughters
HECTOR HUSHABYE, Hesione's husband
ELLIE DUNN, a guest in Captain Shotover's house
MAZZINI DUNN, her father
BOSS MANGAN, an industrialist
RANDALL UTTERWORD, Lady Ariadne's brother-in-law
NURSE GUINESS, a servant
BILLY DUNN, an ex-pirate and burglar

Heartbreak House has always held an equivocal place in the Shavian canon. Its admirers—and they are many—bracket it with Shaw's best, beside such acknowledged masterpieces as *Man and Superman* and *Saint Joan.* Severer critics see it as an unsuccessful attempt to create a mood of Chekhovian melancholy and fatalism within a framework of political allegory and social satire, a mixture of comedy, tragedy, dialectic, and prophecy that never quite coalesces into unity of theme or structure.

Shaw himself was as much to blame as anyone for some of the misconceptions regarding his play. Always ready, even eager, to instruct his public, in this instance he maintained an attitude of reticence toward his work and appeared hesitant to let it pass out of his hands. Although part of it had been written as early as 1913 and it was in its final form by 1916, the play was not published until 1919. Its first performance was the Theatre Guild production on November 12, 1920. Even then Shaw apparently preferred to let his work speak for itself without mediation on his part, for when asked on one occasion to interpret some of his lines he answered brusquely that he was merely the author and therefore could not be expected to know. Perhaps he was still smarting from the abuse he had received following the publication

of his pamphlet, *Commonsense about the War* (1915), read by the jingo-minded wartime public as a piece of pacifist propaganda. Under the circumstances his reluctance to present his most sweeping indictment of a society unable or unwilling to bring its moral judgments and political convictions into balance with its potential of destruction becomes understandable. War, Shaw seems to say, is no longer the trade of the professional soldier or the recreation of the feudal elite; all of mankind is now involved in the common catastrophe and society must perish if it cannot realize its possibilities for good as opposed to its capacities for destruction.

In a way that criticism has not yet fully appraised, *Heartbreak House* presents almost the whole range of Shaw's thought, for few of his plays are more representative or inclusive in the themes and motifs touched upon if not explored: war, love, society, education, religion, politics, and science. The only element lacking is the Shavian principle of the Life Force. As a drama of ideas it looks back to the earlier plays and anticipates *Saint Joan* and *The Apple Cart.* As comment on upper-class life it continues and climaxes the themes Shaw presents in *Getting Married* and *Misalliance.* Shaw himself is present in his various manifestations: the recorder of that verbal interplay which in the Shavian drama often takes the place of conflict, the playwright of ideas, the master of comedy, the maker of epigrams, the teacher, the critic, the philosopher, the parodist, the fabulist, and the poet.

A clue to the meaning of the play is provided in the subtitle: "A Fantasia in the Russian manner on English themes." Following the production of several of Chekhov's plays in London, Shaw had been studying the work of the Russian dramatist and had seen in at least three, *The Cherry Orchard, The Sea Gull,* and *Uncle Vanya,* exempla of the theme he himself had in mind: the disintegration of a society from within and its final collapse in the face of forces it had previously ignored or denied. Allowances must be made, however, for Shaw's habit of exaggeration where precedents or sources are concerned. Shaw may have begun his play with a similarity of tone in mind—the atmosphere, he said, was the initial impulse—but he ends with effects quite different from those we find in Chekhov. Partly the difference is one of temperament, the great Russian power of enclosing the poetry of all experience in the single instance, partly the fact that the haunted landscapes of Chekhov's world have little in common with those aspects of British middle and upper-class life that Shaw observed so shrewdly. Shaw's people exist only in the light of his ethical and political values; Chekhov's, entirely within the world of their own moral and spiritual blight. The sound of the ax echoing through the twilight at the end of *The Cherry Orchard* is more portentous and meaningful than the bombs which rain fire and death from the sky at the close of *Heartbreak House.*

The essential differences between these two plays are not altogether to Shaw's disadvantage, for *Heartbreak House,* although it lacks the larger expressiveness of Chekhov's theater, exhibits all the intellectual vigor and wild poetry, the clash of ideas and personalities, of disquisitory drama at its best. A thesis play, it is admitted as such in Shaw's preface, where

he states that Heartbreak House is more than a title: it is the Europe—or England —of culture and leisure in the period before World War I. As the alternative to Heartbreak House he sees only Horseback Hall, peopled by the gentry who have made sport a cult. In either case, true leadership is lacking in this world of cross-purposes, futile desires, and idle talk. These people have courage of a sort, but they are able to do little more than clench their fists in gestures of defiance as the bombs drop from the sky.

The setting of the play is the Sussex home, built like a ship, of Captain Shotover, an eighty-eight-year-old eccentric and retired sea captain credited by hearsay with selling his soul to the devil in Zanzibar and marriage to a black witch in the West Indies. Cranky, realistic, fantastically wise, he drinks three bottles of rum a day, strives to attain the seventh degree of concentration, and spends his time tinkering with death-dealing inventions. To Ellie Dunn, a young singer arriving as the guest of Mrs. Hesione Hushabye, the captain's daughter, the atmosphere of the house seems as puzzling and unpredictable as its owner. No one bothers to greet visitors; members of the family are treated like strangers; strangers are welcomed like old friends. An elderly servant calls everyone ducky. When Lady Ariadne Utterword returns for a visit after twenty-three years in the colonies with her husband, Sir Hastings Utterword, an empire builder, neither her father nor her sister recognizes her. The captain persists in confusing Mazzini Dunn, Ellie's father, with a rascally ex-pirate who had robbed him many years before. Arriving unexpectedly, Boss Mangan, the millionaire industrialist whom Ellie is to marry, is put to work in the captain's garden.

From this opening scene of innocent, seemingly irresponsible comedy the play proceeds to more serious business, and by the end of the first act the characters have assumed their allegorical identities. Lady Ariadne is Empire, the prestige of foreign rule. Hesione Hushabye is Domesticity, the power of woman's love and authority at home. Hector, her husband, is Heroism, a man capable of brave deeds but so tamed by feminine influence that his only escape is through romantic daydreams and Münchausen-like tales of derring-do. Mazzini Dunn is the nineteenth-century Liberal, a believer in progress but too sentimental to be an intellectual force; consequently he has become the tool of Boss Mangan, a figure of capitalistic Exploitation. Randall Utterword, Lady Ariadne's brother-in-law, is Pride, a Foreign Office official symbolically in love with his sister-in-law and filled with snobbish regard for caste. Looming over these figures is old Captain Shotover, the embodiment of Old England and its genius, no longer the captain of the great Ship of State but the half-cracked, drunken skipper of a house built like a ship, suggesting his own and his country's maritime history. Captain Shotover is the triumph of the play. In spite of his allegorical significance he is always superbly himself, a figure larger than life and yet lifelike, reliving his past and creating his future in terms of his own fantastic logic. These people come together in twos and threes to speak in their own and in their allegorical characters. Childlike resentments, old grievances, brooding frustrations, impossible dreams, and unexpected disillusionments break through their masks in the heavily charged atmosphere that the play generates, but all this sound and fury leads nowhere. *Heartbreak House* is idleness dramatized, impotence of mind and will translated into speech and gesture.

In one sense *Heartbreak House* might be described as the story of Ellie Dunn's education. In the first act, although she is engaged to Boss Mangan, she fancies herself in love with Marcus Darnley, a middle-aged man of romantic background, whom she has been meeting secretly. The discovery that Marcus is Hector Hushabye opens her eyes to reality and deceit. Disillusioned with romantic love, she decides to accept Boss Mangan and his money, only to discover that his millions are nonexistent, that he is simply the capitalist who uses the money other men entrust to him. In the end she decides that she will become the white bride of old Captain Shotover because his seventh degree of concentration holds a promise of peace and happiness beyond desire or despair. This time it is the captain who disillusions her; his seventh degree of concentration is rum. Ellie's education is now complete, and she is free to be as practical or aspiring as she desires.

Suddenly, while these people sit on the terrace and talk out their predicament, planes begin to drone overhead. Boss Mangan and a burglar—who had turned out to be Billy Dunn the ex-pirate now reduced to petty thievery and sniveling confession—take refuge in a gravel pit; a bomb falls and kills them. The others survive. Heartbreak House still stands.

All criticism of *Heartbreak House* reduces itself to a single issue: Can comedy, even brilliantly presented, sustain a theme of tragic significance? Shaw, as he declared, was only the writer. The reader or the playgoer has been left to answer this question for himself.

THE HEAT OF THE DAY

Type of work: Novel
Author: Elizabeth Bowen (1899-1973)
Type of plot: Psychological realism
Time of plot: 1942-1944
Locale: London
First published: 1949

Principal characters:
STELLA RODNEY, an attractive widow
RODERICK RODNEY, her son
ROBERT KELWAY, her lover
HARRISON, a British Intelligence agent
LOUIE LEWIS, wife of a British soldier

Critique:

The wartime setting of this book is no more than incidental, for the story treats of contrasting faiths and loyalties which are altogether timeless. Though the general atmosphere is electric with danger, the author muffles the sound of bombs and anti-aircraft guns until they give only a tonal background for the drama of Stella Rodney, Robert Kelway, and the enigmatic Harrison. The problem of Stella Rodney is that of a woman asked to question her own judgment of the man she loves. Miss Bowen is at her best in dealing with complex personal relationships, and here she inspects some barriers to emotional and intellectual harmony that are embodied in a conflict between patriotism and love. Like Henry James, she is interested in the collision of finely-grained personalities; and the very nature of her subject matter demands a style that is sensitive and involved.

The Story:

The first Sunday afternoon of September, 1942, found Harrison sitting at a band concert in Regent Park. But he was not listening to the music. He was, in fact, merely killing time until he could see Stella Rodney at eight o'clock. Thinking of Stella and the awkward subject he must discuss with her, he kept thrusting the fist of his right hand into the palm of his left. This unconscious motion, as well as his obvious indifference to the music, aroused the curiosity of an adjacent listener. This neighbor, Louie Lewis, was a clumsy, cheaply clad young woman with an artless and somewhat bovine expression. Lonely without her soldier husband and entirely a creature of impulse, she offended Harrison by breaking into his reverie with naïve comments which were brusquely rebuffed. Unabashed, she trailed after him when he left the concert, giving up only when he abruptly left her to keep his engagement.

Stella, in her top-floor flat in Weymouth Street, wondered rather idly why Harrison was late. Her attitude of waiting was more defiant than expectant, for she had no love for her visitor. She hardly knew how he had managed to insinuate himself into her life; first, he had turned up unaccountably at the funeral of Cousin Francis Morris, and since then his attentions had shown a steady increase. There had been a subtle shade of menace in his demand that she see him that night, and a curious sense of apprehension had prompted her to consent. As she awaited his knock, her glance flickered impatiently about the charming flat, and she recalled fleetingly the facts that gave shape to her existence: her young son, Roderick, now in the British army; her ex-husband, long divorced and dead;

her own war work with Y.X.D.; and her lover, Robert Kelway, also in government service.

When Harrison arrived, he received a cool and perfunctory greeting. His first remarks were hesitant and enigmatic, but he soon launched into words that left Stella wide-eyed with shock and disbelief. Her lover, he told her, was a Nazi agent passing English secrets on to Germany. Harrison himself was connected with British Intelligence and he had been assigned to cover Kelway's movements. There was just one way to save the traitor. Stella must give him up, switch her interest to Harrison. Then Kelway's fate might be averted, or indefinitely postponed.

The blunt proposition unnerved Stella. She refused to believe in Kelway's guilt, for Harrison did not impress her as a man to trust. She played for time, winning a month's delay in which to make up her mind. Harrison sharply advised her not to warn Robert; the slightest change in his pattern of action would result in his immediate arrest. As the interview ended, the telephone rang. At the other end was Roderick, announcing his arrival for leave in London. Upon Harrison's departure, Stella pulled herself together and made quick preparation to receive her son.

Roderick's coming helped a little; temporarily it deprived Stella of the time to worry. Roderick was young and vulnerable, and his father's early abdication had made Stella feel doubly responsible for her son. Roderick wanted to talk about his new interest in life, the run-down estate in Ireland recently bequeathed him by Cousin Francis Morris. The boy was determined to keep his new property, but, until the war was over, the task of looking after it would be largely Stella's responsibility.

Roderick's leave expired. The next night Robert Kelway came to Stella's flat. She gave no hint of her inward agitation, though she casually inquired if he knew Harrison. Gazing at her attractive, considerate lover, Stella silently marveled that he should be a suspect—he, a lamed veteran of Dunkirk! Considering, however, that she knew nothing about his family, she renewed her request that they visit his mother and sister in the country. A subsequent Saturday afternoon at Holme Dene revealed nothing strange about Robert's background. On the night of her return from Robert's home, she found Harrison waiting at her apartment; he confirmed his watchfulness by telling her where she had been, and why.

Roderick's interests intervened by summoning Stella briefly to Ireland. Robert protested at losing her for even a few days and they parted affectionately. In Ireland, Stella's distrust of Harrison received a jolt; he had been truthful, she learned, in telling her that he had been a friend of Cousin Francis Morris. She resolved that she would acquaint Robert with Harrison's accusation. When she returned to London, Robert met her at the station. Minutes later, in a taxi, she revealed what she had heard; and Robert, deeply hurt, made a complete denial. Later that night he begged her to marry him, but Stella, surprised and disturbed, succeeded in parrying the proposal.

A few nights later Harrison had dinner with Stella in a popular restaurant. She stiffened with apprehension as he told her that she had disobeyed him by putting Robert on his guard. Before Stella could learn what Harrison intended to do, she was interrupted by the untimely intrusion of Louie Lewis, who crudely invited herself to their table after spotting Harrison in the crowd. Nevertheless, Stella managed to intimate that she would meet Harrison's terms if he would save Robert from arrest. Angry at Louie, Harrison made no response; roughly dismissing the two women, he stalked off, leaving them to find their way home through blacked-out London. Louie, fascinated by the superior charm and refinement of Stella, accompanied her to the doorway of her apartment.

Robert was at Holme Dene, so that not until the next night did Stella have a chance to warn him of his danger. In the early morning darkness of Stella's bedroom, they renewed their love and confidence with a sense that it was to be their last meeting. When Robert finally revealed that he was an ardent Nazi, prizing power above freedom, Stella found no way to reconcile their views. Faint footsteps, as of outside watchers, were heard as Robert dressed and prepared to leave. He climbed up the rope ladder to the skylight in the roof, then came back down again to kiss Stella once more. He told her to take care of herself as he hurriedly disappeared through the skylight. The next morning Robert's body was found lying in the street where he had leaped or fallen from the steeply slanting roof.

More than a year passed before Stella saw Harrison. There were Allied landings in Africa; there was the invasion of Italy; there was the ever-growing prospect of a Second Front. Finally Harrison came back. Stella had had questions to ask him, questions about Robert, but now it seemed pointless to ask them. An air of constraint hung over their conversation, a feeling that Robert's death had removed any real link between their lives. Harrison made no romantic overtures; he even seemed faintly relieved when Stella told him that she was soon to be married.

Further Critical Evaluation of the Work:

Elizabeth Bowen often expressed her concern for the disintegration of tradition and value in the twentieth century by depicting the discrepancy between modern woman's changing aspirations and her felt desire for the traditional roles. In *The House in Paris* (1936) and *The Death of the Heart* (1938), heroines are restless or dissatisfied in the roles of wife or mother, and in *The Heat of the Day* Stella tests "free womanhood." *The Heat of the Day* combines the portrayal of modern woman's dilemma with two other representations of Bowen's concern—the neglected family estate and the events of World War II.

Stella Rodney is Bowen's "free woman." She is a professional working in military intelligence, a longtime divorcée, and the mother of a grown son. She has a lover whom she has known for two years, but she dates and knows other men. Still, the relationship with Robert is the most important. Stella is sensitive, strong, and articulate, not only about others, but also about her own problems. She has let her son and others believe for years that she left her husband, that she was the *femme fatale,* the self-sufficient one. In fact, she was divorced by her husband, who left her for his nurse. Stella's son Roderick discovers this fact and confronts his mother, saying it puts "everything in a different light." She admits that it was a matter of saving face; when most people believed that she was the guilty party, she let the story go on. She says to Harrison that it is better to sound like "a monster than look a fool." That remark suggests the paradox in Stella's psyche: she craves to be identified as a free woman, *"capable de tout,"* but her inner self is not quite in concert with that image. Thus, there is the divorce story, her relationship to Roderick (she takes pains to show that he is not tied to her, but worries a great deal about him), and her attitude to Robert (their relationship is a stable one, but Stella refuses Robert's marriage proposal).

Stella is not alone in her ambivalence about how to react to changes in society. Cousin Nettie Morris is driven to insanity by the difficulties of woman's "place" at the family estate, Mount Morris. It seems she takes refuge in madness. One of the novel's most memorable scenes is the nonconversation between Roderick and Nettie at Wisteria Lodge, the asylum. Nettie is not so mad as others would like to think. Stella, visiting Mount Morris in Ireland, understands how the lack of real choices for the "traditional" woman can drive her insane.

Stella's dividedness is expressed in her attitude toward Mount Morris. She had sold her own house, stored her furniture, and rented a luxury furnished flat in London, thus making herself more independent. Nothing in the flat reflected her personality. But Stella finds herself again saddled with place, family, and tradition when Cousin Francis wills Mount Morris to her son— whom he never met but who was conceived at Mount Morris where Stella and his father Victor honeymooned. Stella's ambivalence begins when she attends Cousin Francis' funeral; it grows as she revisits, after 21 years, Mount Morris, now knowing that Roderick will carry on the tradition she had rejected. (Elizabeth Bowen herself believed that the modern attitude against family estate was erroneous, that indeed it had contributed to the general disintegration of society. She became the first female Bowen to inherit Bowen's Court near Dublin since its construction in 1776. But in 1960 she was forced by financial exigency to sell the house and in 1963 it was torn down.)

Stella is repeatedly characterized as being typical of her generation, and the generation is often described as having "muffed" the century. She became an adult just after World War I, and now there is World War II. The specific details of the war years in London give concrete reality to Stella's own trauma, and are skillfully interwoven in her involvement with Robert. "The heat of the day" is Stella's middle-age, her "noon," and the agony of the decision to question Robert's loyalty. It is also, of course, the height of the war, a turning point in the century.

As Bowen's structure and symbols both clearly suggest, the generation which follows Stella's, that of Roderick and Louie Lewis, represents both a new integration and a rebirth. Stella's story—her "defeat" as a free woman— is framed and intersected by the story of the working-class Louie Lewis, whose vague desires for motherhood culminate in a triumphant pregnancy while her husband is fighting abroad. She is unaware of the identity of the child's father. The novel ends with the birth of her son just after D-Day and her return to the south coast of England where her parents had been killed by a bomb in the early days of the war. Roderick intends to reside at Mount Morris: he has great plans about rejuvenating it with modern farming methods. Both members of the next generation, therefore, are able to resolve the dichotomies that so plagued their parents' generation—dichotomies about family, place, tradition, and role. The three white swans, a recurrent positive symbol in Bowen (they figure in *The Death of the Heart* as well) appear only at Mount Morris and at the end of the book as Louie wheels her new baby. The swans symbolize a positive rebirth, flying straight, and suggest also the resolution of the war in the "direction of the west." Bowen's symbols are more suggestive than absolute, though. Louie's and Roderick's clear choices are more than enough direction for interpreting the novel. Stella's generation has "botched" it; the only hope is in the next.

Margaret McFadden-Gerber

HEAVEN'S MY DESTINATION

Type of work: Novel
Author: Thornton Wilder (1897- 1975)
Type of plot: Social satire
Time of plot: 1930-1931
Locale: Middle West
First published: 1935

Principal characters:
GEORGE MARVIN BRUSH, a traveling salesman
ROBERTA, a farmer's daughter
GEORGE BURKIN, a peeping Tom
HERB, a newspaper reporter
ELIZABETH, his daughter

Critique:

In George Marvin Brush, Thornton Wilder would seem to have synthesized the American character with its many tragic inconsistencies. One admires George Brush one moment and detests him as a prig the next. The irony and the deceptive simplicity of *Heaven's My Destination* are terrifying. Although George Brush is not the picaresque hero-type, the novel, with its many colorful and unprincipled characters and its episodic form, resembles the picaresque genre.

The Story:

George Marvin Brush, a straight-laced, clean-living non-smoker and non-drinker of twenty-three, was a salesman for the Caulkins Educational Press; his territory was the Middle West. He was the amusement and the despair of all the traveling salesmen in the same territory who knew him. One day Doremus Blodgett, a hosiery salesman, caught George in the act of penning a Bible text on a hotel blotter and invited George up to his room to chaff him. The righteousness of George infuriated Blodgett, but the hosiery man was almost reconciled when George admitted to him that he had once wronged a farmer's daughter.

At another time George withdrew all his savings from the bank. In his attempt to explain to the bank president his plan of voluntary poverty, he insulted that executive by saying that banks owed their existence only to man's fear of insecurity.

Being thought mad, George was jailed, but his ingenuousness confounded even his jailers. One of them, after hearing George propound his theories, withdrew his own savings from the bank.

In Oklahoma City George again saw Blodgett and his "cousin," Mrs. Margie McCoy. There he talked of the injustice of his receiving raises in pay, to the utter confusion of Blodgett and Mrs. McCoy. He told them that he had gone through college and had had a religious conversion in order to be of an independent mind. All he wanted, he said, was a perfect girl for his wife, six children, and a real American home. He confessed that he was hindered in his quest for these ideals by his having wronged a Kansas farm girl, one Roberta, whose farm home he had been unable to find since he left it.

George went from Oklahoma City to the Chautauqua at Camp Morgan, Oklahoma, to see Judge Corey, a state legislator who was interested in textbook contracts. There he was shocked by Jessie, a college girl who believed in evolution; he pestered a distraught businessman who wanted to be left alone; and he turned down Judge Corey's offer of thirty-five thousand dollars and a state job if he would marry the judge's daughter, Mississippi.

From Camp Morgan George went to Kansas City, where he stayed in Queenie's boarding-house with his four wild friends,

HEAVEN'S MY DESTINATION by Thornton Wilder. By permission of the author and the publishers, Harper & Brothers. Copyright, 1935, by Harper and Brothers.

Herb and Morrie, reporters; Bat, a motion picture mechanic; and Louie, a hospital orderly. Accord lasted between the four and George as long as George did not preach his anti-tobacco and anti-alcohol creeds. They, in turn, restrained their actions and their speech in his presence. Three of them and George, who had a beautiful voice, formed an expert barbershop quartet. In Kansas City George became the victim of an elaborate practical joke arranged by his friends. After they had tricked him into drunkenness, the five went on a rampage. The second step in their plan to lead George to perdition came when Herb tricked George into going to dinner one Sunday at a brothel. Herb represented the house to George as an old mansion, its proprietor, Mrs. Crofut, as a pillar of Kansas City society, and the troop of prostitutes as her daughters. George, completely duped, was impressed by the graciousness of Mrs. Crofut and by the beauty of her daughters. He treated the girls to a neighborhood movie.

Back at Queenie's, George would not believe Herb when his friend told him the truth about Mrs. Crofut's genteel establishment. Irritated by George's priggishness and stupidity, his four friends beat him nearly to death. Later, at the hospital, Louie told George that he ought to live and let live.

Out of the hospital, George continued his book selling. On a train he met an evangelist who said that money did not matter; however, George gave the man money when he learned that the man's family was destitute. In Fort Worth George exasperated a bawdy house proprietor posing as a medium, by telling her that she was a fake.

Having learned that Roberta had taken a job as a waitress in Kansas City, George went there and forced himself upon the girl, who wanted nothing to do with him. He adopted Elizabeth, the daughter of his friend Herb, who died with few illusions about life.

In Ozarkville, Missouri, George an-gered a father when he talked to the man's young daughter in the street. Then he went to a country store to buy a doll for the girl and became involved in a hold-up. Carrying out one of his strange theories, he assisted the amazed burglar. The storekeeper, Mrs. Efrim, thought that George was out of his mind. Arrested, he was put in jail, where he met George Burkin, a movie director who had been arrested as a peeping Tom. Burkin explained to George that he peeped only to observe unself-conscious human behavior.

George's trial was a sensation in Ozarkville. The little girl and Mrs. Efrim lied in their testimony, and George attempted to explain his theories of life to a confounded court. When he explained what he called ahimsa, or the theory of reacting to every situation in a manner that was the exact opposite from what was expected, the bewildered judge released him, telling him to be cautious, however, because people were afraid of ideas.

After George and Burkin had left Ozarkville in Burkin's car, they picked up a hitchhiker who turned out to be the burglar whom George had tried to help. George attempted to work his radical theory for the treatment of criminals on the burglar, but the man only fled in confused anger. George and Burkin argued about George's theories, Burkin saying that George had never really grown up, and George claiming that Burkin had thought too much and had not lived enough.

Back in Kansas City, George met Roberta and her sister Lottie for the purpose of reaching a decision in his relationship with Roberta. Lottie suggested that the couple marry and get a divorce as soon as possible, so that Roberta could be accepted again by her family. George, however, could not countenance divorce. Being finally persuaded, Roberta married George and the couple moved into a flat over a drug store. But their married life grew more and more trying. George found himself taking notes for topics that he and Roberta could safely discuss. They competed for Elizabeth's affections. At last Roberta decided to leave George and return to the farm.

George, unhappy, continued to sell books. He lost his faith and began to lead what many people would call a normal life. At length he fell sick and was hospitalized. In the hospital he admitted to a Methodist pastor that he had broken all but two of the ten commandments but that he was glad he had broken them. He shocked the pastor by saying that one cannot get better and better. While in the hospital he received a spoon which had been willed to him by a man whom he had never met but whom he had admired reciprocally through a mutual friend. He recovered, left the hospital, and reverted to his old ways. George Brush was incurable.

Further Critical Evaluation of the Work:

Heaven's My Destination is structured around its main character, George Brush, and it is in many ways an involved and complicated study of an all-too-familiar comic hero. Brush is motivated by one outstanding desire, and that is to have a "fine American home." His exploits put him into contact with people and situations which thwart his search; but through these encounters, Wilder develops a George Brush whom we look at humorously and sympathetically. The reader would probably find Brush's evangelism obnoxious if he thought Brush to be consciously hostile and aggravating. But it is clear from the beginning that George Brush is motivated by a sincere desire to do good. For this reason he is pathetic. The causes of Brush's misery lie in his own method of reasoning and coming to conclusions. He bases his principles on Christian morality, but tries to interpret them strictly and apply them to all people—there is no flexibilty in the substance of Brush's ethics. He aspires by his example to change everyone with whom he comes in contact and he is repeatedly shattered when people laughingly reject him. Yet the impact of their rejection never truly scars George Brush, for he bounces back for more, oblivious to the reasons why people think him such a fool.

This novel is quite different from any other Thornton Wilder literary work. In many ways it is Wilder's way of immortalizing his own belief that eternity is all-important to the activities of man, and that Heaven is truly man's destination. Wilder uses plain descriptive prose in this novel, and remains fairly objective, allowing the reader to make his own inferences and observations. Wilder is not the philosopher he appears to be in other works. Rather, he attempts to reveal the influences upon him in his own youth and the results of his own religious upbringing. In *Heaven's My Destination* he tries to put these ideas into perspective in terms of a believable character. There are times in the novel when the thoughts and actions of George Brush are very funny, contemporary, and exceedingly familiar. His experiences cannot help but reinforce one's faith in goodness, no matter what the penalties are for trying to achieve it.

Brush is seen in the final pages of the novel as unchanged. Throughout he has been at odds with what is considered "normal" behavior, and there is no reason to expect that anything will be different in his future life style. He will continue his travels as a textbook salesman, probably never settling in that "fine American home." His failure is pathetic, and the routineness of his life and search are apparent. But it is difficult to put George Brush into a category and unequivocally say we like or dislike him. Wilder asserts that he has portrayed Brush with realism, not satire. It is not impossible, however, to see Brush in a highly satiric light today in terms of religious enthusiasts and their programs for salvation. Brush, like many with missionary intent, demands a great deal of acceptance and understanding and offers very little in return.

HEDDA GABLER

Type of work: Drama
Author: Henrik Ibsen (1828-1906)
Type of plot: Social criticism
Time of plot: Late nineteenth century
Locale: Norway
First presented: 1890

Principal characters:
GEORGE TESSMAN, a scholar
HEDDA TESSMAN, his wife
MISS JULIANA TESMAN, his aunt
MRS. ELVSTED, Hedda's old schoolmate
JUDGE BRACK, a friend of the Tessmans
EILERT LOVBERG, Hedda's former suitor

Critique:

Hedda Gabler has in it most of the elements of good theater which Ibsen painstakingly learned from the popular French playwrights of the last half of the nineteenth century. In Hedda, he created a woman with hardly one redeeming virtue. She is spiritually as empty as she assumes her environment to be. Nearly every great actress of the last half-century has played Hedda and audiences have always been attracted to her powerful but ruthless personality.

The Story:

When aristocratic Hedda Gabler, daughter of the late General Gabler, consented to marry Doctor George Tessman everyone in Hedda's set was surprised and a little shocked. Although George was a rising young scholar soon to be made a professor in the university, he was hardly considered the type of person Hedda would marry. He was dull and prosaic, absorbed almost exclusively in his dusty tomes and manuscripts, while Hedda was the beautiful, spoiled darling of her father and of all the other men who had flocked around her. But Hedda was now twenty-nine, and George was the only one of her admirers who was willing to offer her marriage and a villa which had belonged to the widow of a cabinet minister.

The villa was somewhat beyond George's means, but with the prospect of a professorship and with his Aunt Juliana's help, he managed to secure it because it was what Hedda wanted. He arranged a long wedding tour lasting nearly six months because Hedda wished that also. On their honeymoon George spent most of his time delving into libraries for material on his special field, the history of civilization. Hedda was bored. She returned to the villa hating George. Then it began to look as if George might not get the professorship, in which case Hedda would have to forego her footman and saddlehorse and some of the other luxuries she craved. George's rival for the post was Eilert Lovberg, a brilliant but erratic genius who had written a book, acclaimed a masterpiece, in George's own field. Hedda's boredom and disgust with her situation was complete. She found her only excitement in practicing with the brace of pistols which had belonged to General Gabler, the only legacy her father had left her.

George discovered that Eilert had written another book, more brilliant and important than the last, a book written with the help and inspiration of a Mrs. Elvsted, whose devotion to the erratic genius had reformed him. The manuscript of this book Lovberg brought with him one evening to the Tesman villa. Hedda proceeded to make the most of this situation. In the first place, Thea

HEDDA GABLER by Henrik Ibsen. Published by Charles Scribner's Sons.

Elvsted was Hedda's despised schoolmate, and her husband's former sweetheart. The fact that this mouse-like creature had been the inspiration for the success and rehabilitation of Eilert Lovberg was more than Hedda could bear. For Eilert Lovberg had always been in love with Hedda, and she knew it. In the distant past, he had urged her to throw in her lot with him and she had been tempted to do so but had refused because his future had been uncertain. Now Hedda felt a pang of regret mingled with anger that another woman possessed what she had lacked the courage to hold for herself.

Her only impulse was to destroy, and circumstances played into her hands. When Lovberg called at the Tessman Villa with his manuscript, George was on the point of leaving with his friend, Judge Brack, for a bachelor party. They invited Lovberg to accompany them, but he refused, preferring to remain at the villa with Mrs. Elvsted and Hedda. But Hedda, determined to destroy the handiwork of her rival, deliberately sent Lovberg off to the party. All night, Hedda and Mrs. Elvsted awaited the revelers' return. George was the first to appear with the story of the happenings of the night before.

The party had ended in an orgy, and on the way home Lovberg had lost his manuscript, which George recovered and brought home. In despair over the supposed loss of his manuscript, Lovberg had spent the remainder of the evening at Mademoiselle Diana's establishment. When he finally made his appearance at the villa, George had gone. Lovberg told Mrs. Elvsted he had destroyed his manuscript, but later he confessed to Hedda that it was lost and that, as a consequence, he intended to take his own life. Without revealing that the manuscript was at that moment in her possession, Hedda urged him to do the deed beautifully, and she pressed into his hand a memento of their relationship, one of General Gabler's pistols—the very one with which she had once threatened Lovberg.

After his departure, Hedda coldly and deliberately thrust the manuscript into the fire. When George returned and heard from Hedda's own lips the fate of Lovberg's manuscript, he was unspeakably shocked; but half believing that she burned it for his sake, he was also flattered. He resolved to keep silent and devote his life to reconstructing the book from the notes kept by Mrs. Elvsted.

Except for two circumstances, Hedda would have been safe. The first was the manner in which Lovberg met his death. Leaving Hedda, he had returned to Mademoiselle Diana's, where instead of dying beautifully, as Hedda had planned, he became embroiled in a brawl in which he was accidentally killed. The second was the character of Judge Brack, a sophisticated man of the world, as ruthless in his way as Hedda was in hers. He had long admired Hedda's cold, dispassionate beauty, and had wanted to make her his mistress. The peculiar circumstances of Eilert Lovberg's death gave him his opportunity. He had learned that the pistol with which Lovberg met his death was one of a pair belonging to Hedda. If the truth came out, there would be an investigation followed by scandal in which Hedda would be involved. She could not face either a public scandal or the private ignominy of the judge's proposal. So while her husband and Mrs. Elvsted were beginning the long task of reconstructing the dead Lovberg's manuscript, Hedda calmly went to her boudoir and with the remaining pistol she died beautifully—as she had urged Lovberg to do —by putting a bullet through her head.

Further Critical Evaluation of the Work:

In *Hedda Gabler,* Henrik Ibsen constructed a complex play which caused considerable bewilderment among his contemporary critics. Some found fault; some simply confessed puzzlement. *Hedda Gabler,* as one of Ibsen's later plays, was, for example, often judged in the context of his earlier work instead of evaluated on its own merits. Hence, when the broad social issues treated in earlier plays were found lacking or deficient in *Hedda Gabler,* the latter play was pronounced inferior. The most common misperception of *Hedda Gabler,* however, stemmed from a tendency to see the play through its title and hence its protagonist. "How," it was asked, "could Ibsen present a 'heroine' so totally devoid of any redeeming virtues?" Again, critics who raised the question misconstrued the play—and drama criticism, as well— for a protagonist need not be a heroine or a hero.

Modern critical opinion has focused more carefully on the structure of the play. Hence, one critic has called attenion to a typical Ibsen device which the critic characterizes as "retrospective action"—a theatrical method noted by many other critics but without the apt label. As a thearical device, Ibsen's dramatic innovation operates thus: the problem of exposition—revealing the crucial events which preceded the present action in the play (motion pictures solve the problem through flashbacks)—is handled in the first few scenes by having the major characters, reunited with other characters after a long absence, recapitulate past activities to bring the other characters up to date. Hence, the Tessmans, returning from their extended honeymoon, reveal much of themselves in conversation with Juliana and others. Yet, despite this sophisticated surmounting of theatrical obstacles, the play is not without structural weaknesses. Lovberg's apocalyptic attitude is unconvincing; Ibsen's view of scholarly enterprise as a batch of notes in someone's briefcase is ludicrous; and Hedda's potential disaffiliation with the play poses a threat to dramatic unity. These disabilities notwithstanding, the play holds up under critical review because dialogue, characterization, and theme carry it through.

For the verbal polish and linguistic sensitivity of the dialogue, Ibsen's method of playwrighting is largely responsible. After completing a play, Ibsen would rest, letting his mind lie fallow. Then he would begin incubating ideas for his next play. When he was ready to write, he wrote quickly, completing his first draft in about two months. Next, the draft was set aside for another two months or so to "age" properly, whereupon Ibsen would then attack the final job of refining each nuance to perfection, completing the job in two to three weeks and having the copy ready for the printer within a month's time; the following month, the play was off the press and ready for distribution. It was in the refining process, however, that Ibsen sharpened his dialogue to crystal-clear perfection. Thus it was that he added to the play George Tessman's fussy expostulations—the characteristic, questioning "Hmm's?" and "Eh's"; Brack's inquisitorial manner; the fillips of imagery such as "vine leaves in his hair"; and so on. Out of such stuff truly poetic dialogue is made, and Ibsen certainly made it. Few playwrights can match the exquisitely fine-tuned dialogue of *Hedda Gabler.*

As for characterization, one is hard put to resist the temptation to concentrate exclusively on Hedda without touching upon at least George, Lovberg, and Judge Brack. Yet the character of Hedda stands out in bold relief only by contrast with these other characters in the play. Thus the others must be given serious consideration at least as the medium for Hedda's development. Hedda's three major counterfoils are George Tessman, Eilert Lovberg, and Brack, but all of the men are rather static characters in the play. Although their personalities are revealed to us gradually as the play progresses, none of them undergoes any fundamental change. Thus, George Tessman begins and ends as a somewhat distracted "Mr. Chips" personality; Lovberg is revealed as an incurable incompetent; and Brack is exposed for the coldly calculating, manipulative Svengali he wants to be, on the face of it a perfect match for Hedda's own apparently predatory instincts. But against this background, Hedda dominates the scene: a creature of impulse and indulgence, her father's spoiled darling. Let us remember that the play is titled *Hedda Gabler,* not Hedda Tessman! Let us also remember Hedda's growing contempt for Tessman and her opportunism as it grows in inverse ratio to his declining prospects. And let us not forget that in the matrix of Lovberg's inelegant death, Tessman's ineffectuality, Brack's obscene proposition, and Hedda's unwanted pregnancy with Tessman's child, Hedda prefers an efficient suicide to a messy life. Hedda's life does not meet her exacting standards, but her suicide fulfills her sense of style in a way that living cannot. Ibsen's vivid insight into Hedda's personality thus constitutes the real meat of the play, for it is Hedda as an individual—not Hedda as a "case study" or Hedda as a "social issue" or Hedda as anything else—that constitutes the play *Hedda Gabler.*

If Hedda's character dominates the play, what does this have to do with the theme of the play itself? If the answer were as simple as the question suggests, long explanations would be unnecessary. But the theme of *Hedda Gabler,* like Hedda herself, is complex. It is complex because Hedda's personality is the theme of the play; because Hedda's personality is complex; and because complex personalities—instead of easily distilled social issues—are difficult to convey sympathetically to an audience of diverse and equally complex personalities. How can we understand Hedda? Certainly she is more substantial than a mad housewife or an ex-prom queen. Inchoately, she desires, but she has not the sophistication to focus her desires. She is thus directionless. Her *angst* is as much an identity crisis as a lack of goals. She does not know what she wants, much less how to get it. Her apparent hardheadedness, which so attracts Brack, is no more than a mask for her own insecurity. Hers is not a problem of social justice but of private insight. She knows nothing of personal or political power; hence, she appears to use people, to exploit them—but, in reality, more out of naïveté than cold calculation, for she does not recognize or appreciate her influence. The metaphorical evolution of Hedda's personality—from self-indulgent child, to falsely confident adolescent, to desperate and despairing (and pregnant) woman who puts a bullet through her head—starkly depicts the life of an individual, not a symbol of a social issue. As such, *Hedda Gabler* is a problem play, not a social-problem play.

Joanne G. Kashdan

THE HEIMSKRINGLA

Type of work: Sagas
Author: Snorri Sturluson (1179-1241)
Type of plots: Historical chronicles
Time of plots: Legendary times to twelfth century
Locale: Norway
First transcribed: Thirteenth century

Principal characters:
ODIN, ancestor of the Northmen
ON JORUNDSSON, of Sweden
HALFDAN THE BLACK, of Norway
HARALD THE FAIRHAIRED, his son
AETHELSTAN, of England
HAKON THE GOOD, Harald's son
ERIC BLOOD-AX, Hakon's brother
OLAF TRYGGVESSON, Christianizer of Norway
OLAF THE SAINT
MAGNUS THE GOOD, his stepson
HARALD SIGURDSSON THE STERN, Olaf the Saint's brother
OLAF THE QUIET, Harald's son
MAGNUS BAREFOOT, Olaf's son
EYSTEIN.
SIGURD, and
OLAF, Magnus' sons
MAGNUS SIGURDSSON
HARALD GILLE, Sigurd Magnusson's half brother
INGE,
SIGURD, and
EYSTEIN, Harald's sons
HAKON SIGURDSSON
ERLING SKAKKE, counselor to Inge
MAGNUS, his son

Critique:

The Heimskringla, a collection of traditional sagas of the Norwegian kings, was first transcribed by Snorri Sturluson, an Icelandic bard and chieftain. Interested in the stories handed down by word of mouth in the houses of chieftains in the northern countries, he wrote them down in Old Norse, the language understood by all Scandinavian peoples at that time. Snorri Sturluson began writing in 1220. Beginning with the Yngling Saga, which traces the descent of the Northmen from the legendary god Odin, *The Heimskringla* contains fifteen other sagas covering the historic period between 839 and 1177. Each saga tells of the life and achievements of one man; in *The Heimskringla* each man represented is the chief king of Norway at a time when several men usually fought for the title. These are only a few of the hundreds of sagas known to Scandinavian literature. While the time of sagas in general runs from the sixth to the fourteenth centuries, *The Heimskringla* covers the Viking Age, dating roughly from the eighth century, when Norwegians came into historical significance because of their raiding expeditions, through the years of Norwegian occupation of foreign lands, the Christianizing of their own country, and finally the consolidation of Norway.

The Stories:

In Asaland in Asia near the Black Sea lived Odin, the conqueror of many nations, and a great traveler, whose people believed he would have success in every battle. When a neighboring people beheaded his friend Mime as a spy and sent the head to Odin, he smeared the head with herbs to keep it from rotting and sang incantations over it. Thereafter the head could speak to Odin and discover secrets for him. While the Romans were subduing the world, Odin learned that he was to rule the northern half. Traveling through Russia and northern Germany, he finally settled in the Scandinavian peninsula. There he appeared handsome to his friends and fiendish to his enemies. He used magic against his foes so that they were helpless in battle against him, for he could change his own shape and wish himself from place to place. He made laws for his people: that the dead should be burned, that blood-sacrifice be made for good harvests, and that taxes be paid yearly. When he was near death, Odin said that he would go to Valhalla and wait there for all good warriors. Then he died quietly in his bed, and afterward the rulers of the northland claimed descent from him.

The sacrifices his people made to Odin were sometimes great. When King On Jorundsson of Sweden was sixty years old, he made an oracular sacrifice of a son to Odin. His answer from Odin was that he would live sixty years longer if he sacrificed a son every ten years. He sacrificed as he was told until he had given up nine out of his ten sons. By that time he was so old and weak that his people refused to let the tenth son be sacrificed, and so On died of extreme old age. After that people dying from weakness of age were said to have On's sickness.

After twenty generations of Yngling rulers in the Scandinavian countries came Halfdan the Black, born about 820, King of Norway. In those days a king was an intermediary between the people and the supreme powers, whose favor he courted by sacrifices. Halfdan was considered a good king because the harvests were plentiful during his lifetime. He died young in a sleighing accident while crossing thin ice. His people begged so hard for his body to insure continued good seasons that finally the body was quartered, and each quarter and the head were sent

to separate provinces to spread his good influence.

Harald the Fairhaired was Halfdan's son. He sent some of his henchmen to bring to him a girl to be his concubine, but she refused to bow to a king of any territory so small and sent word that she would consider him when he ruled all of Norway. His attendants thought her attitude warranted punishment; Harald considered it a challenge. Ten years later, after he had conquered all of Norway, he sent for the girl and married her. He had many children by her and other women. When he was fifty years old, he divided his kingdom among his sons and gave them half the revenues.

At that time Aethelstan, King of England, sent Harald a sword. When Harald accepted it, however, Aethelstan's messengers claimed that he was then subject to their king. The following summer Harald sent his nine-year-old son Hakon to Aethelstan to foster, as a foster father was always subject to a real father. Each king tried to outdo the other, but each ruled in his own kingdom until his dying day. When he was seventy-nine years old, Harald died in his bed.

Hakon went from England to Norway when he heard of his father's death. He was then fifteen years old. At the same time the chief Norse king had sailed west to ravage England; he was Hakon's brother, Eric Blood-Ax, so called because he had slain at least four of his brothers. Eric was killed in England and Hakon subdued Norway. Hakon, who had been converted to Christianity while in England, began to practice Christian habits of fasting and prayer in Norway. Although he did not insist on forcing Christianity on his followers, many of them, out of friendship for him, allowed themselves to be baptized. Hakon wanted to forego sacrifices to the gods, but a counselor persuaded him to humor the people who still believed devoutly in blood sacrifice. Known to his country as Hakon the Good, he was killed in battle with Eric's sons, to whom he left the kingdom. The years during which Eric's sons ruled Norway were so bad that fish as well as corn were lacking and the people went hungry. Among other petty kings, the sons killed Tryggve Olafsson, whose wife escaped to bring Olaf Tryggvesson to birth.

As a child Olaf Tryggvesson spent six years in slavery before his uncle learned where marauding Vikings had sent him after capturing the boy and his mother as they were on their way to a place of safety in Russia. By the time he was twelve, Olaf himself was a Viking chieftain. After harrying various parts of England he made peace with Aethelred, the English king, and thereafter always kept the peace with England. By that time his aim was to be a crusader, for he had come under the influence of Christianity during his raids on England. Having been converted and baptized by the English priests, he wanted to Christianize his own land as well. He set sail for Norway in 995. Between that date and 1000, when he was decoyed into a one-sided battle with the kings of Denmark and Sweden and lost his life at Svolder, he converted all of Norway as well as many of the outlying islands, either by the force of his own personality, or, when that did not suffice, by force of arms. Norway was a Christian land by the time Olaf died, but there was no Norwegian king strong enough to rule its entirety while the Danes and Swedes laid claim to various parts of the country.

While he was very young, Olaf Haraldsson joined Viking expeditions to England, Jutland, Holland, France, and Spain. In England, where the Norwegians were fighting the Danes who were then in power in England, he was present at the stoning to death of the archbishop who had confirmed Olaf Tryggvesson. It was said that in Spain Olaf Haraldsson dreamed of a fearful man who told him to give up further travel to the Holy Land and to go back to Norway. In 1015 he sailed for Norway to reëstablish Christianity and to regain the throne once held by his ancestor, Harald the Fairhaired. Though he did not have the strik-

ing personality of Olaf Tryggvesson, Olaf Haraldsson had persistence enough to spread Christianity by his bands of missionaries, to win control over Norway, and to set up a central government. The latter was his hardest task, as it meant taking away some of the traditional powers of the chieftains. He created a form of justice that worked equally for the chieftains and the common people, and because of their resentment the chieftains rose against him at last. With a superior force they fought him at Stiklestad, in 1030, when he was cut down. His hope for national union and independence seemed doomed until suddenly rumors were spread that miracles had occurred where his body had fallen. People began to give Olaf Haraldsson a new name, Olaf the Saint, and the whole Norwegian people suddenly craved the independence he had fought for.

Olaf the Saint's stepson, Magnus, obtained the title of King of Norway without much trouble. Afterward he made a treaty with King Hardacanute of Denmark to keep the peace as long as they both should live, the one surviving to become the ruler of the other's country. When Hardacanute died, Magnus thereupon became King of Denmark. Since Hardacanute had also become King of England after the death of his father, Magnus laid claim to England when Edward the Good became the English king; but he was prevented from invading England by trouble stirred up in Denmark by a false friend whom he had made earl there. Letters were exchanged between Magnus and Edward over Magnus' claim to England. Edward's reply was so sensible and courageous that Magnus was content to rule in his own land and to let Edward reign in England.

Greater troubles beset Magnus when his uncle, Harald Sigurdsson, returned north after many years in Russia, Constantinople, and the Holy Land. Harald had left Norway after the battle of Stiklestad, when his brother Olaf the Saint was killed. He plundered all through the south lands and at Constantinople joined the royal guard called the Vaeringer. Meanwhile he had collected much booty, which he sent to the Russian king for safekeeping until he should have finished his wanderings. When he tired of life in Constantinople, he traveled north to Russia. There he married Ellisiv, the king's daughter, and then traveled with her and his booty toward Norway. Eventually he made a deal with Magnus. He received half of Norway in return for half his booty. When Magnus, called the Good, died of illness, Harald, in contrast called the Stern, ruled alone. He was a harsh ruler and he met his death in England while trying to unthrone Harald Godwinsson, Edward's successor.

Through these times miracles continued to be credited to Olaf the Saint. Sometimes he appeared to people in dreams, as he did to Magnus the Good just before his death. Sometimes a pilgrimage to his shrine cured people who had been crippled from birth or who had been maimed in fighting. It was even said that Olaf could pull the root of a tongue so that a man whose tongue had been cut out could speak again. His shrine was in Nidaros.

After Harald the Stern, his sons Magnus and Olaf ruled Norway, but Magnus soon died of a sickness. Olaf, called the Quiet, reigned for twenty-six years. There was peace in Norway during that time, and the country gained in riches and cultivation.

Thereafter Olaf's son Magnus and his nephew, Hakon Magnusson, ruled Norway, but Hakon soon died of an illness. Magnus' reign was of ten years' time, most of which he spent in expeditions to reduce the island possessions to full submission to the central government in Norway. Under Magnus, for the first time, the government became a strong power. Because Magnus returned from one of his expeditions to Scotland wearing the Scottish national costume, his people called him Magnus Barefoot. On a foraging expedition, in 1103, Magnus was killed in Ireland before he was thirty years old.

From that time until 1130 peace descended on Norway and the Church increased its powers. In the early days the Norwegian churches had been under the archbishopric of Bremen, but during that time they gained an archbishopric of their own at Lund in Skane. Magnus' sons, Eystein, Sigurd, and Olaf, ruled the country, but Olaf was only a small boy. Those years were also the period of the crusades. Sigurd took men and ships to the Holy Land while Eystein ruled at home. Sigurd was gone three years and gained much glory in England, Spain, Constantinople, and Palestine. He was afterward called the Crusader. When he came back to Norway, he and Eystein were jealous of each other's powers. Olaf died young and Eystein died before Sigurd. Sigurd had strange fancies before he himself died, but he had done much to improve the legal system of the country by increasing the powers of the Things. The congregation of people at the Things became the highest authority in the land, and even the kings argued their cases before those representative bodies.

Neither Olaf nor Eystein had sons. Magnus, Sigurd's son, became king, but his sole rule was threatened by Harald Gille, who came from Ireland and claimed to be Sigurd's half-brother. Harald passed an ordeal by hot iron to prove his paternity. After Sigurd's death Harald was proclaimed king over part of Norway. It was said that Magnus was foolish, but Harald was cruel. A series of civil wars ensued, ending when Harald captured Magnus and had him blinded and otherwise mutilated. Thereafter Magnus was called the Blind. He retired to a monastery. Harald was killed by the order and treachery of Sigurd Slembedegn, a pretender to the throne.

In the days when Harald's sons reigned there were more civil wars. Crippled Inge was the most popular of Harald's three sons. Sigurd and Eystein led separate factions, and so there was always unrest in the country.

In 1152, Cardinal Nicholas came to

Norway from Rome to establish an archbishopric at Nidaros, where King Olaf the Saint reposed. Cardinal Nicholas was well loved by the people and improved many of their customs. When the pope died suddenly, Nicholas became Pope Adrian IV. He was always friendly with the Norsemen.

After Sigurd and Eystein had been killed in different battles, Inge ruled alone. He was twenty-six when he was killed in battle with Hakon Sigurdsson, who had claimed Eystein's part of Norway. Hakon was little to be trusted. Erling Skakke, previously a power behind Inge's throne, then took it upon himself to create a strong party which could put upon the throne whomever it chose. None of his party favored Hakon, called the Broad-Shouldered, who was defeated in battle within a year, when he was only fifteen, in 1162.

Erling Skakke's party finally decided to put Erling Skakke's son Magnus on the throne. The child was five years old at the time. He was a legitimate candidate, however, for his mother was a daughter of Sigurd the Crusader. Erling Skakke was jealous of power, yet he gave much of the traditional authority of the throne to the bishops in exchange for their blessing on Magnus as king; and he made an agreement with King Valdemar of Denmark under which he gave Valdemar a part of Norway as a fief under the Danish crown in exchange for peace. It had been a long time since a foreign king had claim to part of Norway. Erling Skakke spent much of his time wiping out the descendants of Harald Gille, and in time he became a tyrant in order to hold the throne safe for his child, Magnus Erlingsson.

Further Critical Evaluation of the Work:

Though his name is hardly well known today, Snorri Sturluson was one of the foremost authors and politicians of the thirteenth century. He came from a rich and politically influential family in Iceland and was very active in the political intrigues of the Norwegian court which ruled Iceland. So much was he involved in politics, that he was assassinated in 1241 by an agent of his enemy, King Hakon of Norway. His political life notwithstanding, it was his role as historian and mythographer for which he is most remembered among scholars today. He wrote and compiled several works on Norse history/mythology, the most famous being *The Heimskringla*. In this work he combined his earlier *Olaf Saga* with stories of the ancient Norwegian kings which were part of Norse tradition to create *The Orb of the World,* which is the English translation of *The Heimskringla*. (Another title by which *The Heimskringla* is known in English is *The Lives of the Kings of Norway;* this is a translation of the work's title as it appears in other Old Icelandic versions of the saga.)

From evidence obtained from careful study of Snorri's works, we know that he was familiar with other historical works, and he made an attempt to be "scientific" in his writings. He was, however, what would be called a "vernacular" historian, that is, he took much of his writings from oral tradition rather than previous written sources. He cannot be called a complete mythographer, however, since, unlike other mythographers, he did not add any myths to his work which had never previously been written down.

In the twelfth and thirteenth centuries Iceland was alive with literary activity. There was great interest among Icelandic people in the myths and history of their own country and also in its ties with their rulers, the Norwegians. Many of the known sagas of Icelandic tradition were written down during this period. The early kings of Norway, the legendary heroes and gods, were dramatized in these writings so that the real people and the actual facts were difficult to separate from legend. One of the most important examples of this is the tradition created around the Norse God Odin. His story was told time and again throughout Norse history in various oral and written forms. There are numerous variations on Odin's story as one can see by comparing several of the written sources in existence today. Snorri explained Odin as one of the earliest kings of Norway who was glorified to such an extent that after his death he was deified by the Norwegian people. This is the "euhemeristic" interpretation of Norse history. Euhemeres was a fourth century B.C. Greek writer who was the first person to propose the theory that all mythological characters are actually based on real people who were deified and glorified after their deaths. Snorri was a follower of this theory. He said that he wrote "biographies" rather than mythological stories. In *The Heimskringla* he wrote sixteen such biographies to give a historical basis for Norse mythology. There are many other interpretations of these stories, however, and it should be noted that the problem of historicity versus mythology is something which cannot be definitely solved in this case.

Snorri did not simply treat the ancient, unreliable accounts of history. He intended to make his work an interpretation of more recent history as well. His work traces Norwegian history down to Snorri's own time, something which again adds to the dispute about how *The Heimskringla* should be categorized. He pays much attention to the part that Christianity played in Norwegian history, although he spends very little time moralizing or even discussing the effects of the Christian religion upon the Scandinavian peoples.

Because of the combination of myth and history in Snorri's work, it reads almost like a novel. He treats the ancient kings the way classical authors such as Plutarch did, glorifying their lives and interpolating anecdotes which are often missing from "textbook" treatments of history. He has been called the Scandinavian Herodotus because of his keen ability to combine myth with history and create an entertaining chronicle, but it is a rather high compliment to pay to Snorri.

A careful reading of *The Heimskringla* indicates that Snorri thought of himself certainly more as a historian than a mythographer. Compared to other treatments of Odin, for example, *The Heimskringla* is quite believable. Odin here is neither an amorphous being nor a sun-god. There are no religious connotations at all attached to his life. One can read this work as a piece of plausible history if one does not have previous knowledge of the flimsy historicity of the "facts" presented therein.

Perhaps it is best simply to define *The Heimskringla* as a "saga" in the traditional meaning of the word: a medieval treatment of sweeping magnitude which describes the history of various aspects of Scandinavian society. The saga usually included numerous battles and conquests, as does *The Heimskringla,* and was written for no other purpose than to illustrate history and increase national pride. It is perhaps difficult for readers more familiar with traditional histories to see the significance of the saga, but to medieval Norsemen it was an important cultural as well as educational device. This is important for modern readers to keep in mind, for *The Heimskringla,* like all sagas and most histories, was written more as an edification of past events than an explanation. It represented the themes which the author wanted to have illuminated and those are often different from the interpretations of other authors.

Patricia Ann King

HELEN

Type of work: Drama
Author: Euripides (c. 485-c. 406 B.C.)
Type of plot: Romantic adventure
Time of plot: Seven years after the sack of Troy
Locale: Egypt
First presented: 412 B.C.

Principal characters:
HELEN, wife of King Menelaus
MENELAUS, King of Sparta
THEOCLYMENUS, King of Egypt
THEONOE, a prophetess, sister of Theoclymenus

Critique:

There is some disagreement among Greek scholars as to whether *Helen* is a serious play or, because of its anticlimactic happy ending, merely Euripidean self-parody. The line of action seems to build toward tragedy, from which it is averted at the last moment by a *deus ex machina* in the form of the Dioscuri. The story is taken from a tradition established in the sixth century B.C. by the Greek poet Stesichorus, who believed that Paris had carried off to Troy only a phantom Helen fashioned by Hera, while the real Helen was taken to Egypt by Hermes. H. D. F. Kitto praises this play, asserting that it has appropriate rhetoric throughout, consistent characterization, and a faultless plot. Perhaps the only exceptions to its comic tone are the first ode of the chorus and the murder of the fifty Egyptian galley-men.

The Story:

Helen prayed before the tomb of Proteus, late King of Egypt, who had protected her from any dishonor while her husband Menelaus was leading the Greek hosts at the siege of Troy in the mistaken belief that the phantom Helen carried off by Paris, son of the Trojan king, was really his wife. She recalled that when the three goddesses, Hera, Cypris (Aphrodite), and Athena had appeared before Paris and asked him to judge which was the fairest, Cypris had promised him Helen as a prize for choosing her. But Hera, enraged at being rejected, had caused a phantom Helen to be carried

off to Troy. In Egypt the real Helen prayed for the safety of her husband and for protection against Theoclymenus, son of Proteus, who was determined to marry her.

She was accosted by Teucer, an exile from Achaea, who brought tidings of the end of the war, the ruin of the Greeks seeking their homelands, the disappearance of Menelaus and Helen, and the suicide of Leda, Helen's mother, who had killed herself because she could not endure her daughter's shame. The anguished Helen then warned Teucer not to seek out the prophetess Theonoe, as he intended, but to flee, for any Greek found in Egypt would be killed. The chorus grieved for Helen, who lamented her miserable fate and threatened suicide. In despair, she took the advice of the chorus and herself sought out Theonoe.

Menelaus, shipwrecked and in rags, appeared before the palace seeking aid, only to be berated and sent off by a portress who warned him that since Theoclymenus had Helen in his possession no Greeks were welcome in Egypt. Menelaus was astounded, for he had just left his Helen secure in a nearby cave. As he stood there in bewilderment, Helen emerged from her conference with Theonoe and confronted amazed Menelaus. Helen could not convince him that she was indeed his wife until a messenger brought word to Menelaus that the Helen he had left at the cave was gone, having soared away into the air. The long separated lovers then embraced, rejoiced, and

2544

told each other of all the adventures that had befallen them. But their immense happiness was darkened by realization of their present plight: Theoclymenus was determined to make Helen his own, and Menelaus was in danger of his life. The two resolved that if they could not concoct some scheme for escape, they would commit suicide rather than be separated again.

Theonoe, aware of the presence of Menelaus, appeared to inform him that, although Hera had relented and was now willing to let him return to Sparta with Helen, Cypris was unwilling to have it revealed that she had bribed Paris to be chosen as the most beautiful of the goddesses. Therefore Theonoe, serving Cypris, felt obliged to expose Menelaus to her brother. Terrified, Helen fell to her knees in tears and supplication, and the enraged Menelaus threatened that they would die rather than submit. Theonoe relented, promised to keep silent, and urged them to devise some way of escape.

After rejecting several of Menelaus' desperate proposals, Helen hit upon a scheme which she put into operation as soon as Theoclymenus returned from a hunting trip. Appearing before him in mourning clothes and addressing him for the first time as her lord, Helen told him in a pitiful voice that a shipwrecked Greek warrior had just brought her word that Menelaus had drowned at sea. She was now ready, she added, to marry Theoclymenus if he would permit proper burial honors, in the Greek fashion, for her husband. Theoclymenus consented and turned to Menelaus, who was posing as the bearer of sad tidings, for instructions concerning Greek burial rites for a

king drowned at sea. He was told that there must be a blood-offering, an empty bier decked and carried in procession, bronze arms, a supply of the fruits of the earth, all to be taken out to sea in a large ship from which the widow must commit everything to the waters. The gullible Theoclymenus, anxious to foster piety in the woman who was about to become his wife, agreed to everything, and preparations were made for both a funeral and a royal wedding.

Later, a breathless messenger came running to Theoclymenus with the news that Helen had escaped with Menelaus. He described in detail how the Greek stranger commanding the ship had permitted a large number of shipwrecked sailors to come aboard and how, when the time came to slay the bull, the stranger, instead of uttering a funeral prayer, had called upon Poseidon to allow him and his wife to sail safely to Sparta. The aroused Egyptians sought to turn back the ship, but they were slaughtered by the Greek warriors whom Menelaus had smuggled aboard. Theoclymenus, enraged, realized that pursuit was hopeless but resolved to avenge himself on his treacherous sister, Theonoe. A servant from the palace tried in vain to convince him that he ought to accept what was obviously an honorable treachery. Both the servant and Theonoe were saved from death when the Dioscuri, the twin sons of Zeus, appeared from the sky to restrain his rage and explain to him that Heaven had ordained the return of Helen and Menelaus to their homeland. Theoclymenus was chastened, and the chorus chanted familiar lines about the irony of Fate.

Further Critical Evaluation of the Work:

A "happy ending" drama such as the *Helen* is as much a "Greek tragedy" as the most typically horrifying and saddening plays. Tragedy meant to the Greeks a dramatic performance drawn from a heroic, that is, mythologically significant, theme; the *Helen* fits that description in that its characters and situation are eminently well known (cf. Euripides *Iphigenia in Tauris* and *Alcestis*). Critics note the resemblance of the *Helen* to the much later love-adventure novels called Greek romances, in which (young) lovers are cruelly separated but are eventually reunited after a tangled succession of trials and misadventures. But in the *Helen*, as in any Greek tragedy, the action is not protracted, nor is the poet's only intention to entertain with spectacle and suspense; on the other hand, we must not try to fit Helen (or any other character) into the mold of the Aristotelian tragic hero.

Broadly this play deals with Helen's rescue-escape from a fate worse than death (widowhood and forced marriage to a *barbaros*). Her gloomy despair is genuine, or at any rate eloquently conveyed. She is a sympathetic character, intelligent as well as beautiful, and she is most exciting when she ruthlessly uses her wit and charm to demonstrate her faithfulness to Menelaus. Nevertheless, Theonoe, not Helen, is the key to this drama. Prophetic powers make her literally the center of attraction, and it is her personal decision of silence which allows Helen and Menelaus to escape. Theonoe enjoys the role of intermediary between men and gods, but as a mortal she is subject to human sympathy, which nearly proves her undoing. Like Helen, Theonoe is rescued from Theoclymenus in the end. All the once-threatening dangers have been removed with much the same ease as had the Helen phantom, which had caused so much death and suffering.

HENDERSON THE RAIN KING

Type of work: Novel
Author: Saul Bellow (1915-   )
Time: The present
Locale: Central East Africa
First published: 1959

Principal characters:

EUGENE HENDERSON, an American millionaire, a traveler in Africa, a
philosophical clown
ROMILAYU, his native guide and companion
WILLATALE, the queen of the Arnewi tribe
MTALBA, her sister
ITELO, the prince-champion of the Arnewi
DAHFU, chief of the Wariri tribe
HORKO, the king's uncle
THE BUNAM, the chief priest of the Wariri
GMILO, a lion superstitiously believed to contain the spirit of Dahfu's
father
ATTI, a lioness
DAHFU, her cub, as named by Henderson

Although the forms and techniques of
fiction seem capable of almost endless variation, most novelists have only one
main story to tell, and the fortunate
writer is the one who finds his major
theme and fable early in his career. Saul
Bellow did in his first novel, *Dangling
Man.* It is the quest, man's search for
freedom and rest within the fretted human spirit.

For this reason *Henderson the Rain
King* is a Messianic novel, like *The
Plumed Serpent* or *A Fable.* The pattern
it follows—the outsider in search of the
truth which a local African Messiah reveals to him—is as old as Samuel Johnson's *Rasselas: Prince of Abyssinia.* The
theme is the achieving of individual identity, of becoming turning into being. For
a man thus to learn the depths of his own
nature Bellow constructs a situation that
verges on the fantastic: a middle-aged
American millionaire becomes the chief
priest of the rain goddess of a tribe in a
totally isolated region somewhere in East
Africa. The identification of the tribe is
impossible, the geography is unplaceable,
the realities of travel are ignored. The
narrator uses a coarse but effective style;
he is what is technically called an
"unreliable narrator" who must reveal

his character, even when he does not
know his identity, in the earlier chapters;
the redeemed must act as if he were un-
redeemed in telling of the events up to
his redemption. Unlike *Great Expectations,* for example, in which Pip tells us
all after the close of the action, the narrator employs a continuous past tense so
that the narration and the action parallel
each other. Thus neither he nor the
reader is ever in advance of the final revelation.

But the seeker in Bellow's fiction is no
Ulysses, Hamlet, Don Quixote, Gulliver,
Huck Finn, or Ishmael. He is the philosophical clown, the innocent American
and adventurous discoverer of a spiritual
quest which begins with the knowledge
that "man's character is his fate" and
ends with the realization that "man's fate
is his character." He is the *schnorrer* Joseph in *Dangling Man,* Asa Levanthal in
The Victim, and Augie in *The Adventures of Augie March,* that free-swinging,
irreverent, passionate account of one
man's journey on two continents, through
the depression years and a world war, and
within the geography of his own soul. All
of Bellow's heroes are driven by their desires toward some goal where the beginning of wisdom is often indistinguishable

from error and folly. Eugene Henderson, the narrator and central figure of *Henderson the Rain King,* is no exception. In fact, he is the most frantic and grotesque of Bellow's creations.

He is, to begin with, a tremendously comic figure, oversized in physique, great in his appetites, obsessed by the demands of an *I want, I want* that clamors without appeasement within him. He is fifty-five years old when we first meet him. A man with a temper as violent as his physical force, he has more money than even his eccentric needs demand, a second wife, an assorted brood of children. He has turned his home into a pig farm, learned to play the violin, and acquired a reputation for drinking and crude manners. When he tries to sum up his life, it is, as he says, a mess, a fact he realizes acutely without knowing why.

When he can no longer face himself, his family, or his past, he flees to Africa with dreams of becoming another Dr. Grenville or Dr. Schweitzer. Africa, as Henderson sees it, is an empty and secret land, the last outpost of the pre-human past, a land unmarked by the footprints of history.

With a native guide, Romilayu, he arrives at last in the land of the Arnewi, where he engages in a ritual wrestling bout with Itelo, the champion of the tribe. But in that remote place he still cannot escape his past; he remains a millionaire, a wanderer, a violent man looking for peace and happiness. The queen of these gentle people tells him that his malady is the *grun-tu-molani,* the will to live instead of dying. Accepted by the Arnewi and courted by the queen's sister, Mtalba, Henderson plans to cleanse the tribe's sacred cistern, which is infested with frogs. But his homemade bomb blasts away the wall of the cistern and the water seeps into the parched earth. Rather than face the consequences of this disaster he runs away.

Henderson next turns up among the Wariri, a more warlike and savage tribe. The king is Dahfu, a ruler considerably more enlightened than his subjects, for he has studied in a missionary school and can speak to Henderson in English. While watching a tribal festival, Henderson is moved to lift the statue of Mummah, goddess of clouds, after several of the Wariri have failed to budge the massive idol. His act of strength, he soon discovers, is sacramental. When a sudden downpour follows, he is acclaimed as the new Sungo, or rain king, of the tribe, and he is compelled to put on the green silk drawers of his office. But Henderson, elevated to a post in which he becomes a scapegoat for the capricious rain goddess, is no better off than he was before; he is as much governed by ritual as King Dahfu, who will rule only as long as his powers of procreation last. When they fail, he will be strangled and another ruler will be selected.

In the end, Dahfu is the means of Henderson's salvation. In an underground pit he keeps a pet lion, Atti, a creature hated and feared by the Wariri because they believe the beast has bewitched their king. As Dahfu continues to postpone the ritual capture of the wild lion supposed to contain his father's spirit, the chief priest and the king's uncle plot against him. Under Dahfu's tutelage, meanwhile, Henderson learns to romp with the lion and imitate its roars. Dahfu tells him to act the lion's role, to be a beast. Recovery of Henderson's humanity will come later; meanwhile, he is to imitate the lion.

Dahfu's lion cult impresses Henderson. His failure has been his bullish or piggish attempt to alter the world around him, to kick back when he felt kicked by fate. Instead he must alter himself, and in particular cure himself of fear by thinking like a lion, by imagining the lion at the cortex of his brain and making himself over as a lion. In spite of his crushing failure with the Arnewi he has learned two things that help him in his daily lion lessons. First, although a man when struck is likely to strike out in revenge (as the Wariri but not the Arnewi do,) pure virtue can break the chain of blows. The Arnewi, principally Mtalba, the aunt of Prince Itelo who was once the companion of Dahfu, are virtuous but cowlike because they love their cows; hence their virtue is not for Henderson. Second, he has been confirmed in a sneaking sense of his own worth by Mtalba, who oozed the odor of sanctity and was prepared to marry him. The demanding voice of the *I want, I want* within Henderson becomes the roar of the lion as Dahfu instructs him that man is still animal, but that it is possible for him to be a lion and not a pig.

The king's final lesson is that of courage in meeting death, which Henderson has always thought the biggest problem of all. When Dahfu is killed, possibly through the chief priest's conniving, while trying to capture a wild lion, Henderson flees the Wariri to avoid becoming the next king, and he returns with a captured lion cub to America. We get our last glimpse of him at the airport in Newfoundland. He is playing with a little boy, the child of American parents but who speaks only Persian. Dahfu and his lion have done their work. Henderson's spirit is finally at home in the animal housing of his flesh.

No brief outline of Henderson's story can ever adequately convey the gusty, wild humor, sensuous brilliance, abundant sense of life, or stylistic vigor of Saul Bellow's novel. Nor is it profitable to discuss the allegorical or symbolic meanings it contains, for those are matters that each reader must discover for himself. Call the novel whatever one will—a wild burlesque on all the travel books ever written, a comic extravaganza on modern themes, a melodramatic adventure story, a fantasy, an allegory, or the narrative of a symbolic journey into the dark reaches of the soul—*Henderson the Rain King* allows every reader to find a moment of truth. It is not always the same truth because readers look in different directions, but it is some revelation of the comedy and the tragedy of being. We cannot demand more of any novelist.

HENRY ESMOND

Type of work: Novel
Author: William Makepeace Thackeray (1811-1863)
Type of plot: Historical romance
Time of plot: Late seventeenth, early eighteenth centuries
Locale: England and the Low Countries
First published: 1852

Principal characters:
HENRY ESMOND, a Castlewood ward
FRANCIS ESMOND, Viscount Castlewood
RACHEL ESMOND, his wife
BEATRIX, their daughter
FRANK, their son
LORD MOHUN, a London rake
FATHER HOLT, a Jacobite spy
JAMES STUART, the exiled pretender

Critique:

Thackeray did not have high regard for the average historian of his day. To present history as he thought it should be presented, he wrote *The History of Henry Esmond,* a novel which contains a blend of fact and fiction. There is fact in the many historical characters of the book. There is fiction in the love story of Colonel Henry Esmond, who was in love with two women. Today's reader is likely to lose patience with Henry Esmond, whose attempts at winning Beatrix are so ineffectual as to be almost ludicrous; but no reader can escape the witchery of Beatrix's charms. In her, Thackeray has created one of the most delightfully puzzling and fascinating coquettes in all English literature.

The Story:

Henry Esmond grew up at Castlewood. He knew there was some mystery about his birth and he dimly remembered that long ago he had lived with weavers who spoke a foreign tongue. Thomas Esmond, Viscount Castlewood, had brought him to England and turned him over to Father Holt, the chaplain, to be educated. That much he learned as he grew older.

All was not peace and quiet at Castlewood in those years, when his lordship and Father Holt were engaged in a plot for the restoration of the exiled Stuart king, James II. When James attempted to recover Ireland for the Stuarts, Thomas Esmond rode off to his death at the battle of the Boyne. His widow fled to her dower house at Chelsea. Father Holt disappeared. Henry, a large-eyed, grave-faced twelve-year-old boy, was left alone with servants in the gloomy old house.

There his new guardians and distant cousins, Francis and Rachel Esmond, found him when they arrived to take possession of Castlewood. The new Viscount Castlewood, a bluff, loud-voiced man, greeted the boy kindly enough. His wife was like a girl herself—she was only eight years older than Henry—and Henry thought her the loveliest lady he had ever seen. With them were a little daughter, Beatrix, and a son, Frank, a baby in arms.

As Henry grew older he became more and more concerned over the rift he saw coming between Rachel Esmond and her husband, both of whom he loved because they had treated him as one of the immediate family in the household at Castlewood. It was plain that the hard-drinking, hard-gambling nobleman was wearying of his quiet country life. After Rachel's face was disfigured by small-pox, her altered beauty caused her husband to neglect her even more. Young Beatrix also felt that relations between her parents were strained.

When Henry was old enough, he went to Cambridge, sent there on money left Rachel by a deceased relative. Later, when he returned to Castlewood on a vacation, he realized for the first time

2550

that Beatrix was exceptionally attractive. Apparently he had never really noticed her before. Rachel, for her part, had great regard for her young kinsman. Before his arrival from Cambridge, according to Beatrix, Rachel went to Henry's room ten times to see that it was ready.

Relations between Rachel and the viscount were all but severed when the notorious Lord Mohun visited Castlewood. Rachel knew her husband had been losing heavily to Mohun at cards, but when she spoke to the viscount about the bad company he was keeping, he flew into a rage. He was by no means calmed when Beatrix innocently blurted out to her father, in the company of Mohun, that that gentleman was interested in Rachel. Jealous of another man's attentions to the wife he himself neglected, the viscount determined to seek satisfaction in a duel.

The two men fought in London, where the viscount had gone on the pretext of seeing a doctor. Henry, who suspected the real reason for the trip, went along, for he hoped to engage Mohun in a fight and thus save the life of his beloved guardian. The viscount, however, was in no mood to be cheated out of an excuse to provoke a quarrel. He was heavily in debt to Mohun and thought a fight was the only honorable way out of his difficulties. Moreover, he knew Mohun had written letters to Rachel, although, as the villain explained, she had never answered them. They fought, and Mohun foully and fatally wounded the viscount. On his deathbed the viscount confessed to his young kinsman that Henry was not an illegitimate child, but the son of Thomas, Lord Castlewood, by an early marriage, and the true heir to the Castlewood title. Henry Esmond generously burned the dying man's confession and resolved never to divulge the secret.

For his part in the duel Henry Esmond was sent to prison. When Rachel visited Henry in prison, she was enraged because he had not stopped the duel and because he had allowed Mohun to go unpunished. She rebuked Henry and forbade him to return to Castlewood. When Henry left prison he decided to join the army. For that purpose he visited the old dowager viscountess, his stepmother, who bought him a commission.

Henry's military ventures were highly successful, and won for him his share of wounds and glory. He fought in the campaign of the Duke of Marlborough against Spain and France in 1702 and in the campaign of Blenheim in 1704. Between the two campaigns he returned to Castlewood, where he was reconciled with Rachel. There he saw Frank, now Lord Castlewood, and Beatrix, who was cordial toward him. Rachel herself cautioned Henry that Beatrix was selfish and temperamental and would make no man happy who loved her.

After the campaign of 1704 Henry returned to his cousins, who were living in London. To Henry, Beatrix was more beautiful than ever and even more the coquette. But he found himself unable to make up his mind whether he loved her or Rachel. Later, during the campaign of 1706, he learned from Frank that the ravishing Beatrix was engaged to an earl. The news put Henry in low spirits because he now felt she would never marry a poor captain like himself.

Henry's affairs of the heart were put temporarily into the background when he came upon Father Holt in Brussels. The priest told Henry that while on an expedition in the Low Countries, Thomas Esmond, his father, had seduced the young woman who was Henry's mother. A few weeks before his child was born Thomas Esmond was injured in a duel. Thinking he would die, he married the woman so that her child would be born with an untainted name. But Thomas Esmond did not die, and when he recovered from his wounds he deserted his wife and married a distant kinswoman, the dowager viscountess, Henry's stepmother.

When Henry returned to Castlewood, Rachel informed him she had learned his secret from the old viscountess and consequently knew that he, not Frank, was the true heir. For the second time Henry refused to accept the title belonging to him.

Beatrix's interest in Henry grew after she became engaged to the Duke of Hamilton and learned that Henry was not illegitimate in birth but the bearer of a title her brother was using. Henry wanted to give Beatrix a diamond necklace for a wedding present, but the duke would not permit his fiancée to receive a gift from one of illegitimate birth. Rachel came to the young man's defense and declared before the duke, her daughter, and Henry the secret of his birth and title. Later the duke was killed in a duel with Lord Mohun, who also met his death at the same time. The killing of Rachel's husband was avenged.

The Duke of Hamilton's death gave Henry one more chance to win Beatrix's heart. He threw himself into a plot to put the young Stuart pretender on the throne when old Queen Anne died. To this end he went to France and helped to smuggle into England the young chevalier whom the Jacobites called James III, the king over the water. The two came secretly to the Castlewood home in London, the prince passing as Frank, the young viscount, and there the royal exile saw and fell in love with Beatrix.

Fearing the results of this infatuation, Lady Castlewood and Henry sent Beatrix against her will to Castlewood. When a report that the queen was dying swept through London, the prince was nowhere to be found. Henry and Frank made a night ride to Castlewood. Finding the pretender there, in the room used by Father Holt in the old days, they renounced him and the Jacobite cause. Henry realized his love for Beatrix was dead at last. He felt no regrets for her or for the prince as he rode back to London and heard the heralds proclaiming George I, the new king.

The prince made his way secretly back to France, where Beatrix joined him in his exile. At last Henry felt free to declare himself to Rachel, who had grown very dear to him. Leaving Frank in possession of the title and the Castlewood estates, Henry and his wife went to America. In Virginia he and Rachel built a new Castlewood, reared a family, and found happiness in their old age.

Further Critical Evaluation of the Work:

Critical reaction to *Henry Esmond* is as varied as reader reaction to the characters themselves. What Thackeray attempted to do was to offset contemporary charges of his "diffusiveness" by providing a well-integrated novel, sacrificing profitable serial publication to do so. He concluded that *Henry Esmond* was "the very best" he could do. Many critics have agreed with him. Others, however, remain loyal to the panoramic social vision and ironic authorial commentary of the earlier *Vanity Fair*. What makes evaluation of *Henry Esmond* so variable?

Short of a full history of cycles and fashions in fiction, certain features may illustrate the problems. First is the narrative point of view. Thackeray cast *Henry Esmond* in the form of a reminiscential memoir—an old man recounts his earlier life, describing it from the vantage point of a later time and distancing it further with third-person narration. The occasional use of "I" suggests the involved narrator, either at emotional highpoints or moments of personal reflection. The distancing in time is increased by Esmond's daughter's Preface, wherein Rachel Esmond Warrington not only "completes" certain details of the plot but also suggests the ambiguities in characterization of her own mother, Rachel, and of her stepsister, Beatrix. Readers of Henry James may react favorably to this early use of a central intelligence whose point of view, limited not omniscient, can suggest the disparities between appearance and reality. They may also welcome the shifting interpretations readers themselves can form of the "reliability" of the narrator. Is Esmond providing a framework within which to reveal only the exemplary, vindicating himself consciously, or is he recollecting as honestly as the self can permit, with the reader knowing more than he at many points?

Another point of contention involves the historical setting of the novel, which purports to be a historical romance. Thackeray casts the novel in the early eighteenth century and attempts to catch the flavor of the Augustan Age, its military conflicts, its waverings between Church of England and Catholicism, and the problems of its monarchs, William, Queen Anne, George II, and the Stuart Pretender. Most readers laud Thackeray's adept handling of the technical problem of suggesting the language and manners of that earlier time without lapsing into linguistic archness or sending readers to glossaries. It is, then, praised by many as a polished example of the historical romance and relished as many relish Scott or Stevenson—for its adventure and its depiction of society, at least those levels that Thackeray chooses to treat. For as with *Vanity Fair,* he is less concerned with portrayal of the lackeys than of the masters, primarily the newly arrived and still aspiring scions of society. Their foibles were his special target.

Yet for others the novel's fascination lies in its domestic realism. Commentators find much to explore in the rendering of the marriage conventions. Lord and Lady Castlewood, new heirs to Castlewood, befriend the supposedly illegitimate Henry Esmond and gradually reveal the strained bonds which hold their marriage together. Esmond, as narrator, takes sides with Rachel, seeing the husband as carousing, unfaithful, not too intelligent. Readers, however, can also realize, despite the analysis of "domestic tyranny," that Rachel's purity and coldness might lead the husband not only to drink but to other fleshly delights. Devoted Henry Esmond may lament the waste of such a fine woman, but the reader perceives in the dramatic scenes that Rachel, who began by worshiping her husband, is also quite capable of both restrictive possessiveness and emotional repression.

Historical romance, novel of domestic manners—*Henry Esmond* also illustrates a favorite nineteenth century form, the *bildüngsroman,* or novel of development and education, which is also represented in such popular contemporary examples as *David Copperfield* and *Great Expectations.* Henry Esmond remembers his childhood vaguely, a time spent with poor weavers, a foreign language. Brought to Castlewood, he is treated with favor by Lord Castlewood but kept in place as a page. It is only with the death of Lord Castlewood that Henry receives any emotional response, this from the new heirs— and most especially from Rachel, Lady Castlewood. Thackeray carefully distances Esmond to be eight years younger than Rachel and eight years older than her daughter Beatrix. Esmond's growth is the principal subject but readers are also aware of the young son Frank and of Beatrix, both children who are alternately spoiled and then emotionally isolated from Rachel. The much sought after but "loveless" Beatrix reveals how isolated she was made to feel by the possessive nets her mother cast over the father and then over the seemingly favored brother. Momentarily consoling Esmond, Beatrix shows the motivation for her romantic conquests so that readers understand her complexity and ambivalence though Esmond may choose not to do so.

As Esmond progresses through Cambridge, through imprisonment following a duel fatal to Lord Castlewood, through military campaigns, through the loss of one idol after another and on to a slow knowledge of the way of the world, the reader watches for his "present" age to come closer to his recollected past. The reader watches for his insight to develop, for memory and maturity to coincide. Whether or not Esmond achieves that wholeness is yet another point for critics and readers to ponder.

Esmond has virtuously denied himself his birthright as legitimate heir to Castlewood so that young Frank may assume the title and Rachel and Beatrix can stay ensconced in society, but some might think Henry revels in the self-sacrifice. He has also chosen to believe that Beatrix will admire him for military daring and political plotting. Thus when the Stuart Pretender misses a chance for the throne in order to secure an amorous chance with Beatrix, Esmond loses two idols at once. "Good" Henry Esmond is settled at the end of the novel on a Virginia plantation in the New World, his marriage to the widowed Rachel compressed into two pages. All ends happily, except for those strange overtones and even stranger suggestions in the Preface by the daughter of this autumnal marriage. She reminds us that Esmond was writing for a family audience, that his role had been carefully established, and that she, Rachel Esmond Warrington, like Beatrix, had also suffered from her mother's possessiveness and jealousy.

Ultimately, then, what the modern reader may enjoy most is the psychological penetration into love bonds which Thackeray provides through the "unreliable" narrator. Dramatic irony permits the reader more knowledge than Esmond permits himself. And as readers circle back in their own memories to the daughter's Preface, the whole range of interrelationships and the ambivalences of human affairs unfold. The characters, in short, remain fascinating puzzles long after the historical details fade. Emotional life, the subtleties of rejection and acceptance, time rendered both precisely and in psychological duration—these are the elements which will continue to tantalize readers of *Henry Esmond*.

Eileen Lothamer

HENRY THE EIGHTH

Type of work: Drama
Author: William Shakespeare (1564-1616)
Type of plot: Historical chronicle
Time of plot: 1520-1533
Locale: England
First presented: c. 1612

Principal characters:
KING HENRY THE EIGHTH
THOMAS WOLSEY, Cardinal of York and Lord Chancellor of England
CARDINAL CAMPEIUS, papal legate
CRANMER, the Archbishop of Canterbury
DUKE OF BUCKINGHAM
DUKE OF SUFFOLK
DUKE OF NORFOLK
GARDINER, the Bishop of Winchester
THOMAS CROMWELL, Wolsey's servant
QUEEN KATHARINE, wife of Henry, later divorced
ANNE BOLEYN, maid of honor to Katharine, later queen

Critique:

In the prologue to *Henry VIII* the audience is advised that this is not a happy play; it should be received in sadness. The description is incomplete and the advice somewhat misleading. True, the play is sad in its reality of ambition, political maneuvering, misunderstanding, and unhappiness, but, as the story progresses, honesty and altruism predominate. And it is difficult to imagine a Shakespearean audience receiving with sadness Cranmer's eloquent prophecy regarding the newborn princess, known to history as Queen Elizabeth. *Henry VIII* vividly pictures British court life in its spectacular pomp and in its behind-the-throne humanity. Many authorities credit John Fletcher with the part-authorship of this play.

The Story:

Cardinal Wolsey, a powerful figure at court during the reigns of Henry VII and Henry VIII, was becoming too aggressive in his self-aggrandizement. Wolsey was of humble stock, which fact accentuated his personal qualities. Since he had lacked the advantages of family and ancestral office, his political prominence was entirely the result of his own wisdom, manner, and persistence. Unscrupulous in seeking his own ends, he had removed any possible obstacle in his climb to power.

One such hindrance to his ambitious designs was the Duke of Buckingham, accused of high treason. When Buckingham was brought before the court for trial, Queen Katharine, speaking in his defense, protested against the cardinal's unjust taxes and informed the king of growing animosity among his people because he retained Wolsey as his adviser. Wolsey produced witnesses, among them Buckingham's discharged surveyor, who testified to Buckingham's disloyalty. The surveyor swore that, at the time of the king's journey to France, the duke had sought priestly confirmation for his belief that he could, by gaining favor with the common people, rise to govern England. In his lengthy and persistent testimony the surveyor played upon earlier minor offenses Buckingham had committed, and he climaxed his accusation with an account of the duke's assertion that he would murder the king in order to gain the throne.

In spite of Katharine's forthright protestations against Wolsey in his presence, and her repeated contention of false testimony against Buckingham, the accused man was found guilty and sentenced to be executed. The duke, forbearing toward his enemies, recalled the experience of his father, Henry of Buckingham, who had been betrayed by a servant. Henry VII had restored the honor of the family by elevating the present duke to favor. One difference prevailed between the two trials, the duke stated; his father had been unjustly dealt with, but he himself had had a noble trial.

Wolsey, fearing reprisal from Buckingham's son, sent him to Ireland as a deputy; then, incensed and uneasy because of Katharine's open accusations, he pricked the king's conscience by questions regarding his marriage to Katharine, who had been the widow of Henry's brother. Wolsey furthered his cause against Katharine by arousing Henry's interest in Anne Boleyn, whom the king met at a gay ball given by the cardinal.

The plan followed by Wolsey in securing a divorce for Henry was not a difficult one. In addition to his evident trust of Wolsey, the king felt keenly the fact that the male children born to him and Katharine in their twenty years of marriage had been stillborn or had died shortly after birth. Consequently, there was no male heir in direct succession.

The cardinal's final step to be rid of his chief adversary at court was to appeal to the pope for a royal divorce. When Cardinal Campeius arrived from Rome as counsel to the king, Katharine appeared in her own defense. But Wolsey had once more resorted to perjured witnesses. Requesting counsel, Katharine was told by Wolsey that the honest and intelligent men gathered at the hearing were of her choosing. Cardinal Campeius supported Wolsey's stand.

In speeches of magnificent dignity and honesty, Katharine denounced the political treachery that had caused her so much unhappiness. Later, however, Katharine, expelled from the court and sequestered in Kimbolton, was able to feel compassion for Wolsey when informed that he had died in ill-repute; and her undying devotion to Henry was indicated in her death note to him. Altruistic to the last, she made as her final request to the king the maintenance of the domestics who had served her so faithfully. Her strength to tolerate the in-

justices she had endured lay in her trust in a Power which, she said, could not be corrupted by a king.

But ambition overrode itself in Wolsey's designs for power. His great pride had caused him to accumulate greater wealth than the king's, to use an inscription, *Ego et Rex meus*, which subordinated the king to the cardinal, and to have a British coin stamped with a cardinal's hat. These, among many other offenses, were of little importance compared with Wolsey's double-dealing against the king in the divorce proceedings. Because Wolsey feared that Henry would marry Anne Boleyn instead of seeking a royal alliance in France, Wolsey asked the pope to delay the divorce. When his letter was delivered by mistake to the king, Wolsey, confronted with the result of his own carelessness, showed the true tenacious character of the ambitious climber. Although he realized that his error was his undoing, he attempted to ingratiate himself once more with the king.

He was too late to save himself. He could instigate the unseating and banishment of subordinates and he could maneuver to have the queen sequestered, but Henry wished no meddling with his marital affairs. Repentant that he had not served God with the effort and fervor with which he had served the king, Wolsey left the court, a broken-spirited man. He was later arrested in York, to be returned for arraignment before Henry. He was saved the humiliation of trial, however, for he died on the way to London.

Henry, shortly after the divorce, secretly married Anne Boleyn. After Wolsey's death she was crowned queen with great pomp. Cranmer, the new Archbishop of Canterbury, became Henry's chief adviser.

Jealousy and rivalry did not disappear from the court with the downfall of Wolsey. Charging heresy, Gardiner, Bishop of Winchester, set out to undermine Cranmer's position with the king. Accused as an arch heretic, Cranmer was brought to trial. Henry, trusting his favorite, gave him the royal signet ring which he was to show to the council if his entreaties and reasoning failed with his accusers. Cranmer, overcome by the king's kindness, wept in gratitude.

As he stood behind a curtain near the council room, the king heard Gardiner's charges against Cranmer. When Gardiner ordered Cranmer to the Tower, stating that the council was acting on the pleasure of the king, the accused man produced the ring and insisted upon his right to appeal the case to the king. Realizing that they had been tricked by a ruse which Wolsey had used for many years, the nobles were penitent. Appearing before the council, Henry took his seat at the table to condemn the assemblage for their tactics in dealing with Cranmer. After giving his blessings to those present and imploring them to be motivated in the future by unity and love, he asked Cranmer to be godfather to the daughter recently born to Anne Boleyn.

At the christening Cranmer prophesied that the child, Elizabeth, would be wise and virtuous, that her life would be a pattern to all princes who knew her, and that she would be loved and feared because of her goodness and her strength. He said that she would rule long and every day of her reign would be blessed with good deeds.

Further Critical Evaluation of the Work:

Henry the Eighth is a relatively weak play: the relationships between the principal characters tend to be superficial, and the characters themselves are more or less transparent, lacking cogency and complexity. Buckingham, for example, although perfectly consistent, is one-dimensional; he is something of a stock character and finally emerges as little more than a display of Wolsey's corruption. Wolsey himself, whose arrogant cruelty together with a seeming nobility adds to his interest, is more or less a cliché of the steward who abuses his power.

Despite these weaknesess, the play remains historically interesting and significant because of its glorification of Elizabeth's reign, the majesty of which is foretold by Cranmer at the end of the drama. Written during the first decade of James the First's tenure, it reflects England's dissatisfaction with the Scottish monarch and a nostalgia for his predecessor. Throughout his history plays, written for the most part early in his career, Shakespeare had sought to legitimatize and honor the Tudors who had saved England from "Crookback Dick," Richard III, and had brought an end to the War of the Roses. Elizabeth, the Virginia Queen and the last Tudor, is glimpsed in *Henry the Eighth* as the crowning glory of that dynasty.

Henry himself is not presented here as the perfidious tyrant that some later historians recognize. Still the Tudor apologist, Shakespeare suggests Wolsey as the principal villain in the deposition of Katharine Aragon. A Machiavellian, the cardinal seeks to center the power in himself at the expense of the king and the Royal family. His motto, *Ego et Rexmeus,* which puts him above the monarch, insures his ignominious defeat. Despite his hatred of tyrants, Shakespeare, in one of his later plays, remains a Royalist to the end, paying his allegiance to the idea of the Divine Right.

HENRY THE FIFTH

Type of work: Drama
Author: William Shakespeare (1564-1616)
Type of plot: Historical romance
Time of plot: Early part of the fifteenth century
Locale: England and France
First presented: 1600

Principal characters:
HENRY THE FIFTH, King of England
CHARLES THE SIXTH, King of France
PRINCESS KATHARINE, his daughter
THE DAUPHIN, his son
MONTJOY, a French herald

Critique:

In *The Life of Henry the Fifth* Shakespeare skillfully combined poetry, pageantry, and history in his effort to glorify England and Englishmen. King Henry himself represents all that is finest in English royalty; and yet when Henry notes on the eve of the battle of Agincourt that he is also a man like other men, Shakespeare shows us an Englishman who possesses that quality of humility which makes great men even greater. Few can see or read the play without sharing, at least for the moment, Shakespeare's pride in England and in things English, and without sensing the vigor and the idealism that are part of the Anglo-Saxon heritage.

The Story:

Once the toss-pot prince of Falstaff's tavern brawls, Henry V was now king at Westminster, a stern but just monarch concerned with his hereditary claim to the crown of France. Before the arrival of the French ambassadors, the young king asked for legal advice from the Archbishop of Canterbury. The king thought that he was the legal heir to the throne of France through Edward III, whose claim to the French throne was, at best, questionable. The Archbishop assured Henry that he had as much right to the French throne as did the French king; consequently, both the Archbishop and the Bishop of Ely urged Henry to press his demands against the French.

When the ambassadors from France arrived, they came, not from Charles, the king, but from his arrogant eldest son, the Dauphin. According to the ambassadors, the Dauphin considered the English monarch the same hot-headed, irresponsible youth he had been before he ascended the throne. To show that he considered Henry an unfit ruler whose demands were ridiculous, the Dauphin presented Henry with some tennis balls. Enraged by the insult, Henry told the French messengers to warn their master that the tennis balls would be turned into gun-stones for use against the French.

The English prepared for war. The Dauphin remained contemptuous of Henry, but others, including the French Constable and the ambassadors who had seen Henry in his wrath, were not so confident. Henry's army landed to lay siege to Harfleur, and the king threatened to destroy the city, together with its inhabitants, unless it surrendered. The French governor had to capitulate because help promised by the Dauphin never arrived. The French, meanwhile, were—with the exception of King Charles—alarmed by the rapid progress of the English through France. That ruler, however, was so sure of victory that he sent his herald, Montjoy, to Henry to demand that the English king pay a ransom to the French, give himself up, and have his soldiers withdraw from France. Henry was not impressed by this bold gesture, and retorted that if King

Charles wanted him, the Frenchman should come to get him.

On the eve of the decisive battle of Agincourt, the English were outnumbered five to one. Henry's troops were on foreign soil and ridden with disease. To encourage them, and also to sound out their morale, the king borrowed a cloak and in this disguise walked out among his troops, from watch to watch and from tent to tent. As he talked with his men, he told them that a king is but a man like other men, and that if he were a king he would not want to be anywhere except where he was, in battle with his soldiers. To himself, Henry mused over the cares and responsibilities of kingship. Again he thought of himself simply as a man who differed from other men only in ceremony, itself an empty thing.

Henry's sober reflections on the eve of a great battle, in which he thought much English blood would be shed, were quite different from those of the French, who were exceedingly confident of their ability to defeat their enemy. Shortly before the conflict began, Montjoy again appeared before Henry to give the English one last chance to surrender. Henry again refused to be intimidated. He was not discouraged by the numerical inferiority of his troops, for, as he reasoned in speaking with one of his officers, the fewer troops the English had, the greater would be the honor to them when they won.

The following day the battle began. Because of Henry's leadership, the English held their own. When French reinforcements arrived at a crucial point in the battle, Henry ordered his men to kill all their prisoners so that the energies of the English might be directed entirely against the enemy in front of them, not behind. Soon the tide turned. A much humbler Montjoy approached Henry to request a truce for burying the French dead. Henry granted the herald's request, and at the same time learned from him that the French had conceded defeat. Ten thousand French had been killed, and only twenty-nine English.

The battle over, nothing remained for Henry to do but to discuss with the French king terms of peace. Katharine, Charles' beautiful daughter, was Henry's chief demand, and while his lieutenants settled the details of surrender with the French, Henry made love to the princess and asked her to marry him. Though Katharine's knowledge of English was slight and Henry's knowledge of French little better, they were both acquainted with the universal language of love. French Katharine consented to become English Kate and Henry's bride.

Further Critical Evaluation of the Work:

Henry the Fifth is the last play in the cycle including *Richard the Second, Henry the Fourth, Part One* and *Part Two,* and *Henry the Fifth.* The three plays dealing with the reign of King Henry VI, mentioned in the epilogue of *Henry the Fifth,* were written much earlier and are not ordinarily grouped with this cycle. *Henry the Fifth* is itself almost a break with this cycle. However, there are important, if in some ways superficial, elements of continuity.

These elements of continuity are the great historical transition represented by the movement from the reign of Richard II to that of Henry V. Richard and, progressively, the two Henrys, are associated by Shakespeare with the medieval, then the Renaissance, even modern, world views. The second dominant element is the formation of Prince Hal, who becomes Henry V, as a Renaissance king.

In *Richard the Second,* the king, Richard, is deposed by Bolingbroke, who becomes Henry IV. What is important is the act of rupturing, symbolized by this usurpation, of an entire conception of humanity governed by ritual and tradition. This conception is sometimes referred to as "the great chain of being." It asserts an utterly planned cosmos which is considered the manifestation of God. To challenge and finally replace this world is a force not clearly understood by its protagonists, but nevertheless defines their own practical and political ambitions as individuals.

The two *Henry the Fourth* plays are continuations of Shakespeare's exploration of the shift in political perspective. The rebellions which follow Henry IV's usurpation had been predicted by Richard II, and seem, indeed, a kind of natural consequence to the break in the structure of authority.

But while his father is engaged morally by that break even to a death troubled by remorse for his "crime," the education of Prince Hal is pursued in a subplot mainly situated in taverns and places of public amusement. Hal's progress, in a few words, is between two extremes of individualism (characteristic of the Renaissance): the obsessive and bloody quest for glory in the person of Hotspur, and the pleasure-seeking, nearly total, incontinence of Falstaff. What he learns from each of them could be said to be the sense of valor and honor of the one, and the wittiness and humanity of the other. But this is so, in a way, only "theoretically." For the nature of the prince in *Henry the Fifth,* as king, is quite removed from either the thesis or the antithesis which precedes him.

An explanation for this can be found symbolically in the two scenes at the end of *Henry the Fourth, Part Two,* where Hal, after his father's death but before his own coronation, takes as his own his father's Lord High Justice, and banishes Falstaff. The Chief Justice had expected—among all who feared Hal would become an irresponsible king—the worst personal damage, as he had punished Hal's revels in the name of Henry IV. Shakespeare seems to imply, in a very modern sense, that Hal was assuming fully his father's Law. In the historical perspective it is secular law, in contrast to the divine mandate of Richard II.

The opening scenes of *Henry the Fifth* show how secular, indeed, how free-and-easy, the new law has become. Individualism, in the form of self-interest, rules, but in an orderly, legalistic way. The bishops make the ancient laws fit the needs of their own financial interests and the ambition (concerning the French throne) of King Henry V.

These scenes already suggest a sense of *fait accompli* to the broad transitional process which is, at base, the rise of the bourgeoisie. Thus the play is a kind of break with the others. As a whole it is a kind of apotheosis of the powerful though incipient undercurrent of the times, the collective mentality we have come to ascribe to the bourgeoisie. This play has a lack of moral depth, which derives, perhaps, from a contradiction in bourgeois society.

There is the economic base of cut-throat competition and an ideological superstructure of supposedly harmonious relations between men and nations. The loss of the sacred system of exploitation made the contradiction more apparent. The dynamic individualism of the new culture takes on the authority of the old order but sublimates the sense of responsibility into platitudes of doubtful logic.

The bishops are one example of this. The ease with which Henry allows his conscience to be soothed in those scenes is another. Later, he rather cavalierly blames the citizens of Harfleur for the impending destruction of their city, with all the barbaric effects he will not even try to control, by his invading army. Likewise, he shuns, by pure sophistry, any responsibility for the deaths, or souls, of his soldiers. He skirts the question of the justice of the king's cause with the assertion that, in any case, each man's soul is his own worry before God.

Shakespeare presents, then, a society in triumph, but one of atrophied moral sensitivity, escaping always in bad faith. The need to compensate for inner insecurity is shown, for example, in the absurd mortality statistic (twenty-nine to ten thousand). Again, it is shown in the aggressive, even hostile and puerile, clumsiness of Henry's wooing of Katharine. He tells her, on the one hand, that he will not be very hurt if she rejects him, and on the other hand, that she and her father are, in effect, his conquered subjects and have no real choice in the matter. This does not constitute, however, a definite condemnation by Shakespeare, of this society. But he does not wholly praise, either. More than the other plays of this cycle, the conventionality and moral opacity leave judgment to the reader's, or spectator's, understanding of history.

James Marc Hovde

HENRY THE FOURTH, PART ONE

Type of work: Drama
Author: William Shakespeare (1564-1616)
Type of plot: Historical chronicle
Time of plot: 1400-1405
Locale: England
First presented: 1596

Principal characters:
KING HENRY THE FOURTH
HENRY, Prince of Wales
JOHN OF LANCASTER, another son of the king
EARL OF WESTMORELAND, and
SIR WALTER BLUNT, members of the king's party
HOTSPUR, son of Henry Percy, Earl of Northumberland
THOMAS PERCY, Earl of Worcester, Hotspur's uncle
EDMUND MORTIMER, Earl of March, Hotspur's brother-in-law and
    claimant to the throne
SIR JOHN FALSTAFF, a bibulous knight
MISTRESS QUICKLY, hostess of the Boar's Head Tavern in Eastcheap

Critique:

In Part I of *The History of King Henry IV* historical details and dramatic sequences involving affairs of state are secondary to the comic aspects of the plot. Falstaff, Shakespeare's best humorous character, is the figure whose entrances have been anticipated by audiences of every period. Here, within a historical framework, humor exists for its own sake, and in no sense are the humorous details a subplot to the activities of the Crown. Woven into and between the scenes of court and military affairs, the antics of Falstaff and his mates created a suitable atmosphere for showing Prince Henry's character. He entered into their tricks and zaniness with an abandon equal to the irresponsibility of the commonest of the group. Falstaff's lies, thieving, drinking, and debauchery made him the butt of repeated ludicrous situations. He used any reverse to the advantage of obtaining another bottle of sack, of gratifying his ego by attracting the attention of his cohorts, or of endearing himself, with his sly rascality, to the prince. Because of Falstaff, comedy and history join in this play.

The Story:

King Henry, conscience-stricken because of his part in the murder of King Richard II, his predecessor, planned a pil-grimage to the Holy Land. He declared to his lords that war had been banished from England and that peace would reign throughout the kingdom.

But there were those of differing opinions. Powerful barons in the North remained disaffected after the accession of the new king. Antagonized by his failure to keep promises made when he claimed the throne, they recruited forces to maintain their feudal rights. In fact, as Henry announced plans for his expedition to the Holy Land, he was informed of the brutal murder of a thousand persons in a fray between Edmund Mortimer, proclaimed by Richard as heir to the crown, and Glendower, a Welsh rebel. Mortimer was taken prisoner. A messenger also brought word of Hotspur's success against the Scots at Holmedon Hill. The king expressed his commendation of the young knight and his regrets that his own son, Prince Henry, was so irresponsible and carefree.

But King Henry, piqued by Hotspur's refusal to release to him more than one prisoner, ordered a council meeting to bring the overzealous Hotspur to terms. At the meeting Henry refused to ransom Mortimer, the pretender to the throne, held by Glendower. In turn, Hotspur refused to release the prisoners taken at Holmedon Hill, and Henry threatened more strenuous action against Hotspur and his kinsmen.

In a rousing speech Hotspur appealed to the power and nobility of Northumberland and Worcester and urged that they undo the wrongs of which they were guilty in the dethronement and murder of Richard and in aiding Henry instead of Mortimer to the crown. Worcester promised to help Hotspur in his cause against Henry. Worcester's plan would involve the aid of Douglas of Scotland, to be sought after by Hotspur, of Glendower and Mortimer, to be won over through Worcester's efforts, and of the Archbishop of York, to be approached by Northumberland.

Hotspur's boldness and impatience were shown in his dealing with Glendower as they, Mortimer, and Worcester discussed the future division of the kingdom. Hotspur, annoyed by the tedium of Glendower's personal account of his own ill-fated birth and by the uneven distribution of land, was impudent and rude. Hotspur was first a soldier, then a gentleman.

In the king's opinion, Prince Henry was quite lacking in either of these attributes. In one of their foolish pranks Sir John Falstaff and his riotous band had robbed some travelers at Gadshill, only to be set upon and put to flight by the prince and one companion. Summoning the prince from the Boar's Head Tavern, the king urged his son to break with the undesirable company he kept, chiefly the ne'er-do-well Falstaff. Contrasting young Henry with Hotspur, the king pointed out the military achievements of Northumberland's heir. Congenial, high-spirited Prince Henry, remorseful because of his father's lack of confidence in him, swore his allegiance to his father and declared he would show the king that in time of crisis Hotspur's glorious deeds would prove Hotspur no better soldier than Prince Henry. To substantiate his pledge, the prince took command of a detachment that would join ranks with other units of the royal army—Blunt's, Prince John's, Westmoreland's, and the king's

—in twelve days.

Prince Henry's conduct seemed to change very little. He continued his buffoonery with Falstaff, who had recruited a handful of bedraggled, nondescript foot soldiers. Falstaff's contention was that, despite their physical condition, they were food for powder and that little more could be said for any soldier.

Hotspur's forces suffered gross reverses through Northumberland's failure, because of illness, to organize an army. Also, Hotspur's ranks were reduced because Glendower believed the stars not propitious for him to march at that time. Undaunted by the news of his reduced forces, Hotspur pressed on to meet Henry's army of thirty thousand.

At Shrewsbury, the scene of the battle, Sir Walter Blunt carried to Hotspur the king's offer that the rebels' grievances would be righted and that anyone involved in the revolt would be pardoned if he chose a peaceful settlement. In answer to the king's message Hotspur reviewed the history of Henry's double-dealing and scheming in the past. Declaring that Henry's lineage should not continue on the throne, Hotspur finally promised Blunt that Worcester would wait upon the king to give him an answer to his offer.

Henry repeated his offer of amnesty to Worcester and Vernon, Hotspur's ambassadors. Because Worcester doubted the king's sincerity, on account of previous betrayals, he lied to Hotspur on his return to the rebel camp and reported that the king in abusive terms had announced his determination to march at once against Hotspur. Worcester also reported Prince Henry's invitation to Hotspur that they fight a duel. Hotspur gladly accepted the challenge.

As the two armies moved into battle, Blunt, mistaken for the king, was slain by Douglas, who, learning his error, was sorely grieved that he had not killed Henry. Douglas, declaring that he would yet murder the king, accosted him after a long search over the field. He would have been successful in his threat had it not been for the intervention of Prince Henry, who engaged Douglas and allowed the king to withdraw from the fray.

In the fighting Hotspur descended upon Prince Henry, exhausted from an earlier wound and his recent skirmish with Douglas. When the two young knights fought, Hotspur was wounded. Douglas again appeared, fighting with Falstaff, and departed after Falstaff had fallen to the ground as if he were dead. Hotspur died of his wounds and Prince Henry, before going off to join Prince John, his brother, eulogized Hotspur and Falstaff. The two benedictions were quite different. But Falstaff had only pretended lifelessness to save his life. After the prince's departure he stabbed Hotspur. He declared that he would swear before any council that he had killed the young rebel.

Worcester and Vernon were taken prisoners. Because they had not relayed to Hotspur the peace terms offered by the king, they were sentenced to death. Douglas, in flight after Hotspur's death, was taken prisoner. Given the king's permission to dispose of Douglas, Prince Henry ordered that the valiant Scottish knight be freed.

The king sent Prince John to march against the forces of Northumberland and the Archbishop of York. He and Prince Henry took the field against Glendower and Mortimer, in Wales. Falstaff had the honor of carrying off the slain Hotspur.

Further Critical Evaluation of the Work:

Although there is no evidence that the cycle of plays including *Richard the Second, Henry the Fourth, Part One* and *Part Two,* and *Henry the Fifth* were intended by Shakespeare to form a unit, there is much continuity, of theme as well as of personages. There is a movement from one grand epoch to another, from the Middle Ages to the Renaissance. The main aspects of his transition implied at the end of each play are projected into the next, where they are developed and explored.

The reader of *Henry the Fourth, Part One,* should be familiar with some aspects of *Richard the Second,* for in that play the broad lines of the entire cycle are drawn and the immediate base of *Henry the Fourth, Part One,* is formed. In *Richard the Second,* the legitimate king, Richard II, is deposed by Bolingbroke, who becomes Henry IV. This event, to include both historical perspectives, must be viewed as at once a usurpation and a necessary political expediency. It is a usurpation because unjustifiable, indeed unthinkable, from the strictly medieval view of what has been called "the great chain of being." This notion postulates that the universe is ordered, hierarchical, that everything is given a place by God, from angels to ants, and that station is immutable. In this world, formed by ritual, an annointed king is representative of God's Order. To depose him is to call in question all order in the world. Tradition, especially ritual, presupposed and supported fixed order. Ritual in this larger sense is broken in *Richard the Second* first by the excesses of Richard himself and then, in a more definitive sense, by the usurping Bolingbroke. The irony of Bolingbroke's act, and the subject of *Henry the Fourth, Part One,* is the consequences of what was to have been a momentary departure from ordained ritual. As with Eve, the gesture of self-initiative was irrevocable, the knowledge and correlative responsibility gained at that moment inescapable.

At the opening of *Henry the Fourth, Part One,* then, we see the results of rebellion already installed; the security of the old system of feudal trust is forever lost. Those who helped the king to power are men instead of God, the guarantors of the "sacredness" (the term already anachronistic), of the crown. This means political indebtedness and, at this point in history, with the anxiety of lost certainty still sharp, terrible doubt as to whence truth, power, and justice rightfully emanate. The king is no longer sovereign as he must negotiate, in the payment of his political debts, the very essence of his station. At the historical moment of the play, distrust predictably triumphs. Men are guided by the most available counsel, a *personal* sense of justice, or merely, perhaps, their own interests and passions.

In the void left by the fallen hierarchical order Shakespeare dramatizes the birth of modern individualism and, as a model for this, the formation of a Renaissance king (Prince Hal), an entity now of uncertain, largely self-created identity.

Prince Hal's position in the play is central. He represents a future unstigmatized by the actual usurpation. However, he inherits, to be sure, the new political and moral climate created by it. Yet while Henry's planned crusade to the Holy Land will be forever postponed in order to defend his rule from his former collaborators, Hal's life looks to the future.

It is characteristic of Henry's uncertain world that he knows his son only through hearsay, rumor, and slander. Even the Prince of Wales is suspect. He is widely thought a wastrel, and the king even suspects his son would like him dead. But where is the pattern of virtue for Hal? The king, the usurper, is tainted, of ambiguous virtue at best. He has betrayed, perhaps out of political necessity, even those who helped him to the throne.

In this play Hal is clearly attracted to two figures, Hotspur and Falstaff. Both of these are removed from the medieval ritualistic structures that had once tended to integrate disparate aspects of life: courtesy, valor, honest exchange, loyalty, and the like. A new synthesis of this sort is symbolically enacted in Hal's procession through the experience of, and choices between, the worlds of Hotspur and Falstaff.

For Hotspur life is a constant striving for glory in battle. As has been remarked, time for him presses implacably, considered wasted if not intensely devoted to the achievement of fame. But his is an assertion of the individual enacted outside a traditional frame such as the medieval "quest." Hotspur's character is seen to be extremely limited, however breathtaking his *élan* may be. For it is finally morbid, loveless, incourteous, and even sexually impotent. He has not the patience to humor the tediousness of Glendower (which costs him, perhaps, his support); his speech is full of death and death's images; he mocks the love of Mortimer and has banished his wife from his bed, too absorbed by his planned rebellion.

Falstaff, on the other hand, is as quick to lie, to steal, to waste time with a whore or drinking wine, as Hotspur is to risk his life for a point of honor. Hal spends most of his time with him, and he seems at times a sort of apprentice to the older man in the "art" of tavern living. This means, for Hal, living intimately with common people, who naïvely call him "boy," and whose unpretentiousness strips him of the artificial defenses he would have among people who understand protocol.

The adventure with the robbery is the image of cowardice as the reputation of Hotspur is the image of valor. Yet both stories are in their ways celebrative. Falstaff's flexible ways are more human, certainly kinder than Hotspur's, kinder even than Hal's. Hal is awkward at joking sometimes, not being sensitive enough to know what is serious, what light. Hotspur has renounced sensitivity to human love; Falstaff has abandoned honor. In schematic terms, it is a synthesis of these two perspectives that Hal must, and in a way does, achieve.

James Marc Hovde

HENRY THE FOURTH, PART TWO

Type of work: Drama
Author: William Shakespeare (1564-1616)
Type of plot: Historical chronicle
Time of plot: 1405-1413
Locale: England
First presented: 1597

Principal characters:
KING HENRY THE FOURTH
HENRY, Prince of Wales
JOHN OF LANCASTER, another son of the king
EARL OF WESTMORELAND, a member of the king's party
EARL OF NORTHUMBERLAND, enemy of the king
SIR JOHN FALSTAFF, a riotous old knight
SHALLOW, a country justice
THE LORD CHIEF JUSTICE, judge of the King's Bench
MISTRESS QUICKLY, hostess of the Boar's Head Tavern in Eastcheap

Critique:

As in *The History of King Henry IV, Part I*, comedy is an outstanding feature of this sequel. The same devices—puns, hyperbole, coarseness—are used to good effect, and in the earlier scenes of the play the character of Falstaff again sustains the spirit of high comedy. He ambles his way through this second part of *Henry IV* as he did in the first, his lying, drinking, and chicanery still useful to his own ends. In this sequel he becomes further involved with Mistress Quickly, and his promise to marry her is no more binding than are any of his other vows. At the end Falstaff goes on breezily promising great things for his friends, until his death. The pomp and display common to Shakespeare's historical chronicles permeate the serious parts of the drama, and the deathbed scene between Henry IV and Prince Henry is generally considered among the best in dramatic literature.

The Story:

After the battle of Shrewsbury many false reports were circulated among the peasants. At last they reached Northumberland, who believed for a time that the rebel forces had been victorious. But his retainers, fleeing from that stricken field, brought a true account of the death of Hotspur, Northumberland's valiant son, at the hands of Prince Henry, and of King Henry's avowal to put down rebellion by crushing those forces still opposing him. Northumberland, sorely grieved by news of his son's death, prepared to avenge that loss. Hope lay in the fact that the Archbishop of York had mustered an army, because soldiers so organized, being responsible to the Church rather than to a military leader, would prove better fighters than those who had fled from Shrewsbury field. News that the king's forces of twenty-five thousand men had been divided into three units was encouraging to his enemies.

In spite of Northumberland's grief for his slain son and his impassioned threat against the king and Prince Henry, he was easily persuaded by his wife and Hotspur's widow to flee to Scotland, there to await the success of his confederates before he would consent to join them with his army.

Meanwhile Falstaff delayed in carrying out his orders to proceed north and recruit troops for the king. Deeply involved with Mistress Quickly, he used his royal commission to avoid being imprisoned for debt. With Prince Henry, who had paid little heed to the conduct of the war, he continued his riotous feasting and jesting until both were summoned to join the army marching against the rebels.

King Henry, aging and weary, had been ill for two weeks. Sleepless nights had taken their toll on him, and in his restlessness he reviewed his ascent to the throne and denied, to his lords, the accusation of unscrupulousness brought against him by the rebels. He was somewhat heartened by the news of Glendower's death.

In Gloucestershire, recruiting troops at the house of Justice Shallow, Falstaff grossly accepted bribes and let able-bodied men buy themselves out of service. The soldiers he took to the war were a raggle-taggle lot.

Prince John of Lancaster, taking the field against the rebels, sent word by Westmoreland to the archbishop that the king's forces were willing to make peace, and he asked that the rebel leaders make known their grievances so that they might be corrected.

When John and the archbishop met for a conference, John questioned and criticized the archbishop's dual role as churchman and warrior. Because the rebels announced their intention to fight until their wrongs were righted, John promised redress for all. Then he suggested that the archbishop's troops be disbanded after a formal review; he wished to see the stalwart soldiers that his army would have fought if a truce had not been declared.

His request was granted, but the men, excited by the prospect of their release, scattered so rapidly that inspection was impossible. Westmoreland, sent to disband John's army, returned to report that the soldiers would take orders only from the prince. With his troops assembled and the enemy's disbanded, John ordered some of the opposing leaders arrested for high treason and others, including the archbishop, for capital treason. John explained that his action was in keeping with his promise to improve conditions and that to remove rebellious factions was the first step in his campaign. The enemy leaders were sentenced to death. Falstaff took Coleville, the fourth of the rebel leaders, who was sentenced to execution with the others.

News of John's success was brought to King Henry as he lay dying, but the victory could not gladden the sad old king.

His chief concern lay in advice and admonition to his younger sons, Gloucester and Clarence, regarding their future conduct, and he asked for unity among his sons. Spent by his long discourse, the king lapsed into unconsciousness.

Prince Henry, summoned to his dying father's bedside, found the king in a stupor, with the crown beside him. The prince, remorseful and compassionate, expressed regret that the king had lived such a tempestuous existence because of the crown and promised, in his turn, to wear the crown graciously. As he spoke, he placed the crown on his head and left the room. Awaking and learning that the prince had donned the crown, King Henry immediately assumed that his son wished him dead in order to inherit the kingdom. Consoled by the prince's strong denial of such wishful thinking, the king confessed his own unprincipled behavior in gaining the crown. Asking God's forgiveness, he repeated his plan to journey to the Holy Land to divert his subjects from revolt, and he advised the prince, when he should become king, to involve his powerful lords in wars with foreign powers, thereby relieving the country of internal strife.

The king's death caused great sorrow among those who loved him and to those who feared the prince, now Henry V. A short time before, the Lord Chief Justice, acting on the command of Henry IV, had alienated the prince by banishing Falstaff and his band, but the newly crowned king accepted the Chief Justice's explanation for his treatment of Falstaff and restored his judicial powers.

Falstaff was rebuked for his conduct by Henry who stated that he was no longer the person Falstaff had known him to be. Until the old knight learned to correct his ways, the king banished him, on pain of death, to a distance ten miles away from Henry's person. He promised, however, that if amends were made Falstaff would return by degrees to the king's good graces. Undaunted by that reproof, Falstaff explained to his cronies that he yet would make them great, that the king's reprimand was only a front, and that the king would send for him and in the secrecy of the court chambers they would indulge in their old foolishness and plan the advancement of Falstaff's followers.

Prince John, expressing his admiration for Henry's public display of his changed attitude, prophesied that England would be at war with France before a year had passed.

Further Critical Evaluation of the Work:

Henry the Fourth, Part Two is, of course, the second part of the Henry IV narrative. But it is also the third part of the unofficial cycle composed of *Richard the Second, Henry the Fourth, Part One, Henry the Fourth, Part Two,* and *Henry the Fifth.* The continuity should be noted, especially from preceding plays. As a whole the cycle traces the historical transition from the reign of Richard II, a distinctly medieval king, to the reign of Henry V, a distinctly Renaissance king. And while it is an "unofficial" cycle, salient aspects of this transition are implied at the end of each play, projected into the next, and developed and explored. *Henry the Fourth, Part Two,* is, of course, a sequel (although an independent play), to *Henry the Fourth, Part One,* but to place it in its larger frame we must briefly look back to *Richard the Second.*

In *Richard the Second* the legitimate king, Richard II, is deposed by Bolingbroke, who becomes Henry IV. This act must be viewed as a usurpation and also as a necessary political expediency. It is a usurpation because unjustifiable, indeed unthinkable, from the strictly medieval view of what has been called "the great chain of being." This idea holds that the universe is ordered, hierarchical, that everything is given a place by God, and that one's station must not be changed. In this world governed by ritual, an annointed king is representative of God's Order. To depose him is to call in question all order in the world.

And indeed, the effects of Bolingbroke's (Henry IV) revolution initiated in England a new, and less innocent world. *Henry the Fourth, Part One,* presents the immediate political effects, the distrust and further rebellion of Henry's nobility (the men who helped him steal the crown), and the wider effects of the new-found sense of individualism relating to all facets of life. *Henry the Fourth, Part One,* is concerned, in large measure, with the struggle of various individualistic viewpoints trying to absorb the whole, to fill the vacuum left by the fallen absolute denoted by "the great chain of being."

The focus in this play, *Henry the Fourth, Part One,* is on Prince Hal, later Henry V, and his attempt to reconcile, or at least compromise, the conflicting claims upon his person, as a Renaissance man and future king, of attitudes represented on the one hand by the glory-obsessed rebel, Hotspur, and, on the other hand, by the humorous wastrel, Falstaff. The world of the tavern, with its riotous submission to basic appetites, still has wit and irony. The battlefield represents reckless courage and the pursuit of personal honor and glory at any cost, shaming Hal. But he senses the need for an alternative to this sure path to early death. Hal learns to compromise, at least, the needs for rigidity and flexibility. The practical politician that the king, entering modernity, must be, is an eclectic solution rather than a great synthesis.

If in *Henry the Fourth, Part One,* Shakespeare showed the new world mainly as a burst of new energies, in *Henry the Fourth, Part Two,* he explores, we might say, some aspects of its darker side. The new freedom to express individual potential is not without costs at the very heart of things, any more than it had been at the political level. It is a 'fallen" world and diminished too, having realized in some way that the power of the individual had, in fact, been exaggerated, misunderstood. This is not to say, however, that there is the radical loss of moral certainty in the problem comedies. But the characters, or what they represent, become almost travesties of their former selves.

Northumberland, the father of Hotspur, upon learning of his son's death, rages rhetorically, even beyond his son:

> But let one spirit of the first-born Cain
> Reign in all bosoms, that each heart being set
> On bloody courses, the rude scene may end,
> And darkness be the burier of the dead.

The morbidity of Hotspur's obsession for battle-glory is translated now into a manifest call for general slaughter.

King Henry, if he has seemed authoritative before, is now much less sure of himself. He cannot sleep, his worry looks fearfully back to the prediction of King Richard that corruption, "foretelling this same time's condition," would thrive as a result of his usurpation. He faces the rebellion with a fatalistic tone: "Are these things necessities / Then let us meet them like necessities," rather than, as he had said at Shrewsbury in *Henry the Fourth, Part One,* "rebuke and dread correction wait on us, / And they shall do their office," or, "And God befriend us as our cause is just."

The world of the tavern is altered as well. The Boar's Head is now clearly a brothel. The humor now reflects the real corruption of the place. The butt of jokes, more often than not, is now someone unable to defend himself, such as Doll, Shallow, or Mistress Quickly. The Braggart Soldier element in Falstaff is now the frenzied mind and speech of Pistol. Falstaff himself is seen to be the victim of ailments of all sorts, results of his long life of excesses. His lust for Doll, and his callous exploitation of Shallow and (he would hope) of his relation to Hal, are now particularly unseemly.

Perhaps as much as in any other, it is in the person of the Lord Chief Justice that we get an idea of the meaning of the coming society. There is a motto on some court houses that suggests the new orientation: "This is a court of Law, not of Justice." That is, institutions are plainly secular, no longer having pretensions beyond human capabilities to control, through human efforts, a moral order. And it is to him, and his administration of efficient Law, that the new king, Henry V, adheres.

It is in deference to such a conception of order, a legalistic social hierarchy, that Henry V banishes Falstaff at the end of the play. For, as Eric Auerbach has shown (in commenting upon Hal's knowledge of Poins's laundry), the absolute distinction between high and low has been lost (through a process of leveling ultimately engendered in Christian doctrine). Hal, Henry V, represents a firm step on the path that will lead, as a character in Stendhal's *The Red and the Black* laments, to a time when there will be no more kings in Europe, but only prime ministers and presidents.

James Marc Hovde

HENRY THE SIXTH, PART ONE

Type of work: Drama
Author: William Shakespeare (1564-1616)
Type of plot: Historical chronicle
Time of plot: 1422-1444
Locale: England and France
First presented: c. 1592

Principal characters:
KING HENRY VI
DUKE OF GLOSTER, uncle of the king and Protector of the Realm
DUKE OF BEDFORD, uncle of the king and Regent of France
HENRY BEAUFORT, Bishop of Winchester, afterward cardinal
RICHARD PLANTAGENET, who becomes Duke of York
JOHN BEAUFORT, Earl of Somerset
EARL OF SUFFOLK
LORD TALBOT, a general, afterward Earl of Shrewsbury
CHARLES, the Dauphin, afterward King of France
THE BASTARD OF ORLEANS, a French general
MARGARET OF ANJOU, afterward married to King Henry
JOAN LA PUCELLE, commonly called Joan of Arc

Critique:

Replete with political intrigue, courtly pomp, grandeur of battle, and the mystery of witchcraft, *King Henry the Sixth, Part I,* is typically Shakespearean historical drama. Also typical, but more flagrant than in most of the other history chronicles are the playwright's gross distortions and inaccuracies in historical detail. A distinguishing factor in the play is the fuller use of melodramatic devices to further character development in instances in which military prowess or statecraft are hardly adequate. Typical, atypical, or distinctive, *Henry the Sixth* is a rousing play, either in print or upon stage. It is a revision of an earlier drama, known by Shakespeare.

The Story:

The great nobles and churchmen of England gathered in Westminster Abbey for the state funeral of King Henry V, hero of Agincourt and conqueror of France. The eulogies of Gloster, Bedford, Exeter, and the Bishop of Winchester, profound and extensive, were broken off by messengers bringing reports of English defeat and failure in France, where the Dauphin, taking advantage of King Henry's illness, had raised the standards of revolt. The gravest defeat reported was the imprisonment of Lord Talbot, general of the English armies. Bedford swore to avenge his loss. Gloster said that he would also hasten military preparations and proclaim young Prince Henry, nine months old, King of England. The Bishop of Winchester, disgruntled because the royal dukes had asked neither his advice nor aid, planned to seize the king's person and ingratiate himself into royal favor.

In France, the Dauphin and his generals, discussing the conduct of the war, attempted to overwhelm the depleted English forces. Although outnumbered and without leaders, the English fought valiantly and tenaciously. Hope of victory came to the French, however, when the Bastard of Orleans brought to the Dauphin's camp a soldier-maid, Joan la Pucelle, described as a holy young girl with God-given visionary powers. The Dauphin's attempt to trick her was unsuccessful, for she recognized him although Reignier, Duke of Anjou, stood in the Dauphin's place. Next she vanquished the prince in a duel to which he challenged her in an attempt to test her military skill.

The followers of the Duke of Gloster and the Bishop of Winchester rioted in the London streets, as dissension between Church and State grew because of Winchester's efforts to keep Gloster from seeing young Henry. The Mayor of London proclaimed against the unseemly conduct of the rioters.

When the English and the French fought again, Lord Salisbury and Sir Thomas Gargrave, the English leaders, were killed by a gunner in ambush. Meanwhile Lord Talbot, greatly feared by the French, had been ransomed in time to take command of English forces in the siege of Orleans. Enraged by the death of Salisbury, Talbot fought heroically, on one occasion with La Pucelle herself. At last the English swarmed into the town and put the French to rout. Talbot ordered Salisbury's body to be carried into the public market place of Orleans as a token of his revenge for that lord's murder.

The Countess of Auvergne invited Lord Talbot to visit her in her castle. Fearing chicanery, Bedford and Burgundy tried to keep him from going into an enemy stronghold, but Talbot, as strong-willed as he was brave, ignored their pleas. He did whisper to his captain, however, certain instructions concerning his visit.

On his arrival at Auvergne Castle the countess announced that she was making him her prisoner in order to save France from further scourges. Talbot proved his wit by completely baffling the countess with double talk and by signaling his soldiers, who stormed the castle, ate the food and drank the wine, and then won the favor of the countess with their charming manners.

In addition to continued internal strife resulting from Gloster's and Winchester's personal ambitions, new dissension arose between Richard Plantagenet and the Earl of Somerset. Plantagenet and his followers chose a white rose as their symbol, Somerset and his supporters a red rose, and in the quarrel of these two men the disastrous Wars of the Roses began. In the meantime Edmund Mortimer, the rightful heir to the throne, who had been imprisoned when King Henry IV usurped the crown some thirty years before, was released from confinement. He urged his nephew, Richard Plantagenet, to restore the family to the rightful position the Plantagenets deserved.

Youthful King Henry VI, after making Plantagenet Duke of York, much to the displeasure of Somerset, was taken to France by Gloster and other lords to be crowned King of France. In Paris, Talbot's chivalry and prowess were rewarded when he was made Earl of Shrewsbury.

In preparation for the battle at Rouen, La Pucelle won Burgundy over to the cause of France by playing upon his vanity and appealing to what she termed his sense of justice. The immaturity of the king was revealed in his request that Talbot go to Burgundy and chastise him for his desertion.

The Duke of York and the Earl of Somerset finally brought their quarrel to the king, who implored them to be friendly for England's sake. He pointed out that disunity among the English lords would only weaken their stand in France. To show how petty he considered their differences he casually put on a red rose, the symbol of Somerset's faction, and explained that it was merely a flower and that he loved one of his rival kinsmen as much as the other. He appointed York a regent of France and ordered both him and Somerset to supply Talbot with men and supplies for battle. Then the king and his party returned to London.

The king's last assignment to his lords in France was Talbot's death knell; Somerset, refusing to send horses with which York planned to supply Talbot, accused York of self-aggrandizement. York, in turn, blamed Somerset for negligence. As their feud continued, Talbot and his son were struggling valiantly against the better-equipped, more fully manned French army at Bordeaux. After many skirmishes Talbot and his son were slain and the English suffered tremendous losses. Flushed with the triumph of their great victory, the French leaders planned to march on to Paris.

In England, meanwhile, there was talk of a truce, and the king agreed, after a moment of embarrassment because of his youth, to Gloster's proposal that Henry accept in marriage the daughter of the Earl of Armagnac, a man of affluence and influence in France. This alliance, designed to effect a friendly peace between the two countries, was to be announced in France by Cardinal Beaufort, former Bishop of Winchester, who, in sending money to the pope to pay for his cardinalship, stated that his ecclesiastical position gave him status equal to that of the loftiest peer. He threatened mutiny if Gloster ever tried to dominate him again. The king sent a jewel to seal the contract of betrothal.

The fighting in France dwindled greatly, with the English forces converging for one last weak stand. La Pucelle cast a spell and conjured up fiends to bolster her morale and to assist her in battle, but her appeal was to no avail, and York took her prisoner. Berated as a harlot and condemned as a witch by the English, La Pucelle pleaded for her life. At first she contended that her virgin blood would cry for vengeance at the gates of heaven. When this appeal failed to move York and the Earl of Warwick, she implored them to save her unborn child, fathered, she said variously, by the Dauphin, the Duke of Alençon, and the Duke of Anjou. She was condemned to be burned at the stake.

In another skirmish the Earl of Suffolk had taken as his prisoner Margaret, daughter of the Duke of Anjou. Enthralled by her loveliness, he was unable to claim her for himself because he was already married. He finally struck upon the notion of wooing Margaret for the king. After receiving her father's permission to present Margaret's name to Henry as a candidate for marriage, Suffolk went to London to petition the king. While Henry weighed the matter against the consequences of breaking his contract with the Earl of Armagnac, Exeter and Gloster attempted to dissuade him from following Suffolk's suggestions. Their pleas were in vain. Margaret's great courage and spirit, as described by Suffolk, held promise of a great and invincible offspring.

Terms of peace having been arranged, Suffolk was ordered to conduct Margaret to England. Suffolk, because he had brought Margaret and Henry together, planned to take advantage of his opportune political position and, through Margaret, rule youthful Henry and his kingdom.

Further Critical Evaluation of the Work:

Some modern critics see an overall design in the three *Henry the Sixth* plays plus *Richard the Third,* and treat them as an epic of the suffering England must undergo in retribution for the deposition and slaying of a rightful monarch, Richard II. Only with the reign of a legitimate successor—Henry VII, the first Tudor king—can England regain peace and greatness.

Henry the Sixth, Part One, while it may seem fragmented, is actually a well-structured episodic play based on the theme of the loss of France and the ruin of England. A concomitant theme, the breakdown of order, is set in motion early in Act One when the Duke of Gloster and the Bishop of Winchester quarrel, disrupting the solemn order at Henry V's funeral. In contrast to the English disintegration into chaos, the French, under Joan of Arc's forceful leadership, unite; England's weakness, however, results more from her own division than from French strength.

As a contrast to the bickering and deceit which is directly responsible for England's decline, Talbot's role in the play is to provide a picture of what

England's successes could be if the English emulated his loyalty, steadfast-ness, and courage. With no English unity to back him, Talbot falls, and with his fall, the prospects of English strength collapses.

The final scene illustrates the play's unified construction. Margaret, of whom we have seen little, would seem not to belong in the play at all. She does belong, however, primarily so that Suffolk can establish her on the English throne purely to further his own power. At the end of the play, Suffolk's deceitful and self-aggrandizing action mirrors the actions of other nobles, and the final scene reinforces the important theme of English loss through selfishness.

HENRY THE SIXTH, PART TWO

Type of work: Drama
Author: William Shakespeare (1564-1616)
Type of plot: Historical chronicle
Time of plot: 1444-1455
Locale: England
First presented: c. 1592

Principal characters:

KING HENRY VI
DUKE OF GLOSTER, his uncle
CARDINAL BEAUFORT, great-uncle of the king
RICHARD PLANTAGENET, Duke of York
EDWARD, and
RICHARD, York's sons
DUKE OF SOMERSET, leader of the Lancaster faction
DUKE OF SUFFOLK, the king's favorite
EARL OF SALISBURY, a Yorkist
EARL OF WARWICK, a Yorkist
BOLINGBROKE, a conjurer
MARGARET, Queen of England
ELEANOR, Duchess of Gloster
MARGERY JOURDAIN, a witch

Critique:

In addition to those features contained in the first part of *King Henry the Sixth* as described in the critique of that play, there are in this second part scenes reflecting social implications. These scenes, within the limits of the five acts, not only make clear the social strata of commoners and nobles but also point up the principal characters. This fuller realism of historical perspective and social content in no way diminishes the picture of ambition, jealousy, love, and courage among the nobility. As is true of the first part of *King Henry the Sixth,* this drama is a revision of an earlier play.

The Story:

The Earl of Suffolk, having arranged for the marriage of King Henry VI and Margaret of Anjou, brought the new queen to England. There was great indignation when the terms of the marriage treaty were revealed. The contract called for an eighteen-months' truce between the two countries, the outright gift of the duchies of Anjou and Maine to Reignier, Margaret's father, and omission of her dowry. As had been predicted earlier, no good could come of this union, since

Henry, at Suffolk's urging, had broken his betrothal to the daughter of the Earl of Armagnac. But Henry, pleased by his bride's beauty, gladly accepted the treaty and elevated Suffolk, the go-between, to a dukedom.

The voices were hardly still from the welcome of the new queen before the lords, earls, and dukes were expressing their ambitions to gain more control in affairs of state. The old dissension between the Duke of Gloster and Cardinal Beaufort continued. The churchman tried to alienate others against Gloster by saying that Gloster, next in line for the crown, needed watching. The Duke of Somerset accused the cardinal of seeking Gloster's position for himself. And these high ambitions were not exclusively for the men. The Duchess of Gloster showed great impatience with her husband when he said he wished only to serve as Protector of the Realm. When she saw that her husband was not going to help her ambitions to be queen, the duchess hired Hume, a priest, to traffic with witches and conjurers in her behalf. Hume accepted her money; but he had already been hired by Suffolk and the cardinal to work against the duchess.

Queen Margaret's unhappy life in England, her contempt for the king, and the people's dislike for her soon became apparent. The mutual hatred she and the duchess had for each other showed itself in tongue lashings and blows. The duchess, eager to take advantage of any turn of events, indulged in sorcery with Margery Jourdain and the notorious Bolingbroke. Her questions to them, all pertaining to the fate of the king and his advisers, and the answers which these sorcerers had received from the spirit world, were confiscated by Buckingham and York when they broke in upon a seance. For her part in the practice of sorcery the duchess was banished to the Isle of Man; Margery Jourdain and Bolingbroke were executed.

His wife's deeds brought new slanders upon Gloster. In answer to Queen Margaret's charge that he was a party to his wife's underhandedness, Gloster, a broken man, resigned his position as Protector of the Realm. Even after his resignation Margaret continued in her attempts to turn the king against Gloster. She was aided by the other lords, who accused Gloster of deceit and crimes against the State; but the king, steadfast in his loyalty to Gloster, described the former protector as virtuous and mild.

York, whose regency in France had been given to Somerset, enlisted the aid of Warwick and Salisbury in his fight for the crown, his claim being based on the fact that King Henry's grandfather, Henry IV, had usurped the throne from York's great-uncle. Suffolk and the cardinal, to rid themselves of a dangerous rival, sent York to quell an uprising in Ireland. Before departing for Ireland, York planned to incite rebellion among the English through one John Cade, a headstrong, warmongering Kentishman. Cade, under the name of John Mortimer, the name of York's uncle, paraded his riotous followers through the streets of London. The rebels, irresponsible and unthinking, went madly about the town wrecking buildings, killing noblemen who opposed

them, and shouting that they were headed for the palace, where John Cade, the rightful heir to the throne, would avenge the injustices done his lineage. An aspect of the poorly organized rebellion was shown in the desertion of Cade's followers when they were appealed to by loyal old Lord Clifford. He admonished them to save England from needless destruction and to expend their military efforts against France. Cade, left alone, went wandering about the countryside as a fugitive and was killed by Alexander Iden, a squire who was knighted for his bravery.

Gloster, arrested by Suffolk on a charge of high treason, was promised a fair trial by the king. This was unwelcome news to the lords; and when Gloster was sent for to appear at the hearing, he was found in his bed, brutally murdered and mangled. Suffolk and the cardinal had hired the murderers. So was fulfilled the first prophecy of the sorcerers, that the king would depose and outlive a duke who would die a violent death.

Shortly after Gloster's death the king was called to the bedside of the cardinal, who had been stricken by a strange malady. There King Henry heard the cardinal confess his part in the murder of Gloster, the churchman's bitterest enemy. The cardinal died unrepentent.

Queen Margaret became more outspoken concerning affairs of state, especially in those matters on behalf of Suffolk, and more openly contemptuous toward the king's indifferent attitude.

At the request of Commons, led by Warwick and Salisbury, Suffolk was banished from the country for his part in Gloster's murder. Saying their farewells, he and Margaret declared their love for each other. Suffolk, disguised, took ship to leave the country. Captured by pirates, he was beheaded for his treacheries and one of his gentlemen was instructed to return his body to the king.

In London, Queen Margaret mourned her loss in Suffolk's death as she caressed his severed head. The king, piqued by her demonstration, asked her how she would react to his death. Diplomatically evasive, she answered that she would not mourn his death; she would die for him. The witch had prophesied Suffolk's death: she had said that he would die by water.

Returning from Ireland, York planned to gather forces on his way to London and seize the crown for himself. Because he also stated his determination to remove Somerset, his adversary in court matters, the king tried to appease the rebel by committing Somerset to the Tower. Hearing that his enemy was in prison, York ordered his army to disband.

His rage was all the greater, therefore, when he learned that Somerset had been restored to favor. The armies of York and Lancaster prepared to battle at Saint Albans, where Somerset, after an attempt to arrest York for capital treason, was slain by crookbacked Richard Plantagenet, York's son. Somerset's death fulfilled the prophecies of the witch, who had also foretold that Somerset should shun castles, that he would be safer on sandy plains. With his death the king and queen fled. Salisbury, weary from battle but undaunted, and Warwick, proud of York's victory at Saint Albans, pledged their support to York in his drive for the crown, and York hastened to London to forestall the king's intention to summon Parliament into session.

Further Critical Evaluation of the Work:

Henry the Sixth, Part Two, generally considered the best of the three *Henry the Sixth* plays, is, like all of Shakespeare's history plays, a rich mixture of fact and fancy. Shakespeare was not a historian; his main concern was to dramatize a political era and comment upon political processes that seriously weakened England a century and a half before he wrote.

Shakespeare's themes are fully realized in the play. Although the play ends at an inconclusive historical point, with the king in retreat but not entirely defeated, a full dramatic action has been concluded and important themes have been fully explored. The most significant themes are the need for loyalty to the monarch, the danger of a weak sovereign, the dangers of perfidy and rebellion, and the success an evil schemer can achieve if not effectively opposed. Shakespeare, as always in his early career, was in the mainstream of Elizabethan political thought: somewhat conservative, patriotic, and optimistic about man's ultimate potential.

The play's many episodes and characters may best be understood in their relationship to the king: Henry stands at the center of the play. He occupies the office that should lead the nation into harmonious order, but he is pitifully ineffectual. Among the characters there are two chief attitudes toward the throne: selfless devotion to its protection, as embodied in Gloster, and selfish desire to possess it, as embodied in York.

Gloster is a key figure early in the play, as York is later. Many of the play's early episodes are intended to establish Gloster's identity as protector of the throne; while most later episodes, including the Jack Cade affair, identify York as the chief threat. Through these two men Shakespeare successfully presents the problem of how a man of power may use his power either for the enhancement of the national welfare or for his own enrichment. In this world the position represented by York often wins, but clearly Shakespeare had a vision of a political order in which man's higher qualities would prevail.

HENRY THE SIXTH, PART THREE

Type of work: Drama
Author: William Shakespeare (1564-1616)
Type of plot: Historical chronicle
Time of plot: 1455-1471
Locale: England and France
First presented: c. 1592

Principal characters:

KING HENRY VI
EDWARD, Prince of Wales, his son
LOUIS XI, King of France
RICHARD PLANTAGENET, Duke of York
EDWARD, York's son, afterward King Edward IV
EDMUND, York's son, Earl of Rutland
GEORGE, York's son, afterward Duke of Clarence
RICHARD, York's son, afterward Duke of Gloster
LORD HASTINGS, of the Duke of York's party
THE EARL OF WARWICK, a king-maker
MARGARET, Queen of England
LORD CLIFFORD, Margaret's ally
LADY GREY, afterward Edward IV's queen
LADY BONA, sister of the Queen of France

Critique:

Although the third part of *King Henry the Sixth* is not a tragedy in the classical sense, it is more poignant than many tragic dramas. A revision of an earlier play, it is an outstanding example of writing for unity of impression. Infinite and unswerving ambition in the characters, and situations of plot closely knit to reveal this unrelenting aggression are always apparent, making this play a masterpiece of gripping drama. The plot is so developed that King Henry is made a pawn to the wishes of others. The characterization is handled with finesse, an occasional line by King Henry showing his true nature. The labels frequently given him — "poltroon," "weak-willed," "willy-nilly"—are unjust and misapplied. Shakespeare's King Henry in this third part is a man caught in the mesh of circumstances and required to exhibit the qualities of leadership, when his only wish was for contentment and tranquillity. Henry's was a life spent in quiet desperation.

The Story:

In the House of Parliament, York, his sons, and the Earl of Warwick rejoiced over their success at Saint Albans. Riding hard, the Yorkists had arrived in London ahead of the routed king, and Henry, entering with his lords, was filled with consternation when he saw York already seated on the throne, to which Warwick had conducted him. Some of the king's followers were sympathetic toward York and others were fearful of his power; the two attitudes resulted in defection in the royal ranks. Seeing his stand weakened, the king attempted to avert disorder by disinheriting his own son and by pledging the crown to York and his sons, on the condition that York stop the civil war and remain loyal to the king during his lifetime.

Annoyed by the reconciliation and contemptuous toward the king because of her son's disinheritance, Margaret deserted the king and raised her own army to protect her son's rights to the throne. The queen's army marched against York's castle as York was sending his sons to recruit forces for another rebellion. York's sons had persuaded their father that his oath to the king was not binding because his contract with the king had not been made in due course of law before a magistrate.

In a battle near Wakefield, Lord Clifford and his soldiers killed Rutland, York's young son, and soaked a handkerchief in his blood. Later, as he joined Margaret's victorious army, which outnumbered York's soldiers ten to one, Lord Clifford gave York the handkerchief to wipe away his tears as he wept for his son's death. York's sorrow was equaled by his humiliation at the hands of Margaret, who, after taking him prisoner, put a paper crown on his head that he might reign from the molehill where she had him placed to be jeered by the soldiers. Clifford and Margaret stabbed the Duke of York and beheaded him. His head was set on the gates of York.

Hearing of the defeat of York's forces, Warwick, taking the king with him, set out from London to fight Queen Margaret at Saint Albans. Warwick's qualities as a general were totally offset by the presence of the king, who was unable to conceal his strong affection for Margaret and Warwick was defeated. Edward and Richard, York's sons, joined Warwick in a march toward London.

King Henry, ever the righteous monarch, forswore any part in breaking his vow to York and declared that he preferred to leave his son only virtuous deeds, rather than an ill-gotten crown. At the insistence of Clifford and Margaret, however, the king knighted his son as the Prince of Wales.

After a defiant parley, the forces met again between Towton and Saxton. The king, banned from battle by Clifford and Margaret because of his antipathy to war and his demoralizing influence on the soldiers, sat on a distant part of the field lamenting the course affairs had taken in this bloody business of murder and deceit. He saw the ravages of war when a father bearing the body of his dead son and a son with the body of his dead father passed by. They had unknowingly taken the lives of their loved ones in the fighting. As the rebel forces, led by Warwick, Richard, and Edward approached, the king, passive to danger and indifferent toward his own safety, was rescued by the Prince of Wales and Margaret before the enemy could reach him. He was sent to Scotland for safety.

After a skirmish with Richard, Clifford fled to another part of the field, where, weary and worn, he fainted and died. His head, severed by Richard, replaced York's head on the gate. The Yorkists marched on to London. Edward was proclaimed King Edward IV; Richard was made Duke of Gloster, and George, Duke of Clarence.

King Edward, in audience, heard Lady Grey's case for the return of confiscated lands taken by Margaret's army at Saint Albans, where Lord Grey was killed fighting for the York cause. The hearing, marked by Richard's and George's dissatisfaction with their brother's position and Edward's lewdness directed at Lady Grey, ended with Lady Grey's betrothal to Edward. Richard, resentful of his hunchback, aspired to the throne. His many deprivations resulting from his physical condition, he felt, justified his ambition; he would stop at no obstacle in achieving his ends.

Because of their great losses, Margaret and the prince went to France to appeal for aid from King Louis XI, who was kindly disposed toward helping them maintain the crown. The French monarch's decision was quickly changed at the appearance of Warwick, who had arrived from England to ask for the hand of Lady Bona for King Edward. Warwick's suit had been granted, and Margaret's request denied, when a messenger brought letters announcing King Edward's marriage to Lady Grey. King Louis and Lady Bona were insulted; Margaret was overjoyed. Warwick, chagrined, withdrew his allegiance to the House of York and offered to lead French troops against Edward. He promised his older daughter in marriage to Margaret's son as a pledge of his honor.

At the royal palace in London, family loyalty was broken by open dissent when King Edward informed his brothers that he would not be bound by their wishes. Told that the prince was to marry Warwick's older daughter, the Duke of Clarence announced that he intended to marry the younger one. He left, taking Somerset, one of King Henry's faction, with him. Richard, seeing in an alliance with Edward an opportunity for his own advancement, remained; and he, Montague, and Hastings pledged their support to King Edward.

When the French forces reached London, Warwick took Edward prisoner. The king-maker removed Edward's crown and took it to re-crown King Henry, who had, in the meantime, escaped from Scotland only to be delivered into Edward's hands and imprisoned in the Tower. Henry delegated his royal authority to Warwick and the Duke of Clarence, in order that he might be free from the turmoil attendant upon his reign.

Richard and Hastings freed Edward from his imprisonment. They formed an army in York; and while Warwick and Clarence, who had learned of Edward's release, were making preparations for defense, Edward, marching upon London, again seized King Henry and sent him to solitary confinement in the Tower.

Edward made a surprise attack on Warwick near Coventry, where Warwick's forces were soon increased by the appearance of Oxford, Montague, and Somerset. The fourth unit to join Warwick was led by Clarence who took the red rose, the symbol of the House of Lancaster, from his hat and threw it into Warwick's face. Clarence accused Warwick of duplicity and announced that he would fight beside his brothers to preserve the House of York. Warwick, a valiant soldier to the end, was wounded by King Edward and died soon afterward. Montague was also killed.

When Queen Margaret and her son arrived from France, the prince won great acclaim from Margaret and the lords for his spirited vow to hold the kingdom against the Yorkists. Defeated at Tewkesbury, however, the prince was cruelly stabbed to death by King Edward and his brothers. Margaret pleaded with them to kill her too, but they chose to punish her with life. She was sent back to France, her original home. After the prince had been killed, Richard of Gloster stole off to London, where he assassinated King Henry in the Tower. Again he swore to get the crown for himself.

The Yorkists were at last supreme. Edward and Queen Elizabeth, with their infant son, regained the throne. Richard, still intending to seize the crown for himself, saluted the infant with a Judas kiss, while Edward stated that they were now to spend their time in stately triumphs, comic shows, and pleasures of the court.

Further Critical Evaluation of the Work:

In *Henry the Sixth, Part Three,* which belongs to Shakespeare's tetralogy of history plays dealing with the political upheaval that followed Henry Bolingbroke's overthrow and murder of Richard II, England continues to suffer the evils of civil strife and social disorder arising from the war between the houses of York and Lancaster. Shakespeare's general purpose in this series of plays is to reassert the power of Providence, and to glorify England and suggest the nature of her salvation; but only with the restitution of the rightful heir at the end of *Richard III* will England be able to bind her wounds and enjoy peace once again.

Henry the Sixth, Part Three is a powerful study of disorder and chaos; the play interweaves a cohesive body of imagery and symbolism with the action of its plot to create a strong unity of impression centering on the theme of anarchy and disunity. Chaos prevails on all levels of society, from the state, to the family, to the individual. At the highest level of authority and social organization—the throne—anarchy has replaced traditional rule. The king, who must be the center of political strength and embody the sanctity of social duty, oath, and custom, is instead the essence of weakness; Henry not only yields the right of succession to York, but eventually abdicates in favor of Warwick and Clarence. Whenever he attempts to intervene in events, his weak voice is quickly silenced; finally he is silenced permanently, and his murder represents the ultimate overturning of political order and rejection of the divine right upon which his rule was founded. Contrasted to Henry, the representative of rightful power, is Richard, who in this play becomes the epitome of total anarchy. Richard murders the prince, the king, and his brother Clarence, boasting later, "Why, I can smile, and murder whiles I smile"; he scornfully disregards any form of moral obligation; and eventually falls victim to unreasoning fears and nightmares.

The primary social bond—that of the family—is likewise in a state of dissolution. Again, the malady begins at the level of the king; Henry disinherits his own son, the rightful heir, thus causing his wife Margaret to cut herself off from him, sundering their marital bond. York's three sons become hopelessly divided by their conflicting ambitions. And in Act II, scene 5, Shakespeare shows, by means of the morality tableau, that the same family breakdown prevails among the common people as well. Simultaneously with its presentation of political and social chaos, the play dramatizes the disruption that is occurring in individuals' morality. Hatred, ambition, lust, and greed are the keynotes, while duty, trust, tradition, and self-restraint are increasingly lost.

Henry the Sixth, Part Three thus depicts a society in the throes of anarchy and war, a society where kings surrender their duties, fathers and sons murder each other, and brothers vie for power at any cost. Yet the play contains an ocasional feeble ray of light, such as in Henry's weak protests against the cruelty of the usurpers, his pleas for pity for the war's victims, and his ineffectual calls for an end to the conflict and a restoration of peace and order. These scattered flickers, dim as they are, along with several prophecies planted throughout the play, foreshadow the coming hope, resolution of conflict, and return of peace and rightful authority which will follow in *Richard III.*

HERAKLES MAD

Type of work: Drama
Author: Euripides (c. 485-c. 406 B.C.)
Type of plot: Classical tragedy
Time of plot: Remote antiquity
Locale: Thebes
First presented: c. 420 B.C.

Principal characters:
AMPHITRYON, married to Alcmene, the mother of Herakles
MEGARA, wife of Herakles and daughter of Creon
LYCUS, usurper of Kingdom of Thebes
HERAKLES, son of Zeus and Alcmene
THESEUS, King of Athens
IRIS, messenger of the gods
MADNESS
CHORUS OF THE OLD MEN OF THEBES

Critique:

Herakles Mad, one of the most puzzling of Euripides' plays, begins with a stereotyped situation and weak characters, builds to a powerful climax in the mad scene of Herakles, and is followed by one of the most moving tragic reconciliations in all drama. Some critics see in Euripides' treatment of Herakles the suggestion that he has been deluded all his life and has never really performed his twelve great labors; others have suggested that the madness comes not from Hera, but from Fate. In either case he reaches heroic and tragic stature when, after murdering his wife and children in a fit of madness, he refuses to commit suicide and decides to face whatever life has in store for him.

The Story:

Amphitryon, who together with Megara and the sons of Herakles had sought sanctuary at the altar of Zeus, lamented the fact that while Herakles was in Hades performing one of his twelve labors Lycus had murdered Creon and seized the throne of Thebes. The murderer was bent upon consolidating his position by killing Megara and her children, whose only hope lay in the protection of Zeus until Herakles returned. Lycus came to taunt them with the charge that Herakles was a coward who used a bow and killed only animals and that, in any case, he was dead in Hades

and would never return.

Amphitryon, retorting that Lycus was the coward in seeking to kill an old man, a woman, and innocent children, begged that they at least be allowed to go into exile. Enraged, Lycus sent his servants to fetch oak logs in order to burn the relatives of Herakles alive in their sanctuary. The chorus of old men vowed that they would fight with their staves against such a horrible sacrilege.

Megara, however, counseled that it was folly to attempt to escape destiny; Herakles could not emerge from Hades to save them and since they must die they ought to do so without being burnt alive. Amphitryon then begged that he and Megara be killed first so that they would not have to witness the massacre of innocent children, and Megara pleaded for the privilege of dressing the children in the proper funeral robes. Lycus haughtily granted both wishes. As the group left the sanctuary for the palace, Amphitryon cursed Zeus for being a senseless and unjust god. In their absence the chorus chanted an ode on the glories of Herakles and the sadness of old age.

Returning with the children, Megara woefully recounted the marvelous plans she had made for her sons. Meanwhile, Amphitryon fervently prayed to Zeus for deliverance. Suddenly they were startled by the spectacle of Herakles approaching. The great joy of their meeting was darkened by the fearful tale Megara had to tell her husband. Furious with rage, Herakles swore that he would behead Lycus and throw his carcass to the dogs; but Amphitryon cautioned him to curb his reckless haste, for Lycus had many allies in his treachery. Though deeply moved by the fear that made his children cling to his robes, Herakles agreed to plan his revenge carefully and led his family into the palace. The chorus of ancients once again lamented their old age and praised Zeus for sending deliverance in the person of Herakles, his son.

Lycus, upon encountering Amphitryon emerging from the palace, commanded that he bring Megara with him, but Amphitryon refused on the ground that such a deed would make him an accomplice in her murder. Intent on dispatching Megara, Lycus angrily stormed into the palace. Amphitryon followed to watch Herakles' revenge. As the chorus hailed the death cries of Lycus, the specters of Madness and Iris appeared from above. Iris, the female messenger of the gods, pronounced that although destiny had preserved Herakles until he had finished his twelve labors, Hera had decreed that he must now suffer lest the powers of man seem greater than those of the gods. She commanded that Madness force Herakles to murder his own wife and children. Reluctantly, Madness sent out her power and described the horrible seizures of Herakles within the palace. When the two specters disappeared, a messenger emerged from the palace to tell how Herakles in a frenzy of madness had murdered his wife and children, believing them to be the kin of his former master, Eurystheus. Amphitryon was saved only by the intervention of Athena, who put the possessed hero to sleep and had him tied to a pillar.

The doors of the palace were opened, revealing Herakles, now awake and puzzled by the awful scene about him. Informed of what he had done, Herakles crouched in shame and wailed in anguish.

Theseus, who had been rescued from Hades by Herakles, arrived with an army for the purpose of aiding his old friend against Lycus. Crushed by the weight of his dishonor, Herakles could not face his friend, and he announced his intention to commit suicide. His compassionate friend Theseus pleaded with him to live and accept his fate; he offered to take Herakles to Athens where, after being purified of his pollution, he would be given great estates and high status. Though he preferred to grow into a stone oblivious of his horrid deed, Herakles reluctantly agreed to harden his heart against death and rose with profound gratitude to accept his friend's offer. As he left, he urged the sorrowful Amphitryon to bury the dead and to follow him to Athens, where they would live out the remainder of their lives in peace.

Further Critical Evaluation of the Work:

Euripides has deliberately reversed the tradition that Herakles was forced to perform his labors to atone for the murder of his family, thereby achieving ultimate greatness. There is no evidence to assume that in this play Herakles had not actually performed the labors, as has been suggested; nevertheless Euripides has demeaned them as mere feats of strength and cunning by demonstrating the greater strength of soul which Herakles must summon from the depths of his misery. True nobility requires that the hero persevere against the uncontrollable whims of immortals, in this case Hera, who is virtually abstracted into Tyche, or Fortune. Herakles' nobility of soul is contrasted with the wealth and might of his antagonist Lycus ("Wolf"), and his killing of this inhuman creature may be seen, then, as merely a "thirteenth" labor.

The first half of the drama is, therefore, appropriate to the variety of Herakles' glories. Note the ironic dependence of Herakles' family on the hero who will save them by killing Lycus to bring about a "happy ending" to the melodrama; but this glorious figure will promptly be transformed into the pathetic wreck that must be restored in the "tragic" half of the drama (compare lines 631 and 1424).

The fact that Madness seizes the innocent hero without cause shows that man must be prepared for any event in this life ruled by unconcerned or unfriendly external forces. Man's only hope or resolution is to turn to his own kind, not to the gods; this is exemplified by Amphitryon's complaint against Zeus and by Theseus' role in giving aid to his former savior. This friendship, *philia,* is Euripides' answer to the cruel and brutal blows of Fortune, epitomized by the rapid succession of horrors unequaled in any Euripidean play. When man's world is violently turned about, humanity must triumph over inhumanity. This realistic rather than nihilistic philosophy prevents life from becoming absurd.

HERCULES AND HIS TWELVE LABORS

Type of work: Classical myth
Source: Folk tradition
Type of plot: Heroic adventure
Time: of plot: Remote antiquity
Locale: Mediterranean region
First transcribed: Unknown

Principal characters:
> HERCULES, hero of virtue and strength
> EURYSTHEUS, his cousin

Critique:

Hercules is the mighty hero of popular imagination in Western culture. Art galleries feature paintings and sculpture of the splendid body of the hero. The latest engines, the strongest building materials, the most powerful utilities bear his name. Hercules, not born a god, achieved godhood at the time of his death, according to tradition, because he devoted his life to the service of his fellow men. Some authorities link Hercules with legends of the sun, as each labor took him further from his home and one of his tasks carried him around the world and back. His twelve labors have been compared to the signs of the zodiac.

The Story:

Hercules was the son of a mortal, Alcmena, and the god Jupiter. Because Juno was hostile to all children of her husband by mortal mothers, she decided to be revenged upon the child. She sent two snakes to kill Hercules in his crib, but the infant strangled the serpents with ease. Then Juno caused Hercules to be subject to the will of his cousin, Eurystheus.

Hercules as a child was taught by Rhadamanthus, who one day punished the child for misdeeds. Hercules immediately killed his teacher. For this his foster father, Amphitryon, took Hercules away to the mountains, to be brought up by rude shepherds. Early in youth Hercules began to attract attention for his great strength and courage. He killed a lion single-handedly and took heroic part in a war. Juno, jealous of his growing success, called on Eurystheus to use his power over Hercules. Eurystheus then demanded that Hercules carry out twelve labors. The plan was that Hercules would perish in one of them.

The first labor: Juno had sent a lion to eat the people of Nemea. The lion's hide was so protected that no arrow could pierce it. Knowing that he could not kill the animal with his bow, Hercules met the lion and strangled it with his bare hands. Thereafter he wore the lion's skin as a protection when he was fighting, for nothing could penetrate that magic covering.

The second labor: Hercules had to meet the Lernaean hydra. This creature lived in a swamp, and the odor of its body killed all who breathed its fetid fumes. Hercules began the battle but discovered that for every head he severed from the monster two more appeared. Finally he obtained a flaming brand from a friend and burned each head as he severed it. When he came to the ninth and invulnerable head, he cut it off and buried it under a rock. Then he dipped his arrows into the body of the hydra so that he would possess more deadly weapons for use in future conflicts.

The third labor: Hercules captured the Erymanthian boar and brought it back on his shoulders. The sight of the wild beast frightened Eurystheus so much that he hid in a large jar. With a fine sense of humor the hero deposited the captured boar in the same jar. While on this trip Hercules incurred the wrath of the centaurs by drinking wine which they had claimed for their own. In order to escape from them he had had to kill most of the half-horse men.

The fourth labor: Hercules had to capture a stag which had antlers of gold and hoofs of brass. In order to capture this creature Hercules pursued it for a whole year.

The fifth labor: The Stymphalian birds were carnivorous. Hercules alarmed them with a bell, shot many of them with his arrows, and caused the rest to fly away.

The sixth labor: Augeas, king of Elis, had a herd of three thousand oxen whose stables had not been cleansed for thirty years. Commanded to clean the stables, Hercules diverted the rivers Alpheus and Peneus through them and washed them clean in one day. Augeas refused the payment agreed to and as a result Hercules later declared war on him.

The seventh labor: Neptune had given a sacred bull to Minos king of Crete. Minos' wife, Pasiphaë, fell in love with the animal and pursued it around the island. Hercules overcame the bull and took it back to Eurystheus by making it swim the sea while he rode upon its back.

The eighth labor: Like the Stymphalian birds, the mares of Diomedes fed on human flesh. Usually Diomedes found food for them by feeding to them all travelers who landed on his shores. Diomedes tried to prevent Hercules from driving away his herd. He was killed and his body was fed to his own beasts.

The ninth labor: Admeta, daughter of Eurystheus, persuaded her father to send Hercules for the girdle of Hippolyta, queen of the Amazons. The Amazon queen was willing to give up her girdle, but Juno interfered by telling the other Amazons that Hercules planned to kidnap their queen. In the battle that followed Hercules killed Hippolyta and took the girdle from her dead body.

The tenth labor: Geryoneus, a three-bodied, three-headed, six-legged, winged monster possessed a herd of oxen. Ordered to bring the animals to Eurystheus, Hercules traveled beyond the pillars of Hercules, now Gibraltar. He killed a two-headed shepherd dog and a giant herdsman, and finally slew Geryones. He loaded the cattle on a boat and sent them to Eurystheus. He himself returned afoot across the Alps. He had many adventures on the way, including a fight with giants in the Phlegraean fields, near the present site of Naples.

The eleventh labor: His next labor was more difficult, for his task was to obtain the golden apples in the garden of the Hesperides. No one knew where the garden was, and so Hercules set out to roam until he found it. In his travels he killed a giant, a host of pygmies, and burned alive some of his captors in Egypt. In India he set Prometheus free. At last he discovered Atlas holding up the sky. This task Hercules assumed, releasing Atlas to go after the apples. Atlas returned with the apples and reluctantly took up his burden. Hercules brought the apples safely to Eurystheus.

The twelfth labor: This was the most difficult of all his labors. After many adventures he brought the three-headed dog Cerberus from the underworld. He was forced to carry the struggling animal in his arms because he had been forbidden to use weapons of any kind. Afterward he took Cerberus back to the king of the underworld. So ended the labors of this mighty ancient hero.

Further Critical Evaluation of the Work:

Hercules (Latin form of Greek "Herakles," meaning "Hera's (Juno's) fame") rightfully deserved to rule Mycenae and Tiryns, but because of the machinations of Juno, his cousin Eurystheus had become his lord. Driven mad by Juno, Hercules killed his own wife and children, and was required by the Delphic oracle to atone for his crime by becoming King Eurystheus' vassal.

Eurystheus originally assigned ten *athloi* (ordeals for a prize), but he refused to count both the killing of the Hydra, since Hercules had been assisted by his nephew Iolaus, and the cleansing of the Augean stables, since Hercules had demanded payment. These *athloi* required twelve years and are described above essentially according to Apollodorus, the first- or second-century A.D. mythographer (the third and fourth labors are reversed as are the fifth and sixth). Sometimes the last two labors are reversed, which subtracts from the supreme accomplishment of conquering death, as it were, by returning from Hades. The same twelve exploits were sculpted nearly life-size on the metopes of the Temple of Zeus at Olympia in the mid-fifth century B.C.; four scenes have been reconstructed from the fragments. Euripides perhaps reflects an earlier tradition, which begins with Homer, when he lists encounters with the Centaurs, with Cycnus the robber, and with pirates in place of the boar, the stables, and the bull *(Herakles Mad)*.

Nevertheless, the twelve labors are not the extent of Hercules' fame. Apollodorus (*Library* 2.4.8-2.7.7), as well as Pausanias and Diodorus Siculus detail the "life" of this folk-hero; Ovid briefly recounts the labors and death of the hero in Book 9 of the *Metamorphoses*. From their accounts, and from numerous other sources, we have a wealth of exploits accomplished before, during, and after the labors. Among those before is Hercules' fathering a child by each of the fifty daughters of King Thespius. During the labors, Hercules performed a number of well-known *parerga,* or "side deeds," such as joining Jason's Argonauts in quest of the Golden Fleece. He never completed the journey, however, since he was left at Mysia looking for his lost squire and boy-love Hylas. Among other *parerga* are his rescue of Alcestis from Death after she had volunteered to die in place of her husband King Admetus of Pherae (see Euripides *Alcestis*). He also rescued Hesione, daughter of King Laomedon of Troy, who was to have been sacrificed to Poseidon's sea-monster. In Italy he killed the fire-breathing Cacus who had stolen the cattle of Geryon(es) which Hercules was driving back to Eurystheus (see Vergil *Aeneid* 8.193-270). In Libya he lifted the giant Antaeus from his mother Earth, from whom he derived his strength, and crushed him. He rescued Prometheus from the rock in the Caucasus and Theseus from the Underworld.

After the labors, Hercules sought to marry Iole, daughter of Eurytus, King of Oechalia and the man who had taught him archery. Eurytus refused, and Hercules killed the king's son, for which he was sold into slavery to Omphale, queen of Lydia. There he performed numerous feats, including killing a great snake, fathering a child on Omphale, and burying the body of the fallen Icarus, who had flown too near the sun. Freed, Hercules went on to seek revenge on Laomedon and Augeas for their refusal to honor their debts for services rendered. He later married Deianira, whom he soon had to rescue from the lustful Nessus, who instructed Deianira to dip Hercules' tunic into the dying centaur's blood. The wearing of the tunic, she was told, would prevent

Hercules (notorious for his *amours*) from loving another. Soon Hercules returned to Oechalia where he murdered Eurytus and abducted Iole. In desperation and ignorance, Deianira sent the tunic, and as soon as Hercules put it on, it began to sear his flesh (since Nessus' blood had been poisoned by an arrow which long ago had been dipped in the Hydra's blood). Hercules' horrible death is vividly described in Euripides' *Trachiniae.*

By the twelve labors Hercules earned the immortality promised by the Delphic oracle, and so when Hercules died (having mounted his own funeral pyre), Jupiter persuaded all the gods, including Juno, to accept him into the pantheon. He took Hebe ("Youth") to wife and was thereafter universally honored. If Hercules' mythic origins are indeed solar, it is appropriate that he enjoyed *apotheosis,* or deification, and allegorical union with Youth, since the sun, having passed through the twelve zodiacal constellations, returns each year, renewed in strength. On the other hand, Hercules may well have been the original male consort to a pre-Greek mother goddess (Hera) as his name would imply. But whatever his origins, throughout the ancient world in religion and literature, he was welcomed as the ultimate folk-hero, simple but not obtuse, powerful but humane, whose myths symbolized the pains and indignities that even great men, beloved of 'Jupiter, must undergo to attain undying glory. On him, the Athenians modeled their local hero, Theseus. Numerous other localities variously worshiped Hercules as a hero, if not a god. The Cynics and Stoics admired his hardy self-reliance and attention to duty.

In art, Hercules is a favorite subject—his broad, muscled shoulders draped with the skin of a Nemean lion. Although he gained fame for his archery and physical strength, he is usually represented wielding a knotted club. In Roman art representations of his brutality seem to tend toward brutishness, so that he becomes more the gladiator than the noble demigod who courageously submitted to the will and whims of the lesser. More than any other figure, Hercules drew together the mythic experiences of Olympians and Titans, monsters and men, death and immortality.

E. N. Genovese

HEREWARD THE WAKE

Type of work: Novel
Author: Charles Kingsley (1819-1875)
Type of plot: Historical romance
Time of plot: Eleventh century
Locale: England, Scotland, Flanders
First published: 1866

  Principal characters:
  HEREWARD THE WAKE, a Saxon thane and outlaw
  LADY GODIVA, his mother
  TORFRIDA, his wife
  ALFTRUDA, his second wife
  MARTIN LIGHTFOOT, a companion in his wanderings
  WILLIAM THE CONQUEROR, Duke of Normandy and King of England

Critique:

Hereward the Wake is one of the very few stories that deal realistically and credibly with the Anglo-Saxon period of English history. Although elements of the chivalric romance, in the more academic sense of that term, are present in this novel, Kingsley has re-created the age and its people in a believable and highly interesting manner. *Hereward the Wake* is both an interesting story and a valuable historical study.

The Story:

Hereward was the son of the powerful Lord of Bourne, a Saxon nobleman of a family close to the throne. A high-spirited, rebellious youth, he was a source of constant worry to his mother, Lady Godiva. Hereward lacked a proper respect for the Church and its priests and lived a boisterous life with boon companions who gave him their unquestioning loyalty.

One day a friar came to Lady Godiva and revealed that Hereward and his friends had attacked him and robbed him of what the priest insisted was money belonging to the Church. Lady Godiva was angry and hurt. When Hereward came in and admitted his crime, she said that there was no alternative. For his own good, she maintained, he should be declared a wake, or outlaw. Upon his promise not to molest her messenger, for Hereward really did not mind being outlawed as he wished to see more of the world, Lady Godiva sent Martin Lightfoot, a servant, to carry the news of Hereward's deed to his father and to the king. Hereward was then declared an outlaw subject to imprisonment or death.

Before he left his father's house, however, he released his friends from their oath of allegiance. Martin Lightfoot begged to be allowed to follow him, not as his servant but as his companion. Then Hereward set out to live among the rude and barbarous Scottish tribes of the north.

His first adventure occurred when he killed a huge bear that threatened the life of Alftruda, ward of a knight named Gilbert of Ghent. For his valorous deed he achieved much renown. But the knights of Gilbert's household, jealous of Hereward's courage and his prowess, tried to kill him. Though he escaped the snares laid for him, he decided that it would be best for him to leave Scotland.

Accordingly, he went to Cornwall, where he was welcomed by the king. There the king's daughter was pledged in marriage to a prince of Waterford. But a giant of the Cornish court had become so powerful that he had forced the king's agreement to give his daughter in marriage to the ogre. Hereward, with the help of the princess and a friar, slew the giant, whose death freed the princess to marry the prince whom she really loved.

After leaving Cornwall, Hereward and his companions were wrecked upon the

Flemish coast. There Hereward stayed for a time in the service of Baldwin of Flanders and proved his valor by defeating the French in battle. There, too, Torfrida, a lady wrongly suspected of sorcery, schemed to win his love. They were wed after Hereward had fought in a successful campaign against the Hollanders, and a daughter was born of the marriage.

Meanwhile King Edward had died and Harold reigned in England. A messenger came to Hereward with the news that Duke William of Normandy had defeated the English at the battle of Hastings and that King Harold had been killed. Hereward then decided to return to Bourne, his old home. There, accompanied by Martin Lightfoot, he found the Norman raiders encamped. He found too that his family had been despoiled of all its property and that his mother had been sent away. He and Martin, without revealing their identity, secretly went out and annihilated all the Normans in the area. Hereward swore that he would return with an army that would push the Norman invaders into the sea.

Hereward then went to his mother, who received him happily. Lady Godiva accused herself of having wronged her son and lamented the day she had proclaimed him an outlaw. He took her to a place of refuge in Croyland Abbey. Later he went to the monastery where his aged, infirm uncle, Abbot Brand, was spending his last days on earth. There Hereward was knighted by the monks, after the English fashion. Hereward went secretly to Bourne and there recruited a rebel army to fight against Duke William.

Although there were many men eager to fight the Normans, the English forces were disunited. Another king, an untried young man, had been proclaimed, but because of his youth he did not have the support of all the English factions. Hereward had been promised help from Denmark, but the Danish

king sent a poor leader through whose stupidity the Danes were inveigled into positions where they were easily defeated by the Normans at Dover and Norwich. Then, instead of coming to Hereward's aid, the Danes fled. Hereward was forced to confess the failure of his allies to his men, but they renewed their pledge to him and promised to keep on fighting. The situation seemed hopeless when Hereward and his men took refuge on the island of Ely. There, with Torfrida's wise advice, Hereward defeated Duke William's attack upon the beleaguered island. Hereward and his men retreated to another camp of refuge.

Shortly afterward Torfrida learned of Hereward's infidelity with Alftruda, the ward of Gilbert of Ghent. She left Hereward and went to Croyland Abbey, where she proposed to spend the last of her days ministering to the poor and to Hereward's mother. Hereward himself went to Duke William and submitted to him. The conqueror declared that he had selected a husband for Hereward's daughter. In order to free herself from Hereward, Torfrida falsely confessed that she was a sorceress, and her marriage to Hereward was annulled by the Church. Hereward then married Alftruda and became Lord of Bourne under Duke William. His daughter, despite her entreaties, was married to a Norman knight.

But Hereward, the last of the English, had many enemies among the French, who continually intrigued against him for the favor of Duke William. As a result, Hereward was imprisoned. The jailer was a good man who treated his noble prisoner as kindly as he could, although, for his own sake, he was forced to chain Hereward.

One day, while Hereward was being transported from one prison to another, he was rescued by his friends. Freed, he went back to Alftruda at Bourne, but his life was not a happy one. His enemies plotted to kill him. Taking advantage of a day when his retainers were escorting Alftruda on a journey, a group of Norman knights broke into Bourne castle. Though Hereward fought valiantly, he was outnumbered. He was killed and his head was exhibited in victory over the door of his own hall.

When she heard of his death, Torfrida came from Croyland Abbey and demanded Hereward's body. All were so frightened, especially Alftruda, by Tor-frida's wild appearance and her reputation as a witch, that Hereward's first wife got her way and the body was delivered to her. She carried it away to Croyland for burial. Thus did Hereward, the last of the English, die, and thus, too, did William of Normandy become William the Conqueror and King of England.

Further Critical Evaluation of the Work:

In his last novel, *Hereward the Wake,* Kingsley treats a heroic figure whose character and adventures form the core of the *Gesta Hereward.* Based on the past, it is, however, more than an adaptation of existing legends. Kingsley makes the most of the rich material provided by this colorful period in history. He chooses to assign a new past to Hereward, making him the son of Lady Godiva, and he also gives much attention to the courtship and winning of Torfrida, a woman of exceptional virtue and talents, who is reputed to be a witch.

Yet what undoubtedly attracted Kingsley to the legend were the various elements that he himself felt were missing in his own time. An advocate of "muscular Christianity" as well as social benevolence to the poor and under-privileged, the Reverend Kingsley found in Hereward's life an opportunity to champion militant heroism blessed by the Church. After Hereward returns from exile, one spent in reparation for his youthful rebellion, he goes to his uncle, Abbot Brand, and is knighted, literally annointed, as a soldier of the Church to battle the Normans. He displays all the virtues, even in his death, of the medieval soldier whose embassy is charity as well as bloodshed.

Hereward stands for the last "pure" English knight, moreover, because the foreigners, the Normans, are successfully installed as England's rulers after his death. It was also this racial purity which the Saxon represents that led Kingsley to the legend. Unspoiled by any alien influence or blood the knight, although finally defeated by the Normans, is apotheosized and even in death his body is saved from his Norman wife by the mysterious Torfrida. It is these chauvinistic qualities which accounted for the success of the novel in England, a society which felt threatened by the Continental political revolutions of the nineteenth century.

A HERITAGE AND ITS HISTORY

Type of work: Novel
Author: Ivy Compton-Burnett (1884-1969)
Time: Late Victorian period
Locale: England
First published: 1960

Principal characters:

SIR EDWIN CHALLONER, the lord of the mansion
HAMISH CHALLONER, his younger brother
JULIA CHALLONER, Hamish's wife
SIMON SHALLONER, their older son, Sir Edwin's heir
WALTER CHALLONER, Simon's younger brother
RHODA GRAHAM CHALLONER, Sir Edwin's wife, Simon's mistress
HAMISH, the son of Rhoda and Simon
FANNY GRAHAM CHALLONER, Simon's wife and Rhoda's sister
RALPH,
NAOMI,
GRAHAM,
CLAUDE, and
EMMA, the children of Simon and Fanny
MARCIA CHALLONER, the wife of young Hamish Challoner
DEAKIN, the butler who resembles a Greek chorus in his comments
on the novel's events and on life generally

In a sense, *A Heritage and Its History,* because it encompasses more time than any other novel by Ivy Compton-Burnett, is the most representative of all her novels, though it is not quite her best. The heritage, as Miss Compton-Burnett's readers and those who have studied their ancestors' lives will recognize, is the complex genetic and social inheritance of what we call good and evil tendencies. It is the virtues and the sins of the fathers that are visited upon all generations since; though we live in our own day, what we do has been done by all our forebears, as Rhoda and Sir Edwin say and as parts of the Bible imply. In its encompassment of universalized and eternalized human activity in three generations, as in its inclusion of the wise butler and the excessively precocious children as commentators upon the sensational and usual events the dialogue of the novel advances, *A Heritage and Its History* is Miss Compton-Burnett at her most representative. Because in presenting more characters and times than usual, she leaves even the alert reader occasionally baffled, the novel, though excellent, is in-ferior to its immediate predecessor, *A Father and His Fate* and its two successors, *The Mighty and Their Fall* and *A God and His Gifts.*

It is not, as indeed it is not usually, of the utmost importance to give the intriguing complexity of the plot, which as someone once said of another of her novels, combines complexities that might have arisen had Sardou and Sophocles collaborated. Of course things are not what they seem. The apparently healthy Sir Edwin precedes in death his dying brother. The proper son of Hamish, Simon, has children by both the Graham sister he marries and the older one he does not, and he becomes at the close of the novel, Sir Simon. The erratic son, Walter, who did not finish Oxford and who is a poet, leads a proper life. Behind the scenes, as in the Greek tragedies it resembles and, like them, interrupted by comic and satirical interludes, events of plausible sensationalism occur: sudden death, adultery, near incest, a conflict of parents and children, of brother and brother. The story is, in other words, the stuff of human nature told factually and

2594

palatably and wittily and bearably, as it is in all but the first of Ivy Compton-Burnett's novels, the stuff of human nature in action.

Under its Victorian trappings *A Heritage and Its History* retells the ancient dynastic story of the cuckolded king, the dispossessed heir, and usurper; but in this case the heir, Simon Challoner, brings about his own undoing. All of the Challoners live in a large family house over which Sir Edwin Challoner, a bachelor, presides. For years, however, the job of running the estate has been entrusted to his younger brother Hamish. Julia, Hamish's wife, has been the mistress of the household ever since her marriage, and Simon, her older son, is Sir Edwin's heir. Because his uncle is over sixty, Simon seems unlikely to have a long wait before he comes into his expectations. Walter, the younger son is an impractical, frustrated poet. Then Hamish Challoner dies. Sir Edwin, lonely after his brother's death, marries Rhoda Graham, a young neighbor less than half his age. Because of his uncle's advanced years, there is no chance that Simon's prospects will be changed by this marriage. Then Simon, ironically, cuts himself off from his inheritance by fathering a child on Rhoda. To avoid scandal, Sir Edwin claims Hamish as his son and heir after swearing Simon and Walter to secrecy.

Forced to yield his place to his own son, Simon marries Fanny, Rhoda's sister, and Julia goes to live with them in the small house which had belonged to Rhoda and Fanny. Simon continues to help his uncle in administering the estate, but as the years pass and his family grows he becomes more and more a disappointed, embittered man. By the time his sons and daughter are grown he has driven them almost to distraction—certainly to the point of detesting him—by complaining gloomily that his family lives only one step away from the workhouse.

But guilt concealed cannot remain hidden. The secret of Hamish's birth must be revealed to all when he falls in love with Simon's daughter Naomi and the young people tell their parents of their desire to marry. Simon accepts the burden of the story that must be told.

This family situation is further complicated when Hamish marries Marcia after Sir Edwin's death at the age of ninety-four. He dies childless, however, and the estate and title pass to Simon. At the end his children are discussing his change of fortunes. Is he actually noble or merely deceiving himself and the others? A combination of both is the answer.

Counterpointing the Challoners in this grim comedy of possession and dispossession is the figure of Deakin, the butler. His true loyalty is not to the different masters and mistresses he serves but to the house itself, which is a symbol of history, of life in the stream of time. The others are like the creeping vine that grows outside the house, shadowing the rooms within; if they were to be exposed to the light they would be startled.

The plot is not the main thing, but merely an unfolding of events that carries forward the revelation of life the characters enact or put in action. The characters are not the main thing, either, in the individualized sense in which they would be in a novel by William Faulkner or Joyce Cary. Here, as in many of Miss Compton-Burnett's novels, it would be possible to transpose some of the characters without causing the reader, unless he is constantly alert, to notice the difference. This statement does not mean that Miss Compton-Burnett's characters are distinguishable types any more than Hemingway's early characters, who were clarified almost exclusively by dialogue. It does mean that they represent all kinds of people in whom the likeness to ourselves and to the friends we know deeply is more marked than individuality.

Aesthetically speaking, the dialogue is the point at which, more in each novel it seems, Miss Compton-Burnett's originality manifests itself most clearly. As in

Congreve and Etherege and Hemingway and Henry Green, to cite disparate aesthetic cousins, the dialogue is the thing wherein the consciousness of the human predicament and how it may be endured, sometimes with joy, sometimes with anguish, is forwarded and revealed. It is bared to the essential bone, increasingly without conventional props. The characters, never identified by more than a few sentences of description and their age, speak it condensedly and wittily. If the reader is not the co-operator in the aesthetic enterprise Miss Compton-Burnett expects, alert as if it were poetry he is reading, he is likely to miss the plot, lost in a mesh of unidentified time and characters unknown. If he attends well, his reward is the aesthetic delight the most harrowing events, well-told, bring.

What occurs in *A Heritage and Its History* is united in tone by the controlled chorus of butler and children, all of whom keep us aware, as Deakin the butler puts it, that life is not adapted to us and that it is up to us to conform as cheerfully as we can to its conditions if we are permitted to know them. To know all that the main characters and the commenting choruses say about themselves and others is to understand and forgive the facts of human nature as Miss Compton-Burnett recognizes them.

This divine lack of reproof—even more apparent in *The Mighty and Their Fall* and *A God and His Fate*—has been increasing ever since Miss Compton-Burnett published *Mr. Bullivant and His Lambs* in 1947. Evidently this develop-ment has burgeoned from both a growing reconciliation to the worst that may happen to all of us and a slight brightening of her world-view, so that it now approaches what may be called cheerful stoicism or uncritical, nearly omniscient, factualism. All her novels deserve attention, the earliest for what they expose, the latest for what they show of how we may dispose ourselves before what must be exposed. "If way to the Better there be," Thomas Hardy said, "it exacts a full look at the Worst." The early novels show the worst. The later suggest, with diffident hopefulness and no lack of clarity about the Worst we must face, how we may best aim towards the Better.

The kind, hard look the novels give on life and death and her unusual technique that requires a co-operative reader rather than one accustomed to the pap-feeding of popular fiction, has kept Miss Compton-Burnett from popularity in the United States. To a lesser extent this has been true of the public even in England, where she has been honored by royalty, critics, and the awarders of prizes. Not to read Ivy Compton-Burnett is to deprive oneself of a depth of vision comparable with what one finds in Aeschylus, Shakespeare, Tolstoy, and other writers we agree to call great. Not to read her is to deprive oneself of pleasure also, for Miss Compton-Burnett's somewhat hopeful stoicism is always leavened by humor and wit. In her work style and wisdom, within the necessary human limit of fallibility, conjoin beautifully to delight.

A HERO OF OUR TIME

Type of work: Novel
Author: Mikhail Yurievich Lermontov (1814-1841)
Type of plot: Psychological romance
Time of plot: 1830-1838
Locale: The Russian Caucasus
First published: 1839

> *Principal characters:*
> "I" supposedly Lermontov, Narrator One
> MAKSIM MAKSIMICH, Narrator Two
> GRIGORIY ALEKSANDROVICH PECHORIN, Narrator Three, the "Hero of Our Time"
> BELA, a young princess
> KAZBICH, a bandit
> AZAMAT, Bela's young brother
> YANKO, a smuggler
> PRINCESS MARY, daughter of Princess Ligovskoy
> GRUSHNITSKI, a cadet and suitor to Princess Mary
> VERA, the former sweetheart of Pechorin
> LIEUTENANT VULICH, a Cossack officer, a Serbian

Critique:

This realistic novel of social and military life in nineteenth-century Russia well deserves its renown because of its colorful descriptions and sharp delineations of character. Structurally, the novel is made up of five related short stories, with Narrator One (presumably Lermontov), Maksim Maksimich, and Pechorin in the principal roles. The narrative is skillfully constructed. In "Bela," "I" meets Maksim Maksimich, who refers to Pechorin. Maksim Maksimich, Narrator Two, tells the story bearing his name as its title. Pechorin actually appears, but briefly. In "Taman," "Princess Mary," and "The Fatalist," the narrator is Pechorin himself, the stories being told as extracts from his journal. A second notable feature of the writing, in addition to the involuted time sequence, is Lermontov's habit of letting the reader eavesdrop in order to avoid detailed narrative. This device makes for compact writing, since it is a convenient means of letting the principal characters learn of events necessary to an understanding of the story. Lermontov felt compelled to preface his novel with the explanation that *A Hero of Our Time* was not a biography of any Russian person, living or dead. Rather, Pechorin was intended to be a collective personification of all the evil and vice then found in Russian life. In creating his portrait of Pechorin, the "superfluous" man, Lermontov pointed to the development of the Russian psychological novel.

The Story:

The Narrator met Maksim Maksimich while on a return trip from Tiflis, the capital of Georgia, to Russia. The season was autumn, and in that mountainous region snow was already falling. The two men continued their acquaintance at the inn where they were forced to take refuge for the night. When the Narrator asked Maksim Maksimich about his experiences, the old man told of his friendship with Grigoriy Pechorin, a Serbian who had come from Russia about five years before to join a company of cavalry in the Caucasus:

To relieve their boredom on that frontier post, the soldiers played with Azamat, the young son of a neighboring prince. As a result of this friendship, the prince invited Maksimich and Pechorin to a family wedding. At that celebration

A HERO OF OUR TIME by Mikhail Yurievich Lermontov. Translated by Vladimir and Dmitri Nabokov. By permission of the publishers, Doubleday & Co., Inc. Copyright, 1958, by Vladimir and Dmitri Nabokov.

Pechorin and Kazbich, a bandit, met and were equally attracted to Bela, the beautiful young daughter of the prince. Azamat, observing this development, later offered to give Bela to Kazbich in exchange for the bandit's horse. Kazbich laughed at the boy and rode away.

Four days later Azamat was back at the camp and visiting with Pechorin, who promised to get Kazbich's horse for the boy in exchange for Bela. The promise was fulfilled. Kazbich, insane with rage at his loss, tried to kill Azamat but failed.

Suspecting that Azamat's father had been responsible for the theft, Kazbich killed the prince and stole his horse in revenge for the loss of his own animal.

Weeks passed, and Pechorin became less attentive to Bela. One day she and Maksimich were walking on the ramparts when Bela recognized Kazbich on her father's horse some distance away. An orderly's attempt to shoot Kazbich failed and he escaped. But Kazbich had recognized Bela, too, and a few days later, when the men were away from camp, he kidnapped her. As Pechorin and Maksimich were returning to camp, they saw Kazbich riding away with Bela. They pursued the bandit, but as they were about to overtake him, he thrust his knife into Bela and escaped.

Although Pechorin seemed to be deeply grieved by Bela's death, when Maksimich tried to comfort him, he laughed.

The Narrator, having parted from Maksim Maksimich, stopped at an inn in Vladikavkaz, where he found life very dull until, on the second day, Maksimich arrived unexpectedly. Before long there was a great stir and bustle in preparation for the arrival of an important guest. The travelers learned that Pechorin was the guest expected. Happy in the thought of seeing Pechorin again, Maksimich instructed a servant to carry his regards to his former friend, who had stopped off to visit a Colonel N——. Day turned to night but still Pechorin did not come to return the greeting. Dawn found Maksimich waiting at the gate again. When Pechorin finally arrived, he prevented Maksimich's intended embrace by coolly offering his hand.

Maksimich had anticipated warmth and a long visit, but Pechorin left immediately. Neither Maksimich's plea of friendship nor his mention of Bela served to detain Pechorin.

Thus Maksimich bade his friend goodbye. To the Narrator's attempt to cheer him the old man remarked only that Pechorin had become too rich and spoiled to bother about old friendships. In fact, he would throw away Pechorin's journal that he had been saving. The Narrator was so pleased to be the recipient of the papers that he grabbed them from the old man and rushed to his room. Next day the Narrator left, saddened by the reflection that when one has reached Maksim Maksimich's age, scorn from a friend causes the heart to harden and the soul to fold up. Later, having learned that Pechorin was dead, the Narrator published three tales from the dead man's journal, as Pechorin himself had written them:

Taman, a little town on the seacoast of Russia, was the worst town Pechorin had ever visited. For want of better lodging, he was forced to stay in a little cottage that he immediately disliked. Greeted at the door by a blind, crippled boy, Pechorin admitted to a prejudice against people with physical infirmities. To him, a crippled body held a crippled soul. His displeasure was enhanced when he learned there was no icon in the house —an evil sign.

In the night Pechorin followed the blind boy to the shore, where he witnessed a rendezvous that he did not comprehend. The next morning a young woman appeared at the cottage and he accused her of having been on the beach the night before. Later, the girl returned, kissed him, and arranged to meet him on the shore.

Pechorin kept the appointment. As he and the girl sailed in a boat, she tried to drown him; he, in turn, thrust her into the swirling, foaming water and brought the boat to shore. He was stunned to find that she had swum to safety and was talking to a man on shore. Pechorin learned that the man was a smuggler. The blind boy appeared, carrying a heavy sack which he delivered to the girl and the smuggler. They sailed away in a boat.

Pechorin returned to the cottage to find that his sword and all his valuables had been stolen.

Quite a different atmosphere pervaded Pechorin's next experience, as described in his journal. While stopping at Elizabeth Spring, a fashionable spa, he met Grushnitski, a wounded cadet whom he had known previously. The two men were attracted to Princess Mary, and Pechorin was angry—though he pretended indifference—because Princess Mary paid more attention to Grushnitski, a mere cadet, than she did to him, an officer. The men agreed that young society girls looked upon soldiers as savages and upon any young man with contempt.

Pechorin opened a campaign of revenge against Princess Mary. On one occasion he distracted an audience of her admirers; again, he outbid her for a Persian rug and then disparaged her sense of values by putting it on his horse. Her fury at these and other offenses gave Pechorin the satisfaction of revenge for her favor of Grushnitski.

Grushnitski wanted Pechorin to be friendly toward Princess Mary so that the cadet might be accepted socially through his association with her. Having seen Vera, a former lover of his but now married, Pechorin decided to court Princess Mary as a cover for his illicit affair with Vera.

As excitement mounted in anticipation of the ball, the major social event of the season, antagonism between Pechorin and Grushnitski and Pechorin and Princess Mary grew. Grushnitski's excitement and pride were the result of his promotion; Princess Mary would see him in his officer's uniform.

Succumbing to Pechorin's attitude of indifference, Princess Mary consented to dance the mazurka with him. Pechorin did not wish to hurt Grushnitski by divulging this news when the new officer later boasted that he intended to have this honored dance with the princess.

When, after the ball, it was rumored that Princess Mary would marry Pechorin, he fled to Kislovodsk to be with Vera. Grushnitski followed, but not to continue his association with Pechorin, whom he deliberately ignored. A short time later the princess and her party arrived in Kislovodsk to continue their holiday.

Still furious at the affront which had caused his disappointment at the ball, Grushnitski enlisted the aid of some dragoons in an attempt to catch Pechorin in Princess Mary's room. When this effort failed, Grushnitski challenged Pechorin to a duel. According to the plan Pechorin would have an empty pistol. Having discovered the plot, Pechorin compelled Grushnitski to stand at the edge of an abyss during the duel. Then he coolly shot the young officer, who tumbled into the depths below. Pechorin labeled Grushnitski's death an accident.

Princess Mary's mother asked Pechorin to marry the girl. He refused and wrote in his journal that a soft, protected life was not his way.

On another occasion, Pechorin and a group of Cossack officers were ridiculing the fatalism of the Moslems. Lieutenant Vulich, a renowned gambler, offered to prove his own faith in fatalism. While Pechorin and the Cossacks watched, aghast, Vulich aimed a pistol at his head and pulled the trigger. No shot was fired. He then aimed at a cap hanging on the wall; it was blown to pieces. Pechorin was amazed that the pistol had misfired on Vulich's first attempt. He was sure he had seen what he called the look of death on Vulich's face. Within a half hour after that demonstration Vulich was killed in the street by a drunken Cossack.

The next day Pechorin decided to test his own fate by offering to take the maddened Cossack alive, after an entire detachment had not dared the feat. He was successful.

Later, when Pechorin discussed the incident with Maksim Maksimich, the old man observed that Circassian pistols of the type which Vulich used for his demonstration were not really reliable. He added philosophically that it was un- fortunate Vulich had stopped a drunk at night. Such a fate must have been assigned to Vulich at his birth.

Further Critical Evaluation of the Work:

Russian literature came of age during the nineteenth century. Mikhail Lermontov, one of the most seminal writers of that century, produced in *A Hero of Our Time* an insightful social document rarely duplicated during the golden century of Russian literature. It was the author's misfortune—and that of all those interested in the development of Russian literary and social thought—that he died at the age of twenty-seven. While Lermontov's literary followers prostrated themselves before the genius of Gogol, claiming "we all crawled out of Gogol's *Overcoat,*" it is just as likely that they were in fact epigones of Lermontov and very well ought to have said—"it is time we acknowledged Lermontov as our hero."

The Russian literary debt owed to Lermontov was and is great. His steadfast desire to depict accurately Russian social types and social conditions led him to create and develop several Russian literary myths which remain an integral part of the Russian literary imagination today. He created the cultivated yet weak and passive "superfluous man." While Pechorin was a soldier, he was not a man of strength or warrior skills; he was a *bon vivant* on horseback, a gay seducer who genuflected to his own pleasure, not to the needs of society. As the passive exploiter, he became the harbinger for a century of similar literary types. The superfluous hero enjoyed a long life, and perhaps a permanent residency, in Russian literature. The novels of Gogol, Turgenev, and Goncharov, to name but a few of the premier writers of the nineteenth century, perpetuated and therefore reaffirmed the accuracy of Lermontov's creation.

Lermontov also clearly defined the relationship of the Russian writer to his society. Desiring to free the writer from a "superfluous" position *vis à vis* Russian society, Lermontov aimed to criticize conditions in Russia, most notably the serf-landlord relationship which was the basis for Russian social and economic life. Lermontov felt that a society changed only through criticism of existing social conditions and values. Lermontov's *A Hero of Our Time* is the first significant attempt in Russian *belles lettres* to define a social role for the writer. His literary followers have perpetrated, with dogged if unacknowledged faithfulness, the correctness of Lermontov's mission.

HEROIDES

Type of work: Letters in verse
Author: Publius Ovidius Naso (43 B.C.-A.D. 18)
First transcribed: Indefinitely B.C.

In the *Heroides* or *Letters of the Heroines* the Roman poet Ovid composed a series of dramatic letters in elegiac verse (alternating lines of dactylic hexameter and dactylic pentameter). "Elegy," writes one of Ovid's heroines, "is the weeping strain," and the mood of most of these letters is that of sadness. Most of the heroines have been rejected by famous heroes, Dido by Aeneas, Ariadne by Theseus, Hypsipyle by Jason, Oenone by Paris. Some are apprehensive of coming death either for themselves or for their lovers: Canace, Dejanira, Sappho, and Dido are about to commit suicide. Medea is about to kill the new wife of Jason and her own two children. Almost all of the heroines are in hopeless but pitiful situations.

Ovid's heroines are caught at a turning point in their lives, usually when bad is going to worse. But in these turning points there is conflict, both internal and between several people, and we are reminded that Ovid was also a dramatist. (His play, *Medea,* is not extant.) The letters are the ancestors of the familiar dramatic monologues of Robert Browning and also of the interior monologue, as used by Joyce or Dostoevski, since the heroines reveal in their writing their inmost thoughts. Also, what the heroine says usually sets a scene for the reader: she will tell, through reminiscence, the events of the past which led up to her present woe. Sometimes the reader seems to be put in the mind of the heroine, moving rapidly from one of her associations to another, or from a past memory to the present. In telling the different stories dramatically, Ovid remains in the background, almost out of sight.

The *Heroides,* apart from being one source of dramatic and interior monologue, have inspired different generations of English poets, from Chaucer, who felt deep sympathy for Canace, and his contemporary Gower, to John Donne, who imitated several of the letters in his own poetry, and to Alexander Pope, who wrote one of his finest poems, "Eloisa to Abelard," in imitation of the verse epistles.

Ovid's "Canace to Macareus" is one of the finest short dramatic poems in classic literature. As it opens, Canace is telling her brother and lover Macareus that she has been ordered by their father Aeolus to kill herself as punishment for having a child by her brother. She tells in close detail how she had become pregnant by Macareus, how her sympathetic nurse had tried unsuccessfully to abort her, and finally how the new-born baby had betrayed itself by crying as the nurse was trying to carry it, wrapped in a bundle of sticks, past Aeolus. Aeolus, the household tyrant, paradoxically able to control the four winds but not his own passion, is the inflexible villain of Canace's letter. The reader sympathizes with the incestuous couple, and Ovid succeeds in getting us to question any sort of inflexible legal or moral code.

At best Ovid's heroines appeal to our sympathies; however, a poet can say only so much on the theme of rejected love. Ovid sometimes seems bored with his subject matter, especially when he takes his material from another poet. When he borrows Dido from Vergil, his poem becomes only a good but obvious imitation; and Ovid's "Dido to Aeneas" adds almost no new detail to Vergil's story in the *Aeneid.*

Most modern readers will be bored with the majority of the *Heroides,* for the letters often seem sentimental or mawkish by modern standards of taste; but at the same time today's reader is often caught up by Ovid's power as a storyteller and dramatist, and convinced that many of the characters are "true" or "real." One remembers, for instance, the pictures of the indulgent nurse and of Aeolus, the petty tyrant, in "Canace to Macareus"; the picture of Ariadne lying on the rocks of her island watching Theseus' sails disappear in the distance; and the picture of Paris flirting with Helen at the table of her husband Menelaus. The realism in the *Heroides* is psychological: what Ovid's characters think and do seems natural today. Also, Ovid writes sympathetically about the social outcast and the mentally sick: he shows understanding for the close to insane Dido and Medea, and for the incestuous Canace and Phaedra.

Ovid's verse is artificial, however, and he makes no effort to give each of his heroines an individual style or poetic voice; all seem to speak in the same way. Still, they retain a psychological individuality, which is shown through their actions and their thoughts.

Ovid depends on his readers' already knowing his story, and he often builds his poems dramatically on various allusions, so that the modern reader is annoyed by all the unfamiliar names. But in the context of his time Ovid was certainly within his rights in sketching in a character's descent from one of the gods. To make up for what are today obscure allusions, Ovid presents accurate physical detail with vigorous and compelling power.

HERSELF SURPRISED

Type of work: Novel
Author: Joyce Cary (1888-1957)
Type of plot: Social comedy
Time of plot: First quarter of the twentieth century
Locale: London and the English southern counties
First published: 1941

> *Principal characters:*
> SARA MONDAY, a cook
> MATTHEW (MATT) MONDAY, her husband
> GULLEY JIMSON, a painter
> NINA, his supposed wife
> MR. WILCHER, owner of Tolbrook Manor
> BLANCHE WILCHER, his niece by marriage
> MISS CLARISSA HIPPER, her older sister
> MR. HICKSON, a friend of the Mondays

Critique:

Sara Monday, the life-loving, self-indulgent, and generous cook who is the heroine of the first volume of Cary's first trilogy, tells her story sometimes ingenuously, sometimes shrewdly. Both these characteristics are portrayed with Cary's compassion and irony. The vivid, complete characters in Cary's novels are presented through their reactions to difficulties. Thus his books are crowded with incident, but without formal plot. Cary's prose style is simple, his language rich and colorful. Although critics have found it impossible to interpret his philosophy with any certainty, he is considered one of the foremost British novelists of his period.

The Story:

In prison Sara Monday realized that she was indeed guilty as charged. She hoped that other women would read her story and examine their characters before their thoughtless behavior brought them also to ruin.

Sara's first position was that of cook in a medium-sized country house. Matthew Monday, the middle-aged son of Sara's employer, had been dominated all his life by his mother and sister. Then this rather pathetic man fell in love with Sara, who discouraged his attentions, both because she feared he would cause her to lose her job and because she found him slightly ridiculous. Nevertheless, and somewhat to her surprise, when he proposed marriage she accepted him.

At a church bazaar a few months after her marriage, Sara met Mr. Hickson, a millionaire art collector with whom Matthew was associated in business. With Hickson's help she was able to emancipate Matt from the influence of his family. Partly because she was grateful to him for his help, Sara did not rebuke Hickson when he tried to flirt with her. After Sara had been forced to spend a night at Hickson's country house—his car had broken down—Matt supported her against the gossip and disapproval the episode occasioned.

Sara's life with Matt was, except for the death of their son in infancy, a happy one during the first years of their marriage. They had four daughters, and Sara's time was filled with parties, clothes, her nursery, and work on local committees.

Hickson brought an artist to stay with the Mondays. He was Gulley Jimson, who was to compete for the commission to paint a mural in the new town hall. Gulley settled in quickly and soon his forbearing wife, Nina, joined him. After a quarrel over a portrait of Matt, the Jimsons left. Soon afterward Sara visited them in their rooms at the local inn.

In jealousy, Hickson told Matt of these visits and the infuriated man accused his wife of infidelity. After his outburst Matt was very repentant and blamed himself for neglecting Sara. However, the incident caused him to lose all the confidence his marriage had given him.

Sara did not see Gulley for years after this incident. One day during Matt's last illness he reappeared. He looked shabby and he wanted money to buy paints and clothes. After telling her that Nina was dead, he asked Sara to marry him after Matt's death. Although she was shocked, Sara did not stop seeing Gulley immediately. While Matt was dying Gulley repeatedly proposed to her. Finally she sent him away.

After Matt's death and the sale of her house, Sara went to Rose Cottage, where Gulley was staying with Miss Slaughter, one of the sponsors for the church hall in which he was painting a mural. Miss Slaughter encouraged Sara to marry Gulley, and at the end of a week they were engaged. Just before they were to be married, however, Gulley unhappily confessed that he had a wife and had never formally been married to Nina. Sara was furious and also bitterly disappointed, but in the end she agreed to live with Gulley and to say they were married. After an intensely happy honeymoon, they lived with Miss Slaughter while Gulley worked on his mural. During that time Sara tried to persuade Gulley to accept portrait commissions. Infuriated by her interference, Gulley struck Sara, who then left him. She was glad to return, however, when Miss Slaughter came for her.

Although Gulley's completed mural was considered unacceptable, he refused to change it. When Sara wanted him to repair some damage done to the painting, Gulley knocked her unconscious and left. Having exhausted her funds, Sara paid their outstanding bills with bad checks, and she was duly summonsed by the police.

After Sara had thus lost her good character, the only position she could obtain was that of cook at Tolbrook Manor. The owner, Mr. Wilcher, had a bad reputation for molesting young girls and seducing his women servants. Sara, however, pitied him and liked him. Eventually Mr. Wilcher moved Sara to his town house, having persuaded her to serve as housekeeper for both residences. She was glad of the extra money because Gulley had been writing to her asking for loans.

For many years Mr. Wilcher had had a mistress whom he visited every Saturday. During one of many long talks by Sara's fireside, he told her that he was tired of visiting this woman. When he asked Sara to take her place, she was at first slightly hesitant and confused, but in the end she agreed. The arrangement worked well enough for several years.

Mr. Wilcher became worried with family and financial affairs and Sara helped him by economizing on household expenses. At the same time she managed to falsify her accounts and send extra money to Gulley. One day a policeman came to the house with two girls who had complained of Mr. Wilcher's behavior. Mr. Wilcher disappeared, but Sara discovered him hours later hiding behind the chimney stacks on the roof. The family was appalled by this incident. After the impending summons had been quashed, Mr. Wilcher became even more unstable. Haunted by his past misdemeanors, he decided to confess them to the police. He also asked Sara to marry him after he had served his sentence. At this time he had an attack of sciatica. While he was confined to his bed, Blanche Wilcher, his niece by marriage and a woman who had always been suspicious of Sara, dismissed her.

Returning from a visit to her daughter, Sara forgot that she was no longer employed and entered Mr. Wilcher's street. There she found that the house had burned down in the night. Mr. Wilcher had been taken to the house of his niece's sister Clarissa. After he had recovered from shock he continued to see Sara and ignored Blanche. He rushed Sara to a registry office to give notice of their forthcoming marriage and then took a small new house for them to live in.

Sara had recently encountered Gulley once more and had gradually assumed financial responsibility for his new household. She maintained these payments for a time by selling to an antique shop oddments that Mr. Wilcher had told her to throw away.

The evening before her marriage, Sara arrived at the new house to find Blanche and a detective examining her possessions. She did not protest. After they had found receipts from the antique dealer and grocers' bills for supplies for Gulley, she was taken to the police station. She received an eighteen-month prison sentence and did not see Mr. Wilcher again.

A newspaper offered her money for her story. With this she paid Gulley's expenses and planned to become a cook again after she had served her sentence. She knew she could thus regain her "character," and she believed she could keep it now that she had discovered her weaknesses.

Further Critical Evaluation of the Work:

Herself Surprised is the first novel in a trilogy published in the early 1940's (the other titles are *To Be a Pilgrim* and *The Horse's Mouth*). Each novel may be read by itself with satisfaction, but for greatest enjoyment and understanding the trilogy should be experienced as a unit. In the trilogy each novel is given over to a single character who tells his or her story with wonderful personal style and inflection. These novels establish Cary as one of the great mimics of literature. The basic scheme of the trilogy involves the conflict between the conservative attitude represented by the lawyer and landholder Tom Wilcher (*To Be a Pilgrim*), and the liberal attitude represented by the painter Gulley Jimson (*The Horse's Mouth*). Sara Monday, the heroine of *Herself Surprised,* has loved both these men. She stands between them in a mediating position.

Sara is a warm, comfortable woman. She likes to make her men feel at ease. Her narrative is full of the imagery of the home and the kitchen. She has been Jimson's mistress and endured his rages as well as his ecstasies. He has painted some of his finest nude studies using her as a model. Basically, however, he rejects her because she threatens to domesticate him and dampen his creative fires. Her next companion is Tom Wilcher, a fussy old bachelor who is largely concerned with maintaining the traditions represented in the family estate of Tolbrook. Sara soothes and smooths Wilcher's thorny nature. He is a perfect object for her feminine arts.

In Cary's world Sara Monday stands for the womanly virtues of love, acceptance, gratification, and nurturing. She may make her way in the world by employing these skills with some calculation, but it is a kind passage.

HESPERIDES

Type of work: Poetry
Author: Robert Herrick (1591-1674)
First published: 1648

> As thou deserv'st, be proud; then gladly
> let
> The Muse give thee the Delphick Coro-
> net.

This brief epigram, one of hundreds Robert Herrick included in his collection of twelve hundred poems, best describes the pride with which he presented his *Hesperides* and the recognition he received after more than one hundred years of neglect. His subtitle, *The Works both Human and Divine of Robert Herrick Esq.*, indicates the inclusion in one volume of his *Hesperides* and his *Noble Numbers,* a group of ecclesiastical poems, prayers, hymns, and apothegms dated 1647. This collection, together with fifteen or so poems discovered by nineteenth-century scholars and about twice the number recovered recently in manuscript, comprise the literary remains of one of the finest lyricists in the English language.

The arrangement of the poems in *Hesperides* (the name itself is a conceit based on the legend of nymphs who guarded with a fierce serpent the golden apples of the goddess Hera) is whimsical. Most of the lyrics were composed in Devonshire, where Herrick was vicar of Dean Prior from 1629 until the Puritan victories caused his removal from his parish in 1647. Restored to his living in 1662, he lived until his death in the West Country which had inspired his pagan-spirited, rustic verse.

The great Herrick scholar, L. C. Martin, has discovered a chronology, from the collation of many manuscripts, which indicates the four general periods in which these poems were composed, carefully rewritten, and then painstakingly published. From his apprenticeship to his goldsmith uncle at least one poem remains, "A Country Life," which may have been one of the reasons why the youthful poet was allowed to terminate his service and go to Cambridge. Though Herrick's activities during his university period are remembered chiefly for the letters he wrote asking his uncle for money, he also composed a variety of commendatory poems and memory verses. One, the longest poem he wrote, is addressed to a fellow student who was ordained in 1623.

The second period, and perhaps the most important, was from 1617 to 1627, when he became the favorite of the "sons" of Ben Jonson. Herrick's famous poem, "His Fare-well to Sack," epitomizes these formative years of good talk, wide reading, witty writing, and good fellowship. In this poem too are the names of the poets who most influenced him—Anacreon, Horace, and by implication, Catullus and Theocritus. The well-known "The Argument of His Book" echoes the pastoral strain in the poet's declaration of his literary interests:

> I sing of *Brooks,* of *Blossomes, Birds,*
> and *Bowers:*
> Of *April, May,* of *June,* and *July-Flow-*
> ers.
> I sing of *May-poles, Hock-carts, Was-*
> sails. *Wakes,*
> Of *Bride-grooms, Brides,* and of their
> *Bridall-cakes.*
> I write of *Youth,* of *Love,* and have
> Accesse
> By these, to sing of cleanly-*Wanton-*
> nesse.
> I sing of *Dewes,* of *Raines,* and piece
> by piece
> Of *Balme,* of *Oyle,* of *Spice,* and *Am-*
> ber-Greece.
> I sing of *Times trans-shifting;* and I
> write
> How *Roses* first came *Red,* and *Lillies*
> *White.*
> I write of *Groves,* of *Twilights,* and I
> sing

The Court of *Mab*, and of the *Fairie-King*.
I write of *Hell;* I sing (and ever shall)
Of *Heaven,* and hope to have it after all.

The Dean Prior vicar's hope for heaven seems to be based on his "cleanly-Wantonnesse," even if one considers his many mistresses—Corinna, stately Julia, smooth Anthea, and sweet Electra—as imaginary, the idealized woman of poetic tradition. Herrick's philosophy is Anacreontic, the *carpe diem* attitude of the Cavalier poets. The best-known example from his work, in his own time as well as ours, is "To the Virgins, to Make Much of Time," which begins: "Gather ye Rosebuds while ye may."

That Herrick was a man of his time may be ascertained by a glance at the rich variety of his poetic subjects. Set in the form of the madrigal, "Corinna's going a Maying," catches all the excitement of the festival in the most intricate of singing forms. A ballad in the manner of Campion is "Cherrie-ripe," one which deserves to be better known:

Cherrie-Ripe, Ripe, Ripe, I cry
Full and faire ones; come and buy:
If so be, you aske me where
They doe grow? I answer, There,
Where my *Julia's* lips doe smile
There's the Land, or Cherry-Ile:
Whose Plantations fully show
All the yeere, where Cherries grow.

In the manner of Shakespeare he composed "The mad Maids Song," with the same "Good Morrows" and the strewing of flowers for the tomb, but in this instance the lament is for a lover killed by a bee sting. In the style of Marlowe and then Raleigh, Herrick continues the Elizabethan shepherd-maiden debate in "To Phillis to love, and live with him":

Thou shalt have Ribbands, Roses, Rings,
Gloves, Garters, Stockings, Shoes, and Strings
Of winning Colours, that shall move
Others to Lust, but me to Love.
These (nay) and more, thine own shal be,
If thou wilt love, and live with me.

A Master of Arts (1620) and a disciple of Jonson, Herrick never forgot his classical background. As an epigrammatist he was without peer, especially since he injected strong originality into a conventional and satiric form. He often made his parishioners models for these satiric verses, as in this comment on one man's discomfiture:

Urles had the Gout so, that he co'd not stand;
Then from his Feet, it shifted to his Hand:
When 'twas in's Feet, his Charity was small;
Now 'tis in's Hand, he gives no Almes at all.

Nor does he spare himself and his friends:

Wantons we are; and though our words be such,
Our Lives do differ from our Lines by much.

An extension of this mode is Herrick's Anacreontic verse. In "To Bacchus, *a Canticle*" he begs the god of revelry and reproduction to show him the way, among thousands, to have more than one mistress. Somewhat more restrained and in the vein of Catullus are his lyrics to Lesbia and the epithalamia with which he greeted his many friends and relatives who, despite all his verses, insisted on getting married. In "The cruell Maid" he echoes, or is echoed by, his contemporary, Andrew Marvell:

Give my cold lips a kisse at last:
If twice you kisse, you need not feare
That I shall stir, or live more here.
Next, hollow out a Tombe to cover
Me; me, the most despised Lover:
And write thereon, *This Reader, know,*
Love kill'd this man. No more but so.

The more humble and bucolic songs of Horace, however, were the poet's abiding love. While he may have wished for the court rather than the parish, his best work was composed amid peaceful surroundings on pleasant rural subjects. His "To Daffadills" is a more delicate and

subtle poem than the well-known lyric
by Wordsworth:

> Faire Daffadills, we weep to see
> You haste away so soone:
> As yet the early-rising Sun
> Has not attain'd his Noone.
> Stay, stay,
> Untill the hasting day
> Has run
> But to the Even-song;
> And, having pray'd together, we
> Will goe with you along.

In the final period represented in
Hesperides, "His returne to London" is
a significant poem illustrating the sophisticated side of his genius, the pomp
and circumstance which made a lasting
poetry for this faithful royalist. He sings
here of

> O Place! O *People!* Manners! fram'd to
> please
> *All Nations, Customes, Kindreds, Lan-
> guages!*

as he links himself with his Elizabethan
patron saints, the Renaissance man who
took all life and all things for their province.

"And here my ship rides having Anchor cast," he writes in his concluding
poems of the book which he sent forth
to find "a kinsman or a friend." He honestly thought and in fact knew "The
Muses will weare blackes, when I am
dead." Ironically, his death went almost
unnoticed, though his verses were recalled in oral tradition for many years before the recovery of his work by modern
scholarship—a most appropriate tribute to
the man who gives such a vivid picture
of the folk and their wassails, harvests,
wakes, and loves.

> To his Book's end this last line he'd
> have plac't,
> *Jocund his Muse was; but his Life was
> chast.*

A HIGH WIND RISING

Type of work: Novel
Author: Elsie Singmaster (Mrs. E. S. Lewars, 1879-1958)
Type of plot: Historical chronicle
Time of plot: 1728-1755
Locale: Pennsylvania
First published: 1942

Principal characters:
ANNA SABILLA SCHANTZ, a pioneer matriarch
JOHANN SEBASTIAN SCHANTZ, her grandson
OTTILIA ZIMMER, a young German immigrant, loved by Sebastian
MARGARETTA, and
GERTRAUD, their twins
CONRAD WEISER, a famous interpreter and Indian agent
SHEKELLIMY, an Oneida chief, friend of Weiser
SKELET, a half-friendly, half-treacherous Delaware

Critique:

A *High Wind Rising* deals with a phase of American history which most writers have neglected. It is a story of the Pennsylvania settlements beyond the Schuylkill during the decisive years when French and English battled for control of the Ohio and Conrad Weiser helped to determine the fate of a continent by keeping the Six Nations loyal to their British allies. The writer brings the period dramatically to life in her characterizations of pioneers like Conrad Weiser and Sebastian Schantz, of frontier women like resourceful, devoted Anna Sabilla. Those people live with no self-conscious sense of national destiny, as do so many pioneers in lesser fiction. Their lives illustrate what must have been the daily life of the frontier, the hardships and dangers that they faced no more than a part of their everyday existence. Other figures great in Pennsylvania annals are more briefly viewed in this crowded canvas of people and events—Benjamin Franklin, James Logan, John Bertram, Henry Melchior Muhlenburg, Lewis Evans. The passing of time and the pressures of history shape the plot, but the story itself is as simple and realistic as homely family legend. The novel is an example of the historical chronicle at its best.

The Story:

In 1728, Conrad Weiser, white clan brother of the Mohawks, saw Owkwari-owira—Young Bear—for the first time, a naked small boy daubed with clay and running wild in Chief Quagnant's village. Weiser, his quick eye seeing pale skin under the dirt and grease, bartered for the child and took him back to the German settlement at Schoharie. Young Bear was baptized Johann Sebastian, and found in Anna Eve, Conrad's wife, a second mother. The Weisers believed that Bastian was the grandson of Anna Sabilla Schantz, whose daughter Margaretta had followed an English trader into the forest.

Many of the Schoharie community were preparing to move to Pennsylvania, where there was rich land for thrifty, industrious German settlers. Anna Sabilla had already gone to her own cabin in a clearing beside the Blue Mountains. Sturdy, resolute, she cared for Nicholas, her paralyzed brother, tended her garden, called all Indians thieves and rascals, but fed them when they begged at her door. For trader Israel Fitch she carved wooden puppets in exchange for salt, cloth, tools. Weiser took Bastian to her when he went to claim his own lands along the Tulpehocken.

Growing up, Bastian helped his grandmother with plantings and harvests. From

Skelet, a sickly, humpbacked Indian whom Anna Sabilla had nursed back to health, he learned the ways of animals and the deep woods. When old Nicholas died, Bastian moved into his room. Tall and strong for his age, he was the man of the family at fourteen.

The chiefs' road ran through the clearing, and along the trail Delawares and Iroquois traveled to and from the treaty councils in Philadelphia. Bastian knew them all— old Sassoonan of the Delawares, loyal Shekellimy, Weiser's friend, who ruled the Delawares for the Six Nations, Seneca, Oneida, and Mohawk spokesmen —and they remembered Owkwari-owira. Sharp-tongued Anna Sabilla grumbled when he talked with them in their own tongues, but she raised few objections when he went with Weiser and the chiefs to Philadelphia for the great council of 1736.

The city was finer than Bastian had ever imagined it. Whenever he could, he left the State House and wandered through the streets and along the waterfront. He saw a shipload of German immigrants and among them a black-haired girl whose parents had died at sea. Because she had no one to pay her passage, her eyes were like those of a hurt deer, and he gave all his money to a kindly couple who offered to look after her. Bastian heard only that her name was Ottilia before a runner from Weiser summoned him to the council. He went back to look for her later, but the immigrants had gone.

Anna Sabilla hinted that Anna Maria, Weiser's daughter, or the Heils' blonde Sibby would have him quickly enough, but Bastian remembered black hair and dark eyes. Tramping from clearing to clearing looking for her, he found some passengers from the ship who remembered that she had gone away with a family named Wilhelm. Again he went to Philadelphia for a treaty council. There Weiser found the girl's name on a ship's list— Ottilia Zimmer. Bastian's search led him to John Bartram, the Quaker naturalist, along the Schuylkill, beyond the Blue Mountains. Nowhere did he get word of Ottilia or the Wilhelms. Anna Maria Weiser became engaged to marry Henry Melchior Muhlenburg, a young pastor. Anna Sabilla shook her head over Bastian; in her old age she wanted the comfort of another woman and children in the cabin.

The chiefs of the Six Nations and delegates from Pennsylvania, Maryland, and Virginia met in Lancaster in 1744. Weiser was there because he was needed to hold the Long House in friendly alliance, Bastian because, as the years passed, Weiser counted greatly on his help. The weather was hot, the noise deafening. Weiser and Bastian went to a small inn to escape feasting Indians. The waitress had black hair and dark eyes. She was Ottilia, and she rode home with Bastian when the conference ended. Humpbacked Skelet ran ahead to tell Anna Sabilla that Bastian had found his squaw.

Settlers were moving beyond the Susquehanna. While Delawares and Shewanese signed treaties with the French, Weiser worked to keep the Long House neutral. Bastian went with him to Logstown on the Ohio, where Tanacharison and Scarouady promised to keep their tribes friendly toward the English. As Bastian rode home, neighbors called to him to hurry. In the kitchen of the cabin Anna Sabilla rocked a cradle in which slept the newborn *zwillings*, Margaretta and Gertraud. At last, said Anna Sabilla, they were a real family.

But winds of violence blew from the west. Weiser gave presents at Aughwick, at Carlisle, but his arguments, feasts, and gifts could not hold the Shewanese and the Delawares, angry because their hunting grounds had been taken from them. General Braddock, marching to force the French from the Ohio, was ambushed. Fitch, the trader, brought word of burnings and killings beyond the mountains. Because Pennsylvania lay open to war parties of French and Indians, Bastian was glad when Fitch decided to stay; another man might be needed if Indians appeared on the Tulpehocken.

Bastian had gone to help a sick neighbor when the raiders struck, burning the cabin and barn and leaving Fitch's body where it fell. Anna Sabilla, Ottilia, and the twins were gone. Pretending ferocity, Skelet had taken a small part of Ottilia's scalp and left her unconscious. Anna Sabilla and the twins he took with him to Kitanning, calling Anna Sabilla his squaw. She was indignant, but she realized that his claims kept her alive and the twins safe.

Reviving, Ottilia wandered through the woods for days in company with a small boy whose parents had been killed and scalped. At last, with other fugitives, she made her way to the Moravian settlement at Bethlehem. There Bastian found her on his journey back from Philadelphia, where he and other settlers had gone to demand the formation of militia units and forts to protect the frontier. Leaving Ottilia with the Weisers, he joined the garrison at Fort Henry, built where Anna Sabilla's cabin had once stood.

One night he and a friend captured a young Frenchman who carried the carved figure of a little girl, and Bastian, recognizing Anna Sabilla's work, concluded that she and the twins were still alive. He joined a raiding party marching on Kitanning, but Anna Sabilla and the little girls were not among the white prisoners freed in the attack.

Anna Sabilla and the twins were already on the way home. Knowing that Skelet was vain and greedy, she promised money if he would guide them back to the settlements. They set out, Skelet dreaming of the rum and finery he would buy with the old woman's gold. Then, worn out by hardships on the trail, he died on the ridge above her own clearing.

Suddenly Anna Sabilla smelled chimney smoke, heard voices. She ran, urging the girls before her. Safe within the stockade, and grateful, she declared that the old humpback had been a rascal but that he had been helpful. She intended to bury him among her people.

Further Critical Evaluation of the Work:

Elsie Singmaster is an author who has attracted little literary criticism. The bulk of her writing is in the genre of the historical novel, and is either written for juveniles or dealing with youthful heroes. Born in a small town in the German region of Pennsylvania in 1879 and educated at Radcliffe, Singmaster's fiction is largely regional, concerned with the span between colonial times and the mid-twentieth century in America. *A High Wind Rising* is one of her later works, and is set in the years of the French and Indian Wars; it details the efforts of local German settlers to secure the Ohio River Valley for the British during the conflict. The writer's straightforward narrative and careful characterizations downplay the historical importance of these people. Instead, she dramatizes the struggle of their everyday lives as pioneers who must cope with both natural and political forces in order to survive.

The author has clearly been influenced by historical romanticists like James Fenimore Cooper. In contrast to Cooper, however, who creates larger-than-life characters such as Natty Bumppo for the purpose of dramatizing significant historical themes, Singmaster wishes to depict the lives of the early settlers without exaggerating for thematic effect. If Cooper is interested in the ethical, historical, and metaphysical aspects of the frontier, Singmaster is interested in the details of everyday lives; whereas romance is central to Cooper, it is incidental to her.

It is, finally, her attention to the orderly lives of her characters that remains her most modern feature. There is, furthermore, a pervasive tone of good feeling toward humanity in her work. That healthy tone, in *A High Wind Rising* and in her other work as well, undoubtedly accounts for her popularity with the young.

THE HILL OF DREAMS

Type of work: Novel
Author: Arthur Machen (1863-1947)
Type of plot: Impressionistic romance
Time of plot: Late nineteenth century
Locale: England
First published: 1907

Principal characters:
LUCIAN TAYLOR, a would-be author
THE REVEREND MR. TAYLOR, Lucian's father, a rural clergyman
ANNIE MORGAN, Lucian's sweetheart

Critique:

This novel by Arthur Machen, in part an autobiography, received little notice when it was published. During the 1920's, after Machen's books had won him a reputation, this novel also came in for a share of attention and popularity. Machen himself said, in the introduction to a later edition of the book, that he had begun it as proof to the world and to himself that he was indeed a man of letters and that, even more important, he had thrown off the style of Robert Louis Stevenson, whom he had been accused of imitating, and had found a style of his own to express his ideas. He also related that the writing of the novel was imbedded in the work itself: that many of the trials and weird experiences which have been put into the life of the fictional Lucian Taylor were, in reality, the experiences of Machen himself as he wrote the novel. This novel will probably never be a popular one, for it is a somewhat difficult study of a highly introverted character, a man who, while searching for a way to express life, lost both himself and the power to understand humanity. Although such studies are too intense and yet too nebulous to appeal to a widely diversified body of readers, the book is likely to stand as a notable example of its type.

The Story:

Lucian Taylor, son of an Anglican rector in a rural parish, was an extraordinary lad, even before he went to school.

He was both studious and reflective, so much so that he was not accepted readily by the boys of the neighborhood. When Lucian went away to school he did very well in his studies, but he formed an acute dislike for athletics and for social life with his fellow students. In his studies he turned toward the less material preferring to learn of the dim Celtic and Roman days of Britain, of medieval church history, and of works in magic.

In his fifteenth year Lucian returned to his home during the August holidays and found it quite changed. His mother had died during the previous year, and his father's fortunes had sunk lower and lower. As a result his father had become exceedingly moody and Lucian spent much of his time away from the house. His habit was to wander through the rolling countryside by himself.

One bright summer afternoon he climbed up a steep hillside to the site of an old Roman fort. The site was at some distance from any human habitation, and Lucian felt quite alone. Because of the heat, he had an impulse to strip off his sweaty clothing and take a nap. He did, only to be awakened by someone kissing him. By the time he had fully regained his senses, the unknown person had disappeared. Lucian was not sure whether some supernatural being or Annie Morgan, daughter of a local farmer, had awakened him thus.

Soon afterward Lucian went back to

school. At last the rector told his son that he could no longer afford to send him to school and that matriculation at Oxford was out of the question. Lucian was disappointed, but he settled down to studying in his father's library or wandering about the countryside in solitary fashion, as he had done during his vacations from school.

As the elder Taylor's fortunes had declined, his popularity in the parish had diminished. Lucian's own reputation had never been high, and his failure to take a job in some respectable business establishment turned the local gentry against him. Everyone felt that his studies and his attempts to write were foolish, since they brought in no money. Nor could the people understand Lucian's failure to maintain their standards of respectability in dress and deportment.

Lucian felt, however, that he could stand beyond such criticism of his habits, but his self-respect suffered a blow when he tried to sell some of his writings. Publishers, refusing to accept his work, pointed out to him that what they wanted was sentimental fiction of a stereotyped kind. Lucian, not wishing to cheapen himself or his literary efforts, refused to turn out popular fiction of the type desired. He felt that he had to express himself in a graver kind of literature.

Lucian's social and intellectual loneliness preyed upon him, plunging him at times into the deepest despair. One afternoon, while sunk in a mood of depression, he went out for a long walk. By dusk he was far from home, or so he thought, and in the midst of a wood. Finally fighting his way clear of the dense brush, Lucian blundered onto a path and there met Annie Morgan. She sensed his mood and fell in with it. Both of them announced their love and pledged one another. Lucian went home feeling better than he had in months.

As the days passed Lucian fell into the habit of putting himself in a world apart, a world of the past, when Rome held Britain as a distant province. He dreamed

that the modern town of Caermaen, near which was his father's rectory, was once again the Roman settlement it had been centuries before. Lucian called his land of make-believe Avallaunius and spent most of his time there, peopling it with men and women, buildings and customs, that he had learned of through his exhaustive studies of Roman times in Britain. He went wandering through the modern town, imagining that the people he met and the scenes before his eyes were those of ancient times. Even Annie Morgan's announcement that she was going away made little impression upon him, for he felt that she had accomplished her mission in his life by showing him how to escape into a better world.

People wondered at the strange behavior of the young man; even his father, not given to noticing anything, became worried because Lucian ate little and grew thin. People who knew him only by sight suspected him of being a drunkard because of his odd behavior and absent-mindedness.

But at last Lucian escaped physically from Caermaen; he received notice that a distant cousin who had lived on the Isle of Wight had died and left him two thousand pounds. He immediately gave five hundred pounds to his father and invested the remainder for himself. With the assurance of a small, regular income, Lucian left Caermaen behind and went to London. There he felt he could escape from the moodiness which had held him prisoner in the country. He also hoped that the different mental atmosphere would prove helpful to him in his attempts at writing.

Upon his arrival in the city Lucian found himself a single room in a private home. He soon settled down to a regular existence, writing late each night, sleeping late in the morning, reading over his work of the night before, and walking, in the afternoons. His meals were sketchy, for he was forced to live on as little as fifteen shillings a week. But the regular schedule was not to hold for long. His inspiration was not a regular thing, and Lucian felt that he had to make his writings perfection itself. He threw away as much as he wrote. Disappointment over his efforts soon began to drive him into worse moods than he had known before.

Having been impressed as a boy by the work of De Quincey in *Confessions of an English Opium Eater,* Lucian turned to that drug for solace and inspiration. After he began taking drugs, he knew little that was going on in the world about him. He spent much of his time lying quietly in his room and reliving the past in visions. Once he had a real inspiration to write; his story about an amber goddess was the product of true imagination. But publication of the story did little to generate ambition and the will to create; he was too far gone in his addiction to opium.

A heavy snow and a severe wave of cold struck London and southern England, but the weather made little impression on him he might just as well have been living in a ghost city. Then one night he took too much opium. His landlady, not hearing him stir for many hours, looked into his room and found him dead at his desk, his writings spread about him. Even she felt little sorrow for him, although he had made over his small fortune to her.

Further Critical Evaluation of the Work:

The Hill of Dreams is the depressing but haunting tale of an apparent failure. Lucian Taylor dreamed impractical dreams, failed to earn a "respectable" living, failed in his writings (which were plagiarized by unscrupulous publishers), and died unnecessarily, having ruined his own health. He was not liked by "respectable" people, even by his landlady to whom he left money, and he had been the cause of strain to his father. Yet, through the story of Lucian, Machen tells us that many *apparent* failures at the time of their deaths, such as Jesus Christ or Lucian, are the *eternal* victors. Lucian's neighbors in his home town and in West London could well be the eternal failures, for they fail to see the proverbial beam in their own eyes, and ignore the Biblical injunction to "judge not, that ye be not judged."

Although Lucian is the target of criticism and condemnation throughout the novel, and although this condemnation seems justified and crushingly final when he is found dead in his dismal rented room amidst his illegible scribblings, *The Hill of Dreams* is not, ultimately, a novel of failure. It breathes of another life beyond the grave, a life that Lucian might have won, for he was loyal to his tortured dreams until the end. Lucian seemingly succumbed to satanic visions only under the unnatural influence of opium, when he had lost his reason. The real Lucian, however, is the youth of the early parts of the novel, who hates cruelty and mediocrity, who has not yet known opium, and who one afternoon walks up an old, neglected country lane when the air is still and breathless. He walks up his "hill of dreams" where wild, bare hills meet a still, gray sky. It is on such occasions, when his sensitive spirit vanquishes harsh reality and the ugly purgatory that enshrouds him in the "real" world, that the reader sees the victorious Lucian Taylor.

HILLINGDON HALL

Type of work: Novel
Author: Robert Smith Surtees (1803-1864)
Type of plot: Comic romance
Time of plot: Nineteenth century
Locale: England
First published: 1845

> *Principal characters:*
> JOHN JORROCKS, a wealthy cockney grocer and sportsman
> MRS. JORROCKS, his shrewish wife
> EMMA FLATHER, a country girl
> MRS. FLATHER, her mother
> THE DUKE OF DONKEYTON, Jorrocks' neighbor
> THE MARQUIS OF BRAY, his son

Critique:

Hillingdon Hall, Or, The Cockney Squire is the final novel of the Jorrocks series. Here the emphasis is on country life and its charms and oddities. John Jorrocks, a London grocer turned sporting country proprietor and agriculturist, is less a clown than he was in previous volumes, although he does meet with many undignified adventures; and the whole tone of the book is more sympathetic than picaresque. There is some good satire in the electioneering scenes and in Emma Flather's attempts to get a husband, and some current farming fads come in for good-natured ridicule. *Hillingdon Hall* is one of the better constructed works in the series, and the cockney speech, as in all of Surtees' work, is accurately represented.

The Story:

Hillingdon Hall was a charming example of the old-style manor house with its many haphazard additions and types of architecture. It was set in a pretty village and the nearby river added to its attractions. Mr. Westbury, the former owner, had been an old-fashioned gentleman of talent and learning who spent his whole time in the country. Since he was a kind of patriarch for the district, the village wondered after his death who would be the new owner of the hall.

When the carriage drew up at the door, curious eyes were fastened on the new arrivals. The chaise was covered with dust. A package of apple trees lay on the roof, the coach boy clutched a huge geranium, and flowers and plants of all kinds were sticking out of the windows. A huge, fat man with roses in his back pocket got out, followed by his wife in stiff brocade. John Jorrocks, the new owner, had arrived.

Mrs. Flather announced the news to her blooming daughter Emma. The two ladies thought it would be only neighborly for them to call right away, especially since there might be a son in the family. Emma at the time had an understanding with James Blake, who had the living at Hillingdon, but she was always on the alert for a better match. Mrs. Trotter, who was, if anything, quicker at gossip than Mrs. Flather, brought the news that Jorrocks was old and married and had no children.

Jorrocks tried hard to be a good gentleman farmer. He visited his tenants faithfully but found them a poor lot. They could scarcely understand his cockney accent and they were full of complaints; besides, they knew much more than he did about farming. Mrs. Jorrocks got on better at first with her country folk. Traditionally the lady of Hillingdon Hall was the patroness of the local school. When she visited the establishment, she was appalled at the drab uniforms worn by the girls. Forthwith she had a friend in London, an actress, design new costumes in the Swiss mode. These she forced on the protesting girls. Unfortunately, when she had a new sign put up at the school the spelling was bad; it announced to the world that the institution was "founder'd" by Julia Jorrocks.

One memorable day a magnificent coach drove up and an impressive footman left a card from the Duke of Donkeyton. The duke fancied himself as a politician. Thinking that Jorrocks might become a person of standing, and feeling sure that he must be a Whig, the duke wanted to make certain of his allegiance. The Jorrockses were still more astounded to receive an invitation to dine and stay the night at Donkeyton. Although much puzzled by the initials R. S. V. P., Jorrocks wrote a formal acceptance. Mrs. Flather and Emma were also invited, but characteristically they were thinking of the duke's son, the Marquis of Bray, as a possible suitor for Emma.

On the way to Donkeyton, Jorrocks contrived to get in the same carriage with Mrs. Flather and squeezed that poor lady and stole a kiss or two. He continued his boisterous tactics at the castle. The duke was much impressed by Jorrocks' appetite for food and drink. After dinner he made the mistake of trying to keep up with Jorrocks in drinking toasts; consequently, he had to retire early and was unable to appear in time for breakfast.

The elegant and effeminate Marquis of Bray was quite taken with Emma. He fell in with a scheme that Jorrocks and the duke had for founding an agricultural society with Bray as president and Jorrocks as vice-president. He readily agreed to come to an organizational meeting, since there he would see Emma again.

The meeting was a great success. Bray was horrified at the amount of food put away by Jorrocks and his farmers, but he did his best to keep up appearances. Jorrocks' speech sounded good, although some of the farmers did not follow him very well. He advocated the growing of pineapples and the making of drain tile with sugar as the principal ingredient. Bray topped off the occasion by a speech lauding the ancient Romans. Afterward

he was able to visit Emma and capture that girl's willing heart.

For some time Jorrocks had had as estate manager a jack-of-all-trades named Joshua Sneakington—Sneak for short. After he had arranged for fees and bribes to add to his income, Sneak thought himself well off. One morning, however, Jorrocks rose very early and decided to make a tour of inspection. In a secluded spot he came upon Sneak netting pheasants. Furious at the trickery, he had Sneak sent to jail. His new manager was a doughty North Countryman, James Pigg, who had been with Jorrocks at Handley Cross.

The duke showed favor to Jorrocks by giving him a prize bull, which won a ribbon at a fair, and by appointing him magistrate. Bray came again to visit, mostly to see Emma, but Jorrocks dragged him off to a rough farmers' masquerade. Bray, who was a slender youth, made the mistake of dressing as a woman. A loutish farmer who would not be put off tried to kiss him. The boisterous treatment startled Bray so much that he wandered off in the night and got lost. He came upon a sleeping household and, after awaking the inhabitants, found he had blundered on the Flather's house. After staying the night with the family, he had a chance to flirt with Emma at breakfast.

After that adventure Emma and her mother confidently expected an offer from Donkeyton. When no word came, the desperate Mrs. Flather herself went to the castle. The duchess was amused at the idea of her son's marriage with a commoner, but the duke was incensed; he knew that Bray had conducted himself properly, for he had read Chesterfield. The son had no voice in the matter at all. Later Emma and her mother had to admit he had never made an outright profession of love.

The member of Parliament from the district died. The duke immediately sent out a bid for Bray to fill the vacancy, and no opposition was expected. The Anti-Corn-Law League wrote several times to Bray asking his stand on repeal of the grain tariff, but Bray knew nothing of the matter and did not reply. Thereupon the League put up its own candidate, Bill Bowker, a grifting friend of Jorrocks. To avoid a campaign, the duke bought off Bowker for a thousand pounds and endorsed the proposals of the League.

It was a shocking thing for the duke to advocate removal of tariffs on grain. When next the farmers tried to sell their produce at market, they found that prices had tumbled. In their anger they put forth the willing Jorrocks as their candidate. The duke was hurt that a man to whom he had given a bull and whom he had elevated to a magistracy should run against his son, but Jorrocks was obdurate. At the hustings, although the Marquis of Bray won, Jorrocks' supporters demanded a poll.

The farmers all worked to get every eligible voter to vote. Pigg was a little tricky because he persuaded the Quakers to vote for Jorrocks on the grounds that his candidate was a teetotaler. When the votes were counted, Jorrocks won by a margin of two. Elated at beating a marquis, and glad to go back to London, Jorrocks left Pigg in charge of Hillingdon Hall and went on to bigger things.

Further Critical Evaluation of the Work:

The third of Surtees' novels treating the comic misadventures of "Cockney sportsman" John Jorrocks, *Hillingdon Hall* is somewhat less episodic and more conventionally plotted than the picaresque *Jorrock's Jaunts and Jollities* (1838) or *Handley Cross* (1843). The author continues the career of Jorrocks, now in his late middle age and fairly prosperous from the success of his London grocery business, who determines to settle down with his wife and hounds at a country estate in order to enjoy the vigorous life of a sporting squire. By placing his parvenu hero among the landed gentry, Surtees is able to develop the amusing possibilities of an idea that he had proposed in his first novel: that if Jorrocks' lot had been "cast in the country instead of behind a counter, his keenness would have rendered him as conspicuous— if not as scientific—as the best of them."

The test of this proposition occurs at Hillingdon Hall, where Jorrocks, in spite of his urban background in vulgar commerce, is entirely at ease among both the aristocrats and simple country folk of the vicinity. Jorrocks is, after all, "frank, hearty, open, generous, and hospitable"—possessing virtues certain to prevail no matter where fortune leads him. There is no question that the onetime grocer is shrewder than his lordly neighbors, the effete Duke of Donkeyton and his blue-blooded but insipid son, the Marquis of Bray. And Jorrocks is honest enough to recognize his own limitations in dealing with farm matters that he cannot comprehend. So he allows the pragmatic James Pigg—another of Surtees' memorable creations—to manage the business part of the estate.

Thanks to his common sense (along with a measure of luck and the political acumen of Pigg), Jorrocks even wins a contested Parliamentary seat from his highborn rival Bray. Although the issue at stake in the election —the question of repealing the Corn Laws—is treated farcically, Surtees was in earnest about the matter in his personal life. A staunch conservative, he feared that a rising middle class would destroy the privileges of wealth and the stability of country life as he had known it. Jorrock's Hillingon Hall, to be sure, is a very modest estate compared to Surtees' own inherited properties: Milkwellburn, Byerside Hall, Espershields, and Hamsterley Hall in Durham.

Because of his experience in public life as well as his high social station, Surtees could view Jorrocks from two vantages: that of an aristocrat laughing at the common man's foibles, but also that of an adopted Londoner who appreciates the rugged strengths of the ambitious middle class. Consequently, he treats his hero both as bumpkin and solid citizen—or "cit." In the third novel of the Jorrocks series, the grocer is not so much a sportsman as he is a landholding squire. Much of the impetuous hilarity of the hunting scenes from the other two novels is missing. But in its place is a fuller portrait of the "cit" as a man of warmth and dignity. By the time Surtees takes his leave of Jorrocks, the master of Hillingdon Hall, he seems to resemble less Dickens' Sam Weller, the Cockney who similarly confuses his *v*'s and *w*'s, and more the great-hearted gentleman Pickwick.

HIPPOLYTUS

Type of work: Drama
Author: Euripides (480-406 B.C.)
Type of plot: Classical tragedy
Time of plot: Remote antiquity
Locale: Troezen in Argolis
First presented: 428 B.C.

Principal characters:
THESEUS, King of Athens
HIPPOLYTUS, son of Theseus and Hippolyta, Queen of the Amazons
PHAEDRA, wife of Theseus
APHRODITE, goddess of physical love
ARTEMIS, goddess of spiritual love

Critique:

The *Hippolytus* is probably one of the most provocative of Greek tragedies, and Phaedra, despite her comparatively brief appearance in the play, is one of the most pitiful of tragic heroines. Hippolytus himself is an insufferable prig; but because Phaedra and Theseus are victims of relentless fate our sympathies go out to them. It has been said that this play is Euripides' dramatic treatment of the conflict in the human between physical and spiritual love, although this theory may attribute too much importance to the traditional rivalry between Aphrodite and Artemis in Greek mythology. Racine treated this story in the baroque manner in his *Phèdre.*

The Story:

Aphrodite, goddess of physical love, became angry because Hippolytus, offspring of an illicit union between Theseus and Hippolyta, Queen of the Amazons, alone among the citizens of Troezen refused to do her homage. Instead, the youth, tutored by holy Pittheus, honored Artemis, goddess of the chase and of spiritual love. To punish him for his disdain of love and marriage, Aphrodite, jealous of Artemis and incensed at his neglect of her altars, vowed revenge: she would reveal to Theseus the love his wife, Phaedra, had for her stepson.

Some time before, Hippolytus had gone to the country of Pandion to be initiated into the holy mysteries. There Phaedra, seeing him, had fallen in love with the handsome youth, and because her heart was filled with longing she had dedicated a temple to the Cyprian goddess. Poseidon, ruler of the sea, had once promised Theseus that three of his prayers to the sea god should be answered. Through that promise Aphrodite planned to accomplish her revenge.

Now it happened that Theseus had killed a kinsman, and as punishment for his crime he had been exiled for a year in Troezen. There Phaedra, who had accompanied her husband when he left Athens, was unhappy in her secret love for the young huntsman.

Hippolytus, returning from the chase, paid his respects with song and garlands before the altar of Artemis. Reminded by a servant that an image of Aphrodite stood nearby, he answered impatiently that he acknowledged the power of the Cyprian goddess, but from afar. Dedicated to chastity, he had no desire to become her devotee. The attendant, after Hippolytus had left the shrine, asked Aphrodite to indulge the young man's foolish pride.

Phaedra, meanwhile, moped in her hopeless passion for the young prince, so much so that her servants expressed deep concern over her illness and wondered what strange malady affected her. A nurse, alarmed at Phaedra's restiveness and petulance, was the most concerned of all. When her mistress expressed a desire to hunt wild beasts in the hills and to gallop horses on the sands, the nurse decided that Phaedra was light-headed because she had not eaten food for three days.

At last the nurse swore by the Amazon queen who had borne Theseus a son that Phaedra would be a traitor to her own children if she let herself sicken and die. At the mention of Hippolytus' name Phaedra started; then she moaned pitifully. Thinking how horrible it was that she had been stricken with love for her husband's son, she bewailed the unnatural passions of her Cretan house. At the nurse's urging she finally confessed her true feelings for her stepson. The nurse, frightened at the thought of the consequences possible because of that sinful passion, was horrified. The attendants mourned at what the future seemed to hold for all concerned. Phaedra told them that she was determined to take her own life in order to preserve her virtue and to save Theseus from shame.

But the nurse, having reconsidered, advised her mistress to let matters take a natural course; she would offend Aphrodite if she were to resist her love for Hippolytus. Phaedra was quite scandalized, however, when the nurse suggested that she even see Hippolytus. The nurse said that she had a love charm that would end Phaedra's malady. As it turned out, the potion was ineffectual without a word from Hippolytus' mouth or an item of his clothing or personal belongings.

Phaedra's attendants melodically invoked Aphrodite not to look askance upon them in their concern for their mistress.

The nurse, eager to aid the lovesick woman, went to Hippolytus and told him of Phaedra's love. The young huntsman, shocked, rebuked the nurse for a bawd and expressed his dislike for all mortal womankind. Phaedra, having overheard her stepson's angry reproaches and his condemnation of all women, feared that her secret would be revealed. To make Hippolytus suffer remorse for her death, she hanged herself.

Theseus, who had been away on a journey, returned to discover that Phaedra had taken her life. Grief-stricken, he became enraged when he read a letter clenched in his dead wife's hand. In it she wrote that Hippolytus had caused her death by his attempts to ravish her. Wild with sorrow and rage, Theseus called upon Poseidon to grant the first of his requests: he asked the god to destroy Hippolytus that very day. His attendants, shocked, implored him to be calm, to consider the welfare of his house, and to withdraw his request.

Hippolytus, returning at that moment, encountered his father and was mystified by the passionate words of Theseus. Standing over the body of his dead wife, the king reviled his bastard son and showed him the letter Phaedra had written. Hippolytus, proudly defending his innocence, said that he had never looked with carnal desire upon any woman. Theseus, refusing to believe his son's protestations, banished the young man from his sight. Hippolytus departed, still insisting to his friends that he was the purest of mortals.

Going down to the seashore, Hippolytus entered his chariot after invoking Zeus to strike him dead if he had sinned. As he drove along the strand, on the road leading to Argos, an enormous wave rose out of the sea and from the whirling waters emerged a savage, monstrous bull whose bellowing echoed along the shore. The horses drawing Hippolytus' chariot panicked and ran away, the bull in pursuit. Suddenly one of the chariot wheels struck a rock and the car overturned. Hippolytus, dragged across the rocks, was mortally injured.

Theseus, learning with indifference that his son still lived, consented to have him brought back to the palace. While he waited, Artemis appeared and told him of his son's innocence and of Phaedra's guilty passion for Hippolytus. Aphrodite, she declared, had contrived the young hunter's death to satisfy her anger at his neglect of her shrines.

Hippolytus, his body maimed and broken, was carried on a litter into his father's presence. Still maintaining his innocence, he moaned with shameless self-pity and lamented that one so pure and chaste should meet death because of his frightened horses. They were, he said, the principal means by which he had always honored Artemis, goddess of the hunt. When she told him that Aphrodite had caused his death, he declared that he, his father, and Artemis were all victims of the Cyprian's evil designs.

Knowing the truth at last, Hippolytus, humbled, took pity on broken-hearted Theseus and forgave his father for his misunderstanding and rage. Theseus, arising from the side of the dead prince, miserably faced the prospect of living on after causing the destruction of his innocent, beloved son.

Further Critical Evaluation of the Work:

Hippolytus is an intriguing play from both a religious and a psychological standpoint. Euripides dramatizes the traditional rivalry in Greek religion between Aphrodite, the goddess of love, and Artemis, the goddess of chastity. The three major characters—Phaedra, Hippolytus, and Theseus—are caught in that antagonism and must suffer for it. Just as a statue of each goddess frames the stage, so the dramatic action is set between the appearance of Aphrodite in the prologue and the appearance of Artemis at the end. The contrast between these two, as Euripides shows it, however, is not between carnal love and spiritual love, but between uncontrolled passion and artificial restraint.

Aphrodite is an intense, volatile goddess who does not hesitate to destroy her own devotee, Phaedra, in order to wreak vengeance upon Hippolytus, who, she believes, has deeply offended her by his conduct and attitudes. Artemis appears, however, as the revealer of truth, the calm reconciler of father and son. After passion wreaks its damage only a clear-eyed view of things is left, sobering and immeasurably sad.

The goddess of passion works her will through two violently emotional people, Phaedra and Theseus. Although perhaps not technically incestuous, Phaedra's love for the young man is clearly immoral and wrong. However, the intensity of her feelings—they are obviously beyond her control—and the sincerity of her guilt and anguish, make her the most sympathetic and moving figure in the play. Hippolytus, on the other hand, is innocent of any actual wrongdoing, but his self-righteous moralism and abnormally rigid sexual behavior not only render him personally unsympathetic, but, more important, are major stimulants to the sequence of actions that lead to the final catastrophe. Theseus' impulsive vengeance adds the third element to the drama. Thus, uncontrollable passion, arrogant self-righteousness, and mindless revenge combine to provoke multiple tragedy.

From a dramatic standpoint, the main problem in the play is that the most important character, Phaedra, dies when the action is little more than half over. Her tragedy finished, the intensity of the play flags. The debate between Theseus and Hippolytus over the causes of her death and Theseus' subsequent condemnation of Hippolytus lack the feelings present in Phaedra's scenes, although they do resolve the action and grant to the males, especially Hippolytus, a measure of sympathy and tragic stature absent earlier. But it is the vividness, intensity, and tragic ambiguity of Phaedra's character that makes *Hippolytus* one of Euripides' greatest and most provocative plays.

HISTORIA CALAMITATUM

Type of work: Autobiography
Author: Pierre Abélard (1079-1142)
Time: 1079-c.1132
Locale: Paris, Melun, Laon, and St. Gildas, France
First transcribed: c. 1132

Principal personages:
>PIERRE ABÉLARD, philosopher, theologian, churchman
>FULBERT, Canon of Notre Dame
>HÉLOÏSE, Canon Fulbert's niece
>WILLIAM OF CHAMPEAUX, Abélard's teacher, a philosopher
>ANSELM OF LAON, a teacher
>BERNARD OF CLAIRVAUX, Abbot of Clairvaux

Abélard's *History of My Calamity* is an account of the romantic and intellectual misfortunes of one of the significant philosophers of the Middle Ages. As a moderate realist Abélard upheld the Aristotelian idea that names of characteristics do not name independently real universals but merely call attention to certain resemblances in things. This opinion made him a philosophical opponent of his teacher, William of Champeaux. Abélard's reliance on logic and dialectic together with his love of debate resulted in his antagonizing many churchmen, Bernard of Clairvaux in particular, and he was condemned for heresy. This misfortune took second place to the castration which he suffered as the result of having seduced Héloïse, niece of the Canon of Notre Dame. Abélard's story of his misfortunes is at the same time a personal statement from the Middle Ages and a timeless expression of human trials.

Pierre Abélard was born in the village of Pallet, about eight miles from Nantes. His father was a soldier who had studied letters, and through his influence Abélard acquired a passion for learning. In particular, he delighted in philosophy and in the logical exercise of disputation.

In Paris he studied under William of Champeaux, whom he irritated by besting him in a series of debates. Abélard set up a school of his own at Melun and, later, at Corbeil, near Paris, until he was forced by illness to return to his native province for several years. When he returned to Paris, he resumed study with William of Champeaux, but once again Abélard's skill in overthrowing his master's philosophy of universals gained the enmity of that cleric. Consequently, Abélard reëstablished his school at Melun and attracted many of William's students to his own school. Later, he moved closer to Paris, conducted his school on Mont Ste. Geneviève, and carried on a philosophical feud with William.

After the conversion of his parents to the monastic life, Abélard decided to study under Anselm of Laon, but he was disappointed to discover that Anselm's fame was more a result of custom than of intellect. Anselm had a great flow of words, but the words were all meaningless. Taunted by Anselm's admirers for his desultory attendance at the lectures, Abélard invited the students to hear his own exposition of the Scriptures. The presentation was so successful that, like William, Anselm began to persecute Abélard for surpassing him. When Anselm ordered Abélard to cease the work which was embarrassing him, Abélard returned to Paris.

In Paris he completed the glosses on Ezekiel which he had begun at Laon. As his philosophical fame grew and the numbers of his students increased, his pride and sensuality grew accordingly. Attracted by Héloïse, the young niece of a canon named Fulbert, Abélard determined to possess her. Having persuaded her uncle to take him in as a lodger, he agreed to become Héloïse's tutor and guide.

Abélard's objective was soon reached. Pretending to be engrossed in study, the lovers explored all the avenues of love, and Abélard gave less and less time to philosophy and to teaching. Instead of writing new lectures, he wrote love poetry which became famous among those who loved the delights of this world. Fulbert dismissed the rumors which came to him because he loved his niece and had faith in the continence of Abélard. The truth becoming finally apparent, even to Fulbert, the lovers were forced to part. Their separation brought them shame, but shame gave way to increased desire. When Héloïse discovered that she was pregnant, Abélard arranged to have her taken to his sister's house. There Héloïse gave birth to a son, Astrolabe.

Fulbert, nearly mad with grief, would have killed or injured Abélard had he not feared that Héloïse might suffer from the vengeance of her lover's family. Then Abélard begged the canon's forgiveness and declared his intention to marry Héloïse. Fulbert agreed to the offer and sealed their agreement with a kiss.

When Abélard told Héloïse of his intention, she objected strenuously, arguing that it would be a loss to the Church and to philosophy if he were to disgrace himself by marrying a girl he had seduced. Furthermore, she argued, if he were to marry he would be going against the advice of the most eminent philosophers, who argued that no one could devote himself to philosophy while compelled to listen to the disturbances of family life. Finally she referred to the examples provided by those who undertook the monastic life in order to serve God.

Abélard refusing to be convinced, he and Héloïse were married secretly in Paris, the ceremony witnessed by her uncle and a few friends. When Héloïse criticized her uncle for telling the secret of her marriage, Fulbert punished her.

Abélard, hearing of the punishment, sent Héloïse to a convent at Argenteuil. This act so angered the canon that he and his kinsmen arranged to have Abélard castrated. Two of those who perpetrated this shameful deed were later apprehended and, as punishment, blinded and also castrated.

Abélard suffered not so much from the physical injury as from the grief of the clerics and scholars of Paris. Héloïse took the vows of a religious life at the convent of Argenteuil, and Abélard became a monk at the abbey of St. Denis. There, deploring the scandalous life of the abbot and other monks, he lured their students from them by teaching secular philosophy as well as theology.

Abélard's rivals at the abbey, through the coöperation of Alberic and Lotulphe, apologists for Anselm, arranged to have him called before an ecclesiastical council at Soissons for writing a tract containing what they regarded as heretical views concerning the unity and trinity of God. Although no case against the book could be made, Abélard's enemies convinced the council that the book should be ordered burned. This decision was carried out and Abélard was sent to the abbey of St. Médard as punishment. After a short period of time, however, all who had been involved in punishing Abélard put the blame on others: Abélard was allowed to return to the abbey of St. Denis.

When the envy of the monks of St. Denis prompted more ecclesiastical quarrels, Abélard secured permission to build an oratory at Troyes. This he named the Paraclete, dedicating the church to the Holy Spirit.

Abélard was then called to be abbot of St. Gildas at Ruits, but his suffering continued because of the undisciplined and immoral behavior of the monks.

When the abbot of St. Denis expelled the nuns from the abbey of Argenteuil, where Héloïse served, Abélard arranged to have her and some of her deposed companions take charge of the Paraclete. In this manner he secured Héloïse's happiness. Rumors began to spread that

Abélard was acting in her behalf because he was moved by lust, but he defended himself by arguing that the damage done to his person made any base act impossible. Furthermore, he regarded it as his duty to supervise the nuns, and he pointed out passages in scripture in support of his action.

Abélard was constantly threatened by the monks of his abbey, who attempted to poison him and to have him murdered by bandits. Only by exercising great care and by excommunicating the most wicked among the brothers was Abélard able to survive. He wrote the letter giving an account of his misfortunes in order to show how much suffering is possible for one who serves God and to argue that, despite suffering, all persons should trust in God's providence.

THE HISTORY OF COLONEL JACQUE

Type of work: Novel
Author: Daniel Defoe (1660-1731)
Type of plot: Picaresque adventure
Time of plot: Late seventeenth century
Locale: England, France, Virginia
First published: 1722

Principal characters:

COLONEL JACQUE, commonly called Jack, a waif
CAPTAIN JACK, his foster brother
MAJOR JACK, another foster brother
WILL, a pickpocket
COLONEL JACQUE'S FOUR WIVES

Critique:

Although in our day Daniel Defoe is remembered chiefly for *Robinson Crusoe*, in its own time *Colonel Jacque* attained great popularity. Defoe declared that his twofold purpose was to show the ruination of youth through lack of proper training and to prove that a misspent life may be redeemed by repentance. The novel opens on a theme similar to that of *Oliver Twist* but follows a line of development modeled after *Gil Blas*. Although a rogue, Colonel Jacque aspires to win back his good name, and in the end he succeeds. Defoe, in the fashion of his day, gave the novel a grandiose title: *The History and Remarkable life of the truly Honourable Colonel Jacque, vulgarly called Col. Jack, who was born a Gentleman, put 'Prentice to a Pick-pocket, flourished six and twenty years as a Thief, and was then Kidnapped to Virginia; came back a Merchant, was five times married to four Whores, went into the Wars, behaved bravely, got preferment, was made Colonel of a Regiment, came over and fled with the Chevalier, is still Abroad Completing a Life of Wonders, and resolves to die a General.* The end of the novel does not fulfill, however, the promise of the title.

The Story:

The illegitimate son of a gentleman and a lady, Colonel Jack, as he was later known, was early in his life given to his nurse to rear. There he was brought up with her own son, Captain Jack, and another unwanted child, Major Jack. She treated the boys well, but she herself had little money and so they were forced to fend for themselves. When Colonel Jack was but ten years of age, the good woman died, leaving the three boys to beg their food. Lodging did not bother them; they slept in ash piles and doorways in the winter and on the ground in summer. Captain Jack soon turned to picking pockets for a living and was so successful that he took Colonel Jack into partnership. The two young rogues preyed on wealthy men who were careless of their money. One of the boys would take the money, extracting only a small note from the whole; then the other would return the rest to its rightful owner and collect a reward for its return. One of the men thus duped was so grateful to honest-seeming Colonel Jack that upon the return of his wallet he agreed to keep the reward money for the boy and pay him interest on it. Since Colonel Jack had no place to keep the stolen goods safely, he had asked the gentleman to do him that service. Later Colonel Jack took more stolen money to the same man for safekeeping and received his note for the whole amount, to be paid only to Colonel Jack himself. In fairness let it be said that after the scamps had robbed a poor woman of all her savings, Colonel Jack was so ashamed that he later returned her money with interest.

Captain Jack, a real villain, was apprehended and taken to Newgate Prison. Colonel Jack then became a partner of a thief named Will, a really vicious rogue

2627

who plundered and robbed and at last killed. He also was caught and taken to Newgate to be hanged, a fate which Colonel Jack knew Will deserved but which made his heart sick and his own conscience a heavy burden.

Captain Jack escaped from prison. Colonel Jack being also in danger because of his deeds, the two journeyed to Scotland. They were almost caught many times, but on each occasion Captain Jack's foresight enabled them to elude capture. When they were ready to return to England, they took work on a ship bound for London, or so they thought. Since they were deserters from the army, which they had joined to save their skins, they could not afford to risk regular means of travel. But the two who had cheated so many were themselves duped. Instead of sailing for England, they found themselves on the high seas bound for America and servitude. Colonel Jack, knowing himself for a villain, accepted his fate calmly, but Captain Jack stormed against it. The defiant Captain Jack abused his master, escaped back to England, resumed his old ways, and some twenty years later was hanged.

In Virginia, Colonel Jack was the property of a good master who told him that after he had served five years he would be freed and given a small piece of land. Thus, if he were industrious and honest, he might benefit from his ill fate. Jack, respecting his master, worked diligently for him. Soon he was made an overseer, and his kind heart and keen mind were responsible for changing the Negro slaves from rebellious fiends to loyal workers. His master was so fond of Jack that he bought for him a small plantation nearby and lent him the money to supply it. He also arranged for Jack to secure his money left in keeping in London. The money was converted into goods for the plantation, goods which were lost at sea. The master offered Jack his freedom before the five years were up, but Jack was loyal and continued to serve his master until that gentleman's death.

Jack's plantation prospered. The original two slaves given to him by his old master were increased by several more slaves and bonded white workers. Jack, always a kind master, won the loyalty of his workmen. Wanting to improve his education, for he could neither read nor write, he took one of his bonded men as a tutor and soon grew to admire him as he himself had been admired by his former master.

Resolving to return to England after an absence of almost twenty years, he tried to get his tutor to travel with him. When the man refused, Jack made him the overseer of his large plantations. It was some time before Jack arrived in his native land. He was first tossed about at sea, then captured by the French, and at last exchanged for a prisoner held by the English.

Soon Jack's heart was taken by a lady who lived nearby and they were married. But she proved unfaithful to him, as well as being a gambler and a spendthrift, and shortly after the birth of their child he left her. He first attacked her lover, however, and so had to flee for his life. Later, learning that she was to have another child, he divorced her and went to France. There he joined an Irish brigade and fought in France, Germany, and Italy. Captured, he was sent to Hungary and then to Italy, where he married the daughter of an innkeeper. Eventually he was allowed to go to Paris with his wife. There he recruited volunteers to fight against the English. Tiring of war, he returned to Paris unexpectedly, only to find that his second wife had also taken a lover. After almost killing the man, he fled to London and then to Canterbury, where he lived as a Frenchman with the English and as an Englishman with the French.

Still desiring a happy home life, he married again. His wife, at first beautiful and virtuous, became a drunkard and finally killed herself. They had had three children. Wishing to provide for them, Jack married an older woman who had cared for them and whom they loved as a mother. But that good woman, after bearing him children, died from a fall, leaving him a widower once more. After smallpox took all but two of his children, he returned to Virginia. His daughter he left with her grandfather; the remaining son he took with him.

In Virginia he found his affairs in good order, the tutor having made a faithful overseer for twenty-four years. Several slaves and servants had been added to the plantations, and Jack found one of them to be his first wife. Since she had repented wholly of her sins, he married her again and lived happily with her for many years.

But he was not always to live in peace. Several captive servants who knew of his part in the rebellion, when he had served with the Irish brigade, were brought to neighboring plantations. His part in the rebellion becoming known, he had to leave Virginia until he could secure a pardon from the king. He and his wife went to Antigua, from which she later returned to Virginia to await the news of her husband's pardon. Pardoned, he was on his way home when he was captured by the Spanish. After many long months as a hostage he was released, having turned the experience into profit by trading with some of his captors. He continued the trade, which was illegal in the eyes of the Spanish government, and made thousands of pounds. He was often in danger during his voyages, even taken, but each time he turned the situation to his own advantage.

At last he left danger behind, returned to England, and sent for his beloved wife. There they remained, leaving the Virginia plantations in the hands of the faithful tutor. In his old age Colonel Jack spent many hours contemplating the goodness of the God he had formerly ignored. He believed that his story was one to make others repent of their sins and mend their broken ways.

Further Critical Evaluation of the Work:

At its very commencement the English novel indicated the direction of its subsequent development. In *The History of Colonel Jacque* as well as in his other novels, Defoe detailed the adventures of the rogue, society's outcast, in his attempt to find station, security, and identity in culture. So even at the beginning of the eighteenth century, the novel was a middle-class, democratic genre, growing out of the political and social rise of that class. It is middle-class in its concern for wealth and station; it is democratic in its insistence that power, which lay in aristocratic hands, be dispersed and allowed to filter down to the parvenu.

Typically, Colonel Jack is an unwanted child who is excluded by his birth from the goods of society. Simply but accurately put, his aim during his adventures is to accumulate wealth, which he soon discovers—and this is of course the edge of Defoe's moral satire—will give him power and place. But it is also a part of Defoe's wisdom, which is as well that of the middle class, that the pleasure goods afford gives man a fundamental nobility. It is a dignity achieved when he frees himself from poverty and gains substance in the eyes of society. Those goods, Defoe also tells us, make possible the pursuit of virtue; for if material security does not necessarily lead to virtue, the moral life is impossible without it.

Colonel Jack's conversion, then, like the more famous one of Moll Flanders, should not be seen as mere hypocrisy. It is a knowledge won at the expense of suffering and deprivation. If one condemn Jack's means to his end, one should be prepared to honor his middle-class sagacity that if man cannot live by bread alone, neither can he live without it.

THE HISTORY OF ENGLAND

Type of work: History
Author: Thomas Babington Macaulay (1800-1859)
Time: 56 B.C.-A.D. 1702
Locale: England
First published: Books I and II, 1848; III and IV, 1855; V, unfinished, 1861

Principal personages:
CHARLES II
JAMES II
WILLIAM III
MARY, wife of William
JOHN CHURCHILL, Duke of Marlborough
WILLIAM PENN

Macaulay knew little about English history before the seventeenth century. He knew almost nothing about foreign history. He was not interested in art, science, philosophy, or religion. As a Whig, he had no sympathy with the Tories and little understanding of James II. He overlooked many of the authoritative books covering the period about which he was writing. Therefore, in *The History of England from the Accession of James the Second* he is sometimes unfair to certain figures or mistaken in facts and interpretations. The result, however, is a vivid and eminently readable history with vivid pictures of the actors and the social and cultural background against which they performed.

Macaulay was a child prodigy who started writing early. Before he was eight, this future historan, poet, and essayist had completed an outline of history and a poem in three cantos modeled after the poetry of Scott. He went to Trinity College, Cambridge, intending to enter law. Before he passed his bar examinations in 1826, he had attracted attention by a critical essay on Milton, the first of many he contributed to the influential *Edinburgh Review*. Later his essays about the Indian question got him an appointment on a commission to India.

While still in India, he wrote in his diary his intention to compile a five-volume history, the first part to cover the thirty years from the revolution of 1688 to the beginning of Walpole's administration. It would end with the death of George IV and achieve unity by covering "the Revolution that brought the crown into harmony with the Parliament and the Revolution which brought the Parliament into harmony with the nation." Further planning convinced him of the need to precede his account of the revolution by the story of the reign of James II.

When he returned to England, he had barely begun his project before he was named Secretary of War, a post which gave him no time for literary work until the elections of 1841 turned him out of office and into his study. He progressed slowly on his history until the return of his party to power in 1846, when he was appointed Paymaster General. In spite of public demands on his time the first two volumes of *The History of England from the Accession of James the Second* appeared in November, 1848.

The ten chapters begin with an account of Roman times and bring the story of England down to the crowning of William and Mary on February 13, 1689. Diary entries reveal Macaulay's worry about how to begin. He had to start somewhere and so, in the first paragraph, he bravely announced his purpose to "offer a slight sketch of my country from the earliest times." Romans, Saxons, and Danes move through the first chapter, bringing the reader up to the general elections of 1660 and the return of Charles II to England. In the next chapter Macaulay followed the career of Charles II until his death in 1685. At this point the historian was ready to

2631

begin his task in earnest. His announced purpose in the third chapter was to "give a description of the state in which England was at the time when the crown passed from Charles II to his brother, James."

First, Macaulay stressed the small population of the British Isles in 1685, perhaps five million, with half living in England. Then he discussed the revenue available. Excise taxes, taxes on chimneys, and the rest brought in hardly a fifth as much to the crown as France was collecting. Then follows a study of the army and the navy on which the money was largely spent. A discussion of agriculture and mineral wealth introduces the country gentlemen and the yeomanry, with a glance at the clergy. Next, the historian's attention fixes on the towns and their growth, following the expansion of trade and manufacturing, with special attention to London. Discussion of communication with London leads to a section on the postal system, inns, and highwaymen. A study of England's cultural status, both literary and scientific, precedes the final section on the terrible condition of the very poor.

The description of the death of Charles II, in Chapter IV, is a sample of Macaulay's style. The ten pages read like a historical novel, except that the historian has footnotes available for the details of the palace room, the visitors at the bedside, and such bits as the king's dying comment about winding the clock at his bedside. The surreptitious visit of the priest, John Huddleston, and the reaction of the crowd outside the palace bring vividness to the event.

The succession of James II to the throne is the theme of the other six chapters of the first two volumes. The new monarch lacked the political acumen and the general knowledge of the world possessed by Charles II; otherwise, he might not have been so easily duped by his Jesuit adviser, for he did possess administrative ability, more, perhaps, than Macaulay grants him.

The exciting part of this section tells of James's following the invasion of England by William of Orange and of his capture by "rude fishermen of the Kentish coast," who mistook the royal party for Jesuits and the monarch for his hated adviser, Father Petre. Then came his flight to France, the Convention that formulated the Declaration of Rights, and the coronation of William and Mary. Because of this stirring material, excitingly told, thirteen thousand copies of the history were sold in four months.

Such success worried Macaulay. Attempting to make the other volumes dealing with William as colorful, he provided himself with a timetable: two book pages a day, two years to finish the first draft, and another year for revision and polishing. He felt the need for making every sentence clear and precise, for seeing that his paragraphs had continuity. Such labor took longer than he had planned. It was nearly seven years before he had the manuscript of Volumes III and IV ready for the printer. Their twelve chapters brought England's story to the end of the war with France in 1697. The public acceptance justified the time taken in its composition. Within two months 26,500 copies were sold, and his royalties amounted to twenty thousand pounds.

Macaulay's diary frequently voiced his desire for fame and immortality. "I think posterity will not let my book die," he wrote in 1838. In addition to the wealth it brought, the success of the work replaced the Tory view of English history, as voiced by Hume in his *History of England* (1754-1761), with the Victorian concept originated with Macaulay.

In the new volumes Macaulay showed himself kindly disposed toward Mary in her trying position between her Catholic father and her Protestant husband, who divided his attention between her and Elizabeth Villiers. But William of Orange did love Mary. The last lines of Macaulay's history tell about "a small piece of black silk ribbon," found next to William's skin when his remains were being laid out. "The lords in waiting ordered it to be taken off. It contained a gold ring and a lock of the hair of Mary."

Macaulay admired William. The Dutch king had an enormous task, organizing England, reconquering Ireland, and subduing rebellious Scotland, all the while carrying on a war in France. Macaulay does seem to overestimate William's political genius, and his account of the king's yearning to return to Holland and leave England for Mary to rule is considered by some scholars an exaggeration of William's basic disillusionment with English life. With a rosy picture of the prosperity amid which William rode into London on Thanksgiving Day in November, 1697, and with the promise of a happier age, the volumes published during the writer's lifetime come to an end.

When Macaulay died he had completed only three chapters of the concluding volume, bringing the story up to the prorogation of Parliament, April 11, 1700. His sister, Lady Trevelyan, prepared this material for publication exactly as Macaulay had left it, with "no references verified, no authority sought for or examined," but she did include several fragments, among them six pages describing the death of William with which Macaulay had probably intended to conclude his work. She also compiled a fifty-page. double-column index of the five books.

In his presentation of his characters, Macaulay was often biased. As one who seemed never in doubt, who decided on one of two conflicting stories and frequently did not mention the existence of the other, he saw a man as good or bad. Historians have pointed out his failure to do justice to William Penn. Being a Whig, he used a more severe criterion toward Tories, as is evident in his discussions of James's relations with Catherine Sedley, and William's with Elizabeth Villiers. What was lamentable in William was a crime in James, whom he portrayed as a libertine and black monster.

His villains are sometimes caricatures. The crafty Robert Ferguson and Titus Oates, whose perjury about the Popish Plot brought death to the innocent, are made physically hideous. In Chapter IV, Macaulay writes of Oates's "short neck, his forehead low as that of a baboon, his purple cheeks, and his monstrous length of chin . . ." and features "in which villainy seemed to be written by the hand of God." For Marlborough, even when he was plain John Churchill, Macaulay turned to lampoons for details, though he must have known they were biased. Perhaps his dislike was based on the unproved accusation that Marlborough had tried to overthrow William.

In a work of such magnitude, errors of fact and interpretation were bound to creep in, but even some that were pointed out to Macaulay during his lifetime remained uncorrected. In other cases, he did not have access to the journals and scholarly research now available. Another source of error arose from Macaulay's attitude toward everything outside the British Isles. Except for India, where he had lived for four years, he practically ignored the colonies. American history is brought in chiefly in connection with happenings in England. Captain Kidd and the piratical activities of New England and New York appear to explain the fate of an English ministry, while the Jamaica earthquake of 1692 serves only as one more reason for the unpopularity of William's reign.

Macaulay's style has also come in for some criticism. His efforts toward clearness lead at times to verbosity and his attempts to emphasize sometimes create a paragraph where a sentence would have served. But its basic flaw is that Macaulay thought as an orator. His history is more impressive when read aloud than when read silently; it is more rhetorical than literary.

But no book lacking in inherent worth can outlast its century, and *The History of England* remains a landmark of its kind. As long as people are moved by an exciting story, interestingly told, they will continue to read Macaulay's history with both enjoyment and profit.

HISTORY OF FREDERICK II OF PRUSSIA

Type of work: Historical biography
Author: Thomas Carlyle (1795-1881)
Time: 1712-1786
Locale: Prussia, Austria, Poland, Hungary, Silesia, Moravia, Saxony, and Friesland
First published: 1858-1865

Principal personages:
FREDERICK II, called the GREAT, born Karl Friederich
FRIEDERICH WILHELM, his father, known as Frederick William I
SOPHIE DOROTHEE OF HANOVER, his mother
WILHELMINA, his older sister
GEORGE II, King of England, his uncle
ELIZABETH CHRISTINA, his wife
FRANÇOIS MARIE AROUET DE VOLTAIRE, his literary confidant and mentor

Sometimes called Carlyle's Thirteen Year War with Frederick of Prussia, the six-volume *History of Friederich II of Prussia Called Frederick the Great* is still a controversial masterwork, more talked about than read. Undisputably original, the work departs radically from the Gibbon-Macauley tradition which Carlyle called the Dryasdusts in order to bring back life to a great man, a hero who exercised the divine right of kings with military and diplomatic might to overcome diabolic wrongs. Such was the belief of Carlyle, a historian who found his theory of history explicit in one great man, and who then accommodated history to fit the thesis, a most objectionable practice to most of his critics, but lively and compelling both as literature of power and literature of knowledge, as De Quincey defined them.

Much of the knowledge, however, is outdated because of recent historical discoveries. Also, the historical method is suspect, Carlyle having explained the past in terms of his present and prejudices. Much of the documentation is edited, especially that concerning Voltaire, to the convenience of the historian. In addition, most of the geneology serves only to confuse without advancing the biography. Careful attention and great ingenuity, however, brings Frederick II to life in his setting, especially on the battlefields which Carlyle traversed with such care and understanding.

The power of the book cannot be overstated; the hundred-year test of a classic has been met. The quality of the framing, the immensity of the design and the execution, the ruggedness of style stand idiosyncratic but firm.

The biography of the author under the stress or the compulsion of writing this work is well known: five years of reading, traveling, and writing and rewriting, to bring out the vigorous first two volumes, the slow, tedious job of digesting and disgorging "truckloads of Dryasdusts" of battles and treaties, the neglecting of his fatally ill wife Jane who saw the hand of God in the enterprise, the fact that his conscience bothered him for the rest of his life.

Frederick II, known in history as Frederick the Great, shaped modern Europe almost single-handedly with his own great strength of character, personality, and resolve. To Carlyle, his might did mean right. No hero, however, made a less auspicious start, and in looking backward to the first volume no hero appeared less impressive in his fullest unpretentious dress. He possessed, however, an internal vigor, a sharp gray eye, and a cloak of inpenetrability learned well in youth.

The protracted opening of the biography traces the history of the Brandenberg and Hohenzollern families back to the Middle Ages, covering both sides of the inbred family.

Emerging from medieval beginnings

born to a militaristically and cruelly imperative father and a seemingly calm but conniving mother, young Frederick, the fourth in the family of ten, seemed destined to failure as a son and prince. His older sister, Princess Wilhelmina, his protector and confidante throughout life, thought him a "dull" student, probably unwilling to learn by rote and drill, and his father discovered him obstinate. He showed an early interest in music (he called the flute his mistress during his lonely and exiled hours), literature, and good conversation. Officially he was exposed to "mathematics, no Latin," science, and military drill.

Before his majority, he revolted against his father's stern measures and planned to flee to England, but this breach in military discipline brought death to one of the conspirators and Frederick himself barely escaped execution. Revolting also against religious conformity, he was compelled to acknowledge the doctrine of Predestination and to swear loyalty to his king before being forced to live in semi-retirement, first in Cüstrin, later in Ruppin, where within four years he had redeemed himself in the King's eyes. "That their method of training-up a young soul, to do God's will, and accomplish useful work in this world, does by no means appear to the royal mind an admirable one," Carlyle adds and explains that this episode, though it brought Frederick to stern self-discipline, caused him to draw a curtain of reticence over all important actions later.

Both Wilhelmina and Frederick were pawns in parental matrimonial machinations, but neither of the hoped-for weddings took place. The sister enjoyed her withdrawal to reading and music; her brother studied to become a monarch, at the same time courting famous literary men by correspondence, Voltaire in particular.

Then followed four years of domestic tranquillity, in which the irascible Friederich Wilhelm had finally to admit "there is much in this Fritz." He married his son to the "Insipidity of Brunswick," as the sharp-tongued Carlyle called Princess Elizabeth Christian, and they lived comfortably in Reinsberg. Apparently this marriage overcame all rumors of the indiscretions of the "foppish" prince. In 1735 he became for some time the virtual ruler during his father's illness.

In 1740 the young king took over a peaceful kingdom into which he brought culture, and Voltaire, for a brief respite. From the three-fold conquest of Silesia to the partition of Poland, King Frederick did not falter in his firm resolve to create, or re-create, an Empire, never holy, and certainly not Roman. The latter three volumes are history: accounts of treaties, battles, entertainments, aggrandizements, pomp and circumstance. With the exception of masterful descriptions of topography and scenes of battle, Carlyle falls into his own dryasdust bin. The affluent and powerful ruler has not the charm of the young prince, though he is vividly portrayed in setback and reversal, and something of his aspiration to glory has majesty in the recounting. His patronage of Voltaire, however, is another matter for discussion.

Prince Frederick had corresponded with Voltaire for several years. When Frederick became king, he invited Voltaire to visit him. The philosopher accepted the invitation because he hoped to convince the new king that peace was the best system for all, and he traveled to Germany as an emissary for Cardinal Fleury. When Frederick realized that Voltaire was acting as a diplomat for the cardinal, his relationship with the philosopher cooled rapidly and soon Frederick was attacking Voltaire's theories. Carlyle, the doughty but dour Scotsman did not like the "crafty" Voltaire or his Madame du Châtelet, even to the point of ridiculing the poor mistress in death. He asks his readers to disregard Voltaire's writings on the subject of Frederick as lies, a request we must in turn suggest in connection with Carlyle on Voltaire.

Embedded in the fourth and fifth volumes are sly though satiric barbs which enliven battles and treaties. On the other hand, there is seldom a question among scholars and none among military men of the worth of these latter volumes, which are carefully composed and documented.

The Seven Years' War and the failure to resolve the Russian problem marks the conclusion of this ambitious work, beginning with the "Afternoon and Evening of Friederich's Life." The repairing of a ruined Prussia, the partition of Poland, and the Bavarian war telescoped into the greater acts of reform, agricultural advances, and stable government. Although the last chapter is an appendix of a day in the life of the great general and ruler, "a Daguerreotype" which repeats something of an opening chapter written years before, the book effectively ends with the death of the monarch, an account of his burial, and a valediction restating the Carlylean thesis.

HISTORY OF KING RICHARD III

Type of work: History
Author: Sir Thomas More (1478-1535)
Time: 1483
Locale: England
First published: 1543

Principal personages:
RICHARD PLANTAGENET, Protector and then King of England, Richard
III
ELIZABETH, wife of deceased King Edward IV
DUKE OF BUCKINGHAM, the ally of Richard

About 1518, at the age of forty, Sir Thomas More stopped work on his *History of King Richard III*. This was the time when he was about to become a valuable member of the Council of Henry VIII, the beginning of a political career that would lead to his death and martyrdom in 1535. The work itself bears the mark of Thomas More the humanist scholar, rather than Sir Thomas the courtier or St. Thomas the martyr. Written in both English and Latin versions, presumably concurrently, the *History* was broken off at the speech of the Duke of Buckingham and Morton, Bishop of Ely, one week after Richard's coronation. The English version was then completed by Richard Grafton and published in the Hardyng and Halle chronicles, before being published in 1557 as a separate work edited by More's nephew, William Rastell. More had planned at first to extend the *History* to include the record of his own times, up to Henry's VII's death, but for reasons of his own he put the work aside.

These reasons may have had their roots in the polemical nature of the work. It is very much a treatise against tyranny and nonmoral statecraft, a refutation of Machiavelli some years before *The Prince* was even completed. Far from being a Tudor apologist, as he is sometimes thought to be, More is nonpartisan. He is against tyranny in any king, whether it be Richard III or Henry VII. A sense of his own well-being, perhaps, is what leads him to draw his moral lesson from Richard alone and not risk extending his

criticism to the kingship under Henry VII. This is the reason why one should remember that it is the Thomas More of the *Utopia* and not the Thomas More of the years of Tudor courtiership who is writing at this time.

The *History of King Richard III* is not only significant as an example of the humanistic education of princes, but it is also important as the model for other histories to follow. Historians tell us it was not equaled in excellence until the appearance of Sir Francis Bacon's *History of the Reign of King Henry VII*, written more than a hundred years later. His historical methodology is not always exemplary, for much of what he says is based on conversations with others and much is used for the polemical thesis he is trying to develop. Though not objective, nor completely accurate, the facts he presents are probably closer to the truth than many scholars in past centuries, notably Horace Walpole, have been willing to admit. Nevertheless, what strikes the reader immediately is the vivid character of the writing and the ability to make the historical characters really seem to have once been alive. The fact that over a third of the work is in the form of speeches and dialogue indicates the book's dramatic character.

The characters are wonderfully alive. Edward IV is not only a model prince who was politic in counsel and who treasured wisdom, thus fitting in well with More's thesis about kingship, but also a lustful king whose youthful excesses are duly recorded yet pardoned by

More because they did not interfere with the ruling of the kingdom. Jane Shore, moralized if not immortalized by Thomas Churchyard in *A Mirror for Magistrates,* is sympathetically drawn and her illustrious past contrasted with her harsh old age, for she was still living at the time of the writing. Henry, Duke of Buckingham, is treated as a surprisingly naïve conspirator, and the gap between his supposed guile and his actual naïveté gives More a chance to exploit fully the irony he sees present throughout the chronicle of the times.

The characters who are drawn in most depth are Queen Elizabeth and King Richard. Elizabeth, the widow of King Edward IV, is sympathetically portrayed. The great scene with her in the sanctuary of Westminster is marked by the pathos and even tragedy of her certain knowledge of what will happen if she allows her younger son to leave the protection of the sanctuary and yet the necessity for her to pretend that she trusts Richard. The verbal jousting between the queen and those trying to pry her son from her could be put almost directly upon the stage, and the final, dramatic separation of mother and son is equal to any scenes on the English stage before Shakespeare. Her clearsightedness, deliberately contrasted with Buckingham's obtuseness, gives her tragic stature while it keeps him a figure worthy of contempt.

The blackness of Richard is dramatically, if not historically, justified. In a world turned upside down by revolt, he is the personification of unnaturalness. Everything about him is unnatural, grotesque, and evil. First, there is his unnatural appearance, his crooked back and malevolent look. More tells us he was born with teeth and came out of the womb feet first. As the unnaturalness extends from his appearance to his actions, we see him causing his blood relatives to be murdered. This evil is illustrated vividly in his scheme to destroy the two princes in the Tower, a deed assigned to Sir James Tyrell and carried out by his two lackeys, John Dighton and Miles

Forest. Finally the poison spreads to the political order itself where the lack of rightful, thus natural, succession leads to many horrors. All this unnaturalness reaches a climax in the nightmares that More says came to Richard as his life drew to its violent close. These terrible dreams disturbed the restful nature of sleep and perhaps inspired Shakespeare in his own handling of the dream scene in *The Tragedy of King Richard the Third.*

The ability to depict vivid scenes such as that of Richard waking trembling from his sleep is another reason for the lasting interest of the history. This scene, the one with the queen, the dream of Stanley about the boar (symbol of Richard) with the slashing tusks, and especially the great "strawberry episode" in which Richard's innocent, offhand request for some strawberries is swiftly followed by his seizure and execution of Hastings, accomplished with a speed that leaves the reader breathless and those around Richard with no time to object, are all examples of how Thomas More is able to develop the dramatic possibilities inherent in the historical situations. Perhaps the most dramatic scene of all, at least the one that best illustrates More's gift for irony and humor, is the one in which the Duke of Buckingham and the Mayor of London are trying to prepare the people for Richard's usurpation. Buckingham is much taken with his flair for rhetoric and expects that after his long speech the people will not only be reconciled to the usurpation but will cry out for Richard to be king. Instead, his speech is met with complete silence. Buckingham turns to the mayor, who tells him that perhaps the people had not understood what he said. Buckingham repeats the whole speech, with several more flourishes, but meets with the same response. Finally some of Richard's men, planted advantageously throughout the audience, cry out for Richard, and the Duke replies that he is happy to see so many behind the new king. Not far behind the ironic detachment in the narration of this scene is a very severe condemnation of usurpation of any sort.

This depiction of character and scene is made possible by the vigorous prose employed by More. The *History of King Richard III* is a fine example of how English could be used for the purposes of rhetoric and represents a considerable prose achievement at a time when English was considered second to Latin as the language of the learned. The style is vigorous, humorous, ironic, and the rhythm is characterized by the balanced cadences. Some of the long sentences, never obscure though sometimes complex, have the balance of the prose of Samuel Johnson. Perhaps this is one of the reasons why Johnson quoted extensively from More in his essay, "The History of the English Language," which he appended to his Dictionary. As a work of prose, the *History of King Richard III* is a landmark.

Thus there seem to be four main facets of the work that demand attention and account for the book's lasting worth. It remains a valuable example of More's own thought and of the humanistic tradition in which he was educated. It is important as an example of English history, both for what it tells us of King Richard III's life and time and for the model it sets for later histories. It is important in that it gave dramatic impulse for one of Shakespeare's early plays and may have had some deeper influence on the development of his thought. But most of all, it is important for the style in which it is written and the dramatic characterization and confrontations which that style brings so vividly to life.

THE HISTORY OF MR. POLLY

Type of work: Novel
Author: H. G. Wells (1866-1946)
Type of plot: Comic romance
Time of plot: Early twentieth century
Locale: England
First published: 1909

Principal characters:
    MR. POLLY, a shopkeeper
    MIRIAM, his wife
    THE PLUMP WOMAN
    UNCLE JIM, her nephew

Critique:

A timeless comedy, as funny now as when it was first published in 1909, *The History of Mr. Polly* has strangely enough not been one of H. G. Wells' most popular novels. It is the story of a gentle man who rebels at last against the insults heaped upon him by the world and finds the peace of mind that few achieve. Wells' special genius here is in the quiet humor that startles even as it amuses. This is a highly original book, funny, moving, and pathetic.

The Story:

Mr. Polly sat on a stile and cursed. He cursed the world, his wife, and himself. For Mr. Polly was thirty-five and buried alive. He hated his slovenly wife, his fellow shopkeepers, and every other person in the world. His life, he felt, had been nothing but one frustration after another, from babyhood into his middle thirties.

Mr. Polly had been the usual adored baby, kissed and petted by his parents. His mother had died when he was seven. After the routine sketchy schooling of his class, he was apprenticed by his father to the owner of a draper's shop.

Mr. Polly was ill-suited to work in that shop or in any other. But he served out his apprenticeship and then began a progression from one shop to another, being unable to hold one position for very long. He hated the bleak life in dreary dormitories. He hated being told to hustle when he wanted to dream beautiful dreams about adventure and romance. He spent most of his money and all his spare time on books which took him away from the humdrum of socks and neckties. He did not know what it was he really wanted, but to anyone who might have studied him the answer would have been simple. He wanted companions.

When his father died, Mr. Polly found himself in possession of several useless bits of bric-a-brac and three hundred and ninety-five pounds. It seemed at first that a whole new world was open to him with this new wealth. Various relatives had sensible suggestions for him, most of them centering on his opening a little shop. He put them off, for he wanted to spend his time in taking a holiday.

At his father's funeral, which was a proper one, Mr. Polly had met aunts and cousins he did not know existed. Three of his cousins, all female, began to set their caps for their rich relative, and before he was sure of what had happened, Mr. Polly found himself in possession of a wife, his cousin Miriam, and a draper's shop. For the next fifteen years Mr. Polly was a respectable though unhappy shopkeeper. He could get on with none of his neighbors, and before long he hated his slatternly wife as much as he hated the other shopkeepers.

For these reasons Mr. Polly sat on the stile and cursed his luck. For the first time in fifteen years he found himself, in addition to his other troubles, unable to meet the forthcoming rent. As well as he could figure, he was in debt sixty or seventy pounds. He knew how Miriam would greet this news; it was just too much for him.

At this point a plan which had been forming in the back of his mind began to take shape. He would kill himself. Then the struggle would be over for him and Miriam would be provided for by his insurance. He would set fire to the shop, for the fire insurance, and before he burned up would cut his throat. Craftily he waited until a Sunday evening, when almost everyone was at church, and then carried out his plan. It worked so well that half the business area of the village was burned. But when Mr. Polly saw flames licking the leg of his trousers, he forgot all about cutting his throat and ran screaming down the street.

It was a beautiful fire, and because of it Mr. Polly was for the first time in his life a hero. He rescued a deaf old lady who lived on a top floor and for whose safety he felt responsible because he had started the fire. When the excitement was all over it dawned on him that he had forgotten to cut his throat. He felt a little guilty.

But that one night of fighting back against the world changed Mr. Polly forever. Taking only twenty-one pounds for himself and leaving the rest for Miriam, he simply disappeared. Wandering through the country, he enjoyed life for the first time. He discovered the world, the beauties of nature, the casual friendship of passing acquaintances. It was wonderful.

After a month Mr. Polly arrived at a little wayside inn run by a cheerful plump woman. They felt an instant closeness, and she offered him a job as handy

man. His duties were endless and varied, but there was an unhurried peace about the plump woman and the inn that brought joy to the soul of Mr. Polly. There was, however, a black spot on the peace. The plump woman had a nephew, called Uncle Jim, who was a brute and a villain. He had run off all other males who had ever stopped there, and he beat his aunt and stole her money. She knew that he would return again when he was out of funds. Mr. Polly knew this was not his fight, but he had started fighting on the night of the fire and he would not stop now. Sometimes running when he should have been chasing, hiding when he should have been seeking his adversary, Mr. Polly nevertheless bested the scoundrel in two encounters. Then Uncle Jim disappeared again, taking Mr. Polly's clothing and leaving in his place an unnecessary peace.

Uncle Jim did not appear again. After five years at the inn Mr. Polly began to think of Miriam and her sadness at losing her husband. Conscience-stricken, he returned to the village and there found that Miriam and her sisters had opened a tearoom, untidy but successful enough to provide their living. They thought him dead, a body wearing his clothing having been fished out of the river. Miriam, recognizing him in terror, began at once to fret about having to pay back his insurance money. She could have spared herself the worry, however Mr. Polly had no desire to reappear. He told her to keep her mouth shut and no one would be the wiser.

Mr. Polly made his way back to the inn and the plump woman. With Uncle Jim gone for good, he knew at last a mellow, wonderful peace.

Further Critical Evaluation of the Work:

Alfred Polly, the English Walter Mitty, closely resembles some of Wells' other protagonists. He is a more middle-class version of Artie Kipps and a less aggressive counterpart of the heroes of *Tono-Bungay* and *Love and Mr. Lewisham.* In *Mr. Polly,* the objects of Wells' attack are the same as in those earlier works: England's stultifying class system; the mind numbing quality of lower-class education; the boredom of "a nation of shopkeepers"; the repression of sexual joy. The novel's humor and pathos derive from Polly's wonderfully confused ways of letting his romantic spirit find expression in such an unfavorable environment.

Like a Don Quixote on a bicycle, Polly seldom discovers a correspondence between his real and imaginary worlds. "The Three P's"—Polly and two fellow apprentices—do enjoy a robust picaresque fellowship. Polly summons up all his malapropistic poetry in wooing his mysterious "lady" in the woods (while her hidden school chums stifle hysterical giggles). But the world of commerce and convention always interrupts such halcyon episodes. So, bewildered Mr. Polly is dragged into matrimony by the heavy tides of custom. His courtship is hilariously painful. Terrified by the proposal he almost offered Minnie, he impulsively proposes to Miriam, only to discover that he would rather have had Minnie. During the wedding, Polly imagines far off "a sweet face in sunshine"; he then awakens to the drab little person next to him: "It was astounding. She was his wife!"

Never quite able to identify the source of his dissatisfaction, Polly nevertheless knows that a change must come. His suicide attempt is successful—in killing the resigned, conformist, "practical" Polly. But what is the connection between the liberated romantic of the final chapters and the earlier spineless protagonist? The world of the Potwell Inn is almost purely feudal; Mr. Polly, now transformed into a latter-day Robin Hood, defends his damsel from the wicked Uncle Jim. The novel remains wonderfully comic, but Wells rather toys with our sense of psychological reality.

A HISTORY OF NEW YORK, BY DIEDRICH KNICKERBOCKER

Type of work: Humorous pseudo-history
Author: Washington Irving (1783-1859)
Time: 56 B.C. to 1664
Locale: New Amsterdam (New York)
First published: 1809

> *Principal personages:*
> HENDRICK HUDSON, the Dutch explorer
> WOUTER VAN TWILLER, the first governor of New Amsterdam
> WILHELMUS KIEFT, the second governor
> PETER STUYVESANT, the last governor
> GENERAL VON POFFENBURGH, Commander of Fort Casimir
> JAN RISINGH, Governor of the Province of New Sweden

The fun of reading a parody is heightened by acquaintance with the material burlesqued. Although Washington Irving confessed, in the "Author's Apology" added to the edition of 1848, that his idea had been to parody Samuel L. Mitchell's *A Picture of New York* (1807), a knowledge of Mitchell's book is not necessary to the enjoyment of the Irving volume. The parody is only part of the humor of *A History of New York, by Diedrich Knickerbocker,* originally begun as a collaboration of Washington and his older brother Peter, and concluded by Washington alone. The original title was *A History of New York from the Beginning of the World to the End of the Dutch Dynasty.*

The book shows the interest of its twenty-five-year-old author in history, customs, and etymology, and the burlesquing of several literary styles reveals Irving as a literary critic. His notebook supplies the names of some of the authors parodied, names now largely forgotten.

While Irving was in the course of completing the book, his fiancée, Matilda Hoffman, died suddenly, and at first he was too stunned to continue his work. Later he returned to the manuscript as an anodyne for his grief, finished it quickly, and delivered it to his publisher. About the same time he conceived the idea of ascribing the authorship of his book to an imaginary and eccentric Dutchman. The hoax was elaborately contrived. First printed in the public press was a story about the disappearance of a man named Diedrich Knickerbocker. A short time later an advertisement appeared, supposedly signed by the owner of the boarding house where Knickerbocker had lived, offering for sale "a very curious kind of written book," printed to reimburse the landlord for the old gentleman's unpaid rent.

On December 6, 1809, *A History of New York, by Diedrich Knickerbocker,* in seven parts and 130,000 words, was first offered for sale. Legends about its reception spread rapidly. A Dutch woman in Albany threatened to horsewhip the author for his slanderous account of an ancestor. A number of famous New York families were reported ready to sue the publisher. On the other hand, Walter Scott was reported with sore ribs from laughing at it.

The style wanders from playful to erudite. Evidence of Washington Irving's wide reading appears on almost every page, and voluminous footnotes clothe it with pseudo-scholarship. At first readers thought that these references were part of the humor; later scholars began tracing them to actual, though minor, Roman and Greek writers.

The author's pleasantries are apparent from the beginning. Book I, according to him, was "learned, sagacious, and nothing at all to the purpose," and he suggested that the idle reader skip it. More precisely, as Irving embarked on a study of cosmogony or creation of the world, he advised the reader to "take fast hold of his skirt or take a short cut and wait for him at the beginning of some smoother chapter."

The first books contain more chatter than matter. It is waggish humor. Noah is mentioned in connection with travel by sea, in order to get the reader to America. In one place the author defends the killing of the Indians because, as the original inhabitants of America, they did not know European procedure to improve ground; therefore they did not use the talents that Providence had bestowed upon them; therefore they had proved careless stewards; therefore they had no right to the soil; and therefore there was Biblical authority for their extermination.

In Book II the author proceeds to the settlement of the Province of Nieuw Nederlandts. He confessed that his was the procedure of Hans von Dunderbottom, who took a running start of three miles to jump over a hill, and arrived at it out of breath. So he "sat down to blow and then walked over it at his leisure."

One source of humor lies in the derivation of names. The four explorers who passed through Hell Gate and reached the Island of Manna-hata ("The Island of Manna") were named Van Kortlandt (Lack-land), Van Zandt (Earth-born), Harden Broeck (Tough Breeches), and Ten Broeck (Ten Breeches or Thin Breeches). Irving usually refers to the governors by his translation of their names. Wouter Van Twiller becomes "Walter the Doubter," living up to his name by smoking his pipe and maintaining silence in every crisis. According to Irving, this man of wisdom, five feet six inches in height and six feet five inches in circumference, settled a suit between debtor and creditor by weighing the papers containing their claims, finding them equally weighty, and decreeing that the accounts were balanced. After he made the constable pay the fees, he had no further law trials.

His successor, Wilhelmus Kieft or "William the Testy," defied the Yanokies ("Silent Men") from Mais-Tchusaeg and Connecticut by bombarding them with proclamations and by building a fortress, garrisoned by a lusty bugler, a flag pole, Quaker guns, and a windmill, to resist them. One of the amusing scenes in the book is the description of the Yankees marching to war at Oyster Bay, where they were defeated by the doughty burghers, who thereupon celebrated on oysters and wine. Later this governor disappeared; either he was lost in the smoke of his pipe or carried away like King Arthur. Peter Stuyvesant, "the Headstrong," then became the governor.

Stuyvesant is the favorite of Diedrich Knickerbocker; three volumes are devoted to him. It was he who built the Battery to hold off the Yankee invasion, though actually their own witch hunting diverted them from their proposed expedition. Then he declared war on Governor Risingh of the Colony of New Sweden, across the Delaware. By treachery Governor Risingh had captured Fort Casimir. (The earlier writer who supplied Irving's model for his flowery description of that campaign is unknown.) The Dutch fighters paused at noon to eat, and the author advised his readers to do the same. Then the battle was resumed, the only casualty being a flock of geese killed by a wild Swedish volley.

Stuyvesant had other troubles, first the Yankees from Connecticut and later the "roaring boys of Merryland"—King Charles II of England who gave New World territory to his brother, the Duke of York, and lent him a fleet to conquer it. Against the arrival of the British ships the Dutch "fortified themselves—with resolution" and burned everything in the colony of British origin. But their defense was futile. Melancholically the white-haired Knickerbocker narrates the end of his "beloved Island of Manna-hata" on August 27, 1664.

In the 1812 edition of his history Irving presents an additional account of his imaginary author and tells of his return to New York, now a British colony, and his death. He was buried, "say the old records," in St. Mark's Cemetery beside his hero, Peter Stuyvesant.

In the revised 1848 edition Irving added an "apology" and an explanation. In setting down the amusing legends of New York, he declared, he had not intended offense to living descendants of any of the old families. His purpose had been to present the history of that remote and almost forgotten age in the spirit of imaginative fancy and legend. This happy blending is his true contribution in his history, accepted by those who have never seen the book or heard of the original Harmen Knickerbocker, who came from Holland about 1674 and settled in Albany, as well as by those who have read with smiles and chuckles this playful but surprisingly accurate history of the Dutch in New Amsterdam.

HISTORY OF THE CONQUEST OF MEXICO

Type of work: History
Author: William Hickling Prescott (1796-1859)
Time: 1519-1525
Locale: Mexico
First published: 1843

Principal personages:
DON DIEGO VELÁSQUEZ, Governor of Cuba
HERNANDO CORTÉS, conqueror of Mexico
PEDRO DE ALVARADO, one of Cortés' lieutenants
MARINA, Cortés' Indian mistress
MONTEZUMA, Emperor of the Aztecs
GUATEMOZIN, Montezuma's nephew and successor
CACAMA, nephew of the emperor
PÁNFILO DE NARVÁEZ, Velásquez' lieutenant

Prescott's observations on Spanish efforts to convert the Aztecs betray his rather marked suspicion of the Catholic Church. His personal biases are less pronounced in other matters. Because Prescott deals with his narrative in dramatic terms and with an abundance of background material, particularly on the Aztec civilization, his *History of the Conquest of Mexico* has remained the classic account of the death of a civilization which in many ways rivaled ancient Egypt's.

The success of the Spanish conquest was aided by the Aztec legend of Quetzalcoatl, a benevolent god who, once having lived on earth and departed, was expected to return: tall, white-skinned, dark-bearded. When the first Spanish expeditionary party, led by Juan de Grijalva, made a preliminary exploration of the mainland, it encountered an unfriendly reception on landing. When the Aztecs happened to associate the Spaniards with the legend of Quetzalcoatl, however, they sent Grijalva away with rich gifts. As a result, Velásquez, Governor of Cuba, immediately organized a second expedition, to be led by Hernando Cortés.

Cortés' armada left Cuba on February 10, 1519, and landed on the island of Cozumel. At that time he acquired two valuable aides: a Spanish soldier named Aguilar, who had been taken captive by the natives of Cozumel during the Grijalva expedition, to serve as an interpreter, and Marina, a girl from the mainland whose mother had sold her on Cozumel. Marina became not only an interpreter but Cortés' mistress.

When the Spaniards moved on to the mainland, landing on Good Friday at what is now Vera Cruz, they stepped ashore in a Mexico significantly disunited. Montezuma, Emperor of the Aztecs, was a good warrior and a just ruler, but he was also superstitious and a lover of pleasure, with numerous enemies. There was in addition to this political unrest a vague feeling among the people that the return of Quetzalcoatl was imminent: since the days of Columbus, there had been rumors of the Spaniards, and these rumors had somehow fused with the ancient legend. Dissension among the lesser kingdoms and tribes of Montezuma's empire and the revival of the Quetzalcoatl myth were of great value to the Spaniards in their invasion of Mexico.

Because he sensed mounting resistance to his leadership, Cortés established Vera Cruz as a civil colony rather than a military base; in this way he made the expedition responsible only to the crown, not to the governor of Cuba. Later, when Juan Díaz conspired to turn the expedition back to Cuba, Cortés ordered the destruction of his fleet. With only one small ship left, the men had little to think about but the march forward.

Leaving some men behind to protect the coastal settlement, Cortés began his march toward the capital, Tenochtitlán, now Mexico City. While one of the original purposes of the expedition was the conversion of the Indians to Catholicism, the expedition, once under way, did not delay for missionary activities. Indeed, Father Olmedo, the expedition's priest, persuaded Cortés not to try to convert all of the heathen along the route.

The first pronounced resistance to the Spaniards took place among the Tlascalans, an agricultural people, but a nation of warriors as well. Two earlier battles with the Tlascalans were indecisive, but a third, fought on September 5, 1519, was in effect a victory for the Spaniards. The Tlascalan leader, Xicotencatl, continued, however, to threaten and to harass the invaders. Cortés forged ahead, his forces plundering as they went, and finally, with Xicotencatl reconciled to submission, the Spaniards arrived at Tlascala itself. In the meantime Montezuma continued in his policy of sending gifts but barring the Spaniards from Tenochtitlán.

At Cholula, Cortés learned through Marina that the natives were planning a conspiracy with Montezuma's help. Profiting from former enmity between the Cholulans and the Tlascalans, Cortés stationed Tlascalans around the city and proceeded to massacre the treacherous Cholulans.

Suspecting still further hostility, Cortés and his men moved on, passing between the mountains named Iztaccihuatl and Popocatepetl. No further resistance was forthcoming, and the expedition was shortly at a point where the fertile Valley of Mexico lay before them. Confounded by their advance and awed by their power, Montezuma at last sent his nephew Cacama with a message of welcome for the conquistadors. On November 8, 1519, Cortés and his men entered Tenochtitlán, a city built in the middle of a great lake, and Montezuma greeted them with pomp and dignity. Although the Aztecs remained outwardly friendly, Cortés continued to be suspicious of his host because he had received reports from Vera Cruz of troubles instigated by the emperor. Quauhpopoca, governor of the coastal province, was burned for his part in the disturbances, and Montezuma, taken by surprise, was seized and removed to the fortified quarters occupied by the Spaniards. Although a hostage, Montezuma conducted the business of the country as usual.

In 1520, Montezuma formally announced his subservience to Spain; the nobles concurred, and the legend of Quetzalcoatl was revived among the people. Though conditions appeared to be stable, Cortés ordered the rebuilding of his fleet.

Cortés' relations with Velásquez had now deteriorated to such an extent that the governor outfitted a rival expedition under the leadership of Pánfilo de Narváez. Gonzalo de Sandoval, the governor appointed by Cortés at Villa Rica, maintained a close watch over Narváez' attempts to establish a settlement, but Cortés felt compelled to deal with Narváez personally. Leaving the capital in the care of an aide, Pedro de Alvarado, he marched to the coast with a detachment of troops and Indian allies.

With his band of only 226 men and five horses, Cortés surprised Narváez and took him prisoner. In Cortés' absence, revolt broke out in Tenochtitlán. Alvarado, plagued by constant fears of conspiracy, had slaughtered several hundred Aztec nobles during the festival of Huitzilopotchli, the Aztec god of war. Earlier, Cortés had allowed Montezuma's brother, Cuitlahua, to act as the imperial representative during Montezuma's captivity. Bitterly vengeful after the massacre, Cuitlahua led the Aztecs in a retaliatory uprising against the Spaniards.

With his own band reinforced by two thousand Tlascalans, Cortés returned hurriedly to the capital. During the first stages of hostilities following the return of Cortés, Montezuma attempted to intercede and pacify the embattled Aztecs, but his people turned on him and he was fatally wounded. Broken and in despair, Montezuma died on June 30, 1520.

During the uprising the Aztecs had destroyed all bridges on causeways leading to the mainland, and the Spanish retreat from the city became chaotic, with heavy losses. On the plains of Otumba, however, the Spaniards and their Tlascalan allies managed to put the Aztecs to flight. The Spaniards retreated into Tlascalan territory, where they could feel safe once more. But the troops were restless after their harrowing retreat, and for a time there seemed to be some chance that the Tlascalans might join the Aztecs in common cause against the invaders. Fortunately, the Tlascalans remained friendly; in fact, their chief, before he died of smallpox, became a Christian—the first successfully converted heathen.

Guatemozin, Montezuma's nephew and successor, had sworn to drive the Spaniards from his country. As Cortés marched back toward the capital, however, he gathered from friendly tribes more Indian auxiliaries to lead against the Aztecs. Welcomed in Tezcuco by the new prince, Ixtlilxochitl, an enemy of Montezuma, Cortés' forces advanced for the final subjugation of the Aztec civilization.

More cohesive than Prescott's companion study on the conquest of Peru, *History of the Conquest of Mexico* is the author's most brilliant work. Though the book may lack profound philosophical insight, it is a vivid portrayal of a fascinating historical fact: the subjugation of a whole people by a mere handful of alien adventurers—cruel, daring intriguers who played upon the religious superstitions of their victims.

THE HISTORY OF
THE DECLINE AND FALL OF THE ROMAN EMPIRE

Type of work: History
Author: Edward Gibbon (1737-1794)
Time: 180-1461
Locale: Italy, Persia, Germany, Constantinople, Greece, Africa, Arabia, Turkey
First published: 1776-1788

Gibbon's *The History of the Decline and Fall of the Roman Empire* is the definitive history of the Roman empire from the end of its golden age to its final political and physical disintegration. The massive character of the work, testifying to the years devoted to its composition by its scholar-author, is the first, but most superficial sign, of its greatness. The style—urbane, dramatic, polished— assures its eminent place in literature. Finally, as history, the work stands or falls on the accuracy and depth of its report of events covering more than twelve centuries; and in this respect *The Decline and Fall of the Roman Empire* continues to prevail as the most authoritative study on this theme ever written. Later scholars have challenged minor points or added to the material of the history, but Gibbon's work stands as the source of all that is most relevant in the story of Rome's declining years.

The account begins with a critical description of the age of the Antonines. Gibbon concentrates on the period from 96 to 180, a time which he describes as "a happy period," during the reigns of Nerva, Trajan, Hadrian, and the two Antonines. The first three chapters are prefatory to the body of the work; they establish the claim that Rome was then at the height of its glory as an Empire— it was strong, prosperous, active, with world-wide influence. After the death of Marcus Aurelius, and with the ascent of Commodus (180-192), the Empire began its long and gradual decline. The body of Gibbon's work is devoted to a careful recital of the events that followed.

Gibbon was more interested in recounting the principal events of the Empire's history than he was in analyzing events in an effort to account for the downfall of Rome. But he did not entirely ignore the question of causes. At the close of his monumental history he reports four principal causes of Rome's decline and fall: "I. The injuries of time and nature. II. The hostile attacks of the barbarians and Christians. III. The use and abuse of the materials. And, IV. The domestic quarrels of the Romans."

It is customary for commentators on Gibbon to emphasize the reference to the opposing influences of Christianity and barbarism; and, in particular, some critics have been inclined to charge Gibbon with a lack of sympathetic understanding of the early Christian church. It is clear from Gibbon's narrative and summary statement, however, that the Christian contribution to the eventual downfall of Rome was only part of a complex of causes, and it seems unlikely that the Christian effort would have succeeded if the Roman Empire had not already been in decline.

In any case, it is not so much what Gibbon says as his way of saying it that has proved irritating. In the first place, Gibbon writes as if he were located in Rome; his view of events is from the Roman perspective, although it does not always exhibit a Roman bias. Secondly, his objectivity, when it is achieved, has been offensive to some who so cherish the Christian church that they cannot tolerate any discussion of its faults; it is as if such critics were demanding that Gibbon maintain historical impartiality about the Romans but not about the Christians.

When the *Decline and Fall* first appeared, the chapters on Christianity— Chapters XV and XVI—immediately became the objects of critical attack. Gibbon seems to have anticipated this response, for he wrote, "The great law of impartiality too often obliges us to reveal the imperfections of the uninspired teachers and believers of the Gospel; and, to a careless observer, *their* faults may seem to cast a shade on the faith which they professed." Perhaps this word of caution would have pacified the critics had not Gibbon immediately brought into play his urbane sarcasm, so distasteful to the insistently pious: "The theologian may indulge the pleasing task of describing Religion as she descended from Heaven, arrayed in her native purity. A more melancholy duty is imposed on the historian. He must discover the inevitable mixture of error and corruption which she contracted in a long residence upon earth, among a weak and degenerate race of beings."

Obviously, there is no truly impartial judge. Gibbon's tone is acceptable, even proper, to those who share his skepticism; but to others more emotionally involved in the Christian faith Gibbon seems cynical to the point of gross distortion.

Gibbon asks how the Christian faith came to achieve its victory over Rome and the other religions of the world. He rejects as unsatisfactory an answer which attributes Christianity's force to the truth of its doctrine and the providence of God. Five causes of the rapid growth of the Christian church are then advanced: "I. The inflexible, and, if we may use the expression, the intolerant zeal of the Christians. . . . II. The doctrine of a future life. . . . III. The miraculous powers ascribed to the primitive church. IV. The pure and austere morals of the Christians. V. The union and discipline of the Christian republic, which gradually formed an independent and increasing state in the heart of the Roman empire."

In his comments on these five causes Gibbon discusses Jewish influences on the Christian faith and explains how the Roman religion had failed to be convincing in its mythology and doctrine of a future life; but although he admits the persuasive power of the Christian use of the claim of immortality, he speaks with skeptical condescension of the efforts of philosophers to support the doctrine of a future life, and he is sarcastic when he mentions "the mysterious dispensations of Providence" which withheld the doctrine from the Jews only to give it to the Christians. When he speaks of the miracles, Gibbon leaves the impression that the pagans failed to be convinced because no such events actually took place. "The lame walked, the blind saw, the sick were healed, the dead were raised," he writes; but he adds that "the laws of Nature were frequently suspended for the benefit of the church."

Gibbon argues that the emperors were not as criminal in their treatments of the Christians as some Christian apologists have argued. He maintains that the Romans acted only with caution and reluctance after a considerable amount of time and provocation, and that they were moderate in their use of punishments. He offers evidence in support of his claim that the stories of martyrdom were often exaggerated or wholly false, and that in many cases the Christians sought martyrdom by provoking the Romans to violence. Gibbon concludes by casting doubt on the numbers of those punished by death, and he insists that the Christians have inflicted more punishments on one another than they received from the Romans.

Discussion of Gibbon's chapters on Christianity sometimes tends to turn attention away from the historian's virtues: the inclusiveness of his survey, the liveliness of his account, and his careful documentation of historical claims. Gibbon did not pretend that he was without moral bias, but his judgments of the tyrannical emperors are defended by references to their acts. It was not enough for Gibbon to discover, for example, that Septimus Severus was false and insincere, particularly in the making of treaties; the question was whether Severus was forced, by the imperious demands of politics, to be deceitful. Gibbon's conclusion was that there was no need for Severus to be as false in his promises as he was; consequently, he condemns him for his acts.

In similar fashion he reviews the tyrannical behavior of Caracalla, Maximin, and other emperors before the barbarian invasion of the Germans.

Gibbon names the Franks, the Alemanni, the Goths, and the Persians as the enemies of the Romans during the reigns of Valerian and Gallienus, when a weakened Empire was vulnerable to attack both from within and without. Perhaps the Empire would have wholly disintegrated at that time had not Valerian and Gallienus been succeeded by Claudius, Aurelian, Probus, and Diocletian, described as "great princes" by Gibbon and as "Restorers of the Roman world."

Several chapters of this massive work are devoted to a recital and discussion of the acts and influence of Constantine I, who reunited the Empire which had been divided under Diocletian and, as a consequence of his conversion to the Christian faith, granted tolerance to the Christians by the Edict, of Milan. One result of the consequent growth of Christianity was a growing emphasis upon the distinction between temporal and spiritual powers; the result was not that Church and state remained apart from each other, but that the bishops of the Church came to have more and more influence on matters of state. The date 476 is significant as marking the end of the West Roman Empire with the ascent to power of Odoacer, the barbarian chieftain.

The remainder of Gibbon's classic story of Rome's decline is the story of the increase of papal influence, the commencement of Byzantine rule, the reign of Charlemagne as emperor of the West, the sacking of Rome by the Arabs, the retirement of the popes to Avignon, the abortive efforts of Rienzi to restore the government of Rome, the return of the popes and the great schism, and the final settlement of the ecclesiastical state.

HISTORY OF THE PELOPONNESIAN WAR

Type of work: History
Author: Thucydides (455?-c. 400 B.C.)
Time: 431-411 B.C.
Locale: Greece and the Mediterranean
First transcribed: c. 431-400 B.C.

Principal personages:
PERICLES, founder of Athenian democracy
THUCYDIDES, an Athenian general and historian
DEMOSTHENES, the famous orator
ALCIBIADES, an Athenian general and turncoat
NICIAS, an Athenian general
ARCHIDAMUS, King of Sparta
BRASIDAS, a Spartan general

In writing his *History of the Peloponnesian War,* Thucydides, content to look for human causes behind results, refused to credit the gods with responsibility for the acts of man. Impartially he chronicled the clash of a military and a commercial imperialism: the land empire of the Spartans confronting the Athenian maritime league. Some have attributed to him an attitude of moral indifference, such as is revealed in his report of the debate between Athenian and Melian ambassadors, but he wrote with no intention of either moralizing or producing a cultural history. He was a military man interested in the vastly different political and economic patterns of Athens and Sparta. Seeing in the modes and ideals of their cultures an explanation of their ways of warfare, he wrote for intelligent readers rather than the ignorant masses.

The eight books of Thucydides' history, divided into short paragraph-chapters, provide a few facts about their author. For instance, in Book IV, he refers to himself as "Thucydides, son of Olorus, who wrote this history." He must have been wealthy, for, discussing Brasidas' attack on Amphipolis, he states that the Spartan "heard that Thucydides had the right of working goldmines in the neighboring district of Thrace and was consequently one of the leading men of the city." He also tells frankly of his failure as the commander of a relief expedition to that city and of his twenty years' exile from Athens as punishment. Appar-

ently he spent the years of his exile in travel among the sites of the battles he describes, thereby increasing the accuracy of his details. Students of warfare find that he gives descriptions of the tricks and stratagems of both siege and defense. Not until 404, after the war had ended, did he return to Athens. By tradition he was killed about 400 B.C., either in Thrace for the gold he carried, or in Athens for publicly writing his opinions.

"Thucydides the Athenian wrote the history of the war in which the Peloponnesians and the Athenians fought against one another" are the opening words of this masterpiece of Greek history. "He began to write when they first took up arms, believing it would be great and memorable above all previous wars." After this beginning Thucydides drops into the first person to explain the rivalry of Athens and Sparta, the two great states of Hellas then at the height of their power. He was proud of the advances made by his native Athens over the ways of the barbarians. "In ancient times the Hellenes carried weapons because their homes were undefended and intercourse unsafe." But swords, like the old-fashioned linen undergarments and the custom of binding the hair in knots, had gone out of style by his time.

Rivalry between the two cities was an old story; it had kept Spartans from fighting beside Athenians at Marathon. It took a commercial form, however, when the Lacedaemonians demanded that their

2652

allies, the Megarians, be allowed to market their products in Athens. Pericles, orator, statesman, and patron of the arts, took the first step toward breaking his own Thirty Years' Truce, agreed upon in 445 B.C. In a fiery oration he declared that to yield to the Spartans would reduce the Athenians to vassals.

The final break, according to Thucydides, came later. He dates the year (431) according to the calendars of the three leading states: Chrysis had been high priestess of Argos for forty-eight years; Aenesias was ephor of Sparta; and Pythodorus was concluding his archonship in Athens. In that year Thebes, at the invitation of disgruntled Plataean citizens, made a surprise attack on Plataea, a Boeotian ally of Athens.

To understand the situation fully, it is necessary to keep in mind a clash of political concepts that the historian does not mention. In 445 B.C., under Pericles, Athens had become a radical democracy whose policy was to send help to any democratically-inclined community. Sparta and its allies were just as eager to promote their conservative oligarchy. To both, self-interest was paramount.

Violation of the truce by Thebes, says Thucydides, gave Athens an excuse to prepare for war. Its walled city could be defeated only by a fleet and Sparta had no fleet. On the other hand, landlocked Sparta could withstand anything except a full-scale land invasion, and Athens had no army. The Lacedaemonians begged their friends in Italy and Sicily to collect and build ships, and Athens sent ambassadors to raise armies and completely surround Sparta. Thucydides was honest enough to admit that public opinion largely favored the Spartans, who posed as the liberators of Hellas.

Sparta moved first by invading the Isthmus of Corinth in 431 B.C. Strife during the winter and summer of the first year (as the historian divided his time) consisted largely of laying waste the fields around the fortified cities. Like many primitive peoples, the Greeks stopped fighting during planting and harvesting. (The entries frequently begin with: "The following summer, when the corn was coming into ear.") The war was also halted for their games, not only the Olympic games of 428, but the Delian, Pythian, and Isthmian games as well.

In the summer of the next year a plague broke out in Athens and raged intermittently for three years. Seven chapters of Book II provide a vivid description, "for I myself was attacked and witnessed the suffering of others." The seriousness of the plague protected Athens because enemy troops were afraid to approach its walls.

The most vivid part of Thucydides' history deals with the Syracuse campaign of 416. An embassy from Egesta, Sicily, sought Athenian help against its rival city of Selinus. The ambitious Alcibiades thought this would be a good excuse for Athens to annex Syracuse. With Alcibiades, Nicias, and Lamachus sharing the command, the best-equipped expeditionary force ever sent from a Greek city sailed for Sicily with 134 triremes, 5,100 hoplites or heavy-armed infantry, 480 archers, and 820 slingers.

Alcibiades had left behind bitter enemies who accused him of defacing sacred statues on the day the fleet sailed. Though there was no evidence against him, he was ordered home to defend himself. Fearing treachery, he fled to Sparta, where he was warmly welcomed. Informed of the Athenian expedition, the Lacedaemonians sent a military adviser to Syracuse. The Persians offered to outfit a fleet for Alcibiades to lead against Athens. His patriotism outweighed his injured pride, however, and eventually he returned to Athens and won several victories for the city before another defeat sent him again into exile. This occurred, however, after the period covered by Thucydides' history.

Meanwhile, in the campaign before Syracuse, Nicias disregarded the advice of Demosthenes and was defeated on both land and sea. "Of all the Hellenic actions on record," writes Thucydides, "this was the greatest, the most glorious to the victor, and the most ruinous to the vanquished. Fleet and army vanished from the face of the earth; nothing was saved, and out of the many who went forth, few returned home. This ended the Sicilian expedition."

The account of the expedition practically ends Thucydides' history. There is another book, but it does not rise to the dramatic pitch of Book VII. Though he lived eleven years after these events and four years after the end of the war, Thucydides did not chronicle its last stages, perhaps because they were too painful. After Alcibiades had been exiled a second time, Sparta starved the Athenians into surrender, and with this defeat their glory faded. For the next thirty years Sparta was the supreme power in Hellas.

As Macaulay wrote, Thucydides surpassed all his rivals as the historian of the ancient world. Perhaps not as colorful as Herodotus, "the Father of History," he was certainly more accurate; and while the annals of Tacitus contain excellent character delineation, the Roman's pages are "cold and poor." Thucydides may be superficial in his observations and shallow in his interpretation of events, but he did accumulate facts and dates and he presented them in a three-dimensional picture of people and places. For this reason his work has survived for more than twenty-three hundred years.

THE HISTORY OF THE PERSIAN WARS

Type of work: History
Author: Herodotus (484-c. 425 B.C.)
Time: 500-479 B.C.
Locale: Greece, Egypt, Asia Minor
First transcribed: c. 430 B.C.

Principal personages:
  CROESUS, King of Lydia
  SOLON, an Athenian statesman
  CYRUS THE GREAT, King of Persia
  DARIUS, Cyrus' cousin
  XERXES, Darius' son and successor
  LEONIDAS, King of Sparta

"Herodotus, beyng of the citye of Halicarnassus in Greece, wrote and compiled an History to the end that nether tract of time might overwhelme and bury in silence the actes of humayne kind; nor the worthye and renowned adventures of the Grecians and Barbarians (as well others as chiefly those that were done in warre) might want the due reward of immortale fame." So did the unknown "B.R." begin his translation of two of the nine books of Herodotus, "entitled with the names of the nine Muses," in 1584.

As the first to use the word "history," Herodotus deserves Cicero's title, "Father of History." To be sure, this son of wealthy upper-class parents did not have the historian's critical attitude toward his sources. Interesting anecdotes of the wars between the Greeks and the Persians of the fifth century B.C. found their way into his pages whether he could verify them or not, but he does sometimes hedge and tag certain items as hearsay. From his quotations, he must have read widely. From the details in his descriptions and the comments like "this I saw," he must have visited most of the places he mentions. The true greatness of Herodotus lies in the fact that he was the first important writer to depart from the verse of Homer and others, to produce Europe's first prose literature. Some predecessors had chronicled the beginnings of their small communities or states, but the writings of Herodotus embrace a vaster panorama, not only Greece, but Egypt, Sardis, and Babylon as well. And he looked for the reasons back of the events. His aim was to trace the early rivalries between Greek and barbarian; in the process he recounted the story of many tribes, described the lands they inhabited, and reported many of their interesting customs. Those who want greater accuracy can consult Thucydides (c.455-400 B.C.), who wrote a half-century later. His work is more objective, but it lacks the color of Herodotus' account.

The Persians maintained that the Phoenicians originally started the quarrel by kidnapping women from Argos. Later the Hellenes raided the port of Tyre and abducted Europa, the king's daughter. The wars actually started, however, when Croesus, whose magnificent court was visited by Solon, desired to enlarge his empire by conquering some of the Ionian cities of Asia Minor. When he consulted the oracles, he was persuaded at Delphi to gather his allies for an attack on the mainland. The invasion resulted in a stalemate, however, and Croesus returned to Lydia, where his capital, Sardis, was surprised and captured by the Persians. Only a rainstorm, sent by the gods, saved him as he was being burned to death. The same miracle persuaded Cyrus to free his captive after taking possession of some of his vassal states. With them, Cyrus went on to capture Babylon. However the Massagetae, under Queen Tomyris, were too strong in their resistance and strategy. Book I, titled Clio, ends with the death of Cyrus. Book II, called Euterpe, tells how

Cambyses, the son of Cyrus, became king and planned to march against Egypt. The rest of the book is a tourist's guide and history of Egypt from its beginnings to the coronation of Amasis.

Book III, called Thalia, tells how Cambyses marched against Amasis. The Egyptian king having died in the meantime, the mercenary army of his son was no match for the Persian, who then betrayed his incipient insanity by dishonoring his slain enemies.

Book IV, called Melpomene, introduces Darius, cousin of and successor to Cambyses, who let the barbarous Scythians outwit him into making peace with them.

The next volume, whose Muse is Terpsichore, begins with a plan that failed. Two Paeonian nobles, wishing to be named rulers over their people, brought their beautiful sister to Sardis, where Darius saw her, carrying water on her head, leading a horse, and spinning. Anxious to spread such industry throughout his empire, he had the Paeonians sent throughout Asia Minor. But the book deals largely with the revolt in Ionia, the growth of Athens, and its expedition, encouraged by Aristagoras, against Sardis. Although the capital was captured and burned, Darius rallied and defeated the invaders at Salamis, in Cyprus.

Erato is the Muse of Book VI, which tells of a battle fought between 353 Ionian triremes and six hundred Babylonian ships. By dissension among the enemy rather than by his strength Darius defeated them and went on to besiege and conquer Miletus. Again Greek bickering helped him during his march to Athens, but the Athenians, rallying and with a few Plataeans, successfully engaged the forces of Darius at Marathon, on September 14, 450 B.C. The Persians were driven back with a loss of 6,400 dead. The Athenians lost only 192 in the battle.

Book VII, named after Polymnia, Muse of the Sublime Hymn, tells in considerable detail how Darius prepared to revenge his defeat. Fate delayed him; re-bellious Egypt sidetracked him, and death ended all his plans. The uncertain Xerxes, succeeding his father to the throne, undertook the Egyptian campaign. After a quick victory, at the head of twenty thousand soldiers he marched on Athens. It took seven days for his army to cross the Hellespont bridge, erected by his engineers, and he, reviewing them, lamented that none would be alive a hundred years hence.

Many Greek cities were quick to surrender. Only Athens, as Herodotus boasts, dared confront the host of Xerxes. Themistocles interpreted the oracle's counsel to defend the city with "wooden walls" as advice to use the two hundred warships originally built for an attack on Egypt. Nature, however, provided a better defense in an east wind that wrecked four hundred Persian galleys along with uncounted transports and provision carriers. However, neither armed forces nor natural obstacles halted Xerxes' army until it reached the Pass of Thermopylae. There, for a day, the Athenians and Spartans checked the Persian host until a traitor revealed another path to the invader. The next day the Persians were again on the march, leaving all the defenders and twenty thousand of their own troops dead behind them.

In Book VIII, titled Urania, there is an account of Xerxes' march into Athens and the firing of the Acropolis. But the "wooden walls" of the Athenian fleet were victorious at Salamis on September 20, 480 B.C. Winner of the greatest glory was the Persian queen Artemis, who used the confusion of battle to get revenge on another Persian by ramming and sinking his ship. Because Xerxes thought she was attacking an enemy and the Athenians believed she had changed loyalties, everybody lauded her.

Fearing that the Greeks might sail on to destroy his bridge, Xerxes ordered a retreat. From the Asian mainland he sent demands for a peace treaty, promptly refused by both Athens and Sparta.

Calliope is the Muse presiding over Book IX. Here the account tells how Mardonios renewed the attack against the Greeks in the hope of sending word of victory back to Xerxes in Sardis. Though temporarily checked by the Thebans, he again entered Athens, whose citizens had fled to Salamis to assemble their allies. When they marched back, Mardonios burned what was left of Athens and retreated.

Except for cavalry skirmishes, neither side wanted to engage in battle until the sacrifices were propitious, but Mardonios' patience broke first, and he fell into a trap at Plataea, where he was killed and his army routed; there were twenty thousand Persian and Boeotian casualties against ninety-one Spartans and fifty-two Athenians killed.

At Thermopylae, Leonidas, the Spar-

tan king, had been crucified and beheaded by the Persians. Certain Greeks wanted to dishonor Mardonios in the same way, but they were told that dishonoring a dead enemy was worthy only of barbarians. Some of the fleeing Persians were pursued and killed at Mycale. Their defeat ended Xerxes' ambitious plan to crush the Hellenes.

Modern historians have honored Herodotus by translating his history into English. Littlebury's version (1709) is outstanding in style, but reveals the writer's imperfect knowledge of Greek. George Rawlinson translated the work in 1858. The most satisfactory translation is the two-volume work published by G. C. Macaulay in 1890.

HISTORY OF THE REBELLION AND CIVIL WARS IN ENGLAND

Type of work: History
Author: Edward Hyde, Earl of Clarendon (1609-1674)
Time: 1625-1660
Locale: England, Scotland, Ireland, Holland, France, and Spain
First published: 1702, 1703, and 1704

Principal personages:
CHARLES I,
CHARLES II,
EDWARD HYDE, Chancellor of the Exchequer, later Lord High Chancellor, Earl of Clarendon
LUCIUS CARY, Lord Falkland
WILLIAM LAUD, Archbishop of Canterbury
OLIVER CROMWELL,
GENERAL GEORGE MONK

The *History of the Rebellion and the Civil Wars in England* has been called the first great English history, without which Macaulay's famous continuation would not have been possible. Clarendon's work was first published in three volumes, in 1702, 1703, and 1704, at Oxford, through the effort of his second son. *The Life of Edward, Earl of Clarendon, . . . Written by Himself,* a companion volume, was written expressly for his children and was not published until 1759. The history was begun informally, being compiled during his two periods of exile in which the earl hoped that something could be learned to improve the future from the "wicked times" of vindictive lawlessness. As an Anglican, loyalist, and legalist he acted always out of high principles during the exasperating Short and Long Parliaments, in exile, and in the Restoration court "full of excess, idleness, and luxury; and the country full of pride, mutiny, and discontent."

The work is not known for its accuracy, although the first draft was completed when state documents were available, nor is it known for its completeness; Clarendon was biased and treated in detail the Royalist argument, to the neglect of the Commonwealth's. However, he was aware that his art and method were different, full, vigorous, "with fidelity and freedom of all I know of persons and things."

As an Oxford bachelor of arts in the Middle Temple, he had moved among the literati and intelligentsia; Ben Jonson and Lord Falkland were his mentors and friends. For twelve years a member of the House of Commons, he was quick to follow the lead of Falkland, learning statesmanship under his tutelage. Clarendon was inspired by the feeling of the revolutionary times, by classical historians whom he knew well, and by historians of his own time, notably Hooker. The history proper begins with his own removal from Parliament to the position of trusted adviser, chief defendant and speech writer, and Chancellor of the Exchequer for the ill-fated but kingly Charles I. Clarendon's advice to Charles I, which was not heeded, was to bring about a conciliation of the factions of Puritans, Royalists, Levellers, Catholics, and Presbyterians. As Chancellor of the Exchequer, Clarendon raised money to support the royal cause and provide a government in exile. During this time he also wrote defenses of the king against the scurrilous accusations of Cromwell's faction. When King Charles delivered himself to the Scottish army at Newark in 1646, his trusted adviser turned to the aid of the exiled Prince of Wales. After a break with Queen Henrietta Maria in France, he went to Spain in an attempt to enlist Catholic forces in a restoration of the monarchy.

In exile in Jersey, the great statesman continued his defense of the king while writing his great work. Clarendon advised Charles II at the time of the Restoration in 1660, and it is here that the *History of the Rebellion* comes to a conclusion, although during his banishment in 1668 Clarendon replaced some of the documents with portraits of influential and pivotal figures of the period. Clarendon never deserted his friends. He defended them against malicious slander, high treason, and any false charges made in the heat of the emotional times. The portraits were deeply and artistically conceived in their candor and touching in their defence of innocence, particularly in death of King Charles I, the Archbishop of Canterbury, and Lord Falkland, who were executed at the time of the regicide.

The overcoming of his wise counsel through malicious mischief on the part of his highborn enemies, and in the face of thirty years of service to two monarchs, is characterized by restraint even when he faced a doubtful posterity. His autobiography, written in the third person and for his family, extends the history, recounts the disappointment of his daughter's marriage to the Duke of York, later King James II, contains his praise of General George Monk, his elation over the return of the monarchy, his disappointment in the "French-influenced" court of Charles II, his good advice for avoiding the Dutch menace, and his sincere praise of crown and church.

The keynote to this remarkable work is Clarendon's respect for and adherence to constitutional law: he opposed Parliament when it became dictatorial and the king when he became irresponsible. Clarendon's reputation, then as now, was clear of any taint of self-serving, although his banishment seemed to be the result of overuse of power and complicity in the war with the Dutch. His judgment, discounting his own claims, always was enlightened and his conciliatory manner as exemplary as that of Sir Thomas More; but always his conscience was clear and his Anglican, Royalist, legalistic actions were consistent with his views.

In that "fit season" of the publication, his sons were loyal servants of the king, his daughter was the Queen of England and later the mother of queens, and his reputation was cleared. His grand canvas of cause and effect, together with his insight into men and their motives, has produced a monumental work almost without parallel in history and letters. He was aware that his panoramic view was an innovation, that his analyses of personages manipulating events with such dire consequences were literary as well as historical; and he wrote a rhythmic prose, perhaps too antithetical and parenthetical even for the convoluted style of those times, yet with verve and directness. His work looks toward the Age of Reason.

HISTORY OF THE REIGN OF KING HENRY VII

Type of work: Biographical history
Author: Sir Francis Bacon (1561-1626)
First published: 1622

> *Principal personages:*
> HENRY VII, the first Tudor monarch of England
> CHARLES VIII, King of France
> FERDINAND OF ARAGON, King of Spain
> LAMBERT SIMNELL and
> PERKIN WARBECK, impostors claiming the English throne

Sir Francis Bacon wrote in his *Advancement of Learning* of the importance of biography as a branch of historical writing, pointing out that it is individuals who direct the actions that are recounted in historical chronicles and suggesting that these events can be best examined in the light of the characters of the men who make them. It is this principle that underlies Bacon's *History of the Reign of King Henry VII*, which is one of the first analytical biographies in the English language.

Bacon wrote his history of Henry VII in a few months during the year following his impeachment in 1621. He was exiled from London, and therefore from many of the sources that would have enabled him to produce new information about Henry's reign. He depended heavily upon the sixteenth century chronicles, especially the history of the early years of the century written by Polydore Vergil. What is original and noteworthy in Bacon's volume is his study of the personality of his subject and its effect upon the course of the English nation during his reign. Bacon is original, too, in his strong emphasis upon the laws of Henry's day; as a distinguished lawyer and Lord Chancellor of England at the height of his career, he was thoroughly familiar with the statute books and the development of the common law, and he felt the significance of innovations in the reign he chronicled. He praised Henry's laws as "deep, and not vulgar; not made upon the spur of a particular occasion for the present, but out of providence of the future, to make the estate of his people still more and more happy; after the manner of the legislators in ancient and heroical times."

Bacon follows a chronological plan in his history, concentrating upon the years after the Battle of Bosworth Field, where Henry dethroned Richard III in 1485. His account alternates between narration and set speeches in the manner of the classical historians; the conversations between important personages add considerable interest to the book.

Bacon presents many facets of Henry's personality as he relates his actions on first gaining the throne. There is a masterful analysis of the king's deliberations about the wisest grounds for claiming royal power, which he held by conquest; through his wife, the eldest surviving child of Edward IV and the heir through the Yorkist line; and in his own right, less clear, through the Lancastrian line. Bacon pictures Henry's reasoning in this manner: "the inconveniences appearing unto him on all parts, and knowing there could not be any interreign, or suspension of title, and preferring his affection to his own line and blood, and liking that title best which made him independent; and being in his nature and constitution of mind not very apprehensive or forecasting of future events afar off, but an entertainer of fortune by the day; resolved to rest upon the title of Lancaster as the main, and to use the other two, that of marriage and that of battle, but as supporters, the one to appease secret discontents, and the other to beat down open murmur and dispute."

Through his account of the major

events of the reign—the successive uprisings of discontented commoners and fractious noblemen; invasions by impostor-Plantagenets who claimed to be true heirs to the throne; lengthy negotiations with Emperor Maximilian, the ineffectual ruler of the Holy Roman Empire, and with King Charles VII of France, a considerably more formidable foe; and the slow formation of an alliance with the politically sagacious Ferdinand of Spain, whose throne rested on foundations almost as uncertain as Henry's—emerges a picture of the English king as a man cautious and deliberative, reluctant to fight, yet skillful in using the threats of war to fill his own coffers, merciful to most of his rebellious subjects, but ruthless in the extermination of others, notably Edward Plantagenet, one of the few surviving Yorkist claimants to the throne, when their deaths seemed expedient.

Henry's skill in the game of statecraft is evident in Bacon's discussion of the lengthy and somewhat confusing conflict with Charles of France over the control of the Duchy of Brittany. The author cites a message from Henry to Charles proclaiming the English monarch's friendship for both the French king and the Duke of Brittany and offering his services as mediator. Bacon explains Henry's desire to avoid military conflict whenever possible: "A fame of a war he liked well, but not an achievement . . . and he was possessed with many secret fears touching his own people, which he was therefore loath to arm."

The liveliest portions of Bacon's narrative are the accounts of the uprisings on behalf of Lambert Simnell and Perkin Warbeck, boys brought forth by opponents of the king, the former as Edward Plantagenet, the latter as Richard, Duke of York, one of the princes murdered in the Tower of London. Both impostors were supported by English noblemen and by Continental sympathizers with the Yorkist cause, especially Margaret, Duchess of Burgundy, a close relative of Edward IV. Henry coped skillfully with

both plots, punishing their instigators and trying to make examples of the youthful conspirators. Simnell was made a kitchen boy; Perkin, whose campaign came far nearer success and lasted for several years, became a juggler at court for a time. However, after he had escaped, been arrested again, and been imprisoned in the tower, he initiated a new and far more threatening conspiracy with the real Edward Plantagenet, Earl of Warwick, who, as the nephew of Edward IV, had a legitimate claim to the throne. As a result of their plot both Warbeck and the prince were executed. Henry incurred considerable public displeasure by his severity with them, though he tried to place the blame on his ally, Ferdinand, who co-operated by saying that he could not allow his daughter, Katherine of Aragon, to wed the Prince of Wales so long as Warwick lived as a threat to the succession of his future son-in-law.

Bacon does not gloss over the later years of Henry's rule, when his henchmen Empson and Dudley perverted the laws of the realm to confiscate land and wealth from subjects all over the kingdom. Henry's avarice increased with his age, and he left enormous wealth at his death, riches soon to be dispersed by his pleasure-loving son, Henry VIII.

Bacon concludes his account of Henry's reign with a character sketch of the king. He summarizes the traits of character that he has shown influencing English policy throughout the reign, portraying Henry as a shrewd ruler, a crafty statesman who calculated the effects of all his actions and "knew the way to peace was not to seem to be desirous to avoid wars." He was his own chief counselor, a man who had no really close friends or advisers. Empson, Dudley, and others who performed his less attractive tasks served him only as the "instrument" does the "workman." Henry's independence is clear in this comment: "To his confederates abroad he was constant and just, but not open. But rather such was his inquiry, and such his closeness, as they stood in the light towards him, and he stood in the dark to them; yet without strangeness, but with a semblance of mutual communication of affairs."

Henry chose his ministers generally for their cleverness rather than for their birth; he commanded the grudging respect of the nobility, but he was never certain of their loyalty. Yet, unlike many monarchs of his era, he could trust his closest counselors implicitly; only one betrayed him during all the years of his reign.

The king emerges from Bacon's account as a clever man, but a cold and withdrawn one; he seems also to have been a dutiful husband and father. He was far from the most appealing of men, but Bacon, whose temperament was in some ways like Henry's, recognized his greatness: "Yet take him with all his defects, if a man should compare him with the Kings his concurrents in France and Spain, he shall find him more politic than Lewis the Twelfth of France, and more entire and sincere than Ferdinando of Spain. But if you shall change Lewis the Twelfth for Lewis the Eleventh, who lived a little before, then the consort is more perfect. For that Lewis the Eleventh, Ferdinando, and Henry, may be esteemed for the *tres magi* of the kings of those ages. To conclude, if this King did no greater matters, it was long of himself: for what he minded he compassed."

THE HIVE

Type of work: Novel
Author: Camilo José Cela (1916-   )
Time: 1943
Locale: Madrid
First published: 1951

Principal characters:
DOÑA ROSA, owner of the café "La Delicia"
MARTIN MARCO, a poor poet
JULITA, the niece of Doña Rosa
CELESTINO ORTIZ, the owner of the café "Aurora"
DON IBRAHIM DE OSTOLANZA Y BOFARULL, the candidate for the Royal
Academy

"The Hive" is the name Cela gives Madrid, specifically in a passage describing dawn breaking after the turgid night life of the city. The book is a latticework, a crisscrossing of innumerable lives; the number of characters has been estimated at some one hundred and sixty. Not all of them are principals, of course, but even where only brief glimpses are given of some of them, they all serve to illuminate the whole fabric of shifting contacts. In fact, in any sense of a structured novel, there are not even any principals. Some characters merely appear more often than others.

In some ways *The Hive* resembles the picaresque novel. The majority of the characters are down-and-outers, or on the verge of poverty. Those who are managing to make a prosperous or respectable living are largely grasping or mean. Hunger is always present. The need for the peseta haunts the lives of the Madrileños. Where can one get the most for it? Who does not have it and is trying to get by without it, bluffing or hoping? But the work is not the traditional picaresque novel with an anti-hero whose personality, in the service of many masters, holds the work together. Here there are only recurrent situations, without either the peripatetic progress of the *pícaro*, or the attainment by him, sometimes, of respectability. No narrative unfolds. None of the characters shows spiritual change. Thus the book is more like Pío Baroja's kind of picaresque world, formless but revealing the swarming life of the city.

The two characters most often seen are the domineering Doña Rosa and the shabby Martin Marco, the nearest thing to an anti-hero. Doña Rosa, owner of the café "La Delicia," is the presiding genius of the book. She is in a sense the queen bee of the hive, although there is nothing regal about her. She is avaricious, a slave driver, and a bully. When young, she had been courted by the wastrel son of a marquis. Today, though she is fat and dirty, she is a rich woman, covered with diamonds. In addition to the café, she owns the house it is in and four apartment buildings, located in other parts of Madrid, whose tenants she terrorizes. She is shareholder in a bank, and it is rumored she has trunks full of gold scattered here and there.

The public that visits Doña Rosa's comes in two waves, as is the case, Cela says, with all cafés: the after-lunch group, around three o'clock, for coffee and, he adds, bicarbonate, and the after half-past-seven group. Early arrivals of the latter receive angry looks from the former; and the same thing happens to stragglers from the afternoon group. Each group likes to feel that it is the Old Guard.

But although the action centers mainly around Doña Rosa's café, other places figure frequently in the kaleidoscopic shifts of scene—the café "Aurora" owned by Celestino Ortiz, who had fought in an anarchist unit during the Civil War and who keeps a copy of Nietzsche under the bar; the house of assignation of the widow Doña Celia Vecino de Cortés, who keeps the portrait of her dead husband Don Obdulio Cortés López on the wall of the most expensive bedroom; the dairy of Doña Ramona Bragado, which is a cover-up for the same line of business, purchased by her out of money left her by the Marquis de Casa Pela Zurana, a senator and twice Undersecretary of Finance, whose mistress she had been.

Still other cafés are visited, as well as the interiors of people's apartments; for example, that of Doña María Morales de Sierra, who spies on everybody in the neighborhood and reports all she sees or hears to her bored husband, a technical assistant at the Ministry of Public Works. Cela likes to insert sly references to important-sounding positions (a dig at Spanish *empleomanía* or urge for government employment).

Martin Marco is a poet who writes (for warmth) either in the Central Post Office or the Bank of Spain; paper is plentiful in both places—telegraph or deposit forms. He carries cigarette stubs in an envelope. He sleeps on a cot in a storeroom of the apartment of Pablo Alonso, and sometimes when his brother-in-law, Roberto González, is not at home, he cadges a meal from his sister Filo, with whom it is strongly suggested he has had incestuous relations in the past.

Roberto is a free-lance bookkeeper who works for, among others, Señor Ramón, a baker. Pablo Alonso is in business but apparently does nothing much about it; he spends most of his time with his mistress Laurita, who is beginning to bore him with her doglike devotion.

One of the regulars at Doña Rosa's is Señorita Elvira, a poor drab who maintains some of her liaisons through correspondence, cadges cigarettes, dines on a *peseta*'s worth of chestnuts, and suffers horrifying nightmares. In the past, one of her patrons was Don Pablo (not Pablo Alonso) who still watches her with interest at Doña Rosa's, much to his wife Pura's disgust.

The manager of Doña Rosa's is Consorcio López, who came to Madrid from the town of Tormelloso; there he had seduced Marujita Ranero and, threatened by her brother, had fled the town. Marujita later gave birth to twins and sent pictures of them to Consorcio, who is quite proud of his unofficial family. Marujita, now Doña María Ranero de Gutiérrez, and rich, comes to Madrid with her husband. Because he is an invalid, she packs him off to a nursing home and loses no time in renewing her affair with Consorcio. She also offers to buy out Doña Rosa.

One of the most amusing characters is the pompous Don Ibrahim de Ostolanza y Bofarull, who is practicing his speech of acceptance into the Royal Academy. A neighbor in his apartment building, Don Leoncio Maestre, bursts in to tell him that Doña Margot, another neighbor, has been strangled with a towel. She was the mother of Julián Suárez Sobrón, an effeminate character known as The Lady Photographer. Unknown to his neighbors, he had come home, found his mother dead, and rushed out in panic to a meeting with his friend Señor Giménez Figueroa, known as The Chip. These two end up in jail for questioning, while Don Ibrahim presides over a meeting of the tenants of the building to decide what to do. The Judge Magistrate has already been to the scene, arrested Don Leoncio Maestre, who after discovering the body is in a state of shock, and told the rest to go home; he will call them if he needs them. However, Don Ibrahim feels the need for the meeting, and here again Cela reveals his extraordinary flair for assembling resounding names and variegated backgrounds.

Among those present we find Don Antonio Pérez Palenzuela, an employee of the National Syndicates, who feels that he should be in charge of the proceedings; Don Camilo Pérez, a chiropodist; Don Exuperio Estremera, a priest; Don Lorenzo Sogueiro, the owner of the Fonsagradino café; Doña Juana Entrena de Sisemón; Don José María Olvera, a captain in the Army Ordnance Corps; Arturo Ricote, a clerk in the Banco Hispano Americano; Don Julio Maluenda, a retired merchant marine officer; and Pedro Tauste, the owner of a shoe repair shop called "The Footwear Clinic."

Don Ibrahim, continuing to make long-winded speeches, proposes that they all mention Doña Margot in their prayers and pay for a funeral mass. This they all vote enthusiastically to do.

Doña Rosa's sister, Doña Visitación, is married to Don Roque, and they have three daughters—Julita, Visi (or Visitación, named for the mother), and Esperanza. They have a maid with the engaging name of Escolástica. Esperanza is the only one of the daughters engaged; she is to marry Agustín Rodríguez Silva, the owner of a drugstore and fifteen years her senior. Julita is in love with Ventura Aguado, a law student who has failed the examinations for public notary for seven years, not counting—Cela inserts—the war years. The two end up in a liaison at Doña Celia's, under the eyes of Don Obdulio's portrait. An ironic touch is that Julita's father, with Lola, maid to Doña Matilde, a pensioned widow, patronize the same establishment. They pass each other on the stairs. Julita says she has just been to the photographer. Don Roque is on his way to see a sick friend. The only one blissfully unaware of all that is going on is Visitación, the mother.

Petrita, the maid to Filo and Don Roberto, is sent to Celestino's café on an errand. When mention is made of recent peevishness on Martin Marco's part and the fact that he is in debt to Celestino, she sells herself to the latter for the twenty-two pesetas owed, because she is fond of Marco.

Victorita, a packer at a printer's, is in love with the sickly Paco, and shamelessly earns money through the offices of the go-between Doña Ramona, in order to keep him alive. Paco is the brother of Eloy Rubio Antofagasta, a poor ex-student who has just been given a job by Don Mario de la Vega, the owner of a

printing shop. Don Mario is also the one making a financial deal for Victorita's favors.

Martin encounters an old friend from the university, Nati Robles, who had been an earnest, political-minded, unattractive girl. Now she is a beauty, elegantly dressed. Martin asks Nati for five pesetas, so that he can pay for standing her a treat. She gives him fifty and tells him to buy her a present. When he finally selects a print for her at the bookshop of a friend, he learns that he has lost what was left of the money. Seoane, the violinist at Doña Rosa's, finds it and is thus able to buy some dark glasses for the weak eyes of his sickly wife.

There are many more characters in Doña Rosa's gallery: Don José Rodríguez de Madrid, a magistrate's clerk, is held in envy by all his friends because he has won a prize in the lottery. The fact that it was only forty pesetas does nothing to dispel their wonder; there is a young poet, given to fainting spells in cafés, who must be carried, unconscious to the lavatory, where the smell of the disinfectant revives him; there is another pensioned widow, Doña Asunción, the friend of Doña Matilde. Besides visiting Doña Rosa's they play cards at Doña Ramona's dairy. Doña Asunción has two daughters, one married to a clerk in the Ministry of Public Works, the other living with a university professor in Bilbao, a fact of which Doña Asunción is very proud. Doña Matilde has a son who is an impersonator in Valencia; his stage name is Florentino de Mare Nostrum.

The staff at Doña Rosa's is as varied as the clients: Padilla, a kind-hearted cigarette boy who lends cigarettes to Señorita Elvira; Luis and Pepe, hardened waiters, indifferent to Doña Rosa's tirades; Alfonsito, the messenger who goes out for the newspapers and is always scolded by Doña Rosa for staying away too long; and the musicians—Macario, the pianist, and Seoane, the violinist. Their czardas and Viennese waltzes are a particular delight to Doña Matilde and

Doña Asunción. Macario is engaged to a girlish, homely woman, thirty-nine years old. Seoane and his sickly wife live in a damp, basement flat they rent for seventy-five pesetas a month. But the apartment is close to the café and he can walk to work.

There is also a little gipsy boy, six years old, a flamenco singer, who haunts the neighborhood. He is self-supporting and, in the midst of all the tawdriness he witnesses, curiously innocent. When kicked by a drunken prostitute early in the day, his only thought is that it is a terrible time of day to be drunk. He collects the copper coins flung to him by his audiences, and by the time he has sung from one to eleven he has enough to get his supper at an inn where he is known —a plate of beans, bread, and a banana, for three pesetas, twenty céntimos. After his supper, he sings until two in the morning. He sleeps under a bridge on the outskirts of Madrid.

There is some resemblance in the pictures of Madrid night life between *The Hive* and José Suárez Carreño's *The Final Hours*. But the latter centers around three main figures, and lacks the amused satirical outlook of Cela. In *The Hive* the handling of personal and local names is one aspect of Cela's attitude. "Dons" and "Doñas" are sprinkled among the resounding names of the pretentious, the mediocre, and the disreputable. One firm mentioned is that of "Casimiro Pon's Widow and Sons, Threads and Yarns." A man who inherited a cakeshop called "The Sweetener" from a brother who died in the Philippines changed its name to "The Site of Our Forefathers." The

final heir changed this to "The Golden Sorbet." A fairly successful bar called "The Earthly Paradise" became run-down and the woman owner ran off with a drunken guitar player. There is even a profane parrot named Rabelais.

In the end, Martin Marco appears to have done something shocking, but the reader does not know specifically what it is. From the timing and from the sequences one can read between the lines, and from what we know of his inherent nature, it would not seem to be connected in any way with Doña Margot. But a newspaper item indicates to his friends and sister and brother-in-law that something must be done for him, that he must be got out of the way. The book ends with Martin's visit to the grave of his mother; he is filled with thoughts of reforming his life and still unaware himself of what he has done. The author leaves him with a sense of foreboding. He has read all of the newspapers which he carries in his pocket except the part concerning himself.

This book is a long way from the contrived *tremendista* cynicism of Cela's *The Family of Pascual Duarte*, published in 1943. (*Tremendismo* was a popular literary trend of the 1940's which emphasized the horrifying mainly for its own sake.) Here, in spite of his sardonic attitude, and the possibility that he himself might be the first to disavow it, Cela reveals a compassion for the unfortunates, the failures, the outcasts that inhabit the "hive", and along with it, in spite of the world of venality and sometimes cruelty displayed, there is always present the Spanish sense of decorum.

HIZA-KURIGE

Type of work: Tales
Author: Jippensha Ikku (1765-1831)
Time: Late eighteenth and early nineteenth centuries
Locale: Japan
First published: 1802-1814

Principal characters:
YAJIROBEI (YAJI), a picaresque traveler
KITAHACHI (KITA), his companion

The first of this series, which was published in eight sections, was titled in various ways, the common part being *Hiza-kurige* (literally, "Knee-chestnut-horse"), usually translated as *Shank's Mare.* The publication dates of these sections are (1) 1802; (2) 1803; (3) in two volumes, 1803; (4) in two volumes, 1805; (5) in two volumes and a supplement in one volume, 1806; (6) in two volumes, 1807; (7) in two volumes, 1808; and (8) in three volumes, 1809. The Prologue, in one volume, was published in 1814.

This work was so popular that it is supposed to have raised the price of paper in the city of Edo, now Tokyo, where it was first published. Ikku's important contribution to Japanese literature through this work was the creation of a fresh type of popular literature—the comic novel. Travel accounts had been written ever since the tenth century, but these early models extolled the beauties of nature, emphasized poetry, and appealed to readers among the educated aristocracy. Ikku turned this form into a popular one for the commoner.

The use of two traveling companions was by no means a new device, but whereas in previous works they were merely mechanical and shadowy, Ikku's two characters are robustly alive. They are not even the better educated, more refined of the commoners living and working in the bustling streets of Edo, but deliberately chosen stereotypes of the lower classed Edo-ite: exuberant, emotional, quick to anger and as quick to forget, with little strength of character to resist temptation, whose wit and skills are untrained, but yet knowing and

shrewd with a shallow wisdom. By making these two characters fall into predicaments of their own making, Ikku created a broad humor, often bawdy but always good, a humor that was mirth-provoking without the sting of satire.

The story line is extremely simple, the treatment episodic. In downtown Edo there lived one Yajirobei, called Yaji for short. He had been born into a merchant family of some means in the town of Fuchû, in the province of Suruga (Ikku's own birthplace), but indulgence in worldly pleasures involving women and wine had greatly reduced his circumstances. Taking with him an actor named Hana-no-suke (which in modern idiom might be translated "Schnozzola"), later renamed Kitahachi, or Kita for short, whom he patronized, Yaji had come to live in Edo. For a time he sent Kita out in servitude, but the poverty of such circumstances proved boring and anyway, Kita was soon discharged. Yaji then sold the belongings he still possessed and with the proceeds set out with Kita on an extended journey. The route they chose was the Eastern Sea Circuit (Tôkai-dô), extending from Edo to Kyoto, including a trip to Japan's holy Great Shrine of Ise, and ending in the commercial city of Osaka.

Ikku himself had made the same trip.

Using material from his own experience, perhaps, he added episodes and occurrences of which he had only heard, and he was not above using material found in the *Kyôgen*, those comic interludes performed in programs of the *Nô* drama, some almost in their entirety, others only thinly disguised. These episodes introduce the reader to particular places of interest along the Eastern Sea Circuit, and each ends with a line or two of humorous verse which greatly points up the humor. This humor is also expressed in play on words, puns, and the clever use of pivotal words joining one phrase to the next. The work has been translated into French and into English. An English translation by Thomas Satchell is titled *Hizakurige* (*Tokaido Circuit*) (Kobe, Chronicle Press, 1929). One section of this translation is included in Donald Keene's *Anthology of Japanese Literature* (New York, 1955).

The twelve parts of the *Zoku Hiza-kurige* (*Shank's Mare, Continued*) were published under various titles, each applicable to the part which it represented. Only Parts 11 and 12 contain the title *Zoku Hiza-kurige*. Each part is in two volumes, with the exception of Part 12, which was published in three volumes. The publication dates were: (1) 1810; (2) 1811; (3) 1812; (4) 1813; (5) 1814; (6) 1815; (7) and (8) 1816; (9) 1819; (10) 1820; (11) 1821; and (12) 1822. This work has not yet been translated.

In Ikku's sequel, the two companions go to the island of Shikoku to worship at the Kompira Shrine, back to Honshū to visit Miyajima, then eastward over the back way, the Kiso Road, to Zenkô-ji in Shinano Province, on to the famous Kusatsu Hot Springs, and finally back to Edo. The style and the format of the continuation remain the same as in the original series.

H. M. S. PINAFORE

Type of work: Comic opera
Author: W. S. Gilbert (1836-1911)
Type of plot: Humorous satire
Time of plot: Latter half of the nineteenth century
Locale: Portsmouth harbor, England
First presented: 1878

Principal characters:
JOSEPHINE, the Captain's daughter
RALPH, the lowly sailor who loves Josephine
SIR JOSEPH PORTER, First Lord of the Admiralty, and Josephine's suitor
THE CAPTAIN, Josephine's father
LITTLE BUTTERCUP, who loves the Captain

Critique:

W. S. Gilbert shared the honors of this operetta with his composer-partner, Sir Arthur Sullivan. *H. M. S. Pinafore; or, The Lass That Loved A Sailor* was written to be sung and acted on the stage; it was not meant to be published and read by itself. Gilbert and Sullivan obviously were poking fun at the extravagances of grand opera, and at the improbable plots in particular. The plot of *Pinafore*, which effectively disregards the element of time, is a successful vehicle of comedy and satire. Every song, every scene is full of mischievous and clever rhymes, adroit and ingenious dialogue.

The Story:

Lying at anchor in Portsmouth harbor, the *Pinafore* was the scene of hectic activity, for Sir Joseph Porter, K.C.B., First Lord of the Admiralty, had announced his intention to visit the ship. The sailors swabbed the decks and were inspected by the Captain, who was as content with them as they were with him. One member of the crew, however, was far from happy. Ralph, the lowly foremast hand, was sunk in gloom and despair. He loved Josephine, the Captain's daughter, but because of his low rank she repulsed his advances and rejected his love.

Before Sir Joseph's arrival, Little Buttercup came on board, plying her trade as a seller of ribbons and laces, scissors and knives, treacle and toffee. In a conversation with the Captain she hinted that appearances are often deceiving. The

Captain noticed that Little Buttercup had physical charms not displeasing to him.

Sir Joseph's barge approached, and the First Lord was soon on board, accompanied by his sisters, his cousins, and his aunts. After inspecting the crew, he gave them instructions for success. His own formula had been simple enough. He had polished door handles, stuck close to his desk, and never gone to sea. Sir Joseph then proceeded to the purpose of his visit. He had come to ask Josephine to marry him.

Josephine had no intention of marrying Sir Joseph, whom she disliked. Not able to give an outright refusal, she informed him that marriage with such a high-ranking officer was impossible because she was only a captain's daughter. Sir Joseph admired her modesty, but brushed the objection aside. Rank, he assured her, was absolutely no barrier, for love leveled all rank. Josephine hastened to agree with him, and everyone immediately assumed that a marriage would soon take place.

Giving up all hope of winning Josephine, Ralph put a pistol to his head and prepared to pull the trigger. At that moment Josephine rushed in, told him not to destroy himself, and proclaimed her undying love for him. At this turn of events there was general rejoicing among Ralph's messmates, with the exception of an unsavory character by the name of Dick Dead-eye.

The couple laid plans to steal ashore the next evening to be married. Once the ceremony was performed, they reasoned, nobody could do anything about it. But Dick Dead-eye went to the Captain and warned him of the plan. Accordingly, just as the lovers and their accomplices were quietly tiptoeing away, the Captain entered, enraged at Ralph's presumption and at the low company in which he found his daughter. Ralph was thrown into the brig.

Attracted by the Captain's swearing, Sir Joseph came rushing up in time to hear what had happened. The sisters, the cousins, and the aunts were horribly shocked. Sir Joseph was equally shocked, so shocked that he administered a very severe rebuke to the Captain. In the midst of the argument, Little Buttercup appeared. To the astonishment of every-

one, she announced that many years ago she had been a baby-farmer. Two infants had been put into her care, one of lowly birth, the other of high position. Because she was very fond of one of them she had changed them around. The Captain was really of low birth, and Ralph was the patrician.

This astounding announcement resulted in a very odd situation which was quickly and amicably arranged. The Captain changed places with Ralph, who became captain instead. Sir Joseph announced that he could not marry Josephine since she was only the daughter of a common sailor. Accordingly, Josephine married Ralph; the Captain married Little Buttercup, and Sir Joseph had no one to marry except a well-born cousin.

Further Critical Evaluation of the Work:

In December 1878, one year after the moderately successful production of *The Sorcerer,* William Schwenck Gilbert offered his musical collaborator, Arthur Seymour Sullivan, a libretto for a new comic opera, with a note appended: "I have very little doubt whatever but that you will be pleased with it." Sullivan was indeed pleased, and although he was suffering intense pain from a kidney disorder, he composed the music rapidly. On the evening of May 25, 1878, three nights after *The Sorcerer* completed its run, the Comedy Opera Company presented *H. M. S. Pinafore, or The Lass That Loved a Sailor,* which was to become one of the great triumphs of the musical theater.

Curious to say, the opening performance of *H. M. S. Pinafore* was nearly a failure. Even though some scandal attached to the caricature of Sir Joseph, who was clearly a satirical portrait of Sir William H. Smith, a publisher appointed by Queen Victoria as First Lord of the Admiralty, the first season of the production languished during the June heat. Most affluent Londoners simply vacationed outside the city, and the cast and chorus, threatened with cancellation of the whole production, agreed to accept a cut of one-third of their salaries. Eventually, however, *H. M. S. Pinafore* began to attract a following. The Savoy Company, under D'Oyly Carte, performing at such theaters as the (English) Opéra Comique, the Imperial, and the Olympic, enjoyed a London run of two years, and was a remarkable success.

Almost concurrently, *H. M. S. Pinafore* was performed in pirated and often poorly staged versions in America. To secure American royalty rights and correct misconceptions about the quality of the work, Gilbert, Sullivan, Alfred Cellier (another composer for the Carte company), and selected members of the original cast, mounted an impressive production of the comic opera at the Fifth Avenue Theater in New York City, starting December 1, 1879. The authorized version of *H. M. S. Pinafore* was widely hailed, and touring companies performed it throughout the United States as well as England.

Reasons for the popularity of Gilbert's comedy are not difficult to identify. Apart from Sullivan's tuneful score, the book itself is delightfully arch, bubbling over with high spirits and clever invention. Gilbert satirizes with wit, but little malice, pretentions of social superiority in class-conscious Victorian England. In the pecking order of rank, Sir Joseph Porter is superior to Captain Corcoran, and the Captain in turn lords it over his crew. Yet even the lowly British tar is snobbish about his rank. After all, every sailor "is an Englishman," and his national pride, for which he feels superior to seamen of other nations, makes him better than "a Roosian, a French or Turk or Proosian." Even the revelation by Buttercup that the Captain is of lowly birth and Ralph Rackstraw of high, scarcely disturbs the Victorian audience's sense of social justice. Now Sir Joseph, who likes to think of himself as democratic but who is really a snob, will have to marry his cousin Hebe instead of Josephine, who has fallen in class as the daughter of a humble sailor. At the same time the former Ralph, elevated in rank to the Captain of the *H. M. S. Pinafore,* can claim Josephine. As for the one-time Captain (now plain Ralph), he is free to marry at his own social level, and wisely chooses the buxom Little Buttercup.

Buttercup, like the gypsy Azucena in Verdi's *Il Trovatore* or like Miss Prism in Wilde's *The Importance of Being Earnest,* had been slightly addled when she was "young and charming." She had mixed up the infant Ralph and the infant Captain, a worrisome mistake perhaps, but obviously no serious harm was done. No matter what his social caste, each Englishman (and Englishwoman too, including sisters, cousins, and aunts) knows what is the proper duty and decorum for that prescribed caste. And since the crew of the *H. M. S. Pinafore* is happy with Buttercup's mistake, so must the audience be.

THE HOLY STATE AND THE PROFANE STATE

Type of work: Moral discourse
Author: Thomas Fuller (1608-1661)
First published: 1642

Clergyman and moralist, Thomas Fuller was one of the most popular preachers of his age, even though he sided against the Puritans during the Commonwealth and died shortly after the Restoration. He was, in other words, popular despite his opposition to the emotionally charged Puritan overthrow of the monarchy. Such popularity was difficult to obtain, but as Thomas Fuller knew, it was even more difficult to keep. He was a prolific writer, and in his many books he always simplified his presentation of even the weightiest matter so that his books would have profitable sales. The result of this simplification is a style that is at once cogent and austere, instructive and entertaining.

But style is only one cause of his popularity. Fuller's agile mind, quick to penetrate into the core of whatever problem was at hand and slow to embrace any tenet that did not withstand scrutiny, was one that would be rare in any age. Not only did he have discrimination of mind; he was also witty, and he was able to captivate his congregations by his balance of the profound and the humorous. In his writings he preserved this ability, so that *The Holy State and The Profane State,* his first book, is never weighty in spite of its didacticism or trite in spite of the detailed moral rules.

The four books of *The Holy State* and the one of *The Profane State* are composed of three major types of prose. First, Fuller lists the traits that best illustrate a certain character. These maxims are pithy, easily remembered statements such as (for an advocate) "He is more careful to deserve, than greedy to take, fees," or (for a statesman) "He refuseth all underhand pensions from foreign princes." But Fuller knew that maxims alone are seldom read and even less frequently obeyed. When he gives a maxim, he im-mediately explains it with a clever anecdote or epigram. Second, after he has listed several of these maxims, he illustrates proper behavior in a "character" or a brief sketch exemplifying ideal types. In these "characters" lie the summations of character-types that were familiar to the Elizabethan theatergoer such as the favorite, the good schoolmaster, or the good servant. In terms of literary history, these "characters" were more than summations of the popular theatrical figures of an earlier age; as the prototypes of the descriptions later to be found in novels, they were influential in the eighteenth and nineteenth centuries as statements of ideal types for the novelist's pen. Third, at times when a historical character will adequately illustrate one of the moral principles, Fuller inserts a terse, greatly stylized biography. In an age when the art of biography was still in its infancy, these biographical sketches helped to form the eulogy into a literary genre that would mature through Walton and Boswell into the psychologically probing biography of the twentieth century. The biographies in this book include such a broad selection of biblical and historical figures that few types of people are neglected.

In Book One of *The Holy State,* Fuller describes domestic relationships. The nine characters are conceived in their widest seventeenth century application so that the twentieth century reader can get a fairly good idea of what the people of that time thought constituted a harmonious home life. The good wife, for example, is properly obedient to her husband, and the good husband is cautioned not to tell secrets to her because she is too frail to sustain the strenuous responsibility of keeping secrets. The good parent is a combination of love and authority, and through his parents' examples the good child can learn to honor and obey them. But Fuller is realistic and cynically adds, "If preserved from the gallows, they are reserved for the rack, to be tortured by their own prosperity." Widening his view to other domestic relationships, Fuller proceeds to describe the good master and the good servant; the first should be stern but just, while the second should be quick to obey. The good widow and the constant virgin are special cases, each demands special consideration, even though Fuller believes that all women should marry and raise large families. The final two relationships, the elder brother and the younger brother, lead Fuller from the immediate family because they concern education and inheritance. Five biographies are inserted into the text to expand the lessons. St. Monica illustrates the good wife; Abraham, the good husband; Eliezer, Abraham's servant, the good servant; Lady Paula, a legendary Christian martyr, the good widow; and Hildegardis, a founder of convents, the constant virgin. The fact that Fuller uses Catholic saints and heroines for his illustrations shows his tolerance in an age of Catholic persecutions, but the fact that none of his examples comes either from England or from contemporary history reveals the severe criticism of his times that makes a moralist concerned enough to take action.

Book Two deals with the citizen, the professional man, and the man of the world. As a moralist, Fuller knew that what began in the home must be extended to society as a whole; therefore the same division into roles and into mutual dependences that he so carefully outlined for the home, he preserves for the business world. The good advocate and the good physician should be servants, not masters; they should think of their clients, not of their purses. But the controversial divine and the true church antiquary should think first of the dogmas rather than pursue far-fetched personal or sectarian ideas. This was especially cogent advice at the time when the Puritans were attempting to justify their recent execution of King Charles I, and Fuller's opinion of such an uncivilized action is clearly, though tactfully, presented. The general artist and the faithful minister are ideal mixtures of learning, moderation, and humility. In these Fuller shows his sensitive awareness of the responsibilities of those men who are in a position to sway public opinion. The good parishioner, the good patron, and the good landlord are also leaders, and since they are closer to the people, their roles are much more important for the maintenance of a "godly" society. The rest of the good citizens—master of a college, schoolmaster, merchant, yeoman, handicraftsman, soldier and sea captain —represent the majority of British wage earners in the 1640's. Their responsibilities can be summed up into a simple dictum: be obedient to your betters and live a Christian life of prayer, industry, and uprightness. The last two citizens are the good herald and the true gentleman, positions that occupy the amorphous gulf between the middle class and the aristocracy and thereby provide the transition to Fuller's discussion of the highest class.

Book Three interrupts the natural progress of the discussion because Fuller thought that it should balance the halves of his folio. This book, subtitled "General Rules," gives moral and social rules that are true for all men regardless of class. Here Fuller covers such broadly different topics as hospitality, self-praising, and tombs. His purpose in this book is to describe the life of moderation in which the individual is neither too proud nor too humble. According to Fuller either extreme in any trait, even religious zeal, is bad; the fully developed Christian gentleman should seek the way of harmony. He should be neither profligate nor unrealistically saintly. The six maxims that Fuller lists in the chapter "Of Moderation" form the philosophical basis to the entire folio: "Moderation is not a halting betwixt two opinions, when the thorough believing of one of them is necessary to salvation. Nor is it a lukewarmness in those things wherein God's glory is concerned. But it is a mixture of discretion and charity in one's judgment. Yet such moderate men are commonly crushed betwixt the extreme parties on both sides. Violent men reel from one extremity to another. Pride is the greatest enemy to moderation." With this enlightened view of moderation, Fuller is almost Aristotelian in his accounts of the general rules that should govern all men.

In Book Four, Fuller treats the aristocracy, and in contrast to Book One most of the biographies are of Elizabethan courtiers and nobles. Also, most of the principles are pointed, for the book was published after the fall of the English monarchy. Fuller discusses ten characters and eleven biographies, each worded in a way that points skillfully to the moral decadence of his own contemporaries. The favorite or court parasite opens Fuller's discussion on the conduct of this class, and his disreputable character is illustrated by the lives of Haman, Cardinal Wolsey, and Charles Brandon, Duke of Suffolk. Fuller's treatment is sarcastic and bitter, for this is one social position with which he has little patience. The wise statesman, on the other hand, is exemplified by William Cecil, Lord Burleigh, Queen Elizabeth's trusted adviser; he is a man who is constant, loyal, and shrewd in the affairs of his monarch. The good judge (Sir John Markham) and the good bishop (St. Augustine and Bishop Ridley)

are men who must maintain the laws and authority of the State and the Church; they must be wise, perceptive, and just. The true nobleman and the court lady are persons of the nobility, but blood alone does not give them their superior graces. That must come from their behavior, for a noble person must act in a noble way. Because the nobility forms the backbone of the nation, it must seek the very best life, or the country will collapse from within. The good ambassador and the good general, the prince and the heir apparent, have the responsibility of holding the country's place in the balance of power both between countries and within the state. Finally, Fuller describes the king, the man who must be virtuous and gentlemanly if the rest of the people are to be the same. Only if the highest member of society is spotless, will the rest be spotless.

The last book is *The Profane State*. Here Fuller describes the behavior that inevitably leads to social, moral, and religious anarchy. The harlot, the witch, the atheist, the hypocrite, the heretic, the liar —these are the types of people whose behavior is sinful and vicious. The traitor and the tyrant, Fuller's last characters, are the two whose actions lead to the end of peaceful Christian society and represent the establishment of Satan's kingdom. This final book shows that, if the moral maxims outlined in the first four books are not obeyed, the result will be a state that no one would willingly choose.

THE HOLY TERRORS

Type of work: Novel
Author: Jean Cocteau (1889-1963)
Type of plot: Psychological fantasy
Time of plot: The present
Locale: Paris
First published: 1929

Principal characters:
PAUL, a sensitive, imaginative boy
ELISABETH, his sister
GERARD, their friend
AGATHA, Gérard's wife, friend of Paul and Elisabeth
MICHAEL, an American

Critique:

Jean Cocteau, a playwright, stage designer, painter, film director, and poet, has been one of the most influential figures in the Paris art world in this century. In this psychological fantasy (*Les Enfants terribles*) he has drawn much on Freudian imagery, and the book is, like his films, informed by romantic imagination. Written with great insight, it is a compassionate account of the creativity and destructiveness of adolescence. The snow scenes at the beginning and the end of the novel provide an image of insulation from the familiar world and of the results of isolation that such alienation may produce.

The Story:

Paul and Elisabeth lived with their paralyzed mother in an old quarter of Paris. They lived as though in a world of vegetable instinct, dissociated from adults by passivity, imagination, and secret, mysterious rites.

One night, when the quarter was transformed by snow, Paul was wandering among the snowballing groups in search of the school hero Dargelos, whom he worshiped. Dargelos, who possessed great charm, was both vicious and beautiful. As Paul moved toward him, Dargelos, perhaps accidentally, knocked him down with a stone-packed snowball. Although he injured Paul, he escaped immediate

punishment but was later expelled from the school. Paul was taken home by Gerard who loved him as much for his weakness as Paul loved Dargelos for his strength. Elisabeth was extremely angry with them when they reached Paul's home. She was then sixteen, two years older than Paul and utterly absorbed by him. She was frequently transported by fury when he appeared to be leaving her sphere of influence.

The three children went into the Room where Paul and Elisabeth ate, slept, read, fought, and played the Game. That Room was the sole material reality in their lives; the Game, their inner world. The Room existed in an established chaos of boxes, clothes, papers, and books. Paul left it only for school and Elisabeth only to look after their mother or to buy magazines. Essentially the Game was daydreaming, a willed withdrawal to an imaginary world of submerged consciousness.

After Elisabeth had sent Gérard away, she undressed Paul and put him to bed. Their doctor decided that Paul was unfit to return to school, a decision which plunged Paul into despair until he learned of Dargelos' expulsion. After that school held no interest for him.

The Room held hidden treasures, the artifacts of their unconscious minds—keys, marbles, aspirin bottles—and when

THE HOLY TERRORS by Jean Cocteau. Translated by Rosamund Lehmann. By permission of the publishers, New Directions. Copyright, 1957, by Rosamund Lehmann.

Gérard told Paul that Dargelos had disappeared, a photograph of him dressed as Athalie was added to the collection.

The mother died suddenly. When Paul and Elisabeth saw her, rigid and transfixed in her chair, staring forward, the picture haunted them; it was the one they retained. The mother's nurse, Mariette, remained in the household, content to care for and love Paul and Elisabeth without altering them.

Now an accepted visitor in the Room, Gérard was aware of the almost tangible tension, expressed in fights, recriminations, and reconciliations, between the two. When Paul was well enough, Elisabeth, surprisingly, accepted an invitation from Gérard's uncle to take a holiday by the sea. On the journey she watched Paul while he was sleeping and was disgusted by the air of weakness which his illness had accentuated. She decided to remold him on her own lines.

Once by the sea, they established a Room as much like their own as possible. Paul gained strength under Elisabeth's tutelage, in part through stealing useless objects from local shops while on raids that she had planned. Their booty formed a treasure imitating that in the Paris Room.

When they returned to Paris, Elisabeth was suddenly aware that Paul had outstripped her and that she had become the subordinate party in their relationship. Paul spent his evenings wandering around Montmartre, watching girls, drinking, and finally meeting Gérard and bringing him home for the night. On these occasions Elisabeth would use him as a means of tormenting Paul. The first time she succeeded in rousing her brother came when she declared that she too would go into the world. Her position, she felt, had become untenable, and she subsequently obtained work as a mannequin. This act enraged Paul, who declared that she was prostituting herself; she thought the same about his nightly excursions.

At the dressmaker's establishment where she worked Elisabeth met Agatha, an orphan whose parents, drug addicts, had committed suicide. For Agatha she felt, for the first time, warm affection; but the girl's introduction to the Room precipitated Paul's and Elisabeth's destruction when Agatha became devoted to Paul. The photograph revealed a startling likeness between Dargelos and Agatha, and Paul enthralled her as he had been in thrall to Dargelos. Agatha felt at home in the Room, but at the same time she recognized the strange, dreamlike existence her friends led.

As they matured, the Game failed to absorb Paul and Elisabeth completely. This situation so distressed Elisabeth that when she met Michael, an American friend of Gérard, she transferred her dream life to him. Paul was excluded from this friendship with Michael, but his anger at learning of it evaporated when he discovered that Michael wanted to marry Elisabeth and not, as he had subconsciously feared, Agatha. Elisabeth did marry Michael, but true to Gérard's vision of her the marriage was never consummated: Michael was killed while driving alone in his sports car a few hours after the wedding.

Elisabeth inherited his fortune and his Paris house, into which the four moved. Lonely and disoriented in separate rooms, they gravitated to the Room that Paul finally established in the dining hall. Their lives moved slowly to a climax from the moment that Paul realized he was in love with Agatha. Afraid to tell each other of their love, they each told Elisabeth. Terrified that Paul might leave her, Elisabeth moved tirelessly between them all one night to dissuade them from marrying. Lying, she told Paul that it was Gérard whom Agatha loved, and told Agatha that Paul was too selfish ever to love anyone. She also convinced Gérard that by friendship he had won Agatha's love and that it was his duty to marry her. Elisabeth was so dedicated to the idea of possessing Paul and so trusted by the others that she succeeded completely in her scheme.

A short time after his marriage to Agatha, Gérard met Dargelos. The former schoolmate sent Paul a gift, part of his collection of poisons. Paul and Elisabeth were delighted with the present which, to Agatha's horror, was added to the treasure.

Weeks later when Paris was again covered in snow, Elisabeth dreamed that Paul was dead. She woke to find Agatha at the door. Agatha was convinced Paul had killed himself; she had received a letter from him threatening suicide. They ran to the Room and found Paul choking in poison fumes which filled the screened-in corner where he lay. Although he could barely speak, with Agatha he reconstructed Elisabeth's scheme. When he cursed her, she felt that her heart had died. After admitting her guilt and jealousy, she snatched a revolver; by that violent act she was able to regain their attention and thus to captivate Paul once more. Elisabeth worked to charm him back into their world of the Room and the Game, far from Agatha, who seemed less real to him than the snowstorm outside. The two women watched each other until Paul fell back exhausted. Thinking him dead, Elisabeth shot herself. Crashing against the screens, she destroyed the Room and let in the enemy world. Paul saw visions of snowballers crowding the windows, watching as he died. Theirs was the tragedy of outcasts who, unaware that they lived on borrowed time, died fighting for their private existence.

Further Critical Evaluation of the Work:

The Holy Terrors possesses many of the qualities of a fairy tale, but it is an erotic and frightening fairy tale. It is a novel which works on the basis of contradictions; little is as it seems in this unusual masterpiece. Layer by layer, reality is stripped away, exposing the fascinating and bizarre personalities of the principal characters. The plot seems almost haphazard, incidents piling up as they are needed (as in the convenient Isadora Duncan-like death of Elisabeth's new husband, Michael). The perverse and yet charming brother and sister never think of the consequences of their actions (for example, Elisabeth's marriage and Paul's letter and, always, the taking of drugs). The characters in the novel seem to plummet forward, toward their ultimately tragic fates.

Cocteau frequently uses the word "devouring" to describe the relationship between the brother and sister. The book begins when they are fourteen and sixteen respectively, and carries them into their early twenties, yet the author always considers them "children." If their actual ages are considered, their actions do not seem so innocent or amusing; their heedlessness becomes selfishness and their games lose the charm of their rather forced spontaneity. Paul and Elisabeth never worry about money, accepting as their due after their mother dies the charity of the Doctor and Gérard's uncle. Michael's convenient death, which results in their inheriting his fortune, seems to them merely an act of the gods, and they refuse to change their morbid existence. Paul and Elisabeth do not care about other people; they never consider the effect they will have on others. They are unnaturallly tied up in themselves, and this obsessive relationship leads to their mutual destruction, carrying along the innocent Gérard and Agatha. They are not likeable, but thanks to the artistry of Cocteau, they are fascinating.

HOMAGE TO MISTRESS BRADSTREET

Type of work: Poetry
Author: John Berryman (1914-1972)
First published: 1956

The admirable Mistress Bradstreet receives in this poem more than homage. The work is a paean of praise to a woman who, as all students of American history and literature agree, was praiseworthy. Her biography, even in a skeletonized version, reveals the causes.

Anne Dudley was born in 1612, presumably in Northampton, England, of a well-read and intelligent non-Conformist father. In 1628, at the age of sixteen, she married Simon Bradstreet, aged twenty-five, a graduate of Cambridge University. They sailed to America on the *Arbella* in 1631. Anne herself was a Puritan of profound religious conviction, but she was intelligent and well-educated, and with her natural stimulus strengthened by her surroundings in the New World she was capable of strong-willed behavior, even to the point of rebellion. Thus she could not accept without questioning the tenets of American Calvinism. She responded energetically to the numerous demands of her father and her husband, both of whom became governors of Massachusetts Colony. Yet she still had time to become the mother of eight children, to overcome illnesses, to be a loving daughter and wife, and to write enough poetry to fill a fat volume. She died in 1672.

John Berryman's response to Anne Bradstreet is one of total approbation. He warms to her with a fervor at times approaches adulation. The poem covers her whole life. But it is not in fact a biography; rather, it is more than a mere account of the external aspects of her life. The work is at the same time a spiritual biography of the woman and of Colonial Massachusetts. Berryman's success in his attempt is notable because of the power of his language and because of the general success of his style.

Berryman catches the essence of his subject's conflicting characteristics, the power of her personality, in the first stanza. She is restless but patient. She was a loving mother but also a scholar of both literature and the Lord. As the stanzas develop, so does her character. She realizes that in the alien New World she and her husband must love each other. They must recognize worldly love and its importance because time is transitory. The years rot away.

The fourth stanza introduces the art and power of the poem. The first three and a half stanzas are spoken by the poet about his subject. At this point the poet's voice blends with that of Mistress Bradstreet, who continues the poem with only occasional interruptions by the poet and with an occasional dialogue between her and someone else. This stylistic technique has been highly praised. It is an effort to push back the horizons of poetic technique begun by the great American innovator Ezra Pound and carried on by various followers. It is a method by which the poet can reach more deeply than common into the very essence of poetry, telescoping statements and feelings, omitting transitions, plumbing to the very axis of poetry. This strength, if misused, can result in mere affectations, in technique for technique's sake and in terribly flat and meaningless statements. Generally, however, the level of poetic accomplishment is effectively high indeed.

The fifth stanza, spoken by Mistress Bradstreet, continues the catalogue of happenings in her world. She recounts the voyage on the *Arbella* and the death of the woman for whom the ship was named. More deeply, the poet touches on her hopes and aspirations and fears, the Puritans' troubles in the New World. All recountings are energized by the subject's strong character, brightened by her personality. She breathes poetry and revels in life. She deftly switches from present to past, effectively overlaying one time with another. She goes back to her youth when smallpox blasted the beauty from her face but when Romance and Mystery were brought to her in the person of Simon, her husband to be.

Her memory is agonized by memory of her revulsion at the Calvinism of John Cotton and her attraction, good Calvinist that she was, to Catholicism; she recognized that she must be disciplined against the easier attraction. The uncertain journey of her life is re-emphasized time and again as she remembers that her patience is short and she revolts from the life around her. The conflict between body and soul—the weakness of the flesh and the hoped-for strength of the spirit—are especially powerful in her memory. Sex pulls her like a magnet, then floods her very being, rising to a crescendo of glory in the accomplishment of having children, especially her first, born when she was twenty-one. Perhaps no lines in the whole poem are superior to the statement of the joy of this accomplishment. She is ecstatic.

The iron bands of her environment are revealed in her reaction to the trial of Anne Hutchinson for her "Antinomianism," her "traducing the ministers and their ministry," and her consequent excommunication and banishment by the synod of churches and by Governor Winthrop. Mrs. Bradstreet's reaction was ambivalent. She despised the mistreatment of Anne Hutchinson for her dissenting views, but she burned more inwardly than outwardly.

As she reveals herself in her examinations of herself, Mistress Bradstreet is of the earth and of the spirit, a balance never firmly and indisputably established, never sure of the ascendency of which. She is also Mother Earth, encompassing the whole of life. Like Walt Whitman at a later period, she is large enough to include all. She renounces nothing, however petty and repulsive. The ending is thus a great affirmation.

In the style and technique of the poem lies its glory, and an occasional lapse into weakness. The language is compact, muscular, powerful. The words are simple, direct, earthy, slangy, idiomatic, and effective. The art of telescoping and compacting sometimes, however, vitiates its own strength, as when, for example a fifty-two-word, eight-line parenthesis separates, for no logical or aesthetic reason, the subject from its verb. But such technical weaknesses are few.

In outline this curious but somberly moving poem of fifty-seven eight-line stanzas is effectively organized as the spiritual autobiography of a complex personality who lived with physical hardship and spiritual travail the double life of a woman and an artist. Readers may be repelled at first by the rough intellectuality of the verse and the elliptical intimacy of the material, but a careful reading is likely to show how apt the writer's form and diction are for his task. In this work the poet shows that the American past may be employed as a subject for serious poetry without reshaping it to the wonder of legend or exploiting it for sentimentality.

THE HONEST WHORE, PART ONE

Type of work: Drama
Author: Thomas Dekker (c.1572-1632?) with Thomas Middleton (1580-1627)
Type of plot: Tragi-comedy
Time of plot: Sixteenth century
Locale: Milan, Italy
First presented: 1604

> Principal characters:
> GASPARO TREBAZZI, Duke of Milan
> INFELICE, his daughter
> COUNT HIPPOLITO, a nobleman in love with Infelice
> MATHEO, his friend
> CANDIDO, a linen-draper
> VIOLA, Candido's wife
> FUSTIGO, Viola's brother
> BELLAFRONT, a harlot

Critique:

Elizabethan dramatist Thomas Dekker was an extremely prolific writer, working often in collaboration with other playwrights. From a passage in Henslowe's diary, it is known that Middleton had a hand in Part One of this play; but scholars are uncertain as to the precise amount that he contributed. The main plot, as will be seen, has a strangely inverted resemblance to that of *Romeo and Juliet*, while the subplot, although the scene is laid in Milan, gives a realistic glimpse of London shop life of that time. Both plots are, by modern standards, exaggerated and improbable. Lamb found the play "offensively crowded" with diatribes against the harlot's profession; the reader of today, however, will not be shocked. Rather, unless he is a specialist in Elizabethan drama, he is likely to be bogged down in the plot complications, and he will hardly agree with Hazlitt that the "contrivance" of the main plot is "affecting and romantic."

The Story:

In Milan, at the funeral of Infelice, daughter of Duke Gasparo, Count Hippolito refused to be restrained by his friend Matheo. Frantic with grief over the death of his beloved, he accused her father of having killed her. After a violent altercation between the two noblemen, the hearse was borne off. In Milan, also, Viola's brother, Fustigo, had returned from sea, to find his sister married to Candido, a linen-draper, and unhappy because her husband was such a model of patience and good temper. In order to make Candido angry, Viola proposed to Fustigo—whom Candido had never seen—that he pretend to be her lover, and this plan was agreed upon.

In the meantime, at the ducal palace, it was revealed that Infelice's death was only a trick produced by a sleeping-potion administered at her father's command. Duke Gasparo admitted that Hippolito was a noble youth whom he would have welcomed as a son-in-law had it not been for a feud between the two families; he had, however, devised the stratagem of her supposed death to break up the love affair between her and the young count. When Infelice awoke, her father told her that Hippolito was dead. He then ordered her to go to Bergamo in order that she might recover from her grief. After she had gone, the duke's physician offered to poison Hippolito and thus relieve the duke's mind forever of the fear of a reunion of the lovers. To this plan the cold-blooded duke assented.

Meanwhile a merry group of Milanese gallants, planning a trick to try the famous patience of Candido, went to his shop and examined his wares, particularly a bolt of lawn at eighteen shillings the yard. When asked the length desired, one of them ordered only a pennyworth and insisted that it be cut from the middle of the piece, thereby ruining the entire bolt. To this fantastic order Candido acceded, to the fury of his wife. But the unruffled Candido served the gallants with wine and even remained calm when one of them walked off with a silver-gilt beaker. He quietly sent for the constable, got his goblet returned, and then invited the gentlemen to dinner.

After the dinner the gentlemen went to the house of a harlot named Bellafront, where they were joined by Hippolito and Matheo. Count Hippolito had never visited the house before and, still in a melancholy mood, he left after a few moments. When he returned to fetch Matheo, he found all the gentlemen gone and Bellafront alone. She immediately fell in love with him, but all she got in return was a long diatribe on the evils of prostitution. Repulsed, she tried to stab herself but was prevented by Hippolito, whose love she vowed to win at any cost.

The attempts to break the patience of Candido continued, as Fustigo put into execution the plan of pretending to be Viola's lover. But the trick miscarried: Candido refused to be offended by his wife's behavior. His loyal apprentices, not knowing the true situation, gave Fustigo a thorough drubbing. Next, the baffled Viola locked up his formal gown, so that, when he was summoned to a meeting of the city Senate, he lacked the proper clothes to wear. But the imperturbable Candido fashioned a gown out of a tablecloth. Wearing this and with a nightcap on his head, he went to the meeting.

Meanwhile Bellafront, chastened by her love for Hippolito, had resolved to give up her shameless life, and so had turned all the gallants out of her house. Her first seducer had been Matheo, who ironically told her that an honest whore is an impossibility. Still determined to win Hippolito's love, Bellafront gained entrance to his house in the disguise of a page. There she found the count gazing at a picture of the supposedly dead Infelice. When Bellafront revealed her identity, he rudely repulsed her again, and she resolved to leave Milan. As she left the house, Hippolito received a note from the duke's physician asking for an interview.

During these events, the drubbed Fustigo had hired two bullies to take revenge upon Candido's apprentices. Viola had ordered one apprentice to dress in his master's clothes, but again Candido, who returned still wearing the tablecloth, refused to take offense and merely changed his own clothes for those of an apprentice. Just as his wife was declaring him insane, the two bullies entered; seeing Candido in the distinctive garb of an apprentice, they started to beat the poor old man. Again the faithful apprentices came to the rescue, but Candido would not let them hurt his assailants. However, Viola entered with two officers and, under the pretext that Candido was mad, had him bound and carried off to Bethlem Monastery—that is, to the London insane asylum. He meekly submitted.

In the meantime the physician informed Duke Gasparo that he had poisoned Hippolito, but he also warned his master that, having done this deed for gold, he might well be hired to poison the duke. Duke Gasparo instantly banished him with the curt statement that rulers often hate the man by whom their plots are carried out. As soon as he was alone the doctor revealed the true situation: he had not poisoned Count Hippolito. He also informed the count of Infelice's feigned death and promised to bring the lovers together in the chapel of Bethlem Monastery, where they could be married.

Viola, beginning to feel that she had gone too far in her efforts to vex her husband, had repaired to Duke Gasparo's palace to seek a warrant releasing Candido from the madhouse. Unfortunately, just as the duke was about to sign the order for the linen-draper's release, a courier brought the news that Hippolito was not dead and that he and Infelice were to meet at the monastery that afternoon for their marriage. Matheo had carelessly revealed the secret. In a desperate attempt to foil the lovers, Duke Gasparo and his courtiers rode in disguise to the monastery, leaving Viola's warrant unsigned.

Hippolito and Infelice had already arrived at the monastery and were planning to be married that evening. When Matheo arrived with the news that the duke had learned of their intention and was on his way to prevent the wedding, the friar who was to marry them promised to perform the ceremony and to get them out of the building disguised as monks. They were hurried out of sight just as

the duke and his followers arrived. The situation became one of great confusion. Bellafront entered, having come to the monastery earlier in the day under pretext of madness. The disguised lovers also came into the room where the duke was, as did Viola, her servant, and Candido. When the various disguises had been thrown off, the duke suddenly relented, forgave Infelice and Hippolito, permitted their marriage, and gave justice to Bellafront by marrying her to Matheo, the man who had first seduced her. Even Viola knelt to ask Candido's forgiveness for the vexations that she had subjected him to. Patient to the end, he forgave her and then delivered to the assembly a long harangue on patience as the greatest of all virtues.

Further Critical Evaluation of the Work:

Although *The Honest Whore, Part One,* taken as a whole, is not a typical comedy of humors, some of its characters display the peculiarities common to the type. Indeed, the advertisement from the title page of the play—"With the Humors of the Patient Man and the Longing Wife"—identifies two characters who suffer from a form of psychological unbalance. Unlike Ben Jonson's comedy of humors, in which the afflicted persons' unbalance often approaches madness, the humors characters in this play appear to suffer milder derangements.

The chief example from the subplot is Candido, the linen draper, whose patience—a Christian virtue usually considered admirable—is exaggerated to the point of stubborn eccentricity. Although Candido has "no more gall in him than a dove, no more sting than an ant," he is rewarded for his meek forbearance with abuse instead of kindness. Candido's problem is that his patient apathy torments his shrewish wife Viola, who is driven nearly lunatic in her futile attempts to rouse him. As the "longing wife," Viola's humor is rage. Nettled, she is ready to bite off her own tongue "because it wants that virtue which all women's tongues have, to anger their husbands." Count Hippolito, the protagonist from the main plot, also suffers early in the play from a humor, that of the "tyrant melancholy." As a dour moralist, he lectures the whore Bellafront on her vice until he reforms her character. Sourly he listens to and rejects her protestations of love. In spite of his otherwise attractive quality as the faithful lover of Infelice, the count is—to modern readers— far too sober a hero to deserve the fullest sympathy.

The strength of the play is, however, in its plot rather than its characters. Complexly structured, *The Honest Whore, Part One* has three distinct actions which are ingeniously entangled and finally unified. In the main plot, Count Hippolito seeks to wed Infelice. Opposed by her father, the Duke of Milan, Hippolito succeeds in his endeavor by overcoming obstacles that, in *Romeo and Juliet*, had proved tragic to the lovers. Though in the first act Infelice appears to be dead, she has merely been drugged. In the high subplot Bellafront, a harlot, first confounds her many lovers and later is driven desperate herself for love of Hippolito. She eventually marries her first seducer, Matheo. In the low subplot Candido, the model of patience, vexes his wife and is in turn persecuted by her. All the plots converge in the triumphant concluding scene at Bethlem Monastery (the madhouse). All the characters are revealed for what they are—virtuous and wise, or vicious and foolish. The ending, undeniably sentimental and pat, is difficult to accept as realistic. But the play, despite a few realistic scenes in the draper's shop, is essentially a romantic entertainment and is meant to be amusingly heartwarming, not perfectly logical.

THE HONEST WHORE, PART TWO

Type of work: Drama
Author: Thomas Dekker (c. 1572-1632?)
Type of plot: Tragi-comedy
Time of plot: Sixteenth century
Locale: Milan, Italy
First presented: c. 1605

Principal characters:
GASPARO TREBAZZI, Duke of Milan
INFELICE, his daughter
COUNT HIPPOLITO, a nobleman, Infelice's husband
BELLAFRONT, a former harlot
ORLANDO FRISCOBALDO, Bellafront's father
MATHEO, Bellafront's husband
CANDIDO, a linen-draper
CANDIDO'S BRIDE

Critique:

Part One of *The Honest Whore* must have been successful on the stage, for Dekker very quickly followed it with a sequel, written entirely by himself. He was obviously endeavoring to capitalize on features of the first play, since in the second part he used all the principal characters save one and continued the subplot of the patient Candido. He ended with a scene in Bridewell, a London prison of his time, to balance the Bethlem Scene in Part One. He also continued the high moral tone of the earlier play, this time, however, making gambling as well as prostitution the object of his strictures. The new character of Friscobaldo, the outwardly stern yet inwardly forgiving father, was extravagantly admired by Hazlitt, and both he and Ernest Rhys considered Part Two superior to Part One. The modern reader will perhaps find that some of the freshness of Part One has worn off and feel that Dekker tried to carry a good thing a bit too far.

The Story:

One day Bellafront, a former prostitute now married to Matheo, the former friend of Count Hippolito, arrived at that nobleman's house with a petition. Her husband had killed a man, but it was in fair fight and the man a notorious villain. Still, Matheo has been condemned to death. Hippolito, who was about to ride

out with his wife Infelice, stayed behind to hear the petition. He took the opportunity to remind Bellafront of their old relationship and promised to help Matheo to a pardon and, if possible, to reconcile her with her unforgiving father. But it was significant that Count Hippolito showed much more interest in Bellafront than she in him.

Meanwhile, at the palace of Duke Gasparo, father of Infelice, the courtiers were talking of the marriage of Candido, an old linen-draper still famous in Milan for his patience. Viola had died, and, to the mystification of the gallants, Candido was marrying a young girl. Just as they had decided to attend the wedding feast, Hippolito entered, followed shortly by Orlando Friscobaldo, Bellafront's estranged father. Their meeting gave Hippolito an opportunity to ask the old man about his daughter. Friscobaldo declared that he had not seen her for seventeen years, that her disgrace had been so great that he no longer considered her his child. But when Hippolito had left, with the parting remark that Bellafront was in dire poverty, the father relented and resolved to rescue his daughter. To this end, he put on the livery of a servant and, thus disguised, went to find his offspring.

At the same time, the wedding of the widowed Candido was taking place, attended by some of the gallants of the city who wished to see what sort of bride the old man had chosen. The first impression was unfavorable: when the bride was handed the wedding goblet, she broke the glass and refused to drink. Candido was as patient as ever, but he did consent to allow a nobleman to disguise himself as an apprentice so that the disguised man might try to cure the bride of her peevishness. The courtiers did not wish to see Candido saddled with another shrew.

Thanks to Hippolito, Matheo had been released from prison and had, somewhat unconvincingly, promised his wife to reform and give up gambling. When Friscobaldo arrived, disguised as a servant, he pretended to be an old family retainer discharged by Bellafront's father. He asked Matheo for a place in his household and insisted on turning over to the latter, for safe-keeping, what he claimed to be his life's savings: twenty pounds. His offer was enthusiastically accepted by Matheo, who took the opportunity to abuse his father-in-law. The outburst was interrupted by the arrival of Hippolito, come ostensibly to congratulate Matheo but in reality to pursue his wooing of Bellafront. He had already sent her gifts; he now left her a purse. To the delight of her disguised father—who was to convey the purse—she rejected all the gifts and resolved to remain honest.

Meanwhile, a rather labored trick was being played at Candido's shop. The nobleman, disguised as an apprentice, arrived as if looking for work. The bride refused to prepare a room for him, whereupon Candido took the unusual step of vowing to tame her. He picked up a yardstick; she armed herself with the longer ell-wand; but before they could come to blows, the bride asked forgiveness and delivered a speech on the proper obedience of wives.

In the interest of saving his daughter from Hippolito's advances, Friscobaldo went to the count's house and revealed to Infelice her husband's infidelity, surrendering to her the gifts sent to Bellafront. When Hippolito returned, Infelice was able to play a neat trick upon him. Kneeling, she made a mock confession of having committed adultery with a servant. The enraged husband delivered a tirade on unfaithful wives, thus giving Infelice the opportunity to turn his own words against him as she displayed the gifts he had sent Bellafront. But her just reproaches succeeded only in making her husband the more determined to pursue his illicit passion.

In the household of Matheo, affairs were going from bad to worse. That unlucky gamester had lost everything at dice, including the money entrusted to him by his feigned servant; so, reduced to nothing, he pawned his wife's clothes and hinted strongly that he would be pleased if she would return to her former profession so as to gain a few ducats. He was, however, temporarily rescued by a friend, who promised to give him both money and clothes fashionable for a gentleman.

Candido's troubles, also, were continuing. Two disreputable characters, Mrs. Horseleech, a bawd, and Botts, a pander, had designs upon his new wife and tried to seduce her for one of their customers; but the plot broke against her honesty. While these events were taking place, Matheo had received his new clothes and was happily showing them to his wife. In the midst of Matheo's display old Friscobaldo appeared, this time in his own person, to be recognized by Bellafront, who asked his forgiveness. The father startled Matheo by his knowledge of the latter's shady dealings and then left in pretended anger, vowing that he would let the couple starve. While Bellafront and Matheo were quarreling, the father returned in his servant's disguise to hear Matheo's very garbled account of what had just happened and his proposal that they rob Friscobaldo's house. The disguised old man agreed to the plan.

After they had left the house, Bellafront appeared with Hippolito, who was still intent on his wooing. A long debate ensued between them, Hippolito urging his suit and Bellafront describing the miseries of a harlot's life. When she repulsed his advances, he swore to continue until he had succeeded. In the meantime, Friscobaldo had been revealing to Duke Gasparo the villainy of Matheo. The duke agreed to aid the plot of catching Matheo in the robbery and also resolved to cure Hippolito by purging Milan of harlots by imposing such strict laws that Hippolito would be afraid to approach a prostitute, no matter how fair she might be.

The young Milanese gallants, never tired of trying to vex the patient Candido, met at Matheo's house to plan another trick. Matheo suggested that, as a bait, he should offer to sell Candido some lawn, thus accomplishing two purposes at once, for he had stolen the lawn from two supposed peddlers—actually men hired by Friscobaldo. Candido arrived and was persuaded to drink a glass of wine. At that moment the constable entered to arrest Matheo for theft and Candido for receiving stolen goods. Both

were taken to Bridewell prison, along with Mrs. Horseleech and Botts, who had been present during the episode. Duke Gasparo, attended by his court, arrived at the prison to administer justice. Hippolito came also, having heard that Bellafront had been arrested in the wholesale sweep of the harlots of Milan. At the trial Matheo's real baseness was revealed: he boldly admitted the robbery but claimed that his wife had inspired it; when this charge was disproved by the disguised Friscobaldo, he accused Bellafront of being a whore and swore that he had found her in bed with Hippolito. To this accusation, Infelice, in order to prolong the stratagem, added that Bellafront had accepted presents from Hippolito. In the midst of these charges and countercharges Friscobaldo at last threw off his disguise and proclaimed his daughter's innocence and Matheo's villainy. All ended happily when, at Bellafront's petition, her unworthy husband was pardoned, Hippolito and his wife were reconciled, and Candido was shown to have been the victim of a cruel joke.

Further Critical Evaluation of the Work:

The Honest Whore, Part Two, continues in a more realistic, indeed often cynical fashion the story of *The Honest Whore, Part One.* As is true of many literary sequels, in the second play Dekker changes his concept of the characters in order to satisfy the demands of his different plot. In *Part One,* Count Hippolito was the melancholy but faithful lover of Infelice; Gasparo Trebazzi was the inflexible father-tyrant who crossed the young lovers until the concluding scene; and Bellafront was the whore reformed through her unrequited but pure love for Hippolito. In *Part Two* Hippolito, now married to Infelice, is no longer the melancholy saint of love: "turned ranger," his passions are roused by Bellafront's beauty; Gasparo is judicious instead of rancorous; and Bellafront is a model of wifely virtue, deaf to Hippolito's seductive entreaties. Only Candido, the patient linen draper, remains quite the same in both plays. His "humor"—an exaggerated meekness and forbearance—is tested by his young skittish bride (his former wife Viola, the shrew, having fortunately expired), by pranksters, a bawd, a pander, and by assorted whores and knaves at Bridewell prison. The single important new character, Orlando Friscobaldo, who is Bellafront's father, is intended to arouse in the audience sentimental affection, but his meretricious disguise and mean intrigues serve only to make his motivation appear inconsistent, and he is ultimately unsympathetic.

To be sure, the major difference between the plays is the change from romantic tragi-comedy approaching comedy of humors in *Part One* to tragi-comic realism in *Part Two*. So far as we can judge from what remains of Dekker's many plays, the author's talents would not appear to run toward authentic tragedy. He is at his best with comic scenes of London lower class or lower-middle class life. In *Part Two*, he is most convincing when he treats Candido in the linen shop, fretted by apprentices; or when he brings all his characters, in the final scene, to Bridewell Prison. Like the conclusion of *Part One* in Bethlem Monastery (a madhouse), the Bridewell scene is vivid with caricatures of the denizens of London's sordid underworld. Unlike such dramatists as Marston, Chapman, or Jonson, who often flail these wretched creatures with indignant satire, Dekker sees them as amusing although pitiful. His humanity rather than moral power is most clearly displayed in the play.

In the character of Matheo, Dekker's failure in moral vision seriously weakens the otherwise happy ending. In *Part One,* Matheo was a minor figure, a friend of the count. In *Part Two,* as Bellafront's husband, he is an evil, scheming, luxurious brute. Contrasted to Hippolito's amateur philandering, Matheo's studied lust and depravity are the greater vices. Yet Matheo is pardoned at the end, thanks to the intercession of Bellafront, who dutifully forgives her husband. Thus the patient generosity of the wife nearly matches the patience of Candido. Nevertheless, for modern audiences, Bellafront sacrifices too much of her self-respect for her worthless spouse; his reformation, it would seem, is only temporary, and he is likely to abuse her afterward—a destiny that any woman, even an "honest whore," should not have to endure.

HONEY IN THE HORN

Type of work: Novel
Author: H. L. Davis (1896-1960)
Type of plot: Regional romance
Time of plot: 1906-1908
Locale: Oregon
First published: 1935

Principal characters:
 CLAY CALVERT, a migrant worker
 WADE SHIVELEY, his stepfather
 UNCLE PRESS SHIVELEY, Wade's father
 LUCE, Clay's woman
 THE HORSE TRADER, Luce's father

Critique:

The story told in this novel is less important than the character studies of some people who settled Oregon in the early part of this century. In his introduction the author states that he is neither criticizing any social group nor suggesting reforms; rather, he attempts to give an accurate picture of the migrants who were always seeking new homes in better lands. The story itself is excellent, however—fast-moving and interestingly told. There have been many novels of pioneers and early settlers during the last two decades, but few surpass *Honey in the Horn.*

The Story:

Wade Shiveley had killed his own brother in a fight over a squaw and had murdered and robbed old man Howell. Now he had been captured. The officers wanted Uncle Press Shiveley, Wade's father, to try to get Wade to say where he had hidden the money. But Uncle Press had threatened to shoot Wade if he ever laid eyes on him again, and so in his place he sent Clay Calvert, the son of one of Wade's wives. Clay did not want to go because he also hated Wade. Uncle Press gave Clay a gun to slip to Wade in the jail. Having loaded the gun with blank cartridges, he hoped Wade would use the worthless gun to attempt an escape and thus be shot down by the officers.

On the way to the jail, Clay met a horse trader and his wife and daughter. When Clay slipped the gun to Wade in the jail, Wade said that he had not killed Howell, that Howell was killed by a bullet that split when it was fired and that such a bullet did not fit his own gun. Wade had always been a liar, but Clay suspected that this time he might be telling the truth.

Clay left town to hide in Wade's abandoned shack until after Wade had been killed and buried. Later Uncle Press sent a half-breed Indian to tell him that Wade had escaped and that the sheriff was now looking for Clay as an accomplice. Clay left the shack with the Indian, taking with him Wade's rifle he had found there, and after traveling awhile they met the horse trader and his women again. Clay learned that the girl was called Luce and that she traveled around with her father and stepmother, trading horses, racing them, and picking hops in season. Since he wanted to get out of the immediate territory and because he was strongly attracted to Luce, Clay decided to travel with the horse trader's family. The Indian stole Wade's rifle from Clay and ran away.

Clay and the horse trader's family worked for a time in the hop fields. The trader was a weak man who lost all he and his family earned by gambling, and Luce took the responsibility for the family on her shoulders. Clay and Luce liked each other very much, but they quarreled frequently, and one day Clay moved away from the wagon. When the sheriff appeared at the field one day, Clay became frightened and left hurriedly, traveling toward the coast.

Luce and her folks found him after awhile, and Luce and Clay decided to stay together. There was no place for them to get married. They spent the winter in a little settlement on the coast, in a cabin apart from the horse trader's. Luce rescued some bags of flour which had floated to shore from a wrecked ship, and with money earned by selling the flour to the Indians she and Clay were able to buy a wagon and start on their own.

Clay and Luce left for eastern Oregon, but Clay refused to let her father and stepmother go with them, for he could not stand the sight of the weak horse trader. They traveled across the mountains and into Looking Glass Valley, where they joined another group of settlers led by Clark Burdon. Burdon described to Clay a stranger who was looking for him, and Clay knew the man was Wade. Clay liked Burdon and told him the story of Wade and his killings and escape. Burdon promised to help him get rid of Wade. That night Clay shot a man he thought was Wade, but the dead prowler turned out to be the son of one of the settlers. When Burdon and Clay declared that Wade had shot the boy, the men formed a posse and captured Wade. After Wade tried to kill Clay, the men believed that the outlaw was trying to keep Clay from testifying against him; and the posse vowed to hang Wade. Clay felt guilty, for he doubted that Wade had killed Howell and he knew that he himself had shot the prowler. But it was his life or Wade's, and so he kept silent. He felt dirty and sick when he saw Wade hanged.

The settlers traveled eastward, Clay and Luce with them. Luce had a miscarriage. She would not let Clay go for a doctor, for she was terrified that he would leave her and never come back.

The rest of the caravan had gone on and they were alone. Clay finally left Luce, promising to return with help as soon as possible. He came back with an Indian midwife, to find that Luce had gone away in the wagon. There were two sets of wagon wheels, and Clay knew instinctively that her father had come by and that Luce had left with him. Angry and hurt by her desertion, Clay decided to go on alone.

He rode his horse into the threshing country and worked with a mowing crew. There he met the half-breed from the Shiveley ranch and told the Indian to be on the lookout for Luce and her father. The Indian did meet the horse trader and made a large wager on a race with him. The horse trader lost the race and the Indian collected the money. Next day the Indian was found with a bullet in the back of his head and no money in his clothing, and the horse trader and Luce had disappeared. Clay helped bury the Indian, but before the burial he shot Wade's rifle, which the Indian had stolen. The bullet did not split. Clay knew then that Wade had been telling the truth about not killing Howell. He suspected that Luce's father had killed and robbed both Howell and the Indian.

Clay joined a party moving on to a railroad construction camp. On their way there was an accident, and one of the horses had to be killed. When Clay saw the horse, he recognized it as one belonging to Luce's father, and he knew that she was in the group. He volunteered to shoot the horse, but first he found Luce and asked for her rifle. With it he killed the animal and later, examining the bullet, he saw that it was split. When he told her that the trader had murdered Howell and the Indian, she claimed she had done the killings. She said that her father, who was now dead, had lost a lot of money to Howell and that her stepmother and Howell had fought. Luce had shot the old man during the fight and had taken the money her father had lost to him. Later she killed the Indian because he had won her father's money in the horse race.

Clay suspected that Luce was trying to protect her dead father. Besides, he still wanted her. He climbed into her wagon and they joined the long line of settlers who were still seeking a place where they could make real homes. Whatever their past, they would always go on together.

Further Critical Evaluation of the Work:

Oregon in the homesteading days was colorful, raw, rollicking, and often brutal. West of the Great Plains meant west of civilization, but the frontier nevertheless profoundly influenced American culture. *Honey in the Horn* is Harold Lenoir Davis' Pulitzer Prize winning attempt to render the unique and captivating quality of that experience.

The title, from a boisterous square dance lyric, introduces a tall-tale dimension popularized by local colorists such as Bret Harte and Artemus Ward. The story derives much of its power and inspiration from the poker-faced comic sketches of the rustic characters the young protagonist encounters. When Clay Calvert flees the ramshackle toll bridge station (under shady circumstances which eventually unfold and help relieve the rambling plot of its dependence on coincidence), his adventures encompass a spectrum of incidents infused with local color, including vivid scenic description, and scenes involving random brutality, frontier lore, backwoods politics, human dignity and degradation, squalor and sensibility.

Davis' story combines authentic frontier language with huge infusions of first-hand knowledge and backwoods lore which are occasionally fabulous, but which nevertheless ring true of human situations. Davis refuses to mythologize his material, but rather allows the tension between the myth and the revealed reality, between the ideal of the Old West and fact, to impel its own conclusions. While his characters tend to be one-dimensional, subtleties of frontier character and nuances of commonplace personal interaction are rendered perceptively and deftly, though without deep probing.

Although his vivid and lovingly rendered descriptions of homesteading life and landscape ranging from Oregon's rain forest to its alkali desert occasionally threaten to overwhelm his story and characters, Davis may be considered a frontier realist of sorts. His honest and authentic portrayal of the scene as it actually was helps to break the grip of the romantic myth on the American imagination.

THE HOOSIER SCHOOLMASTER

Type of work: Novel
Author: Edward Eggleston (1837-1902)
Type of plot: Regional romance
Time of plot: About 1850
Locale: Indiana
First published: 1871

Principal characters:
RALPH HARTSOOK, a young schoolmaster
BUD MEANS, Ralph's pupil and friend
HANNAH THOMSON, the Meanses' bound-girl
DR. SMALL, Ralph's enemy
PETE JONES, Dr. Small's partner in crime
WALTER JOHNSON, Ralph's cousin, one of the robbers
MARTHA HAWKINS, Bud Means' sweetheart
SHOCKY, Hannah's brother

Critique:

Eggleston wrote *The Hoosier Schoolmaster* as a regional study. In it he caught the Hoosiers of his day, with their singular twists of phrasing, their rough frontier conduct. His simple plots, stock characters and thinly-disguised morality were all subordinate to his main purpose. If *The Hoosier Schoolmaster* is not a great book, it certainly is not to be overlooked, for its author faithfully recorded the place and time he wished to describe.

The Story:

Ralph Hartsook had not thought schoolteachers were judged by their muscular ability when he applied for the job as schoolmaster of Flat Creek, Indiana. Before long, however, he learned his competence would be judged by his power to keep his pupils from driving him out of the schoolhouse. His first step was to make friends with Bud and Bill Means, sons of the school trustee, in whose house he was to board for a time. He was tired from the ten miles he had trudged to apply for his job, but he walked almost the same distance that evening when he went coon hunting with the boys.

Ralph Hartsook held his own against the pranks and challenges of his pupils until the night of the big spelling-bee. Then before most of the people in Flat Creek he was defeated by the Means' bound-girl, Hannah Thomson.

Finding himself strongly attracted to the girl, he escorted her home after the spelling-bee.

Kept awake by curiosity about Hannah's past, Ralph had trouble sleeping that night. At two in the morning he got up, restless, and strolled down the road toward the schoolhouse. Three horsemen passed him in the darkness, one riding a horse with white markings. A few minutes later Dr. Small rode by, returning, Ralph supposed, from a night call. He went back to Pete Jones' house, where he was staying at the time. The next morning he discovered that the horse with the white markings stood in Pete's stable, and he learned from Shocky Thomson, Hannah's young brother, that there had been a robbery the night before.

He decided not to tell what he knew. He had no proof that Pete Jones was connected with the housebreaking and it would have been awkward to explain his own ramblings at an early hour. To add to his misery that day, Mirandy Means, who had been casting sheep's eyes at him, informed him that her brother Bud was fond of Hannah.

Squire Hawkins invited Ralph to spend the weekend with him. Walking toward the squire's house with Shocky, who took the same direction home from school, he learned from the boy that his father was dead and his blind mother in the poorhouse. When Hannah went to live with the Meanses, he himself had been taken in by Mr. Pearson, a basket-maker.

That evening Ralph was surprised to see Dr. Small's horse tied in front of Granny Sander's cabin. She had a reputation as a witch among the people of Flat Creek, and she was a malicious gossip. Ralph did not know that the doctor was busy planting the seeds of rumors in Granny Sander's mind, rumors that Ralph had been a philanderer at home, and that he was somehow implicated in the robbery. Small disliked Ralph, though Ralph had never been able to find any reason for it. Rumor had done its ugly work by Sunday morning. At church Ralph's neighbors had little to say to him.

On Christmas Day, which came the following week, the boys did not follow the custom of asking the teacher for a holiday. Instead Bud and others of the older pupils barricaded themselves in the schoolhouse to keep Ralph from entering and had to be forced out by sulphur thrown down the chimney. Later Bud threatened to thrash Ralph because the schoolmaster had taken the squire's niece, Martha, to church the Sunday before. Bud was jealous. Ralph immediately declared he was really inclined toward Hannah, but had avoided seeing her because of Mirandy's statement. He and Ralph quickly became fast friends. Now, the schoolmaster felt, he had a clear field for courting.

Before Bud and Ralph finished their talk, Shocky burst into the schoolhouse with the news that Mr. Pearson was about to be tarred and feathered by the people of Flat Creek, who had been led by Pete Jones to believe the basket-maker was guilty of the robbery. Pearson, too, had seen three men riding by on the night of the robbery, and Jones had decided the best way to divert suspicion from himself would be to accuse Shocky's benefactor.

Hoping to protect the old man, Bud Means started toward the Pearson home. On the way he met Jones to whom he gave a sound drubbing.

That night Bud helped Pearson to escape to his brother's home in the next county. To thwart Pete Jones' efforts to have Shocky Thomson bound out by declaring the Pearsons paupers, Ralph took the boy to stay with his friend, Miss Nancy Sawyer, in his home town of Lewisburg. His aunt, Mrs. Matilda White, refused to have Shocky's mother in her house because she was a pauper, and so, at Miss Sawyer's own suggestion, Mrs. Thomson was brought to the Sawyer home to spend the weekend with her son. Through Miss Sawyer's efforts, a collection was taken up at church that Sunday afternoon, and with that donation and the money she earned knitting socks, Mrs. Thompson was able to make a home of her own for Shocky.

That same Sunday Bud, intending to ask Martha to marry him, visited Squire Hawkins' house. Suddenly bashful, he told her only of the spelling-bee to take place at the schoolhouse on Tuesday night. Shortly afterward the squire received an anonymous letter, threatening him with the burning of his barn if Martha associated with Bud, the implication being that Bud was incriminated in the robbery. The squire persuaded Martha to ignore Bud. Chagrined by her refusal to let him escort her home from the spelling-bee, Bud began to cultivate Pete Jones and his friends, among them Dr. Small and Walter Johnson, Ralph's cousin.

Bud soon proved he was still Ralph's friend. One day Hannah brought Ralph a letter Bud had sent warning him that he was suspected of the robbery and that there was a plan afoot to tar and feather him that night. Ralph saved himself from the mob by going to a nearby town and giving himself up to the authorities there. His trial was held the next day.

All of Flat Creek was present to see the schoolmaster convicted. Mrs. Means and Pete Jones, particularly, were willing to offer damaging testimony, the former because Ralph had spurned Mirandy's attentions. It was Dr. Small who vindicated Ralph, however, by overshooting the mark in his anxiety to clear himself of Ralph's testimony that the doctor had been out on the night of the robbery.

Small had Walter Johnson called to the stand to testify they had spent the evening together in the physician's office. But Johnson, at a prayer meeting he had attended with Bud, had been deeply impressed by the minister's warning of eternal damnation for sinners. Summoned before the court, he gave way to his guilty conscience and declared that he, Small, Pete Jones, and Pete's brother had committed the robbery, and that Ralph and Mr. Pearson were innocent.

Walter Johnson went free because of his testimony, but Dr. Small, who had been the ringleader of the band, was hanged. Jones and his brother were given prison sentences.

Ralph Hartsook returned to Lewisburg to teach in a new academy there. Shortly afterward he married Hannah. At Ralph's wedding Bud found his courage at last and proposed to Martha.

Further Critical Evaluation of the Work:

As one of America's early literary realists, Edward Eggleston was part of a movement to counter the excesses of bucolic romanticism with "truth-telling" about the bleakness of agrarian life, the bitter—and often petty—rivalries of small-town life, and the very real hatreds and resentments of class conflicts. Influenced by the French critic Hippolyte Adolphe Taine, Eggleston—like such contemporaries as Hamlin Garland and William Dean Howells—followed the dictum, "he writes best who writes about what he knows best." Thus, in *The Hoosier Schoolmaster,* Eggleston based his novel upon the experiences—with which he was intimately familiar—of his brother George, a teacher in his early years and later a noted journalist, biographer, historian, and novelist in his own right. Edward Eggleston also made a special effort, in all of his work, to capture accurately and reflect the peculiar speech and behavior patterns of the people he depicted.

A direct offshoot of this particular version of realism was Eggleston's regionalism, for in writing of what he knew best, he wrote of his native Indiana whose residents were called Hoosiers. The Hoosiers who people the novel are dour, small-town folk preoccupied with the façade of respectability. Accordingly, since pauperism is construed as a major social transgression, Pete Jones' attempt to have the Pearsons declared indigent so that Shocky Thompson could be indentured is a deliberate expression of the region's value system, as is Matilda White's refusal of shelter to Shocky's "pauperized" mother who is subsequently aided by Nancy Sawyer and other members of Miss Sawyer's church.

But Eggleston softened the rigid mores of the region with his own uncompromising morality. Tempered by his ministerial experience and his Christian commitment, Eggleston gave high priority to the didactic value of his work. Swift and sure justice was thus meted out to malefactors according to the severity of their offenses. The repentant Walter Johnson was therefore spared punishment; the guilty Jones brothers were sentenced to prison, and the nonparticipating mastermind of the robbery scheme, Dr. Small, was hanged. The implacable vengeance of a wrathful Christian God was accomplished.

One need not accept or reject the demanding moral code of Eggleston or of the characters he so vividly portrayed. It is sufficient to recognize the existential mode of life which Eggleston filtered through his own sensibility in *The Hoosier Schoolmaster,* for that lifestyle was a distinct reality as the author related it. As such, the novel contributes both to our knowledge and to the author's goal of contributing to the history of civilization in America.

HORACE

Type of work: Drama
Author: Pierre Corneille (1606-1684)
Type of plot: Neo-classical tragedy
Time of plot: Remote antiquity
Locale: Rome
First presented: 1640

Principal characters:
> HORACE, the most courageous of the Roman soldiers
> SABINE, his Alban wife
> OLD HORACE, his father, formerly a soldier
> CAMILLE, Horace's sister
> CURIACE, Sabine's brother, in love with Camille
> VALÈRE, a Roman soldier in love with Camille
> JULIE, confidante of both Sabine and Camille
> TULLE, the ruler of Rome

Critique:

After the controversy which raged over *The Cid* (1636), an extravagant heroic drama, Corneille turned to Livy for his inspiration. In *Horace,* a tightly constructed play which rigorously followed dramatic precepts, he succeeded in producing a patriotic drama both popular with the audience and acceptable to the critics.

The Story:

Although formerly united by ties of patriotism and blood, for Alba was the birthplace of the founders of Rome, Romulus and Remus, the cities of Rome and Alba were at war. Sabine, the wife of Horace, was divided in her loyalties between the city of her birth, where her brothers still lived, and the city of her famous warrior-husband. The battle was to be decided by armed combat between three heroes from each side. Sabine drew little comfort from the resolution, which meant the defeat either of her kinsman or of her husband. Camille, the betrothed of Curiace, the Alban warrior-brother of Sabine, felt her loyalties divided between her loved one and her brother Horace. Even though the oracles had been favorable toward her coming marriage, her dreams envisioned the imminent horror.

The battle postponed, Curiace visited Camille at the home of Old Horace, her father. He declared his abiding love for her, though he remained an Alban patriot, loyal to his city. They commented on the oracles and wished for a lasting peace. When the two warriors met, however, Horace was insistent on the outcome of the trial by combat. Curiace, who stressed the need for peaceful understanding, was dismayed to hear that his prospective brothers-in-law, Horace and his two brothers, were to represent the Romans. He was even more oppressed in spirit when a messenger announced that he and his two brothers were to defend the honor of Alba.

Horace wanted no sympathy from Curiace, though he bore him no ill will. Curiace saw love of wife and family as paramount over Horace's kind of patriotism.

Horace then gave the lovers a moment together before the debt of honor was to be paid. Camille, mindful of the fact that she was the daughter and the sister of famous warriors, denounced the patriotism that could make her choose between love of family and of her future husband. She begged Curiace to avoid a battle which could only end in tragedy, no matter what the outcome. His first duty, however, was to his country, and he

HORACE by Pierre Corneille, from CHIEF PLAYS OF CORNEILLE. Translated by Lacy Lockert. By permission of the publishers, Princeton University Press. Copyright, 1952, 1957, by Princeton University Press.

brutally asserted this fact. Sabine and Camille then begged the cause of love of home and family, while Horace and Curiace defended honor and patriotism. The women were unsuccessful in their suit, and Old Horace comforted them as the young men went off to prepare for the combat. Young Horace, loving to his sister and kind to his aged parent, sought glory in battle; Curiace, no less patriotic, felt that he had lost wife, brothers, and brothers-in-law by a grim turn of fate.

Sabine, given at first to confusion and later to bitterness, lamented her sad position as the sister of the Alban warriors and the wife of their adversary. When she inquired of her friend Julie whether her husband or her brothers had been vanquished, she was told that no resolution had been reached; the king had just then arranged the combatants and charged them to fight to the death, that the fate of the two principalities might be determined. Camille, wearied by her solitary wonderings and fears, joined the discussion. She renounced the deceptive oracle, and neither the wife nor the prospective bride could find solace for their anxiety and grief. Sabine declared that a wife was the most bereaved, to which Camille replied that her sister-in-law had never been in love. For the moment the controversy was resolved by Old Horace, who declared that Rome suffered most; all else was in the hands of the gods.

Julie then brought word that the Alban brothers had been victorious, that two of Old Horace's sons were dead, and that Horace had fled the battlefield. The old man was appalled that his son could see his brothers die without drawing new courage from such defeat and either go down to death or glory. Camille felt some relief that both her lover and brother were for the moment spared, and Sabine was content that her husband was alive. Old Horace could share none of these sentiments; his loyalties were for honor, country, manliness.

Valère, dispatched by Tulle to bring comfort to Old Horace, told of the outcome of the battle. He said that Horace had retreated as a ruse in order to attack the Albans at a disadvantage and that he had killed all three. The old man, his family honor vindicated, rejoiced in the face of Camille's great sorrow. Left alone, she lamented the death of her two brothers and her lover and reviled Rome as the symbol of patriotic infamy.

Into this scene of unrestrained grief came the victorious warrior accompanied by his faithful soldier-in-arms bearing the swords of the vanquished brothers. Displaying the arms, now the spoils of war, which had killed their brothers, he taunted Camille with the glory of Rome while she declared his deed murder. When he accused her of disloyalty, her replies inflamed him to murder, and with the sword of Curiace he killed his sister, a deed which he defended as an act of justice. Sabine, shocked by her husband's bloody deed, was comforted crudely by her husband, who felt that he had performed an act of patriotism justified by the insult to his country. The deeds of heroism he recounted only heightened the despair of his wife, who declared her only wish was to die.

Old Horace, proud of his son's achievements but saddened by his vindictiveness, was distressed over the sudden turn of events which might now deprive him of his last offspring. The fate of his son he must now leave to his king. Tulle, in response to the eloquent plea by Valère, allowed Horace to speak for himself. The hero and murderer wanted most to die, knowing that his past glory had been dimmed by the murder of his own sister. Sabine begged the king to kill her that her husband might live; Old Horace wished the king to save the last of his sons. Tulle, after he had heard all the pleas, felt that Horace's fate rested with the gods, that a king could only pardon that which he could not condone.

Further Critical Evaluation of the Work:

Horace is typical of Corneille's tragedies in that the tragic hero is caught in a dilemma. He must make a choice, in this case between the exigencies of patriotism and those of familial affection. In this respect, the play belongs to a long classical tradition, exemplified by Sophocles' *Antigone.*

In its construction *Horace* adheres to the dramatic principles generally followed by Corneille and his great younger contemporary, Racine. The plot develops rapidly, with considerable emphasis on suspense. After a brief expository opening, setting the stage for the war between Rome and Alba, there is an initial surprise, or *coup de théâtre*: the war will be averted (in reality, the outcome will be decided by three warriors on each side). Then comes the crisis: the three Horace and the three Curiace brothers have been chosen to represent their respective states. The first news of the struggle indicates that the Curiace brothers have triumphed. Then the truth, the second *coup de théâtre,* is revealed: Horace ran momentarily, merely as a ruse to enable him to eliminate the Curiace brothers one at a time. The struggle is resolved, in favor of Rome. A second crisis now arises, for which Corneille was much criticized by his contemporaries because he appeared to violate the law of the unity of action. Horace's sister Camille bitterly condemns the harsh Roman ethic that has caused her the loss of Curiace. The third surprise is, of course, Horace's unexpected murder of Camille.

Horace is a singularly unattractive hero. One can hardly sympathize with his single-minded approach to glory, ignoring all human sentiment. A hero who murders his own sister inevitably strikes the spectator, or reader, as an impossible extremist. It is difficult to see, at least at first glance, how Horace can qualify as an acceptable tragic hero who inspires any feelings other than disgust.

The circumstances of his struggle with the Curiaces hardly make him hesitate a moment. He never expresses any sense of revulsion at the task facing him, as does Curiace. We can assume that Horace is probably capable of normal human feelings, though he quickly suppresses them in favor of his patriotic proclivities. Lacy Lockert agrees that the conflict in the soul of Horace is not expressed in words; he suggests that it can be revealed by the actor who plays the rôle. This is undoubtedly the locus of difficulty in accepting *Horace* as tragedy: the tragic hero evinces a distressingly low degree of capacity for suffering. Most critics who have written on the nature of tragedy would agree with Cleanth Brooks' assertion that tragedy deals "with the meaning of suffering," and that in no tragedy "does the hero merely passively endure."

About all that can be said in defense of Horace is that after his orgy of blood-letting he seems to be momentarily pervaded by a feeling of despair. To the accusations of Valère, a disappointed suitor of Camille, he responds by agreeing that he deserves death. But it soon turns out that the real reason behind Horace's desire for death is that he feels that anything he does henceforth is bound to be anti-climactic. He has attained the apogee of glory, from which the only path open to him leads downhill, to mediocrity.

Out of frustration with Horace, one is almost tempted to seek the real tragic hero elsewhere. Curiace, for instance, suffers deeply because of the dilemma in which he is caught. Out of the wide range of attitudes toward duty explored in the play, his is the most human. But he is not the active character that Horace is. He does nothing to shape his destiny.

Besides Horace, the only character whose rôle is active is Camille. She resembles the heroines of Racine in that her inability to control her passion results in her destruction. As far as her rôle goes, she is tragic, though she cannot be considered the central character. In reality, the situation in *Horace* is such that everyone's rôle is essentially tragic, since everyone is inextricably caught in a wave of conflicting emotions.

There is, however, no escaping the conclusion that Horace is the central character and that, if this play is tragic, Horace must be considered a tragic hero, in spite of his apparent insensibility. Lockert's view that Horace must force himself to be inhuman can be most helpful here. He says that Horace has had to do violence to his gentler feelings, and as a result he cannot permit any doubt that he is right. Hence the appearance of insensibility. The very fact that he must rationalize his position to himself makes him highly vulnerable to any allegation that his ideal is unworthy. When Camille attacks his patriotism, he reacts violently as a man who will stop at nothing in order to prevent his painfully acquired position from being destroyed.

Horace can be compared to Lady Macbeth, who calls upon the spirits of night to dry up her human feelings, thus revealing that the heartlessness she later displays is not natural to her. This is made manifest in her sleepwalking scene, in which we see the terrible guilt that weighs on her conscience. Of course, it was not Corneille's intention to show such a development in his tragic hero, nor could he have done so in the limits prescribed by the unities, especially of time. Nevertheless, the last scene does present a rather apathetic Horace, disillusioned and doomed to an existence devoted primarily to justifying, at least to himself, what he did.

Robert Eisner

THE HORSE'S MOUTH

Type of work: Novel
Author: Joyce Cary (1888-1957)
Type of plot: Picaresque romance
Time of plot: The 1930's
Locale: London
First published: 1944

Principal characters:

GULLEY JIMSON, an unconventional artist
SARA MONDAY, his one-time model
COKER, a barmaid
NOSY, an aspiring artist
MR. HICKSON, an art collector
PROFESSOR ALABASTER, a critic
SIR WILLIAM BEEDER, Jimson's benefactor

Critique:

The Horse's Mouth is one of several novels depicting the life and times of Gulley Jimson, artist and social rebel. Told in the first person singular, the story is a delightful combination of humor, pathos, and down-to-earth philosophy. Whether Gulley was a genius or the greatest rogue in modern art circles is a question which the writer makes no attempt to settle, but there is no doubt that Gulley is one of the most fascinating figures in modern literature. Here is the familiar picaresque romance brought up to date and enlivened by the supple, witty qualities of Mr. Cary's style.

The Story:

Just out of prison, Gulley Jimson looked up his old friend Coker, the ugly barmaid at the Eagle. Coker wanted him to press a lawsuit over some of his paintings, for if Gulley collected Coker would collect from him. At last Gulley managed to get away from her and return to his studio in an old boat shed.

The shack roof leaked and the walls sagged. His paints and brushes had either been stolen or ruined by rain and rats, but the Fall was there. The Fall, depicting Adam and Eve in their fall from grace, would be his masterpiece.

Gulley had a questionable reputation as an artist. Several years back he had painted some nudes of Sara Monday, startling portraits of a lovely girl in her bath. Sara had lived with Gulley as his wife. When the breakup came she had stolen the pictures and sold most of them to a collector named Hickson. One or two he kept for herself. Gulley, past sixty now, had done nothing since the Sara nudes to add to his reputation, but he still had faithful followers of tramps, beggars, and young Nosy. Nosy, wanting to be an artist, worshiped art and Gulley Jimson.

To complete the Fall, Gulley needed paints and brushes. In order to get Gulley to see Sara Monday and secure evidence for a lawsuit to compel Hickson to return the Sara nudes, Coker bought him some paints and brushes. Off and on he worked on the Fall, driven sometimes by compulsion to paint, sometimes by desire for a beer or two.

When Coker pinned him down and took him to see Sara, Gulley was stunned to find her an old hag to whom he felt drawn even while he pitied and despised her. Sara willingly signed a statement that she had given the stolen pictures to Hickson; then she tried to renew her affair with Gulley. Sara had been badly treated by a succession of men, but, like Gulley, she had few complaints. Both felt that the short-lived prosperity and good times they had enjoyed were now being paid for.

Gulley, working intermittently on the Fall, frequently had to trick Coker into buying him paints. Once she forced him to go with her to Hickson, to try to get the pictures or a settlement for them. When Hickson was ready to settle a small sum on Gulley, even though he had legitimately taken the pictures in return for a debt, Gulley slipped some valuable snuffboxes in his pocket and was caught by Hickson and the police. Although that bit of foolishness cost him six months, he bore no malice toward Hickson.

In jail, Gulley received a letter from Professor Alabaster, who planned to write a life history of the painter of the Sara Monday pictures. Gulley thought the idea ridiculous, until he decided there might be money in it. He had had another idea for another masterpiece, and after his release he hurried back to the boat shed to finish the Fall and get started on his new work. He found Coker pregnant and in possession of the shed. Betrayed by her latest lover, her job at the pub lost, she had moved to the shed with her mother. Gulley had to find some way to get the Fall out. Before he had made any plans, he met Professor Alabaster. Alabaster not only wanted to write Gulley's life history but also hoped to sell some of Gulley's work to Sir William Beeder, a collector who admired the paintings possessed by Hickson. Gulley tried to interest Alabaster and Sir William in one of the new masterpieces he was going to do, but Sir William had a great desire for one of the Sara nudes or something similar.

Gulley still hoped to interest Sir William in the Fall, but when he went again to the boat shed he found that Coker's mother had cut it up to mend the roof. Gulley decided there was no use in getting his temper up and doing something foolish; then he would land back in jail before he could do another masterpiece or make a sale to Sir William. Besides, he suddenly realized that he was tired of the Fall.

In the meantime, if Sir William wanted a Sara nude, perhaps Gulley could persuade old Sara to give him one of the small ones she had kept. But Sara, still vain, loved to take out the portraits of her lovely youth and dream over them. Gulley tried every trick he could think of, without success.

When Sir William left London, Gulley wheedled Alabaster into giving him the key to Sir William's apartment. Needing canvas and paints, he pawned the furniture and art collections, and even grudgingly let a sculptor rent one end of the drawing-room to chip away on a piece of marble. Gulley honestly kept the pawn tickets so that Sir William could redeem his possessions. He used one wall for a weird painting he was sure would please Sir William. But when the owner returned unexpectedly, Gulley decided to talk to him from a distance and ducked out before his benefactor found him.

With faithful Nosy, Gulley went to the country for a time. There he worked a new scheme to get money, but another crook beat him up and sent him to the hospital. While recuperating, Gulley had another vision for a masterpiece and wrote Sir William about his idea. Alabaster replied for Sir William, who still insisted on a nude and thanked Gulley for caring for his furniture.

By the time Gulley got back to the boat shed, Coker had had her baby and was firmly installed there. Gulley moved into another empty building and set about preparing the wall for a painting of the Creation. He was aided by Nosy and several young art students he had shanghaied. He tried again to get a nude from old Sara. When Hickson died and gave the Sara pictures to the nation, Gulley was famous. Alabaster found a backer for the life history, and distinguished citizens called on Gulley to see about buying more pictures from him. Gulley had, in the meantime, copied one of his old pictures of Sara from the original in the Tate Gallery and had sold it on approval to Sir William for an advance payment of fifty pounds.

He made one last try to get a picture from Sara. When she refused, he pushed her down the cellar stairs and broke her back. Knowing the police would soon be after him, he raced back to the Creation and painted like a madman, trying to finish the picture before his arrest. He never completed the painting; his spiteful landlord tore the building down over his head. Thrown from his scaffold, he came to in a police ambulance and learned that he had suffered a stroke. He did not grieve. Rather, he laughed at all the jokes life had played on him, and the jokes he had played on life.

Further Critical Evaluation of the Work:

The Horse's Mouth is the third novel in a trilogy published in the early 1940's (the other titles are *Herself Surprised* and *To Be a Pilgrim*). Each novel may be read by itself with satisfaction, but for greatest enjoyment and understanding the trilogy should be experienced as a unit. In the trilogy each novel is given over to a single character who tells his or her story. These novels establish Cary as a keen observer and a mimic. Gulley Jimson, the hero of *The Horse's Mouth,* stands in conflict with Tom Wilcher, the conservative lawyer and landholder in *To Be a Pilgrim,* with Sara Monday (*Herself Surprised*) mediating between them.

When Cary was a young man, newly graduated from the university, he went to Paris to study art and to perfect his skills as a painter. He continued to draw and paint all his life. His treatment of Gulley Jimson as a painter was thus written from "inside." Many consider *The Horse's Mouth* to be the finest novel about painting and the painter's way of seeing.

In contrast to the traditionalist Wilcher, Jimson is constantly looking for new ways of expression. As an experimentalist he is committed to rejecting the old forms. His early work may hang in the best museums and be worth a great amount of money to collectors such as Hickson, but it is meaningless to Jimson. He confronts the present like an innocent; no past solutions are of any use. His big work on the Creation, which seems so intractable and frustrating (partially because he is too poor to buy proper working materials), is an image of his own creative situation; it is full of the potential risks and problems incurred by any free, creative effort. Gulley Jimson is like the experimental, original writer and artist William Blake, whose poem "The Mental Traveller" is used as a kind of running commentary throughout the novel. In all of Cary's fiction, Jimson is the hero who most meets the demands of Cary's free, creative world.

HORSESHOE ROBINSON

Type of work: Novel
Author: John P. Kennedy (1795-1870)
Type of plot: Historical romance
Time of plot: 1780
Locale: The Carolinas
First published: 1835

Principal characters:
SERGEANT HORSESHOE ROBINSON, a colonial patriot
MAJOR ARTHUR BUTLER, his friend
MR. LINDSAY, a Loyalist
MILDRED, Lindsay's daughter
HENRY, Lindsay's son
WAT ADAIR, a Tory
TYRREL, a British officer
MARY MUSGROVE, a patriot
JOHN RAMSAY, Mary's sweetheart

Critique:

Horseshoe Robinson, A Tale of the Tory Ascendency is a love story and a war story. A good narrative description of the effect of the American Revolution on the people of the Carolinas, the novel is unspoiled by flag-waving sentimentality. Horseshoe Robinson is a hunter and a woodsman with a personality much like that of our common story-book conception of early American pioneers. The love story is important in this novel, but it is trivial compared to the importance of the war itself. From a historical point of view, the book makes a valuable contribution with its portrayal of the confusion caused by divided loyalties between England and the Colonies.

The Story:

In the secluded back country of South Carolina two men in the service of the revolutionary colonial forces were traveling together. They were Major Arthur Butler and his shrewd sergeant, a man known throughout the region as Horseshoe Robinson, because of his former occupation as a blacksmith. Although they passed as chance travelers, they were on a secret mission to trace the movements of the enemy and to enlist aid for the cause of colonial independence.

Before setting out on their dangerous journey, Arthur Butler was moved to stop near Dove-Cote, the residence of Mr. Lindsay, a Loyalist gentleman who had come to this territory to live because he wished to avoid the conflict between the colonists and the British government. He himself was loyal to the crown because of financial interests in England, but his son Henry was sympathetic to the American cause. Mildred, Lindsay's daughter, was in love with Arthur Butler, but because of the major's connections with the colonial army Mr. Lindsay had forbidden her to see Butler. For this reason they met secretly in a grove not far from Dove-Cote. After the meeting she returned unseen to Mr. Lindsay's house, and Butler and Horseshoe Robinson went to the inn of Mistress Dimock, not far away.

That night at the inn Horseshoe encountered a Tory spy named James Curry, a stealthy rascal who was passing as the servant of Mr. Tyrrel, a guest at Dove-Cote. Tyrrel, a disguised British officer, was often at Mr. Lindsay's home, ostensibly to secure that gentleman's aid for the Loyalists, but in reality to court Mildred, who despised him and everything he stood for. Seeing Curry at the inn, Horseshoe knew that Tyrrel was again visiting Dove-Cote. Although he let the fellow escape, he was afraid that Tyrrel and Curry might cause trouble for

Butler and himself on their trip through South Carolina.

Major Butler had been sent by General Gates on a mission to another rebel general in Georgia. With Horseshoe as a companion, the major felt certain that he could complete his undertaking. On their first night in the forest Horseshoe led Butler to the home of Wat Adair, an old friend whom he thought loyal to the rebel cause. However, Wat was not a true friend. Having been bought off by the Tories, he planned that night to direct Butler and Horseshoe to an ambush in the forest. But a relative of Wat, Mary Musgrove, overheard Wat plotting with another Tory, and being loyal to the rebels she whispered to Butler the plans she had learned.

Through her warning Horseshoe and Butler avoided one trap, only to fall into an ambush of some rough Tories, among them Curry. Fearing that the drunken crew planned to murder Butler and himself, Horseshoe escaped, hoping to rescue Butler later.

The family of Mary Musgrove was a rebel family, and Horseshoe proceeded to their home to get help in his plan. In addition, the family of Mary's sweetheart, John Ramsay, was a rebel family. With the Ramsays and the Musgroves, Horseshoe planned to engage the enemy and bring Butler to safety. Mary, pretending to be a vendor of fruit, was to enter the Tory camp where Butler was being held. There she was to communicate with the major and give him word of his rescuers' plans.

James Curry had charged Butler with conspiring to murder Mr. Lindsay, a loyal subject of the king. In order to disprove this charge, Horseshoe returned to Dove-Cote. Mildred's distress at the news of her lover's arrest had caused her father great grief, and he relented his stern stand against Butler and assured Mildred that he would not punish her for her concern over the major. When Horseshoe found Mildred and her brother Henry at Dove-Cote, Mr. Lindsay had

gone off with Tyrrel to a meeting of Loyalists in a nearby town. Having heard Horseshoe's account of the charges against Butler, Mildred resolved to go to Cornwallis, the English general, and plead with him for Butler's life. Mildred was confident she could prove that Butler could never have had designs on the father of the girl he loved. Accompanied by Henry Lindsay and Horseshoe Robinson, she set out for Cornwallis' headquarters.

John Ramsay and Mary were able to effect Butler's escape from the camp where he was held prisoner, but John was killed before they reached a place of safety. Grief-stricken by the loss of her sweetheart, Mary attended the funeral services, which were conducted by her father, Allen Musgrove. While the services were going on, they were interrupted by some British troops, and Butler was once again taken prisoner.

When Mildred and her two companions succeeded in getting an interview with Cornwallis, the courtly general gave Mildred his promise that no harm would befall Butler. While the general was speaking with Mildred, he received a message that Butler had escaped. Mildred set out for Dove-Cote with Horseshoe and her brother. On their way they met Mary Musgrove, her family, and the Ramsays, who told them of Butler's second capture by British troops from a nearby camp. Again Mildred resolved to intercede on behalf of her lover, and Henry and Horseshoe agreed to accompany her.

While Mildred awaited an opportunity to seek Butler, the forces of the Loyalists and the rebels were engaging in the battle of King's Mountain. During the fighting Horseshoe rescued Butler and brought him safely back to Mildred. Then the two lovers revealed that they had been married for over a year, in a secret ceremony witnessed by Mistress Dimock and Henry Lindsay.

Wat Adair was captured, and Horseshoe saw to it that he received just punishment for betraying his American friends. Wat told Horseshoe that Tyrrel was really an English general who had bribed Wat to lead Butler and Horseshoe into a trap. Henry, who had participated in the battle, found Tyrrel's body lying among the dead and wounded. James Curry was captured by rebel forces. It seemed certain that the Tory ascendency in South Carolina was at an end.

But the happy reunion of the lovers was clouded by the death of Mr. Lindsay. When he learned that Mildred had gone to see Cornwallis, he set out to find her before the battle began. Following Tyrrel toward the scene of the fighting, Mr. Lindsay was fatally wounded and Tyrrel killed. Mildred and Henry were able to speak with their father before he died, however, and he lived long enough to take the hands of Mildred and Butler and forgive them for having disobeyed him. He died shortly afterward in a delirium brought on by his fever.

Mildred and Butler returned to Dove-Cote to live a long and prosperous life together.

Further Critical Evaluation of the Work:

John Pendleton Kennedy is principally remembered as a patron of Edgar Allan Poe and for two of his own books—*Swallow Barn* (1832), a loosely linked series of sketches of plantation life in Virginia written in the manner of Washington Irving's *Bracebridge Hall*; and *Horseshoe Robinson: A Tale of the Tory Ascendency,* with a plot reminiscent of James Fenimore Cooper's *The Spy* and a hero who resembles Cooper's Leatherstocking.

Just as Cooper had built *The Spy* upon the theme of divided loyalties of the Tories and the American rebels in New York during the Revolution, so Kennedy pictures a division of loyalties in the Carolinas at a time when any stranger one met might be either a friend or an enemy. Kennedy is unoriginal in his plot development, using both characters and incidents that seem to have been borrowed from Cooper. Major Butler and Mildred Lindsay are conventional romantic lovers such as may be found in many earlier English and American novels. Also as in Cooper's frontier romances, the lower-class characters are more appealing than the genteel upper-class ones.

Horseshoe Robinson has survived mainly because of Horseshoe himself—Kennedy said he modeled him upon a real Galbraith Robinson—and though the modern reader may object to the slow pace and the contrived plot of the novel, he can still enjoy, as did Kennedy's contemporaries, the character of the stalwart soldier whose good heart and stout body were dedicated to the service of the Revolution and the safety of his friends. In addition, the novel offers, to some readers at least, the pleasure of relishing Kennedy's polished narrative and descriptive style marked by touches of genial humor, directed sometimes at Horseshoe himself. William Gilmore Simms, a South Carolina author of later historical romances, complained in 1852 about faults in Kennedy's dialect, history, and geography; but Kennedy has otherwise been praised for the accuracy of his period detail in this, the first novel which dealt with the Revolution in the South.

THE HOUSE BY THE CHURCHYARD

Type of work: Novel
Author: Joseph Sheridan Le Fanu (1814-1873)
Type of plot: Mystery romance
Time of plot: Late eighteenth century
Locale: Chapelizod, a suburb of Dublin
First published: 1863

Principal characters:

MR. MERVYN, son of Lord Dunoran
LORD DUNORAN, an Irish peer convicted of murdering one
    Mr. Beauclerc
PAUL DANGERFIELD, the real murderer of Mr. Beauclerc
ZEKIEL IRONS, Dangerfield's accomplice in the murder
DR. BARNABY STURK, a witness to the murder

Critique:

Le Fanu's career as a novelist dated from the publication of this book, which he began writing after the death of his wife in 1858. He withdrew from society at the time of her death and wrote to keep himself occupied. Le Fanu's novels, including this one, are novels of lush life—and something more. Death, mystery, and the supernatural are the grim twilight materials of his fiction. Constant speculation on death and the supernatural enabled him to communicate a spectral atmosphere to his novels. A master of terror, Le Fanu has been favorably compared in the past with such other masters of the supernatural as Wilkie Collins and Poe. This novel is generally regarded as his masterpiece, although *Uncle Silas* was the most popular during his vogue.

The Story:

Lord Dunoran, an Irish peer, had been executed after his conviction for murdering a man named Beauclerc in London. In addition, his estates were declared forfeit to the crown, and his family was left under a shadow. Eighteen years after his death, his son, who went under the name of Mr. Mervyn, took the body back to Ireland and buried it in the family vault in the Anglican church in Chapelizod, a suburb of Dublin. Following the burial, Mervyn moved into an old house that was reputed to be haunted; several families had moved out of it

after having seen strange apparitions and heard strange noises at night. Mervyn hoped that in the neighborhood he might pick up some clues that would lead him to the true murderer of Beauclerc, for the young man still believed his father innocent of the crime for which he had died years before.

About the same time that young Mervyn took up residence in the haunted house, another stranger came to Chapelizod, a man named Paul Dangerfield, who was looking after the affairs of a local nobleman. Dangerfield was a very rich man, and before long he had ingratiated himself in the hearts of the local people by his apparent good sense and his liberality. Of young Mervyn, on the other hand, the villagers were very suspicious, for he kept to himself, and only a few people knew his real identity.

The appearance of Paul Dangerfield caused fears and apprehensions in the minds of two men who lived in Chapelizod. The two were Zekiel Irons, the clerk at the Anglican church, and Dr. Barnaby Sturk, a surgeon at the garrison of the Royal Irish Artillery. Irons had been the accomplice of the man who had actually committed the murder of which Lord Dunoran had been convicted. Dr. Sturk had been a witness to the murder. They both recognized Paul Dangerfield to be a man named Charles Archer, a ruthless wretch who would think as little of taking their lives as he had of taking those of others.

Zekiel Irons, who wanted to live without fear, resolved to help young Mervyn discover the guilt of Archer-Dangerfield, for Irons knew that he could never live securely until the man was in prison or dead. Irons had been present also when Dangerfield had killed his other accomplice, who had tried to blackmail Dangerfield. On two occasions Irons visited Mervyn and imparted a portion of what he knew; on both occasions he warned Mervyn not to tell anyone at all, lest his informant be killed.

Dr. Sturk, meanwhile, also recognized Dangerfield as Charles Archer, the man he had seen commit a murder. Dr. Sturk, pressed for money, was trying to become an agent for Lord Castlemallard, who was represented by Dangerfield. Dr. Sturk made the mistake, however, of threatening Dangerfield with exposure if the agency were not forthcoming. Dr. Sturk was found terribly beaten about the head one night. Since he was in a deep coma, no one knew who had tried to kill him. Evidence pointed, however, to Charles Nutter, the man Dr. Sturk was trying to replace as the nobleman's agent in Chapelizod, for Nutter had disappeared on the same night that Dr. Sturk was attacked. There was no evidence to indicate that Dangerfield had been the attacker. He had been so helpful to Dr. Sturk that he was under no suspicion.

Dr. Sturk lingered on, and for a time it seemed as if he might recover. Dangerfield arranged for a surgeon to come, at a high fee, to operate on the doctor. Dangerfield had convinced Mrs. Sturk that the operation was the only chance her husband had for life, but actually Dangerfield hoped the operation would be a failure and that Dr. Sturk would die without revealing the identity of his attacker. But the operation was a partial success. Dr. Sturk regained his mind and lived for several days, during which time he made depositions to the magistrates concerning the identity of his attacker and the fact that Dangerfield had mur-

dered another man years before. These events moved Zekiel Irons to go also to the magistrates and tell what he knew about the real identity of Paul Dangerfield and the part he himself had played in the murder of Beauclerc. Even in the face of that evidence, the magistrates found it difficult to believe Dangerfield guilty. The fact that Dangerfield had paid for the operation and had lent money to Mrs. Sturk, as well as the disappearance of Charles Nutter, left them in doubt.

But Charles Nutter, apprehended in Dublin within one day of Dangerfield's arrest, was able to prove that he had been away on other business at the time of the attack on Dr. Sturk. He had, however, gone so close to the scene of the crime that he had frightened off Dangerfield before he could finish the murder.

Nutter had not run away; he had simply been to England and Scotland trying to straighten out his domestic affairs. A woman had attempted to prove he was a bigamist because he had married her several years before his marriage to the woman the people in Chapelizod knew as his wife. He had married the woman, but she herself was a bigamist, having been already married to another man. Nutter had been off to find the true husband, to prove that his marriage to the woman was really no marriage at all. He had been compelled to leave secretly lest he be arrested as a bigamist before he could gather evidence to clear his name.

In another quarter of the village the apprehension of Dangerfield had great implications. He had been engaged to the daughter of the commanding general of the Royal Irish Artillery, even though he was many years older than the girl. Because of his wealth, the general was quite anxious to have his daughter marry Dangerfield. The girl, however, was in love with Mervyn and secretly engaged to him. Dangerfield's arrest prevented the general from marrying his daughter to a man she did not love.

So far as Mervyn was concerned, the apprehension of Dangerfield did more than open the way for his marriage to the general's daughter. The information which Dr. Sturk and Zekiel Irons gave concerning the murder of Beauclerc cleared Mervyn's father, Lord Dunoran. When Parliament met again, it returned to Mervyn his good name, his title, and the estates forfeited at the time of his father's conviction.

Paul Dangerfield, alias Charles Archer, was never convicted, nor was he tried by a court. He died mysteriously in his cell in the county gaol in Dublin while awaiting trial, thus cheating the state of executing him for murder. Not long afterward, the new Lord Dunoran and the daughter of the general commanding the Royal Irish Artillery were married in a great ceremony at Chapelizod.

Further Critical Evaluation of the Work:

Although Joseph Sheridan Le Fanu is best remembered as a master of the psychological horror story, his first literary efforts were in the field of the Irish historical romance. However, since these early works were ignored by critics and readers, Le Fanu abandoned the novel in favor of editing and short fiction. It was not until after the death of his wife in 1858 and the long seclusion which followed that he returned to long fiction and produced the major novels of his last years, the first of which was *The House by the Churchyard*. The major topics of the work, violent murder and retribution, are characteristic of his late novels, but the novel also reflects Le Fanu's earlier interest in historical and social subjects and thus serves as a tranisition book between the two phases of his career.

The setting of the novel, the Dublin suburb of Chapelizod, was an area Le Fanu knew personally and affectionately from his own youth. He clearly demonstrates this intimacy in the way he captures the atmosphere and character of small town Irish life in the late eighteenth century with considerable warmth and humor. Some critics have faulted the novel as too diffuse and fragmentary, but, in fact, Le Fanu carefully balances the activities of the various social and economic groups as he gradually brings the different plot lines together. The "serious" courtship of Mr. Mervyn and Gertrude Chattesworth and the "doomed" love between Captain "Gipsy" Devereux and the Rector's daughter, Lilias Walsingham, are carefully juxtaposed against the farcical romantic entanglements of the clownish members of the Royal Irish Artillery and their equally comic lady friends. Even the primary villainy, Paul Dangerfield's murder of Dr. Sturk, is set opposite Mary Matchwell's absurd attempt to defraud Charles Nutter's widow of her inheritance. It is this balance between the comic and the horrific, coupled with Le Fanu's acute social observations, that gives *The House by the Churchyard* its unique place in the Le Fanu canon.

All of this is not to minimize the "sensation" element in the novel, only to put it into proportion. Murder and violence do dominate the second half of the book, although the comic is never completely subdued. But after Sturk's beating there is a definite acceleration in the pace and intensification of the suspense. While the focus of the novel is constantly shifting in the early sections of the book, the action in the latter half concentrates on a few characters and their activities, notably Mervyn's efforts to vindicate his father's name, Zekiel Irons' sinister partial confession and bizarre actions, Paul Dangerfield's ambiguous machinations, and, most vivid of all, the mute, zombie-like victim, Barnabas Sturk.

Since Sturk alone can unravel the mystery, the question of his recovery, or at least his speaking, comes to dominate the novel. The climax of the book is the "trepanning" scene which gives Sturk the strength and stimulus to expose Dangerfield ("trepanning" is the archaic medical practice of drilling a small hole in the skull to "relieve pressure"). As mystery writer and historian Dorothy Sayers has rightly stated: "For sheer grimness and power, there is little in the literature of horror to compare with the trepanning scene in Le Fanu's *House by the Churchyard.* . . . That chapter itself would entitle Le Fanu to be called a master of murder and horror."

And once the aristocratic Paul Dangerfield is revealed to be the nefarious Charles Archer, he assumes a kind of evil grandeur that makes him almost the equal of Le Fanu's arch Gothic villain, Silas Ruthyn. Trapped and condemned, Dangerfield-Archer confesses and rationalizes his crime with a cool, stylish audacity that places him in the best tradition of the Gothic hero-villain. "I assure you," he tells Mervyn, "I never yet bore any man the least ill-will. I've had to remove two or three—not because I hated them—I did not care a button for any—but because their existence was incompatible with my safety which, Sir, is the first thing to me, as yours is to you." And then he casually commits suicide.

All things considered, although *The House by the Churchyard* may not possess the sustained, mounting terror and the continuing dramatic intensity of Le Fanu's Gothic masterpiece *Uncle Silas,* it has a breadth, scope, humor, and social realism that the later novel lacks. For this reason, in spite of the greater popularity of *Uncle Silas,* many critics and readers consider *The House by the Churchyard* to be the crowning achievement of Le Fanu's career.

THE HOUSE BY THE MEDLAR TREE

Type of work: Novel
Author: Giovanni Verga (1840-1922)
Type of plot: Impressionistic realism
Time of plot: Mid-nineteenth century
Locale: Sicily
First published: 1881

Principal characters:
PADRON 'NTONI, head of the Malavoglia
BASTIANAZZO, his son
LA LONGA, Bastianazzo's wife
'NTONI, their oldest son
LUCA, their second son
MENA, their oldest daughter
ALESSIO, their youngest son
LIA, their youngest daughter
UNCLE CRUCIFIX DUMBBELL, a local usurer
GOOSEFOOT, his assistant
DON MICHELE, brigadier of the coast guard

Critique:

This novel, translated also under the title *The Malavoglia*, is one of the most interesting contributions of Italian literature to modern realism. Its characters are poor, simple people who can never rest from their struggle to keep alive. The message of the novel is that man is continually being pulled apart by his own forces, so that only by working together with his fellow men can he hope to survive. Written in a completely realistic fashion, with no intrusion from the author, this novel bridges the gap between realism and naturalism.

The Story:

In the village of Trezza, on the island of Sicily, the Malavoglia family had once been great. Now the only Malavoglia left were Padron 'Ntoni and his little brood in the house by the medlar tree. But they were happy and prosperous, living well on the income brought in by their boat, the *Provvidenza.*

When the oldest grandson, 'Ntoni, was conscripted, the first sadness fell on the household. In that same year other things went badly, and the market for fish was poor. With 'Ntoni gone, the money that came in had to be divided with extra help that Padron was forced to hire. Eventually Padron 'Ntoni had to arrange a loan with

Uncle Crucifix Dumbbell to buy a shipment of coarse black beans on credit from him. The beans were to be resold at Riposto by Padron's son, Bastianazzo. Although La Longa, Bastianazzo's wife was skeptical of this deal, she kept quiet, as befitted a woman. Soon afterward, Bastianazzo sailed away on the *Provvidenza* with the cargo of beans aboard. All the villagers whispered that the beans were spoiled, that Uncle Crucifix had cheated the Malavoglia. It was well known that Uncle Crucifix was an old fox in all money matters.

Nevertheless, if the beans were sold, Padron 'Ntoni's family would be well off. The man whose son was to marry Mena Malavoglia rubbed his hands in anticipation of his boy's good fortune. The women of the village, and others too, agreed that Mena was everything a girl should be. But luck went against the Malavoglia family. In the early evening a huge storm came up. Down at the tavern Don Michele, the brigadier of the coast guard, predicted the doom of the *Provvidenza.* When word came that the boat had been lost, Bastianazzo with her, grief engulfed the Malavoglia family. To add to their troubles, Uncle Crucifix began to demand his money. All the neighbors who brought gifts of condolence to the house by the medlar tree looked about the premises as if they saw Uncle Crucifix already in possession.

Stubbornly Padron 'Ntoni and his family set to work to repay the loan. It was decided to have Mena married as soon as possible. Alfio Mosca, who drove a donkeycart and often lingered to talk with the girl, was grieved at the news. Then one day the *Provvidenza*, battered but still usable, was towed into port. The Malavoglia rejoiced. At the same time 'Ntoni arrived home. Luca, the second son, was drafted. Each member of the family slaved to make enough money to repay the debt.

Meanwhile Uncle Crucifix was fiercely repeating his demands. At last he decided to pretend to sell his debt to his assistant, Goosefoot; then, when officers were sent to Padron 'Ntoni's house, people could not say that a usurer or the devil's money had been involved in their troubles. A short time later a stamped paper was served on the Malavoglia family. Frightened, they went to a city lawyer who told them that Uncle Crucifix could do nothing to them because the house was in the name of the daughter-in-law, and she had not signed the papers in the deal of beans. Padron 'Ntoni felt guilty, however; he had borrowed the money and it must be paid back. When he asked advice from the communal secretary, that official told him that the daughter-in-law must give dower rights on the house to Goosefoot, who was now the legal owner of the note. Although Goosefoot protested that he wanted his money, he nevertheless accepted a mortgage.

As the family began to gather money to repay the loan, luck again went against them. New taxes were put on pitch and salt, two necessary commodities, and personal relations between Goosefoot and the family were strained when he and young 'Ntoni came to blows over a girl. In the village there was talk of smugglers, and the rumors involved two of 'Ntoni's close friends. Goosefoot enlisted the aid of Don Michele to watch 'Ntoni closely.

When Mena's betrothal was announced, Alfio Mosca sadly left town.

Padron 'Ntoni, happy over the approaching marriage of his granddaughter, offered Goosefoot part of the money on the loan. But Goosefoot, demanding all of it, refused to be moved by the fact that Mena needed a dowry. On top of these troubles the Malavoglia family learned that Luca had been killed in the war. Goosefoot began again to send stamped papers. When Padron 'Ntoni appealed to the lawyer, he was told that he had been a fool to let La Longa give up her dower rights in the house but that nothing could be done about the matter now. So the family had to leave the house by the medlar tree and move into a rented hovel.

Somewhat repaired and on a fishing excursion, the *Provvidenza* ran into a storm. When Padron 'Ntoni was injured by a blow from the falling mast, young 'Ntoni had to bring the boat in alone. After the old man had recovered, 'Ntoni announced his decision to leave home; he could no longer stand the backbreaking, dull work of his debt-ridden family. His mother, grief-stricken by his departure, contracted cholera and soon died. Meanwhile Mena's engagement had been called off by her betrothed's father. Everything was against the Malavoglia. Goosefoot and Uncle Crucifix gave the family no rest, but insisted that they too were poor and needed their money.

When young 'Ntoni returned to his home with no fortune and clothing more ragged than ever, the villagers laughed with derision. Alessio, the youngest son, now began to help with the work, and he and 'Ntoni were able to earn a little money to apply on the family debt. 'Ntoni, still discontented, was often drunk coming home from the tavern.

Don Michele told the boy's young sister Lia, whom he secretly admired, that she and Mena must keep their eyes on 'Ntoni because he was involved with the smugglers. Although the frightened girls tried to remonstrate with their brother, he refused to listen to their pleas. One night Don Michele knocked at Lia's door and told her that she must find her brother, for the police were planning to ambush the smugglers. His warning came too late for the sisters to act, and 'Ntoni was caught after he had stabbed Don Michele in a scuffle during the raid.

Padron 'Ntoni spent all his savings in an attempt to rescue his grandson. Then he was told a false version of the incident, that 'Ntoni had stabbed Don Michele because he had learned of an affair between the soldier and Lia. The old man was so horrified by this news that he suffered a stroke from which he never completely recovered. Lia left home immediately, without attempting to make known the true facts of the case, and young 'Ntoni was sent to the galleys for five years.

Gradually, under the direction of the youngest son, Alessio, the affairs of the family began to mend. Uncle Crucifix and Goosefoot finally got their money, and Alessio and his bride regained possession of the house by the medlar tree.

Further Critical Evaluation of the Work:

The House by the Medlar Tree was designed by Giovanni Verga to be the first of five novels dealing, each in its turn, with the economic, social, and ethical aspirations of the five principal social classes in nineteenth century Italy. It is generally agreed that Verga drew the inspiration for this literary structure from the cyclical works of Balzac and Zola. Only two of Verga's five novels were finished: *The House by the Medlar Tree* and *Maestro-don Gesualdo.* The former is striking for its choral presentation of human relationships, its success in achieving a poetic, eternalizing tone to realistic investigation, and its astounding objectivity. The latter makes near-perfect use of classical novel structure by depicting in a linear manner the inner life of one man through his outward existence. It is common to assume that Italian Realism dealt almost exclusively with the so-called "primitive" classes, wherein, theoretically, the essential nature of man, neither hidden nor distorted by refinement, most clearly manifested itself. The five-volume *I Vinti* ("The Conquered") was, however, to address itself as a realistic study to all of society; and *The House by the Medlar Tree,* while complete in itself, must also be considered as but one level of interest in Verga's vast design.

Notwithstanding the author's objectivity, the central theme common to this design is that a man, no matter what his discomforts and tragedies, is ultimately better off in the position in which he is born. Portrayal of a static world is hardly the result. Verga's characters fight desperately and in infinitely different ways against the cruelty of this state. Nor does Verga pronounce judgment upon their reactions—the heroic, the pathetic, and the cruel are alike portrayed realistically.

The mainstream of criticism on *The House by the Medlar Tree* views the disintegration of the Malavoglia family somewhat in the terms of Greek tragedy. The family, headed by paterfamilias Padron 'Ntoni, who unquestioningly guides their moral, social, and economic life with ancient Sicilian proverbs, begins the novel in a state of relative prosperity on all three levels. A familiar theme of Padron 'Ntoni's proverbs is that prosperity is possible only when the family works together, completely together, at all times, and does not try for more than its due share. Strangely enough, it is he who arranges to buy the black beans on credit. Although La Longa is afraid, almost the entire family is enthusiastic about the possibility of sudden profit; thus the family commits what may be considered an act of collective hubris by trying to gain what is beyond their proper realm. The ensuing shipwreck, in which Bastianazzo dies and the family is literally torn asunder, may be seen as the resultant nemesis. It is only in their working together, unquestioningly, that the family is able to survive economically and retain a portion of their former prestige and dignity in the eyes of their fellow villagers.

The struggle is long, however—too long for some of the family to bear. Young 'Ntoni is the first family member to question the struggle, and the only one to question it on a rational level. Having been conscripted, he has seen other social environments and other values while in service and soon refutes his grandfather's principle that only total loyalty will bring the meager success so long accepted in Trezza as the maximum hope. He abandons the family when they need him most in order to find his fortune in the world outside, thus proving himself unchristian in the eyes of the village and committing hubris on a personal level. When he returns home in failure, he is greeted with ridicule from Trezza and openly displays antisocial behavior.

Lia likewise commits individual hubris when she acknowledges Don Michele's attentions. Because he is of a superior class, the relationship is doomed and can only end in destroying her reputation and that of her family. Yet her desperation and her attraction to his material gifts are overwhelming. While she is rebelling on an emotional rather than a rational level, the result is the same as it was for young 'Ntoni—her own reputation is ruined, her family is dragged further down in the eyes of Trezza, and the beginning of her moral decline occurs. Thus, by a family member again acting as an individual bent on individual survival, the total family unit sinks deeper into extreme poverty.

In the end, the united efforts of the least questioning—La Longa, Mena, Luca, Alessio, and Padron 'Ntoni—reverse the trend. Yet lines of good and evil, reward and punishment, cannot be clearly drawn. La Longa has died from suffering and exhaustion as wife and mother. Gentle and virtuous Mena cannot marry because of her sister's reputation. Luca has been drafted and killed in a war no one in the village really knows about. Padron 'Ntoni has had to be sent to the poorhouse in his last illness. Alessio has inherited the family's somewhat reversed fortunes. And young 'Ntoni, after serving a prison term, has set out for the world again, partly because of village ostracism and partly because he is determined again not to be strangled by life. There is no comment by Verga on his rightness or wrongness, or his chances of failure or success.

In 1881 the author wrote:

This account [*The House by the Medlar Tree*] is the sincere and impartial study of how most probably the first inquietudes for well-being must be born and develop in the humblest of conditions; and what confusion and disturbance the ill-defined desire for the unknown and the realization that one is not well-off, or could at least be better off, must bring into a family which has lived until now in a relatively happy state.

Interpretation and conclusion are the right of the reader; but, in *The House by the Medlar Tree,* Giovanni Verga's contrary purpose of almost scientific objectivity as an author must be kept continuously in mind.

Roberta Payne

THE HOUSE IN PARIS

Type of work: Novel
Author: Elizabeth Bowen (1899-1973)
Type of plot: Psychological realism
Time of plot: After World War I
Locale: France and England
First published: 1936

Principal characters:
HENRIETTA MOUNTJOY, a brief visitor in Paris, eleven years of age
LEOPOLD MOODY, another visitor, nine years of age
MISS NAOMI FISHER, their hostess for a day
MADAME FISHER, Naomi's invalid mother
KAREN MICHAELIS, friend of Naomi, former pupil of her mother
MAX EBHART, a young Parisian, attractive and intellectual

Critique:

Her facility in creating suspense would have stood Elizabeth Bowen in good stead had she chosen to write detective novels. *The House in Paris* gradually unravels a human secret which not only the readers but also the characters of the novel find both absorbing and oppressive. The author's method, however, is not to emphasize physical action but rather to unfold complex relationships of people, evolving slowly into a conclusion that is logical but necessarily incomplete. There are no pat endings to Miss Bowen's books, no perfect dovetailing of desire and fulfillment; as long as people live, she convincingly and calmly implies, there are questions that will be only partially answered, wishes that will be only partially granted. In this book she presents the situation that a child creates by merely existing: an inadvertent love and an inadvertent begetting that become a problem to several people. It is, in short, the problem of an illegitimate boy, and it has rarely been traced with more keenness and candor.

The Story:

Henrietta arrived at the Gare du Nord uncomfortably early in the morning. She had never been in Paris before; and she was not to be there long this time, for one day only, between two night trains. By a previous arrangement, the eleven-year-old girl was met at the station by Miss Naomi Fisher, an acquaintance of Henrietta's grandmother, who would look after her during her day in Paris.

Clutching her plush toy monkey while the taxi bumped through gray Paris streets, Henrietta drowsily absorbed Miss Fisher's nervous chatter. The flow of comments, however, was not entirely pointless: Henrietta was presently made to comprehend that her stopover would be affected by some rather unusual developments at Miss Fisher's house. For one thing, Miss Fisher's mother was ill, though today she was feeling better and Miss Fisher could still hope to take Henrietta out for a short sightseeing expedition after lunch. A more important complication seemed to be the presence of Leopold.

Leopold, Miss Fisher explained with obvious agitation, was an added responsibility which she had not foreseen when she agreed to meet Henrietta. He was nine years old, and he had come from Italy to see his mother, who was a very dear friend of Miss Fisher. Apparently, Henrietta gathered, he had never seen his mother before, a fact which struck the little girl as being quite odd and mysterious. Miss Fisher agreed that the circumstances were rather unusual, but she evaded a more direct explanation. Leopold, she was careful to bring out, was naturally excited and anxious; Henrietta might play with him, if she liked—but she must not question him about his mother.

After arriving at the house in Paris, Henrietta had breakfast and a nap on the sofa before she awoke to find Leopold standing across the salon and gazing at her curiously. The children made wary approaches to acquaintanceship and tentatively compared notes on their respective journeys. In spite of Miss Fisher's injunction, Henrietta managed to learn that Leopold lived at Spezia with his foster parents. Before she could find out more about him, she was summoned upstairs to meet the ill Madame Fisher. The latter seemed a queer person to Henrietta; her manner was ironic and penetrating, and, to her daughter's distress, she insisted on discussing Leopold's father. Once, Madame Fisher intimated, he had broken her daughter's heart. Now he was dead.

Left alone below, Leopold rummaged through Miss Fisher's purse in a vain search for information about his mother. After Henrietta rejoined him, the children had lunch and played aimlessly at cards. While they were thus occupied, the doorbell rang, and Miss Fisher was heard to go to the door. A few minutes later she entered the room, her face suffused with regret and pity. Leopold struggled manfully to affect nonchalance as she told him that, after all, his mother was not coming—she could not come.

Leopold had no way of knowing that his mother was Karen Michaelis, now married to Ray Forrestier. More than ten years earlier, her engagement to Ray had just been announced, and their friends rejoiced in what seemed an ideal match. The marriage was to be delayed, however, until Ray's completion of a diplomatic mission in the East. Shortly after his departure from England, Karen visited her aunt in Ireland. Returning home, she found a pleasant surprise awaiting her; Naomi Fisher was spending a few days in London.

Karen and Naomi had been intimate ever since Karen, an English schoolgirl, had spent a year under the roof of Madame Fisher in Paris. There she had been housed, perfected in French, and given Madame's keen-eyed supervision, along with other English and American girls who were accepted into the establishment from time to time. There, too, she had first become conscious of Max Ebhart, a dark, taut, brilliant young man whose conversation and intellect Madame Fisher found stimulating. Rather unaccountably, Max had now become engaged to the unassuming Naomi and had accompanied her to England to aid in the settlement of an aunt's estate. Karen welcomed the opportunity to see Naomi, but she expressed reluctance to encounter Max, whose strong self-possession and penetrating mind had always affected her strangely.

Naomi's persistence prevailed, however, and on the final day of her stay in London she succeeded in getting Max and Karen together. While Naomi prepared tea inside the almost-emptied house of her dead aunt, Max and Karen sat outside on the lawn. Little was said, but both were conscious of the tension that their presence together always inspired. That night, as Karen said goodbye at the station, she looked at Max, and their eyes exchanged the mutual admission that they were in love.

A month later the Michaelis telephone rang. It was Max, in Paris, asking Karen to meet him in Boulogne the following Sunday. There they walked and talked, the thought of Naomi shadowing their conversation. Before they parted they arranged to meet again, at Hythe, the next Saturday. They spent the night together and decided that they must marry, in spite of their unwillingness to hurt Naomi. Max went back to Paris to impart the difficult news to his fiancée.

Karen never saw Max again; word of his suicide came in a telegram from Naomi. Weeks later Naomi herself crossed the channel to tell Karen how Max had slashed his wrists after a trying interview with Madame Fisher. When Karen confessed that she was going to bear Max's child, the two girls considered the plans she must make. Karen had already tried to break off her engagement with Ray Forrestier, but he had written that he would never give her up. Nevertheless, she intended to be gone when he returned to London; she would travel to Paris with Naomi and then go on to Germany for perhaps a year. She and Naomi would find a good home for the child. Meanwhile no one else—except possibly Karen's mother—should ever know.

These were the facts about his parents that Leopold had never learned. Now, his mother having failed him by not coming to get him at the house in Paris, he stood, for a moment, immovable, lapped in misery. His air of resolution and determined indifference soon gave way. Crossing to the mantelpiece and pressing himself against it, he burst into sobs. Henrietta tried to comfort him, but he ignored her. Recovering from his spasm of grief, he was sent upstairs to endure Madame Fisher's careful scrutiny. He found her surprisingly sympathetic. She told him something of his mother's marriage to Ray Forrestier, and he confided his determination not to return to his foster parents in Italy. Something in the old invalid's inner force seemed to stiffen and encourage him.

Downstairs the doorbell rang once more, and presently Miss Fisher came running swiftly up the steps. She directed Leopold to the salon where he found a tall, pleasant-looking Englishman. It was Ray Forrestier; overruling Karen's doubts, he had come to accept Leopold as his own son and to restore him to his mother.

Further Critical Evaluation of the Work:

Unwed mother and illegitimate child—Elizabeth Bowen uses these traditional social pariahs to express her perennial concern for the value of the child's perspective concerning adult society, the changing role of woman, and the importance of accepting the past.

Even though Henrietta and Leopold seem so at first, the children are not the most important characters in *The House in Paris*. Bowen is capable not only of detailing the consciousnesses of children but of using the child's perspective in her portrayal of adults. Bowen's real concern is with adults, but she is very much aware of the connection of adult reality to the child's world. The structure of *The House in Paris* clearly suggests both the connection between the two realities as well as the absolute gulf separating them. The first and last sections of the book, both headed "The Present," frame the longer middle section, "The Past." The consciousnesses of Henrietta and Leopold dominate "the Present," while those of their parents' generation dominate "The Past." A character like Naomi Fisher, who appears in both parts, is very different when viewed by a nine-year-old child as "Miss Fisher" and when viewed by a contemporary as "Naomi."

A child's loneliness is often Bowen's metaphor for that human loneliness brought about by fate or misfortune. Thus Leopold—abandoned as an infant by his mother, his father dead—sees himself as utterly alone and bereft of identity. He is, therefore, a stranger to the values of his biological family and the community of the "house in Paris." At nine years he expects to be "initiated" into those mysteries, accepted by his mother, and made a part of the community. But instead he must cope with his mother's rejection; he weeps because this is the end of his hopes and plans. Much of the material devoted to Leopold is narrated through the consciousness of the second child, Henrietta. Henrietta's perception of her contemporary helps to balance Leopold's solipsistic self-analysis.

Bowen often uses the discrepancy between women's changing aspirations and the traditional roles assigned by society as metaphor for the disintegration of society as a whole. Karen is ambivalent about the roles of wife and mother. Maturing in an upper-class environment free of anxieties about family or money, she still feels unfulfilled. Even after she becomes engaged to the man she is expected to marry, she keeps asking, "What next? What next?" She wants to escape from the too-secure future which is held out to her, and she complains bitterly to her Aunt Violet that she will be too "safe" with Ray as a husband. Karen thus rebels, taking her best friend's fiancé as lover and cancelling her own engagement. Ironically, Karen had regretted that no one would ever know of her action. She believes that her "revolution" has changed nothing. But consequences do occur: Max and Karen fall in love and want to marry; Karen is pregnant; Max commits suicide when he learns that Madame Fisher had planned for him to break with Naomi, so his rebellion was useless.

Karen gives up Leopold for adoption, but cannot rid herself of ambivalent feelings toward her son and her past. She makes an attempt to see him again —thus the day at the house in Paris. But although she desperately desires this union of her past with Leopold's present to make a new future, she lacks the courage to take the final step.

The House in Paris uses structure, symbol, and plot to achieve a clear statement about the value and organic character of the past. In the book's structure, "the Past" is bounded by "the Present," showing the essential interpenetration of the two. Leopold personifies the past's ongoing character; in him are embodied Madame Fisher and Naomi, Karen, Ray, Max. The house itself is a symbol of the past's inserting itself into the present: the events of the present were begun on their inexorable course by the meeting of the characters in the house when Karen was a schoolgirl.

In her use of enclosed spaces to give meaning to her characters, Bowen reminds one of Jane Austen and George Eliot. Not only in "the house in Paris," but at 2 Windsor Terrace in *The Death of the Heart* (1938), in Stella's apartment and at Mount Morris in *The Heat of the Day* (1949), and in her early works *The Hotel* (1927) and *The Last September* (1929), Bowen places her female and adolescent characters within architectural structures. Rooms, houses, apartments, mansions—these are the spaces where the drama of female lives takes place. Employing little natural description, Bowen fills her works with depictions of interiors.

Here, of course, the house is Madame Fisher's. She is the strongest personality in the book, and both Karen and Max come to realize that if they fail to assert their wills, she will dominate them. Ray also senses this, and takes the courageous step Karen could not: he decides to accept Leopold (and Karen's past). Ray's gesture is not totally romantic; he understands the difficulties involved. But that Karen can reintegrate past and present and break through to the future may now be hoped for. Unwed mother and illegitimate son have been accepted and taken into society; but will that society really change now that the "revolution" has taken place? Or will Karen still be wondering, "What next? What next?" Bowen is not too hopeful here; all that can be said is that a beginning, an attempt at reintegration, has been made.

Margaret McFadden-Gerber

THE HOUSE OF ATREUS

Type of work: Drama
Author: Aeschylus (525-456 B.C.)
Type of plot: Classical tragedy
Time of plot: After the fall of Troy
Locale: Argos
First presented: 458 B.C.

> *Principal characters:*
> AGAMEMNON, the king
> CLYTEMNESTRA, his queen
> CASSANDRA, a Trojan captive
> AEGISTHUS, paramour of Clytemnestra
> ORESTES, son of Agamemnon
> ELECTRA, his sister

Critique:

In the archonship of Philocles, in 458 B.C., Aeschylus won first prize with his dramatic trilogy, *The House of Atreus.* This story of the doomed descendants of the cruel and bloody Atreus is one of the great tales of classic literature. Aeschylus, building his plays upon themes of doom and revenge, was deeply concerned with moral law in the Greek state. For this reason the moral issues of the plays are clear and steadfast, simple and devastating in implication, especially the working of conscience in the character of Orestes. *Agamemnon, The Libation-Bearers,* and *The Furies* are the individual titles which make up the trilogy.

The Story:

The house of Atreus was accursed because in the great palace at Argos the tyrant, Atreus, had killed the children of Thyestes and served their flesh to their father at a royal banquet. Agamemnon and Menelaus were the sons of Atreus. When Helen, wife of Menelaus, was carried off by Paris, Agamemnon was among the Greek heroes who went with his brother to battle the Trojans for her return. But on the way to Troy, while the fleet lay idle at Aulis, Agamemnon was prevailed upon to sacrifice his daughter, Iphigenia, to the gods. Hearing of this deed, Clytemnestra, his wife, vowed revenge. She gave her son, Orestes, into the care of the King of Phocis, and in the darkened palace nursed her consuming hate.

In her desire for vengeance she was joined by Aegisthus, surviving son of Thyestes, who had returned from his long exile. Hate had brought the queen and Aegisthus together in a common cause; they became lovers as well as plotters in crime.

The ship of Menelaus having been delayed by a storm, Agamemnon returned alone from the Trojan wars. A watchman first saw the lights of his ship upon the sea and brought to his queen the news of the king's return. Leaving his men quartered in the town, Agamemnon drove to the palace in his chariot, beside him Cassandra, captive daughter of the king of Troy and an augeress of all misfortunes to come, who had fallen to Agamemnon in the division of the spoils. She had already warned the king that some evil was to befall him.

Agamemnon, however, had no suspicions of his homecoming, as Clytemnestra came to greet him at the palace doorway, her armed retainers about her, magnificent carpets unrolled for the feet of the conqueror of Troy. Agamemnon chided his queen for the lavishness of her reception and entered the palace to refresh himself after his long journey. He asked Clytemnestra to receive Cassandra and to treat his captive kindly.

After Agamemnon had retired, Clytemnestra returned and ordered Cassandra, who had refused to leave the chariot, to enter the palace. When Cassandra persisted in remaining where she was, the queen declared she would not demean herself by bandying words with a common slave and a madwoman. She reentered the palace. Cassandra lifted her face toward the sky and called upon Apollo to tell her why she had been brought to this cursed house. She informed the spectators in front of the palace that Clytemnestra would murder Agamemnon. She lamented the fall of Troy, recalled the butchery of Thyestes' children, and the doom that hung over the sons of Atreus, and foretold again the murder of Agamemnon by his queen. As she entered the palace, those outside heard the death cry of Agamemnon within.

A moment later Clytemnestra appeared in the doorway, the bloody sword of Aegisthus in her hand. Behind her lay the body of the king, entangled in the rich carpets. Clytemnestra defended herself before the citizens, saying she had killed the king for the murder of Iphigenia, and had also killed Cassandra, with whom Agamemnon had shamed her honor. Her deed, she told the citizens defiantly, had ended the bloody lust of the house of Atreus.

Then she presented Aegisthus, son of Thyestes, who asserted that his vengeance was just and that he intended to rule in the palace of Agamemnon. Reproaches were hurled at the guilty pair. There were cries that Orestes would avenge his father's murder. Aegisthus and Clytemnestra, in a fury of guilty horror, roared out their self-justification for the crime and defied the gods themselves to end their seizure of power.

Orestes, grown to manhood, returned from the land of Phocis, to discover that his mother and Aegisthus had murdered his father. He mourned his father's death and asked the king of the gods to give him ability to take vengeance upon the guilty pair. Electra, daughter of Agamemnon, also mourned and cursed the murderers. Encountering her brother, she did not at first recognize him, for he appeared in the disguise of a messenger who brought word of the death

of Orestes. They met at their father's tomb, where he made himself known to his sister. There he begged his father's spirit to give him strength in his undertaking. Electra assured him nothing but evil could befall any of the descendants of Atreus and welcomed the quick fulfillment of approaching doom.

Learning that Clytemnestra had once dreamed of suckling a snake which drew blood from her breast, Orestes saw in this dream the image of himself and the deed he intended to commit. He went to the palace in disguise and killed Aegisthus. Then he confronted Clytemnestra, his sword dripping with the blood of his mother's lover, and struck her down.

Orestes displayed the two bodies to the people and announced to Apollo that he had done the deed required of him. But he realized that he must suffer for his terrible crime. He began to go mad as Furies, sent by his mother's dead spirit, pursued him.

The Furies drove Orestes from land to land. Finally he took refuge in a temple, but the Pythian priestess claimed the temple was profaned by the presence of the horrible Furies, who lay asleep near Orestes. Then Apollo appeared to tell Orestes that he had put the Furies to sleep so the haunted man could get some rest. He advised Orestes to visit the temple of Pallas Athena and there gain full absolution for his crime.

While Orestes listened, the ghost of Clytemnestra spitefully aroused the Furies and commanded them to torture Orestes again. When Apollo ordered the Furies to leave, the creatures accused him of blame for the murder of Clytemnestra and Aegisthus and the punishment of Orestes. The god confessed he had demanded the death of Agamemnon's murderers. He was told that by his demands he had caused an even greater crime, matricide. Apollo said Athena should decide the justice of the case.

In Athens, in the temple of the goddess, Orestes begged Athena to help him. Replying the case was too grave for her to decide alone, she called upon the judges to help her reach a wise decision. There were some who believed the ancient laws would be weakened if evidence were presented, and they claimed Orestes deserved his terrible punishment.

When Orestes asked why Clytemnestra had not been persecuted for the murder of Agamemnon, he was told her crime had not been the murder of a blood relative, as his was. Apollo was another witness at the trial. He claimed the mother was not the true parent, that the father, who planted the seed in the mother's womb, was the real parent, as shown in the tracing of descent through the male line. Therefore, Orestes was not guilty of the murder of a true member of his blood family.

The judges decided in favor of Orestes. There were many, however, who in an angry rage cursed and condemned the land where such a judgment might prevail. They cried woe upon the younger gods and all those who tried to wrest ancient rights from the hands of established tradition. But Athena upheld the judgment of the court and Orestes was freed from the anger of the Furies.

Further Critical Evaluation of the Work:

The House of Atreus (also known as the *Oresteia*) won first prize in the Athenian drama competition when it was initially presented in 458 B.C. This was the thirteenth time Aeschylus had been awarded the highest honors in a career of forty-one years as a tragedian. No one had done as much to establish the drama as a soaring art form capable of exploring the most compelling problems of human existence. And this dramatic trilogy—the only one in Greek drama to survive intact—was a fitting climax to his life. *The House of Atreus* is not merely a magnificent work, it is one of the supreme achievements of classical culture.

In it Aeschylus took up the theme of the ancestral curse, as he had done in *Seven Against Thebes.* But here he uses that theme to probe the metaphysical problem of evil. The question amounts to this: in a divinely ordered universe why are atrocities committed, and what is the reason for human suffering? Aeschylus brought all of his dramatic skill, all of his lofty genius for poetry, and all of his intelligence and feeling to bear on the issue. And he came as close as any writer ever has to expressing the profoundest truths of human life.

The legend of the dynasty of Atreus is a series of crimes, each committed in retaliation against a close relative. The murder of kin was the most hideous sin a person could perform, according to Greek morality. The blood curse was brought on the house of Atreus when Atreus murdered his nephews, and from there on the history of the family is one of slaughter. *Agamemnon,* the first play in the trilogy, reveals the homecoming and murder of Agamemnon by his wife Clytemnestra and his cousin Aegisthus, who is also her lover. The second play, *The Libation-Bearers,* shows Orestes' arrival in Argos and his revenge upon his mother and Aegisthus for killing Agamemnon. Then he is pursued by the Furies. And in the final play, *The Eumenides* (or "The Kindly Ones"), the curse is put to rest when Orestes is absolved from guilt in the Athenian law court of Athena.

The action of this trilogy is simple enough, but it is in the way Aeschylus develops the action, with layer upon layer of meaning, that these dramas engross us. The curse theme operates on several planes at once, and it is given concrete expression in the recurring images of the web, the net, the coiling snake full of venom.

On the simplest level *The House of Atreus* is a revenge trilogy. Agamemnon kills his daughter Iphigenia, which enables him to make war on Troy. When he returns Clytemnestra kills him in retaliation, aided by Aegisthus, who wants to avenge his father, Thyestes. Then Orestes slays the two of them to avenge Agamemnon, for which the Furies persecute him. Conceivably this chain of butchery could continue forever, if it were not for the intervention of the gods.

Yet on the personal plane crime begets crime not because of any abstract law, but because human motives require it. Aeschylus' characters have freedom of choice, and must take full responsibility for what they do. However, their personalities are such that their deeds seem inevitable. On this level character is fate and impels acts of violence. So Agamemnon brings Troy to rubble because family honor and his own pride demand it. But in the process he kills his daughter and nearly wipes out all the youth of Greece. The tragedy of the Trojan War is repeatedly emphasized, and Agamemnon is in large measure responsible for that waste of life. He is rather a monster, grown fat and arrogant in his power.

Clytemnestra is equally prideful. Her vanity is injured when Agamemnon brings his mistress, Cassandra, home. And out of personal honor she avenges Iphigenia. Also, she is tied by sex to Aegisthus, a demagogue who turns tyrant.

Here another level of meaning becomes visible—that of political intrigue and the lust for power. Agamemnon is king. With him out of the way Clytemnestra and Aegisthus become co-rulers of Argos. And we must not forget that Agamemnon went to Troy fully aware of the wealth and fame in store for him. But Orestes knows, as well, that Argos will fall to him when he kills his mother and her lover. Every act of vengeance in these plays carries some motive of gain.

We see the inevitable sequence of events. Power or the drive for power breeds insolence and crime, which brings retribution. But Orestes breaks this chain. Why? Because he was encouraged to the crime by Apollo; because he feels pain and remorse afterward; because he does not take over Argos once the crime is committed; and because the gods feel compassion for such a man, even if the Furies do not.

Now the final level of meaning emerges—the divine revelation. That this occurs in the Areopagus is Aeschylus' patriotic salute to the notion that Athenian law had supernatural sanction. God, or Fate, tempers retribution with mercy in the end. And the vengeful Furies are placated with an honorary position as tutelary goddesses. If Orestes is absolved by a sophism about paternal lineage, this merely underscores the fact that Athena and Apollo, as the agents of Zeus, have compassion for him and would use any legal pretext to get him off the hook. Man must learn by suffering, Aeschylus says, and Orestes has shown himself to be the only character in the trilogy who is able to learn by agony. Success makes men proud and amoral, but pain teaches men the true way to live. As a vindication of divine justice *The House of Atreus* is splendid, and as a depiction of the cumulative power of evil it is unsurpassed.

James Weigel, Jr.

A HOUSE OF GENTLEFOLK

Type of work: Novel
Author: Ivan Turgenev (1818-1883)
Type of plot: Psychological realism
Time of plot: Nineteenth century
Locale: Russia
First published: 1858

Principal characters:
MARYA DMITRIEVNA, a widow
LAVRETZKY, her cousin
LIZA, her daughter
VARVARA, Lavretzky's wife
PANSHIN, an official

Critique:

A House of Gentlefolk, sometimes translated as *A Nobleman's Nest,* belongs with the simple, powerful group of Turgenev's romances. Here are two characters who stand as symbols of Russia: Lavretzky and Liza. Although their lot is a sad one, they are presented in heroic mold. Indeed, the author in this work exhibits a greater degree of Slavophilism than is usually found in his novels. In this work Turgenev shows little patience with the detractors of Russia, those who exalt the worth of French and German culture. Even the glittering Panshin must admit the worthiness of Lavretzky's aim to cultivate the soil.

The Story:

Marya, since the death of her husband, had become a social leader in her small provincial town. Her daughter Liza spoke French quite well and played the piano. Her other children had the best tutors available. She delighted to receive guests, especially Panshin, who had an important position in Moscow. Her evening gatherings were always entertaining when Panshin was there to quote his own poetry.

It was rumored that Lavretzky was returning to the district. Although he was a cousin of the house, Marya scarcely knew how to treat him, for Lavretzky had made an unfortunate marriage. He was separated from his pretty wife, who was reputed to be fast and flighty.

But Lavretzky's visit created no difficulties. He was a rather silent, affable man who noticed Liza with interest. Liza was a beautiful, religious-minded girl of nineteen. It was very evident that the brilliant Panshin was courting her with the full approval of her mother. On the evening of his visit Lavretzky was not impressed with Panshin's rendition of his musical romance, but the ladies were ecstatic.

The following day Lavretzky went on to his small country estate. The place was run-down because it had been uninhabited since his sister's death. Lavretzky, content to sink into a quiet country life, ordered the gardens cleaned up, moved in some newer furniture, and began to take an interest in the crops. He seemed suspended in a real Russian atmosphere close to the land. The new life was particularly pleasing after his residence in France and the painful separation from his wife.

Lavretzky had had a different upbringing. His father, disappointed by his failure to inherit an aunt's fortune, had decided to make his son a strong man, even a spartan. At twelve Lavretzky was dressed in Highland kilts and trained in gymnastics and horsemanship. He ate only one meal a day and took cold showers at four in the morning. Along with the physical culture intended to produce a natural man according to Rousseau's doctrines, the father filled his son full of Voltaire's philosophy.

The father died horribly after enduring pain for two years. During this period he lost all his bravery and atheistic independence; at the end he was a sniveling wreck. His death was a release to Lavretzky, who immediately enrolled, at the age of twenty-three, in a university in Moscow.

At the opera one night he met the beautiful Varvara, daughter of a retired general who lived mostly by his wits. At first the parents had little use for Lavretzky, for they thought him only an unimportant student. When they learned, however, that he came of good family and was a landed proprietor, they favored an early marriage. Since Varvara wanted to travel, Lavretzky wound up his affairs and installed his new father-in-law as overseer of his properties.

In Paris, Varvara began a dizzy social whirl. Her adoring husband, content merely to be at her side, let her indulge her whims freely. She soon had a reputation as a brilliant hostess, but her guests thought her husband a nonentity. Lavretzky had no suspicion that his wife was anything but a devoted wife and mother to their daughter until a letter came by accident into his hands. From it he learned of her lover and their sordid, furtive meetings in obscure apartments. Lavretzky left home immediately and took up separate residence. When he wrote to Varvara, telling her of the reason for the separation, she did not deny her guilt, but only asked for consideration. Settling an income on his wife, Lavretzky returned to Russia.

After spending some time on his estate, Lavretzky began to ride into town occasionally to call on Marya and her family. After he became better acquainted with Liza, the young girl scolded him for being so hard-hearted toward his wife. According to her religious beliefs, Lavretzky should have pardoned Varvara for her sins and gone on with the marriage. Lavretzky, in turn, warned Liza that Panshin was not the man for her. The gay young official was a diplomat, all surface and no substance. Lavretzky had an ally in Marfa, the old aunt who also saw through Panshin's fine manners and clever speeches. When Panshin proposed to Liza by letter, she postponed making a decision.

Liza's music teacher was an old, broken German named Lemm. Although Lavretsky had little ear for music, he strongly appreciated Lemm's talent. He invited the old man to his farm. During the visit the two men found much in common. Lavretsky was saddened to see that the old music teacher was hopelessly in love with Liza.

One night, in Marya's drawing-room, Panshin was brilliantly holding forth on the inadequacies of Russia. The country was much behind the rest of Europe, he asserted, in agriculture and politics. The English were superior in manufacture and merchandising, the French in social life and the arts, the Germans in philosophy and science. His views were the familiar theme of the aristocratic detractors of Russia. The usually silent Lavretzky finally took issue with Panshin and skillfully demolished his every argument. Liza listened with approval.

In a French paper Lavretzky came upon a brief notice in the society section; his wife was dead. For a while he could not think clearly, but as the import of the news came home to him he realized that he was in love with Liza. Riding into town, he gave the paper quietly to Liza. As soon as he could be alone with her, he declared his love. The young girl received his declaration soberly, almost seeming to regard their love as a punishment. Although troubled at first by her attitude, Lavretzky soon achieved a happiness he had never expected to find.

That happiness, however, was short-lived. His servant announced one day that Varvara had returned with their daughter. His wife told him she had been very ill and had not bothered to correct the rumor of her death. Now she asked only to be allowed to live somewhere near him. Suspecting that her meekness was only assumed, Lavretzky arranged for her to live on a distant estate, far from his own house, and went to break the news to Liza.

Liza was controlled. She might almost have awaited the punishment, for she knew that sorrow was the lot of all Russians. Varvara brazenly called on Marya and completely captivated her with her beauty, her French manners, and her accomplished playing and singing. Liza met Lavretzky's wife with grave composure.

For a time Varvara complied with her promise to stay isolated on the distant estate, where she frequently entertained Panshin. In the winter, when she moved to Moscow, Panshin was her devoted follower. At last she went back to Paris. Liza entered a convent. Lavretzky saw her once from a distance as she scurried timidly to a prayer service. Taking what strength he could from the soil, he remained on his farm. When he was forty-five, he visited the house where Liza had lived. Marya and all the older people of the household had died. He felt ill at ease among the younger, laughing generation.

Further Critical Evaluation of the Work:

The publication of *A House of Gentlefolk* established Ivan Turgenev as a great novelist, and although modern critical opinion has generally awarded *Fathers and Sons* the honor of being Turgenev's masterpiece, this earlier novel was for over half a century his most universally acclaimed work. *A House of Gentlefolk* is to be appreciated on two separate, yet interlocking and organically unified levels: the social-historical and the artistic. Although in the novel as a work of art these two aspects are inextricably fused, they may nevertheless be studied individually in order to illuminate more clearly some of the work's underlying themes and to gain deeper insight into its characters.

Any discussion of Turgenev is enriched by a basic understanding of social movements which were under way in Russia in the mid-nineteenth century. A cultural controversy had arisen during the author's lifetime centering around the question of the relative worth of foreign (that is, Western European) versus exclusively Russian ideals. The so-called "Westerners" were a group of Russians who believed in the efficacy of democracy in curing the ills of society; they repudiated Russia's autocratic government as well as her Greek Orthodox religion as outmoded and repressive institutions. They viewed their homeland as morally, intellectually, and politically primitive by comparison with countries such as England, France, and Germany, which had, either through philosophical soul-searching or actual practical experimentation, advanced toward increasingly democratic institutions.

In bitter opposition to the Westerners there grew up a group known as the Slavophiles, composed of many of Russia's finest poets and novelists and the most gifted philosophers and scholars. These men viewed Western European culture as decadent, corrupt, morally rotten; they looked to a new and pure Slavonic race, headed by Russia, to rejuvenate Western philosophy. In their enthusiasm over Slavonic culture, the early Slavophiles often lived among the Russian peasant population studying their way of life, their art and music, their social customs and legal arrangements. Yet ironically, rather than leading to the seemingly obvious conclusion of condemning the tyranny under which the bulk of the Russian population suffered, their near-worship of all things Slavonic led them instead to deny the obvious and condone autocracy and Orthodoxy simply because the masses accepted them unquestioningly.

Although Turgenev is classified as a Westerner in terms of this debate, such narrow categorizing is misleading in that it does not account for his uniquely clear thinking on the issue. With his usual brilliant insight and objectivity, he saw the pitfalls of either camp and avoided the excesses of both; a lover of the people, he was a passionate believer in democracy like the Westerners, but he understood from his heart the deep and powerful force beneath the Slavophile argument. Nowhere is Turgenev's lucidity and freedom of spirit more evident than in *A House of Gentlefolk,* where, in the character of Lavretzky, he has embodied all the emotional and psychological richness of Slavophilism with none of its rigidness or excess. In a lengthy digression about Lavretzky's lineage before he makes his appearance in the novel, the author is careful to stress his hero's dual background: his mother was a peasant, while his father belonged to the landed aristocracy and had become totally cut off from his people because of his extended residence in Europe. Lavretzky himself enters the story just returned from a stay in Paris with his shallow and unfaithful wife, Varvara, which has ended in their separation; he is coming home to his neglected ancestral estate in order to reëstablish closeness to the land. In the sole political scene in the novel, it is Lavretsky who eloquently summarizes Slavophile doctrine, insisting that the essential life and spirit of Russia resides in the common folk; he completely annihilates the feeble platitudes of the unhealthy, superficial, and egotistical bureaucrat, Panshin. It is crucially important, however, that Lavretzky, unlike his real-life counterparts, is a democratic revolutionary spirit in the truest sense of the word, as witnessed in his freedom and individuality, in his abiding love for the land and its people.

The woman who grows to love and be loved by Lavretzky is Liza, the heroine of *A House of Gentlefolk.* Turgenev has endowed her character with all the attributes shared by generations of Russian women and thus given her a timeless and universal quality. Liza's personality, since it represents the spirit which is at the heart of the novel, is of central importance. She is a religious girl, beautiful in her moral strength and purity rather than physical attractiveness, impressive in her calm passivity, her endurance, and her single-minded devotion. She is never revealed directly to the reader by the author, but rather develops as a character through her reflection in the people around her; we learn the most about Liza through the eyes and heart of Lavretzky, but in the last analysis she remains an elusive, if entrancing, figure.

Artistically, *A House of Gentlefolk* is more like an extended short story than a novel. Its plot is slight: in a time span of only two months (not counting the brief epilogue), Lavretzky returns home and falls in love with Liza; his wife returns after she was believed dead; Liza enters a convent and Lavretzky goes to his estate brokenhearted. The central theme is embodied in the love story, around which all the elements in the novel center; setting, atmosphere, and minor characterizations all combine to produce the single effect of the love sequence. This powerful singleness of effect gives the novel an incredible cohesiveness and perfection of structure.

This cohesiveness is perhaps best seen in Turgenev's evocation of a summer atmosphere which coincides throughout the story with the emotions of the hero and heroine; the spirit of summer pervades the scene of Liza meeting Lavretzky in the garden, for example, imbuing the passage with a lyrical beauty unsurpassed in fiction. Likewise, the minor personages in the story, while they are among Turgenev's most brilliant sketches of character, nevertheless owe their foremost importance to their relationship to either the hero or the heroine. The odious Panshin; the passionate old German, Lemm; Liza's mother and her crusty, wise old aunt, Marfa Timofyevna; Lavretzky's worthless and malicious wife, Varvara; all these unforgettable figures serve to reveal something about the two central characters. Along with the summer atmosphere and country landscape, of which they almost seem a part, they set the stage for the love story long before its participants make their entrance. Thus we are given detailed portraits of a collection of minor characters before we receive any more description of Liza than that she is "a slender, tall, dark-haired girl of nineteen"; and Lavretzky's belated appearance is preceded by a nine-chapter (Chapters 8-16) digression on his genealogy.

In his usual fashion, Turgenev in *A House of Gentlefolk* uses his characters' love affairs to test their strength and worth. When in the epilogue Lavretzky returns after eight years to visit the house where Liza used to live, we find that despite his shattering loss of happiness, he has not only survived but emerged from the ordeal a better and kinder man. On one level Turgenev has produced in his hero a symbol of the indomitable strength of the Russian soul; on another he has shown us the capacity inherent in all people for transcendence of pain and growth through suffering. *A House of Gentlefolk* is an elevating tale of melancholy, but not defeat; of sadness mingled with hope.

Nancy G. Ballard

THE HOUSE OF MIRTH

Type of work: Novel
Author: Edith Wharton (1862-1937)
Type of plot: Social criticism
Time of plot: Early twentieth century
Locale: New York
First published: 1905

Principal characters:

LILY BART, a social schemer
MR. SELDEN, her friend
MR. ROSEDALE, a financier
PERCY GRYCE, an eligible young man
GUS TRENOR, a wealthy socialite
JUDY TRENOR, his wife
BERTHA DORSET, who hated Lily
GEORGE DORSET, Bertha's husband

Critique:

The House of Mirth is still popular among readers who enjoy stories about the social life of the early part of this century. The theme of the book is a criticism of the emptiness and folly of life among the idle rich. Lily Bart sacrificed herself, her principles, her chance for real love, and even her life, in a vain attempt to find a life of ease for herself. The conflict arose when her better nature exerted itself. In that respect she was superior to those who scorned her, for most of them had no redeeming qualities of character. The story is easily read, for it is written with Edith Wharton's usual skill.

The Story:

Selden enjoyed watching Lily Bart put a new plan into operation. She was a very beautiful and clever young lady, and no matter how impromptu any action of hers appeared, Selden knew that she never moved without a definitely worked out plan.

Lily had almost no money of her own; her beauty and her good family background were her only assets. Her father had died soon after a reversal of his financial affairs, and her mother had drilled into her the idea that a wealthy marriage was her only salvation. After her mother's death, Lily was taken in by her aunt, Mrs. Peniston. Mrs. Peniston supplied her with fashionable clothes and a good home, but Lily needed jewels, gowns, and cash to play bridge if she were to move in a social circle filled by wealthy and eligible men.

Mr. Rosedale, a Jewish financier, would gladly have married Lily and provided her with a huge fortune, for he wanted to be accepted into the society in which Lily moved. But Lily thought that she still had other prospects less repulsive to her, the most likely one being Percy Gryce, who lived protected from scheming women by his watchful widowed mother.

Lily used her knowledge of his quiet life to her advantage. Selden, Lily, and Gryce were all house guests at the home of Gus and Judy Trenor, and the opportunity was a perfect one for Lily, who assumed the part of a shy, demure young girl. But when Gryce was ready to propose, she let the chance slip away from her, for Lily really hated the kind of person she had become. In addition, although Selden was poor and offered her no escape from her own poverty, she was attracted to him because only he really understood her.

Gus Trenor offered to invest some of Lily's small income, and over a period of time he returned to her more than eight thousand dollars, which he assured her was profit on the transaction. With that amount she was able to pay most of her creditors and reopen her charge accounts. Gus seemed to think, however, that his wise investment on her account should make them better friends than Lily felt was desirable.

In the meantime, Lily unexpectedly got possession of some letters which Bertha Dorset had written to Selden. Bertha had once loved Selden, but George Dorset's fortune was great and she had left Selden for George. She continued to write to Selden after her marriage.

When Gus Trenor began to get more insistent in his demands for Lily's companionship, she became really worried. She knew that people were talking about her a great deal and that her position in society was precarious. She turned to Selden for advice. He told her that he loved her for what she could be, but that he could give her nothing now. He had no money, and he would not even offer her his love because he could not love her as she was, a scheming, ruthless fortune-hunter.

One night Lily received a message that Judy Trenor wanted her to call. When she arrived at the Trenor home, Lily found Gus there alone. He had sent the message. Gus told her then that the money had not been profit on her investment, but a gift from him. When he intimated that she had always known the money was from him personally, Lily was terrified, but at last she managed to get out of the house. She knew then that there was only one thing for her to do. She must accept Rosedale's offer of marriage. But before she wrote to Rosedale accepting his offer, the Dorsets invited her to take a Mediterranean cruise on their yacht. The moment of decision was postponed for a time.

Selden also left New York. Unknown to her, he had seen Lily leave the Trenor house on the night Gus had tricked her into thinking Judy wanted her to call. Selden had always refused to believe the unsavory stories circulating about Lily, but the evidence of his own eyes, he thought, was too plain to be ignored. When he met Lily abroad, he treated her with courteous disinterest.

Lily returned to New York. Her aunt, Mrs. Peniston, had died, leaving Lily ten thousand dollars. Lily planned to repay Gus Trenor with her inheritance, and she found intolerable the delay in settling her aunt's estate. Meanwhile Bertha Dorset's insinuations about Lily's conduct abroad, coupled with the talk about Lily and Gus Trenor, finished Lily's reputation. She took various positions, until at last she was reduced to working in the factory of a milliner. She had first offered to accept Rosedale's former proposal of marriage, but she was no longer useful to Rosedale since her fall from favor, and he refused to marry her. He knew that Lily had the letters Bertha had written Selden, and he also knew that George Dorset no longer loved his wife and would gladly marry Lily. It seemed to Rosedale that Lily had only two alternatives, either to take George Dorset away from Bertha or to go to Bertha with the letters and force her to receive Lily once more.

At first Lily's feeling for Selden made her shrink from doing anything that would harm him. Then she lost her position. Without money to buy food or to pay for her room in a dingy boarding-house, she reluctantly took the letters and started to the Dorset home. On the way she stopped to see Selden. When he again told her that he loved her, or rather that he would love her if she would only give up her greed for wealth and position, she gave up her plan and, unseen by him, dropped the letters into the fireplace. Then she thanked him for the kindness he, and he alone, had given her, and walked out into the night.

When she returned to her room, she found the check for the ten thousand dollars of her inheritance. She sat down at once and wrote a check to Gus Trenor for the amount she owed him and put it in an envelope. In another envelope she placed the ten thousand dollar check and addressed the envelope to her bank. She put the two envelopes side by side on her desk before she lay down to sleep.

But sleep would not come. At last she took from her bureau a bottle of chloral, which she had bought for those nights when she could not sleep. She poured the contents of the bottle into a glass and drank the whole. Then she lay down again upon her bed.

The next morning, feeling a sudden need to see Lily at once, Selden went early to her rooming-house. There he found a doctor already in attendance and Lily dead from an overdose of chloral. On her desk he saw the two envelopes. The stub of the open checkbook beside them told the whole story of Lily's last effort to get her accounts straight before she died. He knew then that his love for her had been justified, but the words he spoke as he knelt by her bed came too late.

Further Critical Evaluation of the Work:

"Life is the saddest thing," Edith Wharton once wrote, "next to death." *The House of Mirth* perhaps comes as close to tragedy as any novel written in America. Neglected by a generation bored with stories of high society, *The House of Mirth* is now recognized as one of Wharton's outstanding works. One reason for this recognition is that the novel deals with more than high society. It contains the very arresting sequence in which Lily Bart works in the millinery factory. Here Wharton examines the oppression of laborers, a recurring theme in her work, although she is not so sentimental as to overlook the cruelty of those same laborers toward one another. She also explores the character of Mr. Selden, who is not a member of the upper class. But Selden and the millinery factory do not alone explain the novel's new-found appeal.

The House of Mirth is primarily about the degradation of the members of the upper class, and it is one of the most powerful novels of its kind. It illustrates, in bold and clear detail, what the members of the upper class—the "right people"—undergo to keep their places in that class: the meaningless rituals, their loveless marriages, their face-saving loans to friends. Also illustrated is the pervasive influence of the "right people" on those who do not belong, and who should be, but are not, able to see the emptiness of class values. Rosedale, an outsider because of his birth and religion, is overpowered by a need to belong. To satisfy this need, he has worked hard to acquire a fortune; to satisfy this need, he is willing to marry Lily Bart, even if he has to assume her debts.

Lily Bart is a victim of her birth into the upper class. Her artistic sensitivity might have developed into a superior talent, but has been allowed to atrophy because of her acceptance of the teaching that ladies of her class have only one destiny—to make a "good marriage." Thus educated, Lily pursues this "good marriage" in the way a businessman would pursue a good investment, passing up Rosedale in the hope that Percy Gryce might be available. Yet her good qualities get the better of her just as she has almost won Percy Gryce. To maintain her contacts and her place in society, she is obliged to play bridge and to gamble away money she does not have. She misses a second chance to marry Rosedale when the Dorsets invite her on a trip to Europe, thinking that they are thus helping out a fellow member of high society by taking her away from her troubles. The trip, however, ends in disaster, causing Lily to feud with Mrs. Dorset and ruin herself as a respectable members of the upper class. No longer eligible for protection by her social peers, or for marriage to the social-climbing Rosedale, Lily must seek a job. She goes to work in the millinery factory, and there discovers that birth and breeding do not provide one with usable skills.

Lily's ruin is partly treated as a naturalistic drama in which the victim of environment and chance is inexorably crushed. A sense of fatality hangs over the book. But throughout, most especially toward the end, the possibility of escape presents itself, in the person of Selden. At the beginning, he is willing to rescue Lily from the emptiness of being one of the "right people." At the end, he tenders an offer, subject to entirely reasonable conditions, to rescue her from poverty and uselessness. But she is essentially unable to communicate with him, despite her concern that he not be victimized by her corrupt entanglements. Such lack of communication is as much a theme of *The House of Mirth* as is criticism of high society.

Like many communicative failures in real life, that of *The House of Mirth* takes many forms. At first, it is Lily who cannot express her love for Selden because he is not one of the "right people." She offends him by offering to be his friend while continuing her mercenary search for a "good marriage." Later, it is Selden who becomes harsh toward Lily because of unfounded suspicion, although he cannot set aside his genuine feeling for her. In the end, and most pathetically, it is Lily who cannot reach out, because she feels unworthy of Selden.

Most of the action is told from Lily's viewpoint. But, at the beginning, the middle, and the end, it is the story of Selden. A sympathetic character because of the genuineness of his love and because of his freedom from the false values of high society, Selden nevertheless suffers from an inability to see things in context, and, no less than Lily, from a failure to make his true feelings known. For this, he assumes a disproportionate share of the blame for Lily's death.

The House of Mirth can be seen as either the story of Lily or the story of Selden. Lily's story is an indictment of a class, and is somewhat limited in its appeal by the subsequent changes which have occurred in our society. The American upper class is no longer as powerful or prestigious as it was in Edith Wharton's time, and its values have changed. Its members betray a certain amount of guilt because of their privileges and the interests of the quest for proper marriages has been mitigated. Even so, Lily's story is relevant so long as meaningless social rituals, class envy, and the belief that women can have only limited destinies continue.

The plight of Selden is universal. Stories of lovers who cannot express themselves are as old as literary history. But the irony and power of Selden's story lie in what the reader knows that Selden does not. Such is the technical brilliance of Wharton's use of point-of-view. The shift to Lily's consciousness for the bulk of the story enables us to know that she is not having an affair with Gus Trenor, and that her love for Selden is what restrains her from trying to ruin Mrs. Dorset. Ironically, the reader understands more than do either Lily or Selden. Edith Wharton's mastery of point-of-view—with the authorial voice always in command in the background—helps make the novel as powerful as it is.

Charles Johnson Taggart

THE HOUSE OF THE SEVEN GABLES

Type of work: Novel
Author: Nathaniel Hawthorne (1804-1864)
Type of plot: Psychological romance
Time of plot: 1850
Locale: Salem, Massachusetts
First published: 1851

Principal characters:
MISS HEPZIBAH PYNCHEON, a spinster
CLIFFORD PYNCHEON, her brother
JUDGE JAFFREY PYNCHEON, a kinsman
PHOEBE PYNCHEON, a distant cousin
MR. HOLGRAVE, Miss Hepzibah's lodger

Critique:

The theme of Hawthorne's justly famous novel is obviously that the sins of the fathers are passed on to the children in succeeding generations. In the ingenious plot of this novel the reader watches the gradual expiation of old Matthew Maule's curse on the Pyncheon family, as youth in the guise of Phoebe and Holgrave enters the old house. Evident in the finely-written pages of *The House of the Seven Gables* is the author's lively interest in New England history, and his increasing doubts about a moribund New England that looked backward to past times.

The Story:

The House of the Seven Gables was a colonial house built in the English style of half-timber and half-plaster. It stood on Pyncheon Street in quiet Salem. The house had been built by Colonel Pyncheon, who had wrested the desirable site from Matthew Maule, a poor man executed as a wizard. Because Colonel Pyncheon was responsible and because he was taking the doomed man's land, Maule at the moment of his execution declared that God would give the Pyncheons blood to drink. But in spite of this grim prophecy the colonel had his house, and its builder was Thomas Maule, son of the old wizard.

Colonel Pyncheon, dying in his great oak chair just after the house had been completed, choked with blood so that his shirt front was stained scarlet. Although doctors explained the cause of his death as apoplexy, the townsfolk had not forgotten old Maule's prophecy. The time of the colonel's death was inauspicious. It was said he had just completed a treaty by which he had bought huge tracts of land from the Indians, but this deed had not been confirmed by the general court and was never discovered by any of his heirs. Rumor also had it that a man was seen leaving the house about the time Colonel Pyncheon died.

More recently another startling event had occurred at the House of the Seven Gables. Jaffrey Pyncheon, a bachelor, had been found dead in the colonel's great oaken armchair, and his nephew, Clifford Pyncheon, had been sentenced to imprisonment after being found guilty of the murder of his uncle.

These events were in the unhappy past, however, and in 1850, the House of the Seven Gables was the home of Miss Hepzibah Pyncheon, an elderly, single woman, who let one wing of the old house to a young man of radical tendencies, a maker of daguerreotypes, whose name was Mr. Holgrave.

Miss Hepzibah was about to open a shop in one of the rooms of her house. Her brother Clifford was coming home from the state prison after thirty years, and she had to earn money in some way to support him. But on the first day of her venture as a storekeeper Miss Hepzibah proved to be a failure. The situation was saved, however, by the arrival of young Phoebe Pyncheon from the country. Soon she was operating the shop at a profit.

Clifford arrived from the prison a broken man of childish, querulous ways. Once he tried to throw himself from a big arched window which afforded him almost his only contact with the outside world. He was fond of Phoebe, but Miss Hepzibah irritated him with her sullen scowling. For acquaintances Clifford had Uncle Venner, a handy man who did odd jobs for the neighborhood, and the tenant of the house, Mr. Holgrave, the daguerreotypist.

The only other relative living in town was the highly-respected Judge Pyncheon, another nephew of the old Jaffrey Pyncheon, for whose murder Clifford had spent thirty years in prison. He was, in fact, the heir of the murdered man and he had been somehow involved with Clifford's arrest and imprisonment. For these reasons Clifford refused to see him when the judge offered to give Clifford and Hepzibah a home at his countryseat.

Meanwhile, Phoebe had become friendly with Mr. Holgrave. In turn, he thought that she brought light and hope into the gloomy old house, and he missed her greatly when she returned to her home in the country. Her visit was to be a brief one, however, for she had gone only to make some preparations before coming to live permanently with Miss Hepzibah and Clifford.

Before Phoebe returned from the country, Judge Pyncheon visited the House of the Seven Gables and, over Miss Hepzibah's protest, insisted on seeing Clifford, who, he said, knew a family secret which meant great wealth for the judge. When at last she went out of the room to summon her brother, Judge Pyncheon sat down in the old chair by the fireplace, over which hung the portrait of the Colonel Pyncheon who had built the house. As the judge sat in the old chair, his ticking watch in his hand,

an unusually strong family likeness could be noted between the stern judge and his Puritan ancestor in the portrait. Unable to find Clifford to deliver the judge's message, Miss Hepzibah returned. As she approached the door, Clifford appeared from within, laughing and pointing to the chair where the judge sat dead of apoplexy under the portrait of the old colonel. His shirt front was stained with blood. The wizard's curse had been fulfilled once more; God had given him blood to drink.

The two helpless old people were so distressed by the sight of the dead man that they crept away from the house without notifying anyone and departed on the train. The dead body of the judge remained seated in the chair.

It was some time before the body was discovered by Holgrave. When Phoebe returned to the house, he admitted her. He had not yet summoned the police because he wished to protect the old couple as long as possible. While he and Phoebe were alone in the house, Holgrave declared his love for her. They were interrupted by the return of Miss Hepzibah and the now calm Clifford. They had decided that to run away would not solve their problem.

The police attributed the judge's death to natural causes, and Clifford, Miss Hepzibah, and Phoebe became the heirs to his great fortune. It now seemed certain that Jaffrey Pyncheon had also died of natural causes, not by Clifford's hand, and that the judge had so arranged the evidence as to make Clifford appear a murderer.

In a short time all the occupants of the House of the Seven Gables were ready to move to the judge's country estate which they had inherited. They gathered for the last time in the old room under the dingy portrait of Colonel Pyncheon. Clifford said he had a vague memory of something mysterious connected with the picture. Holgrave offered to explain the mystery and pressed a secret spring near the picture. When he did so, the portrait fell to the floor, disclosing a recess in the wall. From this niche Holgrave drew out the ancient Indian deed to the lands which the Pyncheons had claimed. Clifford then remembered he had once found the secret spring. It was this secret which Judge Pyncheon had hoped to learn from Clifford.

Phoebe asked how Holgrave happened to know these facts. The young man explained his name was not Holgrave, but Maule. He was, he said, a descendant of the wizard, Matthew Maule, and of Thomas Maule who built the House of the Seven Gables. The knowledge of the hidden Indian deed had been handed down to the descendants of Thomas Maule, who built the compartment behind the portrait and secreted the deed there after the colonel's death. Holgrave was the last of the Maules and Phoebe, the last of the Pyncheons, would bear his name. Matthew Maule's curse had been expiated.

Further Critical Evaluation of the Work:

In reputation *The House of the Seven Gables* usually stands in the shadow of its predecessor, *The Scarlet Letter*. It is, however, a rich and solid achievement, a Gothic romance whose characters are among Nathaniel Hawthorne's most complex. The author himself thought it, in comparison with the earlier work, "more characteristic of my mind, and more proper and natural for me to write."

In his preface, Hawthorne explicitly states his moral: "the truth, namely that the wrong-doing of one generation lives into the successive ones, and, divesting itself of every temporary advantage, becomes a pure and uncontrollable mischief." This of course echoes the Biblical adage that "The fathers have eaten sour grapes, and the children's teeth are set on edge." Hawthorne's interest in the heritage of sin was probably whetted by the history of his own family. His first American ancestor, William Hathorne (Nathaniel himself added the *w* to the family name), was a soldier and magistrate who once had a Quaker woman publicly whipped through the streets. William's son John, having, as Nathaniel said, "inherited the persecuting spirit," was a judge at the infamous Salem witch trials, during which a defendant cursed another of the three judges with the cry, "God will give you blood to drink!" Thenceforth, as Hawthorne noted, although the family remained decent, respectable folk, their fortunes began to decline.

The fate of the Pyncheon family of the novel is considerably more dramatic. Matthew Maule's curse on Colonel Pyncheon, who has persecuted him for witchcraft and wrested from him the land on which the seven-gabled house is to be built, is precisely that which Judge John Hathorne had heard in a similar trial. It is apparently fulfilled on the day of the housewarming, when Colonel Pyncheon dies of apoplexy, the hemorrhage rising through his throat to stain his white shirt. But, Hawthorne would have us believe, such sins as Pyncheon's are not so easily paid for. The family occupies the mansion, but misfortune is their constant lot. There are repeated apoplectic deaths, sometimes heralded by an ominous gurgling in the throat; greed leads Judge

Jaffrey Pyncheon, like his ancestor, to participate in a trumped-up trial, this time against his own cousin; and years of pride and isolation have thinned the family blood so that, like the scrawny chickens that peck in the Pyncheon garden, they are an unattractive, ineffectual lot. Judge Pyncheon is a monster who hides his avarice and callousness behind a façade of philanthropy and civic service. Clifford, like Hawthorne's Young Goodman Brown, is a sensitive soul who is unmanned by his confrontation with evil; after years of imprisonment he is poised on the brink of madness. Hepzibah, a spinster who has spent most of her life waiting for her brother's release, is virtually helpless either to resolve her precarious financial situation or to deal with her malevolent cousin.

Only young Phoebe possesses both goodness and energy. It is significant that she is the "country cousin" whose father married beneath his rank, and that Hepzibah observes that the girl's self-reliance must have come from her mother's blood. Thus Hawthorne casts his vote for the energizing effects of a democratic, as opposed to an aristocratic, social system; he has Holgrave, the daguerreotypist, support this view with the comment that families should continually merge into the great mass of humanity, without regard to ancestry.

The other fully vital character in the novel is Holgrave, the young daguerreotypist. He is one of Hawthorne's most charming creations: a perceptive, adventurous man who has been, it seems, almost everywhere, and done almost everything. His conversations with Phoebe reveal him as a radical who believes that the Past "lies upon the Present like a giant's dead body," preventing any generation's true fulfillment—a thesis frequently expressed by Hawthorne's contemporary, Ralph Waldo Emerson. Holgrave goes so far as to suggest that institutional buildings should "crumble to ruin once in twenty years, or thereabouts, as a hint to the people to examine into and reform the institutions which they symbolize." He is also a psychologist; his daguerreotypes, which inevitably go beyond mere pictorial likeness to expose personality, symbolize his own insight into human nature.

At the end of the novel we are led to believe that the curse is broken as Phoebe, the last of the Pyncheons, plans to marry Holgrave, who turns out to be a descendant of old Matthew Maule. The curse's effects can all be explained naturally: Holgrave observes that perhaps old Maule's prophecy was founded on knowledge that apoplectic death had been a Pyncheon trait for generations. Avarice and cruelty can certainly be passed on by example; and pride, isolation, and inbreeding can account for the "thin-bloodedness" of the once aristocratic family. Now, as Phoebe, whose blood has already been enriched by plebian stock, and Holgrave, who has escaped the stifling influence of his own declining family by traveling widely, replace a tradition of hatred with that of love, it seems plausible that the curse may indeed have run its course. Perhaps the chain of ugly events—what Chillingworth of *The Scarlet Letter* termed "dark necessity"—can be terminated by positive acts of good will.

The novel is replete with Gothic characteristics: mystery, violence, a curse, gloomy atmosphere, archaic diction, and visits from the spirit world. Yet though it is not realistic, it demonstrates what Henry James called Hawthorne's "high sense of reality," in that it reveals profound truths about how the effects of the sins of the fathers are felt by children for generations to come. The ending, however, discloses that although he recognized the deterministic effects of heredity, environment, and man's predisposition to evil, Hawthorne was essentially a hopeful man who believed that the individual does possess a residuum of will that can cope with and perhaps change "dark necessity."

Sally Buckner

THE HOUSE WITH THE GREEN SHUTTERS

Type of work: Novel
Author: George Douglas (George Douglas Brown, 1869-1902)
Type of plot: Regional realism
Time of plot: Late nineteenth century
Locale: Rural Scotland
First published: 1901

Principal characters:
>JOHN GOURLAY, a wealthy merchant
>YOUNG JOHN, his son
>MRS. GOURLAY, his slovenly wife
>JAMES WILSON, Gourlay's competitor

Critique:

Disgusted with the quaint and sentimental novels in which writers of the kailyard school portrayed his native Scotland, George Douglas Brown attempted to present in his work a more realistic picture of Scottish life in the late nineteenth century. *The House with the Green Shutters* is a forceful book, one alive with characters that grip the reader in their problems. Brown's purpose was to show the true Scottish peasant as he saw him.

The Story:

John Gourlay was proud of his twelve wagons and his many business successes, but mostly he was proud of his House with the Green Shutters. Into it he had put all the frustration he felt for his lack of friends, his slovenly wife, his weakling son. Gourlay's was a pride of insolence. He would have more than his neighbors, his betters; he would make them acknowledge him as their superior. Gourlay had not found a golden touch. He had simply worked hard, turning every shilling into pounds by any method open to him. In the process he became mean, stingy, boastful, and evil.

His son John had inherited all of his characteristics except his courage. As a schoolboy, constantly ridiculed by his mates, he took refuge in boasting of his father's wealth and power. He was no good with his fists, and his only revenge after a sound drubbing was to tell his father. Gourlay hated his son almost as much as he hated everyone else, but he could not let his son be laughed at by the sons of his enemies. Thus John was avenged by the father who despised him.

Gourlay also hated his wife. She who had once been a laughing, pretty lass had become a slattern and a bore whose son was her only reason for living. On him she lavished all the love denied her by her husband. There was one daughter. She was ignored by her mother and favored by her father, each parent taking the opposite point of view from the other.

The whole village bowed to Gourlay, even while they prayed that he would one day meet his match. They were not to be disappointed. One James Wilson returned to the village with money he had earned during his fifteen years' absence. One of the first to meet Wilson was Gourlay. When Wilson had left years before, Gourlay had been then as now the big man in the town. Had Gourlay said a kind word or given one bit of praise for the success of his former acquaintance, Wilson would have been flattered and would have become his friend. But Gourlay was not such a man. He immediately ridiculed Wilson and laughed at the idea that he could be a success at anything. Wilson developed a hatred that was to bring the insolent Gourlay to ruin.

Wilson used his money to set up a general store, which he stocked with many items the villagers had formerly had to send away for and pay Gourlay to haul for them. He also delivered items to neighboring towns and farms. Then he started a regular carting service, cutting prices to get business from Gourlay, just as Gourlay had done to his competitors. The townspeople were glad to patronize Wilson in order to get back at Gourlay for his years of dominance and insolence. Indeed, they even gave Wilson new suggestions for expanding his trade. Gourlay's downfall started slowly, but soon it became a landslide. The peasants began to stand up to the old man, even to laugh openly at him. Gourlay's vows of vengeance were empty talk.

Gourlay turned to his son as his only hope. When Wilson's son went away to high school, John was sent, even though he had no head for books and no ambition. John played truant frequently and was a braggart and a coward as before, but his father still had power enough to keep him in school and in money and in some way the boy was graduated. Wilson sent his son to the university. Gourlay decided that John must go too. Never was a boy more miserable, for he knew he was not suited for advanced study. Gourlay hoped to make the lad a minister; his hope was to recoup some respect, if not money, for the family.

At the university John found little stimulation for his sluggish mind. He had one high spot in his career, indeed in his whole life, when he won a prize for an essay. Since that was the first honor he ever won, he swaggered and boasted about it for months. Because of the prize, also, he won his first and only word of praise from his father. In his second term John fell to his own level and became a drunken sot. Books were too much for him, and people scorned him. The bottle was his only friend.

While John was stumbling through his second term at the university, Gourlay's fortunes reached their lowest ebb. The House with the Green Shutters was mortgaged heavily, all Gourlay's other assets having been lost in wild speculations to recoup his fortunes. But Gourlay still pinned his hopes on the son he had always hated. John would save the family name, the lost fortune, the House. Thus when Gourlay learned that John had been expelled for drunkenness and insubordination, and heard that the whole town knew of the disgrace through a letter of young Wilson to his father, the news was too much for the old man. He returned to the House with the Green Shutters like a madman, as indeed he was. The first sight that greeted him was John, who had sneaked into town in the darkness. Like a cat toying with a mouse, Gourlay tortured his son. He pretended to consider him a great man, a hero. He peered at him from all angles, waited on him with strong whiskey, called him a fine son, a credit to the family. Cowardly John rushed from the house in terror, followed by the screams of his mother and sister and the howls of his father. Then his false courage returned, and he went back into the house after fortifying himself with more whiskey. Picking up a large poker which had been one of his father's prideful purchases, John swung at his father and crushed in his head.

The mother and sister convinced the authorities that Gourlay, falling from a ladder and striking his head, had died accidentally. But John was lost. For days he was haunted by red eyes glaring at him out of space, by unknown things coming to get him. His mother and sister, dependent upon him for their livelihood, tried to get him out of his madness, but nothing soothed him except whiskey, and that only briefly. One day he asked his mother for money, bought his last bottle of whiskey and a vial of poison, and ended his wretched existence.

Completely alone now, aware that even the house must go to the creditors, dying themselves of cancer and consumption, the mother and daughter divided the rest of the poison and joined Gourlay

and John in death. The pride, the lust,   the Green Shutters had claimed them all.
the greed were gone. The House with

Further Critical Evaluation of the Work:
    George Douglas Brown's reputation rests on this single novel, *The House with the Green Shutters*. Born at Ochiltree in Scotland, to a poor family, he managed to attend Glasgow University and Oxford, and in 1895 went to London as a freelance writer. Not until 1901 with *The House with the Green Shutters* did he win recognition. The novel was praised by Andrew Lang and was well received in England and the United States. His royalties in the summer of 1902 brought him the only financial ease he ever knew, but in August of that year he suddenly died.
    This one great novel is modeled on classical Greek tragedy. It is a vivid picture of cottage life in a Scottish village, with finely drawn characters and realistic atmosphere; the peasant humor running through the book has been compared to that of Hardy. The citizens of Barbie are preoccupied with scandal when they are not grubbing for an existence. Beyond work, their concerns are narrow and petty; they are malicious, often from mere boredom. The villagers act as a Greek Chorus, standing around the square commenting on the principal characters and the life in the village. They also fill in background for the reader.
    The author places a heavy emphasis upon "character." If a person is weak, he is doomed. As hubris might cause the fate of a Greek tragic hero, so stupidity or moral weakness causes the fate of these Scottish villagers. John Gourlay is proud and ambitious, eager to make a big showing; his house is a symbol for him of his place and dignity. But he is a stupid man and is easily provoked. Understanding nothing, he is able to sneer at everything. His son cannot build upon his first success at college. Young Gourlay is morally weak and lazy, and must inevitably come into conflict with his father.
    The relentless realism of the narrative, detailing every grimy inch of the town and the house and mercilessly describing the characters as if they are under a microscope might be too much for some readers. (Some critics of 1901 thought the grimness of the tale overdone, while others compared its effect with that of Balzac's *Father Goriot*.) The dialect is not easy for modern readers, but it lends a richness and verisimilitude to the tale, if the reader is patient enough to stick with it. The story moves forward to its tragic conclusion sweeping the reader along. If the narrative does not quite evoke the "pity and terror" of a Greek tragedy, it does provide the reader with a rich and rewarding emotional and intellectual experience. Although the novel seems to be a "slice of life," it is a highly sophisticated and artfully structured book, ingeniously creating a calculated effect, and thus is a work of art of a very high order.

HOW GREEN WAS MY VALLEY

Type of work: Novel
Author: Richard Llewellyn (Richard D. V. Llewellyn Lloyd, 1907-   )
Type of plot: Domestic realism
Time of plot Nineteenth century
Locale: Wales
First published: 1940

Principal characters:
   GWILYM MORGAN, a Welsh miner
   BETH MORGAN, his wife
   HUW MORGAN, their son and the narrator
   IVOR,
   DAVY,
   OWEN,
   IANTO, and
   GWILYM, other sons
   ANGHARAD, their daughter
   BRONWEN, Ivor's wife
   MARGED, Gwilym's wife
   IESTYN EVANS, Angharad's husband

Critique:

How Green Was My Valley is a story of the life of a Welsh boy, seen through the eyes of an old man who has only memory to sustain him. The novel was published during the war years, and perhaps the strife that was everywhere then accounted somewhat for its great popularity. There was trouble in the lives of the people we meet in this story, but the kindness of the main characters was so great that even death seemed gentle and not to be feared. The novel is simply and beautifully told.

The Story:

How beautiful and peaceful the valley looked to Huw Morgan when he was ready to leave it! All the memories of a long lifetime came back to him.

Huw's earliest memories were of his father and brothers when they came home from the mines on Saturday night There was trouble brewing at the mines. The men talked of unions and organizing, and the owners were angry.

Huw loved his family very much, and when he learned that his brother Ivor was to marry he was sorry to lose his brother. But from the first moment Huw saw Ivor's Bronwen, he loved her, and that love for his sister-in-law stayed with him all of his life.

Another brother, Ianto, married soon afterward. His wife was a girl from the village, where Ianto went to live.

Trouble came at last to the mines. The men in the pits went on strike for twenty-two weeks, but the owners were the stronger because they were not watching their families starve. The men finally went back to work for less money than before. After that first strike, the father would never again join the men trying to form a union, for he could not bring himself to lead men out of work. Davy and the other boys, however, were more bitter than ever. When the father ordered his sons never to attend another meeting, Davy, Owen, and Gwilym left home and took a room in a lodging-house. Their mother cried all night, but the father would not change his mind. It was a miserable time for six-year-old Huw. When his sister Angharad found that the three boys were living in filth, she went to the rooming-house to take care of them. Then the father relented and allowed the boys to come home, but he said that they would be lodgers only, not sons.

After the father became superintendent at the mine, Huw heard some of the miners say that his father and Ivor, who agreed with him, might be beaten or even killed by some of the more violent miners. Frightened, he told his mother what he had heard. One winter night she and Huw went to the mountain where the miners were meeting, and she told the men there that she would kill anyone who harmed her husband. On the way home his mother slipped on the bank of a little river. Huw, standing in the icy water, supported his mother on the bank until help came. After that he knew nothing until he awoke in his bed and his father told him that he had saved his mother's life and the life of his new baby sister. Huw had fever in his legs for almost five years and never left his bed during that time.

During his sickness Bronwen nursed him and his brothers read to him until he was far beyond his years in learning. While he was in bed, he first met the new minister, Mr. Gruffydd, who was to become his best friend.

Huw's brother Owen fell in love with Marged Evans. When Marged's father found Owen kissing Marged, he said terrible things to the boy, so that Owen would have nothing more to do with Marged. Gwilym married her, for he had always loved her.

Ianto's wife died and he came home to live. By this time Huw, well once more, went to the National School, over the mountain. He had many fights before he was accepted by the other boys.

Angharad and Iestyn Evans, the son of the mine owner, began to keep company, but Angharad did not seem to be happy. It was some time before Huw learned that Angharad loved Mr. Gruffydd but that he could not take a wife because he was poor. Huw began to think love caused heartache instead of happiness.

One day he took a basket of food to Gwilym's house, and there he found Marged completely mad. Thinking he was Owen, she told him she could not live without him. Huw ran to find Gwilym. Before he returned with his brother, Marged had thrown herself into the fire and burned to death. Afterward Gwilym and Owen went away together, no one knew where.

Iestyn Evans' father died, and soon after Iestyn and Angharad were married in London. Davy was married before they came home, and for the wedding Huw had his first long trousers. Bronwen told him that he was now a man.

Shortly afterward Huw was put out of school for giving the teacher a beating because he had made a small child wear around her neck a sign announcing that she was Welsh. Huw went to work in the pits with his brothers. Owen and Gwilym had returned home and all the boys lived again in the valley. But soon Owen had a telegram from London about an engine he was trying to perfect, and he and Gwilym left again. From London they went to America. Soon afterward Davy went to London on mine union business.

Angharad came home from London alone, Iestyn having gone to Cape Town on business. Soon gossip started because Mr. Gruffydd and Angharad often took carriage rides together. Finally Angharad left the valley and went to Cape Town. Mr. Gruffydd also left the valley.

When Ivor was killed in a cave-in at the mine, Huw's mother sent him to live with Bronwen in her loneliness. Discharged from the mines for striking one of the workmen who made a slurring remark about Angharad and Mr. Gruffydd, Huw became a carpenter. Ianto had already left the pits and only his father and Davy were left in the mines. Davy decided to go to New Zealand. Ianto went to Germany, where he thought he could do better in his trade. The family was now scattered.

One day the workers flooded the mines and Huw's father was crushed by a cave-in. Huw crawled to his father and stayed with him until he died. Huw's heart was as empty as his mother's when he told her the terrible news.

Everyone of whom Huw had thought during this reverie was now dead. He walked slowly away from his valley and from his memories.

Further Critical Evaluation of the Work:

How Green Was My Valley is part of a large body of literature which has developed in England since the end of the eighteenth century. It is a literature of nostalgia; a longing for the past where all *was* (and this is the significant word in the title of Llewellyn's novel) peaceful, ordered, and tranquil. It is associated with the literature of arcadia, possessing a pastoral quality that is inevitably contrasted to the blight of the new industrial city. Goldsmith's "The Deserted Village," bemoaning the rural life that has been destroyed, is one of the earliest and best known poems in the same tradition as *How Green Was My Valley.*

In particular, Llewellyn's novel, narrated by Huw Morgan, is a lament for a Welsh valley with all its connotations of Eden. Moreover, it is a dirge for his own childhood, secure in a large family headed by his temperate and wise father, Gwilym. The principal foe is the mine, or rather the miners who insist upon breaking down the traditional relationship of employer-employee, that of patronage, by forming a modern union. Huw's brothers, enraged by the owners' treatment of the men and their own father's abandonment of the union, leave the family, making the first crack in Huw's happiness and the first step toward the fragmentation of the family. It is, metaphorically, the beginning of the end of the valley life. From that point the modern world with its new ideas of family, work, and society continues to impinge on Huw.

When the Morgan family disintegrates either through death or immigration, Huw is left absolutely alone. What begins as a powerful celebration of a family whose members are deeply in touch with one another and the community, ends in a lament of a single voice: a pattern repeated so often in modern literature that it has become an identifying characteristic.

HOWARDS END

Type of work: Novel
Author: E. M. Forster (1879-1970)
Type of plot: Domestic realism
Time of plot: Early twentieth century
Locale: England
First published: 1910

Principal characters:
HENRY WILCOX, a British businessman
RUTH WILCOX, his first wife
CHARLES WILCOX, his older son
PAUL WILCOX, his younger son
MARGARET SCHLEGEL, Henry Wilcox's second wife
HELEN SCHLEGEL, Margaret's sister
THEOBALD SCHLEGEL, Margaret's brother
LEONARD BAST, a poor young man
JACKY BAST, Leonard's wife

Critique:

E. M. Forster is not a prolific author. He is well known to students of fiction, however, as a thorough critic, as well as an important novelist in his own right, and his *Aspects of the Novel* is a major contribution to study in that field. Prior to his best work of fiction, *A Passage to India, Howards End* was ranked as his most mature novel. Particularly important in Forster's fiction are his subtle and complete characterization, his deft use of irony, the careful plotting of action, the eternal contrast between illusion and reality. *Howards End* is second only to *A Passage to India* in illustrating these characteristics.

The Story:

The Wilcox family met Margaret Schlegel and her sister Helen while both families were vacationing in Germany. Neither group expected the chance acquaintance to amount to anything more, but later, after all had returned to England, Helen Schlegel was invited to visit the Wilcox family at Howards End, their country home near London. While there, Helen fell in love with Paul Wilcox. Both families disapproved of the match, and after hard words on both sides it was broken off.

A few months later the Wilcoxes rented a town flat across the street from the Schlegel home. Both young people were out of the country. Mrs. Wilcox and Margaret Schlegel met and became friends.

Also acquainted with the Schlegels was a young man named Leonard Bast, a seedy fellow whose umbrella had been accidentally taken by Helen at a concert. The young man had interested the girls and their brother by his conversation when he had called to reclaim his umbrella. They did not know that he had an exceedingly frowsy wife, a woman some years older than he who had trapped him into a distasteful marriage.

Some months after the acquaintance between Mrs. Wilcox and Margaret Schlegel had ripened into friendship, Mrs. Wilcox became ill and died. Much to her husband's and sons' surprise, she left a note, in addition to her will, leaving Howards End to Margaret. In their anger at the prospect of letting the house go out of the family, the Wilcoxes disregarded the note, since it was not a part of the official will.

Margaret Schlegel, knowing nothing of the bequest, was really glad that the tie between herself and the Wilcox family had been broken, for she was afraid that her sister was still in love with Paul Wilcox and suffered when she came into contact with other members of the family.

One evening, long after Mrs. Wilcox's death, Margaret and her sister were sitting in the park. There they met Mr. Wilcox, who told them that the firm for which Leonard Bast worked was unreliable. Acting on that information, the girls advised the young man to change jobs. He did so. They did not know that Mr. Wilcox, in love with Margaret, had given them bad advice in order to get rid of a young man he saw as a possible rival for Margaret's love.

A few weeks later the long-term lease on the Schlegels' house was up and they were forced to move. Although they searched a long time, they found nothing suitable. Mr. Wilcox, hearing of their predicament, sent a letter to Margaret offering to lease them his house in London. Margaret went with him to look at the house. While they were there, Mr. Wilcox declared his love. Margaret, who was well into her thirties, was surprised, but without embarrassment or shock. She asked only for a few days to think over the rental of the house and the proposal of marriage. After considering both problems, she agreed to marry Mr. Wilcox, thus making any decision about the rental unnecessary.

Before Margaret's marriage to Mr. Wilcox, his daughter was also married at a house owned by the Wilcoxes near Wales. Shortly after the daughter's wedding Helen Schlegel, who had disapproved of Margaret's approaching marriage, appeared at the house with Leonard Bast and his wife. Helen had learned that through their bad advice Bast had lost everything he had, including his job. Helen thought that Mr. Wilcox ought to recompense the young man. When Mrs. Bast was discovered, rather tipsy, on the lawn, she revealed to Mr. Wilcox and Margaret that she had been Mr. Wilcox's mistress many years before. Margaret was willing to forgive Mr. Wilcox, but she resolved not to help the Basts. Under the circumstances, she felt it was unnecessary and in poor taste to do so.

Helen, who had unwittingly fallen in love with Bast, felt sorry for him. She spent part of one night with him and then remorsefully left England. She tried to give Bast five thousand pounds, most of her fortune, but he refused to accept her aid.

The relationship between her sister and Leonard Bast was unknown to Margaret, who went ahead with her marriage to Mr. Wilcox, despite the fact that his sons did not approve of their father's second marriage. Helen's refusal to return for the ceremony did not surprise her sister. Eight months went by. Helen still had not returned, and Margaret began to worry about her sister.

Helen finally came back to England and sent word that she wanted some books stored in the house at Howards End. She acted so mysteriously that Margaret and Mr. Wilcox planned to encounter her at the house. Because she refused to see them directly, Margaret, worried, thought that Helen might need mental treatment. When Margaret saw Helen, however, the reason for the mystery was plain: Helen was pregnant as the result of the night she spent with Leonard Bast. Helen asked to be permitted to spend one night with her sister in the unoccupied house at Howards End. Mr. Wilcox refused to allow Margaret to do so.

The two sisters stayed in the house in spite of Mr. Wilcox's refusal. The following morning Mr. Wilcox's older son, Charles, went to the house to get them out. A minute or two after his arrival Leonard Bast came to the house in search of Margaret, from whom he hoped to get money. As soon as he saw him, Charles seized a saber that hung on the wall and struck Bast on the shoulders with the flat of the weapon several times. The shock of seeing Helen and the beating were too much for Bast's weak heart. He died suddenly.

Charles was tried for manslaughter and sentenced to three years in prison. The disgrace was too great for his father, who became an invalid. Margaret moved her husband and her sister into the house at Howards End, where Helen's child was born. Mr. Wilcox came to love the baby during his illness and convalescence, and so Helen and the child, much to the displeasure of the other Wilcoxes, were permitted to remain. A few months before Charles' release from prison, Mr. Wilcox called a family conference. He had made a new will giving all his money to the children by his first marriage, but the house at Howards End was to go to Margaret and after her death to Helen's illegitimate child. Thus the mansion, which had played so great a part in all their lives, eventually came to Margaret Schlegel, just as the first Mrs. Wilcox had wished before her death.

Further Critical Evaluation of the Work:

The country house has long been an important image and symbol in English literature. From its appearance in such an early seventeenth century poem as Jonson's "To Penshurst," to its celebration by Pope in the eighteenth century, to its centrality in the nineteenth century fiction of Jane Austen, Anthony Trollope, and Henry James, to its prominence in the modern works of E. M. Forster and Evelyn Waugh, the manor house has provided not only a dramatic setting, but also an embodiment of certain social, moral, and spiritual values. Despite its various literary manifestations, the apotheosis of the country estate is in essence a reaction against the introduction of the mercantile ethic, its manifestation in the phenomenon of industrialism, and the consequent growth of large cities. It is, in brief, a nostalgic image for a way of life, based on the land, that possessed a definite social hierarchy and took its rhythms from nature. While it pays special homage to individuality, intellect, and imagination, its chief virtues are the classical ones of restraint and moderation. The country house, then, is a correlative for a human ideal which found its first flowering in the Renaissance.

Besides these attributes, the house in Forster's novel, Howards End, represents an image of cultural unity. The book's epigraph, "only connect . . . ," suggests the major theme and describes the prescription required to bring about moral health to Edwardian England. To Forster this society, on the verge of becoming completely urbanized and industrialized, is fractured, lacking order and direction. For a solution to this dilemma he looks toward the traditional values embodied in Howards End.

Three principal forces are at work in *Howards End.* The first is embodied in the Schlegel family, which stands for the past, art, imagination, and culture; second, there are the Wilcoxes, representing the present, practical intelligence, and business acumen. The third force points to the future and is found in the parvenu, Leonard Bast. The drama of the novel resides primarily in the conflict between the Schlegels and the Wilcoxes, both solid middle-class families, for the right to direct England's future—or at least to determine its dominant values. Leonard Bast, a member of the working class and always on the periphery, is seemingly lost in the shuffle. He is without manners, culture, or any business sense. Yet he aspires to the center of power, held jointly by the Schlegels and the Wilcoxes. And, after his ignominious death "resolves" the conflict between the two families, it is, ironically, his illegitimate child, conceived by Helen Schlegel in an act of moral protest against the establishment, who will inherit Howards End and—we may infer—the spoils of the battlefield, the future of England.

From the beginning it appears that these three forces have nothing in common. Margaret, Helen, and their brother celebrate the "poetic" inner self, the passion of existence, while despising the world of telegrams, profit and loss, and machines. That world, peopled and directed by their rivals, Henry Wilcox and his son, Charles, dedicates itself to practicality, to the "prose" of life, as Forster phrases it.. Although he is not fully a part of either, Leonard does have one foot in each; he is a small business clerk, yet, he ravenously and superficially fills his life with cultural items, books, concerts, and intelligent conversations.

But as the novel unfolds, the deep connections between these three forces begin to appear: in a private will Ruth Wilcox leaves Howards End to Margaret in recognition of their mutual identities and Jacky, Leonard's wife, is revealed to have been Henry's mistress. These connections are further strengthened by the real attractions that grow up among them. Initially Paul Wilcox and Helen fall in love; the engagement, however, is broken off as unseemly. Later Henry and Margaret discover in each other a passionate need—a fact apparently recognized by the late and mysterious Mrs. Wilcox—and eventually marry. And last, there is the fruitful if misdirected union of Helen and Leonard. Thus, *Howards End* describes a society which on the surface seems fractured and disjointed, but as it is gradually revealed, one which is fundamentally joined by needs and desires of love and fellowship. All that is required to cement the connection is human will and a place to validate the union.

Under the influence of Ruth Wilcox, Margaret provides the will which is constantly directed to the acquisition of Howards End, her rightful legacy. But it finally takes the tragic-comic death of Leonard at the hands of Charles Wilcox to force the principal characters into making *all* of the "connections." With Charles imprisoned and the Wilcox clan disgraced, Henry Wilcox, the practical man-of-action, is thoroughly deflated and it remains for the "poetic" Margaret to assume the leadership and direction of the family.

In the denouement Forster gathers all his principal characters at Howards End for one last conversation. The atmosphere is of peace and joy, not unlike the aftermath of a wedding in which all tensions are abated and passion, fruitfulness, and unity are celebrated. The house itself, cut off from the asservations of culture and the workaday, allows its inhabitants to feel the rhythms of nature and the ties which bind them. It is autumn and around them a bountiful harvest proceeds; it is a time of expectations, further attested by the health of Helen and Leonard's child. Yet Forster is too much of a realist to conclude on a note of simple optimism. For he sees, like Helen and Margaret, that the smog of London is encroaching on the house. It is a complete moment, to be sure, but one stolen from the past. At last Forster knew that it was also the autumn of the country house as well as of the Renaissance and that it was the spring of the modern world.

David L. Kubal

HUASIPUNGO

Type of work: Novel
Author: Jorge Icaza (1906-   )
Type of plot: Social criticism
Time of plot: Twentieth century
Locale: Ecuador
First published: 1934

> *Principal characters:*
> ALFONSO PEREIRA, a debt-ridden landowner
> BLANCA, his wife
> LOLITA, his daughter
> DON JULIO, his uncle
> POLICARPIO, an overseer
> ANDRÉS CHILIQUINGA, an Indian laborer
> CUNSHI, his wife
> PADRE LOMAS, the village priest
> JUANCHO CABASCANGO, a well-to-do Indian tenant farmer

Critique:

Stark, brutal realism overlies the artistry of this novel of protest against the enslavement of the Indian in rural Ecuador. Icaza is only one of many Latin-American novelists who, influenced by Dostoevski, Gorky, and other European realists, have used the indigenous theme and shown the white man's cruelty toward the Indian, but his *Huasipungo* is the best of these polemic works. Greater as a social document, perhaps, than as a work of fiction, it is made up of a series of episodes whose power lies in a graphic account of the lives and trials of the Indian. Icaza writes carelessly, with a scorn of syntax, but with a keen ear that reproduces the difficult dialect of the Quichua-speaking inhabitants of the Andean region near Quito. Types symbolizing classes rather than clearly realized individuals fill his pages, and in this novel the avaricious, lustful priest has been made especially hateful. In spite of its defects *Huasipungo* is a powerful novel, with many pirated editions in Spanish, an English translation printed in Russia, and even a version in Chinese.

The Story:

Alfonso Pereira was an Ecuadorian landowner plagued by domestic and financial troubles. His wife Blanca nagged him and he was worried over his seventeen-year-old daughter Lolita, who wanted to marry a man who was part Indian. Don Julio, his uncle, added to his difficulties by demanding repayment of a loan of ten thousand sucres, a debt already three months overdue.

When Pereira confessed himself unable to pay the loan, Don Julio suggested that his nephew try to interest Mr. Chapy, a North American promoter, in a timber concession on Pereira's mountain estate. Privately the old man suspected that Mr. Chapy and his associates were on the lookout for oil and used their lumber-cutting activities in the region as a blind. In order to interest the North Americans, however, it would be necessary to build fifteen miles of road and get possession of two forest tracts. Also, the Indians must be driven off their *huasipungos*, the lands supplied to them in return for working on the master's estate.

Pereira assured his uncle that such a course would be difficult. The Indians, having a deep affection for their lands along both sides of the river, would never willingly give them up. Old Julio ridiculed Pereira's sentimentality and told him to return to the estate at Tomachi and build the road.

Back home, Pereira discussed his problem with Padre Lomas, the village priest. The padre agreed to persuade the Indians to work on the road; he would tell them that the labor was the will of God. They also tried to determine how many *mingas*, brawls in which Indians were plied with drink to make them willing to work, would be necessary before the road could be completed. Jacinto Quintana, proprietor of the village store and saloon, promised that he and his wife Juana would make the home-brew for the first of the *mingas*.

Andrés Chiliquinga, an Indian workman, was unhappy because Pereira had returned, for he had gone against his master's and the priest's wishes by taking Cunshi as his wife. He was one of thirty Indians sent to start cutting wood and clearing the roadbed.

To find a wet nurse for her baby, Blanca Pereira examined some of the dirty Indian mothers. Their undernourished babies were diseased, some with malaria or dysentery; others were idiotic or epileptic. Policarpio, the overseer, finally chose Cunshi, mother of the healthiest child in the village, and took her to the Pereira house. The master, seeing the young Indian woman, forced her to sleep with him.

One night Andrés made the long trip home to see his wife. Finding no one in their hillside shack, he became suspicious and angry. The next day he deliberately let his ax fall on his foot. The Indians treated the cut with spiderwebs and mud, but when the bandage was removed, three days later, the foot was so badly infected that Andrés was sent home. A medicine man who poulticed the sore saved Andrés' life, but the wound left him lame.

One day, while Pereira and the priest were at the Quintana store discussing the building of the road, they sent Jacinto on an errand. After his departure both men forced Juana to accept their attentions.

Pereira gave Padre Lomas' one hundred sucres for a big mass. Then he held a *minga* and work on the road was speeded up. Storms made life miserable for the Indians, unprotected as they were in their camps. Some died when they tried to drain a swamp. Others perished in quicksands. Pereira, choosing to risk the Indians rather than follow a longer, safer route, kept the workmen drunk and entertained them with cockfights. The ignorant laborers continued to toil.

The priest went to Juancho Cabascango, an Indian with a prosperous *huasipungo* beside the river, and asked for one hundred sucres to pay for another mass. When the Indian refused, Padre Lomas cursed him. A short time later a flash flood drowned some of the Indians and their cattle. Blaming the disaster on Juancho, his superstitious neighbors beat him to death. The priest declared the affair the will of God and easily collected several hundred sucres for his mass.

At last the road was completed, but the Indians received none of the benefits Padre Lomas had promised. He himself bought a bus and two trucks that took away all transport from those who used to drive mule teams into Quito with the products of the region. Young Indians rode the bus to the city and there ended up as criminals and prostitutes.

Because of easy transportation and the possibility of a profitable sale in Quito, Pereira decided not to give the Indians their customary grain from his plentiful harvest. Policarpio's protests did no good. When the hungry Indians went to Pereira's patio and begged their master to relieve the hunger of their families, he told them that their daily pay of fifty centavos was generous enough. Besides, the ton and a half of corn needed to feed the Indians would help considerably in reducing his debts. He did, however, heed his overseer's warning and asked that guards for his estate be sent from Quito.

Hunger stalked the region and babies and old people perished. When one of

Pereira's cows died, the famished Indians begged for the carcass. He refused because they might be tempted to kill other cows, and ordered Policarpio to bury the dead animal. Desperate, Andrés dug it up. After he and his family ate some of the meat, the tainted flesh killed Cunshi. Padre Lomas demanded twenty-five sucres, more than the Indian could ever earn, in payment for burying the dead woman. That same night Andrés stole one of his master's cows and sold it to a nearby butcher. Tracked down by dogs, the Indian was captured and flogged in Pereira's patio. There was no one to protest except his small son, who was almost killed by the white men when he tried to help his father.

A score of foreigners arrived in Tomachi. The Indians welcomed them timorously, thinking that these new white men could certainly be no more cruel than their Spanish masters. But Mr. Chapy's first act was to order the Indians driven from their *huasipungos* to make room for company houses and a sawmill.

When Andrés' son brought news of the order, the Indians rebelled. They had stolidly accepted the white man's cruelty, even his lechery toward their women, but they felt that the land was theirs. Jacinto vainly tried to stop them when they marched on the village. The enraged Indians killed six of the white men. The others, including Mr. Chapy, fled in their autos.

They returned, over the road the Indians had built, with three hundred soldiers under a leader who had killed two thousand Indians in a similar rebellion near Cuenca. Troops hunted down and machine-gunned Indians of all ages and sexes. The few survivors, taking refuge in Andrés' hillside shack, rolled down rocks on the soldiers and shot at them with birdguns. Finally the soldiers set fire to the thatched roof. When the Indians ran from the burning house, the troops shot them without mercy.

Further Critical Evaluation of the Work:

This brutal novel flows swiftly. Technically, it is one of the better Spanish-American novels. Its virtues are legion, as are its defects, and among the former are interesting dialogue, bitter irony, sardonic humor, interesting plot, effective use of detail, exposure of social injustice, and crispness of style with short sentences that get to the point. *Huasipungo* presents the Ecuadorian Andes so clearly that we see them in stark detail. Even the sounds of the sierra are heard, while the odors, temperature changes, and direction of the night wind are experienced. Nevertheless, *Huasipungo's* crowning virtue is its defense of Ecuador's oppressed Indians. For this reason it has been considered Jorge Icaza's most significant novel, and has attained Continental prestige. It helped launch the cycle of so-called *Indianista* novels, devoted to telling the story of the long-abandoned Indians. The novel's protagonist, thus, is the Indian, who is characterized collectively but clearly, even to the peculiar flavor of his Spanish.

Decay is a prominent and depressing note in *Huasipungo;* images of garbage, filth, mold, slime, and rotten meat are frequent. Trash, dirt, and profanity are always present; everything is sloppy and unkempt, reflecting life's hopelessness. Depression is thus a constant note, accentuated by dismal mountain fogs, clammy cold, foul speech, and superstition. *Soroche* (altitude sickness) occasionally strikes, as do other afflictions. Alcoholism is the

Indian's bane, for the *huasipunguero* abandons everything—chickens, corn, potatoes, children—for alcohol. The characters of *Huasipungo* generally fail to change or develop. At the novel's end they are almost the same personalities and characters that they were at its start. The principal exception is the Indian community itself, for "from all corners of the soul, from every pore, grow the secret rebellions of a slave." Icaza also implied that the mestizo or mulatto suffers from a psychological inferiority complex in Ecuador, as is exemplified by Juana la Chola's (Juana the Half-breed) inert submission to rape by a landowner and a cleric. The latter villains, unfortunately, are crudely drawn. Don Alfonso Pereira is a second-rate Simon Legree, a consistent rascal, self-server, hypocrite, and uncomplicated brute from start to finish of the novel. He snarls, curses, and brutalizes Indians, but cringes from those above him. The priest is worse; he is so utterly depraved as to be comical. He extorts money from hungry Indians; sells passages out of purgatory or burial plots "close to Heaven" at alarming prices; builds a lucrative trucking business on ill-gotten money; and commits ridiculous rascalities too numerous to mention, including the drunken rape of Juana the Half-breed. Referred to as "the Cassocked One," the priest is a symbol of Icaza's disenchantment with religion, and it is puzzling that this "larger-than-life" caricature has not aroused disdain or even criticism from many generations of college students and professors.

Other ogres in *Huasipungo* are wealthy people, businessmen, whites, property owners, and Gringo capitalists. The Gringoes career about in Cadillacs oblivious to Indians; they relish money and lack human feelings. It is possible that they were grotesquely overdrawn by Icaza to appeal only to readers blinded by prejudice, but it should also be recalled that the novel was intended as a tirade against the social injustice that then blighted Ecuador. Icaza possibly had the illusion that his novel would bring a better life to the Indians, but initially his work was better received and lauded abroad than it was in his own country. In any event, Icaza exposed the plight of Ecuador's peons and also the decay of the rural aristocrats, who had left the work of their fathers to live luxuriously in the city. The novel also promotes the conflict of red race against white. White aristocrats are portrayed as hard, unfeeling, and cruel. They are contemptuous of Indians and exploit the poor. Some critics feel that Icaza's work had political motivations, others compare him to John Steinbeck (*The Grapes of Wrath*) and consider him a social reformer.

No one in *Huasipungo* apparently wishes to live in the country, since life in Quito is much richer. The countryside is backward, isolated, and uncomfortable; the city is cultured and far superior. Nature is unattractive; its beauties are unmentioned and unextolled. Nature's dangers are stressed, however, such as the scene where a man dies horribly by drowning in mud. Little interest is shown in animals, birds, or plants. The novel is almost devoid of color. Tints of sunrises, sunsets, mountains, skies, fields, or towns are generally lacking, and even the grayness of the constant mountain mist is assumed rather than described. The author's treatment of color is a deliberate stylistic device to increase the feeling of dismal hopelessness.

Although of Spanish blood and comfortable background, Icaza decided as a youth to champion Ecuador's poor of all races. Having attracted international attenion, his novel *Huasipungo* eventually won acceptance in Ecuador and undoubtedly helped the Indian. It has therefore helped to implement some social reform and to attract attention to the cause of the Indian. Some of the political attention has been lip-service, but the life of Ecuador's highland Indians is today improved over that described in *Huasipungo*. Thus, like *Uncle Tom's Cabin,* Icaza's novel has, in spite of its propagandistic qualities and superficial characterization, attracted much attention through its literary readability, and has made considerable impact on Ecuador and Spanish America in general.

William Freitas

HUCKLEBERRY FINN

Type of work: Novel
Author: Mark Twain (Samuel L. Clemens, 1835-1910)
Type of plot: Humorous satire
Time of plot: Nineteenth century
Locale: Along the Mississippi River
First published: 1884

Principal characters:
HUCKLEBERRY FINN
TOM SAWYER, his friend
JIM, a Negro slave

Critique:

Not to have read *The Adventures of Huckleberry Finn* is nearly as sad as never having been to a circus or never having played baseball with the neighborhood gang. Huck is every young boy who ever lived, and he is also an individual worth knowing. He swears and smokes, but he has a set of ethics of his own. Reared haphazardly in the South, he believes that slaves belong to their rightful owners, yet in his honest gratitude toward his friend Jim, he helps him escape his slavery. Huck could not bear to cheat the three Wilks girls, but he did not hesitate to steal food when he was hungry. Huck talks with a lowbrow dialect, but he is keen-witted and intelligent. He tells his story with a straight-faced forwardness, but the reader finds laughter and shrewd, sharp comment on human nature in every chapter of his adventures along the Mississippi.

The Story:

Tom Sawyer and Huckleberry Finn had found a box of gold in a robber's cave. After Judge Thatcher had taken the money and invested it for the boys, each had a huge allowance of a dollar a day. The Widow Douglas and her sister, Miss Watson, had taken Huck home with them to try to reform him. At first Huck could not stand living in a tidy house where smoking and swearing were forbidden. Worse, he had to go to school and learn how to read. But he managed to drag himself to school almost every day, except for the times when he sneaked off for a smoke in the woods or to go fishing in the Mississippi.

Life was beginning to become bearable to him when one day he noticed some tracks in the snow. Examining them closely, he realized that they belonged to the worthless father whom Huck had not seen for over a year. Knowing that his father would be back hunting him when the old man learned about the six thousand dollars, Huck rushed over to Judge Thatcher and persuaded the judge to take the fortune for himself. The judge was puzzled, but he signed some papers, and Huck was satisfied that he no longer had any money for his father to take from him.

Huck's father finally showed up one night in Huck's room at Widow Douglas' home. Complaining that he had been cheated out of his money, the old drunkard took Huck away with him to a cabin in the woods, where he kept the boy a prisoner, beating him periodically and half starving him. Before long Huck began to wonder why he had ever liked living with the widow. With his father, he could smoke and swear all he wanted, and his life would have been pleasant if it had not been for the beatings. One night Huck sneaked away, leaving a bloody trail from a pig he had killed in the woods. Huck wanted everyone to believe he was dead. He climbed into a boat and went to Jackson's Island to hide until all the excitement had blown over.

After three days of freedom, Huck

HUCKLEBERRY FINN by Mark Twain. Published by Harper & Brothers.

wandered to another part of the island and there he discovered Jim, Miss Watson's Negro slave. Jim told Huck that he had run off because he had overheard Miss Watson planning to sell him down south for eight hundred dollars. Huck swore he would not report Jim. The two stayed on the island many days, Jim giving Huck an education in primitive superstition. One night, Huck rowed back to the mainland. Disguised as a girl, he called on a home near the shore. There he learned that his father had disappeared shortly after the people of the town had decided that Huck had been murdered. Since Jim's disappearance had occurred just after Huck's alleged death, there was now a three hundred dollar reward posted for Jim's capture, as most people believed that Jim had killed Huck.

Fearing that Jackson's Island would be searched, Huck hurried back to Jim and the two headed down the Mississippi. They planned to leave the raft at Cairo and then go on a steamboat up the Ohio into free territory. Jim told Huck that he would work hard in the North and then buy his wife and children from their masters in the South. Helping a runaway slave bothered Huck's conscience, but he reasoned that it would bother him more if he betrayed such a good friend as Jim. One night as they were drifting down the river on their raft, a large boat loomed before them, and Huck and Jim, knowing that the raft would be smashed under the hull of the ship, jumped into the water. Huck swam safely to shore, but Jim disappeared.

Huck found a home with a friendly family named Grangerford. The Grangerfords were feuding with the Shepherdsons, another family living nearby. The Grangerfords left Huck mostly to himself and gave him a young slave to wait on him. One day the slave asked him to come to the woods to see some snakes. Following the boy, Huck came across Jim, who had been hiding in the woods waiting for an opportunity to send for Huck. Jim had repaired the broken raft. That night one of the Grangerford daughters eloped with a young Shepherdson, and the feud broke out once more. Huck and Jim ran away during the shooting and set off down the river.

Shortly afterward, Jim and Huck met two men who pretended they were royalty and made all sorts of nonsensical demands on Huck and Jim. Huck was not taken in, but he reasoned that it would do no harm to humor the two men to prevent quarreling. The Duke and the King were clever schemers. In one of the small river towns they staged a fake show which lasted long enough to net them a few hundred dollars. Then they ran off before the angered townspeople could catch them.

The Duke and the King overheard some people talking about the death of a Peter Wilks, who had left considerable property and some cash to his three daughters. Wilks' two brothers, whom no one in the town had ever seen, were living in England. The King and the Duke went to the three daughters, Mary Jane, Susan, and Joanna, and presented themselves as the two uncles. They took a few thousand dollars of the inheritance and then put up the property for auction and sold the slaves. This high-handed deed caused great grief to the girls, and Huck could not bear to see them so unhappy. He decided to expose the two frauds, but he wanted to insure Jim's safety first. Jim had been hiding in the woods waiting for his companions to return to him. Employing a series of lies, subterfuges, and maneuverings that were worthy of his ingenious mind, Huck exposed the Duke and King. Huck fled back to Jim, and the two escaped on their raft. Just as Jim and Huck thought they were on their way and well rid of their former companions, the Duke and King came rowing down the river toward them.

The whole party set out again with their royal plots to hoodwink the public. In one town where they landed, Jim was captured, and Huck learned that the Duke had turned him in for the reward. Huck had quite a tussle with his conscience. He knew that he ought to help return a slave to the rightful owner, but, on the other hand, he thought of all the fine times he and Jim had had together and how loyal a friend Jim had been. Finally, Huck decided that he would help Jim to escape.

Learning that Mr. Phelps was holding Jim, he headed for the Phelps farm. There, Mrs. Phelps ran up and hugged him, mistaking him for the nephew whom she had been expecting to come for a visit. Huck wondered how he could keep Mrs. Phelps from learning that he was not her nephew. Then to his relief he learned they had mistaken him for Tom Sawyer. Huck rather liked being Tom for a while, and he was able to tell the Phelps all about Tom's Aunt Polly and Sid and Mary, Tom's brother and sister. Huck was feeling proud of himself for keeping up the deception. When Tom Sawyer really did arrive, he told his aunt that he was Sid.

At the first opportunity Huck told Tom about Jim's capture. To his surprise, Tom offered to help him set Jim free. Huck could not believe that Tom would be a slave stealer, but he kept his feelings to himself. Huck had intended merely to wait until there was a dark night and then break the padlock on the door of the shack where Jim was kept. But Tom said the rescue had to be done according to the books, and he laid out a most complicated plan with all kinds of story-book ramifications. It took fully three weeks of plotting, stealing, and deceit to let Jim out of the shack. Then the scheme failed. A chase began after Jim escaped, and Tom was shot in the leg. After Jim had been recaptured, Tom was brought back to Aunt Sally's house to recover from his wound. Then Tom revealed the fact that Miss Watson had died, giving Jim his freedom in her will. Huck was greatly relieved to learn that Tom was not really a slave stealer after all.

To complicate matters still more, Tom's Aunt Polly arrived. She quickly set straight the identities of the two boys. Jim was given his freedom and Tom gave him forty dollars. Tom told Huck that his money was still safely in the hands of Judge Thatcher, but Huck moaned that his father would likely be back to claim it again. Then Jim told Huck that his father was dead; Jim had seen him lying in an abandoned boat along the river.

Huck was ready to start out again because Aunt Sally said she thought she might adopt him and try to civilize him. Huck thought that he could not go through such a trial again after he had once tried to be civilized under the care of Widow Douglas.

Further Critical Evaluation of the Work:

Little could Mark Twain have visualized in 1876 when he began a sequel to capitalize on the success of *Tom Sawyer* that *Huckleberry Finn* would evolve into his masterpiece and one of the most significant works in the American novel tradition. Twain's greatest contribution to the tradition occurred when, with an unerring instinct for American regional dialects, he elected to tell the story in Huck's own words. The skill with which Twain elevates the dialect of an illiterate village boy to the highest levels of poetry established the spoken American idiom as a literary language, and earned for Twain his reputation—proclaimed by Ernest Hemingway, William Faulkner and others—as the father of the modern American novel. Twain also maintains an almost perfect fidelity to Huck's point of view in order to dramatize the conflict between Huck's own innate innocence and natural goodness and the dictates of a corrupt society.

As Huck's own story, the novel centers around several major themes, including death and rebirth, freedom and bondage, the search for a father, the individual versus society, and the all-pervasive theme of brotherhood. Huck's character reflects a point in Mark Twain's development when he still believed man to be innately good, but saw social forces as corrupting influences which replaced with the dictates of a socially determined "conscience" man's intuitive sense of right and wrong. This theme is explicity dramatized through Huck's conflict with his conscience over whether or not to turn Jim in as a runaway slave. Huck, on the one hand, accepts without question what he has been taught by church and society about slavery. In his own mind, as surely as in that of his southern contemporaries, aiding an escaped slave was clearly wrong both legally and morally. Thus, Huck's battle with his conscience is a real trauma for him, and his decision to "go to Hell" rather than give Jim up is made with a certainty that such a fate awaits him for breaking one of society's laws. It is ironic, of course, that Huck's "sin" against the social establishment affirms the best that is possible to the individual.

Among the many forms of bondage, ranging from the widow's attempt to "civilize" Huck to the code of "honor" which causes Sherburn to murder Boggs and the law of the vendetta which absolutely governs the lives of the Grangerfords and Shepherdsons, that permeate the novel, slavery provides Twain his largest metaphor for both social bondage and institutionalized injustice and inhumanity. Written well after the termination of the Civil War, *Huckleberry Finn* is not an anti-slavery novel in the limited sense that *Uncle Tom's Cabin* is. Rather than simply attacking an institution already legally dead, Twain uses the idea of slavery as a metaphor for all social bondage and injustice. Thus, Jim's search for freedom, like Huck's own need to escape both the Widow and Pap Finn, is as much a metaphorical search for an ideal state of freedom as mere flight from slavery into free-state sanctuary. Thus it is largely irrelevant that Twain has Huck and Jim running deeper into the South rather than north toward free soil. Freedom exists neither in the North nor the South, but in the ideal and idyllic world of the raft and river.

The special world of raft and river is at the very heart of the novel. In contrast to the restrictive and oppressive social world of the shore, the raft is a veritable Eden where the evils of civilization are escaped. It is here that Jim and Huck can allow their natural bond of love to develop without regard for the question of race. It is here on the raft that Jim can become a surrogate father to Huck, and Huck can develop the depth of feeling for Jim which eventually leads to his decision to "go to Hell." But, while the developing relationship between Huck and Jim determines the basic shape of the novel, the river works in other structural ways as well. The picaresque form of the novel and its structural rhythm are based upon a series of episodes on shore, after each of which Huck and Jim return to the peaceful sanctuary of the raft. It is on shore that Huck encounters the worst excesses of which "the damned human race" is capable, but with each return to the raft comes a renewal of spiritual hope and idealism.

The two major thrusts of Twain's attack on the "civilized" world in *Huckleberry Finn* are against institutionalized religion and the romanticism which he believed characterized the South. The former is easily illustrated by the irony of the Widow's attempt to teach Huck religious principles while she persists in holding slaves. As with her snuff taking—which was all right because she did it herself—there seems to be no relationship between a fundamental sense of humanity and justice and her religion. Huck's practical morality makes him more "Christian" than the Widow, though he takes no interest in her lifeless principles. Southern romanticism, which Twain blamed for the fall of the South, is particularly allegorized by the sinking of the Walter Scott, but it is also inherent in such episodes as the feud where Twain shows the real horror of the sort of vendetta traditionally glamorized by romantic authors. In both cases, Twain is attacking the mindless acceptance of values which he believed kept the South in its dark ages.

Many critics have argued that the ending hopelessly flaws *Huckleberry Finn* by reducing its final quarter to literary burlesque. Others have argued that the ending is in perfect accord with Twain's themes. But all agree that, flawed or not, the substance of Twain's masterpiece transcends the limits of literary formalism to explore those eternal verities upon which great literature rests. Through the adventures of an escaped slave and a runaway boy, both representatives of the ignorant and lowly of the earth, Twain affirms for us that true humanity is of men rather than institutions, and that we can all be aristocrats in the kingdom of the heart.

William E. Grant

HUDIBRAS

Type of work: Poem
Author: Samuel Butler (1612-1680)
Type of plot: Satirical burlesque
Time of plot: 1640-1660
Locale: England
First published: 1663-1678

Principal characters:
    SIR HUDIBRAS, a Presbyterian knight
    RALPHO, Sir Hudibras' squire, a religious Independent
    THE WIDOW, a wealthy woman who befriended Sir Hudibras
    SIDROPHEL, an astrologer
    CROWDERO, a fiddler
    TRULLA, a woman who subdued Sir Hudibras

Critique:

Butler's *Hudibras* was intended to ridicule the Presbyterians, Dissenters, and others who had fought against the crown in the conflict between Charles I and Oliver Cromwell. Published shortly after the restoration of Charles II, the poem had immense popularity for a time. The king himself, one of its most ardent admirers, carried a copy in his pocket and quoted from it. *Hudibras* has sometimes been called a mock-epic. It is more accurate, however, to say that the poem is to an epic what farce is to tragic drama. The burlesque is used with telling effect. Mean and low persons, things, and situations are described in pompous language. By so doing, Butler hoped to unmask the hypocrisy and absurdity of Dissenting reformers in seventeenth-century England and to show them as ridiculous, odious, and obnoxious. He also wanted to draw attention to the pretensions of the false learning rampant in England at the time. Astrology, fortune-telling, alchemy, "sympathetic" medicine, and other pseudo-sciences were presented in such fashion as to show the readers of his time the absurdity of practices and practitioners alike. To *Hudibras* can be ascribed little organization; the best qualities of the poems lie in isolated passages devoted to the satire.

The Story:

Sir Hudibras, a Presbyterian knight, was one of those who had ridden out against the monarchy during the civil war. He was a proud man, one who bent his knee to nothing but chivalry and suffered no blow but that which had been given when he was dubbed a knight. Although he had some wit, he was very shy of displaying it. He knew Latin, Greek, and Hebrew; indeed, his talk was a kind of piebald dialect, so heavily was it larded with Greek and Latin words and tags. He was learned in rhetoric, logic, and mathematics, and he frequently spoke in a manner demonstrating his learning. His notions fitted things so well that he was often puzzled to decide what his notions were and what was reality.

In figure he was thick and stout, both before and behind, and he always carried extra victuals in his hose. He rode a mealy-mouthed, wall-eyed, skinny old nag whose tail dragged in the dust, and he encouraged his horse with a single old spur.

Sir Hudibras had a squire named Ralpho, who was an Independent in religion —a fact which accounted for his partisanship and dogmatic approach to the many discussions and arguments he had with his master on matters of faith. Ralpho was a tailor by trade, but his belief in the efficacy of divine revelation to the individual had made him something of a religious oracle, at least in his own satisfied opinion.

Sir Hudibras and Ralpho rode forth

from the knight's home to reform what they called sins and what the rest of the world regarded as mild amusement. After they had gone a few miles on their journey they came to a town where the people danced enjoyably to a fiddle and, worse in Sir Hudibras' eyes, indulged themselves in the sport of bearbaiting. To the knight's resolve to end these activities Ralpho added his agreement that they were certainly unchristian. When the knight advanced, however, he was met by an unsympathetic crowd. With the rabble were several leaders. One was Crowdero, a fiddler wtih one wooden leg, who played his instrument for the mob in the absence of more martial fifes and drums. Another leader was Orsin, the bear keeper, who led his charge at the end of a rope fastened to the creature's nose. Talgol, a butcher, was also in the van, as was a woman named Trulla, an Amazon of a damsel. When Sir Hudibras called upon the people to disperse and return quietly to their homes, leaving Crowdero a prisoner, a fight began.

Ralpho was soon bucked off his horse when some one put a burr under the animal's tail. Sir Hudibras, pulled from his steed, fell on the bear, who became enraged and escaped from his keeper. The bear's escape scattered the crowd and Crowdero was left behind, the prisoner of Sir Hudibras and Ralpho, for the fiddler's wooden leg had been broken in the melee. Having swooned from fear, Hudibras also lay helpless for a time, but he was soon revived by Ralpho. The pair took their prisoner to the end of the town and placed his good leg in the stocks. They hung his fiddle, bow, and case above the stocks as a trophy of victory.

The people who had been dispersed by the enraged bear, overcoming their fright, planned to attack the knight and release his victim. Hudibras and Ralpho sallied out of their quarters to the attack. A blow on Ralpho's horse caused the animal to unhorse his rider. Hudibras, at first frightened, summoned his courage and charged. The crowd dispersed once again,

and Hudibras went to the aid of his squire. When the knight's back was turned, Trulla attacked him from behind and quickly overpowered him. Rejoined by her friends, the woman marched Hudibras to the stocks to take the place of Crowdero. Placed in the stocks, Hudibras and Ralpho discussed and argued their situation and what had occasioned it. Then a widow who had heard of the knight's plight came to see him in the stocks. After much discussion, she agreed to have Hudibras set free if he would consent to a whipping. He agreed to the condition and was released.

Sir Hudibras, once out of the stocks, was reluctant to keep the bargain he had made. He was anxious for her hand, too, but for her money rather than her love. Hudibras and Ralpho argued long about flagellation. Hudibras suggested that the whipping be administered to Ralpho, as a proxy for the knight. Ralpho refused and an argument ensued. When the two were almost at swords' points, they heard a terrible din. They looked about and saw coming down the road, a party of people making a noisy to-do over a poor man who had let his wife take over his authority. Sir Hudibras tried to break up the crowd, but a volley of rotten eggs and other filth defeated him and cooled his ardor for reform. The knight, going to clean himself after his most recent encounter with sin, decided to lie to the widow about having received a whipping.

Before approaching the widow's house, Sir Hudibras went to consult Sidrophel, an astrologer. Hudibras and Ralpho agreed that a godly man might reasonably consult with such a man if he were on a Christian errand. Hudibras, soon convinced that Sidrophel and his apprentice, Whachum, were frauds, perhaps dabblers with the devil, sent Ralpho off to find a constable. Meanwhile, Hudibras overcame the pair and went through the astrologer's belongings. Instead of going for a constable, however, Ralpho decided to go to the widow. He was afraid that the authorities might think Hudibras involved in black magic.

Ralpho, telling all to the widow, revealed that Hudibras was going to lie about having received a whipping and that he was only after the widow's money. When Hudibras arrived a short time later, the widow hid Ralpho and let the knight tell his long string of half-truths and lies. The widow, knowing the truth, treated him to a somewhat frightening masquerade, with Ralpho as the chief sprite. Hudibras and the squire decided to escape before worse could happen to them. They went hugger-mugger through a window and escaped on their saddleless horses.

The poet then turned in the last part of the poem to talk directly about the religious groups for which Ralpho and Hudibras stood—the Independents and the Presbyterians—and how they had fallen out with one another after the end of the Civil War and had eventually, in their weakness, paved the way for the Restoration of the Stuart line in the person of Charles II.

Further Critical Evaluation of the Work:

Hudibras opens with terse, end-stopped couplets that immediately impede the building of an epic narrative's flow; the impatient reader may be lost in this awkward beginning that sounds to the modern ear like a succession of commercial jingles. Butler, however, redeems himself after this perfunctory start by proving the necessity of that form in establishing a tonal solidity of ridicule toward Sir Hudibras, magically sustained throughout the long poem. About line 300, the couplets open up, assuming a near-speech rhythm in spite of the archaic diction and syntactical inversions; Butler executes this loosening and subsequent flow through frequent use of enjambment.

The paradoxical ridicule of a hero in his own epic poem is accomplished by the successful juxtapositioning of crude, occasionally vulgar language with overblown rhetoric and empty terms. Use of the latter group of words allows Butler to satirize the overly ambitious pedantry of his time; his use of the former group constitutes a strong argument for the stupidity and commonness of man. Butler's contention that moderation is the proper course unfolds as the only alternative to the ludicrous extremes. Other purposeful travesties against a "natural-ness" of language include obscure references to tax even the most resourceful historian of trivia, and heavy use of Latin words and idioms. Both allude to the many quackeries that were springing up in the guise of scientific fields, and the arbitrariness that gave these fields their minute substance. In addition, the characters' epigrammatic speech parodies the religious dogma responsible for the bitter conflict that Butler found so deplorable.

One should note the interesting and unorthodox invocation of the Muse that suggests the unheroic doings through which Fate will drag the knight and his squire. In the same passage (little escaping the satirical sweep), Butler even takes a swipe at the art of writing itself.

HUGH WYNNE, FREE QUAKER

Type of work: Novel
Author: Silas Weir Mitchell (1829-1914)
Type of plot: Historical romance
Time of plot: 1753-1783
Locale: Colonial America
First published: 1897

Principal characters:
JOHN WYNNE, a Quaker
MARIE, his wife
HUGH WYNNE, John's son
JACK WARDER, Hugh's friend
ARTHUR WYNNE, Hugh's cousin
DARTHEA PENISTON, who marries Hugh
GAINOR WYNNE, John's sister

Critique:

Hugh Wynne, Free Quaker is one of the best novels of the American Revolution. The veracity of its events in the historical sense can be judged by any student of history, and its faithfulness to the social history of the time can be judged by reading diaries and chronicles of those who lived through the war years. More than historical fiction, however, the novel is a touching revelation of a child-parent relationship and of the consequences of too much doctrinal discipline.

The Story:

The Wynne family had descended from an ancient Welsh line. That part of the family which had remained in Wales now held the family estate of Wyncote. The American branch, being Quaker, had dissociated itself from the more worldly family at Wyncote, and Hugh Wynne grew up under the stern discipline of John Wynne's orthodoxy. John's sister, Gainor Wynne, had not become a Quaker. Because Hugh was his aunt's favorite, early in his life he fell under the influence of those who were outside the ways of the Quakers. Jack Warder was Hugh's closest friend, the two boys having gone to school together. Aunt Gainor often invited both boys to her home in Phila-

delphia, where she was surrounded by a worldly group of English officers, men upon whom the Quakers frowned. Hugh enjoyed their society, to the delight of his aunt, who wished her nephew to break his Quaker ties. Jack Warder, however, did not like Gainor Wynne's friends. When he and Hugh were old enough to judge moral values for themselves, their friendship became strained. Hugh's father was never fully aware of the way Hugh spent his time away from home.

One night, while drinking and gambling with his worldly friends, Hugh met a cousin, Arthur Wynne, of the family at Wyncote. He instinctively disliked his relative because of his superior ways and his deceitful manner. During the evening Hugh became very drunk. Suddenly his mother and Jack Warder burst into the room.

This incident marked the beginning of Hugh's break with his father's church and the renewal of his friendship with Jack Warder. Hugh, realizing his folly, was thankful that Jack had seen him on the streets and had led his mother to rescue him from the drunken party. He began to realize the depth of his mother's love and understanding. John Wynne was quite different in his attitude. A few nights later he took Hugh to a

HUGH WYNNE, FREE QUAKER by Silas Weir Mitchell. By permission of the publishers, Appleton-Century-Crofts, Inc. Copyright, 1896, by The Century Co. Renewed, 1923, by Langden Elwyn Mitchell.

Quaker meeting, where public prayers were offered to save Hugh's soul. Hugh's embarrassment caused him to lose all of his love for the Quaker religion and to bear a deep resentment against his father.

At Gainor Wynne's home, Jack and Hugh heard much conversation about disagreement between the Americans and the British. Gainor was a Whig, and under her influence Jack and Hugh gained sympathy for their American compatriots. Arthur Wynne too had become part of the society that gathered at Gainor Wynne's house. Jack and Hugh had never liked Arthur, but now they had a new cause for their dislike. Arthur made no secret of his admiration for Darthea Peniston, a schoolmate of Jack and Hugh, and his bragging about Wyncote seemingly won her interest, thus arousing Hugh's jealousy. When Hugh told Darthea of his love, she insisted that she did not love him.

Meanwhile Hugh's parents went abroad. During their absence he stayed with Gainor Wynne. Claiming that the time was not far off when he would need such a skill, she urged him to take fencing lessons. Jack practiced the sport with his friend, although he knew it to be contrary to the laws of the church. Hugh and Jack both knew that soon they would join the American cause for liberty.

While John Wynne and his wife were abroad, Hugh received a letter telling that his mother had died. On his return John showed no signs of his grief at the loss of his wife. Hugh himself felt her loss deeply.

At Gainor's home, where he spent more time than ever since the death of his mother, Hugh quarreled with an English officer and was challenged to a duel. With Jack as his second, Hugh answered the challenge. As a result the Quakers notified both boys that unless they changed their ways and repented for their sins, they could no longer belong to the Society of Friends. Jack and Hugh announced that they intended to join the American army; fighting had already begun at Lexington.

Jack went to join the troops. After a short time Hugh decided to follow him, in spite of his father's crafty excuses that he needed Hugh to conduct his business affairs for him. When he did join the army, Hugh was captured by the British and sent, wounded and sick, to a filthy prison. In the prison Arthur Wynne, now a Tory captain, saw his cousin, but left Hugh to die. Hugh never forgave him for this cruelty and for his subsequent lie concerning the meeting.

Hugh recovered and escaped from prison to return to Gainor Wynne's house. Arthur Wynne was staying at the home of John Wynne and ingratiating himself in the eyes of the old man. Hugh knew that there was something mysterious in relation to the Welsh estate of Wyncote. Supposedly Arthur's father owned the estate, having bought it from John's father. Gainor Wynne urged Hugh to investigate the title of the estate. John Wynne, it seemed, still possessed the title, and out of sympathy for Arthur's alleged poverty had promised to give it to him. Hugh was unable to change his father's decision, even after he told of Arthur's cruel desertion when Hugh lay near death in prison. His father refused to believe Hugh's story.

Hugh could not tell Darthea about Arthur's behavior, for he felt that she would rush to Arthur's defense if he said anything against his cousin.

Once, while Hugh was at home, his father, thinking Hugh was Arthur, handed him the deed to Wyncote. Knowing that his father's mind had often misled him of late, Hugh tried to convince the old man that he was not Arthur, but John insisted that Hugh take the deed. Hugh took it to Gainor Wynne.

After a rest of a few months, Hugh rejoined the American troops. He was able to perform a courageous service for General Washington, for which he received praise and a captaincy. Jack, too, had become an officer.

When Hugh and Jack returned to

Philadelphia on leave, Gainor Wynne managed to expose Arthur to Darthea. Although the young girl had lost her earlier love for the Tory officer, she had been unwilling to break her promise to him. But with proof of Arthur's villainy before her, she felt that she was free at last to break her engagement.

Again Hugh asked her to marry him and she surprised him by accepting. Hugh still did not want the title to Wyncote, and Darthea agreed with him that after he had taken Arthur's betrothed it would not become Hugh to take his inheritance from him as well. Although Gainor Wynne wished to press the legality of the ancient deed, Darthea threw it into the fire, and so destroyed any claim Hugh might have upon the ancestral estate.

John Wynne, who had ceased to live for Hugh when he had lost his mental faculties, died soon after the war ended. Darthea and Hugh were happily married, and they lived long years together to watch their children and their grandchildren grow up unburdened by the rigorous religious control which Hugh had known in his youth.

Further Critical Evaluation of the Work:

Written more than a hundred years after the Revolution, Mitchell's historical romance recaptures the tone as well as the letter of the Philadelphia scene before and during the struggle with Great Britain. Tolstoy recreated the time of the Napoleonic invasion of Russia and its effects on the aristocracy with brilliantly conceived characterizations and dramatized historical events. Mitchell's method is modest by comparison, and if not as effective as Tolstoy's, is curiously satisfying in its own right.

What Mitchell does is play memoirist. His main character, Hugh Wynne, begins by apologizing for "having no gift in the way of composition" and a distaste for fiction. By chance, his friend Jack Warder, a major character in the novel, bequeaths Hugh his diary which is as fulsome and sensitive as Hugh is forgetful and unliterary. This "convenient" bequest does not seem contrived because it is a reflection in point of view of one of the novel's central themes: Warder's protection, through thought and deed, of his less perceptive friend.

The memoir style is very well done: cooly observant, precise in detail and limpidly clear throughout. The eighteenth-century elegance of the tone forms a poignant counterpoint to the emotional turmoil of the irrational relationship between father and son, Hugh and John Wynne. The portrait of Washington is meticulously historical, but the vindictiveness with which Mitchell attacks the zeal of conservative Quakerism mars his pretension of complete historical objectivity. The characters are largely wooden, and motivation is mechanical rather than psychological; Darthea's love is a thing difficult to believe in. Perhaps spirited Gainor Wynne, with her Whig independence and brashly lovable integrity, is the novel's best creation: "The good old lady was lamenting her scanty toilet, and the dirt in which the Hessians had left her house. 'I have drunk no tea since Lexington,' she said, 'and I have bought no gowns. My gowns, sir, are on the backs of our poor soldiers.' "

THE HUMAN COMEDY

Type of work: Novel
Author: William Saroyan (1908-   )
Type of plot: Sentimental romance
Time of plot: Twentieth century
Locale: Ithaca, California
First published: 1943

Principal characters:
KATEY MACAULEY, a widow
HOMER,
ULYSSES, and
MARCUS, her sons
BESS, her daughter
MARY ARENA, Marcus' sweetheart
THOMAS SPANGLER, manager of the telegraph office
MR. GROGAN, assistant in the telegraph office
TOBEY GEORGE, Marcus' friend from the army
LIONEL, Ulysses' friend

Critique:

This novel has for its theme the idea that no human can ever die as long as he lives in the hearts of those who loved him. The story deals with the family of a soldier who died in the war. Frankly sentimental, *The Human Comedy* is one of the most touching of Saroyan's works.

The Story:

Mr. Macauley was dead and his wife and children had to take care of themselves. When Marcus went into the army, Homer, the next oldest, obtained a job on the night shift in the telegraph office at Ithaca, California. He worked at night because he was still attending school during the day. Little Ulysses watched his family and wondered what was going on, for his baby's mind could not comprehend all the changes that had taken place in his home.

Every morning Homer arose early and exercised in his room so that he would be physically fit to run the two-twenty low hurdles at high school. After he and Bess had eaten their breakfast, Mary Arena, who was in love with Marcus, came from next door, and she and Fess walked to school together.

In the ancient history class, taught by Miss Hicks, Homer and Hubert Ackley the Third insulted each other, and Miss

Hicks kept the boys after school. But Coach Byfield had picked Hubert to run the two-twenty low hurdles that afternoon, and Hubert told Miss Hicks that the principal had asked that he be excused. Indignant at the deceit, Miss Hicks also sent Homer to run the race. Although Hubert was the winner, Homer felt that justice had been done.

Thomas Spangler was in charge of the telegraph office and Mr. Grogan, an old man with a weak heart, was his assistant. Because Mr. Grogan got drunk every night, one of Homer's duties was to see to it that Mr. Grogan stayed awake to perform his duties. A problem which had weighed on Homer's mind ever since he had taken his new job and had grown up overnight was whether the war would change anything for people. Mr. Grogan and Homer often talked about the world, Homer declaring that he did not like things as they were. Seeing everyone in the world mixed up and lonely, Homer said, he felt that he had to say and do things to make people laugh.

Mrs. Macauley was happy that her children were so human. Ever since her husband had died, Katey Macauley had pretended to see him and discuss with him problems that arose concerning the rearing of her family. She felt that the father was not dead if he lived again in the lives of his children. One afternoon she had a premonition of Marcus' death, for she imagined that her husband came to her and told her he was going to bring Marcus with him.

Little Ulysses had a friend, Lionel, who was three years older than Ulysses. The older boys chased Lionel away from their games because they said that he was dumb. When Lionel came to Mrs. Macauley to ask her whether he was stupid, the kind woman assured him that he was as good as everyone else. Lionel took Ulysses to the library with him to look at all the many-colored books on the shelves. Ulysses, who spent his time wandering around and watching everything, was pleased with the new experience.

Marcus wrote to Homer from an army camp somewhere in the South, and Homer took the letter back to the telegraph office with him. The letter told about Marcus' friend, an orphan named Tobey George. Marcus had described his family, Homer, Ulysses, Bess, his mother, and his sweetheart, Mary, to Tobey. Because Tobey had no family of his own, he was grateful to Marcus for bringing to him second-hand the Macauley family. Marcus had told Tobey that after the war he wanted Tobey to go to Ithaca and marry Bess. Tobey was not so certain that Bess would want to marry him, but he felt for the first time in his life that he had a family that was almost his own. Marcus had written to Homer, as the new head of the family, to tell him about Tobey George and to ask him to look after his mother and Bess.

Homer was moved by his brother's letter. When he had finished reading it, he told Mr. Grogan that if Marcus should be killed he would spit at the world. Homer could express his love for Marcus in no other way.

The same events repeated themselves many times in Ithaca. Ulysses continued to watch everything with increasing interest. Mary and Bess sang their songs and went for their evening walks. Telegrams came, and Homer delivered them. Soldiers began coming home to Ithaca, to their mothers and to their families.

Homer had been working at the telegraph office for six months. One Sunday night, while he was walking downtown with Lionel and Ulysses, he saw through the window of the telegraph office that Mr. Grogan was working alone. He sent the two small boys home and went in to see if Mr. Grogan needed him. The old man had suffered one of his heart attacks, and Homer ran to the drug store to get some medicine for him. Mr. Grogan attempted to type out one more telegram, a message for Katey Macauley telling her that her son Marcus had been killed in action. When Homer returned with the medicine, he found Mr. Grogan slumped over the typed-out message. He was dead. Homer went home with the message that Marcus had been killed.

That night a soldier had got off the train at Ithaca. He was Tobey George. He walked around for a time before he went to see Marcus' family. When he came to the Macauley porch, he stood and listened to Bess and Mary singing inside the house. Bess came outside and sat next to him while he told her that Marcus had sent him to be a member of the family. When Homer came to the porch with the telegram, Tobey called him aside and told him to tear up the message. Tobey assured him that Marcus was not dead; Marcus could never die. Mrs. Macauley came onto the porch, and Ulysses ran to Tobey and took his hand. For a while the mother looked at her two remaining sons. Then she smiled at her new son as the family walked into the house.

Further Critical Evaluation of the Work:

In *The Human Comedy* William Saroyan details the life of a small town during World War II. The book is full of vignettes which recall such homey matters as Homer buying the day-old pies; Ulysses waving to the train; and Ma Macauley comforting her working son with late night conversations. There is, then, a noticeable mixture of child-like innocence and adult homily in Saroyan's book. The world is seen through the eyes of children, and yet we are always aware of the author whose presence adds complexity to the experience just as we are always aware of the fact of war. While the ordinary problems of human existence, such as school rivalries, adolescent love, and the first experience of evil, are being dealt with by the Widow Macauley and her children, the larger world drives toward cataclysm and challenges the pieties and conventions of innocent, rural America. To be sure Ithaca, an ancient symbol of home itself, comes no closer to actual hostilities than its Greek namesake came to the battlements of Troy. But the arrival and departure of the daily train and the ominous click of the telegraph bring the outside world very close to Ithaca's consciousness.

Saroyan's conclusion is positive if it is melodramatic and sentimental. While Homer is conveying the message of Marcus' death in battle to his family, pensation, Katey Macauley finds comfort, sustenance, and belief in the continuity of human experience. By the title of the novel itself, Saroyan seems to suggest that all tragedy, finally viewed from a wide enough perspective, dissolves into a comedy of joy and affirmation. If we are uncomfortable with this philosophy, it may be we have lost the innocence of faith which Saroyan finds so sustaining in Ithaca.

HUMPHRY CLINKER

Type of work: Novel
Author: Tobias Smollett (1721-1771)
Type of plot: Social satire
Time of plot: Mid-eighteenth century
Locale: England, Scotland, Wales
First published: 1771

Principal characters:

MATTHEW BRAMBLE, a Welsh squire
MISS TABITHA BRAMBLE, his sister
LYDIA MELFORD, his niece
JERRY MELFORD, his nephew
WINIFRED JENKINS, a maid
HUMPHRY CLINKER, a servant, discovered to be Mr. Bramble's natural son
LIEUTENANT OBADIAH LISMAHAGO, an adventurer and sportsman
MR. DENNISON, a country gentleman
GEORGE DENNISON, his son, the actor known as Wilson

Critique:

This novel, written in the form of letters, is easy to read and continually amusing. The characters of the writers of the letters are shown by the variation of their descriptions of the same events. The picture is one of a realistic if somewhat eccentric family, whose members display the manners and customs of eighteenth-century society. *The Expedition of Humphry Clinker,* to use its full title, has often been called the greatest of the letter-novels, and an outstanding example of English humor.

The Story:

Squire Matthew Bramble was an eccentric and skeptical gentleman with large estates in Wales. With him lived his sister, Miss Tabitha Bramble, a middle-aged maiden of high matrimonial hopes that were greater than her expectations. Painfully afflicted with the gout, the squire set out for Bath to try the waters, but with few hopes of their healing properties. With him went his sister; her servant, Winifred Jenkins; his own manservant, and, at the last minute, his niece and nephew, Lydia and Jerry Melford.

The young Melfords were orphans and Squire Bramble's wards. Lydia had been in boarding-school, where, unfortunately, she had fallen in love with an actor—a circumstance Squire Bramble hoped she would soon forget among the gay and fashionable gatherings at Bath. Her brother, who had just finished his studies at Oxford, had tried to fight a duel with the actor, but an opportunity to defend his sister's honor had not presented itself to his satisfaction.

On the way to Bath a Jewish peddler made his way into Squire Bramble's lodgings on the pretext of selling glasses, and in a whisper made himself known to Lydia as George Wilson, the strolling player. The lovesick girl ordered Winifred Jenkins to follow the actor and talk with him. The maid came back in a great flurry. He had told her that Wilson was not his real name, that he was a gentleman, and that he intended to sue for Lydia's hand in his proper character. But, alas, the excited maid had forgotten Wilson's real name. There was nothing for poor Lydia to do but to conjecture and daydream as the party continued on toward Bath.

Arriving at Bath without further incident, the party entered the gay festivities there with various degrees of pleasure. Tabitha tried to get proposals of marriage out of every eligible man she met, and the squire became disgusted with the supposed curative powers of the waters which were drunk and bathed in by people with almost any infirmity in hopes of regaining their health. Lydia was still languishing over Wilson, and Jerry enjoyed the absurdity of the social gatherings. In an attempt to lighten his niece's spirits, Squire Bramble decided to go on to London.

They had traveled only a short way toward London when the coach accidentally overturned and Miss Tabitha's lapdog, in the excitement, bit the squire's servant. Miss Tabitha made such loud complaint when the servant kicked her dog in return that the squire was forced to discharge the man on the spot. He also needed another postilion, as Miss Tabitha declared herself unwilling to drive another foot behind the clumsy fellow who had overturned the coach. The squire hired a ragged country fellow named Humphry Clinker to take the place of the unfortunate postilion, and the party went on to the next village.

Miss Tabitha was shocked by what she called Humphry's nakedness, for he wore no shirt. The maid added to the chorus of outraged modesty. Yielding to these female clamors, the squire asked about Humphry's circumstances, listened to the story of his life, gruffly read him a lecture on the crimes of poverty and sickness, and gave him a guinea for a new suit of clothes. In gratitude Humphry refused to be parted from his new benefactor and went on with the party to London.

In London they were well entertained by a visit to Vauxhall Gardens as well as by several public and private parties. Squire Bramble was disconcerted by the discovery that Humphry was a preacher by inclination, and had begun giving sermons in the manner of the Methodists. Miss Tabitha and her maid were already among Humphry's followers. The squire attempted to stop what he considered either hypocrisy or madness on Humphry's part. Miss Tabitha, disgusted with her brother's action, begged him to allow Humphry to continue his sermons.

The family was shocked to learn one day that Humphry had been arrested as a highway robber, and was in jail. When the squire arrived to investigate the case, he discovered that Humphry was obviously innocent of the charge against him, which had been placed by an ex-convict who made money by turning in criminals to the government. Humphry had made a fine impression on the jailer and his family and had converted several of his fellow prisoners. The squire found the man who supposedly had been robbed and got him to testify that Humphry was not the man who had committed the robbery. In the meantime Humphry preached so eloquently that he kept the prison taproom empty of customers. When this became evident he was hurriedly released, and Squire Bramble promised to allow him to preach his sermons unmolested.

Continuing their travels north after leaving London, the party stopped in Scarborough, where they went bathing. Squire Bramble undressed in a little cart which could be rolled down into the sea, so that he was able to bath nude with the greatest propriety. When he entered the water, he found it much colder than he had expected and gave several shouts as he swam away. Hearing these calls from the squire, Humphry thought his good master was drowning, and rushed fully clothed into the sea to rescue him. He pulled the squire to shore, almost twisting off his master's ear, and leaving the modest man shamefaced and naked in full view upon the beach. Humphrey was forgiven, however, because he had meant well.

At an inn in Durham, the party made the acquaintance of Lieutenant Lismahago, who seemed somewhat like Don Quixote. The lieutenant, regaling the company with tales of his adventures among the Indians of North America, quite captured the heart of Miss Tabitha. Squire Bramble was also charmed with the crusty conversation of the retired soldier, and made plans to meet him later on in their journey. The group became more and more fond of Humphry as time went on, especially Winifred. After a short and frivolous flirtation with Jerry's part-time valet, she settled down to win Humphry as a husband.

The party continued its trip through Scotland. In Edinburgh Lydia fainted when she saw a man who looked like Wilson, an action which showed her uncle that she had not yet forgotten the affair. After visiting several parts of Scotland and enjoying the most gracious hospitality everywhere, they continued by coach back to England. As they were traveling south, Lieutenant Lismahago rejoined the party and Miss Tabitha renewed her designs on him.

Just outside Dumfries the coach was overturned in the middle of a stream. Jerry and Lismahago succeeded in getting the women out of the water after a struggle, and Humphry staged a heroic rescue of the squire, who had been caught in the bottom of the coach. They found lodgings at a nearby inn until the coach could be repaired. While all were gathered in the parlor of a tavern, Squire Bramble was accosted by an old college friend named Dennison, a successful farmer of the county. Mr. Dennison had known the squire only as Matthew Lloyd, a name he had taken for a while in order to fulfill the terms of a will. When Humphry heard his master called Lloyd, he rushed up in a flutter of excitement and presented the squire with certain papers he had always carried with him. These papers proved that Humphry was the squire's natural son. In a gracious way, Squire Bramble welcomed his offspring, and presented him

to the rest of his family. Humphry was overcome with pleasure and shyness. Winifred was afraid that his discovery would spoil her matrimonial plans, but Humphry continued to be the mild religious man he had been before.

The squire was also surprised to learn that the actor who had called himself Wilson was really Dennison's son, a fine proper young man who had run away from school and become an actor only to escape a marriage his father had planned for him long before. He had told his father about his love for Lydia, but Dennison had not realized that the Mr. Bramble who was her uncle was his old friend Matthew Lloyd. Now the two young lovers were brought together for a joyous reunion.

Lieutenant Lismahago was moved to ask for Miss Tabitha's hand in marriage, and both the squire and Miss Tabitha eagerly accepted his offer. The whole party went to stay at Mr. Dennison's house while preparations were being made for the marriage of Lydia and George. The coming marriages prompted Humphry to ask Winifred for her hand, and she also said yes. The three weddings were planned for the same day.

George and Lydia were a most attractive couple. The lieutenant and Tabitha seemed to be more pleasant than ever before. Humphry and Winifred both thanked God for the pleasures He saw fit to give them. The squire planned to return home to the tranquility of Brambleton Hall and the friendship of his invaluable doctor there.

Further Critical Evaluation of the Work:

Humphry Clinker is considered by many critics to be the best of Tobias Smollett's works. First published in the very year of the author's death, the lively novel was written while Smollett was, like his character Matthew Bramble, in retirement seeking recovery from his failing health. Despite the novel's artful treatment of the effect of health on the individual's mentality, *Humphry Clinker* caters delightfully to the tastes of its eighteenth century audience. It focuses primarily on travel, distant societies, and manners since eighteenth century readers thrived on novels of the exotic. Smollett, however, lent that same exotic excitement to the travels of Bramble and his party as they made their excursion through England, Scotland, and Wales. Smollett combined, then, his audience's thirst for the remote with their increasing desire to learn more of history and social structure, particularly their own.

The structure of *Humphry Clinker* is at first glance deceptively simple. It is an epistolary novel, a genre very popular during its time, and as such, it lends itself readily to a straightforward, chronological structure. Dates and locations are given with every letter; even directions are given about where the author will be to receive an answer by return mail. Yet it is not the passing of time that is important for, during any particular period of time, nothing really changes; no one's opinions metamorphose from one point to another. Lydia continues to love "Wilson"; Jerry continues to despise him; Tabitha continues to struggle for masculine attention; Clinker continues to devote himself to a humble way of life; and Matthew Bramble continues to reaffirm above all else a distinct social division. Instead, action is of prime importance. Although there appears to be a tremendous change of orientation toward life at the conclusion of the novel, there is not. The social structure, having been tampered with by chance, has been rectified, and all continue to love and despise as before, now that the labels of the objects have been returned to normal.

Another characteristic of the structure is its semblance of the picaresque. Although it is quite clear that the novel fulfills many of the requirements of the picaresque novel—it is episodic and treats various levels of society—one is asked to question, who is the picaro? He is not the titular hero, who actually appears long after the novel is under way. The "picaro," then, is Bramble. Bramble is a particular type of picaro who appeared often in the eighteenth century. He is not a criminal, loose in his morals, nor is he an anti-hero; he is a reflection of the author, Smollett himself. Most important of all, Smollett-Bramble is a moralizer.

Bramble's moralizing is Smollett's avenue for displaying one of the novel's unifying features—humor. Above all, Smollett-Bramble is a special kind of moralizer—an idealist. According to Bramble's view of humanity, society is to be separated into strict social classes. The classes give society order, and through order men are essentially safe from the many bothersome problems which could prevent them from pursuing the style of life to which they feel entitled. Such is the latent subject of the majority of Bramble's letters to his dear Dr. Lewis. But the ironic and humorous vehicle for these moralistic treatises is his encounters with the oddest assortment of "originals." Although, for the most part, they concur with Bramble's views of society, socially they are not what they seem. Sons of refined blood appear to be lowly; people of adequate means conduct themselves only with the richest of tastes; worthy gentlemen are treated ill by life and reduced to poor, nearly inescapable circumstances. Most of Bramble's acquaintances are eccentrics and as such they are "humorous" in the true sense of the word. Each has a master passion that he fervently pursues, often to ludicrousness. And Bramble, in his effort to comprehend them in a magnanimous manner, is equally humorous—the conflict between his head and his heart is never resolved, and his endearing desire to help everybody is obviously his own master passion.

Humor, in *Humphry Clinker,* eventually lends itself to satire, and at this task Smollett is at least partially successful. Unfortunately Smollett's satire is often against personal enemies, and one of his faults is that his allusions are too obscure to be appreciated. But one means through which his more appreciable satire is executed is that of opposites. Town *versus* country, commoner *versus* gentleman are both opposite extremes which at first appear to have one side clearly preferable to the other. But one soon sees that Smollett does not present his reader with logical alternatives when opposites are in conflict. We know, for example, that the characters have common views of propriety because of their actions and, especially, their verbalized reactions. But the result when the reader tries to reconstruct what these guidelines are, is elusive. What are they based on? And what really are the consequencs if they are ignored? Although we know that the commodities used in pursuit of propriety are good favor, a good name, and money, it is difficult to see what it is these commodities secure when put to use.

Above all, what makes *Humphry Clinker* the successful novel it is, is Smollett's reaffirmation of the genuine emotional response. Bramble is a man of sensitivity to his physical and social surroundings and experiences. He is tempted, for example, to believe that his trip through Scotland is a glimpse into the ideal way of life he has been both proselytizing and searching for. However, Bramble senses that modernization threatens Scotland with the laziness and complacency that consume England. In addition, Smollett emphasizes how a man's character is shaped by his experiences and emotional responses, by anticipating the very responses a reader might have to such a travel novel. But most important, Bramble's solitary reflections imply that the most intense and meaningful emotions a person might have are those he does not feel obligated to verbalize. In this way Smollett's characters are safe from both our pity and our ridicule.

Bonnie Fraser

THE HUNCHBACK OF NOTRE DAME

Type of work: Novel
Author: Victor Hugo (1802-1885)
Type of plot: Historical romance
Time of plot: Fifteenth century
Locale: France
First published: 1831

Principal characters:
QUASIMODO, the hunchback of Notre Dame
ESMERALDA, a gipsy dancer
CLAUDE FROLLO, archdeacon of Notre Dame
PHOEBUS DE CHATEAUPERS, Esmeralda's sweetheart
GRINGOIRE, a stupid and poverty-stricken poet

Critique:

Victor Hugo, leader of the French romantic movement, not only could tell a gripping story, but also could endow his essentially romantic characters with a realism so powerful that they have become monumental literary figures. *The Hunchback of Notre Dame* has every quality of a good novel: an exciting story, a magnificent setting, and deep, lasting characterizations. Perhaps the compelling truth of this novel lies in the idea that God has created in man an imperfect image of Himself, an image fettered by society and by man's own body and soul, but one which, in the last analysis, has the freedom to transcend these limitations and achieve spiritual greatness.

The Story:

Louis XI, King of France, was to marry his oldest son to Margaret of Flanders, and in early January, 1482, the king was expecting Flemish ambassadors to his court. The great day arrived, coinciding both with Epiphany and the secular celebration of the Festival of Fools. All day long, raucous Parisians had assembled at the great Palace of Justice to see a morality play and to choose a Prince of Fools. The throng was supposed to await the arrival of the Flemish guests, but when the emissaries were late Gringoire, a penniless and oafish poet, ordered the play to begin. In the middle of the prologue, however, the play came to a standstill as the royal procession passed into the huge palace. After the procession passed

the play was forgotten, and the crowd shouted for the Prince of Fools to be chosen.

The Prince of Fools had to be a man of remarkable physical ugliness. One by one the candidates, eager for this one glory of their disreputable lives, showed their faces in front of a glass window, but the crowd shouted and jeered until a face of such extraordinary hideousness appeared that the people acclaimed this candidate at once as the Prince of Fools. It was Quasimodo, the hunchback bellringer of Notre Dame. Nowhere on earth was there a more grotesque creature. One of his eyes was buried under an enormous wen. His teeth hung over his protruding lower lip like tusks. His eyebrows were red bristles, and his gigantic nose curved over his upper lip like a snout. His long arms protruded from his shoulders, dangling like an ape's. Though he was deaf from long years of ringing Notre Dame's thunderous bells, his eyesight was acute.

Quasimodo sensed that he had been chosen by popular acclaim, and he was at once proud and suspicious of his honor as he allowed the crowd to dress him in ridiculous robes and hoist him above their heads. From this vantage point he maintained a dignified silence while the parade went through the streets of Paris, stopping only to watch the enchanting dance of a gipsy girl, La Esmeralda, whose grace and charm held her audience spellbound. She had with her a little trained goat that danced to her tambourine. The pair were celebrated through-out Paris, though there were some who thought the girl a witch, so great was her power in captivating her audience.

Late that night the poet Gringoire walked the streets of Paris. He had no shelter, owed money, and was in desperate straits. As the cold night came on, he saw Esmeralda hurrying ahead of him. Then a black-hooded man came out of the shadows and seized the gipsy. At the same time, Gringoire caught sight of the hooded man's partner, Quasimodo, who struck Gringoire a terrible blow. The following moment a horseman came riding from the next street. Catching sight of Esmeralda in the arms of the black-hooded man, the rider demanded that he free the girl or pay with his life. The attackers fled. Esmerelda asked the name of her rescuer. It was Captain Phoebus de Chateaupers. From that moment Esmeralda was hopelessly in love with Phoebus.

Gringoire did not bother to discover the plot behind the frustrated kidnaping, but had he known the truth he might have been more frightened than he was. Quasimodo's hooded companion had been Claude Frollo, archdeacon of Notre Dame, a man who had once been a pillar of righteousness, but who now, because of loneliness and an insatiable thirst for knowledge and experience, had succumbed to the temptations of necromancy and alchemy.

Frollo had befriended Quasimodo when the hunchback had been left at the gates of Notre Dame as an unwanted baby, and to him Quasimodo was slavishly loyal. He acted without question when Frollo asked his aid in kidnaping the beautiful gipsy. Frollo, having admired Esmeralda from a distance, planned to carry her off to his small cell in the cathedral, where he could enjoy her charms at his leisure.

As Quasimodo and Frollo hurried back to the cathedral, Gringoire continued on his way and found himself in a disreputable quarter of Paris. Captured by thugs, he was threatened with death if none of the women in the thieves' den would marry him. When no one wanted the pale, thin poet, a noose was lowered about his neck. Suddenly Esmeralda appeared and volunteered to take him. But Gringoire enjoyed no wedding night. Esmeralda's heart belonged to Phoebus; she had rescued the poet only out of pity.

In those days the courts of Paris often picked innocent people from the streets, tried them, and convicted them with little regard for justice. Quasimodo had been seen in his role as the Prince of Fools and had been watched as he stood before the gipsy girl while she danced. It was rumored that Esmeralda was a witch, and most of Paris suspected that Frollo, Quasimodo's only associate, was a sorcerer. Consequently Quasimodo was brought into a court, accused of keeping questionable company, and sentenced to a severe flogging and exposure on the pillory. Quasimodo endured his disgrace, stoically, but after his misshapen back had been torn by the lash, he was overcome with a terrible thirst. The crowd jeered and threw stones. They hated and feared Quasimodo because of his ugliness.

Presently Esmeralda mounted the scaffold and put her flask to Quasimodo's blackened lips. This act of kindness moved him deeply and he wept. At that same time Frollo had happened upon the scene, caught sight of Quasimodo, and departed quickly. Later Quasimodo was to remember this betrayal.

One day Phoebus was entertaining a lady in a building overlooking the square where Esmeralda was dancing. The gipsy was so smitten with Phoebus that she had taught her goat to spell out his name with alphabet blocks. When she had the animal perform this trick, the lady called her a witch and a sorceress. But Phoebus followed the gipsy and arranged for a rendezvous with her for the following night.

Gringoire, meanwhile, happened to meet Frollo, who was jealous of the poet because he was rumored to be Esmeralda's husband. But Gringoire explained that

Esmeralda did not love him; she had eyes and heart only for Phoebus.

Desperate to preserve Esmeralda for himself, Frollo trailed the young gallant and asked him where he was going. Phoebus said that he had a rendezvous with Esmeralda. The priest offered him money in exchange for an opportunity to conceal himself in the room where this rendezvous was to take place, ostensibly to discover whether Esmeralda were really the girl whose name Phoebus had mentioned. It was a poor ruse at best, but Phoebus was not shy at love-making and he agreed to the bargain. When he learned that the girl was really Esmeralda, Frollo leaped from concealment and wounded Phoebus with a dagger. Esmeralda could not see her lover's assailant in the darkness and when she fainted Frollo escaped. A crowd gathered, murmuring that the sorceress had slain Phoebus. They took the gipsy off to prison.

Now tales of Esmeralda's sorcery began to circulate. At her trial she was convicted of witchcraft, sentenced to do penance on the great porch of Notre Dame and from there to be taken to a scaffold in the Place de Greve and publicly hanged.

Captain Phoebus was not dead, but he had kept silence rather than implicate himself in a case of witchcraft. When Esmeralda was on her way to Notre Dame, she caught sight of him riding on his beautiful horse, and called out to him, but he ignored her completely. She then felt that she was doomed.

When she came before Frollo to do penance, he offered to save her if she would be his; but she refused. Quasimodo suddenly appeared on the porch, took the girl in his arms, and carried her to sanctuary within the church. Esmeralda was now safe as long as she remained within the cathedral walls.

Quasimodo hid her in his own cell, where there was a mattress and water, and brought her food. He kept the cell door locked so that if her pursuers did break the sanctuary, they could not reach her. Aware that she would be ter-

rified of him if he stayed with her, he entered her cell only to bring her his own dinner.

Frollo, knowing that the gipsy was near him in the cathedral, secured a key to the chamber and stole in to see Esmeralda one night. She struggled hopelessly, until suddenly Quasimodo entered and dragged the priest from the cell. With smothered rage, he freed the trembling archdeacon and allowed him to run away.

One day a mob gathered and demanded that the sorceress be turned from the cathedral. Frollo was jubilant. Quasimodo, however, barred and bolted the great doors. When the crowd charged the cathedral with a battering ram, Quasimodo threw huge stones from a tower where builders had been working. The mob persisting, he poured melted lead upon the crowd below. Then the mob secured ladders and began to mount the facade, but Quasimodo seized the ladders and pushed them from the wall. Hundreds of dead and wounded lay below him.

The king's guards joined the fray. Quasimodo, looking down, thought that the soldiers had arrived to protect Esmeralda. He went to her cell, but to his amazement he found the door open and Esmeralda gone.

Frollo had given Gringoire the key to her chamber and had led the poet through the cathedral to her cell. Gringoire convinced her that she must fly, since the church was under siege. She followed him trustingly, and he led her to a boat where Frollo was already waiting. Frightened by the violence of the priest, Gringoire fled. Once more, Frollo offered to save Esmeralda if she would be his, but she refused him. Fleeing, she sought refuge in a cell belonging to a madwoman. There the soldiers found her and dragged her away for her execution the next morning at dawn.

Quasimodo, meanwhile, roamed the cathedral searching for Esmeralda. Making his way to the tower which looked down upon the bridge of Notre Dame, Quasimodo came upon Frollo, who stood shaking with laughter as he watched a scene far below. Following the direction of the priest's gaze, Quasimodo saw a gibbet erected in the Place de la Grève and on the platform a woman in white. It was Esmeralda. Quasimodo saw the noose lowered over the girl's head and the platform released. The body swayed in the morning breeze. Then Quasimodo picked up Frollo and thrust him over the wall on which he had been leaning. At that moment Quasimodo understood everything that the priest had done to ensure the death of Esmeralda. He looked at the crushed body at the foot of the tower and then at the figure in white upon the gallows. He wept.

After the deaths of Esmeralda and Claude Frollo, Quasimodo was not to be found. Then in the reign of Charles VIII the vault of Montfaucon, in which the bodies of criminals were interred, was opened to locate the remains of a famous prisoner who had been buried there. Among the skeletons were those of a woman who had been clad in white and of a man whose bony arms were wrapped tightly around the woman's body. His spine was crooked, one leg was shorter than the other, and it was evident that he had not been hanged, for his neck was unbroken. When those who discovered these singular remains tried to separate the two bodies, they crumbled into dust.

Further Critical Evaluation of the Work:

Victor Hugo was inspired to write *The Hunchback of Notre Dame (Notre Dame de Paris* in the original) when he accidentally discovered the Greek word for "fate" carved into an obscure wall of one of Notre Dame Cathedral's towers. Each personality is built around a "fixed idea": Claude Frollo embodies the consuming, destructive passion of lust; Esmeralda, virgin beauty and purity; Quasimodo, unshakeable devotion and loyalty. Hugo's characters do not develop but simply play out their given natures to their inevitable conclusions.

In analyzing the character of archdeacon Claude Frollo, it is helpful to understand Hugo's theory that the advent of Christianity in Western Europe marked a new era in literature and art. Because Christianity viewed man as a creature half animal and half spirit—the link between beast and angel—writers could present the ugly and lowly as well as the beautiful and sublime. They could attain a new synthesis, more meaningful because realistic, not achieved by writers of antiquity, who only depicted idealized, larger-than-life subjects on the grounds that "Art should *correct* nature." Claude Frollo excludes all human contact from his life and locks himself up with his books; when he has mastered all the legitimate branches of knowledge, he has nowhere to turn in his obsession but to the realm of alchemy and the occult. He is ultimately destroyed, along with those around him, because in denying his animal nature and shutting off all avenues for the release of his natural drives and affections, he falls into the depths of a lustful passion that amounts to madness.

As the novel develops, Quasimodo, the hunchback of the novel's title, is increasingly trapped between his love for the gipsy girl, Esmeralda, and his love for the archdeacon, his master and protector. These two loyalties finally create an irreconcilable conflict; a choice must be made. When the priest destroys the gipsy, the bell ringer hurls his master from the heights of Notre Dame: a fitting death for Frollo, symbolic of his descent in life from the sublime to the bestial. In Quasimodo, Hugo dramatized his belief that the grotesque and the sublime must coexist in art and literature, as they do in life; the modern writer, he says, "will realize that everything in creation is not humanly beautiful, that the ugly exists beside the beautiful, the unshapely beside the graceful . . . and [he] will ask . . . if a mutilated nature will be the more beautiful for the mutilation." Esmeralda is the embodiment of innocence and beauty. She is held in reverence even by the criminal population of Paris, who vaguely equate her in their minds with the Virgin Mary. But her beauty is too innocent and pure to exist amid the brutality and sinfulness of her world. Of all the men in the book, only one is worthy of Esmeralda: the hunchbacked Quasimodo, who loves her so totally and unselfishly that he would rather die than go on living after she is executed. Appropriately, it is Esmeralda and Quasimodo who are finally "married" in the charnel-house at Montfaucon; theirs is the perfect union of physical and spiritual beauty.

Almost more than by any of the human characters, the novel is dominated by the presence of the cathedral itself. The hero, Quasimodo, understands Notre Dame: he is in tune with her "life." Like her deformed bell ringer, Notre Dame is both ugly and beautiful, both strong and vulnerable, both destructive and life-giving. Quasimodo's monstrous face hides a loving, faithful spirit, while his twisted body conceals a superhuman strength; Notre Dame's beautiful sanctuary is enclosed by a rough exterior encrusted with gargoyles, while her vulnerable treasures are guarded by doors that six thousand maddened vagrants cannot batter down. The cathedral and the ringer work together, almost as one entity, to protect Esmeralda in her room hundreds of feet above the city; to repulse invaders with hurled stones and molten lead; to dash the blasphemous student, Jehan, to death against the massive walls; and to cast off the priest whose lustfulness defiles the purity of the place.

Setting was all-important to Hugo. As the foremost French Romanticist of the nineteenth century, he was fascinated by the medieval period, and strove to reconstruct it in such a way that it would live again in his novel. Hugo believed that a description built on exact, localized details would recapture the mood of a historical period; that setting was as crucial as characterization in engraving a "faithful representation of the facts" on the minds of his readers. Early in the novel, therefore, he devotes an entire section (Book Three) to a description of the cathedral and the city of Paris; and throughout the book, he offers brief passages of historical background which add verisimilitude to his narrative.

In the Preface to his play *Cromwell,* Hugo wrote, "The place where this or that catastrophe took place becomes a terrible and inseparable witness thereof; and the absence of silent characters of this sort would make the greatest scenes in history incomplete in the drama." Thus, in *The Hunchback of Notre Dame,* not only does the cathedral live almost as a personality; so also does the Place de la Grève spread its influence over the lives of all the characters. The cathedral and the square are the two focal points not only of the setting, but of the plot and the theme of the novel; the former embodies the spiritual and beautiful, the latter the lowly and cruel. It is the cathedral that enfolds the humble and loyal Quasimodo and the Virgin-like Esmeralda, while the square, the scene of poverty, suffering, and grisly death, with its Rat-Hole and its gibbet, claims Esmeralda, her lunatic mother, and Claude Frollo as its victims.

Nancy G. Ballard

HUNGER

Type of work: Novel
Author: Knut Hamsun (Knut Pedersen Hamsund, 1859-1952)
Type of plot: Impressionistic realism
Time of plot: Late nineteenth century
Locale: Norway
First published: 1890

Principal character:
THE NARRATOR, a young writer

Critique:

Hunger was the work that immediately brought Hamsun to the attention of a wide literary audience, and the novel has been reprinted and translated many times. Realistic in subject, its form and treatment are highly impressionistic. Hamsun has given us a striking study of a man's mind under stress, but it is not a clinical study; it is an artistic piece of literature.

The Story:

I awoke at six o'clock and lay awake in my bed until eight. Hungry, I searched in my packet of odds and ends, but there was not even a crumb of bread. I knew that I should have gone out early to look for work, but I had been refused so often I was almost afraid to venture out again.

At last I took some paper and went out, for if the weather permitted I could write in the park. There were several good ideas in my head for newspaper articles. In the street an old cripple with a big bundle was using all his strength to keep ahead of me.

When I caught up with him he turned around and whined for a halfpenny to buy milk. Not having a cent on me, I hurried back to the pawnbroker's dark shop. In the hall I took off my waistcoat and rolled it in a ball. The pawnbroker gave me one and six for it. I found the old cripple again and gave him his halfpenny. He stared at me with his mouth open as I hurried away.

Two women, one of them young, were idly strolling about. When I told the young woman that she would lose her book, she looked frightened and they hurried on. Seeing them standing before a shop window, I went up to them again and told the younger woman that she was losing her book. She looked herself over in a bewildered way; she had no book. I kept following them, but they put me down as a harmless madman.

In the park I could not write a thing. Little flies stuck to my paper. All afternoon I tried to brush them off. Then I wrote an application for a job as bookkeeper. After a day or two I went to see the man in person. He laughed at my desire to become a bookkeeper because I had dated my letter 1848, years before I was born. I went home discouraged.

On my table was a letter. I thought it a notice from my landlady, for I was behind in my rent. But no, my story had been accepted. The editor said it would be printed right away. He had included a half sovereign in payment. I had written a masterpiece and I had a half sovereign.

A few weeks later I went out for an evening walk and sat in a churchyard with a new manuscript. At eight o'clock, when the gates were closed, I meant to go straight home to the vacant tinker's workshop which I had permission to occupy, but I stumbled around hardly knowing where I was. I felt feverish because I had not eaten for several days. At last I sat down and dozed off. I dreamed that a beautiful girl dressed in silk waited for me in a doorway and

HUNGER by Knut Hamsun. Translated by George Egerton. By permission of the publishers, Alfred A. Knopf, Inc. Copyright, 1920, by Alfred A. Knopf, Inc. Renewed, 1948, by Alfred A. Knopf, Inc.

led me down a hall, she holding my hand. We went into a crimson room where she clasped me tightly and begged me to kiss her.

A policeman woke me up and advised me to go to the police barracks as a homeless man. When I got there, I lied about my name and said that it was too late for me to get back to my lodgings. The officer believed me and gave me a private room. In the morning, thinking I was only a young rake instead of a destitute, the police gave me no breakfast ticket. I drank a lot of water but I could scarcely keep it down.

Faint with hunger, I cut the buttons from my coat and tried to pawn them, but the pawnbroker laughed at me. On the way out I met a friend bringing his watch to pawn. He fed me and gave me five shillings.

I went to see an editor who critically read my sketch on Correggio. He was kind, saying that he would like to publish my work but that he had to keep his subscribers in mind. He asked if I could write something more to the common taste. When I prepared to leave, he also asked me if I needed money. He was sure I could write it out. Although I had not eaten a real meal for some time, I thanked him and left without an advance payment.

A lady in black stood every night on the corner by my tinker's garret. She would look intently at my lodging for a while and then pass on. After several days I spoke to her and accompanied her on her walk. She said she had no special interest in my poor garret or in me. When she lifted her veil, I saw she was the woman I had followed and spoken to about the book. She was merry with me and seemed to enjoy my company.

One night she took me to her home. Once inside, we embraced; then we sat down and began to talk. She confessed that she was attracted to me because she thought I was a madman. She was an adventurous girl, on the lookout for odd experiences. I told her the truth about myself, that I acted queerly because I was so poor. Much of the time I was so hungry that I had a fever. She found my story hard to believe, but I convinced her. She was sympathetic for a moment. I had to leave, for her mother was returning, and I never saw her again.

I awoke sick one morning. All day I shivered in bed. Toward night I went down to the little shop below to buy a candle, for I felt I had to write something. A boy was alone in the store. I gave him a florin for my candle, but he gave me change for a crown. I stared stupidly at the money in my hand for a long time, but I got out without betraying myself.

I took a room in a real hotel and had a chamber to myself and breakfast and supper. About the time my money was gone I started on a medieval play. The landlady trusted me for quite a while, for I explained that I would pay her as soon as my play was finished. One night she brought a sailor up to my room and turned me out, but she let me go down and sleep with the family.

For some time I slept on a sofa in the entryway, and once in a while a servant gave me bread and cheese. In my nervous condition it was hard to be meek and grateful. The break came one evening when the children were amusing themselves by sticking straws into the nose and ears of the paralyzed grandfather who lay on a bed before the fire. I protested against their cruel sport. The landlady flew at me in a rage and ordered me out.

I wandered down to the docks and got a berth on a Russian freighter going to England. I came back to the hotel for my possessions and on the step met the postman. He handed me a letter addressed in a feminine hand. Inside was a half sovereign. I crumpled the envelope and coin together and threw them in the landlady's face.

Further Critical Evaluation of the Work:

Knut Hamsun's works have been neither well-known nor popular for almost a generation. When the Germans invaded Norway during World War II, Hamsun lent his support and prestige to the Quisling government. The reaction against him both during and after the war helps to explain in part why Hamsun's works are no longer popular. But more to the point is the fact that his style of novel writing, impressionistic realism, fell out of favor after World War II. Hamsun's *Hunger* is part of the literary tradition leading to Steinbeck and other writers of the first part of the twentieth century. This so-called "modernistic" school deals in part with subjective reality and it is particularly in this regard that Hamsun's position in the movement is most secure.

Hunger grew out of the same general environment that produced at the end of the nineteenth century Sigmund Freud and his works. Hamsun delves into the subconscious of his protagonist and comes up with an excellent depiction of madness as seen from inside the mind of the madman. The fact that this madness derives from hunger is significant because this story of a young journalist literally starving to death is autobiographical to some extent. When Hamsun first presented the manuscript of his work for publication, the editor was so struck by his emaciation that he paid Hamsun an advance on the work, without even bothering to read the title. The story told by the editor is closely paralleled in the novel.

On one level, this is a madman's story of a madman, but on another it is an account of life in a large city of the industrial age. The city where the action takes place, Christiania, is like any city where people try to sell their art, their literature, or their journalism and discover that there is no market for the best they have to offer. Like modern day Los Angeles and New York, Christiania is presented as a city full of people who seek fame and fortune but who find instead they are not capable of reaching their goals. Characteristically, this sort of person often becomes discouraged and is obliged to seek employment in a field far removed from his original ambition. The protagonist of *Hunger* finds himself in just this situation. He is unable to make a career for himself in the environment of a large city of the industrial age.

What lifts this novel from a mere story about a poor boy doing poorly in the big city is Hamsun's depiction of the internal workings of the human mind. He demonstrates the foolish pride and motiveless behavior that come from a tenuous existence such as the protagonist of the novel leads. The starving man in this novel is one who lies, as the saying goes, even when it is not necessary. He has no regular habits and is at the mercy of his own strange whims. The incident of his persistence in telling a strange woman on the street that she has lost her nonexistent book is a case in point. He lies to save his pride time and again, even in the face of starvation. Hamsun explains that at the stage when the body is starving, the mind falters and mistakes the inconsequentials of life for life's necessities and cannot distinguish between the two. Hamsun terrifyingly depicts in this book the odd sort of seemingly lucid logic that is to an impartial observer nothing but the worst sort of nonsense.

While Hamsun is able to depict the workings of such a mind broken by the stress of hunger, he does not present a full picture of the book's protagonist. Yet, because of this omission his study of psychological pressure is all the more vivid and effective. We do not know much about the young man in the novel, only that he is starving and periodically reduced to chewing on wood shavings or bits of cloth. Hamsun focuses the reader's full attention upon the issue of the mind, and he does so in a masterful fashion.

On yet a third level this book is also a portrait of a failure. Indeed the book is a collection of episodes that are united only by the underlying themes. The book is divided into four sections, each one describing the thoughts and actions of the protagonist as he suffers the effects of starvation at different times. There is, strictly speaking, no beginning or end to the novel. At the end of each section there is a stroke of good luck. The protagonist sells a story, or gets a loan. Then the novel immediately jumps to the next episode in his life when he is starving, and the cycle begins again.

At the end of the book the young writer joins the crew of a steamship bound for England. The effect of this ending, though, is one not of escape but of pessimism. There is a flaw in this man's character, one that Hamsun only hints at, that damns him to a continuing cycle of luck and hunger. It is a cycle that the reader at the end of the novel feels can lead eventually only to death.

Glenn M. Edwards

HUON DE BORDEAUX

Type of work: Chanson de geste
Author: Unknown
Type of plot: Chivalric romance
Time of plot: Ninth century
Locale: Paris, Jerusalem, Rome, the fairy kingdom of Mommur
First transcribed: First half of the thirteenth century

Principal characters:
HUON OF BORDEAUX, older son of the dead Duke of Guienne
GERARD, his younger brother
CHARLEMAGNE, King of France
CHARLOT, his older son
EARL AMAURY, Charlot's evil adviser
DUKE NAYMES, Charlemagne's adviser
THE ABBOT OF CLUNY, uncle to Huon and Gerard
GERAMES, a loyal hermit
OBERON, king of fairyland
GAWDIS, Amir of Babylon
CLARAMOND, his daughter

Critique:

In this lengthy example of medieval French verse romance, we see a *chanson de geste*—a "tale of a deed"—in a developed and perhaps impure form. The unknown author, thought to be a writer of the first half of the thirteenth century and perhaps a resident of the town of St. Omer, combines in a somewhat ununified tale different sorts of materials. The events are supposed to take place late in the reign of Charlemagne, after the betrayal and defeat of Roland at Roncesvalles and therefore early in the ninth century. The Charlemagne of this poem bears a celebrated historical name but few of the attributes of the great king of the Dark Ages. He is petulant, suspicious, and ill-advised in important decisions; the wisdom, temperance, and heroism of the historcal figure is gone, and a fairy tale personage—an inferior King Lear—remains; on his vacillating decisions much of the story rests. Although the imagination of the author of *Huon de Bordeaux* did respond to the actual social conditions of his time, he drew also on conventional but highly fanciful narrative materials to which any medieval storyteller had access. Stories of the dwarf fairy-king, Oberon, rise from both Celtic tale and Germanic story. Tales about the crusaders made available to the writer confused details about "paynim" countries that bulk large in the main portion of Huon's adventures, but it is plain to any reader that these details mask a very sketchy knowledge. In leaving France behind, the medieval rhymer left reality behind; and the extensive travels of the hero take us into realms as fantastic and nonexistent as those of Prester John.

The Story:

King Charlemagne, grown old and wishing to relinquish the burden of government, summoned his court and consulted with his nobles to determine the succession to his throne. His plan was to abdicate in favor of his two sons, but the nobles of France were not willing to accept his favorite, Charlot, partly because of the young prince's association with Earl Amaury, kinsman of the infamous Ganelon who had betrayed Roland to his death. The earl, the partisan of Charlot, took the occasion to get revenge on the noble house of Guienne. His suggestion was that Charlot be given a province to govern before he took over the responsibilities of a state. It was called to Charlemagne's doting attention—for the king had become violent and unreasonable in his judgments and punishments—that the two sons of the dead duke had not yet come to Paris to pay their respects and render homage. Earl Amaury's hope was to see them dispossessed and their lands given to Charlot.

Sent to conduct the heirs of the dead duke to Charlemagne's court, messengers discovered that what the king's wise adviser, Duke Naymes, had stated was indeed the case: the brothers, Huon and Gerard, had been too young to come to court before. The messengers, pleased with their reception by the duchess, the boys' mother, and with the manly bearing of young Huon of Bordeaux, the older son, returned with word that the young noblemen would soon follow them to swear fealty to the king.

Huon and Gerard set out on their journey to Paris, stopping on the way at the monastery of Cluny where their uncle was abbot. The noble churchman decided to accompany his nephews to Charlemagne's court.

In the meantime Charlot had been persuaded by Earl Amaury to ambush the boys and kill them. Because their lands were extensive and tempting, the prince agreed. But in the fray Charlot was killed when Huon struck him with his sword, severing the prince's helmet. In spite of the abbot's testimony, however, Charlemagne refused to believe that Huon had acted in self-defense and without knowledge of his assailant's identity. In a trial by combat with Earl Amaury, Huon killed that wretched knight before he could gasp out, at death's verge, a true account of his villainy. Still unenlightened, the angry king sent Huon on a pilgrimage to Jerusalem and also ordered him to kiss three times the beautiful Claramond, the daughter of Gawdis, Amir of Babylon, and to return with white hairs from the amir's beard and teeth from his mouth.

Obedient to Charlemagne's command, Huon parted company with his brother Gerard, in whose care he left his lands. Although there had been love between the brothers in the past, Gerard straight-way became false to his trust and plotted great evil against his distant brother. For Huon's return was greatly delayed. Though fortune often favored him and provided him with kinsmen in odd corners of the world, the wicked paynims abused him, imprisoned him, and on many occasions carried him far from his destination. Gerames, a hermit, became his loyal follower after chance threw them together, and he was close at Huon's heels when the Christian knight kissed Claramond and got the teeth and the hair from the several head of the amir after that ruler had received the bowstring from the dread Caliph of Arabia. Huon secreted the teeth and hair in the side of the hermit for safekeeping.

Huon was aided in his adventures by two gifts from Oberon, the dwarf king of the Otherworld, born of an ancient union between Julius Caesar and Morgan le Fay. Gerames, the wise hermit, had warned Huon, not to speak to Oberon, but Huon, ignoring his advice, spoke to the dwarf and so won the protection of the white magic of that strange little creature. Huon was able to carry with him the gifts from Oberon. One was a cup that filled up at the sign of the cross and emptied when it was held in the hand of a wicked person. The other was a horn which Huon was supposed to blow to summon Oberon's help when grave danger threatened. Huon, like the boy who cried wolf in Aesop's fable, blew the horn too frequently, and Oberon was sometimes tempted not to respond. Moreover, Huon's dignity and prudence sometimes left him. Despite warnings, he embraced the lovely Claramond before they were married and so brought about an interminable separation; and he once imprudently allowed a giant to arm himself before a contest. But at last, with the combined help of the hermit and the fairy king, Huon and Claramond reached Rome, where their marriage was blessed by the Pope himself, who was the uncle of Huon.

On his return to France with his bride, Huon found that his brother was now his foe and that well-wishers like Duke Naymes could not protect him from the anger and dotage of Charlemagne. But Oberon could. The fairy king made his appearance, humbled great Charlemagne, and saw to it that Huon and Claramond were secure in all their rights. Though Huon interceded for his brother's life and made the court weep by his display of generosity, Oberon was obdurate, and Gerard and his fellow conspirators were hanged. As a final favor, Huon was promised that he would someday inherit Oberon's kingdom.

Further Critical Evaluation of the Work:

The French romance, of which the *chanson de geste* forms the first example, is part of the earliest major classification of romantic literature. The three categories of romantic literature are traditionally the Matter of Roma, which is based upon classical myth and legend, occasionally utilizing Roman history; the Matter of Britain, which is based upon the Arthurian legends and the courtly love device which was so essentially a part of the Arthurian romances; and the Matter of France. The basis for the Matter of France is the *chanson de geste,* of which about twelve hundred are in existence. These fall into three main groups. The *geste du roi* is centered around the legends and history of Charlemagne. He is usually presented as the champion of Christendom against the heathens. The best known of these is the *Song of Roland.* The second group, the *geste de Donnde Mayence,* is the history of his vassals; the third, the *geste de Garin de Monhane,* is the history of William of Orange.

Huon de Bordeaux was first translated into English in 1530 by John Bourchier, Lord Berners. It remains today as a great translation, one of the earliest in English. Berners had previously translated the works of Jean Froissart, which were to have an immense influence on the late English Renaissance. *Huon de Bordeaux* was no less influential for the course of English literature. In it the English caught their first glimpse of Oberon, king of the fairies, and the entire work proved to be a gold mine of information for English dramatists. The subject matter of *Huon de Bordeaux* is most closely related to the Charlemagne cycles, hence it is considered part of the *geste du roi.* Although the plot bears little, if any, relation to history in its latter part, it is nonetheless an interesting picture of the French general attitude toward, and knowledge of the Near East. From it the modern reader may assume that the information given here is indicative of the level of knowledge of the educated classes in the Middle Ages. That *Huon de Bordeaux* was accepted is proof that this mythical interpretation of what was in the not so distant past was the accepted method of transmitting information.

HYDE PARK

Type of work: Drama
Author: James Shirley (1596-1666)
Type of plot: Comedy of manners
Time of plot: Early seventeenth century
Locale: London
First presented: 1632

Principal characters:
LORD BONVILE, a sporting peer
TRIER, his friend, betrothed to Julietta
FAIRFIELD, favored suitor to Mistress Carol
RIDER, and
VENTURE, her rejected suitors
BONAVENT, a merchant returned after seven years' absence
MISTRESS BONAVENT, his wife, who thinks herself a widow
LACY, Mistress Bonavent's suitor
JULIETTA, Fairfield's sister, pursued by Lord Bonvile
MISTRESS CAROL, Mistress Bonavent's cousin and companion

Critique:

Hyde Park, the second of Shirley's sprightly comedies, paved the way for the later Restoration drama. The play, honoring the opening of Hyde Park to the public by the first Earl of Holland, presented to the audience of that time interesting gaming talk as well as the manners of the fashionable world. Pepys reports that live horses were led across the stage in a production of Hyde Park some years after the playwright's death in the Great Fire of London. Though the play itself looks forward to a more sophisticated drama, it is still firmly based in the delightful fancies of Shakespeare, Jonson, and other Elizabethan and Jacobean playwrights, of whom Shirley was the last of note.

The Story:

Because her husband, a merchant, had been missing for seven years, Mistress Bonavent had for some time considered a second marriage to Lacy, her persistent suitor. Mistress Carol, her cousin and companion, urged her not to give away so lightly the independence she had won. Mistress Carol herself swore never to marry, even though she carried on flirtations with Rider, Venture, and Fairfield. Rider and Venture, vying with each other for the lady's favor, had each given her a gift which she in turn presented to his rival. Comparing notes, they concluded that Fairfield must be the favored suitor.

Lacy, summoned by Mistress Bonavent's servant, felt certain that his suit was now successful. Into this confused arena of love arrived Lord Bonvile, a sportsman who admired both horses and women, and Bonavent, disguised in order to find out what had happened during his absence.

Though Fairfield's overtures to Mistress Carol were rejected, Lacy's to Mistress Bonavent were accepted, and the wedding was set for that very morning. Mistress Carol told her cousin that she was acting rashly, no man being worth the candle.

Bonavent soon learned that the sound of merriment in his own house augured no good for that returned merchant who, held captive by a Turkish pirate, had only recently been ransomed. Lacy, perhaps too merry with wine and anticipation, bade the stranger welcome and asked, then demanded, that he dance with and, finally, for them. Bonavent's dancing was ridiculed, especially by sharp-tongued Mistress Carol. Lacy tried to

2787

make amends by inviting him to join additional revels in Hyde Park that very day.

In the meantime Fairfield, despairing because of his love for Mistress Carol, said farewell to his sister Julietta and wished her well in her coming marriage to Jack Trier. But it was soon apparent to the young woman that her suitor was not in earnest in his avowals of love, for he introduced her to his friend Lord Bonvile and then left them. Before his departure Trier had whispered in the lord's ear that he was in a sporting house and the lady was a person of easy virtue. As a woman of good breeding, and aware only that her fiancé had shown poor manners, Julietta invited Lord Bonvile to accompany her to the park, an invitation which provided her betrothed with an opportunity to try her chastity.

When the two aggrieved lovers, Rider and Venture, appealed to Mistress Carol not to make sport of them by passing their gifts on to their rival, she declared that she had no interest in them and had always told them so; in their persistence, however, they had paid little attention to her. Fairfield, coming to say goodbye, first asked her to swear to one agreement without knowing what it was. Convinced at last that the agreement would not commit her to love, marry, or go to bed with him, she agreed; at his request she then swore never to desire his company again or to love him. The oath sealed with a kiss, he departed, leaving her in a state of consternation.

Julietta, courted by a baffled lord whose very propositions were turned into pleasantries, remained aloof from her still more baffled suitor, who could not determine how far the flirtation had gone in Hyde Park.

Still in disguise, Bonavent learned that Lacy and his wife were indeed married but that the marriage had not yet been consummated—to the pleasure of his informant, Mistress Carol, who by now was distressed by affection for the previously spurned Fairfield. She sent a message by Trier asking Fairfield to come to see her, but on his arrival she denied that she had sent for him. Fairfield, in turn, offered to release her from her oath if she would have him, but she turned coquette and rejected his proposal. Consequently, he refused to believe her when she protested that she now loved him.

Lord Bonvile, torn between his desire to play what he thought was a sure thing and the horses which were a gamble, pushed his suit too far, and for his brashness received a lecture on titles and good breeding, a remonstrance which he took to heart.

The disconsolate Mistress Carol met Julietta, who informed the spurned one that Fairfield was as disconsolate as she. Mistress Carol then concocted a stratagem at the expense of Venture, a poet, horseman, and singer. She goaded him into writing a poem on the lengths to which he would go for her love, and to this effusion she later affixed the name of Fairfield. Meanwhile, in Hyde Park, Bonavent hired a bagpipe and made the bridegroom dance to the tune of a sword at his legs, a return for the courtesy extended at the wedding festivities. In a note to his wife, the merchant informed her of his return but urged her to secrecy for the time being.

Mistress Carol, who now pretended to believe that Venture's hyperbole was a suicide note from Fairfield, summoned her recalcitrant suitor. Thinking that she was still making fun of him, he denied any intention of doing away with himself and in turn accused her of duplicity. He added that he would make himself a gelding so that women would no longer concern him—a threat more real to Mistress Carol than that of suicide. On the spot she abandoned all pride and proposed marriage to him. He immediately accepted.

Lord Bonvile, having learned too late from Trier that he was the victim of a jealous lover, was accepted by Julietta as a worthy suitor, now that his thoughts were as lofty as his position in society

Bonavent, to show himself unresentful, proposed a merry celebration and placed willow garlands on the heads of the disappointed lovers: Trier, Lacy, Rider, and Venture. He received the good wishes of Lacy and pledged himself to entertain the whole party at supper with tales of his captivity.

All this, however, had been prophesied earlier in Hyde Park, when Lord Bonvile and his Julietta, Fairfield and Mistress Carol, and Mr. and Mistress Bonavent had heard the song of Philomel, the nightingale. The others had heard only the cuckoo.

Further Critical Evaluation of the Work:

The most prolific of the later Elizabethan dramatists and the only major surviving dramatist until the Restoration was James Shirley. Although he was equally adept at all forms of drama—tragedy, tragi-comedy, and comedy—comedy was his forte. This can be attested to since of the more than thirty of his plays that remain extant, the largest and most distinctive group is his comedies. His best plays in this grouping deal with London's fashionable life and can be categorized as comedies of manners. *Hyde Park* is a distinguished example of this comedic type.

Hyde Park might be considered at first glance to be a drama written for the stage advertisement of a new popular diversion or as an "occasional piece" because it was written to commemorate the opening to the public, in 1632, of the previously private park by its owner, Lord Holland. The play, however, demands closer scrutiny. It provides an example of the apparent trends within the dramatic writing of the later Elizabethan period as well as a view of the foibles of London society.

Great attention to the use of ceremony and pageantry had been paid within early Elizabethan dramatic writing; however, *Hyde Park* seems representative of the trend away from this practice, having only a half-dozen entrances that ask for formal presentation. This is quite a reduction compared with, for example, Thomas Middleton's *Women Beware Women* (c. 1620) which has twelve formal entrances and as many formal exits, a masque, and a staged banquet which includes a procession to it and formal toasts.

Accompanying these reductions came an attempt to cater to the audience's growing taste for a greater realism on stage through the use of ingenious effects and elaborate settings. The undertaking, therefore, in *Hyde Park* was to make the audience feel as though it was *in* the park; and to this end, contemporary reports say the play was staged with bird song.

The content of *Hyde Park*, in the comedy of manners style, exposes the life style of London during the period. Shirley chose the comedic technique to expose man's foibles and vices, believing, as he expressed later in the prologue of the *Duke's Mistress* (1636):

For satire, they do know best what it means
That dare apply; and if a poet's pen,

Aiming at general errors, note the men,
'Tis not his fault. The safest cure is, they
That purge their bosoms may see any play.

In Act I, through the description of the Cavalier Lord Bonvile, Shirley also remarks on the aristocracy's belief that one's station in life brings with it certain privileges.

The aristocratic life with its promenading, horse-racing, and lovemaking is not the only life portrayed, however. There is a wide representation of the Elizabethan class structure: a milkmaid, a jockey, bagpipers, park-keepers, a merchant, officers, lords and ladies, and so on. The feeling for the country life evidenced by the list of the *dramatis personae* and the treatment of those representative characters was uncommon for Shirley's time, and was one of the few characteristics of his writing not generally adopted by the Restoration dramatists that followed him.

Indeed, James Shirley in *Hyde Park* set the pace for the dramatic writing of the Restoration in his comedy of manners. With his later play, *The Lady of Pleasure* (1635)—which gave the stage the characters of Sir Thomas Bornwell and his lady Aretina, who foreshadow so well Sir Peter and Lady Teazle of Richard Sheridan's *The School for Scandal* (1777)—and *Hyde Park,* perhaps one might remark: James Shirley was to Elizabethan drama the spark that William Wycherley was to Restoration drama. He at least was the bridge over the "void" of the Commonwealth period.

HYDRIOTAPHIA: URN-BURIAL

Type of work: Philosophical essay
Author: Sir Thomas Browne (1605-1682)
First published: 1658

Hydriotaphia: Urn-Burial; Or, a Discourse of the Sepulchral Urns Lately Found in Norfolk is at the same time one of the great glories of Renaissance scholarship and without doubt one of the greatest prose poems in English literature. The work is ostensibly a study on some forty or fifty Roman funeral urns that had been recently discovered near Norfolk. But the whimsical and associative mind of the author immediately reads philosophical implications out of, and rich analogues into, the urns.

In the "Epistle Dedicatory," addressed to "My worthy and Honoured Friend, Thomas Le Gros, of Crostwick, Esquire," Browne sets his tone. He broods on the common fate of all men, asking who can know the fate of his own bones or how often he is to be disinterred and scattered, as the bones in these Roman urns are now being brought again from their private seclusion. The uncertainty of man's ashes depresses his enthusiasm for earthly affairs at the same time that it excites his curiosity. He feels that it is his right and duty as physician, and man, to read the bones of our ancestors and learn from them, to make the living profit from the dead and to keep the living alive as long as possible.

Browne begins with a study of burial customs of ancient times, touching first on Biblical Abraham and the patriarchs, and Adam, then proceeds whimsically to the assertion that God interred but one body, that of Moses. Browne next takes up the subject of the burning of corpses, which he asserts was widespread in ancient times. He begins with Homer's account of Patroclus and Achilles, discusses the older tradition in Thebes, and then ranges to Israel, to the Amazons, and even to the Americas.

Next Browne says he will not discuss the ceremonies and rites of cremation or interment that are generally touched on by authors, but will talk only on the collected bones and ashes of the Romans discovered recently in England. He then moves from this narrower subject to a learned discussion of the burial customs of the peoples loosely associated with, or suggested by, the predecessors of seventeenth century Englishmen—the Romans, Druids, Danes, and others.

He points out that Caesar expressly says that the priests of the Druids used to burn and bury. History is silent on whether this custom held in the land of the early Britons, but since history speaks out clearly that the Romans distinctly influenced these early natives of Britain in many ways, for example, in getting them to build temples and wear gowns and study Roman laws with the intention of following it, probably, Browne feels, these people also followed their religious rites and customs in burial.

Browne further reminds his readers that in Norway and Denmark numerous burial urns obviously not of Roman origin in design are found containing not only bones but numerous other substances such as knives, pieces of iron, brass and wood, and, in Norway, one containing a "brass gilded Jewes-harp."

In the next chapter Browne continues with an inquiry into the various ways people have decorated the insides of sepulchers and tombs. He observes that men, such as Ulysses in Euripides' *Hecuba,* have not been so much concerned with how great they have been in life if they can be richly memorialized in death. He observes that great men affect great tombs, and large urns contain no mean ashes. He observes also the changing customs about the artifacts that have been placed in tombs, from the earliest customs when want dictated that only the most meager items be included to more opulent times when objects of much value were buried with the remains of the great people.

Browne also discusses the inscriptions which have headed graves, what kinds of bones make the best skeletons, the various positions in which peoples have placed their dead, and the time allowed between death and interment.

From the physical facts of life and death Browne rises to the spiritual. In these flights of fancy he, as a good Christian, reaches his greatest heights of philosophy and poetry. He realizes that life is transitory, of short duration, and life after death should be of greater importance than life on earth. He believes, however, that many people, perhaps most people, throughout the ages have failed to anticipate the wonders of the next world because of eagerness to exhaust the pleasures of this world. His feelings on the subject are at the same time an affirmation of faith in religion, which is characteristic of his general attitude, and a horror at those people who are short-sighted in their overall view.

The full value of this magnificent work can be appreciated only by actual reading of some of the great organ-like lines, of which the following are typical:

> Were the happiness of the next world as closely apprehended as the felicities of this, it were a martyrdome to live; and unto such as consider none hereafter, it must be more than death to dye, which makes us amazed at those audacities, that durst be nothing, and return into their *Chaos* again.

. . . . . .

> But to subsist in bones, and be but Pyramidally extant, is a fallacy in duration.

. . . . . .

> To be namelesse in worthy deeds exceeds an infamous history.

One of his most eloquent meditations deserves quotation in full:

> But the iniquity of oblivion blindely scattereth her poppy, and deals with the memory of men without distinction to merit of perpetuity. Who can but pity the founder of the Pyramids? *Herostratus* lives that burnt the Temple of *Diana*, he is almost lost that built it; Time hath spared the Epitaph of Adrian's horse, confounded that of himself. In vain we compute our felicities by the advantage of our good names, since bad have equall durations; and *Thersites* is like to live as long as *Agamemnon*. Who knows whether the best of men be known? or whether there be not more remarkable persons forgot, then any that stand remembered in the known account of time? Without the favour of the everlasting register, the first man had been as unknown as the last, and *Methuselahs* long life had been his only Chronicle.

> Oblivion is not to be hired: The greater part must be content to be as though they had not been, to be found in the Register of God, not in the record of man. Twenty-seven Names make up the first story before the flood, and the recorded names ever since contain not one living Century. The number of the dead long exceedeth all that shall live. The night of time far surpasseth the day, and who knows when was the Aequinox? Every hour adds unto that current Arithmetique which scarce stands one moment. And since death must be the *Lucina* of life, and even Pagans could doubt, whether thus to live, were to dye. Since our longest sunne sets at right descensions, and makes but winter arches, and therefore it cannot be long before we lie down in darknesse, and have our light in ashes. Since the brother of death daily haunts us with dying *memento's*, and time that grows old in it self, bids us hope no long duration: Diuturnity is a dream and folly of expectation.

In many ways the most philosophically incontrovertible and stylistically memorable of Browne's statements in this work is the oceanlike roll of "Grave-stones tell truth scarce fourty years. Generations passe while some trees stand, and old families last not three oaks."

One of the curiosities associated with Browne is the fact that the author of such a work as *Urn-Burial* should himself become a victim of persons interested for other reasons in burial places. His coffin was invaded in 1840 and his skull (a craniological wonder) was stolen and subsequently sold by the sexton of the church in which he was interred.

HYPATIA

Type of work: Novel
Author: Charles Kingsley (1819-1875)
Type of plot: Historical romance
Time of plot: Fifth century
Locale: Egypt and Italy
First published: 1853

Principal characters:
PHILAMMON, a young monk
HYPATIA, a female Greek philosopher and teacher
RAPHAEL ABEN-EZRA, a young Jew, Hypatia's pupil
MIRIAM, an old Jewish crone
AMAL, a young Gothic chief
PELAGIA, Amal's mistress
ORESTES, Roman prefect of Alexandria

Critique:

In Alexandria in the fifth century after Christ's death, there were many forces, Pagan, Christian, and Jewish, all struggling for the souls of men. *Hypatia* is the story of that conflict, which ended with the disintegration of a victorious Christian faction that used violence to gain its ends. The larger background of the novel is the dissolving Roman Empire.

The Story:

Philammon might never have left the little colony of monks three hundred miles above Alexandria if he had not strayed into an ancient temple in search of kindling. There, on the temple walls, he saw paintings of a life undreamed of in his monastic retreat, and he longed to visit the greater outside world. That very day, against the advice of the abbot and Aufugus, a monk whom he highly respected, he started out in a small boat and traveled down the river toward Alexandria.

In that splendid city at the mouth of the Nile lived Hypatia, the beautiful philosopher and teacher, one of the last to champion the ancient Greek gods. As she sat with her books one day, she was visited by the Roman prefect, Orestes, with the news that Pelagia, a beautiful courtesan who was Hypatia's rival for the hearts and souls of men, had left the city. Pelagia had transferred her affections to Amal, a Goth chieftain, and

had joined him on a trip up the Nile in search of Asgard, home of the old Gothic gods.

Cyril, the patriarch of Alexandria, had reported to Orestes that the Jews of the city were about to rise and slaughter the Christians, but Orestes chose to ignore the matter and let events take their course. Hypatia, who also had reason to oppose the Christian patriarch, suggested that Cyril make his charges before the Roman tribunal, which would, of course, postpone action against the Jews.

A wealthy young Jew, Raphael Aben-Ezra, whom Orestes met on his way to the palace, suggested that the prefect plead ignorance of any plot in his reply to Cyril. Raphael disclosed to the Roman that Heraclian, a Roman leader, had recently sailed for Italy, where he planned to destroy the Gothic conquerors of Rome and make himself emperor. His news led Orestes to think of the power he might hold south of the Mediterranean if the expedition succeeded.

Sailing down the Nile, Philammon met Pelagia and the party of Goths traveling in the opposite direction. He helped the men kill a hippopotamus. When he warned them that they could never cross the cataracts to the south, the Goths decided to turn back. Philammon was given a place in their boat.

Orestes sent Hypatia a letter delivered by the old Jewish crone, Miriam. It contained Raphael's news and a proposal that Hypatia marry the prefect and share the throne he was planning to create for himself in Egypt. Hypatia's reply was that she would accept the offer if Orestes would renounce his Christian faith and aid her in restoring the Greek gods.

Orestes, having no desire to face excommunication, was disturbed by her answer. At Raphael's suggestion, he decided to wait for a month in the hope that Hypatia's desire to marry a future emperor would overcome her religious zeal.

When they arrived in Alexandria, Philammon left the Goths and went to deliver to the Patriarch Cyril the letters of introduction he carried. While waiting to see the patriarch, Philammon overheard a plot to raid the Jewish quarter the next day.

That night, as he lay in bed in the patriarch's house, Philammon heard cries that the Jews were burning Alexander's Church. Joining a crowd of monks hurrying toward that edifice, he was attacked by a band of Hebrew marauders. But the report of the conflagration was false; it had been a trick of the Jews to lure the Christians into ambush. During the street fighting the Roman constabulary, which was supposed to keep order, remained aloof.

The next morning Miriam, who took a mysterious interest in Raphael's welfare, hastened to his quarters to warn him to flee. Christians, attacking the Jewish quarter, were pillaging the houses and expelling their inhabitants. To Miriam's exasperation, Raphael showed no interest in the fate of his wealth. Calmly exchanging his rich robes for a Christian's tattered rags, he prepared to leave the city. Miriam was left to save what she could of his possessions.

Philammon was one of the Chirstians who aided in despoiling the Jews. During the rioting he began to compare the conduct of the monks of Alexandria with the principles of charity and good works he himself had been taught. Hearing

of Hypatia and her teachings, he naïvely went to the museum where she lectured, in the hope of converting her to Christianity by his arguments. Nearly put out of the building by her pupils when he rose to dispute with her, he was spared at Hypatia's request. After the lecture she invited him to visit her the following day.

The Alexandrian monks were incensed when they learned that one Philammon had been to listen to the discourse of a pagan. When he visited Hypatia again, they accused him of being a heretic, and the young monk barely escaped being murdered. Philammon, charmed by Hypatia's beauty and purity, begged to become her pupil.

Raphael, who had fled to Italy, found himself in a devastated Rome. Heraclian, after his defeat by the Goths, was preparing to reëmbark for Africa. After Raphael had saved one member of the ill-fated expedition and his daughter, Victoria, from two barbarian soldiers, he sailed with them from Ostia to Berenice, a port on the coast of Africa.

Meanwhile, in Alexandria, Philammon had become Hypatia's favorite pupil. Aufugus, learning that the youth had deserted his Christian brethren, went to the city to find him. One day the two men met in the street. Aufugus, seeing that Philammon was determined to remain with his mentor, declared that the young monk was actually his slave, and he appealed to Orestes, who was passing by, to force Philammon to go with his legal owner. Philammon fled to take temporary refuge with the Goths in Pelagia's house.

After Philammon had returned to his own rooms, he received a summons from Miriam. She confirmed the fact that he was Aufugus' slave, for she had seen Philammon bought in Athens fifteen years before. Although Miriam had received the report of Heraclian's defeat by fast messenger, she wrote a letter which declared that Heraclian had been the victor. She sent Philammon to deliver the letter to Orestes.

The prefect immediately planned a great celebration, in which the beautiful Pelagia should dance as Venus Anadyomene. Philammon hotly objected to the plan, for when Miriam told him he was a slave she had implied also that Pelagia was his sister. Annoyed, Orestes ordered the monk to be thrown into jail. There Philammon was held prisoner until the day of the celebration. Released, he hurried to the arena in time to witness the slaughter of some Libyan slaves by professional gladiators. Orestes, with Hypatia beside him, watched from his box.

When Pelagia was carried into the amphitheater by an elephant and introduced as Venus, Orestes' hirelings tried to raise a cry to proclaim him Emperor of Africa. No one responded. Pelagia danced before her audience until Philammon, overcome by shame, could bear the sight no longer. Running to stop her shameful dance, he was caught up by the elephant's trunk and would have been dashed to death if Pelagia had not persuaded the animal to put him down. Pelagia left the amphitheater. Philammon was hustled away by the guards.

Orestes, however, was determined that his plan should succeed. When the uproar caused by Philammon began to die down, he stepped forward and offered himself as emperor. As had been prearranged, the city authorities began a clamor for him; but hardly had they started their outcry when a monk in the topmost tiers shouted that Heraclian had been defeated. Orestes and Hypatia fled.

Philammon, when he returned home, found Pelagia in his quarters. He begged his sister, as he now called her, to leave the Goth, Amal, and repent her ways, but the courtesan refused. Instead, she entreated him to ask Hypatia to accept her as a pupil, so that Amal, whose affection for her was failing, would love and respect her as the Greek woman was respected. But Hypatia had no pity for her hated rival. Philammon, carrying the news of her refusal to his sister, could not help thinking fondly of his own religion, with its offer of pity to all transgressors.

Hypatia knew the populace would soon be clamoring for her blood and that she would be forced to flee. In one last desperate effort to hold to her creed, she forced herself into a trance that she might have a visitation from the gods. The only face she saw, however, was Pelagia's.

When Miriam visited Hypatia the same day with the promise that she should see Apollo that night if she would visit the house of the Jewess, the distraught philosopher agreed. But the Apollo the crone showed her was Philammon, stupefied by drugged wine. As Miriam had foreseen, Hypatia realized at last that the only gods she would ever see were those that existed in her own mind. Shamed and angry, she went away. The final blow to fall on Hypatia was the news Raphael brought her on his return to Alexandria the next day. Under the persuasion of Augustine the famous philosopher-monk, he had become a converted Catholic before leaving Berenice, and he had married Victoria. That afternoon, as she started for the museum to give her farewell lecture, Hypatia was torn to pieces by some of Cyril's monks.

Philammon, when he learned of Hypatia's fate, visited Pelagia and pleaded with her to flee with him. By chance he met Amal, and in a struggle that ensued they fell from a tower together, and the Goth was killed. After Amal's death. Pelagia was willing to leave the city. Together they returned to the desert, where Pelagia lived in solitary penitence and Philammon became abbot, eventually, of the community he had left. Brother and sister died at the same time and were buried in a common grave.

Before he departed from Alexandria forever, Raphael learned from Miriam that she was his mother. A Jewess by birth, she had been converted to Christianity and had lived in a convent until it was sacked by the heathen. Afterward she had renounced her faith and had sworn the destruction of everyone not of her own race. Raphael had been given to a rich Jewess, who had represented him to her husband as her own child. After confessing her relationship to her son, Miriam died on his shoulder. She had been mortally wounded by the Goths after the death of their leader.

The victory which the Patriarch Cyril gained by Hypatia's death was only temporary. Though it marked the end of her creed in Egypt, it also signified the decline of the Egyptian Church, for the Christians, splitting into many factions, did not hesitate to use on each other the same violence they had once displayed toward the Greek philosopher.

Further Critical Evaluation of the Work:

Charles Kingsley was the son of a clergyman and received his education at King's College and at Cambridge. He chose to follow a religious profession, and he became rector of a Hampshire parish, a position which he held for the remainder of his life. His activities were not limited to the religious, for he acted as an instructor in modern history at Cambridge for nine years. His fields of interest were equally broad. He contributed to political pamphlets under a pseudonym and was active in the area of social reform. He was influenced by Carlyle's writings, and continually opposed the Chartist movement.

In addition to his other obligations, Kingsley somehow found time to work in the literary fields which interested him. He wrote songs and ballads, at least one play, numerous children's books, and several novels. His work *Alton Locke,* which appeared in 1850, is an early treatment of the changing view of the worker in society and reflects his essentially left-wing sentiment which prompted so much of his political activity. His other principle novels include *Hypatia, Westward Ho* (1855), and *Hereward the Wake* (1866), an attempt at the historical novel which is admirably accurate in its portrayal of history, but which suffers greatly from the complexities of plot and custom imposed upon it by the author's attention to detail and meticulous accuracy. Kingsley also published reviews of theological works and several volumes of sermons. It was one of his reviews which prompted Newman to write the *Apologia.*

Like *Hereward the Wake, Hypatia* suffers from the sort of overattention to detail which formed a feature of Kingsley's work. The plot is well worked out and of itself interesting, but the author loads a great deal of philosophical and theological discussion into an already overcomplicated plot structure and the predictable happens: the reader is tempted to gloss over the sometimes three to four page dissertations on Platonic logic as it related to the fundamentals of early Christian thought, and to resume reading where the action begins. This flaw is unfortunate, for Kingsley's sermons—and this is what they are—hold a wealth of information in a reasonably readable style. His classical education made him ideally suited for the sort of essays which he published with success elsewhere, but he was unable to resist the temptation to insert them into his novels.

THE HYPOCHONDRIAC

Type of work: Drama
Author: Molière (Jean Baptiste Poquelin, 1622-1673)
Type of plot: Romantic comedy
Time of plot: Seventeenth century
Locale: Paris, France
First presented: 1673

Principal characters:
ARGAN, an imaginary invalid
BÉLINE, his second wife
ANGÉLIQUE, Argan's daughter
CLÉANTE, her lover
BÉRALDE, Argan's brother
THOMAS DIAFOIRUS, the doctor's son
TOINETTE, Argan's maidservant

Critique:

Turning his satirical pen to the medical profession, Molière almost surpasses even his own bitterness as displayed in his earlier plays. *The Hypochondriac (Le Malade imaginaire)* was his last comedy, and he was unmerciful in his attack on all doctors and pharmacists. His usual wit and humor are not lost in the irony, but they are secondary to it. It is now almost three hundred years since Molière's death, but his literary stature has not diminished with the years. He is still studied and imitated as he was in his own time.

The Story:

Argan was the worst sort of hypochondriac. Each day saw him trying a new drug of some sort, so that the doctor and apothecary could exist almost exclusively on their profits from Argan. Toinette, his maidservant, tried in vain to persuade him to end his worries about his health, for she was certain that there was absolutely nothing the matter with her master. But he would not listen to her; he was determined to be an invalid.

He was encouraged in his supposed illness by his doctor and by Béline, his second wife, who used his weakness to further her schemes to get his money. Because the law said that a second wife could not inherit, it was essential to Béline that Argan make a settlement on her while he still lived. To that end also she tried to get him to place his two daughters in a convent, so that they could not interfere by claiming money for themselves.

Argan had other plans for his older daughter, Angélique. He was going to force her betrothal to his doctor's son in order to have a doctor in the family. He told the girl that a dutiful daughter would take a husband useful to her father. But Angélique, loving a young man named Cléante, begged her father not to force her marriage to Thomas Diafoirus, the doctor's son. Argan was firm because the young man would also inherit a large sum of money from his father and another from his uncle, the apothecary. If Angélique would not obey his wishes, he threatened to place her in a convent, as her stepmother wished him to do. Toinette scolded him severely for forcing his daughter to marry against her wishes, but he would not be moved. Toinette, wishing to help Angélique, got word to Cléante that his beloved was to be given to another.

Cléante disguised himself as the friend of Angélique's singing-master and told Argan that he had been sent to give her her singing lesson. Toinette pretended to change her mind and sympathize with Argan's position regarding the marriage. In that way she could offer to guard Angélique, while in reality giving the young lovers an opportunity to be alone together.

As the supposed teacher, Cléante had to witness the meeting between Thomas and Angélique. Thomas was a great boob of a boy, quoting memorized speeches to Argan, Angélique, and Béline. His father, the doctor, was quite proud that Thomas had always been a little slow in learning and that he followed blindly the opinions of the ancients, not accepting any of the new medical discoveries—for example, the thesis that blood circulated through the system.

Poor Angélique knew that she could never marry such a stupid oaf. She begged her father at least to give her time to become acquainted with Thomas, but the most he would give her was four days. At the end of that period she must either marry Thomas or go into a convent. In order to be assured of Argan's money, Béline continued to plead with him to choose the convent for his daughter.

Argan's brother, Béralde, called on him and also pleaded Angélique's cause. He thought it wicked to force her to marry against her wishes. He knew that Argan was not really ill and did not need a doctor in the family. In fact, he knew that the doctor would soon cause his brother's death by the constant "drenching" of his abdomen. Béralde sent the medicines away, causing the doctor to renounce his patient and to predict his death within four days. The apothecary canceled his contract to give his nephew a marriage settlement, and neither of the professionals would be soothed by Argan's protestations that it was his brother and not he who had denounced them and their treatments. Argan believed that he would surely die without their attention.

Toinette and Béralde then schemed to trick the hypochondriac. Toinette disguised herself as a physician and told Argan that his former doctor had been entirely mistaken in his diagnosis of Argan's illness. His liver and bowels were not ailing, but his lungs were; he must cut off his arm and pluck out his eye because they were drawing all his strength to them. Even Argan would not take such a drastic remedy. The poor man felt that he was doomed.

Still Argan would not relent concerning Angélique. Since the doctor and the apothecary had broken their marriage contracts, Angélique must go to a convent and become a nun. When Béralde accused him of being influenced by his wife, Argan agreed to Toinette's suggestion that he allow his wife to prove her love for him. Toinette knew the greed of Béline, but she pretended to Argan that if he acted dead he would see that she loved him and not his money. In this way he could convince his brother of Béline's true love.

The plan was carried out, but when Toinette cried to Béline that Argan was dead, the wife praised heaven that she was rid of her dirty, disgusting husband. Then she tried to bribe Toinette to help her keep Argan's death a secret until she could get certain papers and money into her possession. At that Argan rose up from his supposed deathbed to confront his wife. She fled in terror.

Toinette persuaded Argan to try the same plan with his daughter. When Angélique was told that her father was dead, she wept for him. Cléante came into the room and Angélique told him that now she could not marry him. Her father was dead, and she could make amends for her previous refusals to obey him only by carrying out his wishes now. Argan again rose from his deathbed, this time to bless his daughter for her faithfulness. Toinette and Béralde reminded him of his daughter's love and of his duty to reward her by allowing her to marry the man of her choice. Argan agreed that she could marry Cléante if he would become a doctor and minister to Argan's needs. Cléante was willing, but Béralde had a better idea. Argan should become a doctor himself; then he could give himself constant attention. All that was needed was for him to don cap and gown. He could then spout gibberish and make it sound learned. So the matter was settled, and the old hypochondriac gave his blessing to the young lovers.

Further Critical Evaluation of the Work:

On February 17, 1673, the fourth performance of *The Hypochondriac* was staged with Molière playing the role of the hypochondriac Argan. Toward the end of the final scene, Molière was seized with a fit of choking brought on by a hemorrhage of the lungs. However, such was his dedication and strength of will, that he managed to finish the scene and take his bows without his fellow actors even realizing his condition. He collapsed immediately after the final curtain call, was carried home, and died within a few hours. It was one of the most dramatic deaths in literary history, and much has been written about it. But aside from its poignancy, the incident reflected the most crucial aspect of Molière's genius: his ability to convert painful realities into joyous farce, to defy the limitations of human life through comedy of the most superb and transcendent quality.

The Hypochondriac, the last of Molière's plays, is the culmination of an art which had its roots both in the traditions of old French farce and in the Italian *commedia dell'arte* form. We can see features of the former in the play's irrepressible high spirits, in its uproarious slapstick, and in its hilarious and rollicking episodes. The influence of the latter shows in Molière's use of masks, a device with which he never ceased to experiment throughout his entire career. Beginning in his first plays with masks adopted from the Italian theater by French neoclassicists, he soon modified and expanded their function until they became a device perfectly suited to the expression of his comic genius; in *The Hypochondriac* they are employed with particular effectiveness in the characterization of the various doctors.

But Molière would not have become the great writer that he was if he had not transcended his artistic origins, transforming his raw materials with the spark of genius. As it was, that spark kindled comedies whose characters are unforgettable and whose themes are universal; it produced plays of unsurpassed comedy inspired by passion, fraught with meaning, and rich with implication.

The Hypochondriac contains some of Molière's most memorable characters; Argan is one of his finest creations. Like all of Molière's comic heroes, Argan has fallen prey to an obsession which dominates his every thought and action. He is a domestic tyrant whose entire household revolves around treatment of his imagined illness, and whose selfishness extends to such a point that he attempts to force his daughter into marriage with a witless doctor, so that he can profit from free medical attention. He is opposed every step of the way and eventually duped by the bold, clever, and inventive maid-servant, Toinette. Surrounding these two central figures are a cluster of minor characters including Argan's lovely and generous daughter Angélique; his scheming and greedy second wife Béline; his practical, sensible brother Béralde; his daughter's suitor, the automaton Thomas Diafoirus; and a motley assortment of doctors and apothecaries such as Monsieur Purgon, Monsieur Fleurant, and Monsieur Diafoirus the elder. In all of these characterizations, Molière presents universal types rather than unique individuals; he concentrates only on the character's dominant traits while he passes over his other qualities, simplifying in order to create a single powerful dramatic effect. As in all his comedies, Molière subordinates plot to characterization in *The Hypochondriac;* he created the roles to fit the actors who were to perform them, supplying them with a plot just sufficient to allow them room to develop those roles. Above all, the plays were written to be performed rather than read; and the plots are marked by their blissful disregard of probability and their constant intrusion of musical interludes, song, and dance.

The Hypochondriac is a play of considerable thematic complexity. On the surface, of course, this comedy is an attack on incompetent doctors and unscrupulous quacks; but many critics have discussed the deeper parallels between the open satire on medicine and a disguised attack on religion which they perceive in the play. Whether or not the author consciously intended any parallels, one can certainly see many analogies between the doctors in *The Hypochondriac,* and priests and theologians. Like Argan's doctors, churchmen preach with unbending dogmatism, summarily condemn anyone who questions their authority, and propagate more of their kind through obscure and inaccessible initiation rites. Just as Monsieur Purgon and Monsieur Fleurant dispense their drugs, priests dispense blessings, and Argan is as dependent on his apothecary as a religious fanatic on his confessor.

Beneath this parallel between medicine and religion lies the crucial theme in the play: blind obedience to fallible authority is dangerous. This theme is conveyed in a number of ways; the primary one is through the characterization of Argan, who is the extreme example of a man who has totally surrendered his free will to others and thereby lost his ability to reason clearly. He is so at the mercy of the doctors that he accepts without question the curse which Monsieur Purgon delivers as punishment when his patient delays taking his enema for several minutes past the prescribed hour: "I will that before four days are up you get into an incurable state." This central power-submission theme is also reflected in several minor relationships as well: Monsieur Fleurant, the apothecary, takes orders blindly from his superior within the medical hierarchy, Monsieur Purgon; Thomas Diafoirus worships the ancients and follows his father's commands as a puppet obeys a puppeteer.

The theme is also conveyed, and the parallel between medical and theological dogmatism stressed, through the dialogue. The Biblical echo is unmistakable, for example, when Toinette, disguised as a doctor, advises Argan to cut off one arm and gouge out one eye; one hears behind the line the admonition to sinners in Mark, 9:43-47, "And if thy hand offend thee, cut it off

. . . And if thine eye offend thee, pluck it out. . . ." The implications are provocative. At least one viable interpretation is that Molière is objecting to the abuse of the body and denial of its natural needs, and consequent warping of the spirit, occasioned both by absurd medical practice and the excesses of Christianity. Also fascinating is Molière's constant use of numbers, suggestive both of meaningless medical jargon and religious superstition. Argan in the opening scene equates the quantity of medicines consumed and enemas administred in a month to the quality of his health, much as a scrupulous devotée might worry that he had recited too few rosaries or lit too few votive candles during the week. Likewise, Monsieur Purgon's absurd formula for the proper number of grains of salt to put on an egg ("Six, eight, ten, using even numbers; just as in drugs, you use uneven numbers.") may be Molière's way of satirizing not only contemporary medical gimmicks but also similar Church practices such as indulgences sold to cut down the length of one's stay in purgatory.

It is Molière's unsurpassed comedy, however, which the viewer remembers, and which insures that future productions of *The Hypochondriac* will always be well attended. Scenes of sheer fun, such as Argan's tabulation of his monthly medical expenses, or Thomas Diafoirus' bungled attempt to recite his memorized avowal of love, are unforgettable; when the invalid flies out of his chair brandishing a stick, to chase a maidservant around the table before he suddenly realizes he cannot walk, the audience today roars with laughter as it did in 1673.

Nancy G. Ballard

I, CLAUDIUS

Type of work: Novel
Author: Robert Graves (1895-   )
Type of plot: Historical chronicle
Time of plot: 10 B. C.-A. D. 41
Locale: Rome
First published: 1934

Principal characters:

TIBERIUS CLAUDIUS DRUSUS NERO GERMANICUS, Emperor of
    Rome after Caligula
AUGUSTUS CAESAR, first Emperor of Rome
LIVIA, his wife, Claudius' grandmother
TIBERIUS, Claudius' uncle, successor to Augustus
GERMANICUS, Claudius' brother
CALIGULA, Germanicus' son, successor to Tiberius

Critique:

I, *Claudius* is a semi-fictional reconstruction of an interesting period in the history of the Roman empire. In it are snatches of history, records of conquest, Roman scenes, and names famous in history books. It is told in an informal manner, Claudius going to great lengths to reveal plot after plot, and the narrative method obscures in part the scholarly research and historical accuracy of the author.

The Story:

Claudius, Emperor of Rome, was held in little esteem because he was a stammerer. He was, moreover, a scholar in a nation which worshipped soldiering. He had compiled state histories but he realized that they were dull, sententious drivel. At last he decided to tell the true story of his own life. As the source of his inspiration he cited the Cumaean sibyl whom he had visited in her inner cavern. She had said that eventually he would speak clearly.

From the beginning, the Claudian family felt ashamed of young Claudius because he was a lame stammerer who seemed unlikely to carry on the family tradition of power. For that reason he developed into a scholarly person interested in the lives of others. His teachers told him stories about famous people and from many sources he picked up stray scraps of knowledge about them as he grew up.

He was greatly interested in his grandmother, the Empress Livia. Bored with her husband, she had secured a divorce, arranged her own marriage with the Emperor Augustus, and poisoned thereafter anyone who interfered with her plans. Power was her sole delight.

Another of the infamous people about him was Tiberius, who was for years the successor-to-be of Augustus. Son of Livia by an early marriage, he married the wanton Julia, daughter of Livia and Augustus. When Tiberius, having offended Augustus, was banished, Livia insisted that Julia be banished too. Tiberius, tired of his banishment, promised that if Livia would secure his return he would agree with her every wish thereafter. About that time the two sons of Julia and Tiberius died mysteriously.

Between Claudius' ninth and sixteenth years he occupied himself with affairs of his older relatives. He was married early to a girl named Urgulanilla, who detested him as much as he detested her. Claudius' first love had been mysteriously poisoned and Claudius suspected Livia, who later forced him to marry Urgulanilla. Claudius' scholarship and

2803

stability eventually brought him into the good graces of Augustus and Livia. They made him a priest of Mars and showed by public interest in him that he was an accepted member of the imperial family. Grain shortage caused rioting accompanied by arson. Augustus distributed grain according to the usual custom, banished such people as did not hold property in Rome, and rationed what food was available. Livia staged a sword fight in the arena to restore the good will of the populace. Because Claudius fainted publicly at the brutal sports, Livia decided that never again might he show his face in public. Soon afterward the last of Augustus' sons was banished for life. Tiberius was proclaimed the adopted son and successor of Augustus.

Tiberius and young Germanicus, brother of Claudius, campaigned against the barbarians, but Tiberius was not popular in spite of his victories with the army. Augustus suffered stomach disorders and died. Claudius knew that about a month before his death he had decided to restore his banished son, Postumus, grant money and honor to Claudius, and replace Tiberius. Claudius suspected Livia of the emperor's death.

Postumus was reported killed by a captain of the guard which had been placed around him. Livia slowly starved Julia to death. Because Germanicus was too honorable to seize the empire from Tiberius, there remained only the proof that Postumus was really dead to make Tiberius safe upon the throne. When Postumus returned, to disprove reports of his death, Tiberius had him tortured and killed.

Germanicus continued his successful campaign against the Germans. Tiberius, jealous, insisted that Germanicus return to Rome for his triumph. In A. D. 17 Germanicus returned. By that time Livia suspected Claudius and Germanicus of plotting against Tiberius. She sent Claudius to Carthage to dedicate a temple to Augustus, who had been deified by the Roman Senate.

Germanicus was next dispatched to the East to command the armies there. But Livia and Tiberius began to fear that Germanicus would win favor in the East as he had already done in the West. Germanicus was finally poisoned. His wife, Agrippina, sought protection from Claudius.

Claudius promised his thirteen-year-old son in marriage to the daughter of Sejanus, the friend of Tiberius. A few days later his son was found dead. Again he suspected Livia. Shortly afterward a divorce was arranged for Claudius by Sejanus, who was anxious to have Claudius marry Aelia, his sister by adoption. Claudius knew better than to oppose the wills of those in power and he accepted his new wife with practically no concern.

Tiberius set Livia aside. She was now growing old and he no longer had great reason to fear her. Bitter at the removal of her power, she began to make plans for his successor. She determined that Caligula, the son of Germanicus, should succeed him. She called in Claudius to declare a truce with him on the condition that he would have her declared a goddess after her death. In return, she told Claudius most of her state secrets; she said that all the murders she had planned were committed solely for the good of the state.

Tiberius, sixty-seven years old, seemed destined to die before long. He was living on Capri with a court of scholars, doctors, confidants, and entertainers, Sejanus having been left in Rome with authority to rule for him. When Livia finally died at the age of eighty-six, Tiberius refused to return to Rome even for her funeral.

Tiberius began a reign of terror against all members of Livia's faction. When Sejanus attempted to rebel against the emperor's cruel decrees, Tiberius ordered his execution. His children were also put to death. Claudius was ordered to divorce Aelia.

At last the mad Tiberius lay dying at

Misenum. Macro, commander of the guards, and Caligula, next in line for the throne, planned to take over the country. Caligula, already infamous among people who knew him, was still popular with the Romans. In too great a hurry they took command of the army. Then, learning that Tiberius was still alive, they smothered him.

In order to establish himself, Caligula pretended sympathy and generosity, but Claudius wrote in his history that Caligula held the record for infamy among princes up to that time. He began by spending the money Tiberius and Livia had hoarded so long. Then he fell ill. When he began to recover, he announced to Claudius that he had been transformed into a god, in fulfillment of the many prophecies that a god was soon to be given to the earth.

Caligula celebrated his godhood by wholesale assassination. Claudius' mother committed suicide because of Caligula's infamies. Soon Macro was forced to kill himself. At last the people began to turn against Caligula because of levies forced from the populace and the indescribable depravities of the palace brothel. Caligula, deciding to become a general, led an expedition into Germany. On his return he forced Claudius to marry his cousin Messalina. Calpurnia, Claudius' only true friend, was banished. The Romans were now plotting, almost openly, the assassination of Caligula. Before long he was murdered, and Claudius, the retiring scholar, was named Emperor of Rome.

Further Critical Evaluation of the Work:

From one of the most violent centuries in Western civilization Robert Graves drew his material for *I, Claudius*. After the rule of Augustus and Tiberius, the Roman empire reached a peak of violence and vulgarity under Caligula and after his death—rather incongruously—fell into the hands of Tiberius Claudius. The protagonist is the son of Germanicus, the noble and virtuous son of Augustus Caesar. As Graves presents him, he is the least blessed of all the imperial family: lame, weak in body, cursed with a stutter and a tendency to drool. Yet he is also a scholar and a historian who is able, because he is an outcast, to record with objectivity the events of his turbulent century. He sees his father poisoned, his various aunts, uncles, and cousins murdered; watches his mother starve to death; and manages to survive Caligula's madness. Indeed, bcause of his knowledge of history, and his position as an outcast, he is able to outlast the insanity of all the Roman power seekers. Ironically, when he is finally made emperor, all he thinks about, like most authors, is that now his books will be read.

Throughout the narration Claudius is fascinated and bemused by the delight his family takes in the pursuit of power. Told in an informal manner, a method which undercuts the apparent horrendous nature of their crimes, the various and complicated plots and counterplots become exercises in the banality of evil. Seen from the long, historical perspective such actions seem monumental, but viewed from the inside as Claudius sees them, they appear all too often petty, all too often the greedy sins of ordinary if perverse human beings. The corruption of the empire does not so much arise out of any grand evil plan of supermen but out of the lust of mere mortals.

I SPEAK FOR THADDEUS STEVENS

Type of work: Biography
Author: Elsie Singmaster (Mrs. E. S. Lewars, 1879-1958)
Type of plot: Historical chronicle
Time of plot: 1792-1868
Locale: Vermont, Pennsylvania, Washington, D. C.
First published: 1947

Principal characters:
THADDEUS STEVENS, lawyer and statesman
SALLY MORRILL STEVENS, his mother
JOSHUA,
MORRILL, and
ALANSON, his brothers
LYDIA SMITH, his housekeeper
ABRAHAM LINCOLN
ANDREW JOHNSON
MEMBERS OF CONGRESS, the CABINET, and the ARMED FORCES

Critique:

I Speak for Thaddeus Stevens is a biography in the form of a novel, a work making understandable as a man the complex and often contradictory character of the famous partisan statesman of the Civil War period. The author tells the story of his life as a series of dramatic episodes, each under its proper date and each presenting some crisis, either a triumph or a defeat, in his private affairs or public career. Much of the material in the book is based upon Stevens letters and papers previously unused by historians; the result is a carefully detailed portrait of the man against the unsettled age in which he lived. A native of Pennsylvania, Elsie Singmaster has presented faithfully in her novels and short stories the regional patterns of Pennsylvania German life and the history of the state through three decisive periods in our national life—the frontier in French and Indian days, the American Revolution, and the Civil War.

The Story:

In a Vermont cabin, on April 4, 1792, neighbor women had looked pityingly at a sleeping young mother while they wrapped the deformed foot of her newborn child. There was no need, however, to pity Sally Morrill Stevens, whose brave spirit was greater than her frail body. She would care for her second son as tenderly as she had looked after little Joshua, his father's namesake and a cripple at birth. She called the baby Thaddeus, after Thaddeus Kosciusko— a hero's name.

When Joshua Stevens, shiftless cobbler and surveyor, disappeared at last into the wilderness, there were two more children in the cabin. Morrill and Alanson stood up straight and were quick on their feet, but lame Thaddeus was Sally's favorite. Ambitious for her sons, she never complained as she worked and planned for their future.

Thaddeus struggled to excel. One day he limped through deep snow, his legs cut and bleeding on the icy crust, to speak before patrons and students of the grammar school in Peacham. His subject was free and universal education. Sensitive because of his own deformity, he learned to hate suffering and to sympathize with the weak. Swimming and riding gave him an athlete's body. His teachers and books borrowed from John Mattocks, Peacham lawyer, had trained him well by the time he was ready for Dartmouth College. Sally had hoped he would preach. He thought of Webster, already famous, and told her that he wanted to be a lawyer.

Vermont seemed a sparse land to her ambitious sons. Crippled Joshua traveled west with his bride. Thaddeus went to York, Pennsylvania, to teach and read for the law. Too impatient and poor to complete another year's residence before he could practice in York County, he rode south across the state line and became a member of the Maryland bar.

Returning, he settled in Gettysburg. At first no clients found their way to his office and few Gettysburgians wanted to hear his frank opinions on slavery and education, but children flocked around him to hear his stories of the Vermont woods. Blacks watched him on the street and whispered that he was their friend as well.

Defense lawyer in a murder trial, he lost his first case in court, but his townsmen praised him after he made his plea for justice and mercy. As his reputation grew men could measure his success by his fine house in Gettysburg and the great tract of mountain land providing ore and charcoal for Caledonia Forge, of which he was a partner. Sally Stevens now owned a fine farm in Peacham; he gave openhandedly to his brothers—Joshua in Indiana; Morrill, a doctor in Vermont; Alanson, with Sally on the farm. He fought Masons and Jackson Democrats and men cheered all night under his windows when he was elected to the Legislature. He was forty-one. There was still time for Washington, for Congress, perhaps the White House.

In 1837 word came to him in Philadelphia that the free education bill was about to be repealed. By train and stagecoach he hurried to Harrisburg and risked his political future with his proposed amendment to strike out the bill of repeal and to insert after the clause, "Be it enacted," the words "To establish a General System of Education by Common Schools." Speaking on that motion, he saved the free school system of Pennsylvania.

His fame spread. Men respected and hated and feared the blunt, shrewd orator whose voice was heard everywhere. In Philadelphia, during the Buckshot War, a mob attacked an assembly hall and he and his friends escaped through a window. Campaigning for Harrison, he hoped for a Cabinet appointment. But Harrison died and Tyler forgot campaign promises. Ruined by his partner's failure in 1842, he moved to Lancaster. There he made money and paid his debts. Young men begged the opportunity to read law in his office. He became an ironmaster, owner of a great furnace at Caledonia. Sometimes Washington seemed a long way off. He waited.

Free-Soil Whigs elected him to Congress in 1848. Fighting the compromise measures and the Fugitive Slave Law, he spoke for gentle Sally Stevens, for old John Mattocks, lover of justice, for slaves fleeing northward along the Underground Railroad. He defended the three white men and thirty-eight Negroes accused after the death of a Maryland farmer in the Christiana riot; later he was to recall how Lucretia Mott and other Quakers had dressed the Negroes alike, to the confusion of witnesses and prosecution. Retired from Congress, he traveled to Vermont in 1854. Sally Stevens was dead, Morrill and Alanson before her. The slander of his enemies could never hurt her now. Joshua was soon to die. Thaddeus was sixty-two and failing, but men were mistaken when they said he was too old for public life.

In 1855 he helped to launch the Republican Party in Lancaster. In 1858 he returned to Congress. In Chicago, in 1860, he heard Abraham Lincoln nominated.

He rode the war years like an eagle breasting a whirlwind. Abraham Lincoln was President, but Thaddeus Stevens spoke for the Republican Party. Often impatient with the sad-eyed, brooding man in the White House, he steered through Congress the bills which gave Lincoln men and money to fight the Civil War. Lydia Smith, the decent mulatto at whom men sneered, kept his house on B Street. Sometimes he thought of the Cabinet post or Senate seat he believed his due, but usually more important matters filled his mind. Confederate troops, marching toward Gettysburg, had burned Caledonia Furnace. A nephew died at Chickamauga. Unbowed by personal misfortune, he argued for the Thirteenth Amendment, insisted upon education and suffrage for the Negro. There was little time for the card games he loved; he read more often when he went to bed at night—Shakespeare, Homer, the Bible.

Hating weakness and compromise, he fought Andrew Johnson after Lincoln's death. Congress, he thundered, should be the sovereign power of the nation. Sick and weak, he proposed Article Eleven by which the House hoped to impeach Johnson. Too ill to walk, he was carried into the Senate to hear that decisive roll call. He heard around him whispers of relief, anger, and despair as the telling votes were cast. Friends asked him if he wished to lie down after his ordeal. He answered grimly that he would not.

Although bitter in defeat, he would not let his fellow Republicans punish Vinnie Ream, the little sculptress involved in Johnson's trial, and he angrily insisted that she keep her studio in the Capitol. His detractors claimed he was too mean to die when he refused to take to his bed during that hot Washington summer, but by August the end was near. Devoted son, generous kinsman, loyal friend, harsh enemy, he died at midnight on August 11, 1868. The telegraph clicked the news to the world.

Further Critical Evaluation of the Work:

Elsie Singmaster's *I Speak for Thaddeus Stevens* is less a work of fiction than a work in which fiction and history compete as standard-bearers for the story of humanity's triumphs and failures. It is the historical novel of the Age of Emancipation and the fictional biography of Thaddeus Stevens, uncompromising champion of the underprivileged and disadvantaged.

In overcoming his own personal weakness, the deformity with which he was born, Thaddeus Stevens found symbolic strength in defending the weak and poor. He championed the rights of Pennsylvanians to have free education, risking his own career in the process; he stood for the rights of black people, and attacked the Fugitive Slave Law when it was politically damaging to do so. Singmaster's portrait of the man, whose uncompromising opinions were "imbibed with his mother's milk," creates a convincing psychological *gestalt* of Thaddeus Stevens, who became a superior man by overcoming his innate feelings of inferiority.

As a historical novel, *I Speak for Thaddeus Stevens* recreates an earlier age by infusing it with life. The Free-Soil Whigs, Masons, and Jackson Democrats come to life as men in a political drama unfolding before Thaddeus Stevens. Singmaster's scrupulous use of historical data sheds new light on the Civil War Congress and the struggle for the Thirteenth Amendment. The novel's climax, the attempted impeachment of Andrew Johnson which failed in the Senate, underscores the tragic theme of Thaddeus Stevens, advocate for the sovereign rights of the people.

Singmaster's style is unobtrusive and sparse, devoid of rhetorical flourish and pretense. She writes in clear, unelaborate language whose intention is to present, close to reality, the struggle of Thaddeus Stevens against the forces of ignorance and oppression. *I Speak for Thaddeus Stevens* is the very personal statement of Elsie Singmaster about man's inhumanity to man, and humane forces which can rise to the challenge.

AN ICELAND FISHERMAN

Type of work: Novel
Author: Pierre Loti (Julien Viaud, 1850-1923)
Type of plot: Impressionistic romance
Time of plot: Nineteenth century
Locale: Brittany and at sea
First published: 1886

Principal characters:
SYLVESTER, a young Breton
YVONNE, his grandmother
GAUD, his cousin
YANN, a fisherman

Critique:

The number of translations and editions of *An Iceland Fisherman* are indicative of the warmth created by the reading of this beautiful story. Pierre Loti, of the French Academy, exemplified in this unadorned tale the virtues of French literature: clarity, simplicity, power. The exotic always appealed to Loti, and *An Iceland Fisherman* reflects this appeal in the descriptions of the fishing fleet in Iceland waters. The love interest is well presented and well within bounds. The characters of little Sylvester, big Yann, and serious Gaud are those of real people, whose fortunes are of genuine concern to the reader.

The Story:

In the foc's'l head, a hollow, pointed room like the inside of a gigantic sea gull, five men were sitting around the massive table which filled almost all the space between the bulkheads. They were waiting to take their turn on watch, for it was nearly midnight. They had cracked some biscuit with a hammer and had eaten. Now they were drinking wine and cider.

Around the room little pigeonholes near the ceiling served as bedchambers, for these fishermen were outside so much they seemed to need no air while they slept. A murky lamp swung back and forth with the gentle swell of the sea.

Sylvester, who was only seventeen, was impatient for the appearance of Yann. They were celebrating in honor of their patron, the Virgin Mary, and Yann had to take part in the toasts. Finally Yann opened the little hatch in the deck and came down the narrow ladder. Yann, in his late twenties, and a giant of a man, was a hero to Sylvester. The whole company brightened on his arrival.

It was midnight. The toasts were quickly drunk. Then the watch went on deck for their turn to fish. Outside it was daylight, for in those latitudes it never got dark in summer. It was monotonous and soothing to fish in the daylight.

At the rail Yann and Sylvester baited their hooks and dropped their lines. Behind them William waited with sheath knife and salt. Regularly, in turn, Yann and Sylvester brought up their hooks, passed the plump cod to William, and rebaited. Quickly William slit the fish, cleaned them, and packed them in the salt barrel. The pile of kegs in the hold represented the income of whole Breton families for a year. For his share of the catch Yann would bring home fifteen hundred francs to his mother.

While they were fishing Sylvester talked of marriage. Although still a boy, he was already engaged to Yann's sister. He did his best, as he had done all summer, to talk Yann into the idea of marriage with Gaud. Always Yann shook his head; he was engaged to the sea, he said, and some day he would celebrate that wedding.

AN ICELAND FISHERMAN by Pierre Loti. Published by Alfred A. Knopf, Inc.

Gentle and serious Gaud, Sylvester's cousin, was attracted to Yann. She was, however, a mademoiselle with fine hands and good clothes. Her father was rich. Yann could scarcely help knowing that Gaud liked him, but with Breton stubbornness and simplicity he could not think of pretending seriously to a young woman of the upper class.

In September the fishing boat returned to Paimpol in Brittany. The return of the Iceland fleet was the signal for quickened life among these simple folk. The women and children and the old men spent the whole spring and summer raising small gardens and waiting. Then in the fall, when the men came back, there were weddings and engagements and feasts and pardons. Too often a ship did not return, and several families would wear black that winter.

That fall there was a big wedding with the traditional procession to the seashore and afterward a ball. Yann went to the ball and danced the whole evening with Gaud. Yann told her of his life at sea and of his big family in Pors-Even. Part of the time Yann watched his little sister, who danced with Sylvester. The seriousness of the engaged children amused Yann. Gaud was greatly pleased, for at last Yann had unbent and his talk seemed to her too gentle for casual conversation.

Gaud waited all that winter in her rich home with its fine furniture, but Yann never came to see her. At length, overcoming her modesty, she went on a business errand for her father to Yann's house, in the hope of seeing him. She paid a sum of money to Yann's father and waited longer than she should have, but Yann did not come home. Later, she knew, Yann would come to see her father to conclude the business, and she resolved to talk with him then. But when Yann came to see her father, he prepared to leave without inquiring for her. As he came into the hall, Gaud stopped him. Yann simply told her he could not court her because she was rich and he was poor.

In the spring Yann and Sylvester sailed again with the Iceland fleet. Gaud, during that summer, felt an occasional thrill when she wrote letters to Sylvester for his grandmother, Yvonne. Often the doting old woman would dictate a short message to Yann. So Gaud was not completely out of touch with her simple, stubborn fisherman.

Events were soon to bring Gaud and Yann close together. Sylvester, the next winter, had to leave for his military service. His grandmother, Yvonne, visited him once at the barracks just before he left for French Indo-China. He was to be gone five years, and Yvonne was inconsolable.

Sylvester made a brave sailor in the French navy. On shore in the East he was sent with an armed patrol to reconnoiter. When the small band was surprised and surrounded by a large detachment of Tonkinese, Sylvester led a spirited counter-attack, until he was cut down by a sharpshooter. He was buried far from the rocky Breton coast in a green, strange land. An efficient, soulless government sent back his poor effects to Yvonne. She was now really alone, with only a memory growing dimmer as time passed.

Gaud's father committed one folly after another and lost more money trying to recoup earlier losses. Finally, at his death, he was a ruined man. Gaud, the rich man's daughter, became a seamstress. With quick sympathy she went to live with Yvonne, so that the two bereft women could comfort each other.

Yvonne, infirm of limb and mind, was unmercifully teased by a group of small boys who thought she was drunk. Falling into the mud, she vainly tried to regain her footing. Gaud came along to set the old woman on her feet again and brush the mud from her clothes. Just then Yann happened on the scene and chased the tormentors away. He escorted the two women home.

Yann was slowly changing his mind. Now that Gaud was poor, he felt a barrier between them had been removed. He also felt a great bond of sympathy for Yvonne because of her grandson, and Gaud was part of that sympathy. At the urging of his relatives and Yvonne, he proposed to Gaud. Much of that winter the couple sat by the fire in Yvonne's poor hut while the old woman slept. Six days before the fleet was to leave in March, Gaud and Yann were married.

When the fishermen departed on their summer cruise, Gaud for the first time was part of the busy, weeping crowd. Yann's ship was towed out into the harbor to wait a favorable wind. During the delay Yann came ashore again for a final three hours. Gaud watched the ship disappear in the twilight.

The summer passed uneventfully enough. Gaud made fair wages from her sewing, enough to refurnish Yvonne's poor cottage. In September the fishing fleet came straggling back. Yann's ship was not among them. At the end of the month Gaud still had hope. Each masculine step along the path sent her scurrying to the window. Yann's father, also worried, called to comfort her. He told her many stories of ships delayed by fog until December. The fall and early winter came and went, and still Gaud waited.

She never saw Yann again. In August his ship had become separated from the others and was blown north. Somewhere off Iceland, Yann had kept a tryst, his wedding with the sea.

Further Critical Evaluation of the Work:

The great popularity of Pierre Loti's exotic works at the close of the nineteenth century and in the early years of the twentieth was in part the result of a reaction to the literary naturalism of Émile Zola, the Goncourts, and other novelists in France and elsewhere. Loti had himself, in his wide-ranging voyages as a French naval officer, seen the people and places he described in his fiction. Various works by him are set in Turkey, Tahiti, Africa, Japan, and Persia.

In *An Iceland Fisherman*, Pierre Loti combines realism and impressionism in a simple tale of primitive people living in an elemental world filled with occasional beauty and many natural dangers. The story's theme of love and separation is one frequently repeated by Loti who in his years at sea had learned how often a sailor's farewell to his loved ones is final though he does not wish it so. The sea dominates most of the scenes in the novel, whether the action is on shipboard or on land. The sea is called "the foster mother and destroyer" of generations of Breton fishermen. It shows a "dark and sinister" look before a storm, and when some drunken sailors drown their cares in mirthful song, the sea, "their grave of tomorrow," sings a booming, dirge-like accompaniment. Such poetic language stems from the author's own nautical impressions, an aspect of the novel that heightens the reader's enjoyment of the story.

Loti's characters are realistic but somewhat sentimentalized. Because the author seems to care so much, though, for these doomed people (he mentions that he himself conducted the sad funeral in Singapore of the valiant young Sylvester), the reader does also. One is touched by the handsome young sailor's death far from home, by the deep grief of his grandmother, and by the desperate, vain longing of Gaud for her drowned husband, taken from her by her cruel rival the sea after Yann and Gaud had spent only one week of happiness together.

THE IDES OF MARCH

Type of work: Novel
Author: Thornton Wilder (1897-1975)
Type of plot: Historical chronicle
Time of plot: 45 B. C.
Locale: Ancient Rome
First published: 1948

> *Principal characters:*
> JULIUS CAESAR
> POMPEIA, his second wife
> CALPURNIA, his third wife
> LADY CLODIA PULCHER, a conspirator
> CATULLUS, a famous poet
> CLEOPATRA, Queen of Egypt
> MARCUS BRUTUS, another conspirator

Critique:

When an author writes a novel whose plot is already well-known, and that novel becomes a best seller, we must assume that his style is superior or that the story is so loved that we want to hear it again and again. In *The Ides of March* we have both factors. Thornton Wilder has retold the events of the last months of Caesar's life with warmth and depth of feeling. From imaginary letters and documents he has reconstructed the plots and intrigues leading to the fatal stabbing of the great Roman.

The Story:

There were so many different groups plotting to assassinate Caesar that it was impossible for him to guard himself from all of them. Each day new leaders rose to incite the people against him. Many of the leaders were friends of Caesar; some were relatives; some were merely ambitious men; and some were citizens who sincerely believed that Rome was suffering under Caesar's rule and wanted to free her. The last group had Caesar's admiration. He knew that he had restricted the freedom of the people, but he knew, too, that the masses of people shrink from accepting responsibility for their actions. They want to be ruled by one who will make all important decisions for them, yet they resent that ruler because he has taken their freedom from them. Caesar knew that he would one day be assassinated, but he hoped that he would see in the face of his murderer a love for Rome.

Among the most persistent of the plotters was the mother of Marcus Brutus. She had long hated Caesar and wanted her son to assume the place of the dictator. Many Romans said that Brutus was the illegitimate son of Caesar, but no one had ever been able to prove the accusation. Brutus was loyal to Caesar until the very end; only his mother's repeated urging led him at last to join the conspirators.

Another important figure among Caesar's enemies was Clodia Pulcher, a woman of high birth, great wealth, and amazing beauty. Because of her ambitions and lusts she had become a creature of poor reputation, so much so that her name was scribbled on public walls, accompanied by obscene verses. She was aided in her plots by her brother and by Catullus, the most famous poet in Rome. Catullus was a young man so much in love with Clodia that he would do anything she asked, and he wrote many poems and tracts against Caesar. Clodia spurned Catullus and his love, but her ridicule of him only strengthened his passion for her.

While all these plots against Caesar were taking shape, he and the rest of

Rome were preparing for the visit of Cleopatra, Queen of Egypt. She, too, suffered from a bad reputation, for her many conquests in love were well-known in Rome. Most of the high ladies planned to receive her only because Caesar had so ordered, among them Pompeia, Caesar's wife, who knew of his earlier relations with the queen. But at Caesar's command Cleopatra was accorded the honor due a queen. He visited her many times, always in disguise, and on one of his visits barely missed being killed. He could never be sure whether Cleopatra knew of the plot. Marc Antony had begun to find favor in the eyes of Cleopatra, and as Marc Antony was involved in the attempted assassination, Caesar suspected that she too might be involved.

After Cleopatra's arrival, all Rome began to plan for the mysteries of the Good Goddess. This festival took place each year on December 11, and every Roman woman of high birth and moral virtue took part in the ceremonies. The Vestal Virgins participated in the festival also, and only women whose reputations were above reproach were allowed to attend the mysteries. Clodia's recent actions had given rise to the possibility that she might be rejected. In fact, petitions had been sent to Lady Julia Marcia, Caesar's aunt and a directress of the mysteries, to debar Clodia. Caesar interfered in behalf of Clodia, however, for just as he could understand the reasoning of his enemies, he could understand Clodia. She felt that she was fated to live the life she did and blamed the gods for her actions rather than herself.

But Clodia was vengeful. When she learned a compromise had been reached —she was to be allowed to attend the mysteries only until the Vestal Virgins appeared—she arranged to have her brother dress in the robes of a woman and attend the ceremonies with her. No man had ever been present at that sacred rite, and the profanation was the greatest scandal ever to reach the streets of Rome. The two criminals, for so they were called, were arrested, but Caesar pardoned them, thus adding another reason for public resentment. Once again it was suspected that Cleopatra knew of the plot, for she too had wanted to attend the mysteries and had been told she would have to leave when the Virgins appeared. It was rumored that Pompeia had known of Clodia's plan, and for these rumors Caesar divorced Pompeia, his reason being that regardless of whether the rumors were true Pompeia should have conducted herself so that no rumors could be started about her.

After his divorce Caesar married Calpurnia. Catullus had died in the meantime, and Caesar reflected much on the poet's death. He was not sure about his own beliefs concerning the gods and their influence on the world. Often he felt that there were no gods, that each man was the master of his own destiny. He wished that he were not guided by fear and superstition concerning life and death, but he continued to employ soothsayers and magicians and hoped daily for good omens from the heavens.

There were few good omens for Caesar at that time. His chief soothsayer had warned him of several dangerous days, but as all of them had passed uneventfully Caesar began to be less careful; and he planned to leave for the Parthian battlefront on March 17. He asked Brutus and his wife to care for Calpurnia while he was gone. He knew Brutus had been among his enemies, but he loved the younger man and believed that Brutus was now his friend.

Brutus promised Caesar to care for Calpurnia; but Brutus was to play a different role within a few days. The fateful Ides of March came. Caesar walked to the Senate chambers to make his farewell speech before leaving for the war. Approaching the capitol, he was surrounded by the conspirators. One plunged his dagger into Caesar's throat as the others closed in. Caesar was stabbed twenty-three times. When he saw that he was surrounded, he sat down and wrapped his robe about him. He did not cry out, but there are those who say that when he saw Brutus he said, "You, too, Brutus?" and ceased to struggle. Perhaps he was satisfied with his assassin.

Further Critical Evaluation of the Work:

Thornton Wilder twice received the Pulitzer Prize for his work as a playwright (*Our Town*, 1938; *The Skin of Our Teeth*, 1943). However, he is also respected as a novelist. His reputation was first made by *The Bridge of San Luis Rey*, a best-selling novel that won him his first Pulitzer Prize in 1928. After the success of this work came a succession of other novels, many of which employed Wilder's characteristic device of centering on a group of persons whose lives at some point in time are all in some way interconnected.

This is also the technique Wilder was to use in *The Ides of March*, a novel whose use of "documents" to tell its story fits it into at least two major novel categories: the historical and the epistolary. Wilder's use of these fictitious documents—only the parts from the Catullus and the last entry are authentic—allows him an omniscient point of view in telling his story. He is thus able at the same time to maintain a sense of unfolding progression, as the same facts are discussed again and again from a different viewpoint, and are filled in more completely by each character's successive letter.

This technique of multiple viewpoints also allows Wilder to present a more comprehensive picture of the novel's characters. Caesar is seen as rational, truly unvengeful, dedicated to the responsibilities he accepts as Dictator, and generally superior in every way to those around him. His virtues are not understood by the other characters because they are incapable of possessing such strengths themselves. Brutus, for example, is incapable of the strong convictions, about Rome or himself, which are needed by a man in Caesar's position. Caesar's private character is revealed through his own letters to Lucius Mamilius Turrinus, but we also see different and complementary sides of him in the letters of Clodia Pulcher, Julia Marcia, Pompeia, and others. These in turn are understood through their own and others' letters, so that the reader has a sense of completeness as well as objectivity in Wilder's characterizations.

Wilder's scrupulous accounting of his "documents' " origins, his knowledge of Roman history and customs, and his ability to simulate the Roman epistolary style and language lend further verisimilitude to the work. His unique talent for weaving several lives and points of view into one coherent, fascinating whole is the novel's strongest structural and stylistic asset.

THE IDIOT

Type of work: Novel
Author: Fyodor Mikhailovich Dostoevski (1821-1881)
Type of plot: Psychological realism
Time of plot: Mid-nineteenth century
Locale: St. Petersburg, Russia
First published: 1868-1869

Principal characters:
PRINCE LEF NICOLAIEVITCH MYSHKIN
PARFEN ROGOZHIN, friend of the prince
MME. EPANCHIN, friend and relative of the prince
AGLAYA EPANCHIN, her daughter
NATASYA FILIPOVNA, Aglaya's rival
GANYA ARDALIONOVITCH, secretary to General Epanchin

Critique:

Because this book was written by the author of *Crime and Punishment* and *The Brothers Karamazov*, it will always have a significant place in literature. Like so many characters in Russian fiction, however, the people in this novel exhibit a behavior so foreign to the American temperament that the majority of readers may find the entire story rather incredible. Perhaps the most serious handicap lies in the author's portrayal of Prince Myshkin. It would seem that he is meant to be the foil for the other characters, the person who seems foolish but is, in reality, very wise and good. But the fact that the prince suffers from epilepsy confuses the issue, and one wonders if he really is an idiot. However, as a panorama of Russian morals, manners, and philosophy of the period, *The Idiot* is an interesting and informative novel.

The Story:

After four years spent in Switzerland, where he was treated for epilepsy at a sanitarium, Prince Myshkin returned to St. Petersburg. On the train the threadbare shabbiness of his clothing attracted the attention of the other passengers. One of these, Parfen Rogozhin, began to question him. By the time they reached St. Petersburg, the prince and Rogozhin were well-informed about one another, and Rogozhin offered to take the prince to his home and to give him money.

Myshkin, however, first wanted to introduce himself to General Epanchin, whose wife was distantly related to him. At the Epanchin home he met the general and his secretary, Ganya, who invited him to become one of his mother's boarders. The prince interested the general, who gave him some money, and he also fascinated the general's wife and three daughters. His lack of sophistication, his naïveté, his frankness, charmed and amused the family. Soon they began to call him "the idiot," half in jest, half in earnest, but he remained on good terms with them.

Ganya, a selfish young man given to all kinds of scheming, wanted to marry the beautiful Aglaya Epanchin, chiefly for her money. At the time he was also involved in an affair with the notorious Natasya, an attractive young woman who lived under the protection of a man she did not love. Extremely emotional and neurotic, Natasya was really innocent of the sins charged against her. Myshkin realized her helplessness and pitied her. At a drinking party one night soon after his arrival, he asked her to marry him, saying that he had received an unexpected inheritance. She refused, declaring that she had no desire to cause his ruin. Instead she went with Rogozhin, who had brought her a hundred thousand roubles.

More than ever, Natasya became the

THE IDIOT by Fyodor Mikhailovich Dostoevski. Published by The Modern Library, Inc.

object of spirited controversy among the Epanchins and their circle. Myshkin alone remained unembittered and always kind-hearted. Ganya and Rogozhin poured out their troubles to him, bared the sordidness and shamelessness of their lives, and swore undying friendship for him. Nevertheless, they distrusted Myshkin and plotted against him. When Natasya left Rogozhin, he swore that he would kill "the idiot" because he was sure that Natasya had fled from him because she really loved Myshkin.

Myshkin then became the victim of an extortion attempt. During a violent, repugnant scene, at which the Epanchins were present, he successfully refuted the charge that he had deprived Rogozhin's supposed illegitimate son of his rightful heritage. Having proved that the individual who sought the money was not the illegitimate son, he then, to the disgust of Mme. Epanchin, offered to give money to the extortionist and to become his friend. Mme. Epanchin considered the prince more of an idiot than ever.

Meanwhile, Aglaya Epanchin fell in love with Myshkin, but she continued to treat him scornfully and at first refused to admit that she was in love with him. When her true feelings at last became apparent, Mme. Epanchin gave reluctant consent to their betrothal and planned an evening party to introduce Myshkin to St. Petersburg society. Worried lest he should commit some social blunder, she and her daughter advised him to sit quietly and to say nothing during the evening. But at the party Mme. Epanchin herself drew out the prince, so that he was soon launched on one of his wild and peculiar conversations. The staid, conservative guests were astounded. In the midst of the discussion he knocked over a huge and priceless vase, then stared at the debris like "an idiot." A few minutes later he fell into an epileptic fit and had to be carried to his home. For several days the Epanchins were cold to him, but Mme. Epanchin finally relented and invited him to

their home once more.

In the meantime Aglaya had been corresponding with Natasya, and a friendship had strangely developed between them. One evening Aglaya asked Myshkin to go with her to see Natasya.

In Natasya's apartment a hectic and turbulent argument developed, so that the two women showed their anger and bitterness against each other. For the first time Aglaya revealed fully her love for Myshkin. During the argument Natasya fainted. When Myshkin rushed to her aid, Aglaya considered herself rejected and angrily left the house. The scene between the two women became a scandal, and the Epanchins barred their home to Myshkin. Natasya agreed to marry him and made preparations for the wedding. But on the day of the wedding, while Myshkin waited at the church, Natasya fled with Rogozhin, still haunted by her own helplessness and his terrible possessiveness.

Myshkin received the news calmly. Although there were many who laughed at "the idiot," there were some who were sorry for him when he attempted to discover Natasya's whereabouts. He left the village where the ceremony was to have been performed and went to the city. There he inquired among Natasya's acquaintances, but nobody knew where she was. Finally he went to Rogozhin's apartment and learned from a porter that Rogozhin had slept there the previous night. Myshkin continued his search, convinced that Rogozhin would kill him if he could. But Rogozhin himself stopped him on the street and took him to the apartment, where Myshkin found Natasya lying on the bed. Rogozhin had killed her.

Filled with compassion for the miserable Rogozhin, Myshkin spent that night with the body of Natasya and her murderer. At daybreak Natasya's worried friends and the police broke into the apartment. Rogozhin confessed to the murder. Myshkin was questioned by the police, but he was not implicated in the crime. He was sent back to the sanitarium in Switzerland, where he was visited, from time to time, by the Epanchin family and other friends. There was little hope that he would ever recover from his epilepsy.

Further Critical Evaluation of the Work:

The Idiot has been faulted for technical imperfections as a novel. Such imperfections do indeed exist. The novel begins well—in fact shows outstanding promise—but as it progresses, the author's control over his material seems to deteriorate. Consequently, the latter part of the novel, despite occasional flashes of brilliance, appears ill-conceived and sloppily written. In all fairness, however, consideration must be given to the circumstances under which Fyodor Dostoevski was working when he wrote *The Idiot*. He was living abroad with his second wife (the first had died in 1864), moving too frequently to put down roots in any one place. During this period, he suffered severe attacks of epilepsy. His first child was born and died hardly three months after birth. He gambled compulsively, was constantly in debt to his publisher for advances on the novel, and felt intermittent guilt about subjecting his wife and child to privation because of his gambling. Shortly after the death of the first child, whom Dostoevski mourned excessively, his wife became pregnant again, adding more worries and responsibilities to Dostoevski's already heavy burden. Under these conditions and demands Dostoevski wrote *The Idiot*. If the novel is technically imperfect, the author is nevertheless entitled to mercy.

The Idiot has also been accused of obscurity. Without a doubt, it has languished in the shadow of its two more renowned siblings, *Crime and Punishment* (1866) and *The Brothers Karamazov* (1879-1880). That kind of obscurity, however, is an equivocation of the term. The obscurity charge leveled at *The Idiot* is really one of impenetrability, the inability of the reader to grasp what is happening in the novel. Much of this confusion is simply a failure not of the novel, but of the Western mind to apprehend the essence of the Russian soul, for *The Idiot* is a quintessentially Russian novel. Its uniqueness—and hence its so-called obscurity—derives from the distinctive qualities of the Russian psyche unfamiliar to Western readers. At least seven such qualities can be identified.

First of all is the concept of Russian brotherhood. It is illustrated, among other places, in Myshkin's return from Switzerland when he is befriended en route by Rogozhin, a complete stranger, and on arrival by the Epanchins. But the concept is not thus limited. Myshkin's enduring reputation as "the idiot" with the Epanchins and others throughout the novel evidences an affectionate alliance or brotherhood often under-appreciated in the West.

Another trait is the unmethodical approach to life. Western people tend to place high value on social ritual and punctuality; however, Russians express themselves spontaneously and observe time schedules only when the schedules do not interfere with the more important business of living. Such a tendency leads to a rather irrational attitude toward handling the necessary trivialities as well as the serious aspects of everyday life. Hence, against all logic and reason, Myshkin proposes marriage to Natasya. Myshkin does not calculate advantages and disadvantages; he simply responds autonomically to what the situation calls for. His impulsive behavior, like the impulsive behavior of many others in the novel, is typically Russian.

The Russian is also compassionate and humble. The Epanchins, with affectionate compassion, refer to Myshkin as "the idiot." Myshkin's own compassion is demonstrated in his impulsive proposal of marriage to Natasya. In fact, Myshkin, throughout the novel, remains kindhearted and compassionate. Likewise, he is humble, just as are—ultimately—Natasya, Rogozhin, Ganya, and the Epanchins.

Religiosity is yet another Russian characteristic manifested in *The Idiot.* This quality is particularly demonstrated in Myshkin's peculiar diatribe at Mme. Epanchin's party when he launches upon a recollection of four conversations which he had concerning the matter of faith. It is evidence of the Russian's unquestioning devotion to Eastern Orthodox Christianity. In fact, Dostoevski even goes so far as to allege that Roman Catholicism and socialism are working conjointly toward imposing authoritarian goals and standards, whereas Eastern Orthodoxy encourages individuality—albeit within a set standard of ethics. This logic can be understood only within the framework of the faithful believer.

The belief in the messianic destiny of Russia adds still another dimension to Dostoevski's view of the Russian soul in *The Idiot.* This belief manifests itself as a sense of honor, which is best displayed when Myshkin goes to Rogozhin's apartment only to find the dead body of Natasya. Myshkin spends the night with Rogozhin, the murderer, and Natasya's corpse—performing his honorable duty. The next morning, Rogozhin confesses to the police that he murdered Natasya. These dutiful observances of honorable behavior are, in the context of the novel, attributed to proper Russian conduct. As such, they are individual contributions to Russia's manifest destiny in fulfillment of her obligation to save the world from perdition.

Closely allied to this Russian mission to save the world is the practice of public confession. This practice, too, is intimately connected with the difference between Roman Catholicism and Eastern Orthodoxy. The former requires whispered revelations to a closeted priest; the latter mandates publicly spoken admission of wrongdoing to the full congregation. Consonantly, Ganya and Rogozhin make "confessions" of misdeeds early in the novel. Other characters as well confess transgressions—as Rogozhin confesses murder to Myshkin—throughout the novel. Everyone, it seems, has some dirty little secret hidden away and, finally, can hide it no longer, "confessing" it to someone else. Such purgation is but another typical Russian trait.

The last essential Russian quality in *The Idiot* is the warping effect of the conflict between humility and pride. On the most literal level, this trait is demonstrated by Rogozhin's vow to kill "the idiot" because Rogozhin is sure that Natasya left him for Myshkin, while, as a consequence, Myshkin becomes an extortion victim for being deluded by the same misapprehensions. On a more sophisticated level, all of the characters in the novel are warped by the conflict between pride and humility. They are, in effect, the double or schizophrenic personalities so typical in Dostoevski's novels. Myshkin, for example, is Dostoevski's penultimate Christ figure as well as the idiot-savant of folklore. Natasya is a sado-masochist, reveling in her exploitation while she revenges it. Other characters follow suit.

These factors make the novel uniquely Russian. Since they differ from conventional Western standards, they make *The Idiot* a novel too dense and too complex for most Western readers; hence, misunderstanding is bound to occur. The novel is, finally, too Russian for the non-Russian reader. It can be appreciated only from the Russian point of view—native or trained.

Joanne G. Kashdan

THE IDLER

Type of work: Periodical essays
Author: Samuel Johnson (1709-1784)
First published: 1758-1760

Joseph Addison and Richard Steele created with their *Tatler* and *Spectator* papers a vogue for the periodical essay that lasted almost to the end of the eighteenth century. One of their greatest successors in this genre was Samuel Johnson, who wrote three series of articles for weekly newspapers, naming them for the *personae* he adopted in each. The *Rambler* essays were published between 1750 and 1752; the *Adventurer,* in 1753 and 1754; and the *Idler,* in the *Universal Chronicle,* in 1758 and 1759.

Throughout his life Johnson lamented his tendency to while away his hours in inactivity, and he must have taken wry pleasure in beginning the third series by assuming the role of one who deliberately devoted his life to useless pastimes. In keeping with his role as the Idler, Johnson tried to keep the tone of these last essays lighter than that of his earlier works. However, he inevitably included some of his characteristic reflections on the burdens of life, commenting on the inevitable disappointments that follow most hopes, on the tendency of friendships to dissolve through suspicion, separation, envy, or competition, and on death and his hopes for immortality.

These serious reflections comprise only a small portion of the *Idler;* more often Johnson comments in an amusing vein on the follies of his age. Even his language is more informal than usual, for he has substituted a flowing colloquial style for the carefully balanced phrases and the Latinate vocabulary of much of his work.

Many of the *Idler* pieces purport to be letters from various readers, and through them Johnson gently satirizes social foibles of the mid-eighteenth century. A merchant, Zachary Treacle, writes to complain that his wife distracts him all day long in his shop, strolling about and asking "a thousand frivolous questions" when she might assist him, leaving the housework to a slatternly maid and spoiling their children. He considers the greatest indignity imposed on him to be their regular Sunday afternoon promenade when he is often forced to carry his child.

Betty Broom, a lady's maid, sends the Idler two letters describing her misfortunes as one who has more education than the world thinks her station in life entitles her. Another mistreated husband, Peter Plenty, complains of a wife who cannot resist sales, with the result that his house is full of unused and useless articles: "the dining room is so crowded with tables, that dinner scarcely can be served; the parlour is decorated with so many piles of china, that I dare not step within the door; at every turn of the stairs I have a clock, and half the windows of the upper floors are darkened, that shelves may be set before them."

Many of the essays are enlivened by briefer portrait-caricatures of familiar types. Tom Tempest and Jack Sneaker are the fanatical Jacobite and Whig, each convinced that the party of the other is the embodiment of all evil. Tempest whispers to his friends that a new monarch will soon replace the Hanoverians whom he despises, while Sneaker devotes his hours to worrying about new Papist conspiracies. Jack Whirler, characterized in another essay, is the man who is perpetually busy, so completely occupied in rushing from one task or engagement to the next that he never has time to accomplish anything. The traveler who finds every step a dangerous adventure is pictured in Will Marvel; he regales his acquaintances with vivid accounts of the perils he barely escaped on journeys that were, in fact, quite uneventful.

One of the most interesting of the portraits, one of Johnson himself, was contributed by his friend Bennet Langton, who submitted to the Idler the journal of a scholar, including the projects he planned to complete in three days and the way his hours actually passed. Distracted by visitors, outings, and new ideas, he made little progress on his proposed works, though sudden inspiration contributed to the creation of other pieces. This sketch fits well with what is known of Johnson, who always had a number of enterprises in hand and completed some of his best essays as diversions from the scholarly labors of his dictionary.

Each of Johnson's volumes of essays included literary criticism. In the Idler he introduces Dick Minim, a young man who, on acquiring an unexpected fortune, set himself up as an arbiter of literary tastes, gathering the bulk of his knowledge in coffee houses and at the theater and picking up a few critical clichés from books he studied when the playhouses were closed. His literary opinions were always those generally accepted. Faced with a new work he inevitably gave an equivocal judgment: "Till he knows the success of a composition, he intrenches himself in general terms; there are some new thoughts and beautiful passages, but there is likewise much which he would have advised the author to expunge." Minim was in his element when he had a pupil to instruct in platitudes, and he had a wide following of those who considered him a paragon of learning.

In several of the later Idler essays Johnson comments on various literary matters, among them biography, language, and the problems of translation. A renowned biographer in his later years, he considered the genre one of the most interesting literary forms, but he points out the difficulty in achieving objectivity and suggests that only in autobiography can a man be seen without the colorings of praise or blame.

In another piece Johnson defends the "use of hard words," noting that especially in specialized subjects precision can only be achieved through "difficult" language. If a man is describing a building he can convey a far clearer picture by using architectural terms than by employing the vocabulary of the layman. On the other hand, Johnson discussed the problems of writing "easy poetry," verse which is clear, simple and unadorned, noting that a colloquial or affected style is often mistaken for the pure one he advocates.

A large number of the Idler essays do not fall into any of the categories outlined above. Johnson seems to have written, usually extemporaneously, on any subject that happened to catch his fancy. Several essays are Oriental tales with moral themes. In others he makes an impassioned plea for the relief of those in the debtors' prison and argues convincingly that the creditors are partially guilty for allowing men to fall into their clutches. He praises the charitable impulses of his time in another paper and commends in particular the work of the charity hospitals. Interspersed among these relatively serious observations are a witty account of the ladies left languishing when the gentlemen go off to war and a mock tribute to the enterprising woman who rode a horse a thousand miles in less than a thousand hours.

Johnson has few compliments for the press of his day. Their treatment of war news is, he says, dull, and sets up a model story in which the events of a battle are carefully spaced out to enlist the readers' interest for a whole week; it is a mistake to put all the available information in the first article, then reiterate it for days afterwards.

In one of the most amusing essays Johnson ridicules the advertising in the papers, scoffing at the large claims made for bed coverings, face creams, and patent medicines: "The vender of the 'Beautifying Fluid' sells a lotion that repels pimples, washes away freckles, smoothes the skin, and plumps the flesh; and yet, with a generous abhorrence of ostentation, confesses, that it will not 'restore the bloom of fifteen to a lady of fifty.' "

The *Idler* reveals many facets of Johnson's talents; he succeeds equally well as a portraitist, a satirist, and a moralist. It is in the last, most familiar and most satisfying guise that Johnson concludes his series. He meditates on the sadness of ending any activity and suggests that all conclusions are little deaths: "An even and unvaried tenour of life always hides from our apprehension the approach of its end. . . . The uncertainty of our duration is impressed commonly by dissimilitude of condition; it is only by finding life changeable that we are reminded of its shortness." Though the *Idler* has been meant as entertainment, Johnson expresses the hope that his readers have come, through reading it, to realize that there approaches "the day in which every work of the hand, and imagination of the heart shall be brought to judgment, and an everlasting futurity shall be determined by the past."

THE IDYLLS OF THE KING

Type of work: Poem
Author: Alfred, Lord Tennyson (1809-1892)
Type of plot: Chivalric romance
Time of plot: Fifth century
Locale: England
First published: Separately, 1859-1885

Principal characters:
KING ARTHUR
QUEEN GUINEVERE
SIR LANCELOT,
GARETH,
GERAINT,
BALIN,
BALAN,
GAWAIN,
SIR GALAHAD,
SIR BORS,
SIR PELLEAS,
SIR PERCIVALE,
SIR MODRED,
SIR TRISTRAM, and
SIR BEDIVERE, Knights of the Round Table
MERLIN, a magician
LYNETTE, who married Gareth
ENID, who married Geraint
VIVIEN, an enchantress
ELAINE, the lily maid of Astolat
ETTARRE, loved by Pelleas and Gawain
ISOLT, of the white hands, Tristram's wife

Critique:

Divided into twelve sections, each symbolic of one month of the year, these poems present to the reader the span of a man's life, extending from the coming of Arthur to his passing. If one cared to search into the symbolism of this long narrative poem, he would find it filled with mystic and spiritual meanings. Although Tennyson's stories of King Arthur and the Knights of the Round Table lack the realism and vitality of Malory's tales, *The Idylls of the King* have a poetic compactness and allegorical significance lacking in the original.

The Stories:

THE COMING OF ARTHUR

Gorloïs and Ygerne had borne one daughter, Bellicent. King Uther overcame Gorloïs in battle and forced the widow to marry him immediately. Shortly afterward King Uther died. Ygerne's son, Arthur, was born at a time when he could have been the son of Gorloïs or the son of Uther born too soon.

The birth of Arthur was shrouded in great mystery. Merlin the magician reared the prince until it was time for him to take over Uther's kingdom and to receive from the Lady of the Lake the magic sword, Excalibur. After the marriage of Arthur and Guinevere, the king and his loyal members of the Round Table, in twelve battles, drove the enemy out of the kingdom.

GARETH AND LYNETTE

Bellicent, Arthur's sister, allowed her youngest son to join his two brothers in King Arthur's court on the condition that Gareth serve as a kitchen knave under the surly directions of Sir Kay the seneschal. When the young boy presented himself to King Arthur, Gareth made the king promise to give him the first quest which came along without revealing his identity. One day Lynette came to the court asking for Sir Lancelot to save her sister from wicked knights who held her captive. King Arthur sent Gareth questing with Lynette, who grumbled disdainfully at the kitchen knave ordered to serve her.

The first knight Gareth overcame was the Morning Star. Lynette still sneered at the knave. After Gareth had defeated another knight, Lynette began to relent. When he conquered a third strong knight, she allowed him to ride at her side. Next Gareth encountered a terrible knight, Death, who proved to be a mere boy forced by his brothers to assume a fierce appearance. Gareth returned to the Round Table victorious and married Lynette.

THE MARRIAGE OF GERAINT and GERAINT AND ENID

Geraint, on a quest for Guinevere, came to the impoverished castle of Earl Yniol and his daughter Enid, a girl whose faded brocades spoke of former wealth and family pride. There Geraint learned that the rejected suitor of Enid had caused the ruin of Yniol. The earl gave Geraint Enid for his wife.

Geraint, fearing that the sin of the queen's love for Lancelot would taint Enid's love, went to his own castle and there idled away the hours in company with his wife until neighbors began to gossip that Geraint had lost his courage. Enid feared to tell her lord about the gossip, and Geraint, observing her strange attitude, decided that she had fallen in love with some knight of the Round Table. One morning, bidding Enid to don her faded brocade gown, Geraint set out with his wife after ordering her not to speak to him. Riding ahead of Geraint, Enid encountered men who would attack her husband, and each time she broke his command by warning him of his danger. After a while Enid was able to prove her love to her suspicious husband. They returned to Camelot, where Guinevere warmly welcomed Enid to the court.

BALIN AND BALAN

Balan left the care of Balin, his mad brother, and went on a mission to quell King Pellam, who had refused to pay his yearly tribute to King Arthur. With his brother gone, Balin was left alone in his gloomy moods. He worshipped the purity of Lancelot and the faithfulness of Guinevere until one day he saw his two idols speaking familiarly in the garden. Disillusioned, Balin fled to the woods. There he met Vivien, a wanton woman of the court, who further poisoned his mind against Lancelot and Guinevere. He left hanging on a tree the shield Guinevere had given him years before. Hearing Balin's mad shrieks among the trees, Balan rushed at Balin, whom he did not recognize without the shield of Guinevere. In the struggle Balin killed Balan and then was crushed by his own horse.

VIVIEN

Vain and coquettish Vivien set out to ensnare the most chivalric man in all the kingdom, King Arthur, but her wiles failed to win the attention of a king whose mind could harbor no evil thoughts. Vivien then turned to Merlin, who she knew possessed a magic spell. She tried to charm the magician with her beauty, pretending to love the ancient, bearded man, but he knew that she was not to be trusted. When she asked him to teach her the spell, he refused. But Vivien was not to be denied. At last, tricked by her beauty, Merlin taught her his magic powers. She enchanted him and caused him to disappear forever, a prisoner in a hollow tree.

LANCELOT AND ELAINE

Lancelot in disguise went to Astolat where he left his shield with Elaine and rode off with her brother Lavaine to the tournaments. Lancelot won the jousts; then, wounded, he fled before anyone could discover who he was. King Arthur sent Gawain to search for the winner of the tournament. Gawain rode to Astolat, where he lingered because he had fallen in love with Elaine. She told him that she loved the knight who had left his shield with her. When Gawain saw the shield, he identified it as that of Lancelot.

Elaine nursed Lancelot back to health in the hope that he would return her love. Recovered, he sadly told her that he could never marry any woman. After he had gone, Elaine became ill and finally died in her grief. Her dying wish was to be put into a boat and sent to Camelot, in her hand a letter to Lancelot.

In Camelot Guinevere coldly rejected Lancelot, for Gawain had told of the affair between Lancelot and Elaine. When the body of Elaine floated to Camelot, King Arthur and Lancelot found the beautiful maiden in her boat, the letter in her hand.

Lancelot authorized a fitting burial for the lily maid. He unhappily lamented his hopeless love for the queen, not knowing that he would die a monk.

THE HOLY GRAIL

One day while Sir Galahad, the youngest and purest of all the knights, sat in Merlin's chair, the Holy Grail descended upon the Round Table in a flash and then was gone. When the knights swore to go on a quest for the Holy Grail, King Arthur gloomily predicted that the search would end in disaster for many of his knights because none was pure enough, save Galahad or Percivale, to see the holy vessel.

To Galahad the Grail appeared in all its splendor. Percivale, who followed him, also saw the holy sign. Sir Bors returned to King Arthur to report that he had viewed the Grail; but Lancelot had seen only a sign of it. Some of the other knights never returned to the Round Table from their perilous quest.

PELLEAS AND ETTARRE

Pelleas had given Ettarre a trophy he had won in a tournament, but she, scorning the young knight, barred him from her court. Gawain, meeting Pelleas in his despair, offered to help him. After telling the knight to hide in the forest, Gawain went to Ettarre and told her

he had killed Pelleas. As the days passed, Pelleas became impatient. One night, stealing into the castle, he found Gawain and Ettarre sleeping together and placed his naked sword across the throats of the sleeping lovers. Then in a mad rage he rode through the forest until he met Percivale, who accidentally revealed to Pelleas the scandal about Lancelot and Guinevere. Disillusioned, the young knight returned to the Round Table, where his rude manner to the queen foreshadowed evil to Lancelot and Guinevere. Sir Modred saw that the ruin of the Round Table was near at hand.

THE LAST TOURNAMENT

To a tournament at Camelot came Tristram, who had left his bride, Isolt of the white hands. Her name was the same as that of his beloved, Isolt, the wife of King Mark of Cornwall. Lancelot, laboring under the guilt of his sinful love for Guinevere, decided to fight with the similarly guilty Tristram, who won the tournament. Tristram then went to Isolt of Cornwall. King Mark was away on a hunting trip. He returned unexpectedly, found the lovers together, and killed Tristram.

In the north a knight rebelled against King Arthur's rule and charged that the Round Table was a thing of falseness and guilt where harlots and adulterers lived disguised as ladies and knights. King Arthur rode to quell the revolt and the guilty man was killed; but King Arthur was heavy in heart when he returned to Camelot.

GUINEVERE

Fearing exposure of her love for Lancelot, Guinevere asked him to leave Camelot. On the night of their farewell Modred trapped the lovers together, and Guinevere, feeling that she was shamed forever, went to Almesbury and took refuge in a nunnery. There she recalled how Lancelot had brought her from her father's home to marry Arthur, how she had thought Arthur cold and had fallen in love with the courtly, gay Lancelot.

King Arthur went to Almesbury. To

Guinevere he spoke of his pride in the marvelous truths which the Round Table had upheld, and which Guinevere had inspired. Now all was lost, but he forgave Guinevere before he went off to fight against Modred and his traitor knights.

Filled with remorse, Guinevere asked the nuns to accept her in their order. There she gave her services until they made her abbess. After three years in that rank she died.

THE PASSING OF ARTHUR

In Modred's revolt King Arthur was wounded. As he lay dying he told Sir Bedivere to cast the sword Excalibur into the lake. When Bedivere finally brought to King Arthur the tale that amid flashing and strange sights an arm reached out from the lake to receive the sword, King Arthur knew that Bedivere had truly sent Excalibur back to the Lady of the Lake. Next King Arthur told Bedivere to carry him to the shore. There three maidens came in a barge to take King Arthur away. As Bedivere stood weeping, King Arthur assured him that the old order of the Round Table must pass to give way to something new.

So King Arthur passed, in the manner of his legendary beginning, back across the waters to Avalon, but many men believed that some day he would return to his people in their need. Bedivere watched on the shore until the wintry dawn broke bringing a new year.

Further Critical Evaluation of the Work:

As England's poet laureate from 1850 until his death in 1892, Alfred Lord Tennyson spoke to a complex and paradoxical age. His widely varied poetry made the author of *Idylls of the King* the most representative poet of the Victorian age. Writing sometimes with the optimism of his contemporary Robert Browning, sometimes with the brooding melancholy of Matthew Arnold, Tennyson wrote of the demands of love and duty, of the conflict between the public and private selves.

Tennyson's own life, particularly the early days, was one of tension and conflict. Born in 1809, he began writing poetry at an early age, stimulated perhaps by his wide reading and by a desire to escape the morbid atmosphere of his home. His father, the rector of Somersby, was a man of erratic behavior, sometimes kind, but more often melancholy and harsh toward his family. Even after Tennyson left home his life was not easy; he suffered from poverty, the lack of public recognition of his poetry, and the death of his friend, Arthur Hallam—events which must be at least partially responsible for the introspective quality of much of the early poetry. The last section of *Idylls of the King*, "Morte d'Arthur," was written during this period of his life.

But most of the poem was written after 1850. This is the great year of Tennyson's life, when *In Memoriam* was published and he was made poet laureate. With public recognition came financial security, and the opportunity to marry Emily Sellwood, his fiancée of fourteen years. But if the main part of *Idylls of the King* took shape after the bitter conflicts (at least the external ones) were past, many of the themes of the early poetry recur in the mature work. Contrasting motifs that surface in the early lyrics (the passive acceptance of the sensual life in "The Lotus-Eaters," the ultimate rejection of that subjective world in "Palace of Art") come together in many of the later poems, including *Idylls of the King*. In "The Coming of Arthur," for example, the young king sees Guinevere, falls in love with her, but rides on to duty and to battle.

The decision and the conflict seem typically Victorian. The years 1837 to 1901 (Victoria's reign ends neatly just as the new century begins) saw change and reform in England. The Chartist Movement of the 1840's and the various Reform Bills (in 1867, 1884, 1885) were real if not entirely effectual attempts to right the wrongs of a world irreparably altered by the Industrial Revolution. For many Victorians, and certainly for Tennyson, a sense of duty was as real and immediate a part of life as love and pleasure.

But there was often a paradoxically introspective quality about the literature of this age of social action. New developments in science and their religious and philosophical implications turned writers away from the outer world and inward to the self as they tried to discover through meditation and reflection the values and the God that, in J. Hillis Miller's sense of the word, seemed to be "disappearing." Tennyson read widely in the sciences, in astronomy and geology, while he was a student at Cambridge. He knew Lyell's *Principles of Geology,* an unsettling precursor of Darwin and the Theory of Evolution. Undoubtedly this reading reinforced his early predilection for subjectivity—an attitude that would always be at war with the demands of the public role of poet laureate.

A problem that arises when analyzing these tensions in *Idylls of the King* is that Tennyson's epic (like the earlier *In Memoriam*) was written over a long period of time. The question must be asked: are the twelve idylls separate, fragmentary, or is there a unifying theme—or set of themes? Taken from a chronological point of view the problem is even more difficult here than in *In Memoriam,* which was written over a period of about sixteen years. Although "The Coming of Arthur" was conceived in 1833, the first idylls (four in number) were not completed and published until 1859; expanded versions followed in 1869, 1871, and 1872. The complete work did not appear until 1885, seven years before the poet's death. Thus the reader is dealing with a poem that was written over a period of fifty years, begun when the poet was twenty-four and finished when he was seventy-four.

There is, of course, one obvious unifying theme—the Arthurian legend which Tennyson derived mainly from Malory's *Morte d'Arthur.* But just as *In Memoriam* transcends its original theme (Tennyson's sense of personal loss at the death of Hallam), *Idylls of the King* becomes more than a re-telling of an ancient romance. Written in the Victorian spirit, the poem speaks not only of the mystique of the Round Table, but of man in and out of society, of what was and what might have been.

The plot centers not on one man, but on a vision of the better world that Arthur and his good knights would create. Tennyson's tale is not of a man who would be king, but of a man who must be king—of a society that is destined to be born, come to fruition, and finally to die because of perfidy from within.

A number of the idylls are concerned with the sharp contrast between the high ideal and the actuality. In "Vivien" Merlin is enticed by the vixenish Vivien into giving up a magic formula known to the magician alone. Merlin sometimes sees Vivien without illusion, but at other times allows himself to be ensnared by her false but charming façade. Even the wise Merlin must be reminded that the world is not always as it seems, that in life exists the potentiality of death, in love the possibility of deceit, and in all idealistic endeavors the opportunity for treachery.

This knowledge of the good in evil, the evil in good, appears throughout the poem. The search for the grail, for instance, is a highly idealistic mission. Through the quest for the cup from which Christ drank and the various tests of character to determine whether he would succeed, the quester is strengthened and purified; he returns a better knight. But the vision can only come to a few; despite the noble motives that initiate the adventure, the end result is the weakening of Cameliard because of the absence of her leaders.

Ultimately, it is not the search for the grail, but Guinevere's guilty love for Lancelot that becomes the catalyst for Cameliard's destruction. But it is only one of a flood of incidents. Many events in the poem lead to the defeat of the Round Table; many perfidies—Tristan's, Gawain's, Modred's—destroy the ideal society. Like the period in which it was written, *Idylls of the King* cannot be interpreted simplistically. The problem it examines is perhaps the basic modern and Victorian dilemma: what is to become of society, and more importantly, what is to become of man, destined to exist simultaneously within himself and among others.

Alice Guise

IF WINTER COMES

Type of work: Novel
Author: A. S. M. Hutchinson (1879-1971)
Type of plot: Social criticism
Time of plot: 1912-1919
Locale: Southern England
First published: 1920

> *Principal characters:*
> MARK SABRE, an idealist
> MABEL SABRE, his wife
> LADY NONA TYBAR, a friend
> MR. FORTUNE, Mark's employer
> MR. TWYNING, a business associate
> HAROLD TWYNING, Twyning's son
> EFFIE BRIGHT, Sabre's friend

Critique:

The very least that can be said about *If Winter Comes* is that it is a beautiful and heart-warming novel. It is the story of a man who loved all humanity, but who was persecuted and betrayed by those who did not understand him. Although the book makes no pretensions to great literature, it is a perennial favorite among all classes of readers.

The Story:

Most of his friends thought Mark Sabre a queer sort, in spite of the normal life he led. He was married to a girl of his own class and he worked in the very respectable firm of Fortune, East, and Sabre, suppliers for the best churches and schools in England. It was his attitude toward life that seemed queer. He had no definite convictions about anything, and he could always see both sides of any controversy. He hated the restrictions that convention placed on people, but at the same time he believed that conventions were based on sound principles. Mabel Sabre, one of the most conventional women alive, was totally unable to understand anything her husband tried to discuss with her.

The only person who understood him well was Lady Nona Tybar, with whom Sabre had once been in love. Nona's husband, Lord Tybar, was a charming man, but completely without moral principles. When he flaunted other women in Nona's face, she turned to Sabre for comfort in his friendship, but Mabel, Sabre's wife, could not understand their friendship any better than she could understand anything else about her husband. After five years of marriage Mabel and Sabre were living almost as strangers under one roof. Mark Sabre's employer, Mr. Fortune, and his business associate Mr. Twyning, despised him because they did not understand him, and so Sabre felt that he lived only as he bicycled between his home and his office, for then he could know himself as he really was. Sabre felt that there was a mystery to life which he could unlock if he found the right key. And his life was almost dedicated to finding that key.

In addition to Nona, Sabre had three friends with whom he liked to spend his time. They were his neighbors, Mr. Fargus and old Mrs. Perch and her son. When the war came, young Perch wanted to enlist, but he could not leave his invalid mother alone. Sabre knew that Effie Bright, daughter of an employee at his office, wanted a position as a companion, and he arranged to have her stay with Mrs. Perch after her son went to the army. Young Perch was killed, and when his mother received the news she died too. Shortly after the old lady's death, Sabre himself joined the army. Because Mabel did not want to stay alone, she employed Effie to stay with her. However, she treated Effie as a servant.

Lord Tybar was a hero in the war, winning the Victoria Cross before he was killed. Nona went to France after her husband's death and drove an ambulance for the rest of the war years. When Sabre came home on leave, Mabel discharged Effie. She said that the girl was impertinent and unreliable.

Late in 1917, Sabre was wounded and sent home to stay. Mabel took no more interest in him than she had before, until the day she received a letter from Effie. Effie begged to come back to the Sabres. She now had an illegitimate child and no one, including her father, would take her in. Mabel was righteously angry at the proposal, and when Sabre tried to defend the girl she began to suspect that he might have a reason to help Effie. Before they reached a decision Effie, having no other place to go, arrived with her baby. When Sabre insisted that she stay, Mabel left, declaring she would not return until the girl and her baby had gone. Mr. Fortune and Mr. Twyning, who had been made a partner in the firm, would not allow Sabre to return to the firm unless he sent Effie away. They feared scandal would hurt their business. But Sabre would not be forced to do what he felt would be an injustice and a sin. For he had found the key to the puzzle; he knew that the solution to the mystery of the world is simply that God is love. Love for one's fellow men could set the world right again. He loved Effie as he loved all mankind, as he loved even his wife and the others who hated him.

But keeping Effie in the face of criticism brought only disaster to him and to the girl. Mabel sued for divorce on grounds of adultery, naming Effie. Sabre was away from his home when the papers were served, and before he could quite comprehend that his wife could believe such a foul thing he was arrested. Effie had taken poison, first killing her baby. She had learned of Mabel's suit and thought she could help Sabre best by committing suicide. Sabre's enemies were not satisfied. He was taken to court and accused of being responsible for her death. Effie's father, Mabel, and Mr. Twyning all claimed that he was the father of Effie's baby and that he had bought the poison which she drank. It was proved that he could have been the father of the child. Only one voice was raised in his defense. Nona returned from France and appeared at the trial. But there was little she could do.

The verdict made Sabre responsible for Effie's suicide. Sabre went home, but he would not allow Nona to go with him. In his house he found a letter from Effie. In it she told him that she was taking her life and that of her baby because she had caused him so much trouble. She also named the father of her baby; it was Harold Twyning, the son of Sabre's enemy. The boy had been afraid of his father's anger and had not claimed his responsibility.

Enraged, Sabre went to his old office prepared to kill Mr. Twyning. But when he reached the office, he learned that his enemy had just received word of Harold's death in battle. Sabre dropped Effie's letter in the fire and offered his sympathy to the man mainly responsible for ruining him. Then he went into his old office and collapsed from a cerebral hemorrhage. Nona found him there and took him home. For many months he could remember nothing that had happened to him, but gradually he began to piece together the sordid, tragic story. He learned that Mabel had secured her divorce and remarried. He learned to know Nona again, but he asked her to go away because he had accepted disgrace rather than reveal the story of Effie's letter. Nona refused to leave him, and after a year they were married. Sabre knew then that he had really found the key to the mystery of existence in that dark season of life before winter gives way to spring.

Further Critical Evaluation of the Work:

A. S. M. Hutchinson's *If Winter Comes* is a prime example of a novel which cannot be called universal in its appeal, yet which has remained a minor classic among twentieth century British and American readers. The simplicity of its theme, man's discovery of universal love and forgiveness, coupled with the overly complex plot puts it more on the level of a daytime television serial than a great work of literature. However, as one critic has put it, Hutchinson's works are second rate, but good second rate, which is a distinction in itself.

One of the principal reasons why *If Winter Comes* is not considered first rate is that it plays entirely too much on the audience's emotions. The tragedies which befall the principal characters border on the maudlin. The reader may become very engrossed in the plot, but he does so on an emotional rather than an intellectual level. It is difficult to relate the bizarre turns of plot to real life.

The best aspect of the novel is the characterization of Mark Sabre, a simple man who appears too complex to his acquaintances because he takes a different view of life from their own. He, like many people, desperately tries to find an uncomplicated existence but is prevented from doing so by the complexities of life. In many respects the characterization of Mark is drawn from Hutchinson's own personality. Although he had a great deal of success from his literary career during his own lifetime, he was somewhat of a recluse and desired to live a very simple, peaceful life, devoid of notoriety.

Aside from the picture of Mark Sabre, the descriptions of life and manners during the era of World War I in the English town are valuable to students of social history. By analyzing situations and the moralistic reactions of the townspeople, an interesting picture of English country life emerges; although chronologically removed from the Victorian era, the people in the novel are basically as staid and unrelenting as their nineteenth century counterparts.

IGNATIUS HIS CONCLAVE

Type of work: Theological satire
Author: John Donne (1572-1631)
First published: 1611

In *Ignatius His Conclave,* the Anglican divine John Donne wrote a satire that is at times fanciful, at times devastating, and on occasion screamingly vindictive against the Jesuits. In the final scene Ignatius Loyola, Spanish founder of the Society of Jesus, seats himself next to Lucifer in Hell. *Ignatius His Conclave* appeared in both Latin and an English "translation." A foreword purported to be by the printer but obviously by Donne states that the author was unwilling to have the book published but finally permitted the printer, who cites the examples of Erasmus and Luther, to publish it.

Intending to annihilate the Jesuits with satire, Donne allows his wit and invention to be overpowered by venom. Ignatius' lengthy oration listing the vices of the Popes becomes tedious. Even tedium, however, cannot darken the flashes of Donne's imagination which dart throughout the satire. The comments of his "disembodied soul" are almost always delightful. His awareness of Galileo's discovery of the telescope made public only a year before this satire was written and his use of the Copernican cosmography set Donne in advance of Milton, who preferred to follow Ptolemy. His conquest of space and awareness of "other worlds" on stars make him sound contemporary. The upside down standards in Hell in which vice becomes virtue foreshadow Fielding.

Donne says that his "little wandring sportful Soule" went traveling through the universe while he lay in an "extasie." He prefers to be silent concerning the Heavens rather "than to do Galileo wrong by speaking of it, who of late hath summoned the other worlds, the Stars to come neerer to him and give him an account of themselves." He "saw all the rooms of Hell open to my sight." In the most remote room, he finds Pope Boniface III and Mahomet contending about the highest room in the secret place of Hell reserved for the greatest innovators. Boniface glories in having expelled an old religion and Mahomet in bringing in a new. Donne thinks that Mahomet has no chance of winning because he attributed something to the Old Testament and his followers live in "barren unanimity." Boniface has a better chance because he had not only ignored but destroyed the policy of the State of Israel established in the Old Testament and his successors in the several orders "have ever been fruitful in bringing forth new sinnes, new pardons, and idolatries and King-killings."

As Donne's soul stands listening, pretenders to the eminence of innovator ask admission. The first is Copernicus, whom Donne is surprised to see until he remembers that the Papists have extended heresy to include almost everything. Copernicus says that, pitying Lucifer thrust into the center of the earth, he raised him and his prison the earth up into the heavens so that God no longer enjoys his revenge on him. He has "turned the whole frame of the world" and is "thereby, almost a new Creator."

Lucifer is in a quandary. He thinks that to deny Copernicus admission would be unjust but to admit one of his ambitions and undertakings is dangerous. Ignatius Loyola, who had subtly worked his way up to the Devil's chair, perceives this perplexity. Although, says Donne, Ignatius in life was ignorant and had never heard of either Ptolemy or Copernicus and might have thought that Almagest, Zenith, and Nadir were saints' names and "fit to bee put in the Litanie, and *Ora pro nobis* joyned to them," he had learned a great deal in Hell from the Jesuits arriving there daily. Ignatius asks

Copernicus if he has invented anything which benefits Lucifer. Ignatius thinks not. He also says that Copernicus' findings may be true. Ignatius thinks that Clavius, who designed the Gregorian calendar and denied Copernicus and "the truth which at that time, was creeping into every mans minde," better deserves admission. The new Calendar has "egregiously troubled" both heaven and earth. The saints no longer know when their days are. St. Stephen and John the Baptist have to be awakened ten days sooner so that they can come down to the places where their relics are preserved and work miracles. "Let, therefore, this little Mathematitian (dread Emperour) withdraw himselfe to his owne company." If the Pope should decree that the earth does not move and that an anathema shall be inflicted on all that hold with Copernicus, then he and his followers "may have the dignity of this place." Copernicus stands as still "as he thinks the sun."

When the next pretender says that he is "Philippus Aureolus Theophrastus Paracelsus Bombast of Hohenheim," Lucifer trembles, thinking this a new exorcism, perhaps the first verse of St. John taken out of the Welsh or Irish Bible. When he understands that the words are the name of a newcomer, he recovers and asks what the new arrival has to say to the Great Emperor Sathan, Lucifer, Belzebub, Leviathan, Abaddon. Paracelsus (a German physician and alchemist, 1493-1541) asks to be admitted because his experiments and medicines have killed many while assuring them that their diseases, especially the pox, were curable. Thinking themselves in no danger, these ill people persevered in licentiousness. Also, Paracelsus made poison tasteless.

Ignatius asks why Paracelsus should be favored when the Jesuits, though untrained, practice medicine? He tells Lucifer that men like Paracelsus tamper with metals belonging to Lucifer. Why should these metals be used to cure disease when they could more fittingly be given as tribute to Lucifer's brother and colleague, the Pope? Paracelsus will have to be content to govern in chief that "Legion of homicide-phisitians, and of Princes which shall be made away by poyson in the midst of their sins, and of woemen tempting by paintings and face-physicke." Paracelsus accepts this decision.

Machiavelli decides to outwit Ignatius, who is making all the judgments. Instead of addressing Lucifer, Machiavelli speaks to Ignatius as next after Lucifer, his "beloved son." He intends to make Lucifer feel that Ignatius threatens his authority. Machiavelli says that Ignatius' sons have brought equivocation into the world. This they learned from "The secretest Records of Hell itselfe: that is out of the minds of Lucifer, the Pope, and Ignatius (persons truly equivocal) [who] have raised the life againe the language of the tower of Babel, so long concealed and brought us againe from understanding one another." Compared to the achievements of the Jesuits, his efforts, Machiavelli says, seem childish; yet he has provided the Jesuits with an alphabet and certain elements and was a schoolmaster to them. He says that he taught not only the prince how to possess a free commonwealth through perfidy and dissembling of religion but also the people under his oppression how to conspire and remove a tyrant "so that from both sides, both from Prince and People, I brought in an abundant harvest, and a noble increase to this kingdom."

Moved by his oration, Lucifer feels that he is bound to reward Machiavelli. Aware of Ignatius' ambition, he thinks Machiavelli a fit "instrument to oppose against him." However, Ignatius, more subtle than the Devil, throws himself at his feet and adores him. Finally, getting control of his voice, Ignatius charged that this "obscure Florentine" has transgressed against Lucifer, the Pope, and the Order of the Jesuits. He says that Machiavelli flatters Lucifer in order to trap him. Machiavelli, he says, in life did not even believe in the Devil, thinking that all his inventions came from his own wit. He has belittled the Popes by attributing to them the sins of common men when, actually, their sins were so enormous and unusual that most men would never have thought of them. He gives a long catalogue of the sins of the Popes, ranging from granting indulgences for twenty thousand years for preposterous sins, to Popes who were guilty of all licentiousness and aberration, and finally to transferring empires, ruining kingdoms, and deposing kings. Also, he says, Machiavelli had said that the Pope is the prime mover of evil and so had bypassed the Devil himself. There is nothing in Machiavelli's commentary which might be of use to the Church. Men knew how to lie long before Machiavelli. After a long discourse on the "reforms" in the Devil's religion comparable to the reformation in the Church, Ignatius concludes, "In all times there have been Friers which have far exceeded Machiavel."

Machiavelli, at last, vanishes. Donne says, "Truely, I thought this Oration of Ignatius overlong, and I began to thinke of my body which I had so long abandoned, lest it should putrefy, or grow mouldy, or bee buried."

When Lucifer decides to withdraw to his room and admit none but Ignatius, he is surrounded by a whole army of souls begging for admission. Among them is Christopher Columbus "who having found all waies in the earth and sea open to him did not feare any difficulty in Helle." Ignatius sees that Columbus and all the rest are turned away to lower regions. Lucifer, fearing for his authority, decides to make one decision of his own, to admit Philip Nerius (Saint Philip, Filippo Nero, 1515-1595, Italian priest, founder of Congregation of the Oratory). After a long debate with Ignatius about Nerius, Lucifer yields when he sees that Ignatius has given a sign and all his Jesuits are ready to support him. The English legion, he notes, is fiercer than the rest.

Seeing no way to leave out Ignatius, Lucifer tells him that he cannot divide his kingdom with him nor can Ignatius inherit it because Lucifer cannot die. However, he will write to the Bishop of Rome who will have Galileo draw the moon like a boat closer to the earth. All the Jesuits will cross to the moon, where they can easily unite and reconcile the "Lunatique Church" to the Roman Church. After the Jesuits have been on the moon a little while, there will grow naturally a Hell over which Ignatius may have dominion. He may even advance to the other stars, "which are also thought to be worlds." Lucifer tells Ignatius that he may "beget and propagate many Hells, and enlarge your empire, and so come nearer unto the high seat which I left at first."

A false rumor reaches Hell that the Pope has canonized Ignatius. Ignatius turns to find the seat next to Lucifer taken by Pope Boniface. Lucifer, afraid of losing his seat to Ignatius, helps him hurl Boniface from this eminence.

Donne's spirit returns to his body. He says that after seeing a Jesuit turn the Pope out of his chair in Hell, he suspects that the Jesuits will try as much in Rome.

THE ILIAD

Type of work: Poem
Author: Homer (c. Ninth century B.C.)
Type of plot: Heroic epic
Time of plot: Trojan War
Locale: Troy
First transcribed: Sixth century B. C.

Principal characters:
PRIAM, King of Troy
HECTOR, a Trojan warrior, Priam's son
HELEN OF TROY
PARIS, Hector's brother and Helen's lover
MENELAUS, Helen's husband
AGAMEMNON, Menelaus' brother
ACHILLES, a Greek warrior
PATROCLUS, Achilles' friend

Critique:

Homer has been hailed as the father of all poetry, and the *Iliad* has survived as a masterpiece for all time. The *Iliad*, within a three-day period of the Trojan wars, tells the story of the wrath of Achilles against King Agamemnon. The battle episodes reveal the true characters of the warriors, their strength and their weaknesses. These figures step out of unrecorded history as human beings, not of one era, but of all eras and for all time.

The Story:

The Greeks were camped outside the walls of Troy, in the tenth year of their siege on that city. Agamemnon, king of the Achaians, wanted the maid, Briseis, for his own, but she was possessed by Achilles, the son of Zeus. When Achilles was forced to give up the maid, he withdrew angrily from the battle and returned to his ship. But he won from Zeus the promise that the wrong which he was enduring would be revenged on Agamemnon.

That evening Zeus sent a messenger to the Greek king to convey to him in a dream an order to rise and marshal his Achaian forces against the walls of Troy. When the king awoke, he called all his warriors to him and ordered them to prepare for battle. All night long the men armed themselves in battle array, making ready their horses and their ships. The gods appeared on earth in the disguise of warriors, some siding with the Greeks, some hastening to warn the Trojans. With the army mustered, Agamemnon began the march from the camp to the walls of the city, while all the country around was set on fire. Only Achilles and his men remained behind, determined not to fight on the side of Agamemnon.

The Trojan army came from the gates of the city ready to combat the Greeks. Then Paris, son of King Priam and Helen's lover, stood out from the ranks and suggested that he and Menelaus settle the battle in a fight between them, the winner to take Helen and all her possessions, and friendship to be declared between the warring nations. Menelaus agreed to these words of his rival, and before the warriors of both sides, and under the eyes of Helen, who had been summoned to witness the scene from the walls of Troy, he and Paris began to battle. Menelaus was the mightier warrior. As he was about to pierce his enemy, the goddess Aphrodite, who loved Paris, swooped down from the air and carried him off to his chamber. She summoned Helen there to minister to her wounded lord. Then the victory was declared for Menelaus.

In the heavens the gods who favored the Trojans were much disturbed by this decision. Athena appeared on earth to

Trojan Pandarus and told him to seek out Menelaus and kill him. He shot an arrow at the unsuspecting king, but the goddess watching over Menelaus deflected the arrow so that it only wounded him. When Agamemnon saw that treacherous deed, he revoked his vows of peace and exhorted the Greeks once more to battle. Many Trojans and many Greeks lost their lives that day, because of the foolhardiness of Pandarus.

Meanwhile Hector, son of King Priam, had returned to the city to bid farewell to Andromache, his wife, and to his child, for he feared he might not return from that day's battle. He rebuked Paris for remaining in his chambers with Helen when his countrymen were dying because of his misdeeds. While Paris made ready for battle, Hector said goodbye to Andromache, prophesying that Troy would be defeated, himself killed, and Andromache taken captive. Then Paris joined him and they went together into the battle.

When evening came the Greeks and the Trojans retired to their camps. Agamemnon instructed his men to build a huge bulwark around the camp and in front of the ships, for fear the enemy would press their attack too close. Zeus then remembered his promise to Achilles to avenge the wrong done to him by Agamemnon. He summoned all the gods and forbade them to take part in the war. The victory was to go to the Trojans.

The next day Hector and the Trojans swept through the fields slaughtering the Greeks. Hera, the wife of Zeus, and many of the other goddesses could not be content to watch the defeat of their mortal friends. But when they attempted to intervene, Zeus sent down his messengers to warn them to desist.

Fearing his armies would be destroyed before Achilles would relent, Agamemnon sent Odysseus to Achilles and begged the hero to accept gifts and be pacified. But Achilles, still wrathful, threatened to sail for home at the break of day. Agamemnon was troubled by the proud refusal of Achilles. That night he stole to the camp of the wise man, Nestor, to ask his help in a plan to defeat the Trojans. Nestor told him to awaken all the great warriors and summon them to a council. It was decided that two warriors should steal into the Trojan camp to determine its strength and numbers. Diomedes and Odysseus volunteered. As they crept toward the camp, they captured and killed a Trojan spy. Then they themselves stole into the camp of the enemy, spied upon it, and as they left, took with them the horses of one of the kings.

The next day the Trojans pressed hard upon the Greeks with great slaughter. Both Diomedes and Odysseus were wounded and many warriors killed. Achilles watched the battle from his ship but made no move to take part in it. He sent his friend Patroclus to Nestor to learn how many had been wounded. The old man sent back a despairing answer, pleading that Achilles give up his anger and help his fellow Greeks. At last the Trojans broke through the walls of the enemy, and Hector was foremost in an attack upon the ships.

Meanwhile many of the gods plotted to aid the Greeks. Hera lulled Zeus to sleep, and Poseidon urged Agamemnon to resist the onrush of the Trojans. In the battle that day Hector was wounded by Aias, but as the Greeks were about to seize him and bear his body away the bravest of the Trojans surrounded their hero and covered him with their shields until he could be carried to safety.

When Zeus awakened and saw what had happened, his wrath was terrible, and he ordered Apollo to restore Hector to health. Once again the walls were breached and the Trojans stormed toward the ships, eager to fire them. Zeus inspired the Trojans with courage and weakened the Greeks with fear. But he determined that after the ships were set afire he would no longer aid the Trojans but would allow the Greeks to have the final victory.

Patroclus went to his friend Achilles

and again pleaded with him to return to the fight. Achilles, still angry, refused. Then Patroclus begged that he be allowed to wear the armor of Achilles so that the Greeks would believe their hero fought with them, and Achilles consented. Patroclus charged into the fight and fought bravely at the gates of the city. But there Hector mortally wounded Patroclus and stripped from his body the armor of Achilles.

All that day the battle raged over the body of Patroclus. Then a messenger carried to Achilles word of his friend's death. His sorrow was terrible, but he could not go unarmed into the fray to rescue the body of Patroclus.

The next morning his goddess mother, Thetis, brought him a new suit of armor from the forge of Hephaestus. Then Achilles decked himself in the glittering armor which the lame god of fire had prepared for him and strode forth to the beach. There he and Agamemnon were reconciled before the assembly of the Greeks, and he went out to battle with them. The whole plain was filled with men and horses, battling one another. Achilles in his vengeance pushed back the enemy to the banks of the River Xanthus, and so many were the bodies of the Trojans choking the river that at length the god of the river spoke to Achilles, ordering him to cease throwing their bodies into his waters. Proud Achilles mocked him and sprang into

the river to fight with the god. Feeling himself overpowered, he struggled out upon the banks, but still the wrathful god pursued him. Achilles then called on his mother to help him, and Thetis, with the aid of Hephaestus, quickly subdued the angry river god.

As Achilles drew near the walls of Troy, Hector girded on his armor. Amid the wailing of all the Trojan women he came from the gates to meet the Greek warrior. Not standing to meet Achilles in combat, he fled three times around the city walls before he turned to face Achilles' fatal spear. Then Achilles bound Hector's body to his chariot and dragged it to the ships, a prey for dogs and vultures.

In the Trojan city there was great grief for the dead hero. The aged King Priam resolved to drive in a chariot to the camp of Achilles and beg that the body of his son Hector be returned to him. The gods, too, asked Achilles to curb his wrath and restore the Trojan warrior to his own people, and so Achilles received King Priam with respect, granted his request, and agreed to a twelve-day truce that both sides might properly bury and mourn their dead. Achilles mourned for Patroclus as the body of his friend was laid upon the blazing funeral pyre. In the city the body of mighty Hector was also burned and his bones were buried beneath a great mound in the stricken city.

Further Critical Evaluation of the Work:

The earliest extant work of European literature, Homer's epic poem, the *Iliad,* is also one of the most enduring creations of Western culture. Of the author, or possibly authors, we know nothing for certain. Tradition says that Homer was a Greek of Asia Minor. Herodotus surmised that Homer lived in the ninth century B.C., which seems reasonable in the light of modern scholarship and archaeology. The poet drew on a large body of legend about the seige of Troy, material with which his audience was familiar, and which had been part of a bardic tradition. Homer himself may not have transcribed the two epics attributed to him, but it is probable that he gave the poems their present shape.

The *Iliad* was originally intended to be recited or chanted, rather than read. Its poetic style is vivid, taut, simple, direct, full of repeated epithets and elaborate visual similes. The treatment is serious and dignified throughout, and the total effect is one of grandeur. With Homer we are clearly in the presence of a great poet.

His greatness also reveals itself in the action of the *Iliad,* where, within the scope of a few weeks in the tenth year of the seige of Troy, Homer gives the impression of covering the whole scope of the war by a few deft incidents. The appearance of Helen on the walls of Troy forcibly reminds the reader that she was the cause of the war. The catalogue of ships and warriors calls to mind the first arrival of the Greek army at Troy. The duel between Paris and Menelaus would properly have come in the first years of the war, but its placement in the poem suggests the breakdown of diplomacy which leads to the bloodbath of fighting. And Hector's forebodings of his own death and of the fall of Troy as he talks to his wife, not to mention his dying forecast of Achilles' death, all point to the future of the war and its conclusion. Homer thus gives the rather narrow scope of the poem's immediate action much greater breadth.

However, the *Iliad* is not a mere chronicle of events in the Trojan War. It deals with one specific, and crucial, set of sequences of the war: the quarrel of Achilles with his commander, Agamemnon; Achilles' withdrawal from the war; the fiighting in his absence; Agamemnon's futile attempt to conciliate Achilles; the Trojan victories; Patroclus' intervention and death at Hector's hands; Achilles' re-entry to the war to avenge his friend's murder; the death of Hector; and Priam's ransom of Hector's body from Achilles. The poem has a classical structure, with a beginning, middle, and end.

This sequence is important in its effect on the war as a whole for two reasons. Without Achilles, the ablest fighter, the Greeks are demoralized even though they have many powerful warriors. It is plain that Achilles will die before Troy is taken, so the Greeks will have to capture Troy by other means than force in his absence. The second reason is that the climax of the poem, the killing of Hector, prefigures the fall of Troy, for as long as Hector remained alive the Greeks were unable to make much headway against the Trojans.

Achilles is the precursor of the tragic hero according to Aristotle's definition. Young, handsome, noble, courageous, eloquent, generous, and of unsurpassed prowess, his tragic flaw lies in the savage intensity of his emotions. He knows he will die young. In fact, he has chosen to die at Troy, and thereby win a lasting reputation, rather than to grow old peacefully. It is precisely his pride, his supreme skill in warfare, and his lust for future glory that makes him so ferocious when he is crossed. He has a hard time restraining himself from killing Agamemnon, and a harder time bearing Agamemnon's insult. He puts pride before loyalty when his Greek comrades are being overrun.

And only when the war touches him personally, after he has allowed his friend Patroclus to enter the combat and be slain, does he come to terms with Agamemnon. Then his rage against the Trojans and Hector consumes him, and he is merciless in his vengeance, slaughtering Trojans by scores, gloating over Hector's corpse and abusing it, and sacrificing twelve Trojan nobles on Patroclus' funeral pyre. His humanity is restored in the end when, at Zeus' command, he allows old King Priam to ransom Hector's body. Trembling with emotion, he feels pity for the old man and reaches out his hand to him. It is the most moving moment in the epic.

If Achilles lives by a rigid code of personal honor and fights to win a lasting reputation, he has nothing to lose by dying. Life is worthless to him except insofar as it allows him to prove his own value. Yet, paradoxically, this very ethic makes his life more intense and tragic than it might have been. Hector, by contrast, is fighting on the defensive for a city he knows is doomed, and his responsibilities as a leader tend to burden him. He has others to think about, even though he foresees their fate, and all of this hinders his becoming a truly effective warrior like Achilles. Whereas Achilles' life seems tragic, Hector's life is one of pathos, but the pathos of a man fighting heroically against overwhelming odds.

The gods play a prominent part in the *Iliad,* and they are thoroughly humanized, having human shapes, sexes, and passions. Although they have superhuman powers, they behave in an all-too-human fashion—feasting, battling, fornicating, cheating, protecting their favorites from harm. Just as the Greek army is a loose confederation under Agamemnon, so the gods are subject to Zeus. What is interesting is the way superhuman and human forces interact. Divinity penetrates human action through oracles, dreams, visions, inspiration; it shows itself in inspired warfare where a hero seems invincible, and in miraculous interventions where a wounded hero is spirited away and healed. However, the gods are not omnipotent. Zeus can merely delay the death of a man, but in the end must bow to Fate. Further, men have free will; they are not mere puppets. Achilles has deliberately chosen his destiny. Men, finally, have more dignity than the gods because they choose their actions in the face of death, while the gods have no such necessity, being immortal. It is death that gives human decisions their meaning, for death is final and irrevocable. The *Iliad* is a powerful statement of what it means to be human in the middle of vast and senseless bloodshed.

James Weigel, Jr.

IMAGINARY CONVERSATIONS

Type of work: Dialogues
Author: Walter Savage Landor (1775-1864)
First published: 1824-1848

Landor once said, "Poetry was always my amusement, prose my study and business." When he was forty-five, after having devoted many years to poetic composition, he began the *Imaginary Conversations*, and in this work he found the form best suited to the peculiar aim and direction of his art. His poetry, although some of it attains a gem-like perfection, suffers by comparison with the work of his more famous contemporaries. While the major Romantic writers, with their emphasis on imagination, were bringing new life to poetry, Landor chose not to go beyond ideas that could be clearly grasped. Thus his poetry lacks the emotional appeal necessary to the highest attainment in this form. In prose writing, however, where clarity and restraint are more to be desired, Landor deserves consideration with the best of his age.

By the very nature of his character Landor was drawn for guidance and inspiration to the classical tradition. One side of his personality admired balance, moderation, and precision, qualities admirably displayed in his writing. The other side was irascible, impractical, and impulsive; these traits are revealed in some of his personal relationships. Like Mozart, Landor appears to have found in his restrained and faultless art a counterpoise to his external world of turbulence.

Landor was a true classicist, not a belated adherent of neo-classicism with its emphasis on rules over substance. He was rigorously trained in youth and continued his scholarly pursuits throughout his adult life. His knowledge was no mere surface phenomenon; he was so immersed in the ancients that he took on their characteristic habits of thought. Thus the volumes of the *Imaginary Conversations* not only make use of events and characters from the Greco-Roman civilization, but are infused with classical ideals of clarity and precision in style and tough intellectualism in content.

The *Imaginary Conversations*, written in five series, are grouped into classical dialogues, dialogues of sovereigns and statesmen, dialogues of literary men, dialogues of famous women, and miscellaneous dialogues. The conversations, usually between two people, cover many centuries, ranging from the time of the Trojan War to Landor's own period, and they include people from many geographical areas. Many of the scenes are based on suggestions from history or mythology, but the actual remarks of the individuals are never used. Landor did not attempt to re-create a sense of the past by use of artificial or archaic language. He did, however, endeavor to represent faithfully the spirit of the age and the essential nature of the personage presented.

In the *Imaginary Conversations*, Landor was above all concerned with interpretation of character. While he displayed brilliant insights into human nature, his aim was not toward fully developed characters, but for abstractive idealizations. They are products not of observation directly reported but of observation, especially that gained from reading, filtered through a long process of reflection. Never are the predilections of the author —his sympathies and his aversions—far from the surface.

The manly, heroic character is depicted in many of the dialogues. Two examples of this type are found in "Marcellus and Hannibal." History records the death of Marcellus in the Second Punic War and the respect paid him by Hannibal. Landor created a scene in which Marcellus survived long enough to converse with the Carthaginian leader. When the wounded Marcellus was brought to the camp, Hannibal made every effort to save his life and to make him comfortable. A contrast to Hannibal's chivalric behavior was provided by that of his ally, a Gallic chief who thought only of revenge and of glory to Gaul. Marcellus welcomed death as an escape from capture and politely declined Hannibal's request that Rome agree to a peace treaty. Although under great suffering, he avoided any outward expression of pain. In return for Hannibal's kindness, Marcellus presented him with a ring that might benefit him with the Romans, if his fortunes changed. As Marcellus was dying, the two men were more closely united by their common nobility and respect for nobility in others than were they divided by the exigencies of war.

Women of praiseworthy character are depicted in several of the conversations. In "Lady Lisle and Elizabeth Gaunt," Landor portrayed the remarkable idealism of two women who were condemned to death for sheltering adherents of Monmouth. They had acted through simple Christian charity. Confronted with a choice between the law of the king and the commandment of Jesus, they embraced the latter. Lady Lisle had no blame for the jury that under duress had convicted her. Elizabeth, serene about her own fate, felt sorrow for her companion. Betrayed by the very man she had concealed, she felt no anger toward him, but pitied him for his having to suffer a guilty conscience. Both viewed execution as the avenue to eternal bliss and wished that others might have their perfect serenity.

A more complex character study is found in "Oliver Cromwell and Walter Noble." Cromwell was controlled by conflicting emotions—ambition, pride, compassion, vindictiveness, humility, fear. In response to the practically irrefutable arguments of Noble against regicide, Cromwell constantly shifted position and even contradicted himself. As a last refuge, he justified his proposed action as the carrying out of God's will.

Although Landor sometimes used crucial situations as settings for his conversations, he seldom revealed character in truly dramatic fashion. His dialogues, unlike Browning's monologues, do not have a close causal relationship between the stresses of the moment and the disclosures of the speaker. Nor do Landor's speakers often reveal their inner natures unwittingly. While Browning's works are subtle and require reading between the lines, Landor's are direct and leave little to implication. In the treatment of characters with whom he was unsympathetic, Landor used an irony that is unmistakable, even too obvious at times.

In some of the dialogues, especially the long discursive ones, the characters are not important in themselves, but serve as vehicles for the ideas of the author. Not a systematic philosopher nor a highly original thinker, Landor was alive to the whole range of man's thought, past and present. A wise and judicious man, he expressed his opinions felicitously.

Love of freedom is a leading theme in the *Imaginary Conversations*. Fighters for liberty, such as Washington and Kosciusko, who combined modesty with valor, evoked Landor's highest admiration. Equally fervid was his detestation of tyrants, as expressed. for example, in "Peter the Great and Alexis," a dialogue in which Peter, having failed to make his son as brutal as he, callously orders the boy's execution. Landor believed in a republican form of government and opposed pure democracy because of the corruption, intemperance, and anti-intellectualism that such a system fostered. His expression of political ideas seldom went beyond a statement of general principles.

Landor was often critical of religious leaders and he showed his antipathy to fanaticism in such dialogues as "Mahomet and Sergius" and "Melanchthon and Calvin." Hypocrisy is attacked in other dialogues, such as "Fra Filippo Lippi and Pope Eugenius IV," which is, in part, a satire on the Pope, who makes an outward show of piety and displays great zeal in maintaining the forms of religion, but who is essentially a worldly and sensual man. Also, in this conversation, the Christian-spirited barbarians of Tunisia are, with heavy irony, contrasted with the barbaric Christians of Rome. Landor favored a simple religion that stayed close to its basic tenets. Believing in the limitation of human reason in such matters, he disliked dogmatism and theological quibbling.

His philosophy was influenced by Epicurus and by the Stoics. He believed in meditation, in detachment, in freedom from the ambition and envy of the world. These sentiments are expressed in "Epicurus, Leontion, and Ternissa." Feeling that man's happiness depends on his use of reason to overcome doubts and worries, in many of his character portrayals Landor revealed his belief in self-control, fortitude, sympathy, and humanitarianism.

A significant part of the *Imaginary Conversations* is devoted to literary criticism. Classical standards were Landor's guide. He disapproved of unnecessary ornamentation in writing. "Never try to say things admirably, try only to say them plainly." "Whatever is rightly said, sounds rightly." But Landor was not a narrow classicist in his tastes; he admired a variety of authors, his favorites being Milton, Bacon, Shakespeare, Dante, and Pindar. Among his contemporaries he most respected Wordsworth and Southey.

Landor predicted that only a small, select group of people would prize his writings. He was correct. One reason for the failure of the *Imaginary Conversations* to attract a large audience is the fact that the dialogues lack direction and cohesive development. The absence of dramatic motivation and the presence of disconcerting gaps and shifts in argument create difficulties for the reader.

This weakness, which is a considerable one, has prevented the high merits of the *Imaginary Conversations* from being widely appreciated. The aphorisms scattered throughout the work are among the best in the language. The range of Landor's thought is impressive. His prose style is unexcelled in vigor and purity.

THE IMITATION OF CHRIST

Type of work: Religious meditations
Author: Thomas à Kempis (c. 1380-1471)
First transcribed: c. 1400

Although arguments have been brought forward through the centuries in an effort to show that Thomas à Kempis did not really write *The Imitation of Christ* (*Imitatio Christi*), evidence to the contrary has never been widely accepted and Thomas à Kempis is usually regarded as the author of the famous work. Aside from the Bible, *The Imitation of Christ* is undoubtedly the most famous religious work of the Christian world, having been translated into more than fifty languages and printed in more than six thousand editions. Widely known in manuscript, it was being circulated as early as 1420. Its first publication in English was in 1696. The original language of *The Imitation of Christ* was Latin, not the classical Latin of Rome, but medieval Latin considerably changed from the language of Cicero and Vergil. Many later writers have praised it. Fontenelle said it was the finest piece of writing ever done by man. John Wesley thought so highly of it that he published an English translation under the title *The Christian's Pattern* (1735). Matthew Arnold thought that it was, next to the Bible, the most eloquent expression of the Christian spirit ever penned.

The substance of *The Imitation of Christ* is that God is all and man is nothing, that from God flows the eternal Truth which man must seek, and that by imitating the spirit and actions of Christ man may be helped to achieve a state of grace with God. But as many writers have pointed out, the greatness of Thomas à Kempis' book does not lie in any originality, for there is little that is new in the matter of the work. It is the expression of a spirit that makes *The Imitation of Christ* a piece of great religious literature. Traceable are most of the strands of Christian philosophy and theology of the time, including those which Christians took over, at least in part, from the great pagan thinkers of Greece and Rome. The book has sometimes been described as a mosaic of matter and ideas taken from the early and medieval Christian mystics, the Bible, and writings of the Church fathers. Borrowings from St. Bernard, St. Gregory, St. Ambrose, St. Thomas Aquinas, Plato, Aristotle, Seneca, and even Ovid can be found within the pages of *The Imitation of Christ,* each contributing in a way to the spirit of Christian example. No reader can ever miss, even within a few pages, the eloquence and sincerity of the author. The religious feeling has been expressed so ardently that it is unmistakably a call to the reader to heed the call of Christ and to follow in His steps.

Although he calls the reader to a Christian, hence otherworldly, life, Thomas à Kempis is eminently practical in his insights into human beings, their motivations, and their psychology. More than once the author points out that virtue is only to be claimed by those who have been tempted and have proved themselves equal to denying worldly vanities and other devil's snares in order to remain in act, thought, and spirit a follower of Christ's doctrines and example. Thomas à Kempis also realized that established custom is not easily relinquished by the individual or the community and is thus always a means of keeping one from a Christian life. Thomas certainly was not a man to truckle to the moment; relativism and Christianity could not go hand in hand in his philosophy. Though strict in his admonitions that there was no worldly good, nor any love of man, which could be sufficient reason for doing evil, he admitted that for the help of the suffering, or for a better work, a good work might sometimes be postponed.

The palpable faith of Thomas in philosophical idealism is constantly before the reader. There may be doubt, however, as to whether this idealism is entirely Christian or whether there is a direct influence from Plato or the later neo-Platonists of Alexandria. Though the author's faith in the ideal of God is a mystic belief, intuitive in nature, with little of the rational core of thought behind it upon which Plato insisted, Thomas à Kempis, like Plato, believes that the real world, the world of ideality, is the only true world. But in Thomas' case the method by which Truth is achieved is not through reason; rather, the immediate source is grace acquired through the sacraments of the Church, and through revelation acquired by abstinence from worldly matters, the application of prayer, and the use of contemplation. In answer to his own rhetorical question as to how the Christian saints became so perfect, Thomas points out the fact that their perfection lay in their contemplation of divinity. The greatness of the saints, he adds, came from the fact that they steadfastly sought to abstain from all worldly considerations and to cling with their whole hearts to God and thoughts of Him.

The power of God is, for Thomas à Kempis, in divine love, a good above all others which makes every burden light and equalizes all opportunity. He wrote:

Love is swift, sincere, pious, pleasant, gentle, strong, patient, faithful, prudent, long-suffering, manly, and never seeking her own; for wheresoever a man seeketh his own, there he falleth from love. Love is circumspect, humble, and upright; not weak, not fickle, nor intent on vain things; sober, chaste, steadfast, quiet, and guarded in all senses. Love is subject and obedient to all that are in authority, vile and lowly in its own sight, devout and grateful towards God, faithful and always trusting in Him even when God hideth His face, for without sorrow we cannot live in love.

The pious author suggests in *The Imitation of Christ* that there were four rules for the accomplishment of peace and true liberty: that we should try to do another's will rather than our own, that we should seek always to have less than more, that we should seek the lowest place, and that we should wish and pray always to fulfill the will of God.

The Imitation of Christ was arranged in four parts. Book I deals with "Admonitions Profitable for the Spiritual Life"; Book II, "Admonitions Concerning the Inward Life"; Book III, "On Inward Consolation"; Book IV, "Of the Sacrament of the Altar." The last, a kind of manual for the devout, gives instruction, advice, and guidance on preparing for the sacrament of communion. In the third book are many prayers noted for their eloquence and sincerity of devotion. The last paragraph of a prayer for the spirit of devotion is one of the best examples:

How can I bear this miserable life unless Thy mercy and grace strengthen me? Turn not away Thy face from me, delay not Thy visitation. Withdraw not Thou Thy comfort from me, lest my soul 'gasp after Thee as a thirsty land.' Lord, teach me to do Thy will, teach me to walk humbly and uprightly before Thee, for Thou are my wisdom, who knowest me in truth, and knewest me before the world was made and before I was born into the world.

Although a monk, devoted to his order, his vocation, and God's service through most of his life, Thomas à Kempis was gifted with a keen insight into the world and what it can do to men. He inculcated submission to divine will and recognized at the same time that most men would have difficulty in making such submission. He advocated an ascetic, other-worldly life and point of view, and yet he also recognized the worth of practical goodness. The rules and suggestions he wrote in *The Imitation of Christ* are clear-sighted; the analysis is keen; the tone is humane. The seriousness of its message, the sincerity of its tone, and the humility and compassion of its author make understandable the place that this great devotional work has held in the hearts of men for generations.

THE IMPORTANCE OF BEING EARNEST

Type of work: Drama
Author: Oscar Wilde (1856-1900)
Type of plot: Comedy of manners
Time of plot: Late nineteenth century
Locale: London and Hertfordshire
First presented: 1895

Principal characters:
ALGERNON MONCRIEFF (ALGY), a man about town
LADY AUGUSTA BRACKNELL, his aunt
GWENDOLEN FAIRFAX, her daughter
JACK WORTHING, in love with Gwendolen
CECILY CARDEW, his ward
MISS LETITIA PRISM, Cecily's governess
THE REVEREND CANON CHASUBLE, D.D.

Critique:

This play is built on a pun and the plot turns on a misunderstanding over the name Ernest. The theme is an attack on *earnestness,* that is, the Victorian solemnity of a false seriousness which results in priggishness, hypocrisy, and so-called piety. Unlike Shaw, who used his conventional plots to reinforce his iconoclastic ideas, Wilde used his wit as an ironic counterpoint to the absurdity of the action.

The Story:

Algernon Moncrieff, nephew of the aristocratic Lady Bracknell, was compelled by necessity to live a more or less double life, or he would have been completely at the mercy of his Aunt Augusta. To escape from her incredibly dull dinner parties, he had emulated that lady's husband by inventing a wholly fictitious friend named Bunbury, whose precarious state of health required Algy's absence from London whenever his aunt summoned him to attendance.

Algy's friend, Jack Worthing, was also forced by circumstances into a similar subterfuge for quite a different reason. He had under his care a young ward named Cecily Cardew, who lived at Jack's country place in Hertfordshire under the admirable tutelage of a stern governess, Miss Prism. Jack thought it necessary to preserve a high moral tone in the presence of Cecily and her governess. To escape from this atmosphere of restraint, he in-vented an imaginary brother named Ernest, who was supposed to be quite a reprobate, and whose name and general mode of behavior Jack took over during his frequent trips to London.

To complicate matters, Jack had fallen in love with Gwendolen Fairfax, the daughter of Algy's aunt, Lady Bracknell. Moreover, Gwendolen had fallen in love with him, particularly with his name, Ernest, of which she was very fond. When Lady Bracknell learned "Ernest's" intentions toward Gwendolen, she naturally wanted to know something of his family history. But since "Ernest" could supply nothing more definite than the fact that he had been found in a leather bag at the Victoria Railway Station, and that his true parentage was quite unknown, Lady Bracknell refused to consider his marriage to her daughter.

Jack realized that the time had come to put an end to Ernest. He even went so far as to appear at the manor house in Hertfordshire in deep mourning for his brother Ernest. But his friend Algy, "Bunburying" as usual, had preceded him, posing as Ernest. Cecily took an immediate interest in Algy, the supposed brother of her guardian. When Jack and Algy came face to face, Jack promptly announced that his brother Ernest had been unexpectedly called back to London and was leaving at once. But Algy, having fallen in love with Cecily, refused to leave. Cecily, in turn, confessed that it had always been her dream to love someone whose name was Ernest.

Algy, realizing that his hopes of marrying Cecily depended on his name, decided to have himself rechristened Ernest, and to that effect he called upon the local clergyman, the Reverend Canon Chasuble, D.D. But Jack had preceded him with a like request. Dr. Chasuble had an engagement for two christenings at five-thirty that afternoon.

In the meantime Gwendolen arrived at the manor house. Because of the mix-up in names, both Gwendolen and Cecily believed that they were in love with the same man, the non-existent Ernest.

When Jack and Algy appeared together, the real identities of the two pretenders were established. Both girls became furious. At first Jack and Algy upbraided each other for their mutual duplicity, but they finally settled down to tea and consoled themselves by vying with one another to see who could eat the last muffin on the plate. Cecily and Gwendolen at last decided to forgive their suitors, after Algy had admitted that the purpose of his deception was to meet Cecily, and Jack maintained that his imaginary brother was an excuse to go to London to see Gwendolen. Both girls agreed that in matters of grave importance—such as marriage—style and not sincerity was the vital thing.

Lady Bracknell, arriving in search of her daughter, discovered her nephew engaged to Cecily. Afraid that the girl, like her guardian, might possibly have only railway station antecedents, Lady Bracknell demanded to know Cecily's origin. She was informed that Cecily was the granddaughter of a very wealthy man and the heiress to one hundred and thirty thousand pounds. When she willingly gave her consent to the marriage, Jack refused to allow the match, pointing out that Cecily could not marry without his consent until she came of age, and that according to her grandfather's will she would not come of age until she was thirty-five. However, he said he would give his consent the moment Lady Bracknell approved of his marriage to Gwendolen.

There were, however, some objections to Jack as a suitable husband for Gwendolen, the main one being the question of his parentage. But the mystery was cleared up to Lady Bracknell's satisfaction by the revelation that Miss Letitia Prism, Cecily's governess, was the nurse who had left Lord Bracknell's house with a perambulator containing a male infant which she had placed in a leather handbag and left in the cloakroom of the Victoria Station. The infant was the son of Lady Bracknell's sister, a circumstance which made Jack Algy's older brother. Jack's Christian name still had to be determined. It turned out to be—Ernest. The Reverend Chasuble was relieved of his two christenings that afternoon, and Gwendolen was happy that she was actually going to marry a man named Ernest.

Further Critical Evaluation of the Work:

Oscar Wilde, the leading spokesman for the so-called Yellow Nineties, stood at the end of the nineteenth century and jeered at his Victorian forefathers. All their sacred values—name, position, and money—are ridiculed in his most popular work, *The Importance of Being Earnest*. Turning on a play of words, the drama also satirizes the idea of earnestness. If there were any virtue to which the Victorians attached the greatest significance, it was that of earnestness. To work hard, to be sincere, frank, and open with a high degree of seriousness was a social ideal which underpinned their whole notion of society and religion. Wilde not only satirized hypocrisy and sham virtue, but also mocked its authentic representation.

If the play has any heroes at all, they are Algernon Moncrieff and Jack Worthing, the two dandies; neither are what they seem. The polar opposites of earnestness, placing no value on sincerity or work, they create "night identities" to live out their instinctual life which is forbidden in society. Algy invents a sick friend and goes "Bunburying," while Jack assumes the identity of his nonexistent brother, "Ernest," for his London escapades. It is while they are engaged in such masquerades that they feel themselves to be real and authentic. It is only when they take on their social identities, Jack as the warden of Cecily Cardew, and Algy as the nephew of the fearsome Lady Augusta Bracknell, that they are unreal and hypocritical. The play, however, does not pursue the serious implications of these circumstances and dissolves into a comic farce where Jack and Algy struggle to convince everyone, even Miss Letitia Prism, that they are their social identities, in order to win Cecily and Gwendolen, two empty-headed Victorian maidens. They fall victim, in fact, to the attractions of earnestness and are appropriately rewarded.

IN DUBIOUS BATTLE

Type of work: Novel
Author: John Steinbeck (1902-1968)
Type of plot: Social criticism
Time of plot: The 1930's
Locale: California
First published: 1936

Principal characters:
    MAC, a Communist labor organizer
    JIM NOLAN, his assistant and friend
    LONDON, leader of the fruit pickers
    DOC BURTON, a friend of the strikers
    AL TOWNSEND, a man sympathetic to the strikers

Critique:

With the possible exception of *The Grapes of Wrath, In Dubious Battle* is the most successful proletarian novel yet written in the United States. More sharply focused than the former, and more vivid in its characterizations, its effect is probably more forceful. Although the story springs directly from the clash of social and economic forces during the early part of the depression decade, it remains considerably more than a propaganda piece. An intensely vital narrative, exhibiting both the social awareness and artistic craftsmanship of the author, this book stands among the best of Steinbeck's novels.

The Story:

Jim Nolan's father was a workingman driven to his death by the blows of police clubs and pistol butts. As a youngster Jim witnessed both his father's courage and his despair; he saw his mother lose even her religious faith as poverty and starvation overwhelmed the family.

Older, but still keenly remembering his youth, with the scars of brutality and starvation deeply embedded in his heart, Jim Nolan became a member of the Communist Party. He was assigned to work with Mac, an able, experienced organizer. Together they became fruit pickers, at a time when the fruit growers had cut wages even lower than the workers had thought possible. A strike was brewing and Mac and Jim determined to hurry it along and to direct its course.

Luck was with them. Shortly after their arrival at the camp of the workers, Mac, by giving the impression that he was a doctor, delivered Lisa, daughter of the camp leader, of a baby. Word of his accomplishment spread throughout the area. After Mac and Jim became friendly with London, leader of the camp, and the other workers, they persuaded the fruit pickers to organize and to strike for higher wages and better living conditions. This was not easy to do. As usual, the orchard owners had made effective use of Communism as a bogey. Furthermore, the vigilantes were a constant menace, not to mention deputies, troops, and strikebreakers, all hirelings of the fruit growers. In addition, the authorities could always close down the camp by maintaining that it violated the sanitation laws and was a menace to public health. There was also the problem of money and food; the poor migrant workers desperately needed work to supply their daily necessities.

But at last a strike was called. On the night that the strikers were to sneak out to meet the strikebreakers called in by the owners, Mac and Jim were ambushed by vigilantes. They succeeded in escaping, but Jim was shot in the arm. Word of their plan for the next morning had leaked out, and they suspected that a stool

IN DUBIOUS BATTLE by John Steinbeck. By permission of the publishers, The Viking Press, Inc. Copyright, 1936, by John Steinbeck.

pigeon was in their midst. Nevertheless, the next day they marched out to meet the strikebreakers at the railroad station, and to implore them not to fight against their fellow workers.

Although the police had assembled in force, they seemed afraid of the strikers. During the encounter, Joy, an old and crippled comrade, was shot and killed. The strikers carried the body back to the camp, and over the body of their comrade Mac delivered a fiery and eloquent speech, exhorting the strikers to carry on and to fight to the finish. This action proved to be the best of all possible spurs to bring the workers together, and the strikers were aroused to carry on the struggle even more fiercely.

Luck was with them in other ways. They had persuaded the father of Al Townsend, who owned a lunch cart and gave handouts to Party members, to allow them to camp on his farm, after they promised him that his crop would be picked and that his property would be protected. Doc Burton, a philosopher and skeptic, took charge of the sanitation, thus protecting the camp against the health inspectors. Dick, a handsome comrade, used his charms on women in order to get money and food for the strikers.

Meanwhile the owners tried everything to break up the strike. They attempted to intimidate the workers, to divide them, to bribe London, but all their efforts failed. Then another problem arose. The owners had an article published in which it was stated that the county was feeding the strikers. The report was not true, but those who sympathized with the strikers believed it and stopped helping them altogether. Dick was getting far fewer results from his endeavors, and the situation became desperate.

Mac was often on the point of losing his head, of letting his anger get the best of him, so that the strategy of the strike was sometimes imperiled. By contrast, Jim grew more able, more hardened. He ignored the women of the camp who sought to lure him into their tents, and did not allow his feeling for Lisa to become anything more than a casual, friendly relationship. Thus he provided a sort of balance for his emotional comrades.

Conditions grew worse. The strikers had practically no money, no food. Dick finally managed to get a cow and some beans, but the food sufficed for only a few days. Meanwhile, Doc Burton had vanished. Without his help, the sick and the wounded could not be attended to, and the sanitation of the camp grew progressively worse. One night someone managed to outwit the guards and set a barn afire. The barn and an adjacent kennel housing some favorite pointers were totally destroyed. The next day the owner called in the sheriff to evict the strikers.

The strike seemed lost. The spirits of the men were at a very low ebb, and they gave signs of yielding. On the following night a boy came and told Jim and Mac that Doc Burton was lying wounded in a field. They rushed out, only to realize, when they were fired upon, that they had fallen into a trap. Mac called out a word of warning and fell to the ground. When he got up, after the firing had stopped, he called out to Jim. He got no answer. Jim was dead. By that time the shots had aroused the others and they came forward. Over the body of his comrade and friend, Mac made a strong and rousing speech, urging the workers to stick together, to fight on, and to win the strike.

Further Critical Evaluation of the Work:

In Dubious Battle, Steinbeck's fifth book—the first after *Tortilla Flat* (1935), which had brought him immediate fame—solidified his literary reputation. As an embodiment of the author's reforming vision, derived from the explosive social and economic problems of California in the 1930's, this novel is his most obviously "proletarian" comment on class struggle. It has been looked upon by critics as the source for his Pulitzer Prize-winning masterpiece, *The Grapes of Wrath* (1939). Although its dialogue captures the rough idiom of the migrant workers and strike organizers, the novel is too "pat" in the inevitability of plot and abrupt character development to be considered among Steinbeck's best work.

Yet it is notable for Doc Burton's expression of the concept of "group-man," an organic, animal-like entity which Jim, the hero, learns to recognize as something quite apart from the individual men who compose it. Jim realizes that "the Holy Land, Democracy, Communism," are only words invented by group-man to "reassure the brains of individual men" and that the group has a will of its own that no individual can discern accurately. The novel's major theme is the organizers' recognition that anger must be sublimated into wrath; only then can it be dispassionate and indifferent enough to become mechanistically effective. Steinbeck presents his story with the stark realism of the muckrakers. The idyllic pastoral vision of Frost's "After Apple Picking" is trampled by the actual brutality of the applepickers' lives; only at the end does Mac even taste an apple—and that is a withered one. Jim, a person of feeling and dreams contrasted to Mac who is "too busy to feel" because he is always planning, moves from frustrated bystander to charismatic leader to symbolic martyr. And Mac, the pragmatist, finally realizes that Jim is more useful dead than alive.

IN MEMORIAM

Type of work: Elegy
Author: Alfred, Lord Tennyson (1809-1892)
First published: 1850

In Memoriam A.H.H., Obiit MDCCC-XXXIII, unquestionably one of the four greatest elegies of English literature, records the intellectual, emotional, religious, and aesthetic changes Tennyson underwent throughout a sixteen-year period following the early and tragic death of his closest friend, Arthur Henry Hallam in Vienna, on September 15, 1883. The year *In Memoriam* was first published, 1850, was also the year Tennyson married Emily Sellwood and succeeded Wordsworth as Poet Laureate.

In Memoriam as truly represents the chief Victorian conflict of science and faith as any work of its era; and Tennyson's attempt to reconcile the religious doubts arising from his personal sorrow and the effects of pre-Darwinian theories of evolution was hailed by thinkers of his time as an intellectual landmark. The cyclic change, the turn from private grief and despair to the larger public vision and concern for wider, social issues, that can be found in this poem reflects Tennyson's growing acceptance and reconciliation with the problems of his age.

It appears that Tennyson did not conceive publishing the one hundred thirty-one lyrics of *In Memoriam* until late in the 1840's, when he brought them together as one poem, arranging them so as to reflect in the three-year time scheme of the poem the sixteen-year period of his life which they actually represent. Since these lyrics were written over a long time span, they vary considerably in the tone and mood of reaction to Hallam's death, thus dramatizing lyrically Tennyson's psychological condition. Though many organizational schemes have been offered, the most generally accepted views the poem as illustrating a movement from initial grief (I-XXVII); to philosophic doubt and despair (XXVIII-LXXVII); to rising hope (IXXVIII-CIII); to affirma-

tion of faith (CIV-CXXXI). But the actual growth is more subtle than this and requires close attention to repeated images, such as the two yew tree poems or the two visits to Hallam's house.

The "Prologue," dated 1849, and addressed to "Strong Son of God, immortal Love," expresses the poet's conviction that faith, not knowledge, leads to a harmonious union of the intellectual and the spiritual. The first section then relates the poet's nearly complete self-absorption in grief, but even here we notice a change, evident for example in the difference between "I held it truth" (I) to "I hold it true" (XXVII). Though Love provides a "higher life" for man hereafter, few can find immediate comfort for present loss in this promise of future tranquility. Nevertheless, the poet affirms his belief that " 'T is better to have loved and lost / Than never to have loved at all." This acceptance of his experience despite its accompanying sorrow comes only after intervening poems reveal the true depth of his despair; his identification, for instance, with the yew tree, a symbol of death, shows the poet's marked conviction that he, like the yew tree which is not subject to seasonal changes, is imprisoned in grief and can merely endure in "stubborn hardihood."

This fellowship with "Sorrow" (III) induces an intellectual despair and alienates him from comforting Love.

> "The stars," she whispers, "blindly run;
>   A web is woven across the sky;
>   From out waste places comes a cry,
> And murmurs from the dying sun. . . ."

In one sense this conception of the universe as a blindly run mechanism is the central intellectual conflict of the poem. In his deep melancholy, Tennyson questions not only the justice of Hallam's tragic death, but also the justice of the entire creation.

Like a passenger of a "helmless bark" Tennyson moves alternately from numbed despair to self-awareness (IV), and finds composing poetry an anodyne for pain (V). Poems IX-XVII constitute a group unified by the poet's meditation upon the return from Italy by ship of Hallam's body. A "calmer grief" now pervades his heart (XI).

The pain of grief "slowly forms the firmer mind" (XVIII), but locked in his heart remain the deeper sorrows that words cannot relieve (XX). He writes not to parade his emotions publicly, but because he must (XXI).

The second section commences with the first Christmas celebration some three months after Hallam's death. The poet hears the bells' message of "peace and goodwill" but almost wishes never to hear them again. Yet even in his despondency, the bells recall his happy youth, and, touching pain with joy, ease his misery. In the renewal of "old pastimes in the hall" they make a "vain pretense" (XXX), but find consolation in the thought of an afterlife for the dead, though what that afterlife may be "remaineth unrevealed" (XXXI).

The second yew tree poem illustrates a lightening of his burden, for he now sees the tree with "fruitful cloud," subject to change like his grief. The group of poems from XI to XIVIII represents Tennyson's attempt to resolve the question about afterlife and also the possibility of a reunion with Hallam. These speculations are not meant to solve the problems, he tells us (XLVIII), but were "Short swallow-flights of song" which soothed his mind.

In LIV Tennyson expresses the vague "trust that somehow good/Will be the final goal of ill." But the two following poems call in doubt this qualified optimism, so that all he can permit himself is to "faintly trust the larger hope" (LV). In his agitated state of mind the poet views Nature "red in tooth and claw" (LVI). The remaining portion of this section deals with the former relationship of the poet with Hallam.

The third section opens with the second Christmas and finds the poet with the sense of the abiding presence of his friend. His subdued grief allows him to treasure their friendship.

> Which masters Time indeed, and is
> Eternal, separate from fears.

Tennyson contemplates the possibility of a visitation by Hallam and experiences a "mystic trance" in XCV, when "The dead man touch'd" him "from the past." The third section concludes with a four-poem series relating to the Tennyson family's removal from Somersby, with its pleasant and sorrowful associations.

With the fourth and final section the poet turns from the past and his personal grief to the future of mankind; this change is signaled by the famous lyric "Ring out, wild bells" (CVI). Tennyson resolves not to allow sorrow to alienate him from society (CVIII). Hallam's qualities emerge clearly for the first time; in a series of poems Tennyson praises his friend, particularly for his attributes of leadership and dedication to social good.

Tennyson draws an important distinction in CXIV of the difference between knowledge and wisdom; with wisdom man does not fear death since wisdom is "of the soul," while knowledge must learn to submit to wisdom and "know her place." "Acknowledging "Love" as his "lord and king," Tennyson proclaims that "all is well" (CXXVII). His optimism is buttressed by his knowledge that Hallam

> O'erlook'st the tumult from afar,
> And smilest, knowing all is well.

As the elegy draws to a close the poet more strongly feels the certainty of cosmic design: "That all, as in some piece of art,/Is toil coöperant to an end." (CXXVIII). He feels more confident of Hallam's omnipresence: "Thy voice is on the rolling air;/I hear thee where the waters run" (CXXX). His love, though founded on their previous earthly relationship, is "vaster passion" now that Hallam's presence is spiritual and diffused through "God and Nature." The elegy concludes with the poet's self-confident assertion of the permanence of the "living will" which purifies our "deeds" and of the "faith" in truths not to be "proved" until our deaths.

In the "Epilogue" Tennyson celebrates the marriage of his friend, Edward Lushington, to the poet's sister.

IN THE AMERICAN GRAIN

Type of work: Historical narratives and essays
Author: William Carlos Williams (1883-1963)
Time: The tenth century to the 1860's
Locale: The Americas
First published: 1925

Principal personages:
ERIC THE RED
CHRISTOPHER COLUMBUS
HERNANDO CORTEZ
JUAN PONCE DE LEON
HERNANDO DE SOTO
SIR WALTER RALEIGH
SAMUEL DE CHAMPLAIN
THOMAS MORTON
COTTON MATHER
PÈRE SEBASTIAN RASLES
DANIEL BOONE
GEORGE WASHINGTON
BENJAMIN FRANKLIN
JOHN PAUL JONES
JACATAQUA
AARON BURR
EDGAR ALLAN POE
ABRAHAM LINCOLN

History, to paraphrase Corinthians, is many things to many men. It is the record of what really happened and also the story of what men in later times have believed really happened. It is the story of what men thought and felt and did under the pressure and crisis of decisive action. It is concerned with the noble, the foolish, the violent, the base. It is the careful untangling of political, social, and economic motives and forces in the national experience. It is the unvarnished record of fact and it is also the romantic dream of something men have believed in and died for. It is a record of truth but never the final truth, for each age interprets the events and personalities of history according to its knowledge or need. So it becomes almost meaningless to talk about the "lessons" of history or their meanings: history is a story that is never quite finished because it is always open to reappraisal or new conclusions. The many-sided aspects of history provide one reason for the appeal it holds for its writers, professionals, and amateurs alike.

In the American Grain, one of the au-thentic classics of the 1920's, is a poet's venture into historiography. As such, it is unstaled by conventional theory, without debt to academic authority, and as brilliant and idiosyncratic in purpose, insights, and structure as D. H. Lawrence's *Studies in Classic American Literature.* Also, like Lawrence's critical essays, it is a book written before its proper period. Only in recent years has it been recognized as a revitalizing view of the American past, an original work of considerable magnitude and weight.

At the same time, it was never without influence during the years when it was out of print and neglected by both the critics and the public. One literary debt that comes quickly to mind is found in Hart Crane's *The Bridge.* Traces of Williams' insights and idioms run through the poem. The half-title page of "Powhatan's Daughter," for example, requotes a passage from Thomas Morton's *The New England Canaan,* and there are obvious likenesses between the vision of Columbus in the opening "Ave Maria" section of *The Bridge* and Williams' essay title

"The Discovery of the Indies." Another poet who may have been influenced by *In the American Grain* is Archibald Mac-Leish in *Conquistador,* especially by Williams' description of the destruction of Tenochtitlan and his accounts of the *conquistadores*—Cortez, Ponce de Leon, and De Soto. There may be echoes also in the closing paragraphs of Fitzgerald's *The Great Gatsby,* in the reference to Henry Hudson and his sailors when they saw for the first time the green shores of the New World and were filled with wonder at the promises the new continent held for men's westering dreams. All of this is not to say that these writers were guilty of plagiarism, only that *In the American Grain* offered to perceptive readers images and impressions to be held in memory and knowledge until they could be released in fresh works of the imagination.

Despite its significance as a seminal work, *In the American Grain* is even more important for the function it performs. Williams' purpose, briefly, was not to give a new interpretation of history or to consider its uses, but to discover the thing itself, its nature and the conditions under which it took shape. In "Père Sebastian Rasles" he set forth his aim in a discussion with Paul Valéry, who in the essay is called Valéry Larbaud. Impressed by the other man's knowledge of and interest in American history, Williams claims that everything which has happened or been produced in America springs from discoverable roots, rests on ground capable of being explored and mapped. In the face of the other man's urbane probing into Williams' mind and attitude, the poet insists that it is not possible to trust the men who have interpreted history, from the time of Cotton Mather on. He will go to the sources, he declares, not to uproot history but to make history reveal itself, to trace to their past beginnings the obscurities and partisan views that oppress him, to uncover in the documents of the time the evidence needed to separate fact from myth.

Williams' reordering of the American experience from the century of the Norseman to the Civil War is symbolic rather than philosophical. Clearly, his task involved more than the retrieving of a usable past from the leveling action of time and from legends growing out of the common imagination, or the attempt to find in the meaning of the past a way out of the unsettled present into the future. Exploratory in nature, the book is first of all an act of discovery and recovery, two aspects of the single process of knowing and understanding. Some events or personalities that most historians gloss over or ignore have been brought into the foreground; others recede into it. For Williams is not tracing the development of a society or justifying the culture it created. To speak of a culture implies an abstraction, a phenomenon of cause and consequence which allows no place within its long perspective for the accidental, the discrete, the contingent. This view reduces all history to a concept free of all the rich confusion of chance and circumstance that is life itself. Instead, Williams employs what Allen Tate has called the "Short View" of history, the particular stories of the particular lives of man engaged in contemporaneous interactions of place, time, and personality. Believing, like Emerson, that history is a record of the lengthened shadows cast by men on the earth, Williams reveals in this book the same qualities that we find in his poetry, a strong sense of the "Local"—which is not to be confused with local color—and a ruling passion to express his vision of the world as concisely and concretely as possible. To the poet who declared that there is no reality except in things, no other course was possible.

His experiment in historiography involved also an experiment in style. To give richness of historical content to his book he borrowed lavishly from his sources. Quotations from letters, chronicles, and journals are scattered through the sketches—passages from Columbus' journals, reports of the Salem witchcraft trials, letters written by Benjamin Franklin and John Paul Jones—to color the prose and give it vitality and the ring of truth. Sometimes this quoted matter complements Williams' own prose; sometimes it clashes with dramatic vigor. One is reminded throughout of one of Williams' statements on the writing of poetry: his declaration that the writer takes words as he finds them but transforms them, without destroying their clarity and passion, into an expression of his own feelings and perceptions so presented that they become revelation. It is not what a writer says, he claimed, that is important as a work of art, but the thing he makes with such intensity that it lives by its own force of outward movement and wild inward logic. In the brief narratives and essays making up *In the American Grain* the writer's historical imagination holds revelation of personality and meaning of situation in delicate but compelling balance, while the language gives the whole resonance and depth.

The book is divided into twenty chapters—dramatic narratives, lyric interludes, brief character sketches—ranging in space and time from the settlement of Greenland through the voyages of Columbus and the exploration of Kentucky to the Civil War, and dealing with such representative or illustrative figures as the *conquistadores*, Sir Walter Raleigh, Cotton Mather, George Washington, John Paul Jones, Aaron Burr, Poe, and Lincoln. The arrangement is chronological, but the scale of values accorded to the men and events is quite different from that found in the history texts. Benjamin Franklin, for instance, is no longer the wise founding father but the great apostle of catchpenny materialism and opportunism whose face, appropriately, now decorates the one-cent stamp. Aaron Burr, on the other hand, is not the self-seeking man who tried to upset the established order of government because of personal ambition; Williams sees him as a good soldier who brought into politics an element of democratic theory necessary to the times but neglected by other men already in power or aspiring to office, a champion of liberty at a time when freedom was subverted to bureaucratic tyranny, a man finally driven to the imprudence and excesses of which his opponents had already accused him.

Two themes run through the book. One is the failure of Americans to create for themselves a sense of place. The early settler on these shores was already an alienated man, an exile from European society, and on the new continent his feeling of separation became complete. He saw America not as a place to be sensed and assimilated but as a land to be conquered for selfish ends. The forces motivating him were external circumstances of time and place on the one hand, the opportunity to exploit a vast and rich continent, and on the other inward necessity, the need to justify his own identity as a new man in a new land. The first of these drives was public and pragmatic; it hastened the westward movement, created the myth of scientific progress, and laid the foundation for an industrial society and the comforts of an expanding, affluent technical economy, all the while ignoring the cost in terms of individual hardship, economic waste, and the erosion of human values. The other was private and moral. From it we get in part the restlessness, the violence, the communal guilt and shame, the inner fears, the secret loneliness and desire that agitate our society today. Only at rare intervals, in Williams' view, does history present an individual so completely and individually himself and so much at ease in his environment that he shows himself capable of acting as an American, not as a transplanted European or an alien in his own society: Daniel Boone as the explorer and settler, Aaron Burr as the politician, Edgar Allan Poe as the artist, Abraham Lincoln as the leader of a divided nation in conflict with itself. This conflict is implicit in the beginnings of our history. Columbus sensed without re ally understanding the meaning of America and saw with bright vision the possibilities of place and life in the New World. The opposite side of the picture is the story of the Spanish conquerors, the impact of the cross and sword of feudal Spain upon a pagan society. Occasionally the exploited land revenged itself on its despoilers; the disappointments of Cortez and the secret river burial of De Soto are in effect payment for the destruction of Tenochtitlan and the rape of Mexico and Peru.

Williams' second theme is the blight of Puritanism over the American land. Like Hawthorne, he viewed the Puritans as "miserable wretches" who possessed strength of purpose and will but not the tolerance of strength or the wisdom of purpose. Puritan bigotry and ignorance were demonstrated in the treatment of Quakers in New England and the Salem witchcraft trials. The abstract ideal of purity and salvation almost entirely excluded from Puritan life the idea of place or a sense of beauty as a concrete, natural thing. Williams finds Cotton Mather niggardly and narrow, a man of great but unassimilated learning, whose belief in the supernatural often verged on superstition. Hostile to a flowering of the spirit, the Puritans tried to convert all life into facts and figures, and Benjamin Franklin, as revealed in his maxims, was the inheritor of their materialism and morality. If *In the American Grain* contains a major flaw, it is found in Williams' treatment of the Puritan. Although he does not succumb to the Puritan-baiting popular among intellectuals in the 1920's, he sometimes criticizes Puritanism, or expresses his grudging admiration, for the wrong things. Today we realize that Puritanism was more than an abstract ideal of an earthly paradise, a theocracy of dogmatic belief and practice; it was also a seedbed of political freedom and independence of mind and spirit.

Because he himself was a poet, perhaps, the true hero of Williams' argument is Edgar Allan Poe, whom he calls the first writer to recognize the possibilities of American life in art and to give shape in language to the spirit of place and time. For Poe, culture was not something to be brought into the national experience but something to be revealed because it was already present in the conditions and circumstances of the world around him. In his poems, short stories, and criticism, he tried to find universal meanings in the local, not in setting alone, but in the American psyche, in apocalyptic visions of the American soul. In the end he was defeated by the forms and forces of culture inherited from the past, and he retreated into a region of grotesques. But at best he expressed with originality and vigor the spirit of place, used the creations of his imagination to suggest that literature is a serious business as logical and depth insighted as science or philosophy. He tried to clear the ground of colonial imitation and the growing belief that material advance was the only possibility offered by American life. His effort was moral as well as aesthetic, and for this reason Williams regards him not as a frustrated genius but as a heroic figure deserving the highest praise.

The book ends with a brief appreciation of Abraham Lincoln. The choice is an appropriate one. For Lincoln was our president in the period of the Civil War, the most deeply felt and possessed experience in our national life, the violent summation of all that had gone before and the adumbration of everything that has happened since. Lincoln is here a symbolic figure, an image of the shortcomings and possibilities in our history, a figure of tragic failure as well as a promise of hope. This impingement of the present upon the past gives *In the American Grain* an added dimension, a deeper relevance in our own understanding of the events and the men who have shaped our history. This is a poet's book as well as an amateur historian's, a work in which the writer's vision provides new insights into historical truths imaginatively viewed and passionately re-created in language. In it the local view strikes deep into the shape and meaning of the American past.

IN THE WILDERNESS

Type of work: Novel
Author: Sigrid Undset (1882-1949)
Type of plot: Historical chronicle
Time of plot: Early fourteenth century
Locale: Norway
First published: 1927

Principal characters:
OLAV AUDUNSSON, master of Hestviken
EIRIK, his heir
CECILIA, Olav's daughter
BOTHILD ASGERSDATTER, Olav's foster daughter
LADY MÆRTA, Bothild's grandmother
TORHILD BJÖRNSDATTER, mother of Olav's son Björn
SIRA HALLBJÖRN, a priest

Critique:

When Sigrid Undset was awarded the Nobel Prize for Literature in 1928, that award was made, according to the citation, "principally with regard to her powerful pictures of Northern life in medieval times." No one who has read Kristin Lavransdatter or The Master of Hestviken will deny the justice of that statement. Those not familiar with her novels must be prepared to find a writer who, while true to the life and spirit of a past age, pays little attention to the historical personages and actual events as necessary to the historical romancer. Madame Undset's stories of medieval life are so full-bodied and rich in detail that there is little need in her books for a parade of names and dates. In the Wilderness, the third volume of the Hestviken series, is the one exception to her usual practice, however, for the closing episode of this novel deals with the invasion of Norway by Duke Eirik of Sweden in 1308.

The Story:

Olav Audunsson had little desire to stay on at Hestviken through the summer following his wife's death, and when the sons of the English armorer in Oslo asked him to be shipmaster of their boat on a trading voyage to London it was plain that the idea pleased him. Eirik, Ingunn's son by the Icelander, wanted also to go on the trip, but Olav told him nay—he must remain at Hestviken and be companion to little Cecilia, the daughter Ingunn had borne in her last years.

In England two adventures befell Olav. At evensong in the Dominican's church he saw a woman so much like dead Ingunn that for a moment his breath failed him. So like she was, and yet young enough to be his daughter. With her was a blind man, apparently her husband. Olav saw her again, at mass and evensong, and after a time they began to exchange glances and smiles. One night her serving-woman stopped him after the service and led him to a great house outside the walls. The strange woman was in the garden, her only dress a thin silk shift. For a moment Olav felt that he was about to clasp Ingunn again. Then he realized that she was only a wanton wife seeking sport with a stranger. Thrusting her from him, he ran away.

At another time he went with his shipmates to a famous shrine north of London. Separated from his companions, he wandered in the woods until he encountered some men beside a brook. That night they attacked him for his rich dress and jewels. While Olav fought with the robbers in the dark, he felt the battle-surge he had known in his outlawed youth. Later it

IN THE WILDERNESS by Sigrid Undset. By permission of the publishers, Alfred A. Knopf, Inc. Copyright, 1929, by Alfred A. Knopf, Inc.

seemed to him that he had been tempted by pleasures of the flesh and of violence, sent to lead him from the path of redemption he must follow to atone for the secret slaying of Teit, Eirik's father.

When Olav sailed home in late summer, he found Eirik grown taller and strong for his age and Cecilia fairer than ever, with promise of great beauty. Resolving that Liv, the slatternly serving-woman, was unfit to train the daughter of Hestviken, he wed Liv to Arnketil, his house-carl, and sent the pair to live at Rundmyr, the farm he carried on for Torhild Björnsdatter, who had borne him a son out of wedlock two years before. One day he went across the fjord to Auken, where Torhild was living, to discuss his arrangement. Seeing his son and Torhild again, he was minded to ask the woman to return and keep his house, but he sadly put the thought out of his mind.

After Liv and Arnketil moved to Rundmyr, the place began to have a bad reputation because of the dicing, wenching, and worse that went on there. At last Sira Hallbjörn, the priest, warned Olav to keep Eirik away from that thieves' den. For years Olav had been of two minds about Eirik. He wanted to like the boy whom he had claimed as his heir, yet he could not abide Eirik's insolence and boasting. He realized that he should give more time to his training but shrank from that duty because of the old clash of wills between them. Urged to marry again, he wanted no other wife beside him at table and bed.

His problem was solved in part when Asger Magnusson, an old friend, died in Tunsberg after asking Olav to foster his daughter Bothild and provide for his mother-in-law, Mærta Birgersdatter. Lady Mærta was grim and gaunt but capable. Never had Hestviken been better kept than it was under her charge. Cecilia and Bothild, close in age, lived as sisters. Lady Mærta dressed them well, and people said that in the whole southland there were no fairer maids than those at Hestviken.

But Eirik set himself against Lady Mærta from the first, and Olav was always angry when he was drawn into their rows and forced to rebuke the boy for the sake of a stranger. In the winter of Eirik's sixteenth year they quarreled after Olav found him in rude sport with a serving-girl. That night Eirik left Hestviken without farewell. There was no report of him at Rundmyr or among Olav's distant kin, but at last word came that he was in Oslo, among the men-at-arms who served Sir Ragnvald Torvaldsson. Knowing Sir Ragnvald a gentle knight from whom Eirik would learn the skills of weapons and courtly ways, Olav was satisfied. He went to Oslo and gave the runaway money and a squire's gear. There was much kindness between them when they parted, Olav almost in envy for Eirik's youth.

Three years passed more quietly than any Olav had known since boyhood. Cecilia was his great delight, with little in her nature to recall her weak-willed, sickly mother. One night some men from another parish came to Hestviken. After the drinking in the hall one of the men tried to seize Bothild and Cecilia. Bothild was terrified, but Cecilia drew her knife and slashed at the man until the blade was red. Olav felt that she should have been the boy of the house.

Olav, beginning to grow restless, was often in the company of Sira Hallbjörn, a priestly lover of falconry and hunting. One night, while they supped at a wedding feast, Olav's ancient Viking ax, Kin-fetch, rang. For a moment they saw in one another's eyes old pagan stirrings that neither could have spoken aloud. Riding home later that night, Olav went into the graveyard and called to Ingunn to arise. On another day he went to Auken, where he found Torhild married to Ketil, a young man on the farm. Olav asked her to send Björn, their son, to live with him. She refused.

The snows lay deep that December when Duke Eirik crossed the border from Sweden to lead his troops against his father-in-law, King Haakon. Torhild brought word of the invasion to Hestviken one frosty dawn. After sending Cecilia, Bothild, and Lady Mærta to Auken for safety, Olav rode off to warn his neighbors. When the franklins tried to ambush the Swedes, they were routed by the mailed horsemen. Olav and Sira Hallbjörn were among the few who made their way to the manor at Sundrheim and there spent the Yule. Meanwhile the Swedes occupied Oslo and besieged Akershus, the royal fortress. Olav was in that great fight at Aker church and at Frysja bridge, where there was hard fighting to keep Duke Eirik from taking the castle. Sira Hallbjörn was killed at the bridge, and in the press a crossbow-bolt shattered Olav's jaw.

Olav lay in fever for days. After Duke Eirik withdrew from the siege, a merchant took Olav into Oslo and cared for him there. One day he looked at himself in a mirror. His cheek was furrowed and scarred and his hair was gray. When he went back to Hestviken in the spring, Olav felt that he had become an old man.

Further Critical Evaluation of the Work:

More than the others, this third novel of *The Master of Hestviken* tetralogy depends for its action on the large historical movements of the time. It is vastly interesting, especially since Olav's viewpoint on these events is one not likely to be represented in the actual chronicles of the period, for it is the viewpoint of the rank and file. But the colorful details of war and trade are in fact merely the background for a concentrated examination of Olav's character and spiritual condition.

With Ingunn's death in *The Snake Pit*, Olav had expected to be able to abandon the lie in which he had lived so long; instead, he finds himself more closely bound to it than before, for he must continue in it for Eirik's and Cecilia's sake. When the struggles of his conscience come to a head at the pilgrimage church near London, he decides to resolve the problem by going on pilgrimage to Jerusalem without returning to Hestviken first; but he changes his mind when he realizes that his resolution is prompted as much by his desire to avoid the vexed situation at home as by a wish to humble himself before God and be cleansed of his old sin.

In taking up his old life as a cross to be born for his children's sake, he acts out the Christian precept that sin is its own punishment; his decision not to take Torhild into his house again carries out the penitential theme. But in consciously giving up his soul that his children might thrive, he regresses, in effect, into a pre-Christian state of being. The last part of the book shows him immersing himself in thoughtless paganism: attempting to call Ingunn from her grave, applauding Cecilia's fierceness, and glorying in the panoply and comradeship of war. In a way, he comes full circle, experiencing again the emotions of his youth and young manhood. But with the passing of his physical beauty, the link with his early life with Ingunn dissolves, making way for the renewed Christian conflict of *The Son Avenger*.

INAZUMA-BYÔSHI

Type of work: Novel
Author: Santô Kyôden (1761-1816)
Type of plot: Feudal romance
Time of plot: Fifteenth century
Locale: Japan
First published: 1806

Principal characters:
SASAKI SADAKUNI, feudal Lord of Yamato Province
SASAKI KATSURA, his first-born son, by his deceased first wife
SASAKI HANAGATA, his second son, by his present wife
KUMODE NO KATA (LADY SPIDER), his present wife, Hanagata's mother
ICHÔ NO MAE (LADY GINKGO), Katsura's wife
TSUKIWAKA (YOUNG-MOON), son of Katsura and Lady Ginkgo
FUWA DÔKEN (ROAD-DOG), steward to the House of Sasaki
FUWA BANZAEMON, Dôken's son
HASEBE UNROKU, a disloyal retainer
NAGOYA SABUROZAEMON, a loyal retainer
NAGOYA SANSABURÔ, his son
FUJINAMI (WISTERIA-WAVE), a dancing girl
SASARA SAMPACHIRÔ, a loyal retainer, also known as Namuemon
KURITARO (CHESTNUT-SON), his son
KAEDE (MAPLE), his daughter
YUASA MATAHEI, Fujinami's brother
UMEZU KAMON (GOOD-GATE), a recluse
SARUJIRO (MONKEY-SON), Sampachirô's servant
SHIKAZÔ (DEER), Sansaburô's servant

Critique:

Using the central theme of rivalry for succession to a great feudal house, and the triumph of good over evil, right over wrong, Santô Kyôden took his materials from traditional *Kabuki* plays and wrote *Inazuma-byôshi* (*Trouble in the House of Sasaki*) with stage production obviously in mind. The scenes change rapidly, and the plot is complicated by the appearance of a large number of secondary characters who disrupt the unity of the story. Thus the principal theme tends to move away from the succession intrigues to a depiction of the feudal loyalty of a secondary character, Sasara Sampachirô. That this novel was soon produced on the *Kabuki* stage was a matter of course, and it was staged under various titles, the first being in Osaka in 1808, and in Edo in 1809. As a novel the work comprised a unit in itself, but Kyôden wrote a sequel, the *Honchô Sui-bodai Zenden*, which was published in 1809. This later work, making greater use of syllabic meter, has little in connection with the original, and is thin in plot; but it carries the reader on through the author's sheer writing ability.

The Story:

During the mid-fifteenth century, under the shogunship of Ashikaga Yoshimasa, there lived a warrior lord by the name of Sasaki Sadakuni, lord of the Province of Yamato. He had two sons. One, twenty-five years old and named Katsura, was the son of Sadakuni's first wife; the other, twelve-year-old Hanagata, was the son of Sadakuni's second and present wife, Lady Spider. Katsura, a handsome young man, was taken into the luxurious and self-indulgent service of the shogun at Kyoto. There, at the instigation of one of Katsura's retainers, Fuwa Banzaemon, Katsura fell in love with a dancing girl, Wisteria-wave, and began to lead a life of pleasure.

A retainer of the House of Sasaki, Nagoya Sansaburô, was sent to Kyoto to present a treasured painting to the shogun. Learning how matters stood with Katsura, he did his best to make the young lord mend his ways, but to no avail. Meanwhile, Banzaemon himself had been discovered to be in love with Wisteria-wave, and he was discharged from feudal service. Sansaburô was sent back to the Sasaki provincial headquarters. At the same time a loyal retainer, Sasara Sampachirô, killed Wisteria-wave and went into hiding. On the same night a disloyal retainer, Hasebe Unroku, stole the treasured painting and disappeared.

The next day Banzaemon's father, Road dog, steward to the House of Sasaki, arrived as Sadakuni's emissary, severely reprimanded Katsura for his dissolute ways, and discharged Katsura's retinue as being disloyal. Behind Road-dog's outwardly righteous actions lay a deeper plan, a plot to take over his lord's domain with the connivance of Governor General Hamana. Knowing Lady Spider's hope that her own son Hanagata would succeed to the lordship of Sasaki, Road-dog had joined forces with her. With the backing of an evil sorcerer, the two attempted to do away with Katsura's wife, Lady Ginkgo, and her son Young-moon, who were living in the Sasaki villa in Heguri, guarded by Sansaburô and his father, Nagoya Saburozaemon. Although their plot failed, Sadakuni was deceived and troops were dispatched against Lady Ginkgo and her young son.

In the meantime Banzaemon, who held a grudge against Sansaburô, killed Saburozaemon. Sansaburô placed Young-moon in the care of Young-moon's elderly nurse and helped them escape; he himself fought valiantly in defense of Lady Ginkgo, but in spite of his courage and efforts his lord's lady was abducted. He himself escaped into Kawachi Province.

The old woman in charge of Young-moon had met with difficulty in escaping with her charge. Young-moon was saved, however, by Sasara Sampachirô, who meanwhile had changed his name to Namuemon, and was hidden in Tamba Province.

Namuemon was still haunted by the spirit of the dead Wisteria-wave whom he had killed for the sake of his lord; his son, Chestnut-son, became blind, and his daughter Maple was haunted by a serpent. When it was known that Namuemon was secretly watching Road-dog's movements with the idea of killing him, warriors were sent against Namuemon, who beheaded his own son and then, in order that Young-moon's life might be spared, identified the head as Young-moon's. Namuemon's daughter Maple sold herself for the painting. Namuemon, with his wife and Young-moon, sought refuge in Kawachi Province. Leaving the two in a place of safety, he himself set out to find his master Katsura and Katsura's wife, Lady Ginkgo.

Meanwhile, Lady Ginkgo, who had fallen into Road-dog's hands, was about to be murdered, but she was saved by a hero-recluse by the name of Umezu Good-gate. Katsura, who had become an itinerant Buddhist priest, was about to meet his death at a temple festival in Ômi Province, when his life was saved by Monkey-son, Sansaburô's son who had become a street preacher. After his delivery Katsura was hidden in the home of Wisteria-wave's older brother, Yuasa Matahei, a painter living in Ôtsu. By chance, Namuemon was also staying there. Matahei, becoming aware that Namuemon was his own sister's murderer, was at the same time deeply impressed by the quality of Namuemon's loyalty. Matahei's wife confessed that six years ago she had attempted to hang herself because a ruffian had robbed her of twenty pieces of gold. At the time Namuemon had not only saved her from death but he had even given her twenty gold pieces to make up for her loss. Torn between revenge and gratitude, Matahei drew his sword, cut Namuemon's traveling hat in place of Namuemon's head, and offered the sundered hat to Wisteria-wave's departed but still vengeful spirit. With past wrongs thus redressed, Matahei repaid his gratitude by bringing Namuemon to Katsura. At that point Hasebe Unroku appeared on the scene and was recognized by Matahei's wife as the man who had robbed her six years before. Namuemon forced Unroku to commit suicide to expiate his sins.

Maple, meanwhile, had joined a traveling theatrical troupe which had come to those parts. Namuemon, now revealed as Sampachirô, met his daughter, whose affliction from serpents that always accompanied her had been healed by the painting she had so dearly bought. Matahei, for the first time, realized that he had attained the inner secret which he had striven for in his art—its magical power.

On the following day Katsura and his party left Ôtsu for Kawachi Province. He acquired a book on military strategy and tactics belonging to Good-gate, who had saved Lady Ginkgo's life. Intending to seek the assistance of the new governor general, Katsumoto, the party arrived at Good-gate's secluded abode on Diamond Mountain to find that Katsumoto was already there in an attempt to persuade Good-gate to accept the position of chief of military strategy. It was also revealed that Good-gate was related to Katsura by marriage. Katsura was reunited with Lady Ginkgo, who had been staying there under Good-gate's protection. With the governor general's and Good-gate's backing, Katsura prepared to return to his home province of Yamato.

Meanwhile, in Kyoto, Sansaburô, accompanied by his faithful servant Deer, had been searching for Fuwa Banzaemon and his gang in the brothels of that city. Finally he found them and with the assistance of a courtesan and Good-gate, who had been a friend of his slain father Saburozaemon, Sansaburô achieved his revenge. Good-gate, appointed the governor general's deputy, received orders to go to the headquarters of the House of Sasaki. Requesting the attendance of Sadakuni's wife, Lady Spider, and his steward, Road-dog, as well, Good-gate told Lord Sasaki Sadakuni that Katsura had not only mended his former ways but had displayed great military valor. He requested Sadakuni to pardon his son and to name Katsura his heir and successor; Sadakuni would then retire in Katsura's favor as head of the clan. Good-gate also revealed Lady Spider's and Road-dog's plot to take over the House of Sasaki by conniving for the succession of the second-born, Lady Spider's son Hanagata. With Road-dog under arrest in a caged carriage, and his mission accomplished, Good-gate took his leave amid the low and reverent bows of the House of Sasaki.

Further Critical Evaluation of the Work:

Kyôden, better known in the West by his artist's name of Kitao Masanobu, followed his early successes in both print-designing and fiction, by concentrating his attention on the latter. He was the most versatile and gifted of the popular Edo (modern Tokyo) writers. Besides the picture books and fanciful didactic *yomihon* reading books to which he turned under the pressure of Tokugawa censorship, he wrote many excellent *sharehon* ("books of wit"), sophisticated sketches of manners in the Yoshiwara and other pleasure quarters. Though these were limited in subject matter, their realistic dialogue technique greatly influenced the two leading kinds of realistic Edo fiction of the nineteenth century. This tendency toward realism is evident in *Inazuma-byôshi*.

Like many of Santô Kyôden's works, this novel is written in a vigorous, popular style, simple and direct, and often melodramatic in plot. Because of the skillful handling of action and the true-to-life emotions of the characters, the novel was very widely read in Japan. A somber history of vengeance, the novel abounds in violence, suicides, torture, combat, and rapid shifts of plot. It reads often like an early nineteenth century European romantic novel, filled with Gothic horrors and boiling emotions, but, at the same time, a lusty quality and a certain vigorous humor raises the book to a greater level of realism. Kyôden was considered one of the leaders in Japan in the development of the realistic, romantic school of fiction.

Although the plot at times is confusing, owing partly to the large number of characters, a vigor of style and narrative drive carries the action steadily forward. The minor characters tend to be stylized, boldly-sketched figures, but the principal characters are much more realistically portrayed. *Inazuma-byôshi* possesses an almost cinematic sweep and power of movement, and the Western reader should not become sidetracked by attempting to follow every minute plot thread; the novel's romantic vision of feudal life in Japan is rendered in an exciting, enjoyable style.

INCOGNITO

Type of work: Novel
Author: Petru Dumitriu (1924-   )
Time: 1940-1960
Locale: Rumania
First published: 1962

Principal characters:

THE NARRATOR, the unnamed witness to the testimony and a minor
Party official
SEBASTIAN IONESCO, the hero, a storekeeper
ERASMUS IONESCO, a high Party official
CHRISTIAN IONESCO, and
PHILIP IONESCO, Sebastian's brothers
VALENTINE IONESCO MORCOVICI, their sister
BASIL MORCOVICI, her husband
MALVOLIO LEONTE, Morcovici's rival in the Party
ROMEO ROMANESCO, Sebastian's friend
SABINE, Sebastian's wife
ARTHUR ZODIE, Sebastian's friend
LEOPOLD, a cripple

Until 1960, when he escaped to the West, Petru Dumitriu was head of the State Literary Society of Rumania; he was not only the most powerful man in the literary apparatus of Rumania but was also regarded as his country's leading writer on artistic grounds. Since his escape he has become recognized at least in Europe, as one of those few writers whose talents so far transcend the conventions of nationality as to make them something on the order of writers to the world at large. It is obvious in any case that Dumitriu's stature as an artist raises him above any poet or novelist in the entire history of Rumanian literature.

Incognito, like all of the novels of Dumitriu that have been translated into English previously, was written in French. Given the historical sympathy between France and Rumania and the natural desire of a writer to reach as wide an audience as possible, Dumitriu's adoption of this language was natural. Racially, culturally, and linguistically, Rumania is a Latin island in the midst of an Asiatic—Slavonic and Magyar—sea, and it is significant that his characters speak, when they speak of literature, not of Dostoevski and Tolstoy but of the poets of France, Italy, and Spain, while the

first "foreign" author quoted in *Incognito* itself is Tacitus, in whose *Histories* the narrator, apparently intended to stand for Dumitriu himself, finds remorseless parallels with the state of Rumania in 1960.

It is almost as if, indeed, centuries later in the Rumanian microcosm, the Roman Empire had at last found a creative artist capable of capturing the whole sweep of its decadence and downfall, its decline and the subsequent reign of the Eastern barbarians. *Incognito* should not be read alone but in its proper sequence among all the body of Dumitriu's work thus far, that work which, written for the most part within a five-year period, attempts to render the essence of Rumanian history from the nineteenth century to the time of Dumitriu's own escape to the West. In particular, *Incognito* should be read as the companion piece to *Meeting at the Last Judgment,* to which it stands in much the same relationship as a *Purgatorio* to an *Inferno.*

Focused upon a smaller patch of time than *Incognito* and directed at depicting the character of a particular level in the Rumanian governmental hierarchy, *Meeting at the Last Judgment* describes a Hell on earth, Rumania as a colony in the Soviet bloc, and its inhabitants, the damned, many of them disillusioned, many of them still believing in the Marxist-Leninist cause, all of them in greater or less degree responsible for the creation of a country where life is genuinely intolerable, all of them thus genuinely damned. Their suffering, as it should be in Hell, is not physical but psychological, for the soul is where Dumitriu's interest lies: the country they live in, and particularly the social level, as high functionaries in the imperial apparatus, they live at, make such things as love, friendship, loyalty, self-respect, or charity impossible for them. Their Rumania is ruled instead by brutality, greed, lust, jealous hatred, duplicity, and sub-animal ambition, and one by one they take their turns as victims of this Rumania they have made.

In such a country the mere maintenance of sanity is an achievement; the maintenance of any other human characteristics becomes something of a miracle, a miracle which seems to testify in Dumitriu's eyes to the essential truth, despite all his own evidence to the contrary, in a conception of man as a creature at least capable of his own salvation, if not of any very much higher nobility. Consequently, though he is by no means an "optimistic" writer, one feels at the end of *Meeting at the Last Judgment*, as Dumitriu describes in a few quick pages the narrator's escape with his wife —Dumitriu's child was allowed to join her parents in 1964, having been held hostage for four years—a sudden sense of exaltation.

Incognito may be read as a kind of gloss on this exaltation. All of the characters in the book have already appeared in *Meeting at the Last Judgment*, the difference being that whereas in the previous novel we see them in their basest, most abject, and most superficial aspect, in *Incognito* we see into the secret nobility of their real selves, where it exists, or into the fear of self that creates a Judas. The central figure of *Incognito*, Sebastian Ionesco, is, in fact, a kind of Christ.

The major part of the novel is his autobiography, which he has handed over to the narrator, who has been entrusted by the hierarchy with the job of gathering evidence of a secret conspiracy against the state. This conspiracy actually exists. It is not, however, the kind of conspiracy which the state, thinking only in terms of dialectical materialism, can understand. It is a conspiracy of the soul itself, or of the spirit, and its situation, Dumitriu intends us to see, is exactly like that of primitive Christianity under the Caesars.

It has been customary since Gibbon to treat the conversion of Rome to Christianity as the result of a kind of bribe, the bribe of "everlasting life." Such an interpretation of this major event in Western history is naïve in the extreme, ignoring as it does the testimony of the Roman Empire itself. From the melancholy of Vergil and the despair of Horace's Roman odes to the agonizing self-reappraisal of St. Augustine, the Latin writers bear increasing witness to an unease of the spirit which only Christianity, of all the hundreds of available religions (all of them equally profferring the offer of resurrection), could assuage. Rome chose Christianity, one may conclude, because it was "truer," because it replaced some form of consciousness which had been lost in the process of "civilization," because its implied description of human nature fitted with what seemed to be the human facts. Like primitive Christianity, Sebastian Ionesco's secret sect is thus a conspiracy of truth, a conspiracy against the mechanical lie of Rumania's Oriental masters.

Sebastian's narrative begins with his describing a day in his adolescence, when his country was still a kingdom and a kingdom still renowned for the paganism of its ways. Over every doorway might have been hung the mottoes *"Si piace e lice"* or *"Fayce que vouldras"*: life on a Danube estate like Sebastian's father's was a perpetual Thélème, a pastoral idyl as it might have been painted by some post-Giorgionesque Italian. In this setting we are reintroduced to Sebastian's brothers and to his sister Valentine, who figure in *Meeting at the Last Judgment* largely as promiscuous, ambitious schemers.

The real leader of the family, dominating the others not only through his own talents and strength of character but also through their pagan capacity to be intimidated by his beauty, is Philip, brilliant and licentious, a symbol, perhaps, of prewar Rumania, doomed to die in the wreckage of the house during a bombardment. The hint of incest, lurking in his younger brother Christian's relationship with their mother, becomes an apparent actuality, during the course of the day, in Philip's seduction of Valentine, which Sebastian stumbles on as a witness. It is this event, as much as any other, that drives him away from the comforts of home to join the army, then allied with the Germans in forcing the Soviets out of Rumanian territory and invading Russia.

Captured by the Russians, Sebastian is converted to Communism and repatriated by the Red Army's victorious drive to the West. What he hopes to find in Communism, just as he had hoped to find it in heroic sacrifice to patriotism, is purity; his conversion is an attempt to atone for the sins of his people. Nothing deludes like success and for a while, as he becomes one of the leaders in the movement to overthrow the kingdom and establish a Soviet state, Sebastian believes that he has found the purity he was after. He discovers that Valentine, Christian, and Erasmus, his third brother, have all found their way into the Party apparatus as well, following his lead despite the fact that he is the youngest and least prepossessing of all. Though never a Party member, Valentine in fact is destined to become the wife of one of the most influential men of the new regime, Basil Morcovici.

At the highest peak of his personal success within the Party, Sebastian again becomes disillusioned and resigns his position, a step that puts him automatically under suspicion and leads, by no very circuitous route, to a series of prison camps. It is while working as a slave laborer that Sebastian completes his final conversion, to a vision of life that is analogous to, if not directly derived from, the vision of the New Testament. From this point on his life becomes even more dangerous; persecuted though he has been in his search for his vision, he is now in a position to become a martyr, for his faith demands converts. Meanwhile a plot directed by Malvolio Leonte, one of Morcovici's rivals in the Party, has seen in Sebastian a chance to topple Morcovici through Valentine and the fact that she is Sebastian's sister. The narrator of *Incognito*, "Dumitriu" himself, has been assigned the task of facilitating Sebastian's martyrdom by exposing his creed and denouncing those who adhere to it, a task which he is reluctant to fulfill but which he fears he may have to carry out, to his own shame, for the sake of self-preservation.

In the votaries of Sebastian's sect the narrator finds his allies, in Valentine, Christian, and Erasmus Ionesco, and in Arthur Zodie, a character whose presence in *Meeting at the Last Judgment* always generates suspicion, but whose evasive acts and language are explained to us in *Incognito* as the ambiguous defenses, like Christ's "render unto Caesar," of a man living in a world whose rulers are hostile to his vision of himself. Unfortunately, such allies are powerless against the machinations of Party members more vicious than they. Malvolio Leonte soon finds his Judas in Leopold, a neurotic cripple. At the end of the book, however, we do not know what has happened to Sebastian; Morcovici has managed to turn the tide and Sebastian, now no longer a wanted man, has simply disappeared. In fact, whether Sebastian is dead or alive no longer makes much difference, for the conspiracy of soul of which he was the center has given signs of spreading even into the Byzantine cave of Soviet Russia itself.

In Rumania's recent "thaw" towards the West, as represented chiefly for Dumitriu's readers by the release of his daughter, we may perhaps be witnessing the result of some "conspiracy" like Sebastian's, for Dumitriu himself believes the thaw to be genuine and has remarked further that the people who have created it are the same people who helped put Rumania so firmly behind the Iron Curtain. Regardless of its value, however, as a piece of local prophecy, *Incognito* will remain a considerable work of art, made more considerable by the place it occupies in the total work of a writer who is already recognizably a classic. If Dumitriu has not wholly succeeded in conquering the eternal problem of expressing the experience of religion in words, it must be added that even so *Incognito* dwarfs *Darkness at Noon* and threatens to dwarf *Doctor Zhivago,* the two novels of the twentieth century with which it is most easily compared.

INDEPENDENT PEOPLE

Type of work: Novel
Author: Halldór Laxness (1902-   )
Type of plot: Social chronicle
Time of plot: Twentieth century
Locale: Iceland
First published: 1934-1935

> Principal characters:
> BJARTUR, a crofter
> ROSA, his first wife
> FINNA, his second wife
> ASTA SOLLILJA, Rosa's daughter
> GVENDUR, Bjartur's son
> NONNI, his younger son
> INGOLFUR ÁRNARSON, Asta's father

Critique:

Independent People is one of the few novels to give us a faithful and artistic picture of the essentially unrewarding life in bleak, small Iceland. In addition to the background, Laxness has written in a style and with a scope approaching the epic. We get some of the feeling of the traditions of the Vikings, and we see the old give way to the new. Only the hard, barren life of the crofter is unchanging, for the Icelander in the remoter sections of his country lives on about the plane of the primitive savage.

The Story:

After working for eighteen years for Bailiff Jon, Bjartur was at last able to buy, with a heavy mortgage, the croft called Winterhouses. Proud of his new status as a landowner and fiercely independent, Bjartur promptly renamed the place Summerhouses. It was a poor place, fit only for sheep grazing. The house, which Bjartur rebuilt, consisted of one room over the stable. The walls were of sod, and the roof was made of a few sheets of corrugated iron covered with turf. But it was his own place, and Bjartur was determined to be hired workman for no man and to put his trust in sheep.

For his wife he chose the twenty-six year-old Rosa, a small sturdy girl with a cast in one eye, who had also been in service to the bailiff.

Rosa was disappointed in her house, and Bjartur was disappointed in Rosa. He soon found that she was far from innocent, and worse, she was already pregnant. He suspected, and was sure much later, that the man had been the bailiff's son, Ingolfur.

After a few months of marriage Bjartur left on a cold winter day to look for his sheep. Seeing a buck reindeer in the woods, he jumped on the animal's back and attempted to subdue him. But the reindeer was too strong and took off in mad flight for the river. With Bjartur still holding on, the animal swam downstream and finally landed on the other shore. Bjartur, nearly frozen to death, stayed to recuperate at a nearby croft.

He returned home after several days to find his wife dead from childbirth and a baby daughter still alive. Disregarding the parentage of the girl, he proudly named her Asta Sollilja. The bailiff's wife sent pauper Finna and her mother to look after Bjartur and the baby. Finna was nearly forty but strong and well preserved. To settle the problem of the child's care, Bjartur married her.

Each year Finna had another child, usually stillborn. But after some years there were Helgi, Gvendur, and Nonni,

INDEPENDENT PEOPLE by Halldór Laxness. Translated by J. A. Thompson. By permission of the publishers, Alfred A. Knopf, Inc. Copyright, 1946, by Halldór Laxness.

and their sister Asta. The croft was crowded, and the beds were all dirty and filled with vermin, but the land was clear of debt.

A southerner came to the croft one day to ask permission to camp and hunt. The stranger delighted Asta, who was awkward and uncouth but bursting with love. The stranger hardly noticed her, however, and each night he was gone most of the night. The reason for his visit came out later, when the bailiff's daughter left the country in great haste.

After little Helgi was lost on the moor, the tie between Asta and Bjartur became closer. When Finna died from poor diet and rapid childbearing, the father tried his best to make life easier for the girl. He refused to let Asta go to school, but he did teach her much of the old Icelandic poetry.

Bjartur took Asta on his yearly trip to town, where, after doing the shopping, they stayed overnight in a lodging-house for country folk. To save money, father and daughter both slept in the same bed. Asta was unhappy. The town people had laughed at her homely clothes, and the snores of the drunken farmers in the nearby beds were terrifying. She snuggled closer to her father and kissed him. He put his arms around her, but to his horror found that she was kissing him repeatedly. Abruptly Bjartur got up and went out for their horse. Father and daughter left for home in the rainy night.

Then a series of misfortunes, which the Icelanders laid to a witch buried near Summerhouses, greatly reduced Bjartur's flock of sheep, and he went to town to work. Trying to meet his obligations to his children, Bjartur sent a schoolmaster to instruct Asta, Gvendur, and Nonni during the winter. But Bjartur's choice of teacher was unfortunate. After getting drunk one night the schoolmaster took Asta. When Bjartur came home in the spring, Asta was pregnant. In his rage Bjartur cast out his daughter, who went gladly, full of romantic notions of her lover. She walked to his fine town house, which turned out to be a shack. There she learned that he had many children and that his wife was again pregnant.

Nonni, just before the World War, went to America to join his uncle. Only Gvendur and Bjartur were left, in addition to the old mother-in-law. The war boom raised the price of lambs and Bjartur prospered. He now had two cows and three horses. At the same time, a cooperative movement, with Ingolfur at its head, was organized. In the parish only Bjartur held out; he remained loyal to the merchants who had been gouging him for years.

Nonni sent two hundred dollars from America to pay for Gvendur's passage. In spite of his father's objections, Gvendur, who was seventeen and big and strong for his age, decided to emigrate. He put on his best clothes and went to town to take the coastal steamer. There he was admired because he was going to America. During the day and night Gvendur had to wait before his ship sailed, he met the bailiff's granddaughter. She took him riding on the moor, where they spent the night together. Hoping to win her love, Gvendur renounced his emigration and went back to Summerhouses.

In spite of the depression following the war, Bjartur resolved to build his new house. He went deeply into debt to buy great supplies of stone and timber. That year he got the walls and roof completed, but there were no doors and windows. Before he could finish the house, the mortgage was foreclosed and Summerhouses passed into the hands of the bank.

The only place left for the family was the mother-in-law's old croft, long since abandoned. During the moving Bjartur met Asta and was reconciled to her. Asta had a second child by another man, and she was carrying a third. The family was complete again, except for Nonni.

Asta, like Bjartur, was independent. Ingolfur, now rich and a member of Parliament, had revealed to her that he was her father. His offer of support had been soundly rejected.

Bjartur fell in with some strikers who had struck against the government's low wages. For a while he was sympathetic with the men, who were, in a way, Communist led. Gvendur was even more sympathetic. But they both rejected in principle the idea of collective action. They were independent farmers and herders.

So they moved to the wretched hovel far to the north, with only Blesi, their twenty-five-year-old horse, to do the hauling. By hard work they could continue their old way of life. They would have one room in a turf-covered hut. Their diet would be refuse fish. With luck they would be only a little less comfortable than savages in a jungle.

Further Critical Evaluation of the Work:

Laxness' *Independent People* is an excellent example of the naturalistic novel, for it demonstrates the thesis that man has no connection with a religious or spiritual world and is subject to the natural forces of heredity and environment. According to naturalism, one must confront the social and economic forces of his background which are usually presented by an author of this school with elaborate and minute documentation. The characters usually show strong animal drives, but they are helpless in their fight against sociological pressures. All of these characteristics fit *Independent People.* In it Laxness starkly presents all the grim details of the life of Bjartur, the "independent man," who fights to rise above his environment, becomes successful for a period, and then sinks back into the miserable life he had worked so hard to escape.

Except for occasional references to automobiles and electricity, one would not know that the novel is set in the twentieth century, for the life style of the crofters is no better than that of peasants in medieval times. The poverty of the crofters is almost unbelievable. They live in small, one room hovels above the stables and are plagued by the smoke of peat stoked fires, the dampness of spring, and the bitter cold of winter when snow may cover the entire house. In an environment where humans live little better than beasts, it is almost unavoidable that they become animalistic and lose all compassion and emotion. In *Independent People,* there is no communication nor understanding among the characters, and any attempt at communication is viewed with suspicion.

The role of women in such circumstances is particularly hard. This is shown in the grotesque death of Rosa who, left alone to die in childbirth, is found dead on the croft floor in a pool of blood. Her infant is kept alive by the warmth of the dog that lies upon it until Bjartur returns. The harshness of a woman's life is also seen in the yearly pregnancies of Finna and in the miserable life Asta is forced to live after Bjartur drives her from the house.

But even more interesting is the perverted response man is conditioned to making to the hard life he is locked into. For instance, Bjartur mourns for neither of his wives. When looking for a housekeeper to care for the infant

Asta, he admits that he talks more about animals than about human beings. He dismisses Rosa's death by telling the minister that she just died from loss of blood. No effort to care for her seems to have entered his mind.

There are several prominent themes running through the novel; politics, economics, social reform, and the clash between religion and ancient superstitions are all dealt with in some detail. For years Laxness had searched for a sustaining religious and political ideology, and in *Independent People* the restless energy generated by that search found its first powerful outlet in his bitter attack on materialism. He held the greed and oppression inherent in the materialistic philosophy responsible for the sordidness and suffering which filled the lives of his countrymen in rural Iceland. In exposing the cruelties of rural conditions with all the merciless determination of the naturalist, the author at once enraged many Icelanders—who resented having such a brutal picture of their emerging nation published abroad—and delighted liberals all over Europe and America. Yet for all Laxness' revolutionary vigor, his hatred of power and authority, his scorn for bourgeois morality, and his anger and grim satire, he still was able to express his artist's love of beauty. Alongside scenes of coarseness and themes marked by their bitterness, Laxness displays throughout *Independent People* a great compassion and sensitivity, a capacity for tenderness and concern, and a burning devotion to the spirit of individualism and idealism.

But the center of interest is always the character Bjartur. At times, his seeming indifference is nothing more than an attempt to cope with life's harshness. In the spring following Helgi's disappearance, for instance, Bjartur, looking for a lost ewe, finds the decayed body of a young boy which did not look like a human being. Bjartur touches it once or twice with his stick, takes a good pinch of snuff, and leaves.

Yet Bjartur reveals, at times, that affection is possible in this life. Although he knows Asta is not his child, she is his favorite. He calls her his "little flower" and is horrified when he finds his fingers undoing the fastenings of her undergarment in the townhouse bed they share. He also has a poetic side, for he continually composes complicated verses and teaches the ancient poems of Iceland to Asta. But poetry is the only fancy he allows himself; all else is harsh reality. To Bjartur the sheep and the land are the most important things in the world, for after years of debt his only desire is to be considered an "independent man." When he brings his bride, Rosa, to Summerhouses, he says that independence is the most important thing in life. He intends to maintain his independence. This is the great irony of the book, for his independence is false; he is completely at the mercy of his environment. His stubbornness and false pride lead him to disaster when he refuses to take the advice of wiser men and falls into bankruptcy when he borrows money to build a "real" house which he hopes will rival the Bailiff's mansion. Bjartur defies everything and everyone. He refuses to believe in either the

Christian religion or in the ancient superstitions of the country. In a show of bravado he defies the spirit of Gunnvor, the witch buried upon his land, who was supposed to have killed most of her children and to have drunk the blood of those who survived. Everyone else in the district adds a rock to her grave when they pass, but this Bjartur refuses to do. Instead he purchases a headstone for her grave marked "To Gunnvor from Bjartur." It is after this act of defiance that his financial troubles begin.

Laxness was reared in the country and is able to give an intimate picture of the starkness of Icelandic life on the frontier. This great attention to detail makes the book approach epic proportions. However, there are some flaws in the author's style. He uses the omniscient point of view, but he often violates this with authorial intrusions commenting upon politics, economics, or human nature. The style is also uneven. At times it is smooth and poetic, but at others it is extremely awkward. On the whole, however, the book is valuable both as a social document and as the story of Bjartur, the independent man, who, struggling against impossible odds, is never defeated psychologically even when he loses all he has worked so hard for. Without remorse, he plans to begin again at the wrteched, abandoned croft of his mother-in-law.

Vina Nickels Oldach

INDIAN SUMMER

Type of work: Novel
Author: William Dean Howells (1837-1920)
Type of plot: Domestic realism
Time of plot: Shortly after the American Civil War
Locale: Florence, Italy
First published: 1886

Principal characters:
THEODORE COLVILLE, a middle-aged bachelor
MRS. LINA BOWEN, a middle-aged friend of Colville
IMOGENE GRAHAM, a girl chaperoned by Mrs. Bowen
EFFIE BOWEN, Mrs. Bowen's thirteen-year-old daughter
MR. MORTON, an admirer of Imogene Graham

Critique:

Many readers will find echoes in this novel of *A Hazard of New Fortunes* and the novels Howells wrote featuring Mr. and Mrs. Basil March in their later lives. In novels dealing with cultured older people, Howells was considerably more successful at sympathetic characterization than he was in such novels as *The Rise of Silas Lapham.* That he was infringing on the realm of Henry James, the master of fiction featuring American expatriates in Europe, Howells was well aware, for he comments jokingly about their work in one passage of this novel. As ever, Howells is in this novel a master of the realism of the commonplace. The details of life in the American colony in Florence at the time, the events of the pre-Lenten carnival season, and the background of the city are set forth explicitly.

The Story:

Theodore Colville studied architecture as a young man and in order to continue his professional education he spent some months in Italy. While there he went about with two young women and fell in love with one of them. The girl rejected his suit. Soon afterward he went back to the United States at the request of his older brother, who had recently purchased a newspaper. Returning to America, Colville became the editor of his brother's paper and finally purchased it. He entered politics in his fortieth year. After his defeat he left his home in Indiana and went at once again to Italy.

In Italy he tried to resume the study of architecture, but his interest was soon diverted by his meeting with Mrs. Bowen, who had been one of his companions in Italy years before, the one with whom he had not fallen in love. Mrs. Bowen, now a widow, invited Colville to visit at her home. When he went there, Colville met Mrs. Bowen's thirteen-year-old daughter Effie, who quickly became fond of him, and Imogene Graham, a twenty-year-old American woman whom Mrs. Bowen was chaperoning.

In company with Mrs. Bowen, Imogene Graham, and Effie Bowen, Mr. Colville spent a number of pleasant days and evenings. At first Imogene regarded him as an old man, since he was twice her age, but she soon realized that she enjoyed his company much more than that of many men her own age. In an effort to be companionable with her, Colville danced and went about socially as he had not done for many years. Mrs. Bowen also enjoyed Colville's company; the result was that they were together a great deal.

Mrs. Bowen chose carefully the places where she and her charges went. During the carnival season she permitted Colville to take them all to a masked ball. At the ball little Effie became ill and had to be taken home unexpectedly. As a result, Imogene and Colville were together unchaperoned during much of the evening. At that time they began to realize their affection for each other.

Mrs. Bowen quickly realized that a love affair was developing. She also realized that no one, least of all herself, had expected it. She tactfully pointed out to Imogene the differences between the girl and a man so much older. When she said, rather less tactfully, that she thought Colville had been trying only to be amusing, the girl reported the conversation to Colville. Hurt, he went to Mrs. Bowen and talked with her, finally agreeing to her suggestion that for propriety's sake he leave Florence. Unfortunately, it was a weekend, and Colville, having insufficient funds to leave the city after settling his hotel bills, was forced to wait until the following Monday. By that time Imogene had decided that it was unfair to make him leave the city because of her. She requested that he stay. He decided to do so.

A few days later Colville and Imogene met accidentally in a public park. Quickly coming to an agreement that they loved one another, they went back to Mrs. Bowen's residence and told her that they had decided to be married. Mrs. Bowen, as Imogene's chaperone, told them she would be forced to write immediately to the girl's parents to inform them of this recent development. The lovers, agreeing to her plan, also promised to say nothing about an official engagement until they heard from America. Imogene warned her chaperone, however, that she would marry Colville, even without her parents' consent.

While they were awaiting word from America, a young minister named Morton, also in love with Imogene, returned to Florence to pay her court. Both Colville and Mrs. Bowen wished to let the young man know the state of affairs, but the girl refused to permit them to tell Mr. Morton of her engagement. To make the situation appear normal, the four—Mrs. Bowen, Mr. Morton, Imogene, and Colville—went about together. Finally word came from Imogene's parents. Her

mother had decided to sail for Europe, to see Colville for herself before giving her decision.

During the intervening days before Mrs. Graham's arrival, the four people went on an excursion to Fiesole to see the Etruscan ruins there. At one interval Colville and the young minister walked a short distance beside the carriage. While they were doing so, a peasant driving a band of sheep came over the brow of a hill. The horses, frightened at the sight of the sheep, began to back the carriage dangerously close to a precipitous drop at the side of the road. The two men rescued the women from the carriage. While Mr. Morton was taking Imogene from the vehicle, Colville ran to the horses' heads in an attempt to hold them. Unable to do so, and with his hand caught in the curb strap, he was dragged with the team when the carriage plunged over the edge of the road.

For two weeks Colville lay very ill. When he was finally able to have visitors, Imogene's mother came to see him. She told him that she was taking her daughter to America immediately, even though she felt that Colville had acted as a gentleman in the entire affair. She then gave her reason for preventing the marriage. Her daughter, she said, was not really in love with Colville, although she thought too much of him to break the engagement. The shock was a great one to Colville, but he immediately saw that the girl's departure was the only answer to the problems that the situation had developed. After her mother left, Imogene herself came into the sickroom and bade Colville a hasty goodbye.

Some time later Mrs. Bowen and Colville talked over the affair. During the conversation they both admitted their love for each other. Mrs. Bowen refused to marry Colville, however, because of the embarrassing position in which she had been placed during his affair with Imogene. She had hated herself the whole time she tried to prevent the affair because, although she hoped she could see the situation objectively, she had always feared that her actions and thinking had been colored by her feeling for Colville.

Little Effie Bowen, having formed a very strong attachment for Colville, refused to hear of his departure. Within a few months, under the influence of their mutual love and Effie's attitude toward her mother's suitor, Mrs. Bowen was reconciled to a marriage. They were married quietly and then moved to Rome, where no one who knew them could spread gossip about the affair with Imogene. Not long after their marriage they heard that Mr. Morton, who had been deeply in love with Imogene, had been appointed to a church in a community near Buffalo, where the Grahams lived. Both Mr. and Mrs. Colville hoped that he and Imogene Graham would make a match of their own.

Further Critical Evaluation of the Work:

Indian Summer represents Howells at his best; psychological acuteness, facile development, and deft delineation of character all typify Howells at the top of his form. A European love story in the American mode, the delicate handling of manners, marriage, and travel made *Indian Summer* an immensely popular work.

Howells was well equipped for this particular task. Set in Italy, the novel capitalizes on Howell's experience as consul to Venice during the Civil War. He revisited Italy a few years before writing *Indian Summer,* and worked on that novel concurrently with *Tuscan Cities,* thus keeping the intricacies of the place of Americans in Italian society fresh in his mind. Howells was, in 1886, in the ripe Indian summer of his own career, and the Old World setting and subtle, intricate relationships of the characters provided a most appropriate vehicle for the delicate touch he had perfected in *A Modern Instance* and *The Rise of Silas Lapham.*

Furthermore, while Howells' later fictions were to strain his social consciousness and force him to question the ability of literary realism to deal with real life, *Indian Summer* is a precise embodiment of his own critical theory. It is the commonplace, rather than the fantastic, elaborate, or unusual that provides the material for the novel. The focus of the story is not on plot but rather on the development of character. The story is deliberately antiromantic; real life is shown to be more good than evil, and democracy comes off better than decaying European aristocracy.

Recent criticism, moreover, has uncovered symbolic and even allegorical levels of meaning beneath the quaint and quiet surface of *Indian Summer.* The novel is to be appreciated as vintage Howells, most of all because he was perhaps never to write as well again.

INDIANA

Type of work: Novel
Author: George Sand (Mme. Aurore Dudevant, 1804-1876)
Type of plot: Sentimental romance
Time of plot: Early nineteenth century
Locale: France
First published: 1832

Principal characters:
INDIANA, a young Creole
MONSIEUR DELMARE, her husband
NOUN, her foster sister and maid
RODOLPHE BROWN (SIR RALPH), Indiana's cousin
RAYMON DE RAMIÈRE, her lover

Critique:

Written at the height of the French romantic movement, *Indiana* exhibits all the conventions and idiosyncrasies of the most pronounced romanticism. For this reason modern readers find the characters unbelievable, their words and actions more laughable than tragic, despite the basic tragedy underlying the greater part of the story. The chief value of the book derives from the fact that it typifies a popular literary form and a philosophy which still survive, though in lesser degree, in contemporary literature.

The Story:

Indiana was married to pompous, quick-tempered Monsieur Delmare, a retired army officer no longer young. Loyal to her suspicious and jealous husband, she had lived a discontented, uneventful life. Her cousin, Sir Ralph Brown, himself unhappy and frustrated, was her only companion. Although Monsieur Delmare kept a watchful eye over the young couple, there was nothing untoward in the relationship between them. As a matter of fact, Sir Ralph had secured the good graces of Monsieur Delmare and was accepted as one of the household. If not an intimate friend, he was at least a close companion. Indiana was as reserved in her behavior toward Sir Ralph as she was toward her husband, but to a close observer it was clear that in a friendly, inarticulate manner, Sir Ralph was fond of Indiana.

The submerged tensions of the household erupted one evening when someone was discovered scaling the garden wall and entering the grounds of the estate. Monsieur Delmare rushed out and fired in the darkness at the intruder. When the wounded prowler was brought into the house, he revealed himself as Raymon de Ramière, a young man who, so he maintained, wished to see Monsieur Delmare about the latter's manufacturing enterprise. De Ramière said that his brother had a similar business in another part of the country and would profit by Delmare's information.

Delmare's suspicions were dissolved. He had not, however, noticed the behavior of Noun, Indiana's friend and maid. Noun had become extremely agitated at the entrance of de Ramière, a fact which nobody noticed in the excitement. She knew that de Ramière had come to the estate not to see Delmare on business, but to keep a rendezvous with her. Noun had been his mistress for some time. Once in the house, however, he was immediately attracted to Indiana, especially so since he was already tiring of Noun.

De Ramière began systematically his suit for Indiana's affections and to that end he enlisted the aid of both his mother and Indiana's aunt. Before long Indiana began to reciprocate his attentions and the affair became the subject of much discussion in Parisian salons. Delmare remained ignorant of the gossip. But in spite of de Ramière's urgent avowals and protestations, Indiana refused to yield herself to him because she preferred a pure and spiritual love. Upset by her refusals, de Ramière contracted a fever which kept him confined to his bed for several days. Indiana, too, was strongly affected and experienced several spells of swooning. One night, impatient to achieve his desire, de Ramière impetuously entered the Delmare house. Indiana was away, but Noun was there awaiting the return of her mistress. The two met in Indiana's room and Noun, as passionate as ever, enticed the young man's surrender. Aroused by the return of Indiana, Noun escaped, leaving de Ramière to face her mistress alone. Indiana, disturbed to find her suitor in her room, ordered him to leave before his presence was discovered.

A short time later, Noun's body was discovered floating in a nearby stream. Pregnant, she had taken her life because of de Ramière's refusal to marry her or even to continue their relationship. Indiana was broken-hearted at the death of her maid and de Ramière himself was greatly perturbed. By that time he had tired of his pursuit of Indiana and had determined to forget her. One night Indiana, having decided at last to become his mistress in fact, went to his rooms. Learning that he was not at home, she waited until

he returned at dawn. Then she offered herself to him. Unfortunately, while they were talking, dawn broke. Compromised by her presence in de Ramière's rooms at that hour, Indiana returned to her home, where Delmare, agitated by the discovery of her absence, received her with cold suspicion.

Soon afterward Delmare suffered business reverses and faced complete ruin. Indiana contritely went with him to the Isle of Bourbon, where he hoped to make another fortune. Unhappy in her new home, she lived only for the letters de Ramière wrote her. At last she decided to leave Delmare and arranged for her secret passage back to France. On her arrival in Paris, she learned that fickle de Ramière had recently married.

For weeks she lived a miserable existence. Penniless and starving, she decided to die. When she and Sir Ralph, who had followed her to Paris, were strangely reunited, they agreed to commit suicide by drowning. At the last minute, however, they changed their minds. Moved by Sir Ralph's devotion, Indiana realized that he was the man she truly loved. Together they forsook civilization and lived as recluses, away from all people and society, but satisfied and happy at last.

Further Critical Evaluation of the Work:

Resurgent interest in female and feminist writers ensures that the question of George Sand's literary contribution will again receive attention. Yet it seems likely that her life will remain the central object of controversy and fascination. Calling her a female Lord Byron would not be incorrect, for she scandalized France and England as he had done, and the reading public doted on the autobiographical aspects of her novels. But it is important to recognize the specifically feminist—as opposed to the romantic—dimension of her activities. Her bisexuality, her romantic liaisons, and her opposition to the institution of marriage frequently obscure the fact that she was one of the earliest female writers to make her living by her pen. Her use of a male pseudonym and her masculine dress were occasioned by constraints against women: novels written by women were not often given a fair reading by male editors and critics; likewise, many of the clubs and theaters were closed to women, so her male disguise enabled her to participate more fully in literary Paris. Her first published work under the renowned pseudonym, *Indiana* enjoyed success and convinced Sand that she could support herself and her children by means of her writing.

Indiana, as a heroine of a new order, comes to believe, as did her creator, in the primacy of love over society's moral strictures. The romantic movement, with its emphasis on the individual, championed passionate love as the basis for a relationship—as opposed to the old contractual arrangements based on family, estate, or power. Indiana, says George Sand, "is will battling against necessity . . . love beating its head against the barriers raised by civilization." The novel suggests this new ethic even in the extremes of its romanticism—the suicides and near-suicides, the fainting spells, the exaggerated speech and pleas of everlasting faithfulness. Indiana rebels against the bonds imposed by society, first by refusing to submit her will to her husband, then by offering herself to Raymon, and finally by living in harmony with Sir Ralph, unmarried and away from society's laws ("to resist mentally every species of moral restraint had become with her second nature"). *Indiana* is a good introduction to the concerns and style of George Sand, even though commentary throughout the novel emphasizes differences between males and females, especially of temperament, that a modern reader might find outmoded.

INÊS DE CASTRO

Type of work: Drama
Author: António Ferreira (1528?-1569)
Type of plot: Romantic tragedy
Time of plot: 1354-1360
Locale: Portugal
First presented: c. 1558

Principal characters:
ALFONSO IV, King of Portugal
PRINCE PEDRO, his son
INÊS DE CASTRO, secretly married to Pedro
SECRETARY TO THE PRINCE
DIOGO LOPES PACHECO,
PERO COELHO, and
GONZALVES, King Alfonso's advisers

Critique:

The love story of Inês de Castro was popular with poets and historians long before a Lisbon humanist dramatized it as the first dramatic tragedy in Portuguese, and preceded in all European literature by only one other, *Sofonisba* (1515), by the Italian Gian Trissino (1478-1550). The dramatist, António Ferreira, was the younger son of a noble at the court of the Duke of Coimbra. In construction, *Inês de Castro* follows Greek models, with a chorus that appears in all five acts, both as Ideal Spectator and as the Voice of Fate. This tragedy has flaws. The lengthy exposition by Inês in blank verse is hardly inspiring, and the simple plot allows little on-stage action. Even the murder of Inês must be inferred from the words of the Chorus and the messenger's report. But there are, in spite of these defects, moments of dramatic brilliance and scenes of suspense and charged emotion, with moving poetry to give the drama other reasons for permanence besides its interest as a pioneer effort.

The Story:

On a lovely spring day in the middle of the fourteenth century, Inês de Castro felt especially happy as she walked in her garden in Portugal. Though an illegitimate daughter of a famous Galician noble, she had won the love of Prince Pedro, son of Alfonso IV of Portugal; at last she felt sure the world was about to

learn that he loved her too. Theirs had been a star-crossed love. Pedro's father, trying his best to destroy his son's love for a woman unsuitable to rule Portugal, had compelled his heir to marry the Princess Constanza of Castile. But, as Inês confided to her nurse, fate had been on the side of true love. The birth of Constanza's son, heir to the crown of Portugal, had cost his mother her life. At last Pedro was free. He had carried out his father's command. He had insured a continuation of the dynasty, and now he was coming back to the woman he really loved. Surely King Alfonso would now relent. The beauty of the day seemed an omen, and Inês was weeping with joy as she waited for her lover to appear.

The old nurse was less sure, however, that her mistress' tears were an omen of joy; they might be a foreboding of tragedy. She begged Inês not to count on happiness until everything was settled. Inês, hearing Pedro approaching, would listen to no warnings.

The prince greeted her with an assurance that all would go well. To himself, however, he wondered why he was not loved by the common people of Portugal and why his father had been so incensed by his sincere love for Inês. Nevertheless, he was confident, like Inês, that their four children would move the stern old king to pity. Pedro hoped for the royal acceptance of the love between them and a state wedding to show King Alfonso's recognition of his grandchildren.

Pedro's secretary tried to disillusion him. In spite of the nobility of her famous father, the irregularity of Inês' birth was cause enough for King Alfonso's repeated orders that Pedro must put her out of his mind. The secretary begged Pedro, for the good of the state, to let reason conquer desire and to give up the passion that enslaved him and made him disobedient to the royal will. The prince refused. He had obeyed his father in marrying Constanza. Events had proved that Inês was fated to be his real wife.

King Alfonso, meanwhile, was pacing his throne room. His three advisers, Diogo Lopes Pacheco, Pero Coelho, and Gonzalves, were deaf to his complaints that a king had more woes than pleasures. They preached the obligation of power, pointing out that an officially sanctioned marriage between Pedro and Inês, whose children were older than the recently-born son of Constanza's, might jeopardize the succession of the young child. One of the advisers, the dominating Pacheco, argued that the removal of Inês would solve all difficulties. In spite of King Alfonso's basic agreement with the suggestion, much argument was needed before the king finally gave the trio orders to kill his son's mistress.

That night Inês had a dream in which she was about to die. She interpreted it as proof that Pedro was dead; otherwise he would have been quick to defend her. Before she could discover what truth there was in her dream, the king arrived with a sentence of death. He was accompanied by Pacheco, who intended to block any appeals for royal mercy. Inês pleaded so touchingly, however, insisting on her innocence and the helplessness of her four children related through Pedro to King Alfonso, that the king, reminded of his love for his own child, finally agreed to spare her.

But the reprieve did not last long. Once more the king's advisers, selfishly hoping for more gratitude from the King of Castile than revenge by a mere Galician nobleman, worked on the king, in their determination that Constanza's child should inherit the throne. Though they could not get his consent to the death of Inês, King Alfonso did not actually forbid it. Twisting his indefiniteness into permission, the evil trio hurried away to murder the innocent Inês de Castro.

In the meantime Pedro, hurrying eagerly to join her and confident that the king would consider his son's happiness and permit their official marriage, was met by a messenger who told the prince that the three advisers had sought out Inês and killed her. Out of his mind with grief, Pedro swore to have revenge on all concerned, including his father. He would cast him from the throne and then hunt down and torture the three evil murderers, and he would not only see to it that a child of Inês should be named his successor, but when he was crowned he would also have Inês' corpse exhumed and seated on the throne beside him to receive the honors of a royal coronation.

Further Critical Evaluation of the Work:

This is one of history's most famous love stories, describing "the love that endured beyond the grave." It is set in fourteenth-century Portugal, about a century after the Islamic Moors had been expelled, when Portuguese nobles were still fanatical Christians, wearing chain mail, red crosses on their breasts, and wielding two-handed broadswords.

The counselors of old warrior King Alfonso IV became worried when his son, Crown Prince Pedro, developed an unusually absorbing interest in Inês de Castro, a beautiful lady-in-waiting to the Queen. Many people feared that this union would endanger Portugal, since Inês' brothers were notoriously ambitious. This situation led to a bizarre tragedy, dramatized later by António Ferreira, as well as by Portugal's national poet, Luis de Camoëns, in his masterpiece *The Lusiads*.

Everyone was surprised when Pedro refused to leave Inês, even after pressure had been put upon him. More pressure was exercised, but still Pedro would not abandon Inês. Her enemies finally induced the King to order her assassination, but she made so moving an appeal to Dom Alfonso that he relented—"before the frowning King fair Inês stands, her tears of artless innocence, her air so mild, so lovely, and her face so fair, mov'd the stern monarch. . . . "

The influence of the nobles persisted, however, and she was murdered. As the assassins' swords plunged into the "swan neck" of green-eyed Inês, some small white flowers at her feet, watered with her tears, turned red. Inês is still remembered by the maidens of the university town of Coimbra, where the murder occurred, tradition having it that their tears formed a fountain of love around Pedro's statue there.

Maddened by sorrow, Pedro took the throne in 1357. He exercised ferocious revenge on Inês' killers, staking them out on stone slabs and cutting out their hearts. He then declared that he had been legally married to Inês. Tradition has it that he exhumed her body from the grave, brought it to the palace in Alcobaça, and had her crowned with sumptuous ceremony, obliging the highest nobles of the kingdom to kiss the icy hand of "the Queen after death." Pedro and Inês are buried today in marble tombs in Alcobaça, foot to foot, so that, upon arising on Judgment Day, they will see each other immediately. This tragedy has long been a favorite theme, not only of Portuguese playwrights, but of the playwrights of other literatures.

THE INFORMER

Type of work: Novel
Author: Liam O'Flaherty (1896-   )
Type of plot: Psychological melodrama
Time of plot: The 1920's
Locale: Dublin
First published: 1925

Principal characters:
FRANCIS JOSEPH McPHILLIP, a political murderer
GYPO NOLAN, the informer
DAN GALLAGHER, a revolutionist
KATIE FOX, a prostitute

Critique:

The Informer, an outstanding example
of modern Irish realism and a masterpiece
of suspense, has had a popular as well
as a critical success. Part of its merit consists of its adherence to the classical unities of time, place, and action, for the
entire story covers only a single night in
Dublin. O'Flaherty has given a realistic
picture of the slum and its people, and
of the tight-knit revolutionary organization which could flourish so completely
only in Ireland.

The Story:

Francis McPhillip came to the door
of the public lodging-house. He was un-
obtrusively and shabbily dressed. With
the caution born of necessity, he waited
in the doorway until he was sure he was
not followed. He kept his hand inside
his raincoat to touch the reassuring butt
of his pistol. For six months he had been
a hunted man, hiding out in the wild
mountains.

It was in October that he had killed
the secretary of the Farmers' Union. He
had orders from the revolutionary organization to use his gun only if he had to;
after the killing the organization had
disavowed his act and expelled him. So
he had been a lone fugitive. Now he
was back in Dublin to see his family
once more.

He searched among the public rooms
crowded with Dublin's poor. In the din-
ing-room he found the man he had come

to see: Gypo Nolan. Gypo was eating
from a huge plate of cabbage and bacon
he had stolen from a locker. Francis sat
down and inquired hoarsely of Gypo if
the police were still watching his parents' house. Gypo gave only grunts at
first, and then said he thought the coast
was clear. After eating voraciously from
Gypo's plate, Francis slipped out.

Gypo thought stolidly of his former
companion in the organization. Then he
thought bitterly of his empty pockets;
he could not buy a bed tonight. He tried
to link up these two facts, but Gypo
thought only with great difficulty. The
organization had expelled him too, for
he had been Francis' companion at the
time of the murder. Without Francis'
agile brain he could make no plans. At
last a light came. He marched off to the
police station and told the officers where
they could find Francis. For his information he received twenty pounds. Shortly
afterward, Francis shot himself as police
officers surrounded his father's house.

In a public house Gypo met Katie
Fox, a prostitute who took care of him occasionally when he was destitute. He
bought her a few glasses of gin and told
her he had no need of her bed that night.
She was suspicious because he was in
funds and accused him of robbing a
church. During the quarrel she accidentally let drop the word "informer." Gypo
was startled. He was glad to leave her
and go out in the night.

To keep up appearances, Gypo went to the McPhillip house. He quarreled with Francis' father, who blamed him for the wild life Francis had led. Francis' mother and his sister Mary, however, upheld Gypo for his visit of sympathy. As he left he gave Mrs. McPhillip four silver coins.

Bartly followed him out. Bartly was an organization member sent out to bring Gypo in. After Bartly made a taunting reference to the coins he had given Francis' mother, Gypo choked Bartly, and only the arrival of an armed friend saved his life. By threats and persuasion Gypo was led to the organization headquarters, where he met the feared and respected Dan Gallagher, the revolutionists' leader.

Because of his stupidity and his great strength, Gypo had no fear of men or guns, but Dan was intelligent and soon overcame Gypo's hostility. If Gypo could only give them a lead on the person who had informed the police of Francis' return, he would be taken back into the organization. Dan brought out a bottle and gave Gypo several drinks. Under their influence Gypo concocted a story: Rat Mulligan had a grudge against Francis for betraying his sister, and Gypo declared he had seen Rat following Francis away from the lodging-house. Though he was skeptical, Dan sent for Rat and ordered Gypo to appear for the hearing that night at one-thirty.

Followed by his shadow Bartly, Gypo went out confidently. In a street fight he knocked out a policeman from sheer exuberance. Trailed by an admiring rabble, he went to a lunch stand and bought food for all his admirers. In the confusion he slipped away from Bartly.

Gypo was elated. He had money; he was safe; he would be back in the organization. He went to a superior brothel and spent money recklessly. A well-dressed woman with a scar on her face held aloof. She refused Gypo's advances, saying she was the wife of an army officer and wanted to get back to London. Gypo gave her the fare and accepted the companionship of another girl, Maggie.

Bartly found him with her and reminded him of the inquiry. Gypo gave Maggie a pound to take to Katie and followed Bartly willingly.

Meanwhile Dan had been at the McPhillip house to take the family's statements. He made love briefly to Mary and induced her to accompany him to the inquiry, a kangaroo court held in the wine cellar of a ruined house. Dan acted as prosecutor and three of his men were judges.

First Rat Mulligan was questioned, but it soon developed that Rat could not possibly have been the informer. When Gypo was brought in, Dan made a convincing case: Gypo knew where Francis was going, Gypo had left the lodging-house at the right time, Gypo had been squandering money all night. At last Gypo broke down and confessed his guilt. Dan had him imprisoned in a cellar room with armed guards at the door.

Long ago Francis had discussed with Gypo how to get out of the cell. In the ceiling there was a trapdoor covered with dirt. Exerting his great strength, Gypo seized an iron ring with his hands, and with his legs forced up both trapdoor and covering earth. As he scrambled out the alerted guards shot at him, but he got away. Dan was terrified. Gypo might go to the police and the secret organization would be broken up. Mary was astonished at the weakness of resourceful Dan. When he pulled himself together, he sent agents to cover the roads leading out of the area. Gypo was trapped.

Every time Gypo tried to leave the slum district, he found waiting guards. His only refuge was Katie's room. She let him stay, and he thankfully fell into brutish sleep. Somehow Katie began to think of her own lost and vicious life, and she identified her misery with Gypo. With a notion that she would be canonized, she crept off to inform the organization of Gypo's hiding place.

As four armed men closed in on him, Gypo awoke just in time to fight them off. He crippled two of them in a struggle on the stairs, but he was wounded several times as he ran to escape execution.

Gypo became weaker as he fled. Dan saw him but shrugged as he turned away. He knew the informer was done for. In growing confusion Gypo went into a church where early mass was being celebrated. With dimming vision he made out Mrs. McPhillip. He fell in front of her seat and confessed his treachery. When she forgave him, Gypo stood up and in a loud voice called to Francis that his mother had forgiven him. With a gurgle he fell forward and shivered as blood gushed from his mouth.

Further Critical Evaluation of the Work:

This novel is set in Ireland during the 1920's, in a period when the Irish Republican Army was dormant after its civil conflict with the Free State. There were several isolated bands of rebels still waging a quasi-war. Some of these were units of the IRA and some were communist. Gypo Nolan had belonged to one of these communist groups, but this is not a story about Irish politics or about the way rebels deal with informers. The politics of Gypo Nolan are kept vague by O'Flaherty, partly because Gypo himself understands them so vaguely, and partly because the author wishes to focus his attention, and the reader's, upon the fact of Gypo's abandonment. Gypo's torment, its nature and progress, is the central focus of the novel.

In spite of the fact that relatively little critical work has been done on O'Flaherty, he has long been recognized as one of the central figures of the literary movement called the Irish Renaissance. Seán O'Faoláin felt that O'Flaherty shared center stage in this period with James Joyce only. One of his claims to this honor is *The Informer*. Some feel that of all O'Flaherty's novels this one is the most universal and the least provincial. It, more than any other of his works, is a novel about humanity and the human condition.

O'Flaherty's focus on the human condition in this novel is existential. It is the condition of anxiety. The fact that Gypo Nolan is cut off from human society for being an informer is not as important as the fact that he is cut off. O'Flaherty feels that this is the state of all people. We are all cut off from others to a greater or lesser degree. The purpose of this novel is to explain what the pain of this condition is like, and to describe it as it seems to an observer, to one outside the soul. This same existential loneliness is described internally, as it seems from inside the soul, in one of O'Flaherty's earlier novels, *The Black Soul,* which is the most autobiographical of all his works. He put a great deal of his own loneliness and suffering into the characterizations of *The Black Soul,* and *The Informer* can best be understood as a companion piece. The two novels explore the same problem in different ways.

O'Flaherty makes excellent use of his skill in describing things in order to create atmosphere. He adds to the reader's understanding of loneliness by making him see the misery of Gypo's surroundings. O'Flaherty is able to paint with deft strokes the environment in which Gypo Nolan, Gallagher, and all the other characters operate. He is able to make settings, rooms, household objects, trolley tracks, and paper packages all speak volumes. His use of words is so seemingly magical that he not only can conjure up a scene in the mind's eye of the reader, but also can use this same scene to illuminate the lives, thoughts, and the very essences of the characters in them. It has been said that O'Flaherty writes more for the eye than for the ear. This criticism is all the more appropriate in view of the stunning artistic success of the movie version of this novel. In the motion picture, as in the book, inanimate objects and scenes of action serve only to intensify and illuminate the spiritual lives of the main characters. It is in this visual regard that the movie is most faithful to the form of the novel. Gypo is a miserable man, a fact that we understand more clearly when we see him moving in a miserable world. It is a world that O'Flaherty makes the reader see.

One of the themes runing through the book on several levels is that of New Testament parallels. This is not dissimilar to the existential anxiety which forms the central core of *The Informer,* but rather it is one of the vehicles for its expression. Gypo Nolan can be understood in these terms as a figure of Judas, if one takes Judas also to indicate the nature of Everyman. The parallel with the New Testament is most explicit in the final scene when Gypo, while dying, asks the mother of Francis McPhillip to forgive him. She does so because he did not know what he was doing. This book does not admit of simple substitution of names in order to say that Gypo equals Judas, Gallagher equals Pontius Pilate, and Francis' mother equals the Virgin Mary. O'Flaherty's novel is much too varied and complex for that. Yet Gypo does have much in common with Judas and can be said to be a Judas figure. Gypo turns in his friend to the authorities for a sum of money, and like Judas he finds out that this betrayal cuts him off from his fellow men and women. Neither does the betrayal bring him any sort of happiness. Gypo and Judas both throw the money away and die.

No one, O'Flaherty seems to be saying, can find any sort of happiness if one is cut off from humanity. This is the tragedy of Gypo Nolan, Judas Iscariot, and everyone. Gypo does manage to do some good with the money. He gives a woman in a brothel enough money to enable her to go home, but in the end nothing is left. He has dissipated all the money and is left with only the loneliness that is his birthright, with the existential agony that is the central concern of *The Informer.*

Gypo is not bright. He really was unaware of the consequences of his betrayal. He knew only that he had no money for a bed for the night and that there was a reward of twenty pounds for his friend. By going to the police, he could afford a bed. That was as far as his reasoning went. This lack of intelligence was the immediate cause of his downfall, even though on a deeper level, his humanity made him an outcast from human society. It is important to remember that Gypo is really a very immature person. O'Flaherty is able to build sympathy in the course of this novel, sympathy even for an informer, by gradually pointing out that Gypo is only a child. This is an amazing example of literary skill, for the Irish hate no one so much as an informer. They and their families have for generations suffered too much from traitors for there to be much sympathy left for informers, but O'Flaherty is able to make one see that this informer is still a boy-man torn by the loneliness that all boy-men must live with. And we are all, after all, children in one way or another. Sympathy also arises from the fact that in O'Flaherty's eyes, and ultimately in the eyes of the reader, Gypo Nolan is only incidentally a traitor. He is primarily Everyman, and the author is able to bring about a growing sympathy for him by careful exposition of Gypo's humanity. This special ability was one of the great strengths of O'Flaherty's art.

Glenn M. Edwards

THE INGOLDSBY LEGENDS

Type of work: Comic verse
Author: "Thomas Ingoldsby" (The Rev. Richard Harris Barham, 1788-1845)
First published: 1840, 1842; 1847

Principal characters:
THOMAS INGOLDSBY, Gent., editor of the family legends
CHARLES SEAFORTH, in "The Spectre of Tappington"
LORD TOMNODDY, in "The Execution"
SIR RALPH DE SHURLAND, in "Grey Dolphin"
SAINT DUNSTAN
SAINT GENGULPHUS
SAINT ODILLE
SAINT NICHOLAS
SAINT CUTHBERT
SAINT ALOYS
SAINT MEDARD, in their respective "Lays"

"Captain Swing," the symbol of proletarian revolt in England in the 1830's, makes several appearances in Richard Harris Barham's comic verse, always in a contemptible light. The rick-burning associated with the "Captain" may have been abhorred by the poet and his middle-class public as a foreign import of violence, but it was also a sure sign of the depression which closed the decade and the one which followed. A very different sign of the temper of the times was *The Ingoldsby Legends* themselves; they increased the flow of comic verse initiated by Hood and continued by Lear, Carrol, and Gilbert among a host of minor talents who parodied everything they could lay their hands on and produced comic versions of every familiar object from fox hunting to the history of England. Although the fashion spread to America and the colonies, and lasted into the early decades of this century in *Punch*, it was so much confined to Victorian England as to become a characteristic of that time and place.

The Ingoldsby Legends first appeared in 1837, the year of Victoria's accession, in Richard Bentley's *Miscellany*. This was a new publishing venture, edited by Charles Dickens, which ceased shortly before Barham's death in 1845. The volume now titled *The Ingoldsby Legends* was largely collected from the *Miscellany* pieces which had previously been published in two series in 1840 and 1842. Apart from a few occasional or sentimental pieces, the legends comprise about fifty long poems and six short stories. The best-known of the latter, "The Spectre of Tappington," initiated the *Legends* and explains in a final note that this is a story or legend of the Ingoldsby family of Tappington Everard in Kent, the family mansion of the Barhams. Later the legends continued to be published under the pseudonym of "Thomas Ingoldsby," who was supposed to have found them in an old oak chest in the manor and who edited them for publication in the *Miscellany*.

Barham's pseudonym was preserved for a time and maintained in his letters from "Thomas Ingoldsby" to Bentley prefacing the two series published in his lifetime; but the pretense must soon have been penetrated. Barham in 1837 was forty-nine and well-known in London ecclesiastical, theatrical, and journalistic circles. For sixteen years he had been a Canon of St. Paul's Cathedral and was now also Vicar of St. Mary Magdalene; he is supposed to have been a model parish parson but it is difficult to see how he combined those duties with editing the *London Chronicle* for a number of years and religiously attending the theater. A minister of the Church of England was obviously in the early nineteenth century a gentleman above all else, and as such he was expected to go out in society and to possess some accomplishments such as the ability to turn out light verse. Barham had already shown such ability in the comic verses and the novel he had published before he began the *Legends* which are now his claim to fame.

Some of the *Legends* are still anthologized, "The Jackdaw of Rheims" being the best-known; but the volume as a whole is likely to become wearisome to the modern reader when read right through. The early Victorians found the work amusing because the *Legends* are long stories in comic verse ending in a mock moral: they were intended to occupy one's time, to entertain, and to instruct. The peculiar mode evolved by Thomas Hood and developed by Barham, that of comic verse, accounted for the length of the stories (over one thousand lines in some poems) and for the sly humor of the moral conclusion.

A comparison of "The Jackdaw of Rheims" and "The Spectre of Tappington" will fix most of the qualities of the *Legends*. Both deal with the apparently magical disappearance of objects, in the former the Cardinal's turquoise ring, in the latter Charles Seaforth's whole wardrobe of trousers. Many of the *Legends* deal with the disappearance of treasure— "The Lay of the Old Woman Clothed in Grey," for instance—and that the treasure in one case is trousers is typical not only of oddly coy references to a garment that Barham several times says he can only allude to but also of his general tendency to reduce the exotic and rare to homely proportions. In "The Jackdaw of Rheims" the gorgeous procession of "six little Singing-boys" ends as

One little boy more
A napkin bore,
Of the best white diaper, fringed with
    pink,
And a Cardinal's Hat mark'd in permanent ink.

In both tales there is a rational explanation for the disappearance. Charles Seaforth, for example, in "The Spectre of Tappington" sleepwalks and buries his own trousers. But the Cardinal's curse apparently causes the return of the ring. More than half the *Legends* deal with medieval superstitions, generally ghosts and witches, some of them a retelling of popular stories, as in "The Lay of St. Dunstan," which recapitulates the tale of the sorcerer's apprentice. Most of the *Legends* return to the past rather than dealing with contemporary events; the largest single group is the "Lays" of Saints Dunstan, Gengulphus, Odille, Nicholas, Cuthbert, Aloys, and Medard. The prose "Spectre" reads like one of the comic Irish tales of Charles Lever and restricts Barham's fancy by necessitating dialogue and scenes; he prefers to embroider verbally so that the stanza gradually moves away from the object it is describing and sometimes even returns on itself, as in "The Auto-Da-Fe":

And no one, I am sure, will deny it
    who's tried a
Vile compound they have that's called
    Olla Podrida.
(This, by the by, 's a mere rhyme to
    the eye,
For in Spanish the *i* is pronounced like
    an *e*,
And they've not quite our mode of pronouncing the *d*.
In Castile, for instance, it's given
    through the teeth,
And what we call Ma*d*rid they sound
    more like Marreeth.)

The most obvious feature of comic verse is the complexity of rhyme and meter, providing an elaborate surface to the poems that minimizes their content and is sometimes strained in effect, devices that Gilbert, for instance, gradually toned down in the *Bab Ballads* and was able to use effectively in the dramatic context of his operas. The variety of stanza forms reflects the complexity of other devices, but is also used to change the style of a whole poem, as in the ballad quatrains of "St. Medard," or the tone of a poem when some grave matter must unfortunately be introduced. The grave element in these poems often deals with the deaths of foolish women, such as the Maiden in the mock-ballad, "Bloudie Jack of Shrewsberrie," or of wicked strong men, such as Sir Ralph de Shurland in the prose tale, "Grey Dolphin," and is usually made ridiculous.

One of the shortest *Legends* is "The Execution: A Sporting Anecdote," sometimes anthologized under the name of its hero, Lord Tomnoddy, a young man about town who relieves his ennui by throwing a party for his fellow "sports" to watch a man hang; the party becomes so drunken that all the young men miss the execution, which is described in couplets or triplets without the internal rhyme of the rest of the poem.

In the "Auto-Da-Fe" the mass burning of Jews is described in comic verse:

> While similar treatment is forcing out
> hollow moans
> From Aby Ben Lasco and Ikey Ben
> Solomons,
> Whose beards—this a black, that in-
> clining to grizzle—
> Are smoking, and curling, and all in a
> fizzle;
> The King, at the same time, his Dons,
> and his visitors,
> Sit, sporting smiles, like the Holy In-
> quisitors . . .

But the scene is preceded by a long apostrophe of righteous horror at the tradition of the Inquisition and the cruel auto-da-fe, addressed to Seville and couched in trochaic-iambic tetrameter:

> Those shouts from human fiends that
> swell,—
> That withering scream,—that frantic
> yell,—
> All, Seville,—all too truly tell
> Thou *art* a MARVEL—and a HELL!

The tripping meter is almost always anapaestic tetrameter; to prevent monotony and the effect of doggerel the succes-

sion of twelve-syllable lines is broken by dimeters in the same measure, generally two to a line to give an internal masculine rhyme which is also used by the line or lines that follow:

> But whatever she said, It fill'd him with
> dread,
> And made all his hair stand on end on
> his head. . . .

Barham's verse is chiefly remarkable for its rhyme rather than its meter. He can extend the rhyme of a couplet to eight lines; the triple or feminine rhymes he evolves are his most distinctive feature; usually a polysyllable is made to echo a concluding run of monosyllables or part of another polysyllable which is broken in two. Byron's well-known "intellectual . . . henpecked you all" in *Don Juan* is outdone many times by Barham, as in the following examples, "temper or . . . Emperor," "College, I . . . Acknowledge, I," "in fine a . . . Agrippina," "Rostopchin . . . drop chin," "Apollo, cost . . . holocaust," "condemn none . . . Agamemnon," "dragon he . . . agony," "dupe colour'd . . . pea-soup-colour'd.". It was this verbal dexterity which the Victorians loved, and Barham had a long reign in the parlor, schoolroom, and nursery.

Barham's popularity declined because his verbal dexterity is simply verbal dexterity. When one tires of the juggling virtuosity only the tone and content remain, and both may be distasteful to modern audiences, not because of the constant laughing at church ritual ("Father Fothergill brewed an XXX puncheon of holy water") but for the quality of social and racial snobbery expressed in many of the poems. But these faults are not apparent if the *The Ingoldsby Legends* are read as they should be, at intervals and in the context of Victorian verse. They belong in the anthologies.

THE INHERITORS

Type of work: Novel
Author: William Golding (1911-   )
Time: The Paleolithic period
Locale: A mountainous, wooded countryside not far from the sea
First published: 1955

Principal characters:
THE PEOPLE
MAL, the old leader
THE OLD WOMAN
HA, the wisest of the younger people
NIL, a young mother
THE NEW ONE, Nil's baby
LOK, the People's clown
FA, a young woman
LIKU, a child

THE OTHERS
MARLAN, the leader, called "the old man"
TUAMI, his successor
VIVANI, Marlan's woman, called "the fat woman"
TANAKIL, a child

The *Inheritors*, William Golding's second novel, was first published in England in 1955. Like *Lord of the Flies, The Two Deaths of Christopher Martin,* and *The Spire,* it has a setting remote from our own lives and civilization. In these isolated situations Golding explores man's struggle for survival: the struggle with his fellow men, with his physical environment, and with himself. Although these preoccupations are, in themselves, common to many novels, one of the distinctive features of Golding's work is that at the opening of each novel his characters are already at their hour of reckoning, or, in other words, of extreme peril. The success of Golding's approach is achieved by an exercise of great imaginative power and the ability to create an environment of great solidity and reality, so that what has gone before is apparent through implication and the way in which the characters react to their confrontation with fate in terms of their previous experience. For the Neanderthal people of *The Inheritors* the natural, physical world of tree, mountain, river, and rock is the prime reality; when forces alien to their known world intrude, Gold-

ing begins their story.

Each spring Mal has led his small tribe, the last of their kind, from their winter quarters by the sea to a terrace and overhang above a waterfall that is their summer home. The way leads over a river that divides around a rocky island. "The people" fear water and had never considered going to the island. When they discover that the log by which they have always crossed the river has disappeared, they are confused until Mal "pictures" a past time when wise men took the original log and bridged the water with it.

These "pictures" are the people's embryonic thought processes: they serve both as memories and ideas. The pictures are rarely consecutive and fade as soon as the need for them has passed, for they are an instinctual and not a rational function. The people can share their pictures without words or express them in simple sentences.

The people have retained the strong senses of animals, but they have also developed their own human rituals concerned with food, fire, and burial. The Old Woman always carries the fire from the winter to the summer home. When the smells of smoke and woman come to Lok from the island, he is bemused and, tricked by his senses into following the familiar scent, he almost falls into the river. As the rest of the people have not caught the faint scent, Lok cannot communicate his picture, and this second intimation of otherness is forgotten in their eager journey to the security of the overhang. Lok almost recaptures his experience while guarding the people that night, but the "picture" fades before he can recapture it.

The people's failure to retain ideas not relevant to day-to-day life makes their survival impossible when faced with the existence of "the others." Also, and this is one of the main themes of the novel, their lack of the knowledge of evil inevitably makes them powerless to combat it. When Ha disappears, although the people can tell by the scent that he has encountered another, their emotions are grief at loss rather than abiding fear because people in this simple, distant world understand one another. This simple, moving statement of faith is the pivotal point of the novel. That the remainder of the book proves it false is Mr. Golding's grim assertion that the meek do not inherit the earth.

After Mal's death and Ha's disappearance, Lok is the only surviving adult male; it is his task to seek out the others. These others are true *homo sapiens* with the power of reason, for their senses are reduced, their artifacts far more sophisticated than the people's. They use animal skins for covering, have bows and arrows, canoes, drinking vessels, and crude alcohol. They also know sexual jealousy. However, because they cannot eat the bulbs, slugs, and fungi that sustain the people (who never kill for food) and because hunting early in the year is poor, they are near famine.

When the others capture Liku and the New One on the people's side of the river, Lok hears Liku's screams and tries to reach her. He thus exposes himself to the others' arrows. These weapons merely interest him, although he senses danger when he smells the poison on the barbed heads. Lok's apprehensions of danger are lulled at various times by the others' obvious hunger and by his sympathy for them as they work together.

Finally, only Lok and Fa remain; the old woman was drowned, and Nil slain. Lok rejects Fa's suggestion that they escape and survive (the instinct for the preservation and continuation of life is much stronger in the women, protecting the home and finding food the aims of the men) and insists on trying to rescue Liku and the New One.

The others move their camp from the island to the people's side of the river to hunt for deer. The new camp is made by a hollow tree where Lok and Fa hide from the others. From this tree the two people witness an incomprehensible day of ritual and night of debauchery including, while Lok sleeps, the killing of Liku.

The only communication between the people and the others had been Liku's growing friendship with Tanakil, a girl of her own age. They are able to exchange names and Liku has fed Tanakil fungus when she was hungry. This deed, together with the others' need for a sacrifice to make their hunting successful, caused them to kill her.

In an attempt to snatch the New One from the camp, Lok becomes separated from Fa and, believing that she is dead, mourns for her. Although he feels that he is the last of his people, his hope is still sustained by the presence of the other, and at that moment he reaches his furthest point of comprehension, which he does not have the power to retain. Fa finds Lok again, but during a last effort to recover the New One before the others could take him upstream with them she is stunned and swept away in the falls. After the final disappearance of Fa and the departure of the others, Lok is alone and his humanity leaves him.

Solitary, Lok reverts to an anthropoid state. In a coda passage before the reversal of viewpoint in the last chapter, the first complete physical description of one of the people partly explains the others' destructive terror. The only human aspect remaining to Lok is the tears on his face as he lies down to die on Mal's grave.

In the final chapter, the others are named. Tuami, the younger leader, was known to the people, as was Tanakil. The old man is identified as Marlan; the most important woman, who suckles the New One, is Vivani. As Tuami steers the boat toward the open plains away from "the devils," he and all the others are overcome by grief and bitterness and Tuami cries out to ask what else they could have done. These people are now quite human and understandable, their actions against the Neanderthals having been dictated by the twin evils of fear and ignorance. But some grace has gone out of their lives forever; their slow-moving boat is a point of darkness between the light of sky and water.

This sad and serious novel graphically portrays the destructiveness of fear and the horror of ignorance which together destroyed innocence. But in spite of the irony in the bitter fact that the people and the others, could, together, have improved life, the book is not an allegorical plea. Like William Golding's other novels, it is a fable affirming man's will to survive.

THE INNOCENT VOYAGE

Type of work: Novel
Author: Richard Hughes (1900-   )
Type of plot: Psychological realism
Time of plot: Early nineteenth century
Locale: Jamaica, the high seas, England
First published: 1929

Principal characters:
MR. BAS-THORNTON, a plantation owner in Jamaica
MRS. BAS-THORNTON, his wife
JOHN,
EMILY,
EDWARD,
RACHAEL, and
LAURA, their children
MARGARET FERNANDEZ, Emily's friend
HARRY FERNANDEZ, her brother
CAPTAIN JONSEN, captain of a pirate ship
A DUTCH SEA CAPTAIN, murdered by Emily

Critique:

The Innocent Voyage, equally well-known under its alternate English title, *A High Wind in Jamaica*, is an unusual novel on which the author has realistically shown the effect—or lack of effect —of a series of horrible experiences upon the minds of seven young children. These experiences include a hurricane, capture by pirates, seduction, murder, and a trial at Old Bailey. Written with varied humor that runs from macabre playfulness to biting satire, the novel ranks as a minor classic because of its convincing insights into the childhood psyche. For the world of childhood, as the writer makes plain, is quite different from the adult one, and also different from what most grownups suppose. The Bas-Thornton children are not young monsters, as some mistaken readers have supposed. They are children protected and insulated by the amorality of their own innocence from an adult world of compulsions, frustrations, and fears.

The Story:

Five young Bas-Thorntons lived on the family's run-down sugar plantation in Jamaica. On the day after Emily's tenth birthday they were allowed to make their first visit away from home. They went to meet Margaret and Harry Fernandez, children of creole neighbors, on a nearby plantation. The Fernandez children often ran around barefoot, like Negroes; Emily thought it quite wonderful. During their visit the region was shaken by a slight quake. Emily, wildly excited, galloped her pony into the sea. For the first time she realized that there were forces in the world over which neither she nor adults had any control.

If the earthquake was the most thrilling event of Emily's life, the death of a pet cat was soon to be the most terrible. The next evening, back home, a hurricane struck the island. While the house shook under the force of wind and rain, Tabby streaked through the house and dashed out into the storm pursued by a pack of wild jungle cats. That night the house and the surrounding countryside were blown flat, but the destruction was nothing compared with the mystery of Tabby's horrible fate.

Mr. and Mrs. Bas-Thornton had no way of knowing what was passing through the children's minds. Fearing that the hurricane must have been a shock to them, the parents reluctantly decided to send them back to England to school. They and the Fernandez children were shortly put aboard the *Clorinda*, in care of Captain James Marpole.

Off the Cuban coast pirates boarded the vessel. Her stores and valuables were seized, and the children removed to the marauder for their supper. Captain Marpole, mistaking efforts to return the children for the splash of bodies thrown overboard, left the scene under full sail. Later he wrote the Bas-Thorntons that the pirates had callously murdered the children. Actually, Captain Jonsen, leader of the pirate crew, was surprised to find himself the custodian of seven young travelers.

The *Clorinda's* cargo was auctioned off at Santa Lucia, Cuba. While playing, Emily's older brother John fell forty feet to his death from a warehouse doorway. The vessel presently put to sea with the surviving children.

For weeks the pirate ship sailed aimlessly over the ocean in search of booty. The children, allowed to do much as they pleased, amused themselves with two pigs and a monkey the vessel carried. Emily began to be aware of her identity as a separate personality; shipboard life which she had accepted unquestioningly at first began to disturb her. One night Captain Jonsen, drunk, came into the children's quarters. When he tried to stroke Emily's hair she bit his thumb. Margaret, more mature, was sick after the incident, but a few days later she went to the captain's cabin to live. From that time on she avoided the other children.

As both bore an individual weight of guilt, Emily and the captain evaded each other after the drunken incident, until a thigh wound Emily received from a marlin spike dropped by Rachel brought about a reconciliation. Captain Jonsen carried her to his cabin, dressed the gash, and gave her his bunk.

Emily was still confined to bed, her wound healing, when the pirates captured a Dutch steamer carrying a cargo of wild animals. Her captain was bound and left tied on the floor of Emily's cabin while Captain Jonsen and his crew amused themselves with the animals aboard their prize.

While Emily screamed futilely, the Dutch captain managed to roll toward a knife lying in a corner. He was not a handsome man. He seemed to have no neck and he reeked of cigar smoke; the fact that he was tied up like an animal added to Emily's terror. His fingers were groping for the blade when she threw herself out of her bunk. Seizing the knife, she slashed at him until he was covered with wounds. Leaving him to bleed to death, she then hurled the weapon toward the door and dragged herself back to the bunk.

Margaret was the first to enter the cabin, and so the first boatload of pirates to return from the captured steamer thought she had committed the crime. Horrified, they dropped her overboard to drown. The freebooters in the second boat, assuming that she had accidentally fallen in, picked her up. In the excitement caused by the murder no one noticed her come aboard, and she was not disturbed when she rejoined the younger children in the hold.

With the captain's death hanging over their heads, intimacy between children and pirates came to an end. Realizing the wantonness of her deed, Emily had to bear the double burden of her conscience and the fear that Margaret would identify the real culprit.

The sight of a man-of-war on the horizon finally brought Captain Jonsen to a decision; it was time he and the children parted company. With his ship disguised as a shabby cargo vessel, the *Lizzie Green*, he persuaded the captain of a passing steamship to relieve him of his young passengers. The children were laying their own plans for capturing another prize when the mate called Emily aside to coach her in what he hoped would be the children's story. Emily willingly promised to say that the captain of the *Lizzie Green* had rescued them from pirates; but it was she who, in a childish burst of confidence to the stewardess aboard the steamer, told the secret of the pirate vessel. On that information, a gunboat apprehended Captain Jonsen and his men; they were imprisoned in Newgate. The young Bas-Thorntons were reunited with their parents, who had sold the plantation and moved to England. Margaret and Harry Fernandez went to stay with relatives.

Although Emily had revealed their captors' identities readily enough, the prosecuting attorney had good reason for doubting his ability to obtain a conviction. The children told about the pirates' monkey and some turtles the *Clorinda* had carried, but of life aboard the pirate ship they had little to say. All memory of John seemed obliterated from their minds. It was accepted by the grownups, and gradually by the children, that he had died trying to protect the girls. This conclusion was substantiated by Margaret's condition of shock and loss of memory.

Emily became the chief witness for the Crown. Asked about the Dutch captain and the possibility that he had been murdered, she became hysterical but managed to say she had seen him lying in a pool of blood. Her statement was enough for a conviction. As she left the courtroom she saw in Captain Jonsen's eyes the same desperate and despairing look she had seen in Tabby's the night of the hurricane. Captain Jonsen was condemned to be hanged.

A few days later Emily was taken to her new school by her parents. The head mistress spoke feelingly of the experiences Emily had undergone, but anyone else, looking at her, would have found that Emily's innocent young face blended perfectly with the others as she stood chattering with the quiet-mannered young ladies who were to be her new friends.

Further Critical Evaluation of the Work:

In *The Innocent Voyage* or *A High Wind in Jamaica,* as the novel is now universally known, melodramatic and fantastic events are united with innocence and humor, all blended with craftsmanship and style. A powerful and blunt realism combined with the delicacy of the poetic descriptions gives the narrative a strange, disturbing quality. Yet the author is careful never to overwrite when describing the bizarre incidents of the story. The plot is based upon an actual event related to Hughes by an old lady who had been one of the children. Joseph Conrad previously utilized the same actual happening in *Romance* (1901).

Emily's maturing during the novel is rendered as a symbol, yet Hughes never lets any outside meanings interfere with the tale he has to tell. The sudden awakening of Emily's consciousness is detailed with charming and touching truth. The account of the girl's development is *right,* portrayed with sensitivity and with humor. Her sudden questioning at the age of ten of the universe and its maker and her amazement at her own being are the finest pages in an extraordinary and perceptive novel.

Hughes's attitude toward the children is unique in fiction, never condescending and unusually objective, as if he were writing of a different species being observed under experimental conditions. Because the characters are handled with unassuming honesty, the strange events of the story become almost matter-of-fact. Hughes seems to be implying that, yes, life is bizarre and frightening, but also beautiful and amazing—especially for those with the awareness and fearlessness of children. But with knowledge and maturity must come fear and deception and unhappiness—and the gradual clouding of vision. And this loss of innocence is the real tragedy of human life. (Perhaps the worst aspect of the loss is that adults do not even remember what they have lost, or even seem to realize that they have lost anything.) Yet Hughes does not romanticize either the children or their condition. His power comes from the cleanness of his objectivity and the purity of his prose.

AN INQUIRY CONCERNING POLITICAL JUSTICE

Type of work: Political theory
Author: William Godwin (1756-1836)
First published: 1793

In 1793, William Godwin, the first systematic exponent of anarchism, published his *Inquiry Concerning Political Justice* (its full title *An Inquiry Concerning the Principles of Political Justice, and its Influence on General Virtue and Happiness*). This three-volume work gives evidence of being strongly influenced by the impulses of the French Revolution and argues that the rational being, man, must be given complete freedom to exercise his pure reason. All forms of government, being founded on irrational assumptions, are tyrannical and eventually must be eliminated. Because laws have not been produced by wisdom but by greed and fear, they should be replaced by the products of reasonable men's ability to make decisions. Accumulated property is a means of exploitation and, consequently, must be abolished. This last point was, however, modified in a later edition. With its varying degrees of indebtedness to Aristippus, Plato, Rousseau, and Helvétius, and despite its equivocating alterations in the final revision, Godwin's book gave evidence of original thinking and provided generations of revolutionary thinkers with both stimulation and guidance.

Godwin asserts that the general human objective is happiness, that politics, the promotion of individual good is man's most important pursuit, and that the two traditional articles of political liberty have been (1) "security of our persons" and (2) "security of our property." But, Godwin asks, would not a good government "take away all restraints upon the enquiring mind"? The early chapters of the book develop Godwin's view that all through history government has had a corrupting influence, but only because man has not lived up to his potential truthfulness, his ability to see what is evil and what is good. The assumption is that if man will define clearly to himself the genuinely good principles of life, government will improve.

Godwin surveys historically the destructiveness and futility of war, and to emphasize its irrational causes, he quotes at some length from the satire on war in Book II of Swift's *Gulliver's Travels*. In the present condition punishment is the only means of repressing the violent revolt of the deprived masses. But if government is a subject for discussion, then men might reasonably agree about it some day and see the advantages of freedom and equality.

From these premises Godwin proceeds to demonstrate that, of the three principal causes of moral improvement, both literature and education, though beneficial, have limitations, and that the third cause, political justice, is strong where the first two are weak; that is, in the extent of its operation. When political justice is equally addressed to all, it will impart virtue to all. Since error and injustice tend to destroy themselves, it is doubtful whether they could be perpetuated without governmental support, for government "reverses the genuine propensities of mind, and instead of suffering us to look forward, teaches us to look backward for perfection." To exemplify how political institutions have in the past militated against moral improvement, Godwin points out the destructive passions engendered by the inequality of property, the magnificence accorded to enormous wealth, and the insolence and usurpation of rich persons. Traditionally, both legislation and administration of the law have favored the rich and have repressed the freedom of the poor to stand up to the rich.

Godwin asserts strongly that man's most distinguished and most important characteristic is his perfectability, by which he means not the capacity to become perfect but, rather, the capability of perpetual improvement. Evidences of man's progressive nature are the development of language and the invention of alphabetical writing. Having asserted that all science and all art are capable of further perfection, Godwin asks why the same should not be true of morals and social institutions. On the usefulness of history in this regard, he comments: "Let us look back, that we may profit by the experience of mankind; but let us not look back as if the wisdom of our ancestors was such as to leave no room for future improvements."

The true instruments of moral influence, in Godwin's opinion, are not direct physical causes such as climate but, rather, such concepts as desire and aversion or punishment and reward. Definitely restrictive to moral progress are the institutions or professions which always operate to produce a certain character or stereotype and thus suppress frankness of mind. The example cited by Godwin is the priesthood, which requires that all priests must be alike in their subservience. And Godwin is certain that free men in any country will be "firm, vigorous and spirited in proportion to their freedom," as, conversely, slaves will be "ignorant, servile and unprincipled."

When the magic of the indoctrinated idea is dissolved and the great majority of any society seek true benefits, the struggle need not involve tumult or violence. Indeed, "the effort would be to resist reason, not to obey it." Just views must be infused into the liberally educated, but this process must come about gradually. Man's basic error in politics is the supposition that a change is impracticable, with the result that he does not look forward incessantly to its accomplishment. Men do not choose evil when they see it to be evil. Therefore, once having shaken off an injurious evil, a society will not permit its revival unless its conviction of truth becomes obliterated.

*An Inquiry Concerning Political Jus-*tice develops a theme which is in close agreement with Thomas Paine's belief that society, being produced by our wants, is a blessing, but that government, necessitated by our wickedness, is at its best a necessary evil. Godwin defines the term *justice* as meaning that the individual should contribute everything in his power to the benefit of the whole, not the concept of all for the state but of each individual for the other individuals. The importance to the general weal must be the only standard, and a benefit conferred upon an individual to the detriment of the society is wrong. Even one's self-preservation must be based on the premise of one's good to the society—to all mankind. An important theme in this book is the propriety of applying more justice in order to ascertain political truth.

Society is bound to do for its members everything that can contribute to their welfare. In Godwin's view, that which most enlarges the mind—virtue and consciousness of independence—contributes most to this welfare. Individuals, for their part, must follow the best knowledge obtainable. Regarding the possibility that a wrong action may result even from the individual's best intention, Godwin says: "If the disposition by which a man is governed have a systematical tendency to the benefit of his species, he cannot fail to obtain our esteem, however mistaken he may be in his conduct." Virtue is essentially the incessant search for accurate knowledge about utility and right, in which search the exercise of private judgment and the dictates of individual conscience must be accorded primary importance. Since pleasure is to be desired and pain to be avoided, individuals should contribute to the pleasure and benefit of one another and should oppose the despot's power, which is based on indoctrination and is productive of pain."

Moral equality consists in "the propriety of applying one unalterable rule of justice to every case that may arise." Two persons cannot have opposite rights; men really have no rights. Since *rights* can apply only to totally indifferent things (where to sit and the like), and since intelligent man immediately becomes moral man with duties, rights and duties are absolutely exclusive of each other. Although society, composed of individuals, also has no rights, we must, under the present inadequate government, assert some "rights."

Because judgment is founded on evidence, compulsion cannot bring men to uniformity of opinion. Government needs to be perfected away from the concept of compulsion; the insignificant individual must be made free to criticize the august senate. Countries in which decrees instead of arguments are ultimate contain "mere phantoms of men," who give no indication of what men might be if they were entirely free to follow the dictates of conscience and to speak and act as they think. Finally, individual justice—

equality and freedom—must be the basis and goal of improvement in government.

Having set forth the underlying principles of his theory, Godwin proceeds to criticize existing society, develop his system of social ethics, and predict conditions of the future. His confidence in the power of reason gives the book an optimism which has frequently been criticized as unresponsive to the lessons of history. While it is true that his emphasis on necessity (cause and effect viewed as an invariable sequence) is inconsistent with his simultaneous assertion of the efficacy of education, Godwin has been unfairly criticized for maintaining that enlightened education could rectify the falsity and the ignorance of man's judgments. Such a criticism cannot be fairly administered until after the society has made a concerted effort to educate itself as Godwin proposed.

THE INSPECTOR GENERAL

Type of work: Drama
Author: Nikolai V. Gogol (1809-1852)
Type of plot: Political satire
Time of plot: Early nineteenth century
Locale: Russia
First presented: 1836

> *Principal characters:*
> ANTON ANTONOVICH SKVOZNIK-DMUKHANOVSKY, prefect of a small
> provincial town
> ANNA, his wife
> MARIA, his daughter
> IVAN ALEXANDROVICH HLESTAKOV, a traveler
> OSIP, Ivan's servant

Critique:

This comedy, the high point of Gogol's work in the drama, represents an effective protest on his part against the fumbling, venal bureaucracy of Russia's small towns. Under the tsars, favoritism was rife, and the practice of giving and accepting bribes and favors is here satirized. The characters in the play are numerous but unimportant. The situation, which is credibly presented, and the system of government portrayed are what make this comedy live. The resemblances to modern manners and customs are close enough for us to enjoy the basic similarity to bureaucratic institutions in our own time.

The Story:

The prefect of the town, Anton Antonovich, had received a disquieting letter. A friend wrote that an inspector was coming to visit the province and particularly his district. The inspector would probably travel incognito. The friend advised the prefect to clean up the town and hide evidence of any bribes that might discredit him. Anton in haste called a meeting of the local dignitaries and instructed them how to make a good impression on the official from the capital.

Artemy Filippovich Zemlyanika, the hospital manager, was advised to put clean nightcaps on the patients and take away their strong tobacco for a time. The manager was thoughtful; he had always proceeded on the theory that if a patient were going to die, he would die anyway.

He decided, however, to clean up both the patients and the hospital and to put up a sign in Latin over each bed to tell the patient's malady.

Ammos Fedorovich Lyapkin-Tyapkin, the judge, spent most of his time hunting. He kept a whip and other sporting equipment in his courtroom, and in the vestibule the porter kept a flock of geese. His assessor always smelled of liquor. Ammos protested that the assessor was injured as a baby and had smelled of brandy ever since. Anton suggested that he be made to eat garlic to cover the smell.

Luka Lukich Hlopov, the head of the school, was advised to cover up the more obvious foibles of his teachers. The one with a fat face, for instance, always made horrible grimaces when a visitor came and pulled his beard under his necktie; and the history teacher jumped on his desk when he described the Macedonian wars.

Piqued by a recital of their weaknesses, the others turned on Anton and reminded him that he took money bribes and only recently had had the wife of a noncommissioned officer flogged. During the wrangle the postmaster came in to see they had had any news of the inspector's arrival. Anton advised the postmaster to open all letters in an attempt to discover who the inspector might be and when he would arrive. The advice was superfluous for the postmaster always read all the letters anyway.

Two squires of the town, Bobchinski

and Dobchinsky, rushed in with exciting news. A mysterious stranger, obviously a high-born gentleman, was at that moment lodging in the local inn, and had been there a fortnight. His servant had let it out that his master was from St. Petersburg. Sure that the stranger was the inspector, the company trembled to think what he might already have learned. They scattered to repair any damage they could.

At the inn Osip was lying on his master's bed and ruminating on the queerness of gentlefolk. His gentleman was always gambling, always broke, always selling his clothes to get funds. They were stuck in this wretched inn because there was no money to pay their bill. At this point, Ivan Alexandrovich burst in, loudly calling for supper.

When the waiter was summoned, he insolently refused to serve Ivan until the guest had paid his bill. After a long argument, some watery soup and a tough hen were brought, and perforce Ivan dined poorly. As the dishes were being removed amidst a tussle between Osip and the waiter for the remains of the supper, visitors were announced.

Nervous and apologetic, the prefect stood before Ivan's august person. Ivan thought, however, that he was to be put in jail. For a time the conversation was at cross purposes, but Ivan had the nimbler wit and allowed the prefect to do most of the talking. When he began to suspect what Anton was trying to say, he coolly accepted two hundred roubles to pay his bill, an invitation to stay at the prefect's house, and a nomination as the guest of honor at an official dinner at the hospital.

Anna and Maria were arguing about clothes, as usual, when Dobchinsky rushed in to announce the arrival of the inspector and his fine condescension in coming to stay at their house. Dobchinsky thought that he was being honest when he assured them their guest was a general. Thrilled at the idea of entertaining a general, the two ladies began to primp and preen.

When the men came in, Anton tried to impress the inspector by saying that he never played cards. Ivan approved; he especially abhorred gambling. Osip snickered at his master's remark, but fortunately he was not noticed. To impress the household Ivan then informed them that he was an author; besides writing for the papers he composed poetry and novels. When he referred casually to his high political connections, his hearers were agog, particularly the ladies. Meanwhile Ivan was steadily drinking wine. At last he fell into a drunken sleep in his chair.

With only Osip remaining, Anton tried to pump the servant as to his master's habits and tastes, while the ladies tried to find out something about Ivan's love life. Since Anton kept giving him money, Osip obliged by telling many details of his master's place in high society.

Ivan was put to bed to sleep off the wine. When he awoke, the dignitaries of the town waited on him one by one. Ammos, the judge, introduced himself and asked for the inspector's orders. Ivan carelessly promised to speak well of the judge to his friends, and just as carelessly borrowed money from his suppliant. The postmaster was impressed with Ivan's friendliness and was glad to lend him three hundred roubles. Both Luka and Artemy were glad to lend the inspector three or four hundred roubles, but Bobchinsky and Dobchinsky together could raise only sixty-five roubles.

When the petitioners left, Osip begged his master to leave while the pickings were still good. Ivan, agreeing that immediate departure might be prudent, sent the servant to make arrangements. Osip wangled the best coach the town could offer. In the meantime several shopkeepers also came in to protest against the prefect, who was making them pay tribute. From them Ivan borrowed five hundred roubles.

When Maria came in, Ivan was so elated at his successes that he made love to her and finally kissed her on the shoulder. The daughter scurried away as her mother came in, and Ivan ogled the older lady, too. The daughter came back, full of curiosity, and in his confusion Ivan proposed marriage to Maria, who accepted him graciously. After writing a letter to a friend, in which he detailed his humorous adventures, Ivan left town. He promised, however, to return the next day.

In the morning Anton and his wife received the envious congratulations of friends. The ladies, green with envy, assured Maria that she would be a belle in St. Petersburg society. The parents, much taken with the idea, decided that their new son-in-law would insist on taking the whole family to live in the capital. Anton was sure that he would be made a general at least.

At that moment the postmaster arrived with Ivan's letter. When he read the frank description of the pretended inspector's love-making and his franker opinion of the muddle-headed town officials, the tremendous hoax gradually dawned on the company.

As the crestfallen crowd was counting up the losses, a gendarme came in with an official announcement. An inspector from St. Petersburg had just arrived and desired them all to wait upon him immediately. He was staying at the inn.

Further Critical Evaluation of the Work:

Although most of Nikolai Gogol's highly praised work consists of prose fiction, *The Inspector General* established his reputation in the theater as well. In the history of Russian literature, Gogol was a pioneer of realistic prose. When he turned his hand to playwriting, Gogol set equally important precedents for later Russian drama, for he applied his skills at realistic fiction to the stage. He wrote two other plays and left a dramatic fragment unfinished at the time of his death. But Gogol's theatrical laurels rest on his masterpiece, *The Inspector General*. The play has been translated under several titles: *The Inspector, The Government Inspector,* and *Revizor* (transliterated from the Cyrillic, this is the Russian word for "Inspector" or "Auditor"). But by whatever name it is called, it has deservedly been given unstinting critical acclaim.

This satiric comedy on corrupt bueaucrats in the Russian provinces blazed the trail for the realistic social drama of the later nineteenth and the twentieth centuries. However, Gogol was by no means a doctrinaire realist, nor was he even a devoted social or political reformer in the ideological-polemic sense. In fact, Gogol saw himself not as a social satirist but as a moral satirist, unmasking human frailties and related social imperfections. Yet regardless of his intent, *The Inspector General* is broad social satire, and it set the pace for the realistic comedies of social and political satire which followed.

In addition, lively characterization and spirited language contribute to the play's realistic flavor. The town's minor functionaries, for example, are properly resentful about Anton Antonovich's so-called unwarranted criticism of them and in retaliation endeavor to undermine his reputation with "The Inspector"; and later they are equally indignant about having been bilked of several hundred rubles by "The Inspector"—all of these part of the perdurable behavioral repertoire of civil servants. And the dialogue among these petty bureaucrats and merchants, from Anton Antonovich on down, is likewise authentic: a broad and salty jargon reflected in some of the better translations by such English equivalents as "ain't," the double negative, lack of subject-verb agreement, malapropisms, mangled French expressions, vulgar allusions, pretentiousness, and the like. Here, as nowhere else, Gogol's dialogue is flawless, with never a wrong word or false tone, always with an eye toward intensifying the comic effect. Gogol, in a brilliantly puckish stroke, even named his characters to reflect their qualities. Skvoznik-Dmukhanovsky translates rougly to Rascal-Puffed-up, for instance, and Hlestakov means "Whipper-snapper." Zemlyanika is strawberry; Lyapkin-Tyapkin literally signifies "Bungle-Steal"; and Hlopov designates a "bedbug." Gogol's astute satiric eye, it seems, overlooked no opportunity.

One of Gogol's innovations is the omission of the conventional "love interest," for Ivan's passes at Maria and Anna have nothing to do with love for any of them. And in another departure from convention, Gogol includes not a single sympathetic character in this many-peopled play, a device that his enemies were quick to fault. But serious critics agree about the genius of the ploy, for its satiric quality is enhanced immensely by it. In fact, the play is unerringly constructed from start to finish, and, aside from its topicality, has remained popular because it is plainly and simply good entertainment.

THE INTERPRETATION OF DREAMS

Type of work: Psychological study
Author: Sigmund Freud (1856-1939)
First published: 1900

In March, 1931, in a foreword to the third English edition of *The Interpretation of Dreams*, Freud expressed the opinion that the volume contained the most valuable of all the discoveries he had been fortunate enough to make. The author's estimation of his work concurs with that of most students and critics. The ideas that dreams are wish-fulfillments, that the dream disguises the wishes of the unconscious, that dreams are always important, always significant, and that they express infantile wishes—particularly for the death of the parent of the same sex as that of the dreamer—all appear in this masterpiece of psychological interpretation. Here the Oedipus complex is first named and explained and the method of psychoanalysis is given impetus and credibility by its application to the analysis of dreams.

It is common criticism of Freud to say that the father of psychoanalysis, although inspired in this and other works, went too far in his generalizations concerning the basic drives of the unconscious. Freud is charged with regarding every latent wish as having a sexual object, and he is criticized for supposing that dreams can be understood as complexes of such universally significant symbols as umbrellas and boxes.

Although Freud argues that repressed wishes that show themselves in disguised form in dreams generally have something to do with the unsatisfied sexual cravings of childhood—for dreams are important and concern themselves only with matters we cannot resolve by conscious deliberation and action—he allows for the dream satisfaction of other wishes that reality has frustrated: the desire for the continued existence of a loved one already dead, the desire for sleep as a continuation of the escape from reality, the desire for a return to childhood, the desire for revenge when revenge is impossible.

As for the charge that Freud regarded dreams as complexes of symbols having the same significance for all dreamers, this is clearly unwarranted. Freud explicitly states that "only the context can furnish the correct meaning" of a dream symbol. He rejects as wholly inadequate the use of any such simple key as a dream book of symbols. Each dreamer utilizes the material of his own experience in his own way, and only by a careful analytical study of associations—obscured by the manifest content of the dream—is it possible to get at the particular use of symbols in an individual's dream. It is worth noting, Freud admits, that many symbols recur with much the same intent in many dreams of different persons; but this knowledge must be used judiciously. The agreement in the use of symbols is only partly a matter of cultural tendencies; it is largely attributable to limitations of the imagination imposed by the material itself: "To use long, stiff objects and weapons as symbols of the female genitals, or hollow objects (chests, boxes, etc.) as symbols of the male genitals, is certainly not permitted by the imagination."

It is not surprising that most of the symbols discussed by Freud, either as typical symbols or as symbols in individual cases, are sexually significant. Although Freud did not regard all dreams as the wish-fulfillments of repressed sexual desires, he did suppose that a greater number of dreams have a sexual connotation: "The more one is occupied with the solution of dreams, the readier one becomes to acknowledge that the majority of the dreams of adults deal with sexual material and give expression to erotic wishes." But Freud adds, "In dream-interpretation this importance of the sexual complexes must never be forgotten, though one must not, of course, exaggerate it to the exclusion of all other factors."

The technique of dream-interpretation is certainly not exhausted, according to Freud, by the technique of symbol interpretation. Dreams involve the use of the images dreamed, the *manifest* dream-content, as a way of disguising the unconscious "dream-thoughts" or *latent* dream-content. The significance of a dream may be revealed only after one has understood the dramatic use of the symbolism of the dream, the condensation of the material, the displacement of the conventional meaning of a symbol or utterance, or even a displacement of the "center" of the dream-thoughts; i.e., the manifest dream may center about a matter removed from the central concern of the latent dream. As Freud explains the problems of dream-interpretation, making numerous references to dream examples, it becomes clear that dream interpretation must be at least as ingenious as dream-work—and there is nothing more ingenious.

Freud begins *The Interpretation of Dreams* with a history of the scientific literature of dream problems from ancient times to 1900. He then proceeds to make his basic claim: that dreams are interpretable as wish-fulfillments. To illustrate his point, he begins with an involved dream of his own, justifying his procedure by arguing that self-analysis is possible and, even when faulty, illustrative.

A problem arises with the consideration of painful dreams. If dreams are wish-fulfillments, why are some dreams nightmares? Who wishes to be terrified? Freud's answer is that the problem arises from a confusion between the manifest and the latent dream. What is painful, considered as manifest, may, because of its disguised significance, be regarded as satisfactory to the unconscious. When one realizes, in addition, that many suppressed wishes are desires for punishment, the painful dream presents itself as a fulfillment of such wishes. To understand the possibility of painful dreams it is necessary to consider Freud's amended formula: "The dream is the (disguised) fulfilment of a (suppressed, repressed) wish."

In describing the method most useful in enabling a person to recall his dream both by facilitating memory and by inhibiting the censorship tendency of the person recounting the dream, Freud presents what has become familiar as the psychoanalytic method of free association. He suggests that the patient be put into a restful position with his eyes closed, that the patient be told not to criticize his thoughts or to withhold the expression of them, and that he continue to be impartial about his ideas. This problem of eliminating censorship while recounting the dream is merely an extension of the problem of dealing with the censorship imposed by the dreamer while dreaming. The dreamer does not want to acknowledge his desires; for one reason or another he has repressed them. The fulfillment of the suppressed desire can be tolerated by the dreamer only if he leaves out anything which would be understandable to the waking mind. Consequently, only a laborious process of undoing the dream-work can result in some understanding of the meaning the censor tries to hide.

Among the interesting subsidiary ideas of Freud's theory is the idea that the dream-stimulus is always to be found among the experiences of the hours prior to sleeping. Some incident from the day becomes the material of the dream, its provocative image. But although the dream-stimulus is from the day preceding sleep, the repressed wish which the dream expresses and fulfills is from childhood, at least, in the majority of cases: "The deeper we go into the analysis of dreams, the more often are we put on to the track of childish experiences which play the part of dream-sources in the latent dream-content." To explain the difficulty of getting at the experiences in childhood which provide the latent dream-content, Freud argues for a conception of dreams as stratified: in the dream layers of meaning are involved, and it is only at the lowest stratum that the source in some experience of childhood may be discovered.

Among the typical dreams mentioned by Freud are the embarrassment dream of nakedness, interpreted as an exhibition dream, fulfilling a wish to return to childhood (the time when one ran about naked without upsetting anyone); the death-wish dream in which one dreams of the death of a beloved person, interpreted as a dream showing repressed hostility toward brother or sister, father or mother; and the examination dream in which one dreams of the disgrace of flunking an examination, interpreted as reflecting the ineradicable memories of punishments in childhood.

Of these typical dreams, the death-wish dream directed to the father (by the son) or to the mother (by the daughter) is explained in terms of the drama of *Oedipus* by Sophocles. In the old Greek play, Oedipus unwittingly murders his own father and marries his mother. When he discovers his deeds, he blinds himself and exiles himself from Thebes. The appeal of the drama is explained by Freud as resulting from its role as a wish-fulfillment. The play reveals the inner self, the self which directed its first sexual impulses toward the mother and its first jealous hatred toward the father. These feelings have been repressed during the course of our developing maturity, but they remain latent, ready to manifest themselves only in dreams somewhat more obscure than the Oedipus drama itself. Freud mentions *Hamlet* as another play in which the same wish is shown, although in

Hamlet the fulfillment is repressed. Freud accounts for Hamlet's reluctance to complete the task of revenge by pointing out that Hamlet cannot bring himself to kill a man who accomplished what he himself wishes he had accomplished: the murder of his father and marriage to his mother.

In his discussion of the psychology of the dream process, Freud calls attention to the fact that dreams are quickly forgotten—a natural consequence, if his theory is correct. This fact creates problems for the analyst who wishes to interpret dreams in order to discover the root of neurotic disturbances. However, the self that forgets is the same self that dreamed, and it is possible by following the implications of even superficial associations to get back to the substance of the dream.

Realizing that many persons would be offended by his ideas, Freud attempted to forestall criticism by insisting on the universal application of his theory and by claiming that dreams themselves—since they are not acts—are morally innocent, whatever their content.

There seems little question but that Freud's contribution to psychology in *The Interpretation of Dreams* will remain one of the great discoveries of the human mind. Whatever its excesses, particularly in the hands of enthusiastic followers, Freud's central idea gains further confirmation constantly in the experiences of dreamers and analysts alike.

INTRUDER IN THE DUST

Type of work: Novel
Author: William Faulkner (1897-1962)
Type of plot: Social realism
Time of plot: Early 1930's
Locale: Jefferson, Mississippi
First published: 1948

Principal characters:
CHARLES ("CHICK") MALLISON, a sixteen-year-old boy
GAVIN STEVENS, his uncle, a lawyer
LUCAS BEAUCHAMP, an old Negro
ALECK SANDER, Chick's young colored friend
MISS HABERSHAM, an old woman
HOPE HAMPTON, the sheriff

Critique:

In *Intruder in the Dust,* Faulkner juxtaposed his views regarding the problem of the Negro in the South against a bizarre tale involving murder, grave robbing, and lynching. Before the publication of this novel, in such works as "The Bear" and *Light in August,* he had only hinted at his concept of the problem, with the result that his views were often misunderstood, but in *Intruder in the Dust* he set forth his views boldly, often reinforcing them with italics and using one of his characters as his spokesman. Faulkner's main tenet, developed by Lawyer Gavin Stevens, is that the South must be left alone to solve its own problem; that any interference in the form of federal legislation will only strengthen the South's historic defiance of the North. Lifted from context, however, the plot resembles nothing so much as a rather far-fetched murder mystery; isolated, Gavin Stevens' commentaries on the plot sound like so much propaganda. But within the framework of the novel the plot is credible and Lawyer Stevens' harangues are appropriate. After all, the story is oriented around a boy. It is quite conceivable that a sixteen-year-old could get himself into just such a situation; it stands to reason that a rhetorical lawyer should try to clarify a confused nephew's thinking. *Intruder in the Dust* is a successful novel because Faulkner succeeds in making the reader believe in its central character, understand him, and sympathize with him.

The Story:

On a cold afternoon in November, Chick Mallison, twelve years old, accompanied by two Negro boys, went rabbit hunting on Carothers Edmonds' place. When he fell through the ice into a creek, an old Negro, Lucas Beauchamp, appeared and watched while the boy clambered awkwardly ashore. Then Lucas took the white boy and his companions to the old colored man's home. There Chick dried out in front of the fire and ate Lucas' food. Later, when Chick tried to pay the old man for his hospitality, Lucas spurned his money. Chick threw it down, but Lucas made one of the other boys pick it up and return it. Chick brooded over the incident, ashamed to be indebted to a black man, especially one as arrogant as Lucas Beauchamp. Again trying to repay the old man, he sent Lucas' wife a mail-order dress bought with money he had saved; again refusing to acknowledge payment and thus admit his inferiority as a Negro, Lucas sent Chick a bucket of sorghum sweetening.

Some four years later when Lucas was accused of shooting Vinson Gowrie in the back, Chick still had not forgotten his unpaid debt to the Negro. Realizing that Vinson's poor-white family and friends were sure to lynch Lucas, Chick wanted to leave town. But when Sheriff Hope Hampton brought Lucas to the jail in Jefferson, Chick, unable to suppress his sense of obligation, was standing on the street where the old colored man could see him. Lucas asked Chick to bring his uncle, Gavin Stevens, to the jail.

At the jail the old man refused to tell Stevens what happened at the shooting, whereupon the lawyer left in disgust. But Lucas did tell Chick that Vinson Gowrie had not been shot with his gun—a forty-one Colt—and he asked the boy to verify this fact by digging up the corpse. Although the body was buried nine miles from town and the Gowries would be sure to shoot a grave robber, Chick agreed to the request; he knew that Lucas would undoubtedly be lynched if someone did not help the old man. Barbershop and poolroom loafers had already gathered while waiting for the pine-hill country Gowries to arrive in town.

Stevens laughed at the story, so Chick's only help came from a Negro boy—Aleck Sander—and Miss Habersham, an old woman of good family who had grown up with Lucas' wife, now dead. And so the task of digging up a white man's grave in order to save a haughty, intractable, but innocent Negro was left to two adolescents and a seventy-year-old woman who felt it her obligation to protect those more helpless than she. The three succeeded in opening the grave without incident. In the coffin they found not Vinson Gowrie but Jake Montgomery, whose skull had been bashed in. They filled the

grave, returned to town, wakened Stevens, and went to the sheriff with their story.

This group, joined by old man Gowrie and two of his sons, reopened the grave. But when they lifted the lid the coffin was found to be empty. A search disclosed Montgomery's body hastily buried nearby and Vinson's sunk in quicksand. When the sheriff took Montgomery's body into town, the huge crowd that had gathered in anticipation of the lynching of Lucas Beauchamp soon scattered.

Questioning of Lucas revealed that Crawford Gowrie had murdered his brother Vinson. Crawford, according to the old Negro, had been cheating his brother in a lumber deal. Jake Montgomery, to whom Crawford had sold the stolen lumber, knew that Crawford was the murderer and had dug up Vinson's grave to prove it. Crawford murdered Montgomery at the grave and put him in Vinson's coffin. When he saw Chick and his friends open the grave, he was forced to remove Vinson's body too. Sheriff Hampton soon captured Crawford, who killed himself in his cell to avoid a trial.

At last, Chick thought, he had freed himself of his debt to the old Negro. A short time later, however, Lucas appeared at Stevens' office and insisted on paying for services rendered. Stevens refused payment for both himself and Chick but accepted two dollars for "expenses." Proud, unhumbled to the end, Lucas Beauchamp demanded a receipt.

Further Critical Evaluation of the Work:

Intruder in the Dust is an excellent introduction to William Faulkner's numerous and complex novels of the Deep South. Set in Faulkner's mythical Yoknapatawpha County, his standard fictional location, *Intruder in the Dust* also includes such familiar inhabitants as attorney Gavin Stevens and farmer Carothers Edmonds. But this novel includes only a few examples of such famous Faulknerian stylistic devices as elongated, periodic sentences, disconnected narratives, multiple narrative perspectives, psychological time, and stream of consciousness. While the very substance of *The Sound and the Fury, Absalom, Absalom!, Light in August,* and *As I Lay Dying* consists of these variations in style of form, *Intruder in the Dust* (except for Chick Mallison's meditations and flashbacks) is a relatively straightforward narration. Faulkner novels typically use parable and folklore as a basis for forming a vision of life as a neurotic and involved psychological process. But *Intruder in the Dust* blends folklore and parable with a formula mystery story and strikes a much simpler note than most of Faulkner's work.

Aspects of folklore permeate *Intruder in the Dust*. Faulkner's panorama of rural local color includes a generous sampling of cracker-barrel philosophers, bigoted rednecks, mischievous, shoeless youngsters, and fading ladies of breeding long past their prime. The plot crackles with anecdotes, bits of country wisdom, humor, and superstition. It is thematically enriched by Gavin Stevens' philosophical speeches. After Chick, Aleck, and Miss Habersham discover that Vinson Gowrie's grave contains the body of Jake Montgomery, *Intruder in the Dust* becomes a highly suspenseful mystery story with Sheriff Hampton and Lawyer Stevens solving the crime in barely enough time to prevent Lucas Beauchamp from being lynched by a mob far more interested in violence than justice.

The novel also contains several parables, one of which is a Southern version of the Biblical Cain and Able story. The brothers Vinson and Crawford Gowrie have joined forces in several business ventures including timber dealing. Crawford, increasingly greedy for his own profits, steals timber from his brother and sells it to the shady Jake Montgomery. When Lucas Beauchamp sees Crawford stealing the timber and threatens to expose him, Crawford kills his brother in a way to make Lucas appear as the murderer. Crawford relies on the townspeople's readiness to blame a black man for the murder of a white man. But, like Mink Snopes in Faulkner's *The Hamlet,* Crawford learns too late that violence, instead of eradicating problems, creates more violence, and eventually one's downfall. Truth simply will not stay buried, Faulkner seems to be saying. In a hair-raising midnight scene combining the best of Edgar Allan Poe and Raymond Chandler, plus his own inimitable sense of place and wry humor, the author has three very frightened individuals uncover the truth that frees Lucas.

Beyond the Cain and Abel story, Gavin Stevens' speeches expand *Intruder in the Dust* into a parable about the people's right to govern themselves. Critics have frequently condemned Stevens' rhetoric as the propaganda of an unfeeling and aristocratic bigot. While this interpretation holds some validity, Stevens is not a mouthpiece for Faulkner's views; nor should Stevens' pleadings, however prolix, be discounted. In the filibuster tradition of Southern oratory, he articulates a code of noninterference, following Candide's final words of "till your own garden." The intruder of the title may refer not only to those who open Vinson Gowrie's grave, but also "outlanders" who would dictate moral action to these people. With their own sense of justice, the Southerners close this incident in their own way. They come to realize that Beauchamp could have little to do with what is fundamentally a family feud.

Because of his cruel victimization, Lucas in the future will be shown innumerable courtesies by white people. He has suffered and he is wise. Lucas will endure. The true villains here are the poor whites, those who have perverted the opportunities of their position.

The elderly spinster Eunice Habersham supports Beauchamp enough to rob a grave to prove his innocence. Had Miss Habersham been less sentimental and more skeptical, Crawford Gowrie, guilty and white, would have escaped. On the other hand, Hope Hampton, Sheriff of Yoknapatawpha County, is highly skeptical and totally unsentimental. Hampton seeks justice, not conviction; evidence, not the will of the voters, persuades him to action. He is a diametric opposite to the familiar stereotype of the rural Southern sheriff, a big-bellied bounty hunter who catches victims and tells them "you in a heap of trouble, boy!" The villains of *Intruder in the Dust* behave in predictably stereotyped and evil ways, while the figures in power—Hampton, the prosecutor; Stevens, the defender; and Miss Habersham, the moral sentiment— are humane, rounded characters.

As a story of initiation, the novel is an unqualified success. Young Chick Mallison must unlearn old values as well as learn new ones. In attempting to pay Lucas for his act of kindness, Chick denies the old black man his humanity. What others often interpret as arrogance is really Lucas' unyielding demand that he be treated as a human being, worthy of respect. Gradually Chick comes to realize the moral rightness in the demand Lucas makes. After the death of Mrs. Beauchamp, Chick sees Lucas and understands that grief can come to a black man as well as to a white. By the time Lucas has been accused of committing murder, Chick knows that he must act with the same humanity Lucas showed him. Through Lucas, Chick also learns to accept Aleck as an equal. Thus, through the initiation of Chick Mallison, Faulkner makes a powerful, positive statement about race relations as fundamentally an encounter between one human being and another.

Because *Intruder in the Dust* includes Gavin Stevens' philosophical discourses on the South's ability to handle its own problems *after* the action has essentially been resolved, this novel is too often dismissed as a distasteful polemic, a lapse in Faulkner's series of brilliant novels. Yet, *Intruder in the Dust* is not so much inferior to such works as *The Sound and the Fury* or *Absalom, Absalom!* as it is different in its approach to the genre. Always an experimenter and innovator, here Faulkner turned with considerable success to establishing his vision in formula fiction, as he did earlier with *Sanctuary* (1931), an even more Gothic murder mystery, and *Pylon* (1935), an adventure story about flying. While *Intruder in the Dust* will probably never rank with his greatest fiction, this work, along with *The Reivers* (1962), does present the famous Faulkner world in a form understandable to many readers.

Patrick Morrow

INVISIBLE MAN

Type of work: Novel
Author: Ralph Ellison (1914-   )
Time: The late 1930's
Locale: A small city and a Negro college in the South, and New York City
First published: 1952

Principal characters:
THE NAMELESS NARRATOR-HERO
DR. BLEDSOE, the college president
MR. NORTON, a trustee of the college
BROTHER JACK, the leader of the Brotherhood
RINEHART, a racketeer, lover, minister
RAS THE DESTROYER, the leader of the black nationalists
SIBYL, a married white woman

"Keep this colored boy running" is the theme of both Ellison's *Invisible Man* and William Faulkner's *Light in August.* That Faulkner, a Southern white, published his novel in 1932 while Ellison, a Southern Negro, published his in 1952 is a mark of the important but snail-pace progress from one generation to the next. Yet what distinguishes these novels is not the social protest but the profoundly imaginative use of a particular social injustice to dramatize the outrageous situation of all men. And it is here that we can differentiate the writer of the 1930's and the writer of the 1950's. "Keep this colored boy running" suggests a game which, however malicious, is still a game; both writers see life as a mad game, and both seize on the comic dimensions of situations filled with terror. The signal difference between Faulkner and Ellison is that while Faulkner's attitude toward this grotesque and absurd world is one of outrage, Ralph (Waldo) Ellison's is one of comic acceptance.

Invisible Man is narrated by a nameless Negro living in a coal cellar lighted by 1,369 bulbs. The narrator's background is established in two childhood episodes. First is his brutal initiation into the club world of the Southern white man. Having graduated from high school as valedictorian, he is invited to a gathering of the town's leading citizens to receive a scholarship; but before the award he is mixed into a group of Negro toughs and compelled by the drunken, jeering whites to gaze at a naked blonde, fight a blindfold "battle royal," and grab for coins on an electrified rug. The second episode is a comic introduction to a madhouse world. The boy, now studying at a Negro college, is asked to guide a white trustee through the campus and the neighboring countryside, and they end up at the Golden Day. This is the local roadhouse, where each Saturday a group of disabled Negro veterans are taken for a day of whisky and women. Here the boy and the trustee witness a chaotic orgy, a slapstick but savage rebellion of the inmates against their giant attendant, Supercargo; and they listen to the perceptive ravings of a mad Negro doctor.

The scene at the white man's club ends with the young hero, limp and swollen, enthusiastically delivering again his graduation speech on the social responsibility of the Negro. At the Golden Day, the mad doctor shrewdly observes that the young hero, so dedicated to becoming a leader of his people, has already learned to suppress not only his feelings but his humanity, that he is an invisible, walking personification of negative man. In both scenes Ellison shows great control in moving from an attitude of profound sympathy with his protagonist to one of ridicule, and we see a human victim suddenly turned puppet.

But Ellison does more than satirize the blind self-righteousness of an adolescent. In the white man's club he shows how the boy is forced into the role of the lust-ing, greedy, violent Negro stereotype; how he is compelled to become a puppet by the white gods who manipulate him; how he is denied his identity—his visibility—by the social forces of the American South. In the Golden Day, which is a transmogrification of the white man's club, where the chaos is intensified and expanded, we see that the boy is made a "mechanical man" not just by his blind self-righteousness nor by the white man's injustice, but by an anonymous and generalized authority which the mad doctor sums up in the third person plural pronoun. Now we see that the whole world is governed by wanton powers that make both the Negro and the white man ludicrous puppets. We are now prepared for the novel's conclusion that all men are invisible.

The movement from the white man's club to the Golden Day forms the dominant rhythm of the novel; it is the movement from the local to the universal, from the rational to the grotesque. The hero, expelled from college, leaves his idyllic campus, the comparatively logical South, the relatively simple life of an adolescent for the chaotic adult world, echoing the phrases of Candide as he left the Westphalian castle of his childhood. But unlike Voltaire, Ellison jettisons his logical style. In an interview printed in *The Paris Review*, Ellison explains how he devised three shifts in style to lead the reader of *Invisible Man* from a world that is intolerable but credible and explainable to one that is totally bewildering. In the South, where the hero tries to fit into an unjust but traditional pattern, the style is naturalistic. In New York, where the hero loses his sense of certainty, the style becomes expressionistic. And when the hero falls from grace in the Brotherhood, his last rational grip on reality, the style turns surrealistic. Since the style follows the development of the narrator-hero, it reflects a changing attitude that will finally accommodate and affirm the chaos he encounters.

The Northern city is to the rural South as the Golden Day is to the white man's club. In New York the hero assumes a series of roles: a young man seeking employment, a semi-skilled laborer, the Harlem leader of the Brotherhood, a speaker on women's rights. Blind to the potential of freedom, he is manipulated by an anti-union fanatic, a psychiatrist, a higher official in the Brotherhood, a black nationalist—successive embodiments of the mad doctor's third-person-plural pronoun. The order of events in New York is senseless; it will become meaningful when the hero, like Camus' "stranger," accepts the senseless order as the absurd logic of his life. He is blindly mistaken when he joins the Brotherhood in the belief that history is rational and that human identity and brotherhood can be achieved by a conscious subordination to its logic. But even in his mistake he has advanced beyond the stage where identity equals Negro and where history is limited to the record of his race. And this stage is necessary before he can renounce identity and history altogether, renounce naturalism, determinism, reason, and accept the condition of man as invisible and free.

Before he can accept the outrageous logic of his life he must gain an objective perspective and see the world as ridiculous, as a mad dream filled with grotesque puppets and clowns. The hero begins to see with new clarity when he is made to wonder what the world and life would be like if history were a gambler, if man were not a creature capable of reason but a madman. He becomes a clown in the madman's game when, in order to escape Ras the Destroyer, the black nationalist, he buys the wide hat and green glasses of the zoot-suiter. Mistaken in his new guise for Rinehart, the chameleon-like racketeer, lover, minister, the hero marvels at the man who can assume such varied roles. When he looks at the world through his green glasses and sees the dark merging of shapes, he realizes that this is the way Rinehart must see life, full of possibilities and boundless. And he sees that freedom is not recognition of necessity alone but recognition of possibility as well. Now we come to understand that Ellison's world is chaotic and threatening, but because there is no order there are infinite possibilities for improvising. Seen through the green glasses the absurd world becomes comic and therefore capable of affirmation.

Rinehart exploits the possibilities of the world but also contributes to its destructiveness, and the hero's final step toward independence will be the rejection of Rinehart. This is accomplished in the most purely comic scene in the novel, where he assumes the role of a Rinehart to gain as mistress a spy into the Brotherhood hierarchy. Here he gets his white girl (the promise of his ritual in the white man's club), a married woman who wants only to be raped by a Negro. However, when duty calls him back to Harlem his first thought is to get Sibyl home safely; he instinctively rejects his Rinehart role.

The scene with Sibyl is full of mistaken identity and pantomime, as the hero tries to evade her fanatic desires; a comic version of the scene in the white man's club, its lines recalling the "battle royal," it leads to a more bitter and hilarious version of the Golden Day. The Harlem riot is a re-enactment of the mad veterans' attack on Supercargo, but the figures instead of being madmen are grotesque fantasies in a dream circus. In the description of the looting we see one old woman struggling bowlegged beneath half a cow, and we hear another demand that her husband get only Wilson's bacon. Figures pass in stolen wigs and dress coats, and carry dummy rifles. A huge woman atop a milk cart ladles free beer. A man wearing three hats and several pairs of suspenders leads a group to burn down their rat-infested tenement, ignoring the pleas of a woman about to give birth. Blond mannikins hang from lampposts. Ras the Destroyer, dressed as an Abyssinian chieftain and riding a black charger that had been used the day before to pull a vegetable cart, throws spears at the police.

The hero, running for his life, falls into a coal cellar. In the dark he can recognize that the nightmare circus is reality, and that the joke of the human condition is man's invisibility: the unique self cannot be seen. Now he can renounce all signs of his factitious identities, laughingly accept his ridiculous situation, and prepare to return to the world of light.

There are two insoluble problems in this unusual novel: first, how to develop a hero who until the very end lacks a personality; second, how to make the final affirmation convincing and concrete. If Ellison's hero is shallow, the voice of his narrator is fully developed. If Ellison, as Irving Howe complains, cannot specify the possibilities his hero would find in the world above ground, the narrator does discover and explore a rich range of possibilities in recounting the story of his life from the viewpoint of his final realization. In describing a world where the Negro is kept running, Ellison avoids the narrow view of the protest novel. In describing a world that has long been termed absurd by the Existentialists and to which Faulkner, a more brilliant comic artist, could only respond with outrage, Ellison establishes a new posture. For in a world where both the blind and the rebellious are turned to puppets, one way to maintain independence—identity—is to *play* the puppet, that is to choose the role of clown. Earl Rovit compares the form of the novel to the improvisation of a jazz musician. It is also like the improvisation of Harlequin, who could always turn the tables on Authority and who could survive his beatings with a wry smile.

THE INVISIBLE MAN

Type of work: Novel
Author: H. G. Wells (1866-1946)
Type of plot: Mystery romance
Time of plot: Late nineteenth century
Locale: England
First published: 1897

Principal characters:
GRIFFIN, the Invisible Man
MR. HALL, landlord of the Coach and Horses Inn
MRS. HALL, his wife
DR. KEMP, a Burdock physician
COLONEL AYDE, chief of the Burdock police
MARVEL, a tramp

Critique:

The Invisible Man belongs to that series of pseudo-scientific romances which H. G. Wells wrote early in his literary career. The plot is one of sheer and fantastic invention, but it achieves an air of probability by means of the homely and realistic details with which it is built up. The characters involved in Griffin's strange predicament are also in no way remarkable; their traits, habits, and fears are revealed convincingly. The novel has outlived the time of its publication because of the psychological factors arising from the central situation and the suspense created by the unfolding of an unusual plot.

The Story:

The stranger arrived at Bramblehurst railway station on a cold, snowy day in February. Carrying a valise, he trudged through driving snow to Iping, where he stumbled into the Coach and Horses Inn and asked Mrs. Hall, the hostess, for a room and a fire. The stranger's face was hidden by dark-blue spectacles and bushy side-whiskers.

He had his dinner in his room. When Mrs. Hall took a mustard jar up to him, she saw that the stranger's head was completely bandaged. While she was in his room, he covered his mouth and chin with a napkin.

His baggage arrived the next day— several trunks and boxes of books and a crate of bottles packed in straw. The drayman's dog attacked the stranger, tearing his glove and ripping his trousers. Mr. Hall, landlord of the inn, ran upstairs to see if the stranger had been hurt and entered his room without knocking. He was immediately struck on the chest and pushed from the room. When Mrs. Hall took up the lodger's supper, she saw that he had unpacked his trunks and boxes and set up some strange apparatus. The lodger was not wearing his glasses; his eyes looked sunken and hollow.

In the weeks that followed the villagers made many conjectures as to the stranger's identity. Some thought he suffered from a queer disease that had left his skin black-and-white spotted. Unusual happenings also mystified the village. One night the vicar and his wife were awakened by a noise in the vicar's study and the clinking of money. Upon investigation, they saw no one, although a candle was burning and they heard a sneeze.

In the meantime Mr. Hall found clothing and bandages scattered about the lodger's room; the stranger had disappeared. The landlord went downstairs to call his wife. They heard the front door open and shut, but no one came into the inn. While they stood wondering what to do, their lodger came down the stairs. Where he had been or how he had returned to his room unnoticed was a mystery he made no attempt to explain.

A short time later, the stranger's bill being overdue, Mrs. Hall refused to serve him. When the stranger became abusive, Mr. Hall swore out a warrant against him. The constable, the landlord, and a curious neighbor went upstairs to arrest the lodger. After a struggle, the man agreed to unmask. The men were horror-stricken; the stranger was invisible to their view. In the confusion the Invisible Man, as the newspapers were soon to call him, fled from the inn.

The next person to encounter the Invisible Man was a tramp named Marvel. The Invisible Man frightened Marvel into accompanying him to the Coach and Horses Inn to get his clothing and three books. They arrived at the inn while the vicar and the village doctor were reading the stranger's diary. They knocked the two men about, snatched up the clothes and books, and left the inn.

Newspapers continued to print stories of unnatural thefts; money had been taken and carried away, the thief invisible but the money in plain view. Marvel always seemed to be well-supplied with funds.

One day Marvel, carrying three books, came running into the Jolly Cricketers Inn. He said that the Invisible Man was after him. A barman, a policeman, and a cabman awaited the Invisible Man's arrival after hiding Marvel. But the Invisible Man found Marvel, dragged him into the inn kitchen, and tried to force him through the door. The three men struggled with the unseen creature while Marvel crawled into the bar-parlor. When the voice of the Invisible Man was heard in the inn yard, a villager fired five shots in the direction of the sound. Searchers found no body in the yard.

Meanwhile, in Burdock, Dr. Kemp worked late in his study. Preparing to retire, he noticed drops of drying blood on the stairs. He found the doorknob of his room smeared with blood and red stains on his bed. While he stared in amazement at a bandage that was apparently wrapping itself about nothing in midair, a voice called him by name. The Invisible Man had taken refuge in Kemp's rooms.

He identified himself as Griffin, a young scientist whom Kemp had met at the university where both had studied. Griffin asked for whiskey and food. He said that except for short naps he had not slept for three days and nights.

That night Kemp sat up to read all the newspaper accounts of the activities of the Invisible Man. At last, after much thought, he wrote a letter to Colonel Adye, chief of the Burdock police.

In the morning Griffin told his story to Kemp. He explained that for three years he had experimented with refractions of light on the theory that a human body would become invisible if the cells could be made transparent. Needing money for his work, he had robbed his father of money belonging to someone else and his father had shot himself. At last his experiments were successful. After setting fire to his room in order to destroy the evidence of his research, he had begun his strange adventures. He had terrorized Oxford Street, where passersby had seen only his footprints. He discovered that in his invisible state he was compelled to fast, for all unassimilated food or drink was grotesquely visible. At last, prowling London streets and made desperate by his plight, he had gone to a shop selling theatrical supplies. There he had stolen the dark glasses, side-whiskers, and clothes he wore on his arrival in Iping.

Griffin planned to use Kemp's house as a headquarters while terrorizing the neighborhood. Kemp believed Griffin mad. When he attempted to restrain Griffin, the Invisible Man escaped, and shortly thereafter a Mr. Wicksteed was found murdered. A manhunt began.

The next morning Kemp received a note which announced that the reign of terror had begun; one person would be executed daily. Kemp himself was to be the first victim. He was to die at noon; nothing could protect him.

Kemp sent at once for Colonel Adye. While they were discussing possible precautions, stones were hurled through the windows. The colonel left to return to the police station for some bloodhounds to set on Griffin's trail, but outside the house Griffin snatched a revolver from Adye's pocket and wounded the police officer. When Griffin began to smash Kemp's kitchen door with an ax, the doctor climbed through a window and ran to a neighbor's house. He was refused admittance. He ran to the inn.

The door was barred. Suddenly his invisible assailant seized him. While they struggled, some men came to the doctor's rescue. Kemp got hold of Griffin's arms. A constable seized his legs. Someone struck through the air with a spade. The writhing unseen figure sagged to the ground. Kemp announced that he could not hear Griffin's heartbeats. While the crowd gathered, Griffin's body slowly materialized, naked, dead. A sheet was brought from the inn and the body was carried away. The reign of terror was ended.

Further Critical Evaluation of the Work:

Three factors account for the immense effectiveness and enduring popularity of *The Invisible Man*: its believability, its structure, and the profundity of its main theme.

Wells, a keen observer of English village life, evokes a completely convincing picture of Iping and the people of Sussex. The scenes of Griffin in London—especially the department store incident—are almost photographically vivid. Wells' account of Griffin's transformation abounds in carefully thought out details. Providing enough optical and physiological explanation to gain the reader's confidence, Wells meticulously recounts the difficulties which Griffin must surmount. The iridescent material in the eyes of the experimental cat refuses to become invisible, but since Griffin is an albino, the conversion process is somewhat easier. Yet food shows until it is digested, and sleep is a problem when eyelids are transparent. Rain, fog, and sweat reveal the "glistening surface of a man."

Wells employs a masterful three-part structure. The first part, constituting over half of the novel, presents Griffin through his encounters with the villagers and tells of his unsuccessful attempt to keep his invisibility secret. In the second part, Griffin himself recounts the history of his experiments, describes his motives, and narrates the events which led him to Iping. The final section could be called "The Betrayal of Griffin"; its protagonist is Dr. Kemp. Each of these parts has a dramatic unity with a characteristic tone. The reader is drawn from an almost Dickensian atmosphere into the Kafkaesque nightmare world of Griffin's London; then he is plunged into the frenzied, sunlit action at Burdock. The tension in the novel, broken and reestablished, mounts to higher levels as each section unfolds.

The novel's main ethical concern is revealed in the relationship of Griffin and Kemp. In betraying his guest to the police, Kemp destroys all hope of using Griffin's genius for the benefit of society. Nor does Kemp display sufficient empathy for Griffin's psychological suffering; he therefore ranges himself with the narrow-minded Iping villagers who do nothing to make Griffin feel secure. At the same time, Griffin is clearly a moral monstrosity. He is an archetype of the gifted scientist who craves knowledge for the power it will bring. He disregards "the common conventions of humanity," and Wells introduces the frightening thesis that the process of scientific investigation itself makes men like Griffin possible.

IOLANTHE

Type of work: Comic opera
Author: W. S. Gilbert (1836-1911)
Type of plot: Humorous satire
Time of plot: Nineteenth century
Locale: England
First presented: 1882

Principal characters:
 THE LORD CHANCELLOR
 STREPHON, an Arcadian shepherd
 QUEEN OF THE FAIRIES
 IOLANTHE, Strephon's fairy mother
 PHYLLIS, a shepherdess and ward in Chancery
 THE EARL OF MOUNTARARAT, and
 EARL TOLLOLLER, her suitors
 PRIVATE WILLIS, a palace guard

Critique:

The story of a shepherd lad, the top of him a fairy but his feet mired in human form, *Iolanthe, Or, The Peer and the Peri* is a light-hearted satire on many human foibles. In particular, the drama pokes fun at the House of Lords, but it is such gentle fun that no one in Victorian England could take offense. *Iolanthe* is a delightful comedy, one of many from the pen of Sir William Schwenck Gilbert, whose name will always be associated with that of his composer-collaborator, Sir Arthur Seymour Sullivan.

The Story:

The Fairy Queen had banished Iolanthe because she had married a mortal. Normally the punishment for such an act was death, but the queen so loved Iolanthe that she had been unable to enforce a penalty so grave. Iolanthe had been sentenced to penal servitude for life, on the condition that she never see her mortal husband again. At last the other fairies begged the queen to relent, to set aside even this punishment, for Iolanthe had served twenty-five years of her sentence by standing on her head at the bottom of a stream.

The queen, unable to resist their pleas, summoned the penitent Iolanthe and pardoned her. Iolanthe explained that she had stayed in the stream to be near her son Strephon, an Arcadian shepherd who was a fairy to his waist and a human from the waist down. While they spoke, Strephon entered, announcing that he was to be married that day to Phyllis, a ward of Chancery. The Lord Chancellor had not given his permission, but Strephon was determined to marry his Phyllis anyway. He was delighted when he learned that his mother had been pardoned, but he begged her and all the fairies not to tell Phyllis that he was half fairy. He feared that she would not understand.

The queen determined to make Strephon a member of Parliament, but Strephon said that he would be no good in that august body, for the top of him was a Tory, the bottom a Radical. The queen solved that problem by making him a Liberal-Unionist and taking his mortal legs under her particular care.

Phyllis talked with Strephon and warned him that to marry her without the Lord Chancellor's permission would mean lifelong penal servitude for him. But Strephon could not wait the two years until she was of age. He feared that the Lord Chancellor himself or one of the peers of the House of Lords would marry her before that time had passed.

Strephon's fears were well founded; the Lord Chancellor did want to marry his ward. Fearing that he would have to punish himself for marrying her without his permission, however, he decided to give her instead to one of the peers of the

House of Lords. Two were at last selected, the Earl of Mountararat and Earl Tolloller, but there was no agreement as to the final choice. Phyllis herself did not wish to accept either, for she loved only Strephon. Then she saw Strephon talking with Iolanthe, who, being a fairy, looked like a young and beautiful girl, even though she was Strephon's mother. Phyllis was filled with jealousy, augmented by the laughter of the peers when Strephon in desperation confessed that Iolanthe was his mother. Weeping that he had betrayed her, Phyllis left Strephon. No one had ever heard of a son who looked older than his mother.

The Fairy Queen herself told the Lord Chancellor and the peers that they would rue their laughter over Iolanthe and her son. To punish them, Strephon would change all existing laws in the House of Lords. He would abolish the rights of peers and give titles to worthy commoners. Worst of all, from then on peers would be chosen by competitive examinations. Strephon would be a foe they would not soon forget.

The queen's prediction came true. Strephon completely ruled the House of Lords. Every bill he proposed was passed, the fairies making the other members vote for Strephon even when they wanted to vote against him. The peers appealed to the fairies, but although the fairies admired the peers, they could not be swayed against Strephon.

The Earl of Mountararat and Earl Tolloller tried to decide who should have Phyllis. Each wanted the other to sacrifice himself by giving up all rights to her. Both had a family tradition that they must fight anyone who took their sweethearts, and since a fight meant that one of them would die and the survivor would be left without his friend, each wanted to make the sacrifice of losing his friend. At last the two decided that friendship was more important than love. Both renounced Phyllis.

Strephon and Phyllis met again, and at last he convinced her that Iolanthe was really his mother. Phyllis still could not believe that Strephon looked like a fairy, and she could not quite understand that his grandmother and all his aunts looked as young as his mother. She was sensible, however, and promised that whenever she saw Strephon kissing a very young girl she would know the woman was an elderly relative. There was still the Lord Chancellor to contend with. When they went to Iolanthe and begged her to persuade him to consent to their marriage, Iolanthe told them that the Lord Chancellor was her mortal husband. He believed her dead and himself childless, and if she looked on him the queen would carry out the penalty of instant death.

Iolanthe could not resist the pleas of the young lovers. As she told the Lord Chancellor that she was his lost wife, the queen entered and prepared to carry out the sentence of death against Iolanthe. Before she could act, however, the other fairies entered and confessed that they too had married peers in the House of Lords. The queen grieved, but the law was clear. Whoever married a mortal must die. But the Lord Chancellor's great knowledge of the law saved the day. It would now read that whoever did *not* marry a mortal must die. Thinking that a wonderful solution, the queen took one of the palace guards, Private Willis, for her husband. Knowing that from now on the House of Lords would be recruited from persons of intelligence, because of Strephon's law, the peers could see that they were of little use. Sprouting wings, they all flew away to Fairyland.

Further Critical Evaluation of the Work:

While *Patience* was still enjoying a long run at The Savoy Theatre, William Schwenck Gilbert prepared for his musical callaborator, Arthur Seymour

Sullivan, the libretto for a new comic opera. Sullivan, as usual, was not wholly satisfied with the preliminary draft of the book, and at his urging Gilbert rewrote the first act. Gilbert himself had trouble with the title. Because his last three successful D'Oyly Carte productions had begun with the letter *P*— *Pinafore* (1878), *The Pirates of Penzance* (1880), and *Patience* (1881)— Gilbert thrashed about for another title beginning with the "lucky" initial. He considered and then rejected "Perola," "Phyllis," and "Princess Pearl" before he chose *Iolanthe,* with the acceptable subtitle *The Peer and the Peri.* This last matter settled, Gilbert and Sullivan's "entirely new and original fairy opera" opened at The Savoy on the evening of November 25, 1882, and continued to hold the stage for a year and two months.

No doubt Gilbert wished to emphasize the "fairy" elements of *Iolanthe* in order to soften any possible criticism of his spoof upon the House of Lords. In the course of Parliamentary debates running throughout Victorian England, the House of Lords, a privileged and largely hereditary body lacking any democratic representation, was under constant fire as antiquated, unresponsive to the people, and ultra-conservative. Almost every reform bill intended to widen the franchise, limited at the same time the powers of the Lords, who eventually lost most of their real authority to the House of Commons. Gilbert, clearly on the side of the liberals, wished to satirize the absurdity of the Peers, but not so directly as to excite political controversy. For the framework of his plot, he reworked an old idea from one of his *Bab Ballads* concerning a hero who is the child of a fairy and is, therefore, half fay and half human. Not even a crusty Tory could complain that the adventures of Strephon could possibly insult the dignities of a modern Lord; and when, at the conclusion of *Iolanthe,* all the Peers marry the fairies, the doughtiest Lord in Parliament would have to acquiesce in pleasure to Gilbert's romantic jest.

But behind the jest, Gilbert's satire applies not only to the House of Lords but also to the notion of a privileged class. The Peers announce their arrival ("Loudly Let the Trumpets Bray") with the contemptuous salutation: "Bow, bow, ye lower middle classes . . . ye tradesmen, bow ye masses!" And the powerful Lord Chancellor, who argues that the law is the "true embodiment of everything that's excellent," cynically changes the law to suit himself and insure that every fairy shall die who does *not* marry a mortal. In "Spurn Not the Nobly Born," Lord Tolloller insists that high rank "involves no shame," so women should never withhold affection from "Blue Bloods." Finally, Lord Mountararat, in "When Britain Really Ruled the Waves," looks backward to the good old days of Queen Bess, when the House of Peers "made no pretence to intellectual eminence or scholarship sublime. . . . " By their own merry words, the Peers indict themselves as a class of drones, bores, and fools. And Gilbert, not disposed to press the point, permits the Lords to grow wings to fly off to a fairyland blessedly distant from the responsibilities of office.

ION

Type of work: Drama
Author: Euripides (c. 485-c. 406 B.C.)
Type of plot: Tragi-comedy
Time of plot: Remote antiquity
Locale: The temple of Apollo at Delphi
First presented: Fifth century B.C.

Principal characters:
HERMES, speaker of the prologue
ION, son of Apollo and Creusa
CREUSA, daughter of Erechtheus, King of Athens
XUTHUS, Creusa's husband
AGED SLAVE TO CREUSA
A PRIESTESS OF APOLLO
PALLAS ATHENA, goddess of wisdom
CHORUS OF CREUSA'S HANDMAIDENS

Critique:

In *Ion*, Euripides fashioned a curious and compelling drama out of a legend which, so far as we know, no other ancient playwright touched. Although several lines of action threaten to culminate in tragedy, as when the outraged Creusa sends her slave to poison Ion and when Ion attempts to retaliate, the play ends happily and must be described as a comedy. Indeed some critics claim that the technique of the recognition scene, the identity of Ion being established by his miraculously preserved swaddling clothes, is the basis of the New Comedy which developed in the fourth century B.C. A tantalizing ambiguity in *Ion* concerns Euripides' attitude toward the gods. On the one hand the action of the play demands that we accept Apollo's existence and his power; on the other, the sly way in which he is presented seems to suggest that he is ridiculously anthropomorphic, a knave caught cheating and forced to concoct a way out for himself.

The Story:

Years before Phoebus Apollo had ravished Creusa, daughter of King Erechtheus, who subsequently and in secret gave birth to a son. By Apollo's command she hid the infant in a cave where Hermes was sent to carry him to the temple of Apollo. There he was reared as a temple ministrant. Meanwhile, Creusa had married Xuthus as a reward for his aid in the Athenian war against the Euboeans, but the marriage remained without issue. After years of frustration, Xuthus and Creusa decided to make a pilgrimage to Delphi and ask the god for aid in getting a son.)

At dawn Ion emerged from the temple of Apollo to sweep the floors, chase away the birds, set out the laurel boughs, and make the usual morning sacrifice. Creusa's handmaidens came to admire the temple built upon the navel of the world and to announce the imminent arrival of their mistress. At the meeting of Creusa and Ion, Creusa confirmed the story that her father had been drawn from the earth by Athena and was swallowed up by the earth at the end of his life. The credulous Ion explained that his own birth, too, was shrouded in mystery, for he had appeared out of nowhere at the temple and had been reared by the priestess of Apollo. The greatest sorrow of his life, he said, was not knowing who his mother was. Creusa sympathized and cautiously revealed that she had a friend with a similar problem, a woman who had borne a son to Apollo, only to have the infant disappear and to suffer childlessness for the rest of her life.

Ion, shocked and outraged at the insult to his god, demanded that Creusa end her accusation of Apollo in his own temple, but the anguished woman assailed the god with fresh charges of injustice, breaking off only at the arrival of her husband. Xuthus eagerly took his wife into the temple, for he had just been assured by the prophet Trophonius that they would not return childless to Athens. The perplexed Ion was left alone to meditate on the lawlessness of gods who seemed to put pleasure before wisdom.

Xuthus, emerging from the temple, fell upon the startled Ion and attempted to kiss and embrace him. He shouted joyfully that Ion must be his son, for the oracle had said that the first person he would see upon leaving the temple would be his son by birth. Stunned and unconvinced, Ion demanded to know who his mother was, but Xuthus could only conjecture that possibly she was one of the Delphian girls he had encountered at a Bacchanal before his marriage. Ion, reluctantly conceding that Xuthus must be his father if Apollo so decreed, begged to remain an attendant in the temple rather than become the unwelcome and suspicious heir to the throne of Athens— for Creusa would surely resent a son she had not borne. Xuthus understood his anxiety and agreed to hide his identity; however, he insisted that Ion accompany him to Athens, even if only in the role of distinguished guest. He then gave orders for a banquet of thanksgiving and commanded that the handmaidens to Creusa keep their silence on pain of death. As they departed to prepare the feast, Ion expressed the hope that his mother might still be found and that she might be an Athenian.

Accompanied by the aged slave of her father, Creusa reappeared before the temple and demanded from her handmaidens an account of the revelation Xuthus had received from Apollo. Only under relentless cross-examination did the fearful servants reveal what had passed between Xuthus and Ion. Overcome by a sense of betrayal, Creusa cursed Apollo for his cruelty but dared not act upon the old slave's suggestion that she burn the temple or murder the husband who had, after all, been kind to her.

But the murder of the usurper, Ion, was another matter. After some deliberation Creusa decided upon a safe and secret method of eliminating the rival of her lost son. From a phial of the Gorgon's blood which Athena had given to Creusa's grandfather and which had been passed down to her, the old slave was to pour a drop into Ion's wineglass at the celebration feast. Eager to serve his master's daughter, the slave departed, and the chorus chanted their hope for success.

Some time later a messenger came running to warn Creusa that the authorities were about to seize her and submit her to death by stoning, for her plot had been discovered. He described how at the feast a flock of doves had dipped down to drink from Ion's cup and had died in horrible convulsions and how Ion had tortured a confession out of the old slave. The court of Delphi had then sentenced Creusa to death for attempting murder of a consecrated person within the sacred precincts of the temple of Apollo. The chorus urged Creusa to fling herself upon the altar and remain there in sanctuary.

A short time later Ion arrived at the head of an infuriated crowd, and he and Creusa began to hurl angry charges and counter-charges at each other. Suddenly the priestess of the temple appeared, bearing the cradle and the tokens with which the infant Ion had been found years before. Slowly and painfully the truth emerged: Ion was the lost son of Creusa and Apollo. Creusa was seized with a frenzy of joy, but the astounded Ion remained incredulous. As he was about to enter the temple to demand an explanation from Apollo himself, the goddess Athena appeared in mid-air and confirmed the revelation. She urged that Xuthus not be told the truth so that he might enjoy the delusion that his own son was to be his heir, while Creusa and Ion could share their genuine happiness. Creusa renounced all her curses against

Apollo and blessed him for his ultimate wisdom. As she and Ion departed for Athens the chorus called upon all men to reverence the gods and take courage.

Further Critical Evaluation of the Work:

The *Ion* falls into the category of Euripides' *Helen* and *Iphigenia in Tauris,* since the three dramas bring their principal characters to the brink of destruction before sudden and marvelous rescues resulting in lives lived happily ever after. Into no other play of Euripides are the techniques of reversal and recognition more tightly woven; so too, irony abounds in the actions and intentions of not one but all parties. The sympathetic wishes of Ion and Creusa for each other in the first half of the play are sharply and ironically reversed in the second half to mutual intentions of murder. In the first half Xuthus connives with Ion to hide from Creusa what they believe to be the lad's true identity, but in the second half it is Xuthus who is deceived by Creusa.

This play has been the occasion of much debate since it does not fall neatly into a tragic or comic mold. On the one hand scholars insist that it is a propagandistic piece, aimed at flattering the Athenians by deifying their origins. The traditions of Hesiod and Herodotus had Ion the son of Xuthus and grandson of Hellen, who himself was the grandson of Prometheus. Evidently Euripides borrowed a less-known tradition in order to trace the lineage of the Ionian Athenians directly to the Olympian god Apollo, patron of the arts. The *Ion* seems to be the last of Euripides' so-called patriotic plays, which include the *Herakleidae, The Suppliants,* and *Herakles Mad.* On the other hand, some critics prefer not to attach any real profundity to the play, citing the complexity of the plot and the melodramatic climax as designed solely for the absorbing entertainment of the Athenian audience, unused to plays on the less familiar myths and always expecting a different twist to the Euripidean version of a well-known myth.

IPHIGENIA IN AULIS

Type of work: Drama
Author: Euripides (480-406 B.C.)
Type of plot: Classical tragedy
Time of plot: Beginning of Trojan War
Locale: Aulis, on the west coast of Euboea
First presented: 405 B.C.

Principal characters:
AGAMEMNON, King of Mycenae
CLYTEMNESTRA, his wife
IPHIGENIA, their daughter
ACHILLES, a Greek warrior
MENELAUS, King of Sparta

Critique:

In *Iphigenia in Aulis*, Agamemnon, the co-commander of all the Greek forces in the Trojan War, impresses one as being essentially the civilian executive, the upper middle-class husband and father who would rather be dictating business, not military policies. Likewise, Clytemnestra, his wife, resembles the society-conscious suburban matron, rather than a queen. Hence, despite its heroic background and despite the nominally heroic aspects of its characters, the play is in many respects a domestic tragedy. Lacking are the terrible and compulsive passions which motivate the story of Clytemnestra and Agamemnon in the dramas of Aeschylus.

The Story:

At Aulis, on the west coast of Euboea, part of Greece, the Greek host had assembled for the invasion of Ilium, the war having been declared to rescue Helen, wife of King Menelaus, after her abduction by Paris, a prince of Troy. Lack of wind, however, prevented the sailing of the great fleet.

While the ships lay becalmed, Agamemnon, commander of the Greek forces, consulted Calchas, a seer. The oracle prophesied that all would go well if Iphigenia, Agamemnon's oldest daughter, were sacrificed to the goddess Artemis. At first Agamemnon was reluctant to see his daughter so destroyed, but at last Menelaus, his brother, persuaded him that nothing else would move the weather-bound fleet. Agamemnon wrote to Clytemnestra, his queen, and asked her to conduct Iphigenia to Aulis, his pretext being that Achilles, the outstanding warrior among the Greeks, would not embark unless he were given Iphigenia in marriage.

The letter having been dispatched, Agamemnon had a change of heart; he felt that his continued popularity as co-leader of the Greeks was a poor exchange for the life of his beloved daughter. In haste he dispatched a second letter countermanding the first, but Menelaus, suspicious of his brother, intercepted the messenger and struggled with him for possession of the letter. When Agamemnon came upon the scene, he and Menelaus exchanged bitter words. Menelaus accused his brother of being weak and foolish, and Agamemnon accused Menelaus of supreme selfishness in urging the sacrifice of Iphigenia.

During this exchange of charge and countercharge a messenger announced the arrival of Clytemnestra and Iphigenia in Aulis. The news plunged Agamemnon into despair; weeping, he regretted his kingship and its responsibilities. Even Menelaus was affected, so that he suggested disbanding the army. Agamemnon thanked Menelaus but declared it was too late to turn back from the course they had elected to follow. Actually, Agamemnon was afraid of Calchas and of Odysseus, and he believed that widespread disaffection and violence would break out in the Greek army if the sacrifice were not made. Some Chalcian women who had come to see the fleet lamented that the love of Paris for Helen had brought such stir and misery instead of happiness.

When Clytemnestra arrived, accompanied by Iphigenia and her young son, Orestes, she expressed pride and joy over the approaching nuptials of her daughter and Achilles. Agamemnon greeted his family tenderly; touching irony displayed itself in the conversation between Agamemnon, who knew that Iphigenia was doomed to die, and Iphigenia, who thought her father's ambiguous words had a bearing only on her approaching marriage. Clytemnestra inquired in motherly fashion about Achilles' family and background. She was scandalized when the heartbroken Agamemnon asked her to return to Argos, on the excuse that he could arrange the marriage details. When Clytemnestra refused to leave the camp, Agamemnon sought the advice of Calchas. Meanwhile the Chalcian women forecast the sequence of events of the Trojan War and hinted in their prophecy that death was certain for Iphigenia.

Achilles, in the meantime, insisted that he and his Myrmidons were impatient with the delay and anxious to get on with the invasion of Ilium. Clytemnestra, meeting him, mentioned the impending marriage, much to the mystification of Achilles, who professed to know nothing of his proposed marriage to Iphigenia. The messenger then confessed Agamemnon's plans to the shocked Clytemnestra and Achilles. He also mentioned the second letter and cast some part of the guilt upon Menelaus. Clytemnestra, grief-stricken, prevailed upon Achilles to help her in saving Iphigenia from death by sacrifice.

Clytemnestra then confronted her husband, who was completely unnerved when he realized that Clytemnestra was at last in possession of the dreadful truth. She rebuked him fiercely, saying that she had never really loved him because he had slain her beloved first husband and her first child. Iphigenia, on her knees, implored her father to save her and asked Orestes, in his childish innocence, to add his pleas to his mother's and her own. Although Agamemnon was not heartless, he knew that the sacrifice must be made. He argued that Iphigenia would die for Greece, a country and a cause greater than them all.

Achilles, meanwhile, spoke to the army in behalf of Iphigenia, but he admitted his failure when even his own Myrmidons threatened to stone him if he persisted in his attempt to stop the sacrifice. At last he mustered enough loyal followers to defend the girl against Odysseus and the entire Greek host. Iphigenia refused his aid, however, saying that she had decided to offer herself as a sacrifice for Greece. Achilles, in admiration, offered to place his men about the sacrificial altar so that she might be snatched to safety at the last moment.

Iphigenia, resigned to certain death, asked her mother not to mourn for her. Then she marched bravely to her death in the field of Artemis. Clytemnestra was left in prostration in her tent. Iphigenia, at the altar, said farewell to all that she held dear and submitted herself to the sacrifice.

The Chalcian women, onlookers at the sacrifice, invoked Artemis to fill the Greek sails now with wind so that the ships might carry the army to Troy to achieve eternal glory for Greece.

Further Critical Evaluation of the Work:

This play has been characterized by the best of classical scholars as one of Euripides' finest creations but also a play full of weaknesses. It is formally a tragedy, but it lacks the traditional tragic concentration and heroic figures. Unlike other tragedies which succeed as adaptations of myths, the *Iphigenia in Aulis* seems controlled by the myth, unable to rise above the complexities of the original story. Thus it has been called a "nontragedy" or a "tragedy *manqué."* Nevertheless, an attempt has been made to resolve its appeal with its flaws by finding its structure in the "ironic lack of cohesion" in the various attempts to save Iphigenia; thus the drama reflects the tragic disorder of the world.

The characters themselves are not genuinely "tragic"; that is, both their situations and their reactions seem too incredibly removed from reality. On the other hand, if we look beneath the spectacle of deceptions and discoveries, we may see that the basic notion of the sacrifice is credible and absorbing. Thus the play seems to succeed by a tension between two levels: the intrigues of the relatively dimensionless mythic characters versus the real prospect of a horrifying death, lurking, tugging at the entertainment.

As in so many of Euripides' plays, the vanity of war is thematic to the *Iphigenia in Aulis*. The less than noble characterizations of Agamemnon and Menelaus, revealed particularly in their "contest of words" beginning at line 317, help us to see the baseness of this whole affair. Because of Agamemnon's personal ambition and Menelaus' exaggerated outrage, a protracted, destructive war must be waged. The irony becomes unbearable when Iphigenia selflessly yields herself to sacrifice, apparently influenced by Agamemnon's rationalization that she will be dying for all Greece. At this point, no longer able to identify with the girl, we are dragged into the pathetic plight of Clytemnestra and distracted by the heroic overtures of Achilles, and here the play all but collapses. Evidently the bathos tests even Artemis, who demanded the sacrifice in the first place, since in the final report to Clytemnestra we discover that at the sacrificial blow Iphigenia vanished from view, and in her place lay a bloody deer gasping out its life.

IPHIGENIA IN TAURIS

Type of work: Drama
Author: Euripides (480-406 B.C.)
Type of plot: Romantic tragedy
Time of plot: Several year after the Trojan War
Locale: Tauris, in the present-day Crimea
First presented: c. 420 B.C.

Principal characters:
IPHIGENIA, a priestess of Artemis
ORESTES, her brother
PYLADES, Orestes' friend
THOAS, King of Tauris
ATHENA, goddess of the hunt

Critique:

Actually, *Iphigenia in Tauris* is not a tragedy in the classic sense at all; instead, it is a romantic melodrama. Iphigenia, after years in a barbaric land, may still have felt hatred for the Greeks, but her sentimental longing to return to Argolis, her birthplace and the scene of her happy childhood, was intense. Her feelings are described most touchingly by Euripides. The play abounds in breathtaking situations of danger and in sentimental passages of reminiscence. The recognition scene is perhaps the most thrilling, if not the most protracted in the classic Greek drama. Goethe dramatized this story in his *Iphigenie auf Tauris* (1787).

The Story:

When the Greek invasion force, destined for Ilium, was unable to sail from Aulis because of a lack of wind, Agamemnon, the Greek commander, appealed to Calchas, a Greek seer, for aid. Calchas said that unless Agamemnon gave Iphigenia, his oldest daughter, as a sacrifice to Artemis, the Greek fleet would never sail. By trickery Agamemnon succeeded in bringing Clytemnestra, his queen, and Iphigenia to Aulis, where the maiden was offered up to propitiate the goddess. At the last moment, however, Artemis substituted a calf in Iphigenia's place and spirited the maiden off to the barbaric land of Tauris, where she was doomed to spend the rest of her life as a priestess of Artemis. One of Iphigenia's duties was to prepare Greek captives—any Greek who was apprehended in Tauris was by law condemned to die—for sacrifice in the temple of the goddess.

Iphigenia had been a priestess in Tauris for many years when, one night, she had a dream which she interpreted to mean that her brother Orestes had met his death; now there could be no future for her family, Orestes having been the only son.

Orestes, however, was alive; in fact, he was actually in Tauris. After he and his sister Electra had murdered their mother to avenge their father's death at her hands, the Furies had pursued Orestes relentlessly. Seeking relief, Orestes was told by the Oracle of Delphi that he must procure a statue of Artemis which stood in the temple of the goddess in Tauris and take it to Athens. Orestes would then be free of the Furies.

Orestes and his friend Pylades reached the temple and were appalled at the sight of the earthly remains of the many Greeks who had lost their lives in the temple. They resolved, however, to carry out their mission of stealing the statue of Artemis.

Meanwhile Iphigenia, disturbed by her dream, aroused her sister priestesses and asked their help in mourning the loss of her brother. In her loneliness she remembered Argos and her carefree childhood. A messenger interrupted her reverie with the report that one of two young Greeks on the shore had in a frenzy slaughtered Taurian cattle which had been led to the sea to bathe. The slayer

2931

was Orestes, under the influence of the Furies. In the fight which followed Orestes and Pylades held off great numbers of Taurian peasants, but at last the peasants succeeded in capturing the two youths. The Greeks were brought to Thoas, the King of Tauris.

Iphigenia, as a priestess of Artemis, directed that the strangers be brought before her. Heretofore she had always been gentle with the doomed Greeks and had never participated in the bloody ritual of sacrifice. Now, depressed by her dream, she was determined to be cruel.

Orestes and Pylades, bound, were brought before Iphigenia. Thinking of her own sorrow, she asked them if they had sisters who would be saddened by their deaths. Orestes refused to give her any details about himself, but he answered her inquiries about Greece and about the fate of the prominent Greeks in the Trojan War. She learned to her distress that her father was dead by her mother's treachery and that Orestes was still alive, a wanderer.

Deeply moved, Iphigenia offered to spare Orestes if he would deliver a letter for her in Argos. Orestes magnanimously gave the mission to Pylades; he himself would remain to be sacrificed. When he learned that Iphigenia would prepare him for the ritual, he wished for the presence of his sister to cover his body after he was dead. Iphigenia, out of pity, promised to do this for him. She went to bring the letter. Orestes and Pylades were convinced that she was a Greek. Pylades then declared that he would stay and die with his friend. Orestes, saying that he was doomed to die anyway for the murder of his mother, advised Pylades to return to Greece, marry Electra, and build a temple in his honor.

Iphigenia, returning with the letter, told Pylades that it must be delivered to one Orestes, a Greek prince. The letter urged Orestes to come to Tauris to take Iphigenia back to her beloved Argos; it explained how she had been saved at Aulis and spirited by Artemis to Tauris.

Pylades, saying that he had fulfilled the mission, handed the letter to Orestes. Iphigenia, doubtful, was finally convinced of Orestes' identity when he recalled familiar details of their home in Argos. While she pondered escape for the three of them, Orestes explained that first it was necessary for him to take the statue of Artemis, in order to avoid destruction. He asked Iphigenia's aid.

Having received a promise of secrecy from the priestesses who were present, Iphigenia carried out her plan of escape. As Thoas, curious about the progress of the sacrifice, entered the temple, Iphigenia appeared with the statue in her arms. She explained to the mystified Thoas that the statue had miraculously turned away from the Greek youths because their hands were stained by domestic murder. She declared to King Thoas that it was necessary for her secretly to cleanse the statue and the two young men in sea water. She commanded the people of Tauris to stay in their houses lest they too be tainted.

When Orestes and Pylades were led from the temple in chains, Thoas and his retinue covered their eyes so that they would not be contaminated by evil. Iphigenia joined the procession and marched solemnly to the beach. There she ordered the king's guards to turn their backs on the secret cleansing rites. Fearful for Iphigenia's safety, the guards looked on. When they beheld the three Greeks entering a ship, they rushed down to the vessel and held it back. The Greeks beat off the Taurians and set sail. The ship, however, was caught by tidal currents and forced back into the harbor.

Thoas, angry, urged all Taurians to spare no effort in capturing the Greek ship. Then the goddess Athena appeared to Thoas and directed him not to go against the will of Apollo, whose Oracle of Delphi had sent Orestes to Tauris to get the statue of Artemis. Thoas meekly complied. Iphigenia, Orestes, and Pylades returned to Greece, where Orestes, having set up the image of the Taurian Artemis in Attica, was at last freed from the wrath of the Furies. Iphigenia continued, in a new temple, to be a priestess of Artemis.

Further Critical Evaluation of the Work:

Like Shakespeare, Euripides turned to the romance in his later years to convey a more optimistic view of the world. In fact, he invented this new dramatic form. *Iphigenia in Tauris,* along with *Helen* and *Ion,* are the few surviving examples. As a play *Iphigenia in Tauris* is masterly. It is carefully plotted, full of suspense, and genuinely moving. The setting is distant, dangerous, romantic. And a wistful love for all of Greece illuminates the action, especially in the beautiful choral odes. The characters are realistically drawn, and their reactions at tense moments are both unexpected and credible. The mixture of accurate psychology and miraculous occurrences is typical of Euripides. Further, the long recognition scene between Iphigenia and Orestes is thrilling in its execution. It would be hard to find a better piece of pure theater in the repertoire of classical drama. But this play has the penetrating depth of Euripides' finest works, in addition to being high entertainment.

Euripides seems to have been fascinated by the legend of the House of Atreus. From the final years of his life five plays on the subject have come down to us. *Iphigenia in Tauris, Electra, Helen, Orestes,* and *Iphigenia in Aulis* treat this story in different ways mostly, and sometimes the depiction of a character is inconsistent from play to play, particularly with Orestes and Helen. Of these works *Iphigenia in Tauris* comes closest to *Helen* in mood and plot. Both are romances in which a woman has been supernaturally transported to a remote, barbaric land and there held in chaste captivity. Iphigenia and Helen long for one deliverer whom they believe to be dead. Promptly they meet the man and a recognition scene follows. Then they plot a means of escape, trick the king, and return home by divine intervention. The similarities are remarkable and suggest that one of these plays attempts to repeat the success of the other, although Euripides may have written more plays along these lines.

The plot of *Iphigenia in Tauris* has two major climaxes and can be divided into two parts. The first part begins with Iphigenia believing her brother, Orestes, to be dead and ends with her accepting the captive Orestes. The second part begins with the two of them planning the escape and ends as they overcome all obstacles with Athena's aid.

Euripides uses an interesting technique. Often a character will state a principle by which he intends to act and then immediately betray the principle. Thus, Iphigenia states her intention of being harsh to the Greek captives because of her own misery (lines 350-353), and melts on hearing news of her homeland, offering to spare Orestes. In this case the technique points up her intense homesickness for Greece and Argos, a passion that animates not only her, but the chorus of Greek maidens, Orestes, and Pylades as well.

With Orestes, Euripides varies the technique in relation to a major theme. When Orestes appears before Iphigenia as a prisoner he says he disdains self-pity; and a few lines after, when Iphigenia asks his name, he replies sullenly, "Call me unfortunate." The method indicates his misery. But it also underscores his nobility of character later when he insists on being sacrificed to free his friend, Pylades. Disinterested love is always a sign of redemption in Euripides.

The barbarian king, Thoas, claims no barbarian would murder his mother, as the Greek, Orestes, had done. Yet he has no compunction about ordering a massacre of all Greeks, including the temple virgins. Euripides uses Thoas as a gullible, vengeful foil to the clever Greeks.

However, the most important theme of the play has to do with divine injustice and human suffering. Iphigenia is in thrall to the goddess Artemis, a victim who has been offered up herself for sacrifice, transported far away from home, and then set to aid in the sacrifices of all strangers and Greeks, a task she loathes. Artemis has been the perpetrator of this whole sequence.

But Artemis' twin, Apollo, has visited similar suffering on Orestes, causing him to kill his mother, be pursued and driven mad by Furies, and sent to Colchis (not Tauris), where he is captured for sacrifice. At first glance the gods Apollo and Artemis appear to be arch-villains ruthlessly dealing out anguish.

There is another perspective, however, that mitigates this view. Orestes is working out his redemption and must enter the gates of death almost literally before he can free himself of the guilt of matricide. He is offered a chance to live, but he chooses to save Pylades. Presumably Apollo sent him to Colchis for that very purpose, to act as a free man rather than an embittered victim. Once this choice occurs things begin falling into harmony. Iphigenia accepts him as her brother and contrives an escape. Orestes repays the favor by saving her life as they board the ship. Then in the moment of greatest danger the goddess Athena arrives to rescue the Greeks, showing that the gods give help to those who help others.

Euripides is showing us that as long as a person regards himself as a victim he can only suffer. Only when someone acts freely and unselfishly does their suffering cease and gods come to their assistance. By disinterested love divine injustice is transmuted to true justice.

James Weigel, Jr.

IRISH MELODIES

Type of work: Poetry
Author: Thomas Moore (1779-1852)
First published: 1807-1834; 1835

Few men of letters have been able to write on Thomas Moore without disparaging the financial and social success of his life or the great mass of his work, mostly verse, from which so little of any worth is still remembered except the *Irish Melodies.* The quantity of his work and the ready charm which contributed to his success in London society are largely attributable to the fact that Moore, like many another aspirant from the provinces, had to get on as best he could. Starvation in a garret may be the mark of genius but only posterity can decide between the respective merits of Chatterton and Blake. Moore took no chances; he stuck by the Whigs and forswore his early Republicanism and modulated his Irishness into its most acceptable form in the London drawing room, the real source of political power and hence patronage in Regency England. He sang Irish songs and at the same time gained practically the only claim he has on our memory and affections. The rest of his work fills up that yawning gulf of trivia which kept the publishers of London prosperous, their readers contented, the popular authors wealthy, and the best of contemporary English writers—Shelley, Keats, Blake—out of sight.

Yet Moore was in his way a pioneer. He always claimed to have originated modern Irish poetry, enjoying a personal application of the song which takes its title from the opening words:

Dear Harp of my Country! in darkness
 I found thee,
 The cold chain of silence hung o'er
  thee long,
When proudly, my own Island Harp! I
  unbound thee,
 And gave all thy chords to light, free-
  dom and song!

In the rest of the lyric Moore sums up his subjects—death, love, mirth, and patriotism—and specifies his technique: "wild sweetness." The revolutionary effect of this combination in London when he began the composition of *Irish Melodies* in 1806 (seven years after his arrival there from Dublin) was more noticeable because of the stolidity of the serious verse of the time and popular light verse, to both of which Moore had contributed enough to acquire a lucrative government post in the Bermudas. He left London in 1803 to take up the post, but soon returned and set to work on his *Irish Melodies,* exile from London having apparently sharpened his love for Ireland. The new style of drawing room entertainment Moore often provided in person (he was an accomplished musician) was soon earning him five hundred pounds a year. The lyric was restored to popularity in English literature not by the *Lyrical Ballads* or by Burns or by Blake, all of whom came before Moore, but by the *Irish Melodies.*

Moore had given a sample of his ability to write lyrics to folk tunes in the feebly satirical *Poems Relating to America,* published in 1806: the "Canadian Boat Song" which he heard his "voyageurs" sing as they rowed all the way down the St. Lawrence from Kingston to Montreal. The poems were published in ten parts from 1807 to 1834, words and music, with editions of the words alone appearing from 1820 on. Time has established the concert repertoire selected from the songs: "The Harp That Once Thro' Tara's Halls," "Believe Me if All Those Endearing Young Charms," "She Is Far from the Land," "'Tis the Last Rose of Summer," "The Minstrel Boy," "Sweet Inishfallen, Fare Thee Well," to which may be added the "Canadian Boat Song" and two later songs, the "Vesper Hymn" and "Oft in the Stilly Night" from *National Airs*, lyrics and arrangements of folk songs from most European countries.

Generally only one of the lyrics is now anthologized as a poem apart from its setting: "The Time I've Lost in Wooing." It shows Moore's abilities to advantage: the rhymes are feminine in the longer lines and in triples (*wooing . . . pursuing . . . undoing*); the shorter lines (none is long) end in masculine rhyme; the alternations give a pleasing variation to the run of the poem; the poem in three stanzas reaches a witty conclusion that echoes the Caroline poets. In the conflict between Wisdom and Beauty the poet's time has been wasted in pursuit of the latter; he knows this but still cannot cease his pursuit:

> Poor Wisdom's chance
> Against a glance
> Is now as weak as ever.

Of the language of the lyrics Edmund Gosse observed that "words of a commonplace character are so strung together as to form poetry easily grasped and enjoyed by the ear." The secret of Moore's original and present popularity lies in providing acceptable poetry for the ear, not for the eye, and since we have largely lost that gift so enjoyed by Elizabethans it is little wonder that our ears have to be assisted by folk tunes.

In the collected editions of Moore's works the *Irish Melodies* now number one hundred and twenty-five, beginning with "Go Where Glory Waits Thee" and ending with "Silence Is in Our Festal Halls," Moore's elegy for Sir John Stevenson, who wrote the arrangements for the parts. Most of the parts as they were issued contained dedications to patrons from Moore and advertisements from his publisher, Power, to the general public insisting that there were plenty more "airs" in the treasury of Irish folk song for future parts. A certain amount of national feeling is evident in both advertisements and dedications, especially in that to the first part which includes a letter from Moore referring to the Irish reputation for song as "the only talent for which our English neighbors ever deigned to allow us any credit." A more important preface is that to the third part or number. As well as dealing with the age of Irish songs, their resemblance to Scottish song, and the harmonic peculiarities of Irish music, Moore refers to three aspects which in their way sum up much of the *Melodies*: their national feeling; their peculiar mixture of defiance and despondency; and their being lyrics to songs, not poems as such.

On the last point he begs exemption from "the rigors of literary criticism" because he can "answer for their sound with somewhat more confidence than for their sense." This statement is admirably sensible but makes it difficult to discuss the *Irish Melodies* as if they were poems. If Moore's guiding principle was to make them singable, only a singer can argue the point and many a trite phrase and conventional rhyme can be excused on this ground. Moore's other two remarks point to two obvious features in the lyrics. They often begin strongly and fade into resignation at parting, death, the passage of time, the decay of good customs. Where the poems reach a strong conclusion they do so by denying the resigned close, generally by appeal to the Divine or to Ireland. The endings to two patriotic poems illustrate the difference: "Let Erin Remember the Days of Old" declines into

> Thus, sighing, look through the waves
>   of time
> For the long-faded glories they cover.

On the other hand "Sublime Was the Warning" challenges Irish national aspirations by appealing to the success of Spanish independence after the Napoleonic wars and concludes:

> The young spirit of Freedom shall shelter their grave
> Beneath shamrocks of Erin and olives of Spain.

The Irish quality of the poems is most apparent in their subjects. Some are taken from Irish history; others contain references to Irish legends and customs; but the one thread that runs through the volume is "Erin." Much of the reference to Ireland is a prophecy of longed-for independence; a purely poetic exercise Moore's contemporaries in London must have thought it, but history has realized Moore's longing, and it would be an interesting point to settle how much his songs had to do with maintaining Irish nationalism during the struggles of the nineteenth century—songs like "Where Is the Slave?" "Erin, Oh Erin," "Oh the Shamrock," and the better-known "Minstrel Boy" and "The Harp That Once Thro' Tara's Halls." The most curious of these is "As Vanquished Erin," which describes how the Fiend of Discord persists in sending "his shafts of desolation . . . through all her maddening nation." When Erin asks the "Powers of Good" when this will end, the Demon answers "Never." This is possibly the truest statement Moore made about Ireland.

The phrase that sums up the quality of the lyrics in the *Irish Melodies* is Moore's "wild sweetness," an unusual and romantic combination of opposites, its Irishness, one may say. But the "sweetness" of the verses is obtained by both technical dexterity (Moore maintains, as he must, the rhythm of the melody in a variety of meters) and a neatness of phrasing that might be called Irish wit were it not that, except in a few light pieces of which "The Time I've Lost in Wooing" is the best, this gift is usually spent on general topics and does not show to advantage:

Love, nursed among pleasures, is faithless as they,
But the love born of Sorrow, like Sorrow, is true.

Much of the "wild" note comes from the subjects of war, chains, heroic death, but also from the ecstasy of the love poems, tinged as they generally are with sadness. Oddly enough it is probably the romantic combination Moore achieved which was responsible for the gradual disfavor into which the *Irish Melodies* fell about the turn of the century, though they are still referred to in Joyce and O'Casey. When the Gaelic Revival and the independence of Eire finally arrived, a more genuine folk song with real Irish lyrics seems to have lessened Moore's popularity and reduced it to the proportions of the man himself, whom Scott once called "a little, very little man."

ISRAEL POTTER

Type of work: Novel
Author: Herman Melville (1819-1891)
Type of plot: Social satire
Time of plot: 1774-1826
Locale: Vermont, Massachusetts, England, France, the Atlantic Ocean
First published: 1855

Principal characters:
ISRAEL POTTER, a wanderer
ISRAEL'S FATHER
KING GEORGE III
BENJAMIN FRANKLIN
JOHN PAUL JONES
ETHAN ALLEN
SQUIRE WOODCOCK, an American agent
THE EARL OF SELKIRK

Critique:

Facetiously dedicated to the Bunker Hill Monument, *Israel Potter* is a mock picaresque novel. The hero, Israel Potter, wanders about America and Europe for over fifty years, never settling, never successful, providing a vehicle through which Melville satirizes a great many ideas and institutions. The pious morality of Benjamin Franklin, tidied into sugar-coated aphorisms, is one of Melville's principal targets. Other targets are the brutality of all wars, the idiocy of jingoistic patriotism, the barbarous quality lurking behind supposedly civilized behavior; neither American energy nor European polish can protect man from brutality or from the ridiculous patriotism around him. Despite the serious nature of Melville's theme, the novel is frequently very funny. Israel, the innocent, frequently stumbles into difficult situations and out of them by changing clothes, masquerading as a ghost, feigning madness, or pretending a polite worldliness he does not possess. The novel was not well received when it was written, for mid-nineteenth-century American taste did not relish the picaresque or the mocking treatment of America's noble fight for freedom. Although generally appreciated by those who have read it, *Israel Potter* has not yet received the attention accorded to many of Melville's other novels nor the attention that it deserves because of its genuine comedy and its astringent defense of civilized values.

The Story:

Born among the rugged stones of the New England hills, in the Housatonic Valley, Israel Potter grew up with all the virtues of the hard, principled, new land. After an argument with his father over a girl whom his stern parent did not think a suitable match, Israel decided to run away from home while his family was attending church. He wandered about the countryside, hunting deer, farming land, becoming a trapper, dealing in furs. During his wanderings he learned that most men were unscrupulous. He also hunted whales from Nantucket to the coast of Africa.

In 1775, Israel joined the American forces and took part in the Battle of Bunker Hill. He fought bravely, but the battle, as he saw it, was simply disorganized carnage. Wounded, Israel enlisted aboard an American ship after his recovery. Once at sea, the ship was captured by the British. Israel was taken prisoner and conveyed to England on the British ship, but on his arrival in London he managed to make his escape.

Wandering about London, Israel met various Englishmen who mocked his American accent. Some of the English were kind and helpful to him; others cuffed him about and berated the scurrilous Yankee rebels. He found various odd jobs, including one as a gardener working for a cruel employer. He escaped from this job and found one as a gardener on the king's staff at Kew Gardens. One day Israel met King George III. The king, completely mad, realized that Israel was an American and was ineffectually kind to him. Eventually, in a slack season, Israel was discharged. He then worked for a farmer, but when neighboring farmers discovered that he was an American, he was forced to run away.

Israel met Squire Woodcock, a wealthy and secret friend of America, who sent him on a secret mission to Benjamin Franklin in Paris. Israel carried a message in the false heel of his new boots. On his arrival in Paris, while he was looking for Benjamin Franklin, a poor man tried to shine his boots on the Pont Neuf. Israel, in fright, kicked the man and ran off. At last he found Benjamin Franklin, who took the message and then insisted that Israel return and pay damages to the bootblack.

In this fashion Israel, under the tutelage of Franklin, learned his first lesson in European politeness and consideration. From this incident Franklin proceeded to instruct Israel in the ways of proper behavior, deriving many of his lessons from the simple maxims in *Poor Richard's Almanack*. Israel, still innocent, absorbed the teaching carefully, although none of it ever applied to his later experiences. Franklin promised that Israel would be sent back to America, if he would first return to England with a message. While still in Paris, Israel met the stormy and ferocious Captain John Paul Jones, who also visited Franklin. John Paul Jones found Israel a bright and likely young man.

Israel made his way back across the Channel and went to Squire Woodcock. The squire urged him to hide in the dungeon cell for three days, since their plot was in danger of discovery. When Israel emerged from the cell, he recognized that the good squire must have been killed for his activities in the American cause.

Having appropriated some of the squire's clothes, Israel masqueraded as Squire Woodcock's ghost and escaped from a house filled with his enemies. He then traded clothes with a farmer, wandered to Portsmouth, and signed on as a foretopman on a British ship bound for the East Indies. In the Channel, his ship met another ship whose captain had authority to impress some of the men; Israel was among those taken. That same night the ship was captured by an American ship under the command of John Paul Jones. Having revealed himself to his old friend, Israel soon became the quartermaster of the *Ranger*. With John Paul Jones, Israel engaged in piracy, capturing and looting ships.

In Scotland they called on the Earl of Selkirk in order to rob him, but the nobleman was not at home. Israel impressed the earl's wife with his Parisian manners, drank tea with her, and assured her that he and John Paul Jones did not intend to do the lady any harm. The crew, however, insisted that plunder was a part of piracy, and so Israel and John Paul Jones were forced to allow the men to take the family silver and other valuables. Israel promised to restore all articles of value, and when he received a large sum of money from another exploit, he and John Paul Jones bought back all the earl's articles from the men and returned them to the Selkirk family.

Other adventures did not end so cheerfully. The sea fight between the *Bon Homme Richard* and the *Serapis* was a violent and bloody battle, fought along national lines and devoid of all the amenities of piracy. Both ships were lost, and Israel and John Paul Jones, still hoping to get to America, sailed on the *Ariel*. The *Ariel* was captured by the British and Israel was again impressed into the British Navy. By feigning madness to hide his Yankee origins, he got back to England safely.

In England, Israel met Ethan Allen, a strong, heroic, Samson-like figure, held prisoner by the English. Israel tried to help Allen escape but was unsuccessful.

Disguised as a beggar, he went to London, where he remained for over forty years. During that time he worked as a brick-maker and laborer, always hoping to save enough money to return to America but never finding the economic situation in London stable enough to permit saving. A wanderer in an alien land, he became part of the grime and poverty of London. During those years he married a shopgirl who bore him a son. Finally, in 1826, he secured some credit and, with the help of the American consul, sailed for America with his son.

Israel arrived in Boston on July 4, during a public celebration of the Battle of Bunker Hill. No one recognized him or acknowledged his right to be there. Instead, people laughed at him and thought he was mad. He returned to his father's farm, but the homestead had long since disappeared. Old Israel, his wanderings ended, found no peace, comfort, or friendship in his old age. Although heroes of the Revolution were publicly venerated, the aged man could not even get a small pension.

Further Critical Evaluation of the Work:

"Is civilization a thing distinct, or is it an advanced state of barbarism?" Melville asks the question after describing in vivid detail, but with cynical detachment, the canine ferocity of the fight to the death between John Paul Jones's *Bon Homme Richard* and the British man of war *Serapis*. Joined by their smashed and burning rigging, the two vessels are a fitting symbol of the fratricidal struggle between Britain and the young United States. What bemuses Melville is the insanity of a fight in which both parties literally destroy themselves in pursuit of victory over the other; when the *Serapis* finally strikes her colors, it is almost impossible to determine the true victor because both ships were disemboweled wrecks with half their crews killed or wounded. Ironically, Jones and his men board the *Serapis* the morning after battle because they are unable to put out the flames on the *Richard*.

In *Moby Dick* and *Pierre*, written a few years before *Israel Potter*, Melville had traced the consequences of erratic and self-destructive behavior in titanic and tormented individuals: satanic Ahab and maddeningly idealistic Pierre. In *Israel Potter* Melville broadens his focus to include the world at large; instead of cosmic tragedy, we have cosmic laughter, a kind of grim snicker at the absurdity and contemptuous pettiness of the real world. There is no doubt that this minor work is an important bridge between *Moby Dick* and *The Confidence Man*, that dark social satire which Lewis Leary has called "the inevitable sequel" to *Israel Potter*.

The famous portraits in the novel of actual historical figures (Franklin, John Paul Jones, and Ethan Allen) are artful exercises in debunking and anticipate by more than sixty years the biographical intentions of Lytton Strachey. Great men are mirrors to the corruption and vanities of their time. Israel Potter, the common man, despite the adventurous promise of his youth fails to realize the American imperative of independence and self-realization. Although brave and gifted with the shrewdness necessary for survival, he lives out his days in mediocrity and helpless exile. When he finally does return to America, he is unrecognized and denied his pension—a hero of Bunker Hill!

IT IS BETTER THAN IT WAS

Type of work: Drama
Author: Pedro Calderón de la Barca (1600-1681)
Type of plot: Cape-and-sword comedy
Time of plot: Seventeenth century
Locale: Vienna
First presented: 1631

Principal characters:
CARLOS COLONA, son of the Governor of Brandenburg
DON CÉSAR, a Viennese magistrate
FLORA, his daughter
LAURA, Flora's friend
FABIO, Laura's brother
ARNALDO, Laura's suitor
DINERO, Carlos' servant

Critique:

In his early days, Calderón, as the inheritor of the good and the bad of sixteenth-century drama, followed Lope de Vega's formula for comedy, but with a tightening of the plot and the illumination of some of the extra threads. His cape-and-sword plays dealt with veiled women, secret rooms, and the hoodwinking of fathers and guardian brothers by sweethearts who, like Lope's heroines, are frequently motherless, lest fooling a mother might be regarded as disrespect for womanhood. Calderón's servants, derived from the *gracioso* invented by Lope, are a combination of a shrewd rascal faithful to his master and a character added to the cast to provide humor. During his ten years of service in Spanish armies (1625-1635) Calderón sent back from Flanders and Italy about ten plays, including *It Is Better than It Was*, an optimistic contrast to the earlier *It Is Worse than It Was*. In the celebrated letter to the Duke of Veragua, written ten months before his death and listing the 111 plays from his pen, Calderón mentioned it as among those still unpublished. There is little philosophy in this drama, aside from the shrewd wisdom and salty comments of the skeptical servant. It is a comedy of love-making among the nobility, with the outcome not definitely known until the lines spoken just before the hero puts in a good word for the author to end the play.

The Story:

Flora and her friend Laura, both motherless, went out veiled into the streets of Vienna to witness the city's welcome to the Spanish princess María. Unfortunately, they were recognized by Arnaldo, in love with Laura, and by Licio, chosen by Flora's father as the future husband of his daughter. Flora became intrigued by the attempts of a handsome stranger to talk to her. When a quarrel between him and Licio seemed imminent, both ladies fled to their homes.

Into Flora's home rushed the stranger, Carlos Colona, in search of asylum. He said that he had been forced into a duel over a veiled woman and had killed his challenger. Without identifying herself, Flora promised him protection and hid him in a closet as Arnaldo appeared, seeking to kill the man who had murdered Licio. Her father, Don César, also came in, having learned from Dinero, the stranger's servant, that the murderer was the son of his old friend, the Governor of Brandenburg. He faced a predicament. His ties of friendship required that he help the young fugitive, but as magistrate he must hunt him down and execute him.

In the meantime Arnaldo had carried the news to Laura as an excuse to enter her house without objections from her brother and guardian, Fabio; but Fabio warned the young man never again to try to talk to Laura while she was unchaperoned. Then, seeing in Flora's grief a chance to further his own courtship, Fabio left to visit her and in doing so interrupted her plans to get Don Carlos to a place of safety.

Because there were too many people around the house, visitors come to see the magistrate, Flora and her servant Silvia decided to hide Don Carlos in the tower of the building, formerly the town jail. Later Silvia returned to tell the fugitive that a heavily muffled woman wanted to talk to him. Flora, the caller, knew that it was impossible for her to go openly calling on the man who had just killed her fiancé. Don Carlos decided that the women of Vienna were kind to strangers. The visitor, after making him promise not to try to discover her identity, explained that she had come because she was the cause of all his trouble, the motive for the duel, and she wanted to make amends. He answered that he was leaving Vienna as soon as possible in order not to harm her reputation. But the arrival of Dinero again delayed his escape. The servant, learning Flora's identity, prevented her father's discovery of her secret by claiming that he had brought a cloak which the girl was merely trying on.

Don César having gone to post guards at the gates, Don Carlos gave Flora a jewel as a token and then slipped over the wall into the next house. There he interrupted the love-making of Arnaldo and Laura, but he won their sympathy by telling a story about fleeing from a jealous husband. Arnaldo, having boosted the fugitive over a high fence to safety, was himself caught by Don César, who

was pursuing the fugitive, and by Fabio, who had been awakened by the noise. By keeping muffled, Arnaldo tricked the magistrate into believing him the escaping Don Carlos. Don César ordered a jailer to return the fugitive to the tower prison.

Don Carlos had already taken refuge there, convinced it was the safest place in which he could hide. The young man's presence now offered Don César a triple problem of honor: his conflicting duties as father, friend, and magistrate. Meanwhile, Arnaldo, finding Don Carlos in the tower, started a quarrel. The noise of the fight brought Don César to the scene. He scoffed at Arnaldo's accusations that the young man was secretly visiting Flora; his own jailer had brought the young man there. Denounced as a scandalmonger, Arnaldo was thrown out of the house.

Laura, veiled, was an early morning visitor to the tower. At first Flora, also in disguise, saw in her friend a possible rival; but Laura, thinking that the prisoner was Arnaldo, had come to confess her indiscretion, if necessary, in order to free him. The others, bursting in, found the two veiled women. Arnaldo, realizing that one was Laura, confessed his misdeeds and asked to marry her, but only after he had killed Don Carlos. The prisoner then concocted a story that placated everybody. Laura's honor was now safe. Don Carlos also assured Don César that he had sought asylum in the house of his father's friend, not of his sweetheart's father; and he pointed out his marriage to Flora would resolve all problems. So all ended happily with a double wedding.

Further Critical Evaluation of the Work:

Calderón's *It Is Better than It Was* falls into that subdivision of his cloak-and-sword plays known as the Palace Plays. Although the techniques applied to this type are essentially the same as in the cloak-and-sword plays, the distinguishing feature is that the Palace Plays revolve around incidents in the lives of the upper nobility.

The primary purpose of *It Is Better than It Was* is simple amusement, and consequently there is little of the philosophy of Calderón's later plays.

Yet there are on display many of the traits for which the playwright is noted. The stylization of balance and contrast for which Calderón had so strong a penchant is found not only in the linguistic style and imagery, but also in the arrangement of the plot. The main plot deals with Don Carlos' love for Flora, who is aiding his escape from his pursuers. The secondary plot centers around the love of Arnaldo and Laura. This situation turns on the appearance versus reality theme brought by misunderstanding, deceptions, veiled ladies, and forbidden suitors. Comic situations arise because of the discrepancy between illusion and reality and are accentuated by the compromising circumstances in which the characters find themselves.

The linguistic style and imagery are full of the gyrations of conceptual and formal language, particularly characteristic of the seventeenth century Spanish court. The rigid formality of this style and imagery, although seeming artificial today, served to create the courtly atmosphere of the society in which the action took place and its vogue for expressing matters of the heart in veiled language.

It Is Better than It Was, while not being one of Calderón's most notable plays, was characteristic of his early efforts and was a great favorite of audiences who enjoyed the tricks and deceptions of Calderón's comedies.

IT IS WORSE THAN IT WAS

Type of work: Drama
Author: Pedro Calderón de la Barca (1600-1681)
Type of plot: Cape-and-sword comedy
Time of plot: Seventeenth century
Locale: Gaeta, Italy
First presented: 1630

> Principal characters:
> CÉSAR URSINO, a fugitive from justice
> CAMACHO, his servant
> FLÉRIDA COLONA, whom César loves
> JUAN DE ARAGÓN, Governor of Gaeta
> LISARDA, his daughter
> CELIA, her servant
> DON JUAN, Lisarda's suitor and César's friend

Critique:

In his early days, Calderón imitated the complicated plots of Lope de Vega's cape-and-sword plays with their disguises and mistaken identities. A good example is *It Is Worse than It Was (Peor está que estaba)*, first presented in 1630 and appearing in the first "Parte" of twelve plays by Calderón published in 1635. Later it was corrected and reprinted in 1682 by Calderón's friend, Juan de Vera Tassis. Because many seventeenth-century Spanish dramatists were competing with Lope for popularity, the Jesuit-trained Calderón, to make his plays different, added an interest in philosophy and logic. His characters, as one critic has put it, make love like debaters. Lisarda, inquiring how César can love her without having seen her, is answered by an exposition of how blind people can admire what they cannot see. For additional differentiation, Calderón borrowed from the Gongoristic literary practice, then popular, and provided word puzzles for his audiences, as when he refers to a diamond bribe given a servant as an "errant star," or played with metaphors, as when César speaks of the dawn "crowned with roses and carnations." But Calderón was also a skilled poet and dramatist, even in his early days. His thoughts are clothed in word music, and his plots, in spite of their complications, are mechanically correct and exciting to follow.

The Story:

When Juan de Aragón, Governor of Gaeta, received a letter from his old friend Alonso Colona of Naples, saying that his daughter had run off with a murderer, César Ursino, that official was so upset and incoherent that his daughter Lisarda was sure that her own guilty secret had been discovered, for she had been going veiled to assignations with a romantic wooer. This gallant, who called himself Fabio, was really César. He was deeply interested in the veiled girl whom he was meeting, much to the dismay of his servant Camacho, who remonstrated with his master and reminded him that he was to marry Flérida.

One day César ran across his old friend, Don Juan, who had returned from Flanders to visit an old soldier friend of his and to pay court to Lisarda. About the same time Flérida Colona arrived in Gaeta from Naples and appealed for help to the governor's daughter. Calling herself Laura, she explained that her sweetheart was in flight after having killed a man who had molested her, and that she was following him.

During her next meeting with César, Lisarda was persuaded to unveil herself. Her maid Celia, flirting with Camacho, also revealed herself. At that moment they were discovered by the governor, who was searching for César. The fugitive declared: "Things are worse than they

2945

were." The governor sent him a prisoner to the tower, and ordered the veiled girl, whom he took for the daughter of his old friend, to be taken under guard to his own house.

Returning home before her father, Lisarda was able to make him believe on his arrival that his captive had been Flérida, the girl whom Lisarda was already sheltering in the house. Satisfied with the way matters had turned out, the governor dispatched a messenger to his friend in Naples and promised to keep the runaway girl out of mischief until she was safely married. Meanwhile, Don Juan had been accepted as Lisarda's suitor and was being entertained in the governor's house.

Lisarda, remorseful that César had been jailed because of his passion for her, sent Celia to him with a note arranging for another meeting that night. The servant found him and Camacho comparing Flérida and his new lady. César, immediately accepting the invitation, promised to bribe the jailer for a night of freedom. Bribery was not necessary, however. Don Juan, on his arrival to visit the prisoner, announced that the jailer was his old military comrade, who would let César out on parole. César had hoped to keep his friend from learning about the veiled woman, but was glad of Don Juan's help when his pistol went off unexpectedly, revealing his presence in Lisarda's room. Don Juan, who was staying in the governor's house, arrived first on the scene, recognized César, and aided him to escape.

Don Juan debated all night whether to challenge César as a rival or to aid him

as a friend. Unable to make up his mind, he hesitated about accepting the governor's offer of immediate marriage to Lisarda. While he was debating with himself, the early-rising Flérida found him in the patio. Her general remarks about César and their adventures together in the past convinced Don Juan that she had been the girl in César's company the night before. During their discussion Flérida learned for the first time that César was in the Gaeta jail.

When her attempts to visit him aroused Lisarda's jealousy, the governor, overhearing part of the conversation between the girls, almost uncovered the truth about Lisarda's secret meetings. But Lisarda managed to keep her secret from her father. She also promised Flérida a full explanation of everything that had happened.

Once more Don Juan visited César in jail. Camacho, by his quick wit, managed to save Lisarda's good name, but all was nearly discovered when the governor arrived with news that he had made arrangements for César's immediate marriage to Flérida. Unable to understand the young man's surprise at news of his sweetheart, he insisted that he had found them together the previous night.

To get the truth, Don Juan gathered everyone concerned at the governor's house. There Lisarda, to escape scandal, was compelled to see Flérida paired off with César while she had to be satisfied with Don Juan. To complete the round of weddings, Celia and Camacho were paired off with each other.

Further Critical Evaluation of the Work:

It Is Worse than It Was is a fairly representative example of a cloak-and-sword play, so-called because of the cloak and sword worn by the gentlemen of the era depicted in the play. This type of play, the purpose of which is to amuse, reached its zenith with Calderón de la Barca. *It Is Worse than It Was*, while not being as important as some of Calderón's other cloak-and-sword plays, notably *The House with Two Doors,* excellently showcases the traits of the genre. It contains the zestful ingredients of a romantic love, universal in its appeal: Boy (César) meets girl (Lisarda), all kinds of obstacles arise, especially a vigilant father, and the audience is kept on edge by the rapidity of the action, the excitement of the chase, and the various intrigues, deceits, and misunderstandings.

The character portrayals are the weakest part of the play's fabric, as they usually are in cloak-and-sword plays. César is somewhat insipid in professing to love Lisarda, whose face he has not seen. Lisarda is a little better portrayed. She is forward, clever, bold, and deceitful. She is of major importance in determining the flow of the action.

The play makes use of a number of stock devices inherited from classical Roman comedy as found in the works of Plautus and Terence and continued in the Italian comedies of intrigue. Some of these devices are seen in the manipulation of the intrigue where mistakes, identity, trickery, misunderstanding, and surprise disclosures combine to produce an effect of suspense, bewilderment, and comic irony. The purpose of the intrigue is to create a farcical situation which reveals character and satirizes manners of the day. The audience enjoys sorting out the deceptions, and interest is sustained by the onlookers' natural desire to determine the workings and outcome of the intrigues.

THE ITALIAN

Type of work: Novel
Author: Mrs. Ann Radcliffe (1764-1823)
Type of plot: Gothic romance
Time of plot: 1758
Locale: Italy
First published: 1797

Principal characters:

VINCENTIO DI VIVALDI, a young nobleman of Naples
ELLENA DI ROSALBA, loved by Vincentio
THE MARCHESE DI VIVALDI, and
THE MARCHESA DI VIVALDI, Vincentio's parents
SCHEDONI, the marchesa's confessor, formerly the Count di Bruno
SIGNORA BIANCHI, Ellena's aunt
SISTER OLIVIA, formerly the Countess di Bruno
PAULO MENDRICO, Vincentio's faithful servant

Critique:

In *The Journal of a Tour,* an account of a journey through Holland and Germany with her husband in 1794, Mrs. Radcliffe told how on her trip up the Rhine she had encountered two Capuchins "as they walked along the shore, beneath the dark cliffs of Boppart, wrapt in the long black drapery of their order, and their heads shrouded in cowls, that half concealed their faces. . . ." She saw them as "interesting figures in a picture, always gloomily sublime." This vision is commonly believed to have inspired the character of Schedoni, the most sinister villain in that gallery of villains, the Gothic novel. As in her other books, *The Italian, or, The Confessional of the Black Penitents* mingles the wild or idyllic beauty of nature with scenes of nightmare and terror. The novel is wholly a work of the romantic imagination, lacking both the fantastic supernaturalism and the turgid sensationalism of her rivals in this specialized genre.

The Story:

Vincentio di Vivaldi saw Ellena di Rosalba for the first time at the Church of San Lorenzo in Naples. So impressed was he by the sweetness of her voice and the grace of her person that at the end of the service he followed the girl and her elderly companion in the hope that the fair unknown would put aside her veil so that he might catch a glimpse of her features. When the elderly woman stumbled and fell, Vivaldi seized the opportunity to offer her his arm, a gallant gesture which gave him the excuse to accompany the two women to the Villa Altieri, their modest home on an eminence overlooking the bay of Naples.

The next day he returned to ask after the health of Signora Bianchi, as the older woman was named. Although the matron received her guest courteously, Ellena did not appear. Thrown into a mood of despondency by her absence, he inquired of his acquaintances into the girl's family, but learned only that she was an orphan, the niece and ward of her aged relative.

That night, resolved to see Ellena again, he left a reception given by his mother and repaired to the Villa Altieri. The hour was late and only one window was lighted. Through a lattice he saw Ellena playing on her lute while she sang a midnight hymn to the Virgin. Entranced, he drew near the lattice and heard her pronounce his name; but when he revealed himself the girl closed the lattice and left the room. Vivaldi lingered in the garden for some time before returning to Naples. Lost in reverie, he was passing under a shattered archway extending over the road when a shadowy figure in a monk's robe glided across his path and in a ghostly whisper warned him to beware of future visits to the

2948

villa.

Thinking that the warning had been given by a rival, he returned the next night in the company of his friend Bonorma. Again the dark figure appeared and uttered a sepulchral warning. Later, as the two young men were passing under the arch, the figure showed itself once more. Vivaldi and Bonorma drew their swords and entered the ancient fortress in search of the mysterious visitant. They found no trace of anyone lurking in the ruins.

Still believing that these visitations were the work of a rival, Vivaldi decided to end his suspense by making a declaration for Ellena's hand. Signora Bianchi listened to his proposal and then reminded him that a family as old and illustrious as his own would object to an alliance with a girl of Ellena's humble station. Vivaldi realized that she spoke wisely, but with all the fervor of a young man in love he argued his suit so eloquently that at last Signora Bianchi withdrew her refusal. After Vivaldi had made repeated visits to the villa, a night came when the aged woman placed Ellena's hand in his and gave them her blessing. To Vivaldi's great joy it was decided that the marriage would be solemnized during the coming week.

The Marchese and Marchesa di Vivaldi, in the meantime, had not remained in ignorance of their son's frequent visits at the Villa Altieri. On several occasions the marchese, a man of great family pride and strict principles, had remonstrated with his son and assured him that any expectation of marriage to one so far below him in station was impossible. To this argument Vivaldi answered only that his affections and intentions were irrevocable. His mother, a haughty and vindictive woman, was equally determined to end what she regarded as her son's foolish infatuation. Realizing that the young man could not be moved by persuasion or threats, she summoned her confessor and secret adviser, the monk Schedoni, and consulted him on measures to separate Ellena and Vivaldi.

Schedoni, a monk at the Convent of the Santo Spirito, was a man of unknown family and origins. His spirit appeared haughty and disordered; his appearance conveyed an effect of gloom that corresponded to his severe and solitary disposition. Because of his austere manners, brooding nature, and sinister appearance he was loved by none, hated by many, and feared by most. Vivaldi disliked the monk and avoided him, even though he had no presentiment of what Schedoni was preparing for him and Ellena.

On the morning after his acceptance as Ellena's suitor Vivaldi hastened to the villa. In the darkened archway the ghostly figure again appeared and told him that death was in the house. Deeply disturbed, Vivaldi hurried on, to learn on his arrival that Signora Bianchi had died suddenly during the night. When Beatrice, the old servant, confided her suspicions that her mistress had been poisoned, Vivaldi grew even more concerned. His own suspicions falling on Schedoni, he confronted the monk in the marchesa's apartment on his return to Venice, but the confessor cleverly parried all the questions Vivaldi put to him. Vivaldi, apologizing for his conduct and accusing speech, failed to realize that he had made an enemy of Schedoni and that the monk was already planning his revenge.

Meanwhile, it had been decided that Ellena was to find a sanctuary in the Convent of Santa Maria della Pieta after her aunt's funeral, and Vivaldi was in agreement with her desire to withdraw to that shelter during her period of mourning. While Ellena was packing in preparation for her departure the next day, she heard Beatrice screaming in another room. At that same moment three masked men seized Ellena and in spite of her protests carried her from the house. Thrust into a closed carriage, she was driven throughout the night and most of the next day into the mountainous region of Abruzzo. There her captors conducted her to a strange religious establishment where she was turned over to the care of the nuns. Almost distracted, the girl was led to a cell where she was at last able to give way to the extremities of her terror and grief.

Knowing nothing of these events, Vivaldi had decided that same night to explore the ruined fortress and to discover, if possible, the secret of the strange visitant he had encountered there. With him went Paulo Mendrico, his faithful servant. When they were within the archway the figure of the monk suddenly materialized, this time telling Vivaldi that Ellena had departed an hour before. Paulo fired his pistol, but the figure eluded them. Following drops of blood, Vivaldi and Paulo came at last to a chamber into which the figure had disappeared. As they entered, the great door shut behind them. In the chamber they found only a discarded, bloody robe. During the night they spent as prisoners in that gloomy room Paulo told his master of a muffled penitent who had appeared at the Church of Santa Maria del Pianto and made a confession apparently so strange and horrible that Ansaldo di Rovalli, the grand penitentiary, had been thrown into convulsions. During this recital they were startled by hearing groans close by, but they saw no one. In the morning the door of the chamber stood open once more, and Vivaldi and Paulo made their escape.

Alarmed for Ellena's safety, Vivaldi went at once to the villa. There he found Beatrice tied to a pillar and learned from her that her mistress had been carried off by abductors. Convinced that the strange happenings of the night were part of a plot to prevent his intended marriage, he again confronted Schedoni at the Convent of the Santo Spirito and would have assaulted the monk if others had not seized the distraught young man and restrained him by force. That night, by accident, Vivaldi heard from a fisherman that early in the day a closed carriage had been seen driving through Bracelli. Hopeful that he could trace the carriage and find Ellena, he set off in pursuit in the company of faithful Paulo.

On the fourth day of her imprisonment Ellena was conducted to the parlor of the abbess, who informed her that she must choose between taking the veil or the person whom the Marchesa di Vivaldi had selected as her husband. When Ellena refused both offers she was taken back to her cell. Each evening she was allowed to attend vespers and there her attention was attracted to Sister Olivia, a nun who tried to reconcile her to the hardships of her confinement. For this reason, perhaps, Sister Olivia was the nun chosen by the abbess to inform Ellena that if she persisted in refusing a husband proper to her station she must take holy orders immediately.

Vivaldi, meanwhile, was continuing his search for Ellena. On the evening of the seventh day he and Paulo fell in with a company of pilgrims on their way to worship at the shrine of a convent about a league and a half distant. Traveling with this company, Vivaldi arrived at the convent in time to witness the service at which Ellena was to be made a novitiate. Hearing her voice raised in protest, he rushed to the altar and caught her as she fainted. Unable to secure Ellena's freedom, Vivaldi left the convent in order to try another plan to set her free. Though he did not know it, there was need of haste; the abbess had decided to punish Ellena by confining her in a chamber from which none had ever returned alive. Alarmed for the girl's life, Sister Olivia promised to help her escape from the convent that night.

Dressed in the nun's veil, Ellena attended a program of music given in honor of some distinguished strangers who were visiting the convent. There Vivaldi, disguised as a pilgrim, passed her a note in which he told her to meet him at the gate of the nuns' garden. Guided by Sister Olivia, Ellena went to the gate where Vivaldi was waiting with Brother Jeronimo, a monk whom he had bribed to lead them from the convent by a secret path. Brother Jeronimo tried to betray them, however, and Ellena would have been recaptured if an aged monk whom they disturbed at his solitary prayers had not pitied them and unlocked the last door standing between the lovers and freedom.

Once in the open air, Vivaldi and Ellena descended the mountains to the place where Paulo waited with the horses for their escape. Instead of taking the road toward Naples, the fugitives turned westward toward Aquila. That day, as they were resting at a shepherd's cabin, Paulo brought word that they were being pursued by two Carmelite friars. Eluding their pursuers, they rode toward Lake Celano, where Ellena took refuge for the night in the Ursuline convent and Vivaldi stayed in an establishment of Benedictines.

While these events were taking place, the marchese, who knew nothing of his wife's scheming with Schedoni, was suffering great anxiety over his son's possible whereabouts and welfare. The marchesa, on the other hand, was apprehensive only that Ellena would be found and her plans undone. When Schedoni suggested in his sly, indirect fashion that Ellena be put out of the way for good, she was at first horrified by his suggestion. Later she reconsidered and at last she and the sinister monk came to an understanding. Ellena was to die. Schedoni, who had spies everywhere, was not long in locating the fugitives. As Vivaldi and Ellena were about to be married in the chapel of San Sebastian at Celano, armed men broke into the church and arrested the two under a warrant of the Holy Inquisition. Ellena was charged with having broken her nun's vows and Vivaldi with having aided her escape. Vivaldi, although wounded in his struggle to prevent arrest, was carried to Rome and after a short hearing before the Inquisitor was imprisoned to await future trial and possible torture to extort a confession. Paulo, protesting against separation from his master, was also confined.

After the agents of the Inquisition had taken Vivaldi and Paulo away, Ellena's guards put her on a waiting horse and set out on a road which led toward the Adriatic. After traveling with little interruption for two nights and two days they came to a lonely house on the seashore. There she was turned over to a villainous-looking man whom the guards called Spalatro and locked in a room in which the only furnishing was a tattered mattress on the floor. Exhausted, she fell asleep. Twice during the next day Spalatro came to her room, looked at her with a gaze that seemed a mixture of impatience and guilt, and then went away. At another time he took her to walk on the beach, where she met a monk whose face was hidden by his cowl. The monk was Schedoni. When he spoke to her, Ellena realized that he was neither a friend nor a protector but an enemy; and she fainted. Revived, she was returned to her room.

Schedoni was determined that Ellena should die that night. When Spalatro confessed pity for the girl and refused to be the executioner, Schedoni swore to do the deed himself. Going to the room where the girl was sleeping, he stood, dagger in hand, over her. Suddenly he bent to look closely at a miniature she wore about her neck. Agitated, he awoke Ellena and asked her if she knew whose portrait she wore. When she answered that it was the miniature of her father, Schedoni was even more shaken. He was convinced that he had discovered his lost daughter.

Overcome by remorse for his persecution of Ellena and the accusation which had exposed Vivaldi to the tortures of the Inquisition, Schedoni now tried to make amends. He and Ellena traveled as quickly as possible to Naples. After leaving the girl at the Villa Altieri, the monk hastened to the Vivaldis' palace and in an interview with the marchesa begged, without disclosing his connection with Ellena, that objections to Vivaldi's suit be withdrawn. When the marchesa proved inattentive, he determined to solemnize, without her consent, the nuptials of Vivaldi and Ellena.

Called a second time before the tribunal of the Inquisition, Vivaldi heard again among those present at the trial the voice which had warned him on earlier occasions against his visits to the Villa Altieri. That night a strange monk visited him in his cell and asked how long he had known Schedoni. The monk then instructed Vivaldi to reveal to the Inquisition that Schedoni was actually Count Ferando di Bruno, who had lived fifteen years in the disguise of a Dominican monk. He was also to ask that Ansaldo di Rovalli, the grand penitentiary of the Black Penitents, be called to testify to a confession he had heard in 1752. When Vivaldi was again brought before the Inquisition he did as he had been told, with the result that Schedoni was arrested on his way to Rome to intercede for Vivaldi's freedom.

At Schedoni's trial the mystery that linked the sinister father confessor and the two lovers was made clear. Years before, Schedoni, then a spendthrift younger son known as the Count di Marinella, had schemed to posses himself of his brother's title, his unencumbered estate, and his beautiful wife. He had arranged to have his brother, the Count di Bruno, assassinated by Spalatro and had contrived a story that the count had perished while returning from a journey to Greece. After a proper season of mourning he had solicited the hand of his brother's widow. When she rejected him his passion had caused him to carry her off by force. Although the lady had retrieved her honor by marriage, she continued to look on her new husband with disdain, and in his jealousy he became convinced that she was unfaithful. One day, returning unexpectedly, he found a visitor with his wife. Drawing his stiletto with the intention of attacking the guest, he struck and killed his wife instead. This was the confession which had so agitated the grand penitentiary, for he himself had been the guest and for him an innocent woman had died.

Further proof was the dying confession of Spalatro, whose death had been caused by a wound inflicted by Schedoni. Condemned to die for plotting his brother's death, Schedoni still persisted in his declaration that Ellena was his daughter. This mystery was cleared up by Sister Olivia, who in the meantime had removed to the Convent of Santa Maria della Pieta; the nun was the unfortunate Countess di Bruno and the sister of Signora Bianchi. Her wound had not been mortal, but the report of her death had been given out in order to protect her from her vengeful husband. Wishing to withdraw from the world, she had entrusted her daughter by the first Count di Bruno and an infant daughter by the second to Signora Bianchi. The infant had died within a year.

Ellena, who knew nothing of this story, had been mistaken in her belief that the miniature was that of her father, and it was on her word that Schedoni had claimed her as his daughter. It was also revealed that Father Nicola, who had collected the evidence against Schedoni, had been the mysterious monk whose ghostly warnings Vivaldi heard under the arch of the old fortress. Appalled by the father confessor's villainy, he had turned against him after being wounded by Paulo's pistol on the night of the midnight search.

Schedoni had his final revenge. In some manner he administered a fatal dose of poison to Father Nicola and then died of the same mysterious drug. In his last moments he boasted that he was escaping an ignominious death at the hands of the Inquisition.

Because of Schedoni's dying confession, Vivaldi was immediately set free. During his imprisonment the marchesa had died repentant of the harm she had plotted against Ellena. Now the marchese, overjoyed to be reunited with his son, withdrew all objections to Vivaldi's suit. With all doubts of Ellena's birth and goodness removed, he went in person to the Convent of Santa Maria della Pieta and asked Sister Olivia for her daughter's hand in the name of his son. Vivaldi and Ellena were married in the convent church in the presence of the marchese and Sister Olivia. As a mark of special favor Paulo was allowed to be present when his master took Ellena for his wife. If it had not been for the holy precincts and the solemnity of the occasion the faithful fellow would have thrown his cap into the air and shouted that this was indeed a happy day.

Further Critical Evaluation of the Work:

The Italian is one of the most skillful and successful examples of the Gothic novel, a literary sub-genre whose aim is to astound, terrify, and thrill its readers. More controlled and convincing than her earlier *The Mysteries of Udolpho,* Mrs. Radcliff's novel is filled with the conventional Gothic qualities: a highly melodramatic (and unlikely) plot set in the remote past, a minimal degree of character development, and a painstakingly developed setting and atmosphere.

The plot is a familiar one to readers of the Gothic: a mysterious and black-hearted villain, Schedoni, plots against a beautiful damsel, Ellena, who spends most of the novel either imprisoned or in imminent danger of death, while her chivalrous and faithful lover, Vivaldi, struggles against incredible odds to rescue her. Character delineation is crude, limited primarily to blacks and whites. Predictably, the villainous monk Schedoni is much more fascinating than the somewhat vapid hero and heroine. The air of mystery and terror in the monk is strikingly described: "An habitual gloom and severity prevailed over the deep lines of his countenance; and his eyes were so piercing that they seemed to penetrate, at a single glance, into the hearts of men, and to read their most secret thoughts."

Setting is crucial to *The Italian.* Here are the gloomy monasteries, the dank dungeons of the Inquisition, the dizzying precipes and crags of Abruzzo, as well as scenes of quiet but spine-tingling terror, such as the one between Ellena and Schedoni on the deserted beach. Just as the evil characters are made even more menacing by their contrast to the good characters, the wild landscapes and brooding interiors are made even more threatening by their contrast to the beauty of Naples at the beginning and end of the novel.

The excesses and improbabilities of the lurid plot are tempered by a number of qualities. First, despite the manifold mysteries and hints of ghostly or demonic forces pervading the work, nothing magical or supernatural actually does occur; unlike the events in *The Castle of Otranto,* for instance, there is ultimately a rational explanation provided for everything. Also, Radcliffe's handling of suspense, mystery, dramatic pacing, and realistic detail and description is expert and gripping throughout. Finally, the author displays a serious concern for the main Gothic theme of man's inhumanity to man, as seen, for instance, in Vivaldi's outburst against the brutalities of the Inquisition: "Can this be in human nature!—Can such horrible perversion of right be permitted! Can man, who calls himself endowed with reason, and immeasurably superior to every other created being, argue himself into the commision of such horrible folly, such inveterate cruelty, as exceeds all the acts of the most irrational and ferocious brute . . . !"

Such novels as *The Italian* were adroitly satirized by Jane Austen in her *Northanger Abbey*. But Radcliffe's novel is significant not only in its own right, but for the influence it had on later writers, such as Scott, Charlotte Brontë, Coleridge, Keats, and Poe, all of whom made use of the mysterious and threatening Gothic settings and atmospheres in many of their own works.

THE ITCHING PARROT

Type of work: Novel
Author: José Joaquín Fernández de Lizardi (1776-1827)
Type of plot: Picaresque satire
Time of plot: The 1770's to 1820's
Locale: Mexico
First published: 1816

Principal characters:
PEDRO SARMIENTO, The Itching Parrot, or Poll, a young Mexican
DON ANTONIO, Poll's prison mate and benefactor
JANUARIO, Poll's schoolmate
AN ARMY COLONEL, Poll's superior and benefactor

Critique:

This novel, written by the most rabid controversialist among Mexican authors during the unsettled years when Mexico was seeking to become independent of Spain, was suppressed after the publication of the eleventh chapter in 1816, and the complete novel was not published until three years after the author's death. Scholars have viewed it as the first Spanish-American novel, and it is reputed to have sold over one hundred million copies. Lizardi managed to smuggle into the novel most of the polemical tracts which had earned him nationwide fame as The Mexican Thinker, pamphlets directed against whoever sat at the head of the Mexican government, whether he was Spanish viceroy or revolutionist dictator. Lizardi, like his fictional hero, spent many months in jail. He considered himself a no-party man, and many Mexican regimes resorted to prison sentences to silence him; but Lizardi, always placing Mexico above its rulers, alternately satirized and advised them.

The Story:

Pedro Sarmiento was born to upper middle-class parents in Mexico City between 1771 and 1773; of the actual date, he was not sure. As a child he was willful, and his mother's excessive devotion only made him worse. He became such a scamp that at last his father sent him off to school. At school he was nicknamed Parrot. A little later, when he contracted the itch, his schoolmates nicknamed him The Itching Parrot, or Poll for short, and the name stuck to him through most of his life.

In addition to his nickname, Poll acquired many vicious habits from his schoolfellows. Poll's father resolved to put Poll out as an apprentice in a trade, but Poll's mother, not wishing her son to disgrace her family by becoming a vulgar tradesman, insisted that the boy be sent to college. Against his better judgment, the father agreed, and so Poll was sent off to study for a college degree. After learning some Latin, some Aristotle, some logic, and a little physics, Poll was awarded a baccalaureate degree by the College of San Ildefonso.

Shortly after receiving his degree, Poll went into the countryside to visit a hacienda owned by the father of a former schoolmate. At the hacienda he earned the hatred of his schoolmate, Januario, by making advances to the latter's cousin, with whom Januario was infatuated. Januario took his revenge by tempting Poll into a bullfight. Poll, who lost both the fight and his trousers, became the laughingstock of the hacienda. Still unsatisfied, Januario tricked Poll into trying to sleep with the girl cousin. Through Januario, the girl's mother discovered the attempt, beat Poll with her shoe, and sent him back to Mexico City in disgrace.

Upon his return to the city Poll was told by his father that he had to find some

THE ITCHING PARROT by Jose Joaquin Fernandez de Lizardi. By permission of the publishers, Doubleday & Co., Inc. Copyright, 1942, by Doubleday & Co., Inc.

means of earning a livelihood. Poll, searching for the easiest way, decided he would study theology and enter the Church. Theology quickly proved uninteresting, and Poll gave up that idea. Trying to escape his father's insistence that he learn a trade, Poll then decided to enter a Franciscan monastery. There he soon found that he could not stand the life of a monk; he was glad when his father's death gave him an excuse to leave the monastery. After a short period of mourning Poll rapidly exhausted his small inheritance through his fondness for gambling, parties, and women. The sorrow he caused his mother sent her, also, to an early death. After his mother died, Poll was left alone. None of his relatives, who knew him for a rogue, would have anything to do with him.

In his despair Poll fell in with another schoolmate, who supported himself by gambling and trickery. Poll took up a similar career in his schoolmate's company. A man he gulled discovered Poll's treachery and beat him severely. After his release from the hospital Poll went back to his gambling partner and they decided to turn thieves. On their very first attempt, however, they were unsuccessful. Poll was caught and thrown into prison.

Because he had no family or friends to call upon, Poll languished in jail for several months. He made one friend in jail who helped him; that friend was Don Antonio, a man of good reputation who had been unjustly imprisoned. Although Don Antonio tried to keep Poll away from bad company, he was not entirely successful. When Don Antonio was freed, Poll fell in with a mulatto who got him into all kinds of scrapes. By chance Poll was taken up by a scrivener who was in need of an apprentice and was pleased with Poll's handwriting. The scrivener had Poll released from prison to become his apprentice.

Poll's career as a scrivener's apprentice was short, for he made love to the man's mistress, was discovered, and was driven from the house. The next step in Poll's adventures was service as a barber's apprentice. He left that work to become a clerk in a pharmacy. After getting into trouble by carelessly mixing a prescription, Poll left the pharmacy for the employ of a doctor.

Having picked up some jargon and a few cures from his doctor-employer, Poll set out to be a physician. Everything went well until he caused a number of deaths and was forced to leave the profession.

Trying to recoup his fortunes once more, Poll returned to gambling. In a game he won a lottery ticket which, in its turn, won for him a small fortune. For a time Poll lived well: he even married a girl who thought he had a great deal of money. But the life the couple led soon exhausted the lottery money, and they were almost penniless again. After his wife died in childbirth, Poll set out once again in search of his fortune. His work as a sacristan ended when he robbed a corpse. Poll then joined a group of beggars. Finding that they were fakers, he reported them to the authorities. One of the officials, pleased with Poll, secured him a place in government service.

For a time all went well, but Poll, who was left in charge of the district when his superior was absent, abused his authority so much that he was arrested and sent in chains to Mexico City. There he was tried, found guilty of many crimes, and sent to the army for eight years.

Through his good conduct and pleasing appearance, Poll was made clerk to the colonel of the regiment. The colonel placed a great deal of trust in Poll. When the regiment went to Manila, the colonel saw to it that Poll was given an opportunity to do some trading and save up a small fortune. Poll completed his sentence and prepared to return to Mexico as a fairly rich man. All his dreams and fortune vanished, however, when the ship sank and he was cast away upon an island. On the island he made friends with a Chinese in whose company Poll, pretending all the while to be a nobleman, returned to Mexico. When they reached Mexico the l-was discovered, but the Chinese continued to be Poll's friend and patron.

Poll stayed with the Chinese for some time, but he finally left in disgrace after having introduced prostitutes into the house. Leaving Mexico City, Poll met the mulatto who had been his companion in jail. Along with the mulatto and some other men, Poll turned highwayman but barely escaped with his life from their first holdup. Frightened, Poll went into retreat at a church, where he discovered his confessor to be a boy he had known years before in school. The kind confessor found honest employment for Poll as an agent for a rich man. Poll became an honest, hardworking citizen, even being known as Don Pedro rather than Poll or The Itching Parrot. Years passed quickly. Then one day Don Pedro, befriending some destitute people, found the man to be his old benefactor of prison days, Don Antonio. The other people were Don Antonio's wife and daughter. Don Pedro married the girl, thus completing his respectability. He lived out the rest of his days in honesty, industry, and respect.

Further Critical Evaluation of the Work:

The Itching Parrot is of special interest to literature students. Besides being the first true novel of Latin American literature, and the only important Spanish American representative of the picaresque novel, it is of definite sociological interest. It compares reasonably well in entertainment value with good modern novels. It paints Mexican society in the last phase of the colonial period and the first years of national independence. *The Itching Parrot* is still a widely-read Mexican novel, and has been published in approximately twenty editions.

The novel's primary aim was to satirize socio-economic conditions in Mexico. Lizardi's criticism of the abuses of his time was sound, and he became an apostle of reform. Realism dominates *The Itching Parrot,* making it primarily a call for social reform, but the book has other virtues as well. It not only exposes charlatans and fakes at all levels, but draws them well, whether they be lower social types or aristocrats. The book is not pessimistic, even though its many episodes, mutually independent, are usually depressing. Life is not meaningless to Lizardi, for God is not dead, and good will eventually conquer evil. The novel has a cheerful ending, proving that man is capable of reform, and indeed Lizardi always seems honest and attracted by good. Class hatreds are lacking even while social inequalities and evils are scorched. Religious bias is also lacking even though individual Catholic priests are lampooned. Lizardi's patriotism glows throughout the book, in glaring contrast to the selfishly corrupt politicians who mislead Mexico during the initial years of independence, and whose stupidity leads directly to the loss of half of Mexico's national territory to the Americans.

The book is written in the good, basic Spanish that has almost always characterized Mexican literature. Its one thousand pages and three hundred thousand words expose many evils, not only social but political, for the last Spanish viceroys and the first rulers of independent Mexico were absolute monarchs who failed to use their powers wisely. Lizardi flayed the vicious town bosses, who wallowed in extortion, "bites," and corruption. He also exposed court clerks, tax collectors, police, jailers, the swarms of beggars, and the merchants who used false weights. Even though a Catholic himself, who defended worthy clerics, Lizardi blasted individual priests, such as the one who drank at a party and squabbled over a woman, or another who refused to interrupt his card game to give the last rites to a dying person, and the incredible cad who collected money to pray for the soul of Christ.

Lizardi's arrows did not spare the unsanitary Indian wet nurses who tied the hands and feet of babies to prevent them from striking themselves, nor the ignorant and lecherous teachers, lawyers, and doctors who infested the unhappy Mexico of his days. Hospitals were often horrible; pharmacists gouged for drugs, doctors peddled fake nostrums. Nor was the antiquated university system spared—students argued logic all day, as was done in the Middle Ages, and learned little of practical value. Lizardi especially resented the fact that the aristocracy and even the middle class scorned manual work, causing their young to waste their time as con men, card sharps, embezzlers, pimps, and the laziest of thugs.

The style of *The Itching Parrot* is direct. Action is never lacking, and a sense of anticipation tinges most of the book, along with several episodes of adventure and travel.

IVANHOE

Type of work: Novel
Author: Sir Walter Scott (1771-1832)
Type of plot: Historical romance
Time of plot: 1194
Locale: England
First published: 1820

Principal characters:
CEDRIC THE SAXON, of Rotherwood Grange
WILFRED OF IVANHOE, his disinherited son
THE LADY ROWENA, his ward, loved by Ivanhoe
ISAAC OF YORK, a Jewish money-lender
REBECCA, his daughter
SIR BRIAN DE BOIS-GUILBERT, a Norman Knight Templar
KING RICHARD I, returned from the Third Crusade
ROBIN HOOD, an outlaw

Critique:

For over a hundred years *Ivanhoe* has held its charm in the popular mind as the epitome of chivalric novels. It has among its characters two of the most popular of English heroes, Richard the Lion-Hearted and Robin Hood, and tells a story of chivalric romance. It has sufficient action and color to appeal to a great number of people. Although *Ivanhoe* may not be Scott's greatest novel, it is without doubt his most popular.

The Story:

Night was drawing near when Prior Aymer of Jorvaux and the haughty Templar, Brian de Bois-Guilbert, overtook a swineherd and a fool by the roadside and asked directions to Rotherwood, the dwelling of Cedric the Saxon. The answers of these serfs so confused the Templar and the prior that they would have gone far afield had it not been for a pilgrim from the Holy Land whom they encountered shortly afterward. The pilgrim was also traveling to Rotherwood, and he brought them safely to Cedric's hall, where they claimed lodging for the night. The custom of those rude days afforded hospitality to all benighted travelers, and so Cedric gave a grudging welcome to the Norman lords.

There was a feast at Rotherwood that night. On the dais beside Cedric the Saxon sat his ward, the lovely Lady Rowena, descendant of the ancient Saxon princes. It was the old man's ambition to wed her to Athelstane of Coningsburgh. of the line of King Alfred. Because his son, Wilfred of Ivanhoe, had fallen in love with Rowena, Cedric had banished him, and the young knight had gone with King Richard to Palestine. None in the banquet hall that night suspected that the pilgrim was Ivanhoe himself.

Another traveler who had claimed shelter at Rotherwood that night was an aged Jew, Isaac of York. Hearing some orders the Templar muttered to his servants as the feast ended, Ivanhoe warned the old Jew that Bois-Guilbert had designs on his moneybag or his person. Without taking leave of their host the next morning, the disguised pilgrim and Isaac of York left Rotherwood and continued on their way to the nearby town of Ashby de la Zouche.

Many other travelers were also on their way to the town, for a great tournament was to be held there. Prince John, Regent of England in King Richard's absence, would preside. The winner of the tournament would be allowed to name the Queen of Love and Beauty and receive the prize of the passage of arms from her hands.

Ivanhoe attended the tournament with the word *Disinherited* written upon his shield. Entering the lists, he struck the shield of Bois-Guilbert with the point of his lance and challenged that knight to mortal combat. In the first passage both knights splintered their lances but neither was unhorsed. At the second passage Ivanhoe's lance struck Bois-Guilbert's helmet and upset him. Then one by one Ivanhoe vanquished five knights who had agreed to take on all comers. When the heralds declared the Disinherited Knight victor of the tourney, Ivanhoe named Rowena the Queen of Love and Beauty.

In the tournament on the following day Ivanhoe was pressed hard by three antagonists, but he received unexpected help from a knight in black, whom the spectators had called the Black Sluggard because of his previous inactivity. Ivanhoe, because of his earlier triumphs during the day, was named champion of the tournament once more. In order to receive the gift from Lady Rowena, Ivanhoe had to remove his helmet. When he did so, he was recognized. He received the chaplet, his prize, kissed the hand of Lady Rowena, and then fainted from loss of blood. Isaac of York and his daughter, Rebecca, were sitting nearby, and Rebecca suggested to her father that they nurse Ivanhoe until he was well. Isaac and his daughter started for their home with the wounded knight carried in a horse litter. On the way they joined the train of Cedric the Saxon, who was still ignorant of the Disinherited Knight's identity.

Before the travelers had gone far, however, they were set upon and captured by a party led by three Norman knights, Bois-Guilbert, Maurice de Bracy, and Reginald Front de Boeuf. They were imprisoned in Front de Boeuf's castle of Torquilstone. De Bracy had designs upon Lady Rowena because she was an heiress of royal lineage. The Templar desired to possess Rebecca. Front de Boeuf hoped to extort a large sum of money from the aged Jew. Cedric was held for ransom. The wounded knight was put into the charge of an ancient hag named Ulrica. Isaac and his daughter were placed in separate rooms. Bois-Guilbert went to Rebecca in her tower prison and asked her to adopt Christianity so that they might be married. But the plot of the Norman nobles with regard to their prisoners was thwarted by an assault on the castle by Richard the Lion-Hearted, The Black Sluggard of the tournament at Ashby, in company with Robin Hood and his outlaws. Ulrica aided the besiegers by starting a fire within the castle walls. Robin Hood and his men took the prisoners to the forest along with the Norman nobles. In the confusion, however, Bois-Guilbert escaped with Rebecca, and Isaac made preparation to ransom her from the Templar. De Bracy was set free and he hurried to inform Prince John that he had seen and talked with Richard. John plotted to make Richard his prisoner.

Isaac went to the establishment of the Knights Templar and begged to see Bois-Guilbert. Lucas de Beaumanoir, the grand master of the Templars, ordered Isaac admitted to his presence. Isaac was frightened when the grand master asked him his business with the Templar. When he told his story, the grand master learned of Bois-Guilbert's seizure of Rebecca. It was suggested that Bois-Guilbert was under a spell cast by Rebecca. Condemned as a witch, she was sentenced to be burned at the stake. In desperation she demanded, as was her right, a champion to defend her against the charge. Lucas de Beaumanoir agreed and named Bois-Guilbert champion of the Temple.

The day arrived for Rebecca's execution. A pile of wood had been laid around the stake. Rebecca, seated in a black chair, awaited the arrival of her defender. Three times the heralds called upon her champion to appear. At the third call a strange knight rode into the lists and announced himself as Rebecca's champion. When Bois-Guilbert realized that the stranger was Ivanhoe, he at first refused combat because Ivanhoe's wounds were not completely healed. But the grand master gave orders for the contest to begin. As everyone expected, the tired horse of Ivanhoe and its exhausted rider went down at the first blow, so that Ivanhoe's lance merely touched the shield of the Templar. Then to the astonishment of all, Bois-Guilbert reeled in his saddle and fell to the ground. Ivanhoe arose from where he had fallen and drew his sword. Placing his foot on the breast of the fallen knight, he called upon Bois-Guilbert to yield himself or die on the spot. There was no answer from Bois-Guilbert, for he was dead, a victim of the violence of his own passions. The grand master declared that Rebecca was acquitted of the charge against her.

At that moment the Black Knight appeared, followed by a band of knights and men-at-arms. It was King Richard, come to arrest Rebecca's accusers on a charge of treason. The grand master saw the flag of the Temple hauled down and the royal standard raised in its place.

King Richard had returned in secret to reclaim his throne. Robin Hood became his true follower. Athelstane relinquished his claims to Lady Rowena's hand so that she and Ivanhoe could be married. Cedric the Saxon, reconciled at last with his son, gave his consent, and Richard himself graced their wedding.

Isaac and Rebecca left England for Granada, hoping to find in that foreign land greater happiness than could ever be theirs in England.

Further Critical Evaluation of the Work:

Scott himself wrote that he left the Scottish scenes of his previous novels and turned to the Middle Ages in *Ivanhoe* because he feared the reading public was growing weary of the repetition of Scottish themes in his books. Since he was fascinated with history all of his life, it was logical that Scott should turn to the past for subject matter. Many faults have been found with the historical facts of the book; Robin Hood, if he lived at all, belonged to a later century than that represented in the novel, and by the time of Richard I the distinction between Saxons and Normons had faded. But the thrilling story, the drama and action, still grip the reader, whatever liberties Scott took with history.

Scott's four great chivalric novels all possess similar structures in that they all focus on a moment of crisis between two great individuals, a moment which determines the survival of one of the opposed pair. In *Ivanhoe,* the symbolic contrast is between Richard the Lion-Hearted and his brother John. The struggle between these two helps to raise one of the principal questions of the novel: the decadence of chivalry. For generations of juvenile readers, *Ivanhoe* represented the glory of chivalric adventure, but actually Scott entertained serious doubts about the chivalric tradition. At several strategic points in *Ivanhoe,* passages occur which unequivocally damn the reckless inhumanity of romantic chivalry.

The novel is symmetrically designed in three parts, each reaching its climax in a great military spectacle. The first part ends with the Ashby tournament, the second with the liberation from the castle of Front de Boeuf, and the third with the trial by combat of Rebecca. The beginning chapters draw together all of the character groups for the tournament, Ivanhoe being present only as the mysterious palmer. The problem of seating at the tournament provides a sketch of the cultural animosities that divide the world of the novel.

Richard is the moral and political center of the book, and, therefore, the proper object of Ivanhoe's fidelity. The captive king does not appear until he fights the mysterious Black Knight during the second day of the tournament. He saves Ivanhoe and then disappears until the scene of his midnight feast with Friar Tuck. The reader's impression of him is of a fun-loving, heroic fighter. The friar thinks of him as a man of "prudence and of counsel." Richard possesses a native humanity and a love of life, as well as the heroic chivalric qualities. He is always ready to act as a protector of others.

John, by contrast, is an ineffectual ruler whose own followers despise him. His forces quickly disintegrate, his followers abandoning him for their own selfish ends. He is a petulant, stupid man, incapable of inspiring loyalty. It is inevitable that the historical climax of the novel should be the confrontation between Richard and John. The chivalric code has become completely corrupt in the England left to John's care. Both the narrator and the characters make clear that chivalry is no more than a mixture of "heroic folly and dangerous imprudence."

Rebecca speaks against chivalry, asking during the bloody siege of the castle if possession by a "demon of vainglory" brings "sufficient rewards for the sacrifice of every kindly affection, for a life spent miserably that yet may make others miserable?" (Rebecca is antichivalric, yet she is the most romantic character in the book, suggesting the traditional chivalric attitudes towards women.) The narrator speaks most sharply of the chivalric code at the end of the tournament: "This ended the memorable field of Ashby-de-la-Zouche, one of the most gallantly contested tournaments of that age; for although only four knights, including one who was smothered by the heat of his armour, had died upon the field, yet upwards of thirty were desperately wounded, four or five of whom never recovered. Several more were disabled for life; and those who escaped best carried the marks of the conflict to the grave with them. Hence it is always mentioned in the old records as the 'gentle and joyous passage of arms at Ashby.' "

An argument has been made that Scott's historical novels, such as *Ivanhoe,* are inferior to his earlier novels based on his direct, personal knowledge of the Scottish customs and characters and land. But even in the historical novels, Scott's characters are colorful, full of vitality, and realized with amazing verisimilitude. Scott's knowledge of the past about which he was writing was so deep that he could draw upon it at will to clothe out his fictions. He did not find it necessary to research a novel such as *Ivanhoe* in order to write it; the historical lore was already part of him. Years before, at the time when he was beginning the Waverley series, he had written a study about chivalry. His prolific writing did not seem to exhaust his resources.

Sir Walter Scott was one of the most prolific writers in the history of

British fiction; only Trollope could stand up against his record. Scott's novels were published anonymously, although their authorship came to be an open secret. His friends found it difficult to believe that he was the author of the novels, for he lived the life of a county magistrate and landowner, spending hours daily on these occupations, as well as entertaining lavishly and writing poetry and nonfiction works. His secret was that he would rise early and and finish novel-writing before breakfast. In time, his compulsive working injured his health, and while he was writing *Ivanhoe,* he was tortured by a cramp of the stomach and suffered such pain that he could not physically hold the pen, but was forced to dictate much of the story.

Like many great novels, *Ivanhoe* betrays a complexity of attitude on the part of the author. Although much of the book makes clear Scott's severe view of the code of chivalry, beyond the antichivalric attitude the reader can see a definite attraction on Scott's part for the romantic traditions of the period. It is in Richard that Scott seems to instill the chivalric virtues, although his personality is not romantic. Through the characters of Rebecca and Rowena, Ivanhoe and Richard, Scott dramatized his ambivalent feelings about the chivalric period. The tension created through these mixed feelings, coupled with the dramatic (if historically inaccurate) story and the vast accumulation of detail as to costume and social customs and historical anecdotes, all worked together to create a novel which has remained popular for more than a hundred and fifty years. *Ivanhoe* is no longer considered as seriously as Scott's Scottish novels, but its achievement remains impressive.

Bruce D. Reeves

JACK OF NEWBERRY

Type of work: Novel
Author: Thomas Deloney (1543?-1607?)
Type of plot: Picaresque adventure
Time of plot: Reign of Henry VIII
Locale: England
First published: 1597

Principal characters:
JACK WINCHCOMB, a weaver
JACK'S MASTER'S WIDOW
JACK'S SECOND WIFE
HENRY VIII, King of England
QUEEN CATHERINE, his wife
CARDINAL WOLSEY, Lord Chancellor of England

Critique:

Jack of Newberry, originally titled *The Pleasant Historie of John Winchcomb, in his Younger Yeares called Jack of Newberry, the Famous and Worthy Clothier of England,* is an important work because it marks the first successful attempt of any writer to use the material found in the lives of ordinary working people as the material for prose fiction. For this reason Deloney's book marks a great step toward the novel as we know it today. In a day when authors were writing about the gentry and nobility and were dedicating books to them, Thomas Deloney wrote about the lower classes and dedicated his volumes to them. Since almost no original copies of his publications have come down to modern times, it is a fairly safe guess that Deloney found a ready audience for his materials. Even the style in which he wrote smacked of the language of the people, rather than the absurdly elevated and involved style of such authors as Lyly, author of *Euphues,* and Sir Philip Sidney. Like his own Jack of Newberry, Deloney was a man of the people and a cloth weaver by trade. The pictures Deloney gave of bourgeois England were exaggerated, but highly entertaining. The real Jack of Newberry is known to have died there in 1519.

The Story:

In the days of King Henry VIII there lived in the English town of Newberry a young weaver named Jack Winchcomb. As a young man he was something of a prodigal, spending as much as he made and having a reputation as a gay young fellow, known in all the county of Berkshire as Jack of Newberry. But after his master died, Jack changed his ways, for his mistress, having acquired a fondness for the young man, entrusted to him the entirety of her husband's business. Jack became a careful man, both with his mistress' affairs and with his own, and soon lost his reputation for prodigality. In its place he acquired a reputation as an honest, hardworking, and intelligent businessman.

His mistress thought so highly of Jack that she even made him an adviser in affairs of the heart. His advice was of little value to her, however, for she had already made up her mind, despite the difference in their years, to marry Jack himself. She tricked him into agreeing to further her marriage with an unknown suitor. When they arrived at the church, Jack found that he was the man; thus Jack became her husband and the master of her house and business.

The marriage went none too smoothly at first, for despite her love for Jack the woman did not like to be ordered about by the man who had once been her servant. But at last they came to an understanding and lived happily for several years, at which interval the good woman died, leaving Jack master of the business.

and rich in the world's goods.

Not long after his first wife died, Jack remarried, the second time to a young woman. The wife was a poor choice, even though he had the pick of the wealthy women of his class in the county. Not many months passed after the marriage, which had been a costly one, before James, King of Scotland, invaded England while King Henry was in France. The justices of the county called upon Jack to furnish six men-at-arms to join the army raised by Queen Catherine. Jack, however, raised a company of a hundred and fifty foot and horse, which he armed and dressed at his own expense in distinctive liveries. Jack himself rode at the head of his men. Queen Catherine was greatly pleased and thanked Jack Winchcomb personally for his efforts, although his men were not needed to achieve the English victory at Flodden Field. In reward for his services, Jack received a chain of gold from the hands of the queen herself.

In the tenth year of his reign King Henry made a trip through Berkshire. Jack Winchcomb introduced himself in a witty way to the king as the Prince of the Ants, who was at war with the Butterflies, a sally against Cardinal Wolsey. The king, vastly pleased, betook himself to Newberry, along with his train, where all were entertained by Jack at a fabulous banquet. After the banquet the king viewed the weaving rooms and warehouses Jack owned. Upon his departure the king wished to make Jack a knight, but the weaver refused the honor, saying he would rather be a common man and die, as he had lived, a clothier.

In his house Jack of Newberry had a series of fifteen paintings, all denoting great men whose fathers had been tradesmen of one kind and another, including a portrait of Marcus Aurelius, who had been a clothier's son. Jack kept the pictures and showed them to his friends and workmen in an effort to encourage one and all to seek fame and dignity in spite of their humble offices in life.

Because of the many wars in Europe during King Henry's reign, trade in general was depleted. The lot of the clothiers and weavers being particularly bad, they joined together and sent leaders to London to appeal to the government on their behalf. One of the envoys they sent was Jack Winchcomb of Newberry. The king remembered Jack and in private audience assured him that measures would be taken to alleviate the hardships of the clothiers. Another man who had not forgotten Jack was the Lord Chancellor, Cardinal Wolsey. In an attempt to circumvent the king's promise, he had Jack and the other envoys thrown into prison for a few days. Finally the Duke of Somerset intervened and convinced the cardinal that the clothiers meant no harm.

Some time later an Italian merchant named Benedick came to the house of Jack of Newberry to trade. While there, he fell in love with one of Jack's workers, a pretty girl named Joan. But she paid no attention whatever to Benedick and asked a kinsman to tell the Italian not to bother her. When the kinsman did as he was asked, he angered the Italian, who vowed to make a cuckold of the kinsman for his pains. With gifts and fair speech the Italian finally had his way with the weaver's wife, although the woman was immediately sorry. She told her husband, who had his revenge on the Italian by pretending that he would see to it that the Italian was permitted to go to bed with Joan. The Italian fell in with the scheme and found himself put to bed with a pig, whereupon all the Englishmen laughed at him so heartily that he left Newberry in shame.

Jack's second wife was a good young woman, but she sometimes erred in paying too much attention to her gossipy friends. At one time a friend told her that she was wasting money by feeding the workmen so well. She cut down on the quantity and the quality of the food she served the workers, but Jack, who remembered only too well the days when he had been an apprentice and journeyman forced to eat whatever was placed in front of him, became very angry and made her change her ways again. His workers were gratified when he said that his wife's friend was never to set foot in his house again.

At another time Jack of Newberry went to London, where he found a draper who owed him five hundred pounds working as a porter. Learning that the man, through no fault of his own, had become a bankrupt, Jack showed his confidence in the man by setting him up in business again. Friends warned him that he was sending good money after bad, but Jack's judgment proved correct. The man paid back every cent and later became an alderman of London.

Jack was always proud of his workers. One time a knight, Sir George Rigley, seduced a pretty and intelligent girl who worked for Jack. Jack vowed that he would make it right for her. He sent the woman, disguised as a rich widow, to London. There Sir George fell in love with her, not knowing who she was, and married her. The knight was angry at first, but he soon saw the justice of the case and was very well pleased with the hundred pounds Jack gave the girl as a dower. Still knowing their places in life, Jack and his wife gave precedence to Sir George and his new lady, even in their own house.

Further Critical Evaluation of the Work:

Very little is known about the pamphleteer and balladeer who was Thomas Deloney, the English writer whose works were precursors of the English novel. By trade a silk weaver, probably of Norwich, Deloney wrote topical ballads and, through his pamphlets, took part in the religious controversies of the day. Even the date of his birth is not certain, some sources suggesting 1543, others the more likely date of 1560. But it seems certain that Deloney died early in 1600, after producing at least three "novels" (that is, episodic narratives) in a short but crowded life. He seems to have had more education than most weavers of the time would have had, and he translated from Latin into his uniquely vigorous English. The ballads of the day were the newspapers of the period, and Deloney's apprenticeship, like that of so many novelists, might be said to have been in journalism. Probably, that was how he learned how to write concisely and how to choose popular subjects. He wrote broadside ballads on such subjects as the defeat of the Spanish Armada, great fires, the execution of traitors, and domestic tragedies, but current events were not Deloney's only ballad subjects. Using Holinshed and other sources, he drew on English history for subject matter. A collection of Deloney's ballads titled *The Garland of Good Will* appeared in 1631, and earlier editions, like those of his prose fictions, were probably read out of existence. More than once, Deloney's pamphlets and more than fifty ballads put him in trouble with the authorities, even sending him to spend time in Newgate. One ballad in particular, showing disrespect for the queen, caused him serious difficulties.

Though widely read, Thomas Deloney's novels were scorned by the university educated writers of the day as mere plebian romances from the pen of a ballad-maker, and it was not until the twentieth century that his merits as a writer were recognized. The three novels, all approximately the same length, appeared between 1597 and 1600. Probably, *Jack of Newberry* was the first one written and published. Each novel was in praise of a trade: *Jack of Newberry* of weaving, *The Gentle Craft* of shoemaking, and *Thomas of Reading* of the clothiers' trade.

Deloney's stories contain excellent pictures of contemporary middle-class London life, introducing a variety of quaint characters. But the realism of the novels is only in matter of setting and dialogue; probability is disregarded and wish-fulfillment fantasy prevails as members of the hardworking trade class are rewarded for their diligence by large fortunes. The tales are rich with humor and told in a straight-forward way, except for "ornamental" language used in some romantic passages.

Deloney may have been commissioned by the cloth-merchants to compose a life of one of their order, the result being *Jack of Newberry*. Jack was a real person who lived in Newberry under Henry VII, but his history is merely traditional. Deloney, however, knew the town and had a gift for elaborating a tale with circumstantial facts and humorous episodes.

Despite its popularity in its own day, Deloney's fiction probably had little real effect on the subsequent development of English prose fiction, which had to wait a hundred years and more for the geniuses of Defoe and Richardson to get it off the ground. On the other hand, *Jack of Newberry* may be considered the first really dramatic novel in English. The fictions of Nash and Greene are witty and satirical, but they do not have the dramatic plots of Deloney's work. Sidney's *Arcadia* and John Lyly's *Euphues* were only minor influences, if any, on Deloney, who seems to have been more impressed by the Elizabethan stage than anything else (the widow and the other characters display a sense of rhetoric in their dialogue reminiscent of the stage). Deloney's view of life was essentially dramatic, and the people he wrote about in *Jack of Newberry* and his other novels are people of action, people who set out to accomplish material things.

Deloney's focus is on the details of everyday life. Love and marriage and money and food are the main topics of conversation. Materialist to his heart, he is fascinated by business and household matters. Like Dickens, Deloney plunges into scenes that summarize dramatically an entire situation, painting a picture of an entire culture along the way. There are few irrelevant incidents in *Jack of Newberry*. The story of the middle-aged widow who falls in love with her young apprentice, and of his subsequent adventures (including that concerning the king) is told with great enthuiasm. The widow is portrayed as a lusty, self-sufficient female, a woman who knows what she wants and goes after it—in this case, Jack. Jack is apparently as virtuous and industrious an apprentice as Ben Franklin, but he is not as innocent as he pretends and soon moves up in the world.

The tradesmen heroes such as Jack are rather idealized characters. Jack rises less from his own efforts than from those of the people around him. It almost seems that he is above certain efforts, as the king, himself, is. The women in *Jack of Newberry* are the book's finest characterizations. In creating the gallery of female portraits, Deloney leaves behind him all of his rivals in the prose fiction of the time and approaches the best of Elizabethan stage comedy. Queen Catherine, the first Mistress Winchcomb, and other women in the story are colorful figures, alive with natural vitality. As the plots develop, the women are in the midst of the action. Perhaps it is a man's world, but the wife seems to be responsible for her husband's success. Deloney knew and understood middle-class women, and recorded their foibles and unique characteristics with a sharp eye and a precise pen. For the author, the good wife was one who was never idle, but knew her place and did not "gad about." Jack and his first wife made no headway at all until she decided to stay at home and manage the household.

The minor characters are well drawn, especially Randoll Pert. Recently out of debtor's prison, Pert becomes a porter to support his family. His description is delightful, and his antics add both comic and pathetic touches to the novel. The meeting of Jack and Pert at the Spread Eagle in London is superbly handled. The whole episode, including the part where Jack agrees not to collect five hundred pounds until Pert is sheriff of London, is excellent comedy.

Although the novel is episodic, it forms a coherent and often dramatic whole, and is filled with humorous scenes and witty dialogue. *Jack of Newberry* stands as a good "novel" in its own right, as well as the first example of its kind in English literature.

Bruce D. Reeves

JACK SHEPPARD

Type of work: Novel
Author: William Harrison Ainsworth (1805-1882)
Type of plot: Picaresque romance
Time of plot: 1702-1724
Locale: London and its environs
First published: 1839

Principal characters:
JACK SHEPPARD, a housebreaker and popular jailbreaker
JOAN SHEPPARD, his mother
OWEN WOOD, a London carpenter
MRS. WOOD, his wife
WINIFRED, their daughter
SIR ROWLAND TRENCHARD, an aristocrat
THAMES DARRELL, Sir Rowland's nephew and foster son of Owen Wood
JONATHAN WILD, a thief-taker
BLUESKIN, devoted henchman of Jack Sheppard

Critique:

Jack Sheppard differs from most of Ainsworth's work in that it has a rogue instead of a historical figure for its title character. Extremely popular in its own day, it has remained the most widely read of this author's novels. The plot is based on the life of a famous English criminal who so appealed to the public imagination that both Hogarth and Sir James Thornhill used him as a model in their paintings. Abounding in characters, circumstantial incident, obviously delineated protagonists and antagonists, and scattered references to historical incident, the novel illustrates the typically Victorian treatment of the rogue theme in fiction. Thackeray, critical of Ainsworth's characterization of Sheppard, wrote *Catherine* in protest against this book.

The Story:

When Owen Wood went to offer his condolence to Joan, the widow of Tom Sheppard, who had been executed for stealing from Wood, he found the woman living in misery near the Old Mint, a haven for mendicants, thieves, and debtors. Joan told Wood that Van Galgebrok, a Dutch seaman and conjurer, had prophesied that her baby, Jack, would be executed as his father had been. The prophecy was based on the presence of a mole behind Jack's ear. Wood offered to take the infant out of that sordid environment in order to avert fulfillment of the prophecy, but the mother refused to part with her child.

Left alone with the infant while Joan went to the attic to get a key which her deceased husband had ordered given to Wood, the carpenter was accosted by a mob led by Sir Rowland Trenchard, in pursuit of a young man named Darrell. In the confusion Jonathan Wild, a thief-taker, picked up the key which Joan was to return to Wood.

While a great storm raged, Darrell, the fugitive, with a baby in his arms, was again pursued by Sir Rowland. The chase continued to the flooded Thames, where Darrell was drowned after a struggle with Sir Rowland. Wood, on his way home, rescued the baby from drowning. Some falling bricks saved him and the baby from Sir Rowland's wrath. Wood, understanding little of the night's strange events, took the child home with him. He named the boy Thames Darrell.

Twelve years later Wood had taken Jack Sheppard as an apprentice in his carpenter shop, but he found the boy indifferent and listless in his work. Thames Darrell, reared by the Woods, was a model apprentice. A third child in the household was Winifred, Wood's daughter, a charming, beautiful girl. The three twelve-year-olds were very fond of each other.

Mrs. Wood, a termagant, had long berated her husband for his kindness to Jack and to Joan Sheppard, who lived modestly and respectably in Willesden. Following an episode in which Thames was injured while trying to prevent injury to Jack, Mrs. Wood reprimanded Jack and predicted that he would come to the same end that his father had met. Her chastisement was strong enough to arouse a spirit of misdemeanor and criminality in Jack.

Jonathan Wild, who had hanged Tom Sheppard, boasted that he would hang the son as well. A resolute and subtle plotter, he worked slyly to bring about the boy's ruin. One day he gave Jack the key which he had found on the floor of the Mint twelve years before. It was Wood's master key; his hope was that Jack would rob the carpenter. Investigating Thames' parentage, Wild learned also that Thames was the child of Sir Rowland Trenchard's sister, Lady Alvira, whose husband Sir Rowland had drowned and whose child he had tried to destroy on the night of the great storm. Later Lady Alvira had been forced to marry her cousin, Sir Cecil Trafford. Lady Trafford was dying, in which event the estates would revert to her brother if she left no other heir. Wild promised Sir Rowland that he would remove Thames in order that Sir Rowland could inherit the entire estate. As a hold over the nobleman, he told him also that he knew the whereabouts of Sir Rowland's other sister, Constance, carelessly lost in childhood to a gipsy.

Wild and Sir Rowland trapped Thames and Jack in Sir Rowland's house and accused them of robbery. Imprisoned, Jack and Thames made a jail break from Old Giles' Roundhouse, the first of innumerable and difficult escapes for Jack, and the last for Thames, who was sent off to sea to be disposed of by Van Galgebrok, the Dutch seaman and conjurer.

Jack was soon fraternizing with the patrons of the Mint, much to the pleasure of the derelicts, prostitutes, and gamblers, who gathered there. It was in this environment that Joan saw Jack as the criminal he had become. When she went there to admonish her son to live a life of righteousness, she was answered by the taunts and sneers of the patrons, who reminded her that she had at one time enjoyed the life of the Mint. Jack, egged on by two prostitutes, spurned her pleas. Joan returned to her little home in Willesden to pray for Jack.

Jonathan Wild, having rid himself of Thames, one obstacle in the thief-taker's scheme to get control of the fortune of Sir Montacute Trenchard, Thames' grandfather, set about to remove Sir Rowland as well. Wild, plotting against the aristocrat, had him arrested for treason in connection with a proposed Jacobite uprising against the crown.

Jack Sheppard used the key given him by Wild to rob Wood's house. Caught and jailed in the Cage at Willesden as he was going to visit his mother, he soon escaped from the supposedly impregnable structure. At his mother's house Jack declared his undying love for her but announced that he could not return to honest living. Questioned by Joan as to how long he would wait to execute his threat against Jack, Wild, who had followed Jack to Willesden, answered boldly and confidently, "Nine."

Nine years later, in 1724, Jack had become the most daring criminal and jailbreaker of the day. By that time the Woods were affluent citizens living in Willesden. Joan Sheppard, insane because of worry over Jack, had been committed to Bedlam, a squalid, filthy asylum. Sir Rowland had been released from prison. Thames Darrell, thrown overboard by Van Galgebrok, had been picked up by a French fishing boat and carried to France, where he was employed by and subsequently commissioned by Philip of Orleans. Wild had continued in his pleasures of execution and collecting keepsakes of his grisly profession.

Jack Sheppard and Blueskin, one of Wild's henchmen, quarreled with Wild because he would not help Thames Darrell get his rightful share of the estate which Sir Rowland had confiscated, and Blueskin became Jack's loyal henchman. The two robbed the Wood home again, Blueskin slashing Mrs. Wood's throat as she attempted to detain him.

Jack went to see his mother, a haggard, demented object of human wreckage, in chains and on a bed of straw. Wild followed Jack to the asylum. During a brawl Wild struck Joan and the blow restored the poor woman's senses. After her release from Bedlam, Wild divulged to Sir Rowland Trenchard the fact that Joan was his long-lost sister and an heir to the Trenchard estates.

Wild disposed of Sir Rowland by bludgeoning him and throwing him into a secret well. Sir Rowland, almost dead from the beating, attempted to save himself by catching hold of the floor around the opening of the well, but Wild trampled his fingers until the nobleman dropped to his watery grave. The thieftaker, still plotting to secure the Trenchard wealth, took Joan captive, but she killed herself rather than be forced into a marriage with the villain. At her funeral Jack was apprehended after a jail break that required passage through six bolted and barred doors and the removal of innumerable stones and bricks from the prison walls.

In the meantime Thames Darrell had returned from France to visit in the Wood household. Through information contained in a packet of letters which reached him in circuitous fashion, he learned that his father, the fugitive known only as Darrell, had been the French Marquis de Chatillon. His paternity proved, he inherited the Trenchard estates as well. He married Winifred Wood.

Jack Sheppard, after his seizure at his mother's funeral, was executed at Tyburn. As his body swung at the end of the rope, Blueskin cut him down in an attempt to save his life. A bullet from Wild's gun passed through Jack's heart. The body was buried beside Joan Sheppard in Willesden cemetery; and in later years the Marquis de Chatillon and his wife tended the grave and its simple wooden monument. Jonathan Wild eventually paid for his crimes; he was hanged on the same gallows to which he had sent Jack Sheppard and his father.

Further Critical Evaluation of the Work:

William Harrison Ainsworth held the editorship of *Bentley's Miscellaney* for two years beginning in 1840, and then edited his own publication, *Ainsworth's Magazine,* for eleven years following. It was during these years that some of his best-known novels were written, giving us astounding evidence of this enormous capacity for work. As is to be expected in view of such productivity, not all his works are of even quality.

Jack Sheppard is Ainsworth's attempt at the form already explored in English literature by Smollett, Defoe, and Fielding. He differs from the picaresque form as it existed in English in several ways. The pure picaresque novel is episodic and concerns itself essentially with the rogue figure, but also is a vehicle for satirizing the institutions of the society which exclude the rogue. The rogue generally ends his career in a secure social position which he assumes not as the logical consequence of his own actions, but through the machinations of an irregular and sometimes perverse Fate. The picaresque novel is written from a point of view which expresses sympathy for the rogue, who should be the central point of interest. Ainsworth's narrative point of view is that of the good society; his rogue is neither ironic nor the vehicle for satire, and he does not end in a better position than before, all violations of the picaresque form.

The true hero of the novel, though Ainsworth thought to create the second plot line in him, is Thames Darrell, who in the end rises to inherit untold fortune and marry his true love. This is the picaresque ending, but Thames is a romantic hero, not a picaro. Ainsworth, while using elements of the picaresque, is much more at home with the romantic hero. The characterization of Jack Sheppard is more thorough than that of Thames, but it is generally true of Ainsworth, as with many of his generation, that character development for villains proves much more interesting than for that of romantic heroes.

JALNA

Type of work: Novel
Author: Mazo de la Roche (1885-1961)
Type of plot: Domestic realism
Time of plot: The 1920's
Locale: Canada
First published: 1927

> Principal characters:
> RENNY WHITEOAK, head of the family
> MEG, his sister
> EDEN,
> PIERS,
> FINCH, and
> WAKEFIELD, their half-brothers
> PHEASANT VAUGHAN, Piers' wife
> MAURICE VAUGHAN, her father
> ALAYNE ARCHER, Eden's wife
> GRANDMA WHITEOAK

Critique:

One of a series of novels dealing with the Whiteoak family, *Jalna* describes the violent passions of a household that is as familiar to many readers as John Galsworthy's fictional Forsytes. The brothers and sisters are strangely different from each other, but all are bound together by family ties which few of them can understand. Over all towers the somewhat frightening figure of Grandma Whiteoak, binding them to her with the uncertain terms of her will and her unyielding spirit. This indomitable old woman is a character lifting the Jalna novels above the level of popular fiction.

The Story:

The Whiteoaks of Jalna were quite a family. The parents were dead, and the children, ranging in age from eight to over forty, were held together by Renny, the oldest son, and tyrannized by Grandma Whiteoak, a matriarch of ninety-nine years. The family estate of Jalna had been founded by Grandfather Whiteoak, but it had dwindled somewhat from its original greatness. By common consent Renny managed the farms and the family, although he frequently encountered resistance from both.

Meg, the oldest daughter, had in her youth been engaged to Maurice Vaughan, a neighbor and a friend of the family. But while he waited out the long engagement insisted upon by Meg, he had become entangled with a low-class girl and fathered a child, Pheasant. The girl had disappeared and Maurice had grudgingly raised Pheasant. Meg, deaf to the pleas of Maurice and her family for a forgiving heart, had broken the engagement and gone into almost complete retirement. Maurice was never allowed at Jalna again, although he and Renny served in the war together and remained friends.

Renny had remained a bachelor, the head of the family, and a man with quite a reputation with the women. Only his passions had been involved in these affairs, however, and thus it seemed that he would never marry. Renny accepted his power and his position but seemed not greatly to enjoy either.

The rest of the children were half-brothers to these two. Eden was a poet and a dreamer. Farm life disgusted him, and since he had recently had a book of poetry accepted by a New York publisher, he hoped to get away from Jalna and make his way with his writing. However, work of any kind was so distasteful to Eden that it seemed unlikely he could ever break the ties which held him to Jalna.

Piers was a plodder, with no flights of fancy or dreams of grandeur. Doing most of the manual work on the farms, he took orders from Renny in a lethargic way. Renny, learning that Piers had been seen with Pheasant Vaughan, warned the boy that such an alliance could lead only to trouble for both.

Finch was the real problem. Still in school, he barely managed to return each term. Different from the rest, he had no ambition, no drive of any kind. The family obviously considered him useless, but they stuck by him because he was family. Finch brooded. On his lonely walks through the woods and fields, he often saw through matters other members of the family tried to conceal.

Wakefield was just eight, and thus greatly spoiled. He had a heart condition which allowed him to get his own way without effort.

Over them Grandma Whiteoak held a whip. Her will had been made—and often changed—to be used as a weapon over the children and her two sons, who also lived at Jalna. She was ninety-nine and a despot. In many ways she was evil, using her power to force the children to obey her whims.

The first to cause a real stir at Jalna was Piers. He and Pheasant eloped. When they returned home, both Maurice and the Whiteoaks scorned them. Meg became hysterical and swore she would not have Maurice's daughter in her house. Grandma hit Piers over the head with her cane and would have hit Pheasant, but Renny quieted them and said that Pheasant was now part of the family and would be treated accordingly. Instantly everyone, even Meg, accepted his authority.

Eden went to New York to see his publisher and there met and married Alayne Archer, a reader for the publishing house. She felt she had discovered him through his poetry and could inspire him. An orphan, she looked forward to being part of such a large family. But when they reached Jalna, she felt an unexplained coldness. She was warmly welcomed by all but Piers, who resented the difference between her reception and Pheasant's, but she could feel tensions that were just under the surface. Grandma was revolting to the gentle Alayne, who knew she must make the old tyrant like her if she was to know any peace at Jalna.

With Alayne, Finch found his first real happiness. Seeing the artistic need in the boy, she tried to encourage the others to help him. Only Renny listened to her, and because of her arranged to have Finch take music lessons from a good teacher. The boy drove the rest of the family crazy with his practicing, but for the first time he began to be less restless.

Eden, reluctant to get down to serious writing, began to accuse Alayne of nagging him when she tried to encourage him. She wanted to get away from Jalna, for the place was exerting an uneasy hold on her. Worse, she and Renny were unwillingly drawn to each other. He kissed her once, and although they both pretended it was only a brotherly kiss, each knew it was more. At last they confessed their love for each other, but both knew that they would never bow to it because Eden was Renny's brother.

Eden grew troublesome about working at his writing or anything else. When he was injured in a friendly family scuffle, Alayne nursed him tenderly, hoping to hurry him back to health so that they could leave Jalna and Renny. Pheasant also helped nurse Eden, spending hours in his room. When they fell in love, they too tried to fight it because Pheasant's husband was family. At last Eden was able to be about again. Finch, during one of his wanderings, saw Pheasant in Eden's arms. He ran to Piers and told him about his wife and brother. Piers went prepared to kill them, but Pheasant escaped to her father's house. Renny and Piers followed her there. Piers, deciding that she was his wife and therefore his responsibility, took her back to Jalna, where he locked her in her room and allowed no one to see her for weeks. Eden fled, leaving Pheasant and Alayne to face disgrace alone.

When Piers took Pheasant back to Jalna, Meg, refusing to stay in the same house with Pheasant, moved into an abandoned hut on the farm. After a few weeks, Maurice Vaughan went to see her and persuaded her to forgive him his old sin. Soon afterward they were married, trying to make up quickly for all the years they had lost. Alayne prepared to return to New York alone. There would be no divorce, no marriage to Renny. The scandal would be too much for the family — whose pattern would never change.

Further Critical Evaluation of the Work:

Jalna and all the books of the Jalna series are unusual in that each stands alone on its own merits; the mass of exposition needed to set the stage for the events of the plot is deftly incorporated into the musings of the characters or their dinner-table conversation. Yet we feel from the first that the characters have had a life prior to the novel, just as we feel that their lives continue beyond the end of it. The characters, painted with a critical detachment, are extremely amusing. The author has achieved an impressive balancing of the dozen portraits of hardy egoists going about their nagging, fighting, and loving. But there is too much material in the book—too many characters and a confusion of incident. Some descriptions and scenes are brisk and fresh, but other passages are weak and amateurish in execution. The characters never develop; they are born in full bloom, as it were. It is the sense of *family,* the cumulative effect of the group, that provides the real charm of the novel, despite its shortcomings. The elderly matriarch holds together both the family and the book.

The very quarrelsomeness of the family prohibits us from taking any of the members solely at his own self-estimate. Finch is both a stupid, sulky young whelp and a person of almost clairvoyant sensitivity to the moods and motives of those about him, just as Eden is talented, sinned against, and at times a cad. Neither is readily likable, and the somewhat perverse claims they make upon the reader seem the very essence of their being Whiteoaks. The many-sidedness of these quarrelsome people and the sparks they strike from one another find their synthesis in the character of Grandma Adeline Whiteoak. The living symbol of the family's covenant with the land, she draws warmth from the friction of their communal life, and strength from their vivid physicality. *Jalna* is a well-crafted popular novel that comes close to being literature.

JANE EYRE

Type of work: Novel
Author: Charlotte Brontë (1816-1855)
Type of plot: Psychological romance
Time of plot: 1800
Locale: Northern England
First published: 1847

> *Principal characters:*
> JANE EYRE, an orphan
> MRS. REED, mistress of Gateshead Hall
> BESSIE LEAVEN, a nurse
> EDWARD ROCHESTER, owner of Thornfield
> ST. JOHN RIVERS, a young clergyman
> MARY, and
> DIANA RIVERS, his sisters

Critique:

Charlotte Brontë published *Jane Eyre* under the pseudonym of Currer Bell, a name chosen, she said, because it was neither obviously feminine nor masculine. But the emotions behind the book are purely feminine. Literary criticism may point to the extravagance, melodrama, and faulty structure of the novel, but lasting popularity is sufficient evidence of its charm and character for generations of readers. Charlotte Brontë wrote wisely when she cast her novel in the form of an autobiography. The poetry and tension of *Jane Eyre* marked a new development in adult romanticism, just as Jane herself brought to English fiction a new type of heroine, a woman of intelligence and passion.

The Story:

Jane Eyre was an orphan. Both her father and mother had died when Jane was a baby, and the little girl passed into the care of Mrs. Reed of Gateshead Hall. Mrs. Reed's husband, now dead, had been the brother of Jane Eyre's mother, and on his deathbed he had directed Mrs. Reed to look after the orphan as she would her own three children. At Gateshead Hall Jane knew ten years of neglect and abuse. One day a cousin knocked her to the floor. When she fought back, Mrs. Reed punished her by sending her to the gloomy room where Mr. Reed had died. There Jane lost consciousness. Furthermore, the experi-ence caused a dangerous illness from which she was nursed slowly back to health by sympathetic Bessie Leaven, the Gateshead Hall nurse.

Feeling that she could no longer keep her unwanted charge in the house, Mrs. Reed made arrangements for Jane's admission to Lowood School. Early one morning, without farewells, Jane left Gateshead Hall and rode fifty miles by stage to Lowood, her humble possessions in a trunk beside her.

At Lowood, Jane was a diligent student, well-liked by her superiors, especially by Miss Temple, the mistress, who refused to accept without proof Mrs. Reed's low estimate of Jane's character. During the period of Jane's schooldays at Lowood an epidemic of fever caused many deaths among the girls. It resulted, too, in an investigation which caused improvements at the institution. At the end of her studies Jane was retained as a teacher. When Jane grew weary of her life at Lowood, she advertised for a position as governess. She was engaged by Mrs. Fairfax, housekeeper at Thornfield, near Millcote.

At Thornfield the new governess had only one pupil, Adele Varens, a ward of Jane's employer, Mr. Edward Rochester. From Mrs. Fairfax, Jane learned that Mr. Rochester traveled much and seldom came to Thornfield. Jane was pleased with the quiet country life with the beautiful old house and gardens, the book-filled library, and her own comfortable room.

Jane met Mr. Rochester for the first time while she was out walking, going to his aid after his horse had thrown him. She found her employer a somber, moody man, quick to change in his manner toward her, brusque in his speech. He commended her work with Adele, however, and confided that the girl was the daughter of a French dancer who had deceived him and deserted her daughter. Jane felt that this experience alone could not account for Mr. Rochester's moody nature.

Mysterious happenings occurred at Thornfield. One night Jane, alarmed by a strange noise, found Mr. Rochester's door open and his bed on fire. When she attempted to arouse the household, he commanded her to keep quiet about the whole affair. She also learned that Thornfield had a strange tenant, a woman who laughed like a maniac and who stayed in rooms on the third floor of the house. Jane believed that this woman was Grace Poole, a seamstress employed by Mr. Rochester.

Mr. Rochester attended numerous parties at which he was obviously paying court to Blanche Ingram, daughter of Lady Ingram. One day the inhabitants of Thornfield were informed that Mr. Rochester was bringing a party of house guests home with him. In the party was the fashionable Miss Ingram. During the house party Mr. Rochester called Jane to the drawing-room, where the guests treated her with the disdain which they thought her humble position deserved. To herself Jane had already confessed her interest in her employer, but it seemed to her that he was interested only in Blanche Ingram. One evening while Mr. Rochester was away from home the guests played charades. At the conclusion of the game a gipsy fortune-teller appeared to read the palms of the lady guests. Jane, during her interview with the gipsy, discovered that the so-called fortune-teller was Mr. Rochester in disguise.

While the guests were still at Thornfield, a stranger named Mason arrived to see Mr. Rochester on business. That night Mason was mysteriously wounded by the strange inhabitant of the third floor. The injured man was taken away secretly before daylight.

One day Robert Leaven came from Gateshead to tell Jane that Mrs. Reed, now on her deathbed, had asked to see her former ward. Jane returned to her aunt's home. The dying woman gave Jane a letter, dated three years before, from John Eyre in Madeira, who asked that his niece be sent to him for adoption. Mrs. Reed confessed that she had epidemic at Lowood. The sin of keeping from Jane news which would have meant relatives, adoption, and an inheritance had become a heavy burden on the conscience of the dying woman.

Jane went back to Thornfield, which she now looked upon as her home. One night in the garden Edward Rochester embraced her and proposed marriage. Jane accepted and made plans for a quiet ceremony in the village church. She wrote also to her uncle in Madeira, explaining Mrs. Reed's deception and telling him she was to marry Mr. Rochester.

Shortly before the date set for the wedding Jane had a harrowing experience. She awakened to find a strange, repulsive-looking woman in her room. The intruder tried on Jane's wedding veil and then ripped it to shreds. Mr. Rochester tried to persuade Jane that the whole incident was only her imagination, but in the morning she found the torn veil in her room. At the church, as the vows were being said, a stranger spoke up declaring the existence of an impediment to the marriage. He presented an affirmation, signed by the Mr. Mason who had been wounded during his visit to Thornfield. The document stated that Edward Fairfax Rochester had married Bertha Mason, Mr. Mason's sister, in Spanish Town, Jamaica, fifteen years before. Mr. Rochester admitted this fact; then he conducted the party to the third-story chamber at Thornfield. There they found the attendant Grace Poole and her charge, Bertha Rochester, a raving maniac. Mrs. Rochester was the woman Jane had seen in her room.

Jane felt that she must leave Thornfield at once. She notified Mr. Rochester and left quietly early the next morning, using all her small store of money for the coach fare. Two days later she was set down on the moors of a north midland shire. Starving, she actually begged for food. Finally she was befriended by the Reverend St. John Rivers and his sisters, Mary and Diana, who took Jane in and nursed her back to health. Assuming the name of Jane Elliot, she refused to divulge anything of her history except her connection with the Lowood institution. Reverend Rivers eventually found a place for her as mistress in a girl's school.

Shortly afterward St. John Rivers received from his family solicitor word that John Eyre had died in Madeira, leaving Jane Eyre a fortune of twenty thousand pounds. Because Jane had disappeared under mysterious circumstances, the lawyer was trying to locate her through the next of kin, St. John Rivers. Jane's identity was now revealed through her connection with Lowood School, and she learned, to her surprise, that St. John and his sisters were really her own cousins. She then insisted on sharing her inheritance with them.

When St. John decided to go to India as a missionary, he asked Jane to go with him as his wife—not because he loved her, as he frankly admitted, but because he admired her and wanted her services as his assistant. Jane felt indebted to him for his kindness and aid, but she hesitated to accept his proposal.

One night, while St. John was awaiting her decision, she dreamed that Mr. Rochester was calling her name. The next day she returned to Thornfield by coach. Arriving there, she found the mansion gutted—a burned and blackened ruin. Neighbors told her that the fire had broken out one stormy night, set by the madwoman, who died while Mr. Rochester was trying to rescue her from the roof of the blazing house.

Mr. Rochester, blinded during the fire, was living at Ferndean, a lonely farm some miles away. Jane Eyre went to him at once, and there they were married. For both, their story had an even happier ending. After two years Mr. Rochester regained the sight of one eye, so that he was able to see his first child when it was put in his arms.

Further Critical Evaluation of the Work:

Charlotte Brontë was always concerned that her work be judged on the basis of its art and not because of her sex. Thus the choice of the pseudonym which she continued to use even after her authorship was revealed, often referring in her letters to Currer Bell when speaking of herself as writer. *Jane Eyre,* her first published novel, has been called "feminine" because of the romanticism and deeply felt emotions of the heroine-narrator. It would be more correct, however, to point to the feminist qualities of the novel: a heroine who refuses to be placed in the traditional female position of subservience, who disagrees with her superiors, who stands up for her rights, who ventures creative thoughts; more importantly, a narrator who comments on the role of women in the society and the greater constraint experienced by them. Those "feminine" emotions often pointed to in Jane Eyre herself are surely found as well in Rochester, and the continued popularity of this work must suggest the enduring human quality of these emotions.

Brontë often discussed the lack of passion in her contemporaries' work and especially in that of Jane Austen, about whom she said, "Her business is not half so much with the human heart as with the human eyes, mouth, hands and feet." Coldness, detachment, excessive analysis, and critical distance were not valued by Brontë. The artist must be involved in her subject, she believed, and must have a degree of inspiration not to be rationally explained. Such a theory of art is similar to that of the romantic poets, an attitude not altogether popular by mid-nineteenth century.

In *Jane Eyre*, therefore, Brontë chose the exact point of view to suit both her subject matter and her artistic theory, the first-person narrator. The story is told entirely through the eyes of the heroine Jane Eyre. This technique enabled Brontë to bring the events to the reader with an intensity that involved him in the passions, feelings, and thoughts of the heroine. A passionate directness characterizes Jane's narration: conversations are rendered in direct, not indirect dialogue; actions are given just as they occurred, with little analysis of either event or character. In a half-dozen key scenes, Brontë shifts to present tense instead of the immediate past, so that Jane Eyre narrates the event as if it were happening just at the present moment. After Jane flees Thornfield and Rochester, when the coachman puts her out at Whitcross having used up her fare, she narrates to the moment: "I am alone. . . . I am absolutely destitute." After a long description of the scene around her and her analysis of her situation, also narrated in the present tense, she reverts to the more usual past tense in the next paragraph: "I struck straight into the heath." Such a technique adds greatly to the immediacy of the novel and further draws the reader into the situation.

Jane Eyre, like all Brontë's heroines, has no parents and no family that accepts or is aware of her. She, like Lucy Snowe (*Villette*) and Caroline Helstone (*Shirley*), leads her life, then, cut off from society, since family was the means for a woman to participate in society and community. Lacking such support, Jane must face her problems alone. Whenever she forms a close friendship (Bessie at Gateshead, Helen Burns and Miss Temple at Lowood, Mrs. Fairfax at Thornfield), she discovers that these ties can be broken easily —by higher authority, by death, by marriage—since she is not "kin." Cutting her heroines off so radically from family and community gave Charlotte Brontë the opportunity to make her women independent and to explore the romantic ideal of individualism.

Jane Eyre is a moral tale, akin to a folk or fairy tale, with nearly all ambiguities—in society, character, and situation—omitted. Almost all the choices that Jane must make are easy ones, and her character, although she grows and matures, does not change significantly. Her one difficult choice is refusing to become Rochester's mistress, leaving Thornfield alone and penniless instead. That choice was difficult precisely because she had no family or friends to influence her with their disapproval. No one would be hurt if she consented;

that is, no one but Jane herself, and it is her own self-love that helps her to refuse.

Again like a fairy tale, *Jane Eyre* is full of myth and superstition. Rochester often calls Jane his "elf," "changeling," or "witch"; there are mysterious happenings at Thornfield; Jane is inclined to believe the gipsy fortune-teller (until Rochester reveals himself) and often thinks of the superstitions she has heard; the weather often presages mysterious or disastrous events. And, most importantly, at the climax of the story when Jane is about to consent to be the unloved wife of St. John Rivers, she hears Rochester calling to her —at precisely the time, we learn later, that he had in fact called to her. This event is never explained rationally, and we must accept Jane's judgment that it was a supernatural intervention.

Numerous symbolic elements pervade the novel; most often something in nature symbolizes an event or person in Jane's life. The most obvious example is the chestnut tree, which is split in two by lightning on the night that Jane accepts Rochester's marriage proposal, signifying the rupture of their relationship. The two parts of the tree, though, remain bound, as do Jane and Rochester despite their physical separation.

Likewise, the novel is full of character foils and parallel situations. Aunt Reed at Gateshead is contrasted with Miss Temple at Lowood; the Reed sisters at the beginning are contrasted with the Rivers sisters—cousins all— at the end; Rochester's impassioned proposal and love is followed by St. John's pragmatic proposition. Foreshadowing is everywhere in the book, so that seemingly chance happenings gain added significance as the novel unfolds and each previous event is echoed in the next.

Thus, the novel's artful structure and carefully chosen point of view, added to the strong and fascinating character of Jane herself, make *Jane Eyre,* if not a typical Victorian novel, surely a classic among English novels.

Margaret McFadden-Gerber

JASON AND THE GOLDEN FLEECE

Type of work: Classical legend
Source: Folk tradition
Type of plot: Heroic adventure
Time of plot: Remote antiquity
Locale: Ancient Greece
First transcribed: Unknown

Principal characters:
JASON, Prince of Iolcus
KING PELIAS, his uncle
CHIRON, the Centaur who reared Jason
ÆETES, King of Colchis
MEDEA, his daughter

Critique:

The story of *Jason and the Golden Fleece* has been repeated in story and song for more than thirty centuries. Jason lived when great heroes lived and gods supposedly roamed the earth in human form. The story of the golden ram and his radiant fleece is read and loved by adults as it is by children. The story has been told in many different forms, but its substance remains unchanged.

The Story:

In ancient Greece there lived a prince named Jason, son of a king who had been driven from his throne by a wicked brother named Pelias. To protect the boy from his cruel uncle, Jason's father took him to a remote mountaintop where he was raised by Chiron the Centaur, whom many say was half man and half horse. When Jason had grown to young manhood, Chiron the Centaur told him Pelias had seized his brother's crown. Jason was instructed to go and win back his father's kingdom.

Pelias had been warned to beware of a stranger who came with one foot sandaled and the other bare. It happened that Jason had lost one sandal in a river he crossed as he came to Iolcus, where Pelias ruled. When Pelias saw the lad he was afraid and plotted to kill him. But he pretended to welcome Jason. At a great feast he told Jason the story of the golden fleece.

In days past a Greek king called Athamas banished his wife and took another, a beautiful but wicked woman who persuaded Athamus to kill his own children. But a golden ram swooped down from the skies and carried the children away. The girl slipped from his back and fell into the sea, but the boy came safely to the country of Colchis. There the boy let the king of Colchis slaughter the ram for its golden fleece. The gods were angered by these happenings and placed a curse on Athamus and all his family until the golden fleece should be returned to Colchis.

As Pelias told Jason the story, he could see that the young prince was stirred, and he was not surprised when Jason vowed that he would bring back the golden fleece. Pelias promised to give Jason his rightful throne when he returned from his quest, and Jason trusted Pelias and agreed to the terms. He gathered about him many great heroes of Greece—Hercules, the strongest and bravest of all heroes; Orpheus, whose music soothed savage beasts; Argus, who with the help of Juno built the beautiful ship *Argo;* Zetes and Calais, sons of the North Wind, and many other brave men.

They encountered great dangers on their journey. One of the heroes was drawn under the sea by a nymph and was never seen again by his comrades. They visited Salmydessa where the blind King Phineus was surrounded by Harpies, loathsome creatures, with the faces of women and the bodies of vultures.

Zetes and Calais chased the creatures across the skies, and the heroes left the old king in peace.

Phineus had warned the heroes about the clashing rocks through which they must pass. As they approached the rocks they were filled with fear, but Juno held the rocks back and they sailed past the peril. They rowed along the shore until they came to the land of Colchis.

Æetes, King of Colchis, swore never to give up the treasure, but Jason vowed that he and his comrades would do battle with Æetes. Then Æetes consented to yield the treasure if Jason would yoke to the plow two wild, fire-breathing bulls and sow a field with dragon's teeth. When a giant warrior sprang from each tooth, Jason must slay each one. Jason agreed to the trial.

Æetes had a beautiful daughter Medea, who had fallen in love with the handsome Jason, and she brewed a magic potion which gave Jason godlike strength; thus it was that he was able to tame the wild bulls and slay the warriors. Æetes promised to bring forth the fleece the next day, but Jason saw the wickedness in the king's heart and warned his comrades to have the *Argo* ready to sail.

In the night Medea secured the seven golden keys that unlocked the seven doors to the cave where the golden fleece hung and led Jason to the place. Behind the seven doors he found a hideous dragon guarding the treasure. Medea's magic caused the dragon to fall asleep, and Jason seized the fleece. It was so bright that night seemed like day.

Fearing for her life, Medea sailed away from her father's house with Jason and the other heroes. After many months they reached their homeland, where Jason placed the treasure at the feet of Pelias. But the fleece was no longer golden. Pelias was wrathful and swore not to give up his kingdom. But in the night the false king died. Afterward Jason wore the crown and the enchantress Medea reigned by his side.

Further Critical Evaluation of the Work:

The journey of the Argonauts ("Sailors of the *Argo*") and/or Minyae may well be one of the oldest of Greek adventure myths. Homer alludes to it, and it is placed in the generation preceding the Trojan War (the roster of heroes includes Telamon, the father of Ajax, and Peleus, the father of Achilles). No doubt its folk-tale theme of a sea journey to inhospitable lands in quest of a valuable prize was the model for the adventures of Odysseus, Herakles, Theseus, and others. Compare, for example, the dragon-guarded golden fleece with the dragon-guarded golden apples of the Hesperides (the eleventh labor of Herakles); the beautiful young princess who aids her father's enemy and is eventually cast aside (as was Ariadne by Theseus); the journey to Aeaea, the island of Circe (Odysseus); a kingdom usurped (Herakles) and regained with a vengeance (Odysseus). Typical of such tales is the accomplishment of an impossible task, a confrontation with death and the fantastically inhuman, all to prove one's nobility of birth and right to reign. The retrieval of the fleece, then, is not the subject of this myth, but the occasion; it is a device by which the hero becomes involved with the heroic. Futhermore, the entire expedition would not have come about were it not for Hera, whom Pelias had refused to honor. Her tortuous plan was to have Jason sent off to Colchis so that he would bring back with him the sorceress Medea who would kill Pelias (which she did, by convincing the old king's daughters to kill him so that she might rejuvenate him).

Despite the age of this myth, the earliest extensive literary account is found in Pindar's Fourth Pythian Ode (462 B.C.), and it was not until the third century B.C. that the myth received formal expanded treatment by Apollonius of Rhodes, who revived the epic genre. His romantic effort, the *Argonautica,* would henceforward not only be the model for other versions of the quest, but would greatly influence Roman epic poets, notably Vergil.

Apollonius' work, despite its obvious stylistic and structural inferiority to Homer's poems, nevertheless contains some very charming, if not masterful, descriptions and characterizations. The first two books are devoted to the voyage from Thessaly to Colchis. Among the more prominent episodes are the Argonauts' landfall at Lemnos, where they are entertained for a year by the women who, having once been plagued with a malodor, killed their men because they had taken Thracian brides. Reaching the Asian mainland, they soon were forced to fight six-armed giants and were involved in two other battles before rescuing the prophet-king Phineus. Book III contains the arrival at Colchis and Medea's falling in love with Jason. Unlike the *Iliad,* in which Hera and Athena are at odds with Aphrodite, the *Argonautica* portrays them as allies who instigate the mischievous Eros (Cupid) to fire a shaft into the princess Medea. Torn between filial loyalty and her uncontrollable passion, she soon yields to love. Her escape with Jason and their eventual arrival at Iolchus (Book IV) include the murder of Medea's brother Absyrtus and the necessary expiation on Circe's island, Aeaea. Apollonius has Jason kill Absyrtus through Medea's treachery; in the earlier version Medea herself murders her brother and scatters the butchered remains over the sea in order to delay the pursuing Colchians, who have to gather the pieces for burial.

The exact return route supposedly taken by the Argonauts was disputed in ancient times. Doubtless the various versions were based on the trade routes begun in the Mycenaean age. Apollonius takes the Argonauts from the mouth of the river Phasis on the Black Sea to the Ister (Danube), overland to the Adriatic, where they are confronted by Absyrtus; thence to the Eridanus (Po?) overland to the Rhone to the Tyrrhenian Sea and Circe's island. Other accounts include (1) a return by the same route as they came; (2) sailing east up the Phasis to the world-encircling river Ocean, then southwest to Africa and overland to the Mediterranean (Pindar's version); and (3) up the Phasis, through Russia and over northern sea routes past Britain and through the Pillars of Herakles. Apollonius includes in the journey the perils of the Sirens, Scylla and Charybdis, and the Wandering Rocks; Medea and Jason are, like Odysseus, given refuge in hospitable Phaeacia on the west coast of Greece, but only after the young lovers marry to void Æetes' claim to his daughter.

The myth receives brief attention in Ovid's *Metamorphoses* (Book VII), and would have been retold at length in the Latin hexameters of Valerius Flaccus

(A.D., first century), but his *Argonautica* is incomplete. Jason's adventure is, nevertheless, included in Apollodorus' *Library,* the invaluable (Greek) collection of myths (A.D., first or second century). Like most myths, the search for the fleece was subject to the rationalizing minds of classical writers: Strabo the geographer theorized that the Argonauts were an expedition in search of alluvial gold; but whatever the origins of the myth, it stands out as a magnificent prototype of the perilous search for the marvelous prize. In a sense this is also the theme of the Trojan cycle, in which the greatest figures of a distant glorious age attempt to retrieve the most beautiful mortal woman. But the voyage of the *Argo,* like the wanderings of Odysseus, belongs to that entertaining genre, *Märchen,* which attends to the unnatural, the exotic, the romantic. Jason-like heroes are not only seen in the many local legends of ancient Greece, but in history (Alexander's oriental conquests were romanticized). Comparisons may be drawn between Jason and Celtic heroes, and between the Fleece and the Grail. In 1867, William Morris revived the original myth with a 7,000-line Victorian epic entitled *The Death of Jason.* Robert Graves has authored a novel about the search for the fleece—*Hercules, My Shipmate* (1944).

Classical authors seemed to be more concerned with Medea than with Jason. Euripides' masterpiece tragedy, *Medea,* deals with Jason's cruel rejection of the woman who sacrificed all—even murdered—for him (cf. Ovid *Metamorphoses VII*). Her vengeance, to deprive Jason of the things he loves most, requires that she kill not only the girl he intends to marry, but Jason's (and Medea's) own sons as well. Her refuge in Athens as wife of aging King Aegeus is brief; she escapes to Colchis after an unsuccessful attempt to poison Theseus. Nothing is known of her death—if she died at all. Jason, however, overcome with grief, loneliness, and shame, returned to the rotting hulk of the *Argo* which he had beached at Corinth, and there he was struck by a falling beam and died.

E. N. Genovese

JAVA HEAD

Type of work: Novel
Author: Joseph Hergesheimer (1880-1954)
Type of plot: Period romance
Time of plot: 1840's
Locale: Salem, Massachusetts
First published: 1919

>   *Principal characters:*
>   GERRIT AMMIDON, a Yankee sea captain
>   TAOU YUEN, Gerrit's Chinese bride
>   NETTIE VOLLAR, Gerrit's former sweetheart
>   EDWARD DUNSACK, Nettie's uncle
>   JEREMY AMMIDON, Gerrit's father

Critique:

Java Head is a novel of colorful detail and romantic incident, its scene laid in a historic port town during the period when the clipper ship was making America the mistress of the seas. In this novel Hergesheimer recaptures the spirit of an era, and by placing the exotic Taou Yuen against a late Puritan background he presents also a contrast of civilizations. One of the interesting features of the book is the fact that each chapter is written from the point of view of a different character.

The Story:

In Salem, Massachusetts, one spring in the early 1840's, there was concern because the ship *Nautilus*, owned by Ammidon, Ammidon, and Saltonstone, was seven months overdue. The captain of the ship was young Gerrit Ammidon, son of Captain Jeremy Ammidon, senior partner of the firm. Nettie Vollar grew more disturbed as the weeks passed. On the day the *Nautilus* left Salem, her grandfather had ordered Gerrit from the house before he reached the point of announcing his love for Nettie and asking her to marry him. The old man's reason for his action had been that Nettie was an illegitimate child and, as such, did not deserve to be married and lead a normal life. His theory was that the girl had been placed on earth only as a punishment for her mother.

Old Jeremy Ammidon also awaited the return of the *Nautilus*, for Gerrit was the favorite of his two sons. The other son, William, was primarily a tradesman interested in making money. Old Jeremy and William clashed regularly over the kind of trade the firm was to take, the liberty to be given its captains in trading, and whether the ships of the firm should be replaced by the swift new clippers that were revolutionizing the Pacific trade. William had never told old Jeremy that the firm had two schooners engaged in carrying opium, a cargo the older man detested. The atmosphere at Java Head, the Ammidon mansion in Salem, was kept more or less in a state of tension because of the disagreements between the father and son. Rhoda Ammidon, William's cheerful and sensible wife, was a quieting influence on both men.

Not many days later the *Nautilus* was sighted. When it cast anchor off the Salem wharves, Gerrit asked that the Ammidon barouche be sent to carry him to Java Head. The reason for his request became clear when the carriage discharged at the door of the mansion not only Gerrit but also his Manchu wife, Taou Yuen. The sight of her resplendent clothes and lacquered face was almost too much for Gerrit's conservative New England family. Only William's wife was able to be civil; the father said nothing, and William declared that the painted foreign woman was an unpleasant surprise.

Gerrit's first difficulty came when he assured his family that the Chinese marriage ceremony which had united him with Taou Yuen was as binding as the Christian service of William and Rhoda. The people of Salem wished to look upon the Chinese noblewoman as a mistress rather than as a wife. Nor did they understand that Taou Yuen was from one of the finest families of China, as far removed from the coolies and trading classes of Chinese ports as the New Englanders themselves.

The first Sunday afternoon after the arrival of the *Nautilus* Edward Dunsack appeared to thank Gerrit Ammidon for bringing a chest from China for him. The sight of Taou Yuen stirred Dunsack, largely because he was homesick for China. When he left Java Head, his mind was filled with a sense of injustice that Gerrit Ammidon should have the Manchu woman as his bride instead of Edward Dunsack and that Gerrit had married the Chinese woman instead of Dunsack's niece, Nettie Vollar.

Back in port, Gerrit saw to the refitting of the *Nautilus*. He did not see Nettie Vollar. Then, on the Fourth of July, the Ammidons met Nettie on the street and took her back to Java Head for the evening, lest she be injured or insulted by rough sailors on the streets. She did not see Taou Yuen, however, for the Chinese woman had remained in her room during the day. When it was time for Nettie to return home, Gerrit escorted her. It was the first time they had been alone together since he had been ordered from her home months before. Gerrit returned to the Ammidon house realizing that he had done Nettie a great wrong when he married Taou Yuen.

The following morning misfortune struck the Ammidons. Old Jeremy accompanied his son William down to the offices of the firm to inspect the specifications for two new clipper ships, and among some papers he discovered a bill of lading for one of the firm's two schooners engaged in the opium trade. His anger was roused to such an extent that his heart could not carry the strain. He collapsed and died in the office.

After the funeral, Gerrit, sick of the life ashore, took the *Nautilus* as his share in the estate, left the company, and prepared to return to sea as an independent trader. Even his wife had become unbearable to him since he had renewed his friendship with Nettie. Nevertheless, he determined to take Taou Yuen back with him and to establish their household in Shanghai, where he would no longer face the complications which arose from residence in Salem.

One day Edward Dunsack appeared at the Ammidon home to ask Gerrit to pay a call on his niece Nettie, who had been severely injured by a carriage. Gerrit left immediately, and Dunsack took the opportunity to attempt the seduction of Taou Yuen. Failing in his design, he poisoned her mind with an account of the love affair between his niece and Gerrit. In the meantime Gerrit, after a regretful interview with Nettie, had gone down to the *Nautilus* to regain his peace of mind.

The next day Taou Yuen was driven in the Ammidon carriage to pick up Rhoda Ammidon at the Dunsack home, where the latter had made a call on Nettie Vollar. Rhoda had already left. On an impulse Taou Yuen went into the house to see her rival. Angered because she thought Nettie commonplace and plain, Taou Yuen began to contemplate suffocating the girl. Suddenly Edward Dunsack, drug-crazed, entered the room and locked the door. Nettie fainted. When Taou Yuen repelled Edward, he threatened to strangle her so as to leave marks on her throat. To escape such disfiguration, forbidden by Confucius, Taou Yuen quickly swallowed some opium pills lying on the table beside the invalid Nettie's bed.

When help came a short time later, Taou Yuen was already unconscious. She died soon afterward. Edward Dunsack had gone mad. Several days later, after the Christian burial of Taou Yuen, the *Nautilus* sailed from Salem harbor. It carried its young captain and his new wife, Nettie, to what they hoped would be a happier life.

Further Critical Evaluation of the Work:

Java Head is essentially a novel about the struggles of outsiders with the powerful and closed society in which they find themselves. Although Joseph Hergesheimer did not give full effect to the dramatic possibilities inherent in the story, his feeling for surface impressions and the honesty of his statement produced a vivid spectacle and a thought-provoking book. Technically, the different parts—each from the viewpoint of a different character—remain "set" pieces, never quite fusing into a whole, but the book is worth reading for the skill of the sketching of atmosphere and characterization. Hergesheimer writes of a sailing ship, for example, as if she were a living creature, and conveys great insight into sea psychology. One of the highlights of the narrative is the dramatic and detailed description of the ship *Nautilus* docking in Salem port.

Gerrit Ammidon tends to reduce the other characters to the background. Almost bigger than life, he stands for romance, eternally protesting against the conventional and bigoted, rebelling against the restrictions laid down by others. Only his old father, Jeremy Ammidon, is equal to him. Reliving his past glories and old voyages, and reworking bygone grievances, Jeremy is frustrated by his beached existence. The characters symbolize the conflict of old and new, the struggle between the "clerk-sailors," as Jeremy calls them, and those who would cling to the romance and danger of old ways. The tide of trade is turning from Salem to the railway and docking facilities of larger cities; although Gerrit and Jeremy are noble figures, they cannot win out against the pettiness of the majority and the lure of "progress."

Taou Yuen is presented with subtlety and restraint. Hergesheimer resists the temptation to use her as a mere exotic counterpoint to the other characters. Viewed merely as a study of the ancient opium habit, the section of the book dealing with her is impressive and interesting. She is an outsider by birth, but her husband is an outsider by nature of his character, as his father has become one by virtue of his age. The destiny of the outsiders is martyrdom. Although their story is told in a strangely passive style, it is effective and significant.

JEAN-CHRISTOPHE

Type of work: Novel
Author: Romain Rolland (1866-1944)
Type of plot: Social chronicle
Time of plot: Late nineteenth and early twentieth centuries
Locale: Germany, France, Switzerland
First published: 1904-1912

Principal characters:
JEAN-CHRISTOPHE KRAFFT, a musician
MELCHIOR, his father
JEAN MICHEL, his grandfather
LOUISA, his mother
ANTOINETTE, a French girl
OLIVIER, her brother
GRAZIA, Jean-Christophe's friend

Critique:

Jean-Christophe is a two-thousand-page novel originally published in ten volumes, the painstaking record of the artistic development of a musical genius. Romain Rolland set out to portray the adventures of the soul of his hero and succeeded magnificently; in addition he broke down the artistic barrier between France and Germany. The experiences of Jean-Christophe are those of every genius who turns from the past to serve the future. In 1915 Rolland was awarded the Nobel Prize for Literature, in great part for *Jean-Christophe*.

The Story:

Melchior Krafft was a virtuoso, his father Jean Michel a famous conductor. It was no wonder that Melchior's son, Christophe, should be a musician.

Louisa, Melchior's wife, was a stolid woman of the lower class. Her father-in-law had been furious at his son for marrying beneath him, but he was soon won over by the patient goodness of Louisa. It was fortunate that there was a strong tie between them, for Melchoir drank and wasted his money. Often the grandfather gave his little pension to Louisa because there was no money for the family.

Melchior by chance one day heard his three-year-old Christophe playing at the piano. In his drunken enthusiasm, Mel-chior conceived the idea of creating a musical prodigy. So began Christophe's lessons. Over and over he played his scales; over and over he practiced until he was letter perfect. Often he rebelled. Whipping only made him more rebellious, but in the end the piano always pulled him back.

His grandfather noticed that he would often improvise melodies as he played with his toys. Sitting in a different room, he would transcribe those airs and arrange them. Christophe showed real genius in composition.

At the age of seven and a half Christophe was ready for his first concert. Dressed in a ridiculous costume, he was presented at court as a child prodigy of six. He played works of some of the German masters and then performed with great success his own compositions gathered into an expensive privately printed volume, *The Pleasures of Childhood: Aria, Minuetto, Valse, and Marcia, Opus 1,* by *Jean-Christophe Krafft.* The grand duke was delighted and bestowed the favor of the court on the prodigy.

Before reaching his teens, Christophe was firmly installed as official second violinist in the court orchestra, where his father was concert master. Rehearsals, concerts, composition, lessons to give and take—that was his life. He became

JEAN-CHRISTOPHE by Romain Rolland. Translated by Gilbert Cannan. By permission of the publishers, Henry Holt & Co., Inc. Copyright, 1910, 1911, 1913, 1938, by Henry Holt & Co., Inc.

the mainstay of the family financially, even collecting his father's wages before Melchior could get his hands on them. All the other phases of his life were neglected; no one even bothered to teach him table manners.

When Melchior finally drowned himself, his death was a financial benefit to the Kraffts. But when Jean Michel died, it was a different matter. Christophe's two brothers were seldom home, and only Louisa and her musician son were left. To save money, they moved into a smaller, more wretched flat.

Meanwhile Christophe was going through a series of love affairs which always terminated unhappily because of his unswerving honesty and lack of social graces. In his early twenties he took Ada, a vulgar shop girl, for his mistress. Because of gossip, he found it much harder to get and keep pupils. When he dared to publish a criticism of the older masters, he lost his standing at court. He had almost decided to leave Germany.

At a peasant dance one night he protected Lorchen, a farm girl, from a group of drunken soldiers. In the ensuing brawl, one soldier was killed and two were seriously injured. With a warrant out for his arrest, Christophe escaped to Paris.

Once in France, a country he greatly admired, Christophe found it difficult to acclimate himself. He met a group of wealthy and cynical Jews, Americans, Belgians, and Germans, but he judged their sophistication painful and their affectations boring. His compositions, although appreciated by a few, were not generally well received at first.

After a time, with increasing recognition, he found himself alternately praised and blamed by the critics. But he was noticed, and that was the important thing. Although he was received in wealthy homes and given complimentary tickets for theaters and concerts, he was still desperately poor.

At the home of the Stevens family, where he was kindly received, he in-structed Colette, the coquettish daughter, and the younger, gentler Grazia, her cousin. Without falling in love with Colette, he was for a time her teacher and good friend. Grazia, who adored him, was only another pupil.

One night a blushing, stammering young man of letters was introduced to him. It was Olivier, who had long been a faithful admirer of Christophe's music. Christophe was immediately attracted to Olivier, although at first he was not quite sure why. Olivier's face was only hauntingly familiar.

It turned out that Olivier was the younger brother of Antoinette, a girl whose image Christophe cherished. Before he left Germany, a Jewish friend had given Christophe tickets for a box at the theater. Knowing no one to ask to accompany him, he went alone and in the lobby saw a French governess who was being turned away from the box office. Impulsively, Christophe took her in with him. The Grunebaums, the girl's employers, had expected to be invited also, and they were angry at the fancied slight. Antoinette was dismissed from their employ.

As she was returning to France, Christophe caught a glimpse of her on the train. That was all the contact he ever had with Antoinette. Now he learned that she had worn herself out by supporting Olivier until he could enter the École Normale. When he finally passed the entrance examinations, she had already contracted consumption, and she died before Christophe came to Paris.

Finding a real friend in Olivier, Christophe took an apartment with him. The house was only middle-class or less; but in that house and its inhabitants, and with Olivier's guidance, Christophe began to find the real soul of France. Away from the sophisticated glitter of Paris, the ordinary people lived calm and purposeful lives filled with the ideal of personal liberty.

Olivier became a champion of Christophe and helped establish his reputation in the reviews. Then some one, an important person, worked anonymously on Christophe's behalf. In a few years he found himself famous in France and abroad as the foremost composer of the new music.

Olivier's marriage to the shallow Jacqueline separated the two friends. In his eventful life Christophe made many more friends, but none so dear as Olivier. He did, however, discover his anonymous benefactor. It was Grazia, no longer in love with him and married to a secretary of the Austrian legation.

Jacqueline left Olivier, and he and Christophe became interested in the syndicalist movement. They attended a May Day celebration which turned into a riot. Olivier was fatally stabbed. After killing a soldier, Christophe fled the country.

During his exile in Switzerland, Christophe went through an unhappy love affair with Anna, the wife of a friend, and the consequent sense of guilt temporarily stilled his genius. But with the help of the now widowed Grazia, Christophe spent ten fruitful years in Switzerland.

When he returned to France, he was sought after and acclaimed. He was vastly amused to find himself an established master, and even considered out of date by younger artists.

Although Grazia and Christophe never married, they remained steadfast and consoling friends. Grazia died in Egypt, far from her beloved Christophe. He died in Paris. To the end, Christophe was uncompromising, for he was a true artist.

Further Critical Evaluation of the Work:

The subject matter in *Jean-Christophe* is more important than the technique. The style of composition and manner of construction are straightforward and plain; with few exceptions, the narrative moves smoothly forward, like a river, carrying Christophe through his life. The first sentence establishes the continuous symbolism of the river. Days, weeks, and months are seen as a tide, ebbing and flowing, always beginning anew. First the Rhine and then the Seine dominate the setting. Christophe's first experience of lovemaking, with Ada, is on the river, and his father drowns in the river. When Christophe dies, the image of the river recurs.

The importance of honesty and integrity forms a continuing theme in the novel. Only one thing is asked of a baby, Christophe's grandfather says at his birth: that he grow into an honest man. Old Jean Michel, one of the finest characters in the novel, has a fondness for spouting aphorisms; he suggests many of the thematic beliefs—honesty, duty, industry—that will later be developed in the book.

Rolland effectively attempts to reveal the world from the point of view of the baby and tiny child. From infancy, music has a special, magical effect on Christophe, whether it is the ringing of church bells or the playing of the church organ. He does not understand the feeling, but it foreshadows the dominant influence in his life. An old piano becomes a source of magic and joy to the child and soon is the most important power in his life. Christophe dreams and muses through childhood. The first crisis of his life occurs when he realizes that some men command and others are commanded. Injustice torments him all of his life. The name Jean-Christophe suggests Jesus Christ, and he later thinks that to create music is to be God on earth.

The maturing process is shown in great detail; the reader is spared none of the pains and joys of Christophe's development. Christophe's grandfather set him on the path of composing, and his Uncle Gottfried taught him to respect music. He saw the faults of the composers around him, and labored to avoid those faults in his own work. He struggled always to make his work *true*. He was torn between the instincts of his family and those of his genius; this struggle is at the heart of the novel. Christophe's "progress" seems to move inevitably from the horror of his grandfather's death, to the importance of his first friendship at fifteen with Otto, to the civilizing influence of Frau von Kerich and the beauty and pain of his first love for Minna.

Occasionally, the reader wonders if it is really necessary to learn about each and every quarrel in which Christophe is involved or to see every suffering moment and witness every betrayal and agonized failure. The catalogue of pain is somewhat excessive. The moral growth of the protagonist is shown with special sensitivity, begining with the religious crisis that he experiences in his late teens. Before then, he does not have time or education enough to consider philosophical or religious questions. Sabine's sudden death teaches him another painful lesson about the injustices of life, but, perhaps it is Ada who teaches him the most of the inconsistencies of the human heart and the treacherousness of life. Ada, ignorant and vain, petty and jealous, with nothing appealing about her but her physical appearance, is particularly well-drawn. She hates Christophe's music because she hates anything that she cannot understand, but Christophe is captivated by her until he catches her in an affair with his brother. The least sympathetic characters, such as Ada, are often the best drawn in the book.

The narrator holds up Christophe as an example of a man who refuses to give up in the face of defeat, a man who is made stronger by setbacks. The theme of endurance, survival at all costs, is important in the book. If Christophe can be said to possess any one outstanding characteristic, it is tenacity. Perhaps it begins when his uncle Gottfried tells him that what men *will* and what they *do* are seldom the same, but the important thing is never to give up either. Christophe becomes disillusioned with both German and French music, because he feels it is filled with cheating and superficialities. He realizes that honesty must be everything to him. The novel, in large part, is the story of this honesty confronting the sham and lying of the world. Life is always a struggle for Christophe; without his music and friendships, he would not be able to endure the hardships that he faces. The theme of the importance of friendship runs through the many volumes of *Jean-Christophe*; Olivier recalls Otto of so many years before. But Christophe realizes that he is a man alone; it is the man who counts only on his own efforts in life and does not lean on others who wins the author's respect. Rolland does not moralize, but he makes his opinions clear. *Jean-Christophe* is more than the romantic story of a struggling young musician; intellectual and moral beliefs play an important part in the narrative.

The account of the world of the arts, and particularly music, as no more than a great marketplace is superbly detailed. A better indictment of Philistinism has never been written. Christophe's vain efforts to find an unmercenary musician or writer are poignantly described. The section of Christophe's confrontation with the artistic establishment of Paris is well-written, although at times it turns into a diatribe. The book is filled with many intellectual conversations about the arts, politics, science, and philosophy, as well as about psychology and human nature. Christophe is amazed and horrified, in particular, by French politics. The descriptions of Christophe's first impressions of Paris and later efforts to succeed in the French capital are fascinating, filled with both humorous and pathetic details. Vast numbers of characters pass through the book, many only slightly touching Christophe's life; this device stresses Christophe's immersion in the world. He moves in a complex and real society, and he cannot retreat into isolation.

The frustrations and ultimate successes of the protagonist are detailed fully, but Christophe is one of those true artists who creates without hope of glory. Despite loneliness, illness, and poverty, Christophe is patient; he feels that suffering purifies the soul, a romantic notion that runs throughout the book. *Jean-Christophe* is an immense achievement, perhaps somewhat dated in its romantic attitudes, but nonetheless impressive.

Bruce D. Reeves

JEFFERSON AND HAMILTON:
THE STRUGGLE FOR DEMOCRACY IN AMERICA

Type of work: Political history
Author: Claude G. Bowers (1878-1958)
Time: End of the Eighteenth century
Locale: New York, Philadelphia, Washington, Paris, and London
First published: 1925

Principal *personages:*
GEORGE WASHINGTON
THOMAS JEFFERSON
ALEXANDER HAMILTON
GOUVERNEUR MORRIS
JAMES MADISON
ALBERT GALLATIN, a Jeffersonian from Pennsylvania
AARON BURR
MRS. WILLIAM BINGHAM, a social leader of Philadelphia
JOHN JAY, United States Minister to Great Britain
THOMAS PINCKNEY, United States Minister to Great Britain
CHARLES C. PINCKNEY, Jefferson's opponent for the presidency
JOHN ADAMS, a statesman from Massachusetts

The dramatic and picturesque aspects of the birth of the United States are presented in Claude G. Bowers' book about the political struggle of the last quarter of the eighteenth century. The surrender at Yorktown ended one phase of the Revolution, only to begin another, a battle of fundamentals of government. Should the new republic develop along aristocratic or democratic lines? Leaders in the conflict were Thomas Jefferson, who believed in the political sense of the common people, and Alexander Hamilton, who did not trust an illiterate people to develop government.

Professor Bowers shows how much more logical Hamilton's distrust was than Jefferson's faith in the common man. Yet because Jefferson was willing to try to organize and discipline not only the independent and individualistic towns but the remote farms and the vast open spaces of the West into a unity, he was able, in spite of the weaknesses and lack of ability of his helpers, to achieve success against a powerful opposition. Hamilton, despite his genius and the unquestioned ability of many in the Federalist Party, failed because he did not understand his countrymen and the spirit of the times.

Though Jefferson's name heads the title, Bowers begins his study with a look at Alexander Hamilton after setting the stage in the capital of New York City, on September 12, 1789, as the Congress was about to meet. As he points out, Hamilton looked the born leader. Though he was not of commanding stature, he impressed men by the dignity of his bearing. But Hamilton had other qualities: an ability to write clearly and to assemble and present facts to convince an audience and not merely appeal to their emotions. Strangely, Hamilton was most certain of his genius as a military leader, though never given an opportunity to demonstrate it. He was honest and generally a man of integrity, with a capacity for long stretches of concentrated work.

Bowers also points out his flaws. Perhaps his success, despite his humble origin, and the praise given his brilliant youthful efforts had convinced him that he was superior to most people. Therefore he was unable to inspire enthusiastic co-operation. He showed himself opinionated and dictatorial, and his early insults to Jefferson in Cabinet meetings grew out of his feeling that he was really Washington's Prime Minister. Jefferson disliked him as a man, in addition to distrusting his political beliefs.

The first step in the Jefferson contest with Hamilton was taken when James Madison tried in Congress in April, 1790, to force discrimination between the Revolutionary soldiers holding warrants given in payment of wages, and the speculators who had been buying them at a small portion of their value. After the House voted down his motion, it was learned that nearly half of those opposing had been acquiring warrants, confident that they would be redeemed at full value.

This was a set-back for the Jeffersonians, but the public discussion that followed helped defeat by a few votes Hamilton's next proposal that the government assume the debts of the states. Great was the consternation of speculators who had counted on passage of the proposal.

On March 24, 1790, Thomas Jefferson, Secretary of State for the United States, had arrived in New York. He was willing to agree to a reconsideration of the Assumption Bill, in return for moving the capital out of New York. But following its transfer to Philadelphia, he rarely agreed again with Hamilton. They clashed over Hamilton's plan to use an excise tax on liquor as means of raising money to pay off the states' debts. But when the Federal machine pushed the bill through, Jefferson, having reached the end of his patience, prepared to challenge the policies and powers of his political opponent.

So far there had been no clash over their basic conflict. That came when Jefferson sent to a Philadelphia printer a copy of Thomas Paine's *The Rights of Man*, with a covering note expressing his delight at this reply to the political heresies of the time. The printer used Jefferson's letter, under his signature as Secretary of State, for the preface to the work. Many Americans, to whom democracy was anathema and republicanism was viewed with cynicism, were enraged that a pamphlet suppressed in England should be reprinted in the United States; but

the discussion aroused served Jefferson's purpose and was actually the opening move in the ten-year war between Jefferson and Hamilton.

The Federalists were well organized. The various Chambers of Commerce were like Federalist clubs; the intellectuals mostly championed Hamilton; and the press was generally either for him or indifferent. However, Jefferson believed he could count on the farmers, the ex-soldiers cheated of their war pay, those exasperated by the excise tax, and liberals antagonistic to the aristocratic pose of those governing them.

Earlier, Jefferson had declared that he would rather have a newspaper without a government than a government without a newspaper. Now he set out to find a journal equivalent to the *Gazette of the United States*, edited by John Fenno to extol the Federalist doctrine. For him Madison turned up Philip Freneau, the "poet of the Revolution," who founded *The National Gazette* in Philadelphia. Soon its bold satire had everybody talking.

Angry, Hamilton made anonymous attacks on Freneau, and the struggle became so violent that President Washington tried to bring peace, but the approaching political campaign, which eventually made Adams president, provided more ammunition for the battles between the Federalists and the Jeffersonians.

The outbreak of the French Revolution helped Jefferson, for his was the popular side. Hamilton's followers, on the other hand, sympathized with the French aristocracy. The beheading of the French monarchs swung the scales. The Federalist war party was able to pass the Alien and Sedition Acts giving the President power to expel dangerous aliens and to punish citizens who defamed the government. Jefferson then won a victory over the Federalists by easing tensions caused by the XYZ Papers. But the final confrontation came on the eve of the election of 1800, in the new capital of

Washington.

Most Federalists were scheming to elect Aaron Burr instead of Jefferson. Hamilton was too great a patriot, despite his personal feelings about his rival, to favor Burr, and so he helped make possible the outcome of ten days of balloting, the election of Jefferson to the presidency of the United States.

After that, Hamilton went into isolation. The brilliant party he had created had fallen, as he himself would fall four years later before Burr's pistol. Ex-president Adams, for whom Bowers displays a lukewarm admiration, returned to Massachusetts. But as Jefferson took his oath of office, there was on the political scene evidence of the right of the common people to create their own government and make their own laws.

JENNIE GERHARDT

Type of work: Novel
Author: Theodore Dreiser (1871-1945)
Type of plot: Naturalism
Time of plot: The last two decades of the nineteenth century
Locale: Chicago and various other Midwestern cities
First published: 1911

Principal characters:
JENNIE GERHARDT
WILLIAM GERHARDT, her father
MRS. GERHARDT, her mother
SEBASTIAN GERHARDT, her brother
SENATOR BRANDER, Jennie's first lover
VESTA, Jennie's daughter
MRS. BRACEBRIDGE, Jennie's employer in Cleveland
LESTER KANE, a carriage manufacturer, Jennie's second lover
ROBERT KANE, Lester's brother
MRS. LETTY PACE GERALD, a widow, Lester's childhood sweetheart,
later his wife

Critique:

Jennie Gerhardt, like other of Dreiser's novels, tells the story of a beautiful and vital young girl who is beaten by the forces of life. Jennie's nobility, her willingness to sacrifice herself for her family and others, is part of the reason why she finds herself cast off by society and victimized by the accident of her humble birth. The forces that defeat Jennie are not malign or cruel (her seducers, for example, do not toy with her cynically and cast her aside); rather, these forces are accidental and inevitable, yielding the notion that all human life is diverted from its purpose and its self-control by the casual forces of nature. Jennie, in Dreiser's terms, neither sins nor is overwhelmingly sinned against; things simply do not work out happily for the heroine in Dreiser's naturalistic world. This novel again demonstrates the inevitable play of external forces that are stronger than man's will or purpose. The full social and economic details of the work provide an interesting picture of urban life in the Middle West at the end of the nineteenth century.

The Story:

Jennie Gerhardt, the beautiful and virtuous eighteen-year-old, was the eldest of six children of a poor. hard-working German family in Columbus, Ohio, in 1880. Her father, a glass blower, was ill, and Jennie and her mother were forced to work at a local hotel in order to provide for the younger children in the family. Jennie did the laundry for the kind and handsome Senator Brander (he was fifty-two at the time), and attracted his eye. Senator Brander was kind to Jennie and her family. When he was able to keep Jennie's brother Sebastian out of jail for stealing some needed coal from the railroad, Jennie, full of gratitude, allowed him to sleep with her. Senator Brander, struck by Jennie's beauty, charm, and goodness, promised to marry her. He died suddenly, however, while on a trip to Washington.

Left alone, Jennie discovered that she was pregnant. Her father, a stern Lutheran, insisted that she leave the house, but her more understanding mother allowed her to return when her father, now in better health, left to find work in Youngstown. Jennie's child was a daughter whom she named Vesta. At Sebastian's suggestion, the family moved to Cleveland to find work. While her mother looked after Vesta, Jennie found a job as a maid in the home of Mrs. Bracebridge. One of Mrs. Bracebridge's guests, Lester Kane, the son of a rich carriage manufacturer, found Jennie temptingly attractive. When he tried to seduce Jennie, the girl, though greatly attracted to him, managed to put off his advances.

Mr. Gerhardt was injured in a glass-blowing accident and lost the use of both of his hands. Again, the family needed money badly, and Jennie decided to accept Lester's offer of aid for her family. The price was that she become his mistress, go on a trip to New York with him, and then allow him to establish her in an apartment in Chicago. Although Jennie loved Lester, she knew that he did not intend to marry her because his family would be horrified at such an alliance, but once again she sacrificed her virtue because she felt that her family needed the offered aid. After Jennie had become Lester's mistress, he gave her family money for a house. Jennie was afraid, however, to tell Lester about the existence of her daughter Vesta.

Jennie and Lester moved to Chicago and lived there. Her family began to suspect that, contrary to what Jennie had told them, she and Lester were not married. When Mrs. Gerhardt died, several years later, Jennie moved Vesta to Chicago and boarded the child in another woman's house. One night Jennie was called because Vesta was seriously ill, and Lester discovered Vesta's existence. Although upset at first, when Jennie told him the story, Lester understood and agreed to allow Vesta to live with them. They soon moved to a house in Hyde Park, a middle-class residential district in Chicago. Mr. Gerhardt, now old and ill and willing to accept the situation between Jennie and Lester, also came to live with them and to tend the furnace and the lawn.

Although they were constantly aware of the increasing disapproval of Lester's family, Jennie and Lester lived happily for a time. Lester's father, violently op-posed to the relationship with Jennie, whom he had never met, threatened to disinherit Lester if he did not leave her. Lester's brother Robert urged his father on and attempted to persuade Lester to abandon Jennie. Nevertheless, Lester felt that he owed his allegiance, as well as his love, to her, and he remained with her in spite of the fact that they were snubbed by most of Lester's society connections.

When Lester's father died, still believing that his son's relationship with Jennie demonstrated irresponsibility, he left Lester's share of the estate in trust with Robert. Lester was given three alternatives: he could leave Jennie and receive all his money; he could marry Jennie and receive only $10,000 a year for life, or he could continue his present arrangement with the knowledge that if he did not either abandon or marry Jennie within three years, he would lose his share of the money. Characteristically, Lester hesitated. He took Jennie to Europe, where they met Mrs. Letty Pace Gerald, a beautiful and accomplished widow who had been Lester's childhood sweetheart and who was still fond of him. In the meantime Robert had expanded the carriage business into a monopoly and eased Lester into a subordinate position. When Lester returned to Chicago, he decided to attempt to make an independent future for himself and Jennie. He put a good deal of money into a real estate deal and lost it. Mrs. Gerald also moved to Chicago in pursuit of Lester.

After old Mr. Gerhardt died, Jennie found herself in a difficult situation. Lester, out of the family business because of her, was finding it difficult to earn a living. Mrs. Gerald and Robert's lawyers kept pressing her to release him, claiming this suggestion was for his own economic and social good. Jennie, always altruistic, began to influence Lester to leave her. Before long both were convinced that separation was the only solution so that Lester could return to the family business. Finally Lester left Jennie. Later he set up a house and an income for her and Vesta in a cottage an hour or so from the center of Chicago.

Once more established in the family business, Lester married Mrs. Gerald. Six months after Lester had left Jennie, Vesta, a fourteen-year-old girl already showing a good deal of sensitivity and talent, died of typhoid fever.

Jennie, calling herself Mrs. Stover, moved to the city and adopted two orphan children. Five years passed. Jennie, although still in love with Lester, accepted her quiet life. At last she was able to cope with experience in whatever terms it presented itself to her, even though she had never been able to impose her will on experience in any meaningful way.

One night, Lester, having suffered a heart attack while in Chicago on some business matters, sent for Jennie; his wife was in Europe and could not reach Chicago for three weeks. Jennie tended Lester throughout his last illness. One day he confessed that he had always loved her, that he had made a mistake ever to permit the forces of business and family pressure to make him leave her. Jennie felt that his final confession, his statement that he should never have left her, indicated a kind of spiritual union and left her with something that she could value for the rest of her life. Lester died.

Jennie realized that she would now be forced to live through many years that could promise no salvation, no new excitement—that would simply impose themselves upon her as had the years in the past. She was resolved to accept her loneliness because she knew there was nothing else for her to do.

Jennie went to see Lester's coffin loaded on the train. She realized then, even more clearly, that man was simply a stiff figure, moved about by circumstance. Virtue, beauty, moral worth could not save man; nor could evil or degeneracy. Man simply yielded and managed the best he could under the circumstances of his nature, the society, and the economic force that surrounded him.

Further Critical Evaluation of the Work:

In his second novel, *Jennie Gerhardt,* Theodore Dreiser continues his exploration of themes first introduced in *Sister Carrie.* Central to the novel's vision is Dreiser's belief that the misery in people's lives arises from the conflict between natural human instincts and artificial social and moral standards. Man denies his basic animal appetites, condemning them because they violate the codes of society; yet, ironically, he himself has not only created, but come to believe in, those very social mores which thwart his true desires and bring him great unhappiness. Thus, Jennie is condemned by society for acting on motives of selfless love and generosity. She violates moral codes in becoming Lester Kane's mistress, although she does so in order to save her family from poverty; and when that relationship proves to be a loving and happy one, it is nevertheless considered sinful because it lacks the legal sanction of a marriage license. Likewise, Lester's natural desires are blocked on both sides: if he marries Jennie he will be disinherited and ostracized for marrying beneath his social class, while if he does not, he will be condemned for "living in sin."

In terms of the novel, the people most guilty of perpetuating a social framework so destructive of human happiness are the fathers, who represent the rigid old morality. Mr. Gerhardt, who stands for the blindness and bigotry of religious conviction, turns his own daughter out of her home for trying to help him in a time of financial distress. For similar reasons, Mr. Kane condemns his son's alliance with Jennie, although for his moral arbiter he has replaced the Christian God with the gods of money and respectability.

Within the naturalistic vision embodied in *Jennie Gerhardt,* man is seen as a powerless victim, a creature without free will who therefore lacks the means to control his own destiny. It would be a mistake, however, to assume that, in the absence of free will, chance rules men's lives. It is true that the story of Jennie's career is filled with chance incidents which seemingly bring about important changes in her life; but actually, these chance occurrences are mere catalysts. What really dictates the course which each character's life takes is his or her temperament and personality. Dreiser creates in each character a particular set of limitations which predetermine how he or she will respond to any new circumstances. Thus, when it appears that Jennie or Lester have a free choice to make between two alternatives, what is actually the case is that their respective temperaments cause them to choose as they do. Given Jennie's generous and caring nature, she has no choice but to become Lester's mistress; given Lester's lack of ambition, and his love of an easy life, it is inevitable that he leave Jennie in order to secure his inheritance. By the same token, such seemingly crucial chance events as Senator Brander's untimely death or Letty Pace Gerald's sudden appearance do not materially affect the characters' lives in the long run; if it were not for these *particular* two incidents, some other incidents would eventually occur through which Jennie and Lester would play out the inevitable roles determined for them by the essential qualities of their personalities.

JERUSALEM DELIVERED

Type of work: Poem
Author: Torquato Tasso (1544-1595)
Type of plot: Historical romance
Time of plot: Middle Ages
Locale: The Holy Land
First published: 1580-1581

Principal characters:
GODFREY DE BOUILLON, leader of the Crusaders
CLORINDA, a female warrior
ARGANTES, a pagan knight
ERMINIA, princess of Antioch
ARMIDA, an enchantress
RINALDO, an Italian knight
TANCRED, a Frankish knight

Critique:

Jerusalem Delivered is one of the great poems to come out of the Italian Renaissance, and since that time the work has remained a landmark of heroic literature. The treatment of the Crusades is highly romantic, with both God and Satan freely taking an active part and magicians, angels, and fiends frequently changing the course of events. The descriptions of the fighting are in the typical romantic, chivalric vein. The action is rapid, scene following scene in kaleidoscopic review. In all, we have here an absorbing tale.

The Story:

For six years the Crusaders had remained in the Holy Land, meeting with success. Tripoli, Antioch, and Acre were in their hands, and a large force of Christian knights occupied Palestine. Yet there was a lassitude among the nobles; they were tired and satiated with fighting. They could not generate enough warlike spirit to continue to the real objective of their Crusade, the capture of Jerusalem.

In the spring of the seventh year, God sent the Archangel Gabriel to Godfrey de Bouillon, ordering him to assemble all his knights and encouraging him to begin the march on Jerusalem. Obeying the Lord's command, Godfrey called a council of the great nobles and reminded them stirringly of their vows. When Peter the Hermit added his exhortations,

the Crusaders accepted their charge, and all preparations were make to attack the Holy City.

Within the walls of Jerusalem the wicked King Aladine heard of the projected attack. At the urging of Ismeno the sorcerer he sent soldiers to steal the statue of the Virgin Mary, hoping to make the Christian symbol a palladium for Jerusalem. But next morning the statue had disappeared. Enraged when he could not find the culprit who had spirited away the statue, Aladine ordered a general massacre of all his Christian subjects. To save her co-religionists, the beautiful and pure Sophronia confessed to the theft. Aladine had her bound to the stake. As her guards were about to light the fire, Olindo, who had long loved Sophronia in vain, attempted to save her by confessing that he himself had stolen the statue.

Aladine ordered them both burned. While they were at the stake, Sophronia admitted her love for Olindo. They were saved from burning, however, by the arrival of Clorinda, a beautiful woman warrior who knew that both were admitting the theft to save the other Christians from death. Released, Sophronia and Olindo fled from the city.

Clorinda was a great warrior who scorned female dress. On a previous campaign she had met Tancred, a mighty Christian noble, and Tancred had fall in love with her; but she rejected his love. On the other hand, Erminia of Antioch had become enamored of Tancred when he had taken her city, but Tancred felt only friendship for her.

The Christians came within sight of Jerusalem. A foraging party encountered first a small force under Clorinda. She was so valorous that she defeated them.

The King of Egypt, whose army was advancing to the aid of Jerusalem, sent Argantes to parley with Godfrey. The Crusader chief haughtily rejected the overtures of the Egyptians, and Argantes angrily joined the infidel defenders of the Holy City. Although the Crusaders met with some initial successes, Argantes was always a formidable opponent.

Satan was annoyed at the prospect of the fall of Jerusalem. He induced Armida, an enchantress, to visit the Christian camp and tell a false story of persecution. Many of the knights succumbed to her wiles and eagerly sought permission to redress her wrongs. Godfrey was suspicious of her, but he allowed ten knights chosen by lot to accompany her. In the night forty others slipped away to join her, and she led the fifty to her castle where she changed them into fishes. Their loss was a great blow to Godfrey because the pagans were slaying many of his men.

Rinaldo, one of the Italian knights among the Crusaders, sought the captaincy of a band of Norwegian adventurers. Gernando, who sought the same post, quarreled with him, and in a joust Gernando was killed. For this breach of discipline Rinaldo was banished.

When Argantes challenged to personal combat any champion in the Crusaders' camp, Tancred was chosen to meet him. On the way to the fight, Tancred saw Clorinda and stopped to admire her. Otho, his companion, took advantage of his bemusement and rushed in ahead to the battle. Otho was defeated by Argantes and taken prisoner. Then Tancred, realizing what had happened, advanced to meet the pagan knight. Both men were wounded in the mighty, day-

long duel. They retired to recuperate, agreeing to meet again in six days.

When Erminia heard of Tancred's wounds, she put on Clorinda's armor and went to his camp to attend him. He heard of her coming and waited impatiently, thinking his beloved Clorinda was approaching. But Erminia was surprised by the sentries, and in her maidenly timidity she ran away to take refuge with a shepherd.

When the supposed Clorinda did not arrive, Tancred went in search of her and came to the castle of Armida, where he was cast into a dungeon.

Godfrey received word that Sweno, Prince of Denmark, who had been occupying Palestine, had been surprised by pagan knights and killed with all his followers. The messenger announced that he had been divinely appointed to deliver Sweno's sword to Rinaldo. Although Rinaldo was still absent, Godfrey set out to avenge the Palestine garrison.

Godfrey and his army fought valiantly, but Argantes and Clorinda were fighters too powerful for the shaken Christians to overcome. Then Tancred and the fifty knights, who had been freed from Armida's enchantment, arrived to rout the pagans with great losses. Godfrey learned that the missing men had been liberated by Rinaldo. Peter the Hermit was then divinely inspired to foretell the glorious future of Rinaldo.

In preparation for the attack on Jerusalem the Christians celebrated a solemn mass on the Mount of Olives before they began the assault. Wounded by one of Clorinda's arrows, Godfrey retired from the battle while an angel healed his wound. The Christians set up rams and towers to break the defense of the city.

At night Clorinda came out of the city walls and set fire to the great tower by which the Christians were preparing to scale the wall. She was seen, however, by the Crusaders, and Tancred engaged her in combat. After he had run his sword through her breast, he discovered to his sorrow that he had killed his love.

He had time to ask her pardon and baptize her before her death.

Godfrey was taken in a vision to heaven where he talked with Hugh, the former commander of the French forces. Hugh bade him recall Rinaldo, and Godfrey sent two knights to find the banished Italian. On the Fortunate Islands the messengers discovered the Palace of Armida where Rinaldo, having fallen in love with the enchantress, was dallying with his lady love. The sight of the two knights quickly reminded him of his duty. Leaving his love, he joined the besieging forces of Godfrey.

With the arrival of Rinaldo, the Christians were greatly heartened. Then the Archangel Michael appeared to Godfrey and showed him the souls of all the Christians who had died in the Crusades. With this inspiration, the Crusaders redoubled their efforts to capture Jerusalem.

The walls of the city were breached. Tancred met Argantes and killed him in single combat. Finally the victorious invaders stormed through the streets and sacked the Holy City. When the Egyptians arrived to help the pagan defenders of Jerusalem, they too were beaten and their king was slain by Godfrey. Armida, all hope gone, surrendered herself to Rinaldo, who had been the most valorous of the conquerors.

After the fighting was over, Godfrey and all his army worshiped at the Holy Sepulchre.

Further Critical Evaluation of the Work:

As the son of a poet, Torquato Tasso grew up knowing the hardships and insecurities of the poet's life, but he could not be dissuaded from his own pursuit of poetry and a career as a court poet. After thorough grounding in the classics, Tasso wrote in Italian. Early success with *Rinaldo,* a narrative poem, was followed by his two best works: *Aminta,* a pastoral play, and *Jerusalem Delivered (Gerusalemme Liberata),* a romantic epic completed when he was hardly thirty years old. His later works included a tragic drama, a biblical poem, and *Jerusalem Conquered (Gerusalemme Conquistata),* an ill-advised and best-forgotten revision of his masterpiece. In his lifetime, Tasso also produced a prodigious quantity of lyric poems. But in his thirty-third year, he was afflicted with severe mental illness which required his confinement off and on until his death, only days before he was to be awarded the laurel wreath for poetic achievement.

Jerusalem Delivered is a literary epic divided into twenty cantos of *ottava rima* (an eight-line stanza rhyming abababcc). The historical matter of the poem deals with the First Crusade (1097-1099). In substance, however, it reflects the renewed power of Catholicism in Tasso's time, in the wake of the establishment of the Holy Office. Yet, in structure, it clearly shows the influence of Tasso's classical education as well as the contemporary vogue for classical rules of poetics. The central issues developed in the plot are the effectiveness—or ineffectivenss—of Godfry's military ladership; the banishment and infatuation of Rinaldo; and the three-sided love relationship among Tancred, Clorinda, and Erminia. All of these issues bear on the final victory of Christendom over the pagans. Other aspects of the poem become important as elements in its romantic attitude. Magic, in particular, plays a heavy part in the romantic quality of the poem: the enchantress Armida, the angel who heals Godfrey's wounds, and Godfrey's visions of Hugh and of Archangel Michael. Other super-human (Clorinda's warrior-like skills) and super-natural (Satan's intervention in the early success of the Christian campaign) occurrences contribute to the romantic atmosphere. Likewise, the ultimate triumph of Good over Evil indicates the romantic orientation of the poem. The artful integration of all of these many features places *Jerusalem Delivered* in the front ranks of the Italian epic tradition in the Renaissance.

THE JEW OF MALTA

Type of work: Drama
Author: Christopher Marlowe (1564-1593)
Type of plot: Romantic tragedy
Time of plot: Fifteenth century
Locale: Malta
First presented: c. 1589

Principal characters:
BARABAS, a Jewish merchant
ABIGAIL, his daughter
ITHAMORE, a slave
THE GOVERNOR OF MALTA

Critique:

The Machiavellian character of Barabas dominates *The Jew of Malta;* the other characters are merely sketched in. The plot of the play seems to have come wholly from the fertile mind of Marlowe, whose exotic plots and romantic heroes set a pattern which was followed by subsequent Elizabethan playwrights, including Shakespeare. Mechanically, *The Jew of Malta* begins well, but it degenerates into an orgy of blood after the second act.

The Story:

Barabas, a Christian-hating merchant of Malta, received in his counting-house a party of merchants who reported the arrival of several vessels laden with wealth from the East. At the same time three Jews arrived to announce an important meeting at the senate.

The import of the meeting was that the Turkish masters of Malta had demanded tribute long overdue. The Turkish Grand Seignior had purposely let the payment lapse over a period of years so that the Maltese would find it impossible to raise the sum demanded. The Maltese had a choice of payment or surrender. The Christian governor of the island, attempting to collect the tribute within a month, decreed that the Jews would have to give over half of their estates or become Christians. All of the Jewish community except Barabas submitted to the decree of the governor in one way or another. The governor seized all of Barabas' wealth as punishment and had the

Jew's house turned into a Christian convent.

Barabas, to avoid complete ruin, purposely failed to report part of his treasure hidden in the foundation of his house. Then he persuaded his daughter, Abigail, to pretend that she had been converted to Christianity so that she might enter the convent and recover the treasure. Abigail dutifully entered the nunnery as a convert and subsequently threw the bags of money out of the window at night to her waiting father.

Martin Del Bosco, vice-admiral of Spain, sailed into the harbor of Malta for the purpose of selling some Turkish slaves he had aboard his ship. The governor was reluctant to allow the sale because of the difficulties he was having with the Grand Seignior. Del Bosco, by promising military aid from Spain, persuaded the governor to defy the Turks and to permit the sale.

Barabas bought one of the slaves, an Arabian named Ithamore. During the sale, Barabas fawned upon Don Lodowick, the governor's son, and Don Mathias. He invited the two young men to his house and ordered Abigail, now returned from the convent, to show favor to both. In his desire for revenge, Barabas arranged with each young man, separately, to marry his daughter. He then sent forged letters to Don Lodowick and Don Mathias, and provoked a duel in which the young men were killed. Meanwhile Barabas trained his slave, Ithamore, to be his creature in his plot against the governor and the Christians of Malta. Because of her father's evil intentions, Abigail returned to the convent. Barabas, enraged, sent poisoned porridge to the convent as his gesture of thanks on the Eve of St. Jacques, the patron saint of Malta. All in the convent were poisoned, and Abigail, before she died, confessed to Friar Jacomo, disclosing to him all that Barabas had done and all that he planned to do.

When the Turks returned to Malta to collect the tribute, the governor defied them and prepared for a siege of the island.

Meanwhile the friars, in violation of canon law, revealed the information they had gained from Abigail's confession. Barabas, again threatened, pretended a desire to become a convert and promised all of his worldly wealth to the friars who would receive him into the Christian faith. The greediness of the friars caused differences to arise among them; Barabas took advantage of this situation and with the help of Ithamore strangled a friar named Bernardine. He then propped up Bernardine's body in such a way that Friar Jacomo knocked it down. Observed in this act, Friar Jacomo was accused of the murder of one of his clerical brothers.

Ithamore met a strumpet, Bellamira, who, playing upon the slave's pride and viciousness, persuaded him to extort money from his master by threatening to expose Barabas. His master, alarmed by threats of blackmail, disguised himself as a French musician, went to the strumpet's house, and poisoned Bellamira and Ithamore with a bouquet of flowers.

Before their deaths, they managed to communicate all they knew to the governor, who, despite his preoccupation with the fortifications of Malta, threw Barabas into prison. By drinking poppy essence and cold mandrake juice, Barabas appeared to be dead. His body was placed outside the city. Reviving, he joined the Turks and led them into the city. As a reward for his betraying Malta, Barabas was made governor. He now turned to the conquered Maltese, offering to put the Turks into their hands for a substantial price.

Under the direction of Barabas, explosives were set beneath the barracks of the Turkish troops. Then Barabas invited the Turkish leaders to a banquet in the governor's palace, after planning to have them fall through a false floor into cauldrons of boiling liquid beneath. On signal, the Turkish troops were blown sky-high, but the Christian governor, who preferred to seize the Turkish leaders alive, exposed Barabas' scheme. The Jew of Malta perished in the trap he had set for the Turks.

Further Critical Evaluation of the Work:

Although Marlowe may have found his initial inspiration for the story and its hero in the person of Juan Michesius, recorded in Philip Lonicerus' *Chronicorum Turcicorum* and in Belleforest's *Cosmographie Universelle,* it is clear from a comparison that the character of Barabas in this play owes at least as much to the tradition of Italian revenge tragedy, to the English morality plays, and to his own preferences in characterization as demonstrated in *Faustus* and in *Tamburlaine.* Considered the most important English dramatist before Shakespeare, Marlowe's social background was similar to that of his illustrious successor, although Marlowe's formal schooling was more extensive just as his theatrical career was, unfortunately, much briefer. Perhaps it was because he himself was gripped by a master passion that Marlowe constructed his greatest plays around characters obsessed with one thing or another; for them, the obsession itself is all-imporant, not particularly its object.

Marlowe has been given credit for raising the formerly stilted and academic English theater to the level of a both serious and entertaining art.

Though *The Jew of Malta* is written in Marlowe's most masterful and fully-developed style, it nonetheless remains an enigmatic and difficult play because of the unevenness of its structural impact and emotional effect. Perhaps this is inevitable in the very combination of the morality drama with the drama of personality; it is hard to maintain Barabas as both a typical figure of evil and as a sympathetic, understandable person in his own right. Although the play is usually considered a "romantic tragedy" or a "tragedy of blood," T. S. Eliot considered it a farce, characterized by "terribly serious even savage comic humor." What is certain is its thematic resemblance to Marlowe's other great plays. With *The Tragedy of Doctor Faustus* and *Tamburlaine, The Jew of Malta* shares a concern with exploring the limits of human power; a self-made hero who rises to power from lowly origins, compelled to his own end by an over-arching passion; and the play itself is unified by this hero's personality alone. Moreover *The Jew of Malta* is Marlowe's first Machiavellian play, the first in which the word "policy" appears. As he speaks at the play's opening, Machiavelli embodies in general and final fashion the vices that Barabas' history will reenact: unbounded greed, accompanied by a complete absence of conscience or moral scruples. In many senses, a major theme of the play is amorality rather than immorality—the amorality displayed by Ferneze as a representative of the political realm, or by the friars as representative Catholics, as well as by Barabas himself as a type of the commercial sphere.

The Jew of Malta is critically difficult because of its apparent structural disjunction, as it moves from an emphasis on Barabas' mind and motivations in the first part to a concentration solely upon his evil actions in the second. In the first part, the familiar Marlovian themes are presented. Barabas' Machiavellian egocentrism is apparently well-founded on the hypocrisy of his "Christian" enemies; the splendor of his wealth is delineated, not in the grandiose general terms of *Tamburlaine,* but in appropriate mercantile detail. The scene between Barabas and Ferneze develops the satirical tone, as it seems to contrast the hypocrisy of the Maltese Christians with the Jew's overt wickedness, their greed with his—an extension of the quarrel between Christians and infidels in *Tamburlaine Part Two.* Barabas nearly captures the sympathies of the audience by making us believe that he will suffer from Ferneze's decree; and that decree *is* manifestly unjust.

In the second part, as the play moves from what M. C. Bradbrook calls the "technique of verse" to the "technique of action," we see that Barabas has fooled the audience; his subterfuge thereby exposes him now as the completely villainous Machiavellian. Marlowe therefore no longer presents introspective revelations of Barabas' mental and emotional processes but turns instead to concentrate on verbal and narrative reversals in the last three acts.

The primary interest now is in clever stage situations and adroit manipulation of the narrative, as, for example, when Barabas constantly reverses his overt meaning by his tagged-on asides. The entrapment of Lodowick and Mathias, of the two friars, of Ithamore and Bellamira, and the final series of double-crosses between Ferneze, Calymath, and Barabas, are obviously influenced by the revenge tragedy tradition as brought to England by Kyd's *The Spanish Tragedy*. The plot of *The Jew of Malta*, then, is largely episodic, constructed through the "symmetrical pairing" of a series of figures around that of Barabas: the three Jews at the beginning, the abbess and the nun, Mathias and Lodowick, Friar Bernardine and Friar Jacomo, Bellamira and Pilia-Borsa, the Calymath and Del Bosco.

The focus of the play is Barabas' own character. He is at one and the same time, according to David M. Bevington, the "lifelike Jewish merchant caught in a political feud," an "embodiment of moral vice," and the "unrepenting protagonist in [a] homiletic 'tragedy.'" Once our initial sympathies for Barabas have vanished, we see him only as the heinous culprit who un-intentionally fashions his own downfall by the very complications of his evil schemes and his ultimate inability to control those around him who, in their own lesser ways, are also evil schemers. It would be, clearly, a mistake to consider Barabas as an epitome of a race persecuted by prejudice; he shows, at the very beginning, that he himself has no more respect for Jews than he does for Christians or Turks. Abigail, before entering the convent for the second time, now in earnest, makes this point when she says, "But I perceive there is no love on earth,/Pity in Jews, nor piety in Turks." Barabas, instead, proclaims himself "a sound Machiavell," as the Prologue predicts, when he instructs Ithamore in the ways of evil: "First, be thou void of these affections,/Compassion, love, vain hope, and heartless fear." It is supremely ironic that he calls Ithamore his "second self," since in the end Barabas murders the slave, figuratively revealing the self-destructive bent of his own narcissistic selfish-ness. On a larger scale, the same irony pervading the entire play is proclaimed in the absurdly righteous closing words of Ferneze: "So, march away; and let due praise be given/Neither to Fate nor Fortune, but to Heaven." Heaven has had little hand in this story; instead, the hand of the pessimistic atheist Marlowe leaves its prints everywhere.

Kenneth John Atchity

THE JEWESS OF TOLEDO

Type of work: Drama
Author: Franz Grillparzer (1791-1872)
Type of plot: Historical tragedy
Time of plot: About 1195
Locale: Toledo and vicinity
First presented: 1872

Principal characters:
ALFONSO VIII, King of Castile
ELEANOR OF ENGLAND, daughter of Henry II, his wife
ISAAC, the Jew
ESTHER, and
RACHEL, his daughters
MANRIQUE, Count of Lara, Almirante of Castile
DON GARCERAN, his son
DOÑA CLARA, lady in waiting to the queen

Critique:

Few writers since Shakespeare have managed to use the dramatic form with the poetic clarity and tragic force exhibited by the Austrian playwright, Franz Grillparzer. Usually the form is too much for the content or the content overburdens the play, giving to exposition the prominence that the expression of passion should have. Grillparzer avoids these faults, and contributes new psychological and moral perspectives which give his work its distinctive quality. *The Jewess of Toledo* tells of a monarch's lapse from duty because of his sudden passionate affection for a beautiful but vain young Jewess. With a simplicity of effect that defies analysis, Grillparzer makes the king's discovery of his own foolish bondage credible, without in the least detracting from the impression that Rachel, the Jewess, for all her faults, was undeniably charming and even to be pitied.

The Story:

Isaac, a Jew, found himself in the royal gardens of Toledo with his two daughters, Rachel and Esther. Realizing that the king was about to visit the gardens and that no Jews should be there during the royal outing, he urged his daughters to hurry from the gardens. Rachel laughingly refused, declaring that she would stay and see if the king was

as young and handsome as she had heard. Isaac answered that Rachel was like her mother, for his second wife had found the Christians charming and had had eyes for nothing but fine clothing, jewels, and banquets. Esther, on the other hand, was like her mother, Isaac's first wife, who had been as good as she was poor.

Rachel sang and danced about while waiting for the king. She told her father that perhaps the monarch would find her charming, would pinch her cheek, and make the queen jealous. Isaac, frightened more than ever, hastened to leave the gardens with Esther.

When King Alfonso appeared, he invited the crowds to draw near him. He explained that the people had made him king while he had been still a child, that they had rallied around him in order to depose his uncle, a tyrant, and that they had then taught him the duties of one who would be just and good. Count Manrique turned to Queen Eleanor and told her of the people's affection for their ruler. The count declared that the present king was the noblest of all who ever ruled in Spain, turning aside petty criticism with wisdom and justice. The king, half jesting, replied that he might be an even better king if he were forced to overcome some fault. He suggested that the protection of the people might have kept

THE JEWESS OF TOLEDO by Franz Grillparzer. Translated by Arthur Burkhard. By permission of the publishers, Register Press, Yarmouth Port, Mass. Copyright, 1953, by Register Press.

him from developing the moral strength a ruler should have.

The king also urged everyone to enjoy the respite between wars, for the Moors were about to start another attempt to invade Spain. He called his wife's attention to the English-type garden he had ordered; he was disappointed that she had not noticed it.

A messenger, Don Garceran, the son of Count Manrique, brought news of the military preparations being made by Jussuf, the ruler of Morocco. Don Garceran was making his first appearance before the king since being assigned to a frontier post for having stolen into the women's quarters of the palace to view Doña Clara, his betrothed.

When the king suggested that the peasants pray to God for victory, Don Garceran replied that the churches were crowded, such was the religious zeal of the people. One sign of mistaken zeal, however, was the rough treatment sometimes given the Jews.

As the king was vowing to protect the Jews and all other of his subjects, he received word that a Jew and two girls were being pursued by the guards. Rachel came running to the group for protection. When Queen Eleanor refused to take her hands, she threw down her bracelet and necklace as ransom and clasped the king's knees. King Alfonso asked Esther, who had joined them, whether Rachel was always timid, and Esther replied that her sister was often too bold, too much a clown. The king, attracted by Rachel, ordered Don Garceran to shelter her in one of the garden houses until night, when there would be no danger of mob action.

After Don Garceran had escorted Isaac and his daughters to a shelter in the garden, the king accosted Don Garceran, questioning him about the family, praising the Jews for their long history, and begging for information about the art of casual love. Isaac, scolding his daughters for not attempting to leave, came from the garden house. He told Don Garceran

that Rachel was her old self again, laughing and singing, and amusing herself by dressing herself as a queen with some masquerade costumes she had found.

Vowing Don Garceran and Isaac to silence, the king entered the garden house in time to observe Rachel, dressed as a queen, pretending to address a portrait of Alfonso which she had removed from its frame. In the role of the queen, Rachel accused the king in the portrait of having been attracted to the Jewess. The monarch interrupted this play and assured the frightened girl that he did indeed like her and that after the war he might ask for her. He asked her to return the portrait to its frame, but she refused. At that moment the arrival of the queen and the royal party forced the king to hide in another room. Count Manrique would have discovered him had not Don Garceran intercepted his father and, in the king's name, put an end to the search.

When the king reappeared after the queen's departure, he realized how he had already shamed himself because of the Jewess, and he asked her to return the portrait and leave with Don Garceran. After she had gone, he found that she had put her own portrait in the frame. The king was instantly stirred by the picture as if some magical spell surrounded it. In confusion, he first ordered his servant to go after Don Garceran and demand the return of his portrait; then he decided to go himself. He also asked about the Castle Retiro where a former king had kept a Moorish girl, but he could not copy such baseness. Finally, giving in to his passion, he went after Rachel.

Later, at Castle Retiro, Isaac was dealing with petitioners to the king, forcing them to pay heavily for the privilege of having their messages conveyed. Rachel complained that King Alfonso did not give enough time to her, and she was upset because her dallying with Don Garceran did not make him jealous. Esther arrived with the news that Queen Eleanor, Count Manrique, and other noblemen were joining in counsel, apparently plotting a revolt against the king. The king, already feeling guilty about neglecting the preparation for war, quickly left with Don Garceran for Toledo. Rachel, convinced that the king had never loved her, found no satisfaction in her perfumes and jewels.

Count Manrique and the noblemen, with the queen present, considered how to deal with the Jewess. Buying her off with gold was suggested, but the king had gold to give her. Imprisoning her would be useless, for the king had the power to release her. Finally, Count Manrique turned to the queen, who softly suggested that death was the answer, death for the woman who had broken the laws of God. Don Garceran interrupted the proceedings with an order from the king to dissolve the meeting. Count Manrique, dismissing the nobles, told them to be prepared for action. He then urged his son to join the rebellion, but Don Garceran refused. The count and the others left.

The king then prevailed upon the queen to listen to him. In a heartfelt conversation he admitted his guilt, calling attention to the changes of heart and mind that are inevitable for man. But the queen was reluctant to place the entire blame on her husband. She accused the girl of using shameless magic. In anger, King Alfonso defended Rachel as one who, for all her faults, had never pretended to a lifeless virtue that made life empty of warmth. He criticized the queen for encouraging his nobles to conspire against him.

The king discovered that the queen had left while he was talking. In growing apprehension he pursued the vassals to Castle Retiro. He arrived too late. The castle was in ruins, and Isaac and Esther told him that Rachel had been killed. To fire his desire for vengeance, the king viewed her body, but the sight of her reminded him not of her charm but of her wanton guile. Reaffirming his duty to the people, he forgave Count Manrique and the others when they appeared, swordless, to learn their punishment. He made his infant son king, with the queen as regent, and set forth for war against the Moors. Esther, at first cynical about the quick atonement of the Christian king, was appalled to find that her father was more concerned about his gold than he was over the tragic event that had involved them all. She confessed that she, her father, and Rachel were as guilty as the Christians.

Further Critical Evaluation of the Work:

Although *The Jewess of Toledo* was first performed in 1872, the five-act tragedy had been completed in the 1850's, and the idea dated back to 1824, when Grillparzer read Lope de Vega's *La Judea de Toledo,* upon which *The Jewess of Toledo* is closely based. Into it he wove not only his own experience of an overpowering sensual love, but also his observation of a major political scandal of the day, the passion of King Ludwig I of Bavaria for the Spanish dancer, Lola Montez, which ended in her banishment and his abdication. The play is thus doubly motivated, and has been criticized as falling into two pieces: a love tragedy and a political tragedy.

In fact, the two are inseparably intertwined. The fortunes of the state are inextricably bound up with the personal fate of the naïve king, just awakening to the power of the senses. His English wife, Eleanor, is coldly virtuous, though not above jealousy, but it is Rachel to whose charms he succumbs so utterly as to neglect his duty as king. Rachel is a creature of impulse, not of deep emotion, and embodies the absence of moral obligation. Queen Eleanor places duty above all, but lacks warmth and sensuality. It is the king's tragedy and the tragedy of the state, that this division of attributes places his desire and his duty in conflict. His tragedy is, therefore, personal and political. The throne is as good as vacant as the king forgets his divinely ordained role, and the nobles and the queen have no choice but to act to restore the order of the state. In this play, all incur guilt, not so much legal as moral. Rachel pays with her life, and in a sense, so do the king and nobles, as the king embarks upon a crusade against the Moors to atone his guilt by committing his life to the judgment of God in defense of his state.

JOANNA GODDEN

Type of work: Novel
Author: Sheila Kaye-Smith (1888-1956)
Type of plot: Domestic realism
Time of plot: Early twentieth century
Locale: Rural England
First published: 1921

Principal characters:
JOANNA GODDEN, a wealthy landowner
ELLEN GODDEN, her younger sister
ARTHUR ALCE, Joanna's perennial suitor
MARTIN TREVOR, Joanna's betrothed
ALBERT HILL, Joanna's betrayer

Critique:

Joanna Godden is the powerful story of a strong and vibrant woman who ruled her sister and her farm with an iron hand. She herself, however, was often bewildered by emotions she did not understand. When tragedy involved her, she did not let it ruin her as it might have lesser women. She simply marshaled all her forces and went to meet it. That was Joanna's way. The novel is also notable for its atmosphere of the English countryside in all weathers and seasons.

The Story:

After her father's funeral, Joanna Godden took immediate command of her sister Ellen and of the prosperous farm, Little Ansdore. She had always had many notions about making the farm even more productive, and she proposed now to execute these ideas, even though her neighbors and her advisers thought her a stubborn and foolish woman. Her perennial suitor, Arthur Alce, stuck by her, although he knew he could never change Joanna's mind about the farm or about accepting him as a husband.

In addition to the farm, her sister Ellen consumed much of Joanna's energy Ellen must be a lady. To this end she was sent to school and humored in many other ways. But Joanna was the boss. No matter how much she babied Ellen, Joanna still made all decisions for her. Ellen was pliable, but she secretly planned for the day when she could escape her sister's heavy hand.

Little Ansdore prospered under Joanna. She shocked her neighbors by painting her house and wagons in bright colors and by appearing in loud clothing and jewels as soon as the period of mourning was over. In spite of their distrust of her, they were forced to admire her business acumen. Many men failed while she accumulated money in the bank. Through it all, Arthur stood by her and ran her errands. Once she felt stirrings of passion for one of her farm hands, but she quickly subdued the feeling because the ignorant lad was unsuitable. Joanna knew vaguely that she was missing something every woman wanted, something she did not completely understand but still longed for.

When Joanna met Martin Trevor, the son of a neighboring squire, she knew almost at once that Martin was the kind of man she had waited for. Although they were at first antagonistic, they soon were drawn together in real love and announced their engagement. Joanna was happy; Martin made her feel she was a woman first and a successful farmer second. The sensation was novel for Joanna. Martin's father and clergyman brother accepted her, in spite of a social position lower than theirs. Poor Arthur Alce grieved to lose her, even though he had never possessed more than her friendship. He sincerely wished her happiness.

The only thing that dimmed their happiness was Joanna's insistence upon waiting for the wedding until there should be a slack time on the farm. Martin knew that if he gave in to her he would forever play second fiddle to Ansdore. On a walk, one rainy day, he begged her to marry him at once, both to please him and to show him that he was first in her heart. She refused, but at home a few nights later she knew that she must give in, for herself as well as for Martin. When she hurried to his home to see him the next day, she found Martin gravely ill. He had not been strong and the walk in the rain had caused a serious lung congestion. Joanna, realizing that her happiness was not to last, felt no surprise when Martin died. Her grief was so deep that she could feel nothing, only numbness. She felt that she had missed the only real happiness of her life.

The farm claimed her once more, and to it she gave all her energy and hope. Ellen also felt Joanna's will. Seventeen and finished with school, she was a lady. But Joanna was not pleased with her. Ellen had more subdued taste than Joanna, and the two girls clashed over furnishings, clothing, manners, and suitors for Ellen. Ellen usually submitted, but her one ambition was to get out from under Joanna's domination. Marriage seemed her only course. When Joanna began to ask Arthur to escort Ellen various places so that the young girl would not be so bored, Ellen thought it would be a good joke to take Arthur away from Joanna. However, Joanna herself thought a match between Ellen and Arthur would be a good thing. Unknown to Ellen, she asked Arthur to marry her sister. Arthur protested that he loved and would always love Joanna. She, in her usual practical way, overrode his objections and insisted that he marry Ellen. Finally he proposed to Ellen and was accepted. Ellen believed that she had stolen her sister's lover.

At first Ellen was happy with Arthur, for she was genuinely fond of him, but she resented his continuing to run errands for Joanna. She attributed these acts to Joanna's domineering ways, never realizing that her husband still loved her sister. Because Ellen also resented not meeting any of the gentlefolk of the area, Joanna arranged for her to meet Squire Trevor, Martin's father. It was an unfortunate meeting. Ellen became infatuated with the old man, left Arthur, and followed the squire to Dover. When she asked for a divorce, Arthur refused. Joanna was alternately furious with Ellen for her immorality and sorry for her heartbreak. At last Ellen went home to Little Ansdore. Joanna took her in and treated her like a little girl again.

When a neighboring estate, Great Ansdore, was put on the market, Joanna bought it. Her triumph was now complete; she was the wealthiest farmer in the area. New power went with the land. She chose the rector for the village church and in other ways acted as a country squire. But she still longed for Martin; or perhaps only for love. At any rate, when Arthur refused to stay after Ellen came home, Joanna for the first time saw him as a man she might love. Too sensible to risk more trouble from that quarter, however, she brushed off his goodbye kiss and turned her mind back to Ansdore.

After a time Arthur was killed in a hunting accident at his new home. His will, leaving his old farm to Joanna, made Ellen dependent on her sister as before. Ellen was furious, but Joanna could see no harm in Arthur's having left his money to his friend rather than to his faithless wife. Meanwhile Joanna would take care of Ellen, who would no doubt marry again.

Time began to take its toll of Joanna. Following her doctor's advice, she combined a business trip and a vacation. During that time she met Albert Hill, a young man thirteen years her junior. Thinking herself in love with Albert, Joanna the strong, the moral, the domineering, gave herself to the young man.

They planned to marry, but Joanna, on second thought, realized that she did not love Albert, could never marry him. Learning that she was pregnant, she confessed to Ellen, who demanded that she marry Albert to protect their family name. But Joanna wanted her baby to grow up in happiness and peace, not in the home of parents who did not love each other. She would sell Ansdore and go away. As she made her plans, Martin's face came back to her and gave her strength. He would have approved. The past seemed to fuse with the years ahead. Joanna Godden, her home, her sister, her good name, and her lover all gone, still faced the years with courage and with hope.

Further Critical Evaluation of the Work:

Joanna Godden is a novel about a remarkable woman who not only survives, but thrives through her efforts to carve out a niche for herself within a man's world. Her strength and independence are such that she wastes no time after her father's death in building her inherited property, Little Ansdore, into a prosperous farm. This she manages to do at a time when many men are sinking under financially in similar enterprises. Her gift for management and insight into business matters finally earns her the grudging admiration of her neighbors who had been at first so disapproving of what they considered her indecorous and unfeminine behavior.

Sheila Kaye-Smith creates the character of Joanna with skill and sensitivity; her heroine is a vibrantly real figure who blends both strength and vulnerability, sharp judgment and naïveté, staunch independence and the need for human relationships within her personality. Through an unfolding of her interpersonal relationships with her younger sister Ellen, her devoted admirer Arthur, her fiancé Martin, and the father of her child Albert Hill, the author reveals Joanna as a very complex and deep woman. Her almost paternal relationship with Ellen, for example, brings out both the loving and the controlling, dominating sides of her character. In her tender affection and instinctive desire to protect her weaker sister, she exerts such control that the latter feels stifled and longs to escape into some kind of independence.

Likewise in her relationships with men, Joanna is an odd mixture of strong and weak, sensible and foolish. She feels nothing for Arthur, the man who truly loves her. She is actually able to pressure him into marrying Ellen, yet when he finally leaves Little Ansdore, she begins to see him as more desirable; and after he is dead, it is his memory and the imagined approval of her actions that give her strength in selling the farm and refusing to marry Albert. When Joanna finally does meet a suitable man in Martin Trevor, her tough-minded devotion to the farm causes her to delay the marriage; she decides too late that Martin's love is more important than the farm: he becomes ill and dies. When an undesirable man comes into her life in the form of Albert Hill, the woman who can unerringly choose the best sheep or barter for the highest price is unable to judge a potential lover wisely. And yet it is this very blend of qualities that make Joanna Godden such a human and sympathetic heroine.

Sheila Kaye-Smith, dubbed the "Sussex novelist" by some critics to suggest a comparison to her contemporary, the "Wessex novelist" Thomas Hardy, sets her story against the rural setting of the Sussex countryside. The novel is rich in local-color detail; it abounds with loving descriptions of both the people, their habits and dialect, and the beauty of the land. In *Joanna Godden,* Kaye-Smith realizes her early ambition, recounted in her autobiography, to become an excellent novelist of rural life; in so doing, she brings that life back for her readers.

JOHN BROWN'S BODY

Type of work: Poem
Author: Stephen Vincent Benét, (1898-1943)
Type of plot: Historical romance
Time of plot: 1859-1865
Locale: The United States
First published: 1928

Principal characters:
JACK ELLYAT, a soldier from Connecticut
CLAY WINGATE, a soldier from Georgia
LUKE BRECKINRIDGE, a Southern mountaineer
MELORA VILAS, Jack Ellyat's beloved
SALLY DUPRÉ, Clay Wingate's fiancée
LUCY WEATHERBY, Sally's rival
SHIPPY, a Union spy
SOPHY, a Richmond hotel employee

Critique:

John Brown's Body, which won the Pulitzer Prize for 1929, tells, in free and formal verse, the tragic story of the Civil War and its effects upon the nation. Benét achieves an effective counterpoint by weaving several small plots concerned with fictional characters into the main plot which we know as the actual history of the time. He manipulates his characters so that important phases of the war are interfused with his minor plots, and the two are carried forward simultaneously. His re-creation of the atmosphere of a burgeoning, adolescent United States is excellent.

The Story:

Jack Ellyat, a Connecticut youth, had premonitions of trouble as he walked with his dog in the mellow New England Indian summer. He and his family were Abolitionists. The influence of Emerson and Thoreau was felt in Concord, where they talked about an ideal state. But in Boston Minister Higginson and Dr. Howe waited for reports of a project planned for Harper's Ferry. In Georgia young Clay Wingate also received a premonition of impending disaster and great change.

John Brown, rock-hard fanatic, believing he was chosen by God to free the black man in America, led his troop of raiders to seize the United States arsenal at Harper's Ferry, Virginia. The first man killed in the fracas was Shepherd Heyward, a free Negro. The South was alarmed. Federal troops under Robert E. Lee subdued the Brown party in fifteen minutes; all was ended but the slow, smoldering hates and the deaths to come.

At Wingate Hall in Georgia all was peaceful. Sally Dupré and Clay Wingate were expected to marry. When Cudjo, the major-domo of the Wingate plantation, heard of the Harper's Ferry raid and John Brown, he opined that the Negro's business was not the white man's business. In Connecticut Mrs. Ellyat prayed for John Brown.

Brown was tried at Charles Town, Virginia. During the trial he denied the complicity of anyone but himself and his followers in the raid. He insisted that he had done what he thought was right. A legend grew around his name and mushroomed after he was hanged. Songs were sung. John Brown's body rested in its grave, but his spirit haunted the consciences of North and South alike.

Fort Sumter surrendered, and the Confederate States of America elected gaunt, tired Jefferson Davis president. Lank, sad-faced Abraham Lincoln, the frontier wit and small-time politician, was President of the United States. He ordered conscription of fighting men. Clay Wingate, loyal to Dixie, joined the Black Horse Troop and rode away to the war. Jack Ellyat marched off with the Connecticut volunteers.

Raw soldiers of North and South met at Bull Run under the direction of Generals McDowell, Johnston, and Beauregard. Congressmen and their ladies drove out from Washington to watch the Union victory. While they watched, the Union lines broke and retreated in panic. A movement to treat with the Confederacy for peace got under way in the North. Lincoln was alarmed, but he remained steadfast.

Jack Ellyat was mustered out after Bull Run. Later he joined the Illinois volunteers in Chicago and became known as "Bull Run Jack." Near Pittsburg Landing, in Tennessee, he lost his head and ran during a surprise attack. He was captured but escaped again during a night march. Hungry and worn out, Jack arrived at the Vilas farm, where he stayed in hiding and fell in love with Melora Vilas. At last he left the farm to seek the manhood he had lost near Pittsburg Landing, but not before he had got Melora with child. He was recaptured soon afterward.

Meanwhile Clay Wingate returned to Georgia on leave. At Wingate Hall the war seemed far away, for the successful running of the Union blockade of Southern ports made luxuries still available. Lucy Weatherby, a Virginian whose sweetheart had been killed at Bull Run, attended a dance at Wingate Hall and replaced Sally Dupré in Clay's affections. Spade, a slave on the nearby Zachary plantation, escaped that same night.

New Orleans was captured. Davis and Lincoln began to bow under the burdens of the war. McClellan began his Peninsular campaign. Lee inflicted defeat after defeat on the Army of the Potomac. Jack Ellyat was sent to a prison in the deep South. The fortunes of the Union were at their lowest ebb after the Confederate victory at the Second Manassas, and the spirit of John Brown was generally invoked by editors and preachers. Lincoln issued the Emancipation Proclamation. In the meantime, Spade made his way north and swam across a river to freedom, but when he arrived in the land of the free he was railroaded into a labor gang. McClellan was relieved by Burnside, who, in turn, was relieved by Hooker, as commander of the Army of the Potomac. Jack Ellyat, sick, was returned to the North in an exchange of prisoners of war.

Slowly the Confederacy began to feel the effects of the blockade and the terrible cost of war. Clay Wingate thought of his next leave—and of Lucy Weatherby. Jack Ellyat spent the dark winter of 1862-63 convalescing at his home in the cold Connecticut hills. He had been assigned to the Army of the Potomac as soon as his recovery was complete. In Tennessee, Melora Vilas gave birth to a baby boy.

Grant and Sherman led the Union forces to victory in the West; Vicksburg was surrounded. Hunger and anti-inflation riots broke out in Richmond. America, meanwhile, was expanding. New industries sprang up in the North, and the West was being developed. In Richmond, Shippy, a Union spy posing as a peddler, promised Sophy, a servant at the Pollard Hotel, to bring her some perfume from the North. Sophy knew that Clay Wingate and Lucy Weatherby had stayed together in the hotel. Luke Breckinridge, Sophy's rebel suitor, was a member of a patrol that stopped Shippy to search him. When they found incriminating papers in his boots, Luke gloated, for he was jealous of Shippy.

Stonewall Jackson was killed by his own pickets, and Lee, desperate for provisions, invaded the North. Jack Ellyat was in the Union army that converged on Gettysburg and was wounded during a battle there. After three days of bloody fighting at Gettysburg, Lee fell back to Virginia. Then Vicksburg surrendered. Defeated, the South continued to hang on doggedly. Sheridan marched through the Shenandoah Valley and left it bare and burned. Petersburg was besieged. Luke, along with thousands of other rebel troops, deserted from the Confederate Army, and when he headed back toward his laurel-thicket mountains he took Sophy with him. Melora and her father, John Vilas, traveled from place to place in search of Jack Ellyat; they became a legend in both armies.

General Sherman captured Atlanta and marched on to the sea. During Sherman's march, Wingate Hall caught fire accidentally and burned to the ground. Clay Wingate was wounded in a rear-guard action in Virginia. The war came to an end when Lee surrendered to Grant at Appomattox.

Spade, who had gone from the labor gang into the Union Army and who had been wounded at the Petersburg crater, hired out as a farm laborer in Cumberland County, Pennsylvania. Clay Wingate returned to his ruined home in Georgia, where Sally Dupré was waiting. And in Connecticut Jack Ellyat heard stories of strange gipsy travelers who were going from town to town looking for a soldier who was the father of the child of the woman who drove the creaking cart. One day he was standing beneath the crossroads elms when he saw a cart come slowly up the hill. He waited. The woman driving was Melora.

Further Critical Evaluation of the Work:

Stephen Vincent Benét's poem *John Brown's Body* is the only American poetic work which reaches epic proportions; its nearly fifteen-thousand-line length qualifies it as an epic in the classical sense, and ranks it, in form and purpose at least, with the great epics of Western literature. But although the poem as a whole is traditional in its classic structure, it is distinctly and uniquely American in its atmosphere, imagery, style, and symbolism. In his Invocation, Benét calls upon the American Muse to aid him, providing inspiration for what he humbly acknowledges to be an almost impossible task because of the magnitude of its scope. The poet's Muse becomes a symbol of America, his elusive subject: she is beautiful and strong, colorful and diverse, a unique, mysterious offspring of European and native parentage. Within the poem (line 311), Benét describes his work as a "cyclorama": a series of large pictures of America spread around the reader, who views them from the center.

The major unifying element in this cyclorama is the spirit of John Brown. Based on the historical figure of the man who raided the arsenal at Harper's Ferry, Benét's hero becomes the focal symbol of the epic; although he is condemned and hanged early in the work, his memory grows into the legend that gives hope and inspiration during the dark days of the Civil War. The second unifying thread throughout the loosely-woven eight books is provided in the characters of Northerner Jack Ellyat and Southerner Clay Wingate. Other minor characters help round out the scheme whereby all the regions and social groups of a huge nation are represented: Melora Vilas and her father typify the Border States and the expanding West; Lucy Weatherby is the Southern coquette; Luke Breckinridge, the independent mountaineer;

Jake Diefer, the settled farmer; Spade, the runaway slave, and Cudjo, the loyal slave; and Shippy, the Northern spy. By tracing the fortunes of such diverse people, Benét dramatizes not only how the war affects their lives, but how their lives shape the nation.

One of the greatest achievements of *John Brown's Body* is Benét's accurate and balanced picture of Southern life. With realism and insight he probes the character of John Brown and of his legend; judging the raid as foolish, he sees Brown as a murderer and a fanatic, a man so caught in his zealous dream that he remains coldly unmoved by his son's horrible death. Brown the man was a failure; but dead, he became a crucial legend and symbol. Likewise, the Southern slaves are portrayed in all the complexity, ambiguity, and irony of their situation; and the Wingates embody the dilemma of the genteel Southern aristocrat. Unfortunately, Benét fails to capture the culture and way of life in the North; his portraits of the Ellyat household, in contrast to those of the Wingate plantation, are rather flat and one-dimensional.

JOHN DRYDEN: THE POET, THE DRAMATIST, THE CRITIC

Type of work: Critical essay
Author: T. S. Eliot (1888-1965)
First published: 1932

There is always interest in hearing what one great poet has had to say about an important predecessor, or what one dramatist has had to say about another, or what one influential critic thinks of an earlier critic. When T. S. Eliot wrote about John Dryden he spoke with peculiar and noteworthy authority: he was one famous poet-playwright-critic assessing another famous poet-playwright-critic.

There are many parallels between the careers and reputations of Eliot and Dryden. Both are better known for their poetry than for their plays, and both, perhaps, are as well known for their criticism (or will be, as the long-range influence of Eliot becomes clear) as they are for their poetry. Each man discarded the poetic conventions of a previous age, set the tone for an age to come, and dominated the age in which he lived. (Dryden was the great man of English letters during the last quarter of the seventeenth century; Eliot was his counterpart during the second quarter of this century.) And just as Eliot considers Dryden to be even more important for his influence than for his actual work, so too the generation after Eliot is beginning to focus more and more attention on his historical significance—his influence.

This volume consists of three separate but interrelated essays on the poetry, the plays, and the criticism of Dryden. In the first essay, the main point Eliot makes is that Dryden reformed the language by devising a naturally flowing, speaking form of speech in verse instead of an artificial and dead form. It is a misconception to think of his style as artificial. It is likewise a mistake to make too much of Dryden's debt to his predecessors, for the style was due more to his rebellion against the artificial sounds of the old verse, than to an imitation of it.

In the previous age Donne had also been a reactionary by updating the language, doing away with the conventions of the regular lyric verse of the Elizabethans, and introducing into lyric poetry a conversational flow of normal speech. But by Dryden's time the vitality of Donne's reaction had dissipated and the normal had become false. So it was left to Dryden to restore English verse to normal speech. Dryden's reformation of language, moreover, has been lasting.

Eliot is not primarily concerned in this essay with particular poems of Dryden. Of Dryden's translations he felt only that they aided in forming our present-day language almost as much as did his original poems. Eliot merely mentions the great satires, *MacFlecknoe* and *Absalom and Achitophel.* He lingers briefly over *The Hind and the Panther* and *Religio Laici,* the two poems that kept reason even in verse, observing that in the former, which Eliot considers the greater of the two, political-religious thought is uplifted into poetry for the first and last time. Eliot's only comment on Dryden's lyrics is that, in such poems as "Song for St. Cecilia's Day" and "Alexander's Feast," he perfected the form that was not handled as well by Cowley but which he bequeathed to Gray, Collins, Wordsworth, Coleridge, and Tennyson, who used it with skill. Otherwise, we would not have the *Ode: Intimations of Immortality from Recollections of Early Childhood.*

Although he certainly does not depreciate the poetry, Eliot considers Dryden more important for his influence, particularly on the language, than for his poetry itself. He feels that the reason why Dryden's poetry did influence other poets was the fact that he was not so great as to be unable to influence them. Shakespeare and Milton were greater poets, but because they were greater they were less imitable; they had mimics but not followers. Dryden did not overshadow all followers by being too great; therefore he could influence others. Dryden's influence, in Eliot's view, has been enormous: Dryden felt that the English were without proper speech and so he gave it to them. For this reason no one has dominated English literature for as long or as completely as Dryden.

The least important of the three essays in this volume is that which deals with Dryden as a dramatist, and this is probably a reflection of the fact that Dryden achieved greater success in poetry and criticism than he did in drama. Eliot's main interests in this chapter are, as in the first chapter, Dryden's language and his influence. Eliot wastes little time in dismissing Dryden's comedies. Instead, he gives most of his attention to Dryden's heroic dramas, discussing in turn the plays in blank verse and those in rhymed couplets.

Eliot acknowledges Dryden's skill in blank verse, particularly in *All for Love*, observing that he escaped the sour influence of the final followers of Shakespeare, with their methods of overusing everything to the point of destruction. Dryden accomplished the wonder of reawakening. Eliot hazards the debatable opinion that blank verse dramatists have written better works when they wrote more in the style of Dryden than in the manner of Shakespeare. And yet, he says, there is not a verse in *All for Love* which carries the conversational tone of any of Dryden's best satires. This effect is accounted for by the fact that blank verse was not easy for him.

The rhymed couplet, on the other hand, is perfectly suited to Dryden's abilities, says Eliot; what Dryden could not do with the couplet simply could not be done, and his couplet is living speech. The main reason is that Dryden knew the limits of the rhymed couplet in creating dramatic effects. If Dryden's use of blank verse was an improvement over that of Shakespeare's imitators, his

use of couplets was even more of an improvement, for his firm masculine couplet was better than the feathery Jacobean verse of Fletcher.

The main point Eliot wishes to make in the middle essay is this: although Dryden was not a dramatist in the natural sense, for drama was not a form of literature to which his talents were best suited, and although his plays themselves have but a limited degree of interest, his influence on the history of drama was considerable. This influence was largely negative: he killed off the worn-out Jacobean tradition, substituting for it his own form of heroic play, which was representative of the period.

Dryden's prose writings, says Eliot, are noticeably important in two ways: in the historical development of the style of English prose and in the background of English criticism. The influence of Dryden's prose style on the development of the English language was not, however, "dominant" because his prose influenced prose less than his verse probably did. Nonetheless his prose style is admirable: elegant, urbane, and finely polished. Dryden did not waver in his writing abilities; he kept a wit which overshadowed that of his contemporaries.

But what is chiefly important about Dryden's literary criticism is not the style but the fact that it is the first conscious criticism by an English poet in English on a large scale. English criticism had Dryden as its first master.

Eliot does take exception to some of Dryden's critical pronouncements, referring, for example, to his misunderstanding of the Aristotelian theory of the unities of time and place as absurd. But he explains that here, and in his strictures upon Shakespeare, Dryden's rigid appeals to authority are the outcome of a sense of form and order in conflict with the disorder of the Elizabethan stage. These, in other words, are limitations imposed upon Dryden by the age in which he lived. What is truly praiseworthy about Dryden is that in him we find an almost perfect balance between creative poet and critic.

In contrast with other great poet-critics, Dryden is what Eliot calls "the *normal* critic." Coleridge could not hold himself to plain criticism but ran into discourses on philosophy and aesthetics. Wordsworth was engaged in preserving his own practices, and Matthew Arnold was too busy searching for the moral lesson. Dryden's great merit as an influence in criticism is the fact that he stayed within the bounds of critical poetry. Dryden was a "normal critic" in that his only bias is in favor of common sense. In other words, his theories were all aimed at what the poet could intelligently attempt. And, concludes Eliot, Dryden stands, both as poet and critic, for he practiced in his poetry what he preached in his criticism as the great champion of sanity at a time when English poetry and criticism alike were greatly in need of sanity.

JOHN HALIFAX, GENTLEMAN

Type of work: Novel
Author: Dinah Maria Mulock (Mrs. George Craik, 1826-1887)
Type of plot: Domestic realism
Time of plot: Turn of the nineteenth century
Locale: Rural England
First published: 1857

> *Principal characters:*
> JOHN HALIFAX, one of Nature's gentlemen
> URSULA, his wife
> GUY, their oldest son
> MAUD, a daughter
> ABEL FLETCHER, John's benefactor
> PHINEAS FLETCHER, his invalid son
> LORD RAVENEL, a landowner

Critique:

The story of John Halifax is one depicting the simple pleasures of lower middle-class life in rural England. In the book there is also a plea that a man be judged by his merits, not by his social class or his birth. But primarily the story is one of simple domesticity, of the real love that exists among members of a simple family who place the happiness and security of others above themselves. The theme was common among nineteenth-century authors, one that found immediate reception from readers who were slowly awakening to a new social order. Shortly after its publication the book was translated into French, German, Italian, Russian, and Greek.

The Story:

When Phineas Fletcher and his father, Abel, first saw John Halifax, they were immediately struck with his honest face and worthy character. For although the boy was only fourteen and an orphan, he would accept help from no one. Instead, he preferred to make his own way, even though it meant that he was always half-starved. Phineas, just sixteen, and an invalid, would have enjoyed having John for a companion, but Abel Fletcher, a wealthy Quaker, put the boy to work in his tannery. Although Abel was a real Christian and wanted to help others, he knew that the boy would be better off if he helped himself. Then, too, there was a class distinction between Phineas and John that even Abel could not entirely overlook.

Phineas and John became good friends, the orphan being the only friend Phineas ever loved as a brother. John rose rapidly in the tannery because of his honesty and his willingness to work at any job. He also had the ability to handle men, an ability ably proved when a hungry mob would have burned down the Fletcher home and the mill which the Quaker owned. John arranged to have the workers get wheat for their families, and from then on they were loyal to him through any crisis.

When they were in their early twenties, Phineas and John took a cottage in the country so that Phineas might have the advantage of the country air. While there they met a lovely girl, Ursula March, who had taken her dying father to the same spot. John was from the first attracted to the modest girl, but since she was a lady he felt that he could not tell her of his feelings. After the death of her father, it was learned that she was an heiress, and to John even more unattainable. However, John knew himself to be a gentleman, even if others did not, and at last circumstances brought him an opportunity to let her know his heart. When Ursula saw his true character and gladly married him, everyone was shocked but Phineas. Ursula's kinsman, a dissolute nobleman, refused to give her

her fortune, and John would not go to court to claim the fortune, as was his legal right as Ursula's husband.

After the death of Abel Fletcher, Phineas lived with John and Ursula and their children, the oldest of whom was a lovely blind girl. Abel had made John a partner in the tannery, and since John did not like the tan-yard and also since it was losing money, he sold it and put the money into the operation of the mill. Times were often hard during the next few years, but finally, for political reasons Ursula's kinsman released her fortune to John. After settling a large amount on his wife and children, he used the rest to lease a new mill and expand his business interests. His hobby was a steam engine to turn the mill, and before long he began to see his project materialize. The family moved to a new home in the country and lived many long years there in peace and happiness. John, becoming influential in politics, used his power by choosing honorable men for office. He made some powerful enemies too, but his concern was only for the right. During this time his income grew until he was a very wealthy man. He continued to use his money to help others.

The steam engine, built and put into operation, gave John new advantages, but he provided generously for his workmen so that they would not suffer because of the machine. Then tragedy struck the family. Shortly after the birth of their last child, a daughter, the blind child was taken by death. It was a sorrow from which John never completely recovered. The years brought other troubles to his household. Two of his sons loved the same girl, the governess of their little sister. The brothers had a bitter quarrel, and the loser, who was the oldest son, Guy, left home and went abroad, almost breaking his mother's heart. After two or three years they learned that Guy had almost killed a man in Paris and had fled to America. From that time on, Ursula aged, for Guy was her favorite son.

Shortly afterward, John learned from Lord William Ravenel that that noble man was in love with the youngest daughter, Maud. Lord Ravenel was not only the son of a worldly family; he himself had led a useless and sometimes wild life. John would not listen to the man's pleas, and Lord Ravenel, agreeing that he was unworthy of her, left without telling Maud of his love. But John was to revise his opinion somewhat when after the death of his father. Lord Ravenel gave up his inherited fortune to pay his father's debts. After this incident Lord Ravenel was not heard from for many years. Maud did not marry. Her parents knew that she had never lost her affection for Lord Ravenel, although she did not know that he had returned her feelings.

Years passed. The married children gave John and Ursula grandchildren. John could have had a seat in Parliament, but he rejected it in favor of others. He continued to do good with his money and power, even when suffering temporary losses. And always he longed for his lost blind child, just as Ursula longed for her missing oldest son. Their own love grew even deeper as they reached their twilight years. John often suffered attacks that left him gasping in pain and breathlessness, but in order to spare his family any unnecessary worry he kept this information from all but Phineas.

Then came wonderful news: Guy was coming home. All of the family rejoiced, Ursula more than any other. They had six anxious months when he did not appear and his ship was not accounted for, but at last he arrived. He had been shipwrecked and lost, but had eventually made his way home. With him was Lord Ravenel, who had gone to America after being rejected by John. Both men had done well there, but had lost everything in the shipwreck. In their happy reunion, the money seemed of little importance. John knew now that Lord William Ravenel had proved himself worthy of Maud, nd the two lovers were at last allowed o express their love for each other. Guy oo, began to show interest in a child- ood friend, and another wedding in the amily seemed likely. John felt that his life was now com- plete, his peace and happiness being broken only by longing for his dead child. He was soon to join her. One day he sat down to rest, and so his family found him in the peaceful sleep of death. That night, as she sat by her husband's body, Ursula must have felt that she could not lose him, for the children and Phineas found her lying dead beside her husband. They were buried side by side in the country churchyard.

Further Critical Evaluation of the Work:

Few readers today probably know this once widely read novel, a domestic idyll extolling Christian virtues and plain values of family life. Its simplicity and seeming artlessness have little appeal for readers who have accustomed themselves to ambiguity, violent realism, and sophisticated innovations of style. But *John Halifax, Gentleman* enjoyed decided popularity in its Victorian milieu. The author, Dinah Maria Murlock, or Mrs. Craik, wrote fifty-two works of fiction, poetry, and children's stories. Whatever judgment modern critics might place upon her output, she was honored by some of the most famous writers of her period. Indeed, after her death, a committee which included Lord Tennyson, Matthew Arnold, Robert Browning, Professor Huxley, James Russell Lowell, and Mrs. Oliphant, erected a marble medal- lion in Tewkesbury Abbey in her memory.

As background for her story of John Halifax and Ursula March, Mrs. Craik chose one of the most picturesque sections of Gloucestershire; she faithfully described the small English homesteads clustered in the pleasant valleys, the softly rolling hills, and the town of Tewkesbury itself, which she terms Norton Bury. Like Hardy and others, Mrs. Craik chose an area with which she was familiar; one who knows the locale easily recognizes Nunnely Hill as Selsley Hill and Enderley Flats as the real Amberley Common.

As a novelist, Mrs. Craik shows herself cognizant of some of the most important principles of the craft, as seen, for instance, in her method of allowing dialogue to carry the plot, instead of relying on authorial reportage. And her characters develop; John Halifax, Ursula, Lord Ravenel, and especially the elder son, Guy Halifax, go through experiences which effect changes in their outlooks or adjustments to society or to themselves. Though the novel emphasizes ideals, the characters are not ideal. They act and react like human beings and are therefore believable. John Halifax must come to terms with his own pride, Ursula with her tendency to direct situations. Lord Ravenel must choose between a decadent luxury which is empty, and effort in a new world which exacts of him his latent strength and belief. A simple story simply told, *John Halifax, Gentleman,* in spite of its quaint Victorian tone and exaltation of old-fashioned ideals, is based upon clear principles of good writing and can still for this reason involve today's reader.

JOHN INGLESANT

Type of work: Novel
Author: Joseph Henry Shorthouse (1834-1903)
Type of plot: Historical-philosophical romance
Time of plot: Seventeenth century
Locale: England and Italy
First published: 1881

Principal characters:

JOHN INGLESANT, an Englishman interested in spiritual affairs
EUSTACE INGLESANT, his materialistic twin brother
FATHER ST. CLARE, a Jesuit and John's mentor
CHARLES I, King of England, who used John's services as an agent
LAURETTA CAPECE, John's Italian wife
CARDINAL CHIGI, John's Italian patron

Critique:

John Inglesant, a philosophical and historical romance, was done, according to its author, in the style of the great American writer of romances, Nathaniel Hawthorne. In all literature there is probably no better picture of the complicated political and ecclesiastical affairs in England luring the stormy years of the reign of Charles I and the ensuing Civil War. In this novel many of the historical personages of the time—King Charles, Archbishop Laud, John Milton, Thomas Hobbes, and others—make their appearance, adding to the realism of the story and demonstrating the parts they played in seventeenth-century England. While Shorthouse, in his author's introduction to the second edition, laid the greatest emphasis on the philosophical content of the novel, the modern reader is likely to find the historical aspects considerably more important and certainly more interesting than the nebulous philosophical gropings adumbrated in the story.

The Story:

The family of Inglesant had long been loyal to the British crown, which had conferred lands and honors upon it, and yet the family also had strong leanings toward the Roman Catholic Church. Such inclinations were dangerous during the sixteenth and seventeenth centuries, when the whole of England was forced to change religions several times, according to the monarch who sat on the throne. In 1622 two sons were born to the family, twins whose mother died at their birth. One was named Eustace, after his father; the other, born a few minutes later and therefore the younger son of the family, was named John.

In boyhood the twins saw little of one another. Eustace, the older, was given a worldly training, for his father, outwardly conforming to the Anglican Church under James I and Charles I, wished him to make a place for himself at court. The younger son, John, was given bookish training in the classics and philosophy by various tutors. At the age of fourteen, John was placed under the tutelage of Father St. Clare, who was in England on a political and ecclesiastical mission for his order. The priest saw in the highly intelligent and cultured young lad the prospects of a fine instrument that his order might use; in addition, he felt that the boy deserved the training which would make him fitted for that unquestioning discipline of the highest order, as the Jesuits saw it: the discipline that is enforced from within the individual but controlled from without.

After several years of study and training, John Inglesant became a page in the train of the queen at the court of Charles I. Father St. Clare had sent him to court that he might come to the attention of the Roman Catholic nobles and serve to further the interests of the Roman Church in England.

As the country became more and more troubled, and civil war threatened because of rivalry between the Puritans and the adherents to the crown and the Anglican Church, the Roman Catholics felt themselves in a rather strong position with the king and everyone loyal to him. It was the dream of Father St. Clare, as a member of the Society of Jesus, to return England to the domination of Rome. With that end in view, he did all he could to aid the crown against the Puritans. Because John Inglesant, who came from a family long noted for its loyalty to the king, was active as an agent between Roman Catholic leaders and the crown, he was often employed on secret missions by the king. Father St. Clare, who saw Inglesant as having greater value as an Anglican communicant with papist leanings, advised the young man against conversion to the Roman Church. Inglesant, puzzled, followed his mentor's wishes.

When fighting broke out between the Cavaliers and the Puritans, Inglesant spent much of his time on missions for the king and Father St. Clare. Eustace Inglesant, after marrying a rich woman some ten years his senior, believed the king's cause doomed to failure and left England for France. John Inglesant was sent on a secret mission to Ireland, where Lord Glamorgan was attempting to raise an Irish army to aid the royal cause in England. From Ireland, young Inglesant was sent to bear tidings of imminent relief to the royal garrison at Chester, which was under siege.

Inglesant reached Chester and gave his message to Lord Biron, the commander. Weeks went by, but the relief did not appear. At last the garrison learned that the king had been forced to deny any part in the plan for an Irish invasion of England, because of popular outcry against the project. Chester was given up to the Puritans, and Inglesant, wishing to protect his monarch, permitted himself to be sent to London as a prisoner charged with treason.

Weeks turned into months; still Inglesant languished in prison. Meanwhile the Puritans were trying to implicate the king in the charge against Inglesant. Finally the king's forces were utterly defeated and Charles I was taken prisoner. In an effort to make him give evidence against the king, Inglesant was condemned and actually taken to be executed, but, true to his Jesuit training, he remained steadfast.

Through the good offices of Father St. Clare, Inglesant was released after the beheading of Charles I. One day Eustace Inglesant, who had returned to England under the protection of his wife's Puritan kinsmen, brought his brother's pardon to the Tower of London. Immediately, the two brothers set out for the estate of Eustace's wife.

Eustace, in the meantime, had been warned by an astrologer that his life was in danger, and he was murdered during the journey by an Italian, an enemy whom he had encountered while traveling in Italy years before. John Inglesant, after a period of sickness and recuperation spent at his sister-in-law's estate, left for France, where he hoped to find Father St. Clare and to gather information about his brother's murderer, whom he had resolved to kill in revenge.

Arriving in France, he was not immediately successful in finding Father St. Clare. In the interval he tried to evaluate his spiritual life. A Benedictine acquaintance tried to encourage him to enter that order, but Inglesant felt that his spiritual answers did not lie in that direction. He believed that somehow he had been singled out by heaven to find salvation more independently. When he finally found Father St. Clare, the priest told him to go to Rome and there continue his spiritual search under the protection of the Jesuits, who were indebted to him for the many missions he had undertaken in their cause.

On the way to Rome, a journey taking several months, Inglesant stopped many times. He spent several weeks in Siena as a guest of the Chigi family. One of the Chigis was a cardinal who had hopes of being elected pope when the incumbent died. From Siena, Inglesant journeyed to Florence. There he met Lauretta Capece, with whom he fell in love.

After his eventual arrival in Rome, Inglesant was sent to the Duke of Umbria on a mission by influential Jesuits who wished the nobleman to turn his lands over to the Papal See after his death. His mission accomplished, Inglesant married Lauretta Capece. He returned to Rome as a temporary aide to Cardinal Chigi during the conclave to elect a new pope. The cardinal was elected. Inglesant retired to an estate given to him by the Duke of Umbria.

Inglesant and his wife lived in Umbria for several years, until a great plague broke out in Naples. Inglesant went to that city in an effort to save his brother-in-law, who had been in hiding there. In Naples, also, he found his brother's murderer; the man had become a monk after having been beaten and blinded by a mob. Now, with his brother's murderer in his power, Inglesant had lost his desire for revenge. In company with the blind monk, he continued his search and finally discovered his dying brother-in-law. After the sick man had died, Inglesant returned home, only to learn that his family had been wiped out by the plague.

Once again he journeyed to Rome in search of spiritual consolation, but because of his independent attitudes he got into serious trouble with the Inquisition. Because of Jesuit influence, he was not condemned to prison or death. Instead, he was sent back to England, where he lived out his days in philosophical contemplation.

Further Critical Evaluation of the Work:

Judged as a philosophical novel, *John Inglesant* is a product of Tractarianism, deriving from the Oxford Movement of mid-nineteenth century England. For his Victorian audience, Shorthouse attempts to mediate between the conflicting claims of Anglicanism and Roman Catholicism. He provides a historical perspective for the conflict by setting the novel in the seventeenth century, a period of great religious upheaval, to show that it is possible to bridge the gap between the two religions and their underlying cultures. In a letter to his friend Dr. Abott, Shorthouse writes that perhaps the chief object of his novel is to "promote culture at the expense of fanaticism."

His spokesman for tolerance, John Inglesant, is trained as a Jesuit by Father St. Clare, but is permitted freedom to exercise his own religious conscience. During the course of his adventures, Inglesant meets representatives of different Christian viewpoints, from those of the High Anglican monastic colony under John Ferrar at Little Gidding to the "Quietist" followers of Michael de Molinos; from Puritans hostile to King Charles I to followers of the Benedictine Order directed by Hugh Paulin Cressy. He comes to understand the intricate politics of electing a Pope and discovers secrets of the Jesuits. Wherever he goes, he meets Christians of principle, conviction, and dignity. Devoted to the "ideal of Christ," he remains to the last a member of the Church of England. Yet he is neither exceedingly zealous in his own faith nor bigoted toward any other. Except for the Puritans, whom he considers narrow-minded fanatics, he finds among all other Christians the same high-minded dedication to Christ's ideal that he professes.

Searching for spiritual perfection, Inglesant moves freely through the different levels of seventeenth century society, both in England and on the

Continent. His quest is also a romantic one. Mary Collet and Lauretta Capace, his two loves, help to perfect his character as a gentleman, just as his religious teachers perfect his moral nature. Always his enemy is Malvolti, slayer of his brother Eustace, master of disguises, resourceful and cunning betrayer. The romantic climax of the novel is Chapter 32, the scene in which Inglesant delivers Malvolti, now in rags and begging for pity, over to the priest of the capella for justice, leaving his sword on the altar. In his letters, Shorthouse reveals that he wrote the entire novel expressly to describe this scene (based upon an historical anecdote concerning one Giovanni Gualberto of Florence). Just as Inglesant foregoes religious fanaticism through love of Christ, so he spares his enemy, making possible Malvolti's later reformation. Thus Inglesant's romantic quest is fulfilled; he becomes a true gentleman in Christ.

Inspired by William Smith's *Thorndale, John Ingelsant* in turn influenced many late-Victorian philosophical novelists, including Mrs. Humphry Ward (*Robert Elsmere*, 1888). Most important, it created an interest in philosophical romance that helped to develop an audience for Walter Pater's *Marius the Epicurean* (1885), probably the most important English work of this genre.

JONATHAN WILD

Type of work: Novel
Author: Henry Fielding (1707-1754)
Type of plot: Social criticism
Time of plot: Late seventeenth century
Locale: England
First published: 1743

Principal characters:
JONATHAN WILD, a "great man"
LAETITIA, his wife
LA RUSE, a rogue
HEARTFREE, a good man
MRS. HEARTFREE, his good wife

Critique:

Although *The History of Jonathan Wild the Great* is possibly the least known of Fielding's novels, it is the one likely to appeal most to those who enjoy barbed satire and pure irony. Jonathan was a "great man"—not a good man. Fielding makes it quite clear that greatness and goodness are never to be found in one person. A "great man" is a pure villain, with none of the minor virtues with which ordinary villains are endowed. The characters are vivid; the plot is sure and swift. *Jonathan Wild* is, in all ways, a delightful book.

The Story:

Jonathan Wild was prepared by nature to be a "great man." His ancestors were all men of greatness, many of them hanged for thievery or treason. Those who escaped were simply shrewder and more fortunate than the others. But Jonathan was to be so "great" as to put his forefathers to shame.

As a boy he read about the great villains of history. At school he learned little, his best study being to pick the pockets of his tutors and fellow students. When he was seventeen, his father moved to town, where Jonathan was to put his talents to even better use. There he met the Count La Ruse, a knave destined to be one of the lesser "greats." La Ruse was in prison for debt, but Jonathan's skill soon secured his friend's freedom. Together they had many profitable ventures,

picking the pockets of their friends and of each other. Neither became angry when the other stole from him, for each respected the other's abilities.

Jonathan, for unknown reasons, traveled in America for seven or eight years. Returning to England he continued his life of villainy. Since he was to be a truly "great" man, he could not soil his own hands with too much thievery because there was always the danger of the gallows if he should be apprehended. He gathered about him a handful of lesser thieves who took the risks while he collected most of the booty. La Ruse joined him in many of his schemes, and the two friends continued to steal from each other. This ability to cheat friends showed true "greatness."

Jonathan admired Laetitia Snap, a woman with qualities of "greatness" similar to his own. She was the daughter of his father's friend, and she too was skilled in picking pockets and cheating at cards. In addition, she was a lady of wonderfully loose morals. But try as he would, Jonathan could not get Laetitia to respond to his passion. The poor fellow did not at first know that each time he approached her she was hiding another lover in the closet. Had he known, his admiration would have been even greater.

Jonathan's true "greatness" did not appear until he renewed his acquaintance with Mr. Heartfree, a former schoolmate. Heartfree would never be a "great" man

3030

because he was a good man. He cheated no one, held no grudges, and loved his wife and children. These qualities made him the sort of person Jonathan liked to cheat. Heartfree was a jeweler who by hard work and honest practices had become moderately prosperous. With the help of La Ruse, Jonathan was able to bring Heartfree to ruin. They stole his jewels and his money and hired thugs to beat him unmercifully, all the time convincing the good man that they were his friends.

La Ruse approached the greatness of Jonathan by leaving the country after stealing most of their booty. Poor Heartfree was locked up for debt after the two scoundrels had ruined him. Then Jonathan performed his greatest act. He had also a strong passion for Mrs. Heartfree, a good and virtuous woman, and he persuaded her that her husband had asked him to take her and some remaining jewels to Holland until her husband could obtain his release. So cleverly did he talk that the woman did not even tell her husband goodbye, though she loved him dearly. Instead, she put her children in the hands of a faithful servant and accompanied the rogue on a ship leaving England immediately.

When a severe storm arose, Jonathan was sure that death was near. Throwing caution aside, he attacked Mrs. Heartfree. Her screams brought help from the captain. After the storm subsided, the captain put Jonathan adrift in a small boat. The captain did not know that Jonathan was a "great" man, not destined to die in ignoble fashion. After a while he was rescued. He returned to England with tall tales of his adventure, none of which were the least bit true.

In the meantime Heartfree had begun to suspect his friend of duplicity. When Jonathan returned, he was for a time able to persuade Heartfree that he had done everything possible to help the jeweler. He told just enough of the truth to make his story acceptable, for in "greatness" the lie must always contain some

truth. But Jonathan went too far. He urged Heartfree to attempt an escape from prison by murdering a few guards. Heartfree saw his supposed friend as the rogue he was and denounced Jonathan in ringing tones. From that time on Jonathan lived only to bring Heartfree to complete destruction.

While Jonathan was plotting Heartfree's trip to the gallows, Laetitia's father finally gave his consent to his daughter's marriage to the rogue. It took only two weeks, however, for his passion to be satisfied; then the couple began to fight and cheat each other constantly.

After his marriage Jonathan continued in all kinds of knavery, but his most earnest efforts were directed toward sending Heartfree to the gallows. At last he hit upon a perfect plan. He convinced the authorities that Heartfree himself had plotted to have his wife take the jewels out of the country in order to cheat his creditors. Mrs. Heartfree had not returned to England. Although Jonathan hoped she was dead, he thought it better to have her husband hanged at once in case she should somehow return. Before Heartfree's sentence was carried out, however, Jonathan was arrested and put in jail. He was surprised by a visit from Laetitia. She came only to revile him. She, having been caught picking pockets, was also a prisoner. Her only wish was that she could have the pleasure of seeing Jonathan hanged before her turn came to die on the gallows.

On the day that Heartfree was to be hanged his wife returned. After many adventures and travel in many lands, she came back in time to tell her story and to save her husband from hanging. She had brought with her a precious jewel which had been given to her by a savage chief she met on her travels. Heartfree was released and his family was restored to prosperity. It was otherwise with Jonathan, whose former friends hastened to hurry him to the gallows. On the appointed day he was hanged, leaving this world with a curse for all mankind. His wife and all his friends were hanged, save one. La Ruse was captured in France and broken on the wheel. Jonathan Wild was a "great" man because he was a complete villain.

Further Critical Evaluation of the Work:

Jonathan Wild is an exceptionally brilliant novel. It reflects and comments upon the life of London and, at the same time, offers a profound moral analysis of human behavior.

The London in which Henry Fielding lived was characterized by wildness, extravagances and corruption. London was a "wide-open" city, a sort of American frontier town on a huge scale. During the years when Fielding was beginning his career, Sir Robert Walpole dominated the Parliament, the King, and the Courts. He stifled opposition and succeeded in amassing enormous power and wealth; he also attracted the brilliant and biting satire of some of England's most talented writers, including Swift, Gay, Pope, and Fielding. Jonathan Wild, a "great man," is intended as a satire of Walpole as well as of the moral position he occupied. Viewing this "great man" as a gangster and an opportunist, Fielding combined him with another personage, an actual small time criminal named Jonathan Wild, who was hanged at Tyburn before a large, interested crowd.

Henry Fielding offers an alternative to the blind respect that those in authority often demand. By stressing throughout the novel the distinction between "greatness" and "goodness," Fielding makes moral judgments independent of social standing. He implies not only that we must distinguish between greatness and goodness, but that the two are mutually exclusive.

But there is a further point that Fielding makes about "greatness": it amounts to nothing but the untrammeled selfish instincts of men. For Jonathan Wild, it means stealing from friend and foe alike, taking advantage of women whenever possible, and, above all, thinking and acting in behalf of no one but himself. This unrestricted and uncivilized behavior accounts for his name: he is wild indeed. But although he is as wild as an animal, he is basically not free. At every step, he is entirely possessed by his own desires and driven by his own selfish instincts. The more he looks after "number one," and the more he lets himself go, the fewer choices he has left open to him. Thus it is philosophically appropriate, as well as morally necessary, for Jonathan Wild to be jailed and hanged at the conclusion of the novel.

Fielding intends Wild to be contrasted with his enemy, Heartfree, who, because he thinks of others and lacks ambition, is basically free as well as morally acceptable. Freedom for Henry Fielding, then, lies not in the possession of power or wealth or license, but in the practice of a simple morality and a consideration for others. Thus, in *Jonathan Wild*, freedom arises from social responsibility and not from individual prerogative.

JORROCKS' JAUNTS AND JOLLITIES

Type of work: Tales
Author: Robert Smith Surtees (1803-1864)
Type of plot: Comic romance
Time of plot: The 1830's
Locale: England and France
First published: 1838

Principal characters:
JORROCKS, a grocer and sportsman
MR. STUBBS, a Yorkshireman
THE COUNTESS BENVOLIO

Critique:

This volume of Jorrocks' adventures differs from the others in that there is no connecting plot; the work is simply a series of tales given unity by the irrepressible and immortal Jorrocks. The satire here is double-edged; first there is the pretentious cockney aping his aristocratic betters; second, sporting life comes in for uncomfortably keen depiction. The wealth of detail furnishes us with a good contemporary account of town and country life in Victorian England.

The Story:

When they went out to hunt, the members of Jorrocks' Surrey fox hunt did not always keep their minds on the sport. As they gathered, their talk included shouts to the dogs and quotations on the price of cotton, advice on horses, and warnings of bank policies. While waiting for the dogs to run the fox closer, they all eagerly pulled out bread and meat from their capacious pockets.

One morning a swell joined the veteran Surrey hunters. He was plainly an aristocrat. While the others were paunchy and stooped, he was thin and straight. His handsome mount contrasted sharply with their skinny nags. They all watched him enviously. He was new in Surrey evidently, for he drove his horse at a fast clip through the bottom lands, heedless of the numerous flints. The riders were glad when he had to retire from the chase with a lame horse.

As he left, Jorrocks rushed up with the news that the stranger was no less a personage than a Russian diplomat. The whole hunt joined in heartily wishing him back in Russia for good.

In town Jorrocks ran into agreeable Mr. Stubbs, a footloose Yorkshireman and invited him to go to the hunt on Saturday morning. So long as Jorrocks paid the bills, the Yorkshireman was glad for any entertainment. On the appointed foggy morning Jorrocks was on time. He was riding his own bony nag and leading a sorry dray horse for his guest. The fog was so thick that they bumped into carriages and sidewalk stands right and left. The Yorkshireman would have waited for the fog to lift, but doughty Jorrocks would countenance no delay. Mrs. Jorrocks had a fine quarter of house-lamb for supper and her husband had been sternly ordered to be back at five-thirty sharp. Jorrocks was never late for a meal.

On the way Jorrocks' horse was nearly speared by a carriage pole. The resourceful hunter promptly dismounted and chaffered a bit with a coach driver. When he remounted, he had a great coach lamp tied around his middle. Thus lighted, the two horsemen got safely out of town.

The hunt that day held an unexpected surprise for both of them. Thinking to show off a little for his younger friend, Jorrocks put his horse at a weak spot in a fence. He wanted to sail over in good time and continue after the fox. Instead, he landed in a cesspool. His bright red coat was covered with slime and mud for the rest of the day. But the Yorkshireman noted that Jorrocks carried on till the end of the hunt and got home in time for his house-lamb.

As usual, Jorrocks went hunting in Surrey on a Saturday. When his horse went lame, he stopped at the smith's shop for repairs, and his five-minute delay made him lose sight of the pack. Consequently, he lost out on a day's sport. As he sat in a local inn nursing a grouch and threatening to withdraw his subscription to the Surrey hunt, in came Nosey Browne. Jorrocks was delighted to see his old friend and willingly accepted an invitation to a day's shooting on Browne's estate.

A few days later he collected the Yorkshireman and set out eagerly for the shooting. He was dashed to find that Nosey's big estate was little more than a cramped spot of ground covered with sheds and other outbuildings. Squire Cheatum, learning that Nosey was a bankrupt, had forbidden his neighbor to hunt in his woods, and so Jorrocks was forced to hunt in the yard behind sheds. Soon he saw a rabbit. In his excitement he took a step forward and shot the animal. As he was about to pick up his prize, a gamekeeper arrived and accused him of trespassing. After an extended argument it was shown that Jorrocks' toe had indeed at the moment of shooting been over the line on Squire Cheatum's land; and so the wrathy Jorrocks was fined one pound one.

He was no man to accept calmly a fine so obviously unfair. He hired a lawyer and appealed the case to the county court. On the day of the trial Jorrocks beamed as his own attorney pictured him as a substantial citizen with a reputation for good works. He squirmed as the squire's lawyer described him as a cockney grocer who was infringing on the rights of countryfolk. At the end the judges woke up and sustained the fine.

After the fox-hunting season ended, Jorrocks accepted an invitation to a stag hunt. The Yorkshireman came to breakfast with him on the appointed morning. Jorrocks led him down into the kitchen, where the maid had set out the usual fare. There were a whole ham, a loaf of bread, and a huge Bologna sausage. There were muffins, nine eggs, a pork pie, and kidneys

on a spit. The good Betsy was stationed at the stove, where she deftly laid mutton chops on the gridiron.

As the two friends ate, Mrs. Jorrocks came in with an ominous face. She held up a card, inscribed with a woman's name and address, which she had found in her spouse's pocket. Jorrocks seized the card, threw it into the fire, and declared it was an application for a deaf and dumb institute.

The men set out for the hunt in Jorrocks' converted fire wagon. Ahead of them was a van carrying a drowsy doe. They were shocked to learn on arriving that their "stag" was that same tame deer imported for the day. She had to be chased to make her stop grazing on the common. Jorrocks' disappointment was complete when he learned that he had been invited only for his contribution to the club fund.

Abandoning the hunt for a while, Jorrocks took a boat trip to Margate with the Yorkshireman. That expedition was also a failure, for he left his clothes on the beach when he went for a swim and the tide engulfed them. The unhappy grocer was forced to go back to London in hand-me-downs.

Seeing numerous books for sale at fancy prices, Jorrocks determined to write a four-volume work on France that would sell for thirty pounds. With little more ado he collected the Yorkshireman and set out for Dover.

He was charmed with Boulogne, for the French were gay and the weather was sunny. On the coach to Paris he met the Countess Benwolio, as Jorrocks, in cockney fashion, called her. She was quite receptive to the rich grocer. The countess seemed a beautiful, youthful woman until she went to sleep in the coach and her teeth dropped down. Once in Paris, Jorrocks was snugly installed as the favored guest in her apartment. He began to collect information for his book.

The countess was avid for presents, and before many days Jorrocks began to run short of money. He tried to recoup at the races, but the Frenchmen were too shrewd for him. Finally he offered to race fifty yards on foot, with the Yorkshireman perched on his shoulders, against a fleet French baron who was to run a hundred yards. Jorrocks took a number of wagers and gave them to the countess to hold. He won the race easily. When he regained his breath and looked about for the countess, she had disappeared.

With little money and no French, the Englishmen were quite some time getting back to the countess' apartment. By the time they arrived, a gross Dutchman was installed as her favorite. When Jorrocks tried to collect his wagers, she presented him with a detailed board bill. Pooling his last funds with the Yorkshireman's hoard, he was barely able to pay the bill. Chastened by his sojourn among the French, Jorrocks returned to England.

Further Critical Evaluation of the Work:

Appearing in serialized form in *The New Sporting Magazine*, the episodic sporting adventures of Mr. Jorrocks, the rich Cockney grocer, captured the English imagination. His exploits were discussed in stable and dining room alike; among sportsmen he enjoyed as great a popularity as Dickens' Mr. Pickwick did in the society at large.

Although Surtees subjects Jorrocks to one social or physical humiliation after another, it would be a mistake to assume that the mudfalls and dunkings, the ridicule in court and the gulling by the French, are calculated primarily to reduce Jorrocks to the level of an exploited clown, or a lower-class trades-man satirized for his social pretensions. He *is* funny, and he is ridiculed for his sports mania, but Surtees' humor is not informed by social snobbery.

Jorrocks suffers from enthusiasm, from an overinvolvement with all forms of sport. He is punished comically for the exaggerated role the hunt and chase play in his life, but at the same time he is humanized by the very weakness that makes him ridiculous. What Surtees seems to be suggesting is that the true sportsman, no matter how disastrous the weather or how foul his luck, is always ready for the morrow, for the next hunt when everything will be perfect. In short, the sheer joy of the sportsman's expectations make him impervious to disappointment. There is greatness in that.

Surtees is the original apologist for the "sporting life." The secret of Jorrocks' appeal lies very much in the way Surtees managed to graft eighteenth century sentimentalism to what is essentially a robust social satire. It is as if Sterne and Smollett had joined forces in the same work. Dickens was to carry that kind of blend to far greater heights than Robert Smith Surtees, a yarn-spinning journalist who stumbled into comic fiction.

JOSEPH ANDREWS

Type of work: Novel
Author: Henry Fielding (1707-1754)
Type of plot: Comic epic
Time of plot: Early eighteenth century
Locale: England
First published: 1742

>*Principal characters:*
>JOSEPH ANDREWS, a footman to Lady Booby
>PAMELA ANDREWS, his sister, wife of Squire Booby
>LADY BOOBY, aunt of Squire Booby
>FANNY, Joseph's sweetheart
>MRS. SLIPSLOP, Lady Booby's maid
>PARSON ADAMS, parson of Booby parish and friend of Joseph

Critique:

The History of the Adventures of *Joseph Andrews, and of his Friend Mr. Abraham Adams* is the full title of the work often called the first realistic novel of English literature. Henry Fielding turned aside from the episodic sentimental writing of the age to give an honest picture of the manners and customs of his time and to satirize the foibles and vanities of human nature. In particular, he ridiculed affectation, whether it stemmed from hypocrisy or vanity. Although the structure of the novel is loose and rambling, the realistic settings and the vivid portrayal of English life in the eighteenth century more than compensate for this one weakness. Joseph is presented as the younger brother of Samuel Richardson's heroine, Pamela.

The Story:

Joseph Andrews was ten or eleven years in the service of Sir Thomas Booby, uncle of the Squire Booby who married the virtuous Pamela, Joseph's sister. When Lord Booby died, Joseph remained in the employ of Lady Booby as her footman. This lady, much older than her twenty-one-year-old servant, and apparently little disturbed by her husband's death, paid entirely too much attention to pleasant-mannered and handsome Joseph. But Joseph was as virtuous as his famous sister, and when Lady Booby's advances became such that even his innocence could no longer deny their true nature, he was as firm in resisting her as Pamela had been in restraining Squire Booby. Insulted, the lady discharged Joseph on the spot, in spite of the protests of Mrs. Slipslop, her maid, who found herself also attracted to the young man.

With very little money and fewer prospects, Joseph set out from London to Somersetshire to see his sweetheart, Fanny, for whose sake he had withstood Lady Booby's advances. The very first night of his journey, Joseph was attacked by robbers, who stole his money, beat him soundly, and left him lying naked and half dead in a ditch. A passing coach stopped when the passengers heard his cries, and he was taken to a nearby inn.

Joseph was well cared for until the innkeeper's wife discovered that he was penniless. He was recognized, however, by another visitor at the inn, his old tutor and preceptor, Parson Adams, who was on his way to London to sell a collection of his sermons. He paid Joseph's bill with his own meager savings; then, discovering that in his absent-mindedness he had forgotten to bring the sermons with him, he decided to accompany Joseph back to Somersetshire.

They started out, alternately on foot and on the parson's horse. Fortunately, Mrs. Slipslop overtook them in a coach on her way to Lady Booby's country place. She accommodated the parson in the coach while Joseph rode the horse. The inn at which they stopped next had an innkeeper who gauged his courtesy according to the appearance of his guests. There Joseph was insulted by the host. In spite of the clerical cassock he was wearing, Parson Adams stepped in to challenge the host, and a fist fight followed, the ranks being swelled by the hostess and Mrs. Slipslop. When the battle finally ended, Parson Adams was the bloodiest looking, since the hostess in the excitement had doused him with a pail of hog's blood.

The journey continued, this time with Joseph in the coach and the parson on foot, for with typical forgetfulness the good man had left his horse behind. However, he walked so rapidly and the coach moved so slowly that he easily outdistanced his friends. While he was resting on his journey, he heard the shrieks of a woman. Running to her rescue, he discovered a young woman being cruelly attacked by a burly fellow, whom the parson belabored with such violence that he laid the attacker at his feet. As some fox hunters rode up, the ruffian rose from the ground and accused Parson Adams and the woman of being conspirators in an attempt to rob him. The parson and the woman were quickly taken prisoners and led off to the sheriff. On the way the parson discovered that the young woman whom he had aided was Fanny. Having heard of Joseph's unhappy dismissal from Lady Booby's service, she had been on her way to London to help him when she had been so cruelly molested.

After some uncomfortable moments before the judge, the parson was recognized by an onlooker, and both he and Fanny were released. They went to the inn where Mrs. Slipslop and Joseph were staying.

Joseph and Fanny were overjoyed to be together once more. Mrs. Slipslop, displeased to see Joseph's display of affection for another woman, drove off in the coach, leaving Parson Adams and the young lovers behind.

None of the three had any money to pay their bill at the inn. Parson Adams, with indomitable optimism, went to visit the clergyman of the parish in order to borrow the money, but with no success. Finally a poor peddler at the inn gave them every penny he had, just enough to cover the bill.

They continued their trip on foot, stopping at another inn where the host was more courteous than any they had met, and more understanding about their financial difficulties. Still farther on their journey, they came across a secluded house at which they were asked to stop and rest. Mr. and Mrs. Wilson were a charming couple who gave their guests a warm welcome. Mr. Wilson entertained the parson with the story of his life. It seemed that in his youth he had been attracted by the vanity of London life, had squandered his money on foppish clothes, gambling, and drinking, and had eventually been imprisoned for debt. From this situation he was rescued by a kindly cousin whom he later married. The two had retired from London to this quiet country home. They had two lovely children and their only sorrow, but that a deep one, was that a third child, a boy with a strawberry mark on his shoulder, had been stolen by gipsies and had never been heard of since.

After a pleasant visit with the kindly family, the travelers set out again. Their adventures were far from ended. Parson Adams suddenly found himself caught in the middle of a hare hunt, with the hounds inclined to mistake him for the hare. Their master goaded on the dogs, but Joseph and the parson were victorious in the battle. They found themselves face to face with an angry squire and his followers. But when the squire caught sight of the lovely Fanny, his anger softened, and he invited the three to dine.

Supper was a trying affair for the parson, who was made the butt of many practical jokes. Finally the three travelers left the house in great anger and went to an inn. In the middle of the night, some of the squire's men arrived, overcame Joseph and the parson, and abducted Fanny. On the way, however, an old acquaintance of Fanny, Peter Pounce, met the party of kidnapers, recognized Fanny, and rescued her.

The rest of the journey was relatively uneventful. When they arrived home however, further difficulties arose. Joseph and Fanny stayed at the parsonage and waited eagerly for the publishing of their wedding banns. Lady Booby had also arrived in the parish, the seat of her summer home. Still in love with Joseph, she exerted every pressure of position and wealth to prevent the marriage. She even had Fanny and Joseph arrested. At this point, however, Squire Booby and his wife Pamela arrived. That gentleman insisted on accepting his wife's relatives as his own, even though they were of a lower station, and Joseph and Fanny were quickly released from custody.

All manner of arguments were presented by Pamela, her husband, and Lady Booby in their attempts to turn Joseph aside from his intention of marrying Fanny. Her lowly birth made a difference to their minds, now that Pamela had made a good match and Joseph had been received by the Boobys.

Further complications arose when a traveling peddler revealed that Fanny, whose parentage until then had been unknown, was the sister of Pamela. Mr. and Mrs. Andrews were summoned at this disclosure, and Mrs. Andrews described how, while Fanny was still a baby, gipsies had stolen the child and left behind them a sickly little boy she had brought up as her own. Now it appeared that Joseph was the foundling. However, a strawberry mark on Joseph's chest soon established his identity. He was the son of the kindly Wilsons.

Both lovers were now secure in their social positions, and nothing further could prevent their marriage, which took place, to the happiness of all concerned, soon afterward.

Further Critical Evaluation of the Work:

Joseph Andrews is many things: a parody of Richardson's *Pamela,* a sentimental tale of virtue rewarded; a realistic portrayal of the English road in the eighteenth century; a resetting of the values of comic epic poetry in prose, resulting in what Fielding calls a "comic epic romance" and by which he has in mind the model of Cervantes' *Don Quixote*; an experiment in social satire which brands affectation as ridiculous. All these characteristics blend in a master function. It is an oversimplification merely to conceive of this function in generic terms, to formulate an all-encompassing descriptive label like "comic epic in prose" or "comic novel" and consider the book defined.

Fielding, along with Richardson, is sometimes called the father of the English novel because he ventilated the concept of narrative itself; his brilliant plotting in *Tom Jones* and the desultory Odyssean travels of *Joseph Andrews* are contrasting patterns for realizing a broadly imagined action rich in human nature. *Joseph Andrews,* then, is one of the earliest examples of modern literature's successful extension of mimetic possibilities beyond the models of classical antiquity and the folk tradition. The novel is a mixed genre; it is composed of tale, parable, ballad, and, of course, epic. But the mixture becomes a whole greater than its parts with true innovators such as Fielding.

What holds Fielding's book together is its cosmic exposure of appearance. Wherever Joseph and Parson Adams go, their naïveté and innocence make them inadvertent exposers of affectation. Affectation is the most ridiculous form of "appearance" among men. It invites derision and must be exposed: the effect is morally healthy, but even more to the point, mimetically revealing. Behind appearance lies the "true springs of human action." The essence of a man is often better than his appearance, even though his vanity may commit him to affectation. Parson Adams is a loveable character mainly because under his pedantries and vanities beats a heart of gold. His naïve trust in human goodness, and his unshakeable belief in practiced Christianity define the true man: the "real" Adam is better than his affectations. Similarly, when Joseph is robbed, beaten, and stripped of his clothes, Fielding takes the opportunity to demonstrate the fact that true human charity may emanate from a person whose appearance and life history would seem to mark him incapable of any kindness: "the postillion (a lad who has since been transported for robbing a hen-roost) . . . voluntarily stripped off a great-coat, his only garment; at the same time swearing a great oath, for which he was rebuked by the passengers, that he would rather ride in his shirt all his life, than suffer a fellow passenger to lie in so miserable a condition."

Fielding trusts in his satiric method—the exposure of affectation and the questioning of appearance—because he senses that it will not ground his comic vision in despair or cynicism. He avoids the satiric fate of Swift, whose contempt for human imperfections of character and principle drove him to contempt for men in general. Fielding maintains a love of life itself, an essential state of mind for an artist who presumes to epic achievements in the imaginative grasp of social reality. Swift could never have written *Tom Jones* (1749), Fielding's great comic novel with its tolerant but firmly objective picture of human nature. *Joseph Andrews* is a preface, in theme and style, to the more carefully plotted masterpiece.

As tolerant as Fielding is of human nature, he is also capable of biting judgment. Not a misanthrope like Swift, as Walter Allen reminds us in *The English Novel* (1954), Fielding is nevertheless a tough-minded moralist who delights in passing harsh comic judgment when it is called for. He was, after all, a court judge in real life. Parson Trulliber is a case in point. Fielding has Parson Adams fall into the mud with Trulliber's pigs, but this embarrassment is typical of the many other physical beatings and discomforts that the good Parson suffers throughout the novel. They are emblematic of Fielding's mild judgment of Adams' clerical vanity. Once the mud is washed off, the naïve but true Christian in Parson Adams is all the more shiningly revealed. Things are exactly the opposite with Trulliber. His Christianity is completely superficial; Parson Adams' innocent request for fourteen shillings of charity is met by cries of thief. Once Trulliber's fake Christianity is exposed, he is all hog's mud underneath. This is established from the beginning of his encounter with Parson Adams, whom he mistakes for a hog merchant. Trulliber sees and feels with the eyes and temperament of a hog. He is stingy with food as well as money and like his angry pigs is quick to belligerence. The only way he can defend himself against Parson Adams' accusation that he is not a good Christian is by clenching his fist. The most telling irony is Trulliber's contempt for Parson Adams' appearance. How can this horseless man with a torn "cassock" call himself a man of the cloth? Because Trulliber's Christianity is all surface, it is he who is dripping in hog's mud from first to last, not Parson Adams.

Fielding's pursuit of essential humanity in his characters, through the stripping away of affectation and appearance, is so successful that by the end of the novel he can indulge in burlesque without dehumanizing. Two chapters from the end, Parson Adams, thinking he is about to rescue Fanny from rape, finds himself wrestling with Slipslop, whom he mistakes for the rapist. Aroused to his mistake by Slipslop's huge bosom and Lady Booby's entrance, he staggers back to what he mistakenly thinks is his own room and lies down beside Fanny. In the morning Joseph discovers them lying together. Everything is explained and everyone is appeased. Even Slipslop seems to have enjoyed the "attention" of both the rapist (Beau Didapper) and her attacker, the Parson. All this is pure farce, a broad joke to usher in the warmly comic conclusion of the novel. It is a measure of Fielding's fictive power that he can people a story with characters rich enough to shift from burlesque to comedy without compromising their credibility. In fact, both plot and character seem to benefit mutually from the author's comic exuberance.

Peter A. Brier

JOSEPH VANCE

Type of work: Novel
Author: William De Morgan (1839-1917)
Type of plot: Simulated autobiography
Time of plot: Mid-nineteenth century
Locale: England
First published: 1906

Principal characters:

JOSEPH VANCE, who wrote his memoirs
MR. CHRISTOPHER VANCE, his father
DR. RANDALL THORPE, Joseph's foster father
LOSSIE THORPE, Dr. Thorpe's daughter
JOE THORPE (BEPPINO), her brother
VIOLET THORPE, her sister
NOLLY THORPE, another brother
BONY MACALLISTER, Joseph's business partner
GENERAL DESPREZ, Lossie's husband
JANEY SPENCER, Joseph's wife
PHEENER, a maid

Critique:

Joseph Vance is an early example of the now popular type of autobiographical novel. It is the story of the life of Joseph Vance from his earliest recollections until the last years of his life. As the author tells us through the words of his main character, there is much that might have been left out, since there are many threads of the plot which are unimportant to the story. Humor and pathos are successfully mixed; the humor particularly is the quiet kind that makes us chuckle to ourselves. It comes largely from the character of Vance's father, whose firm belief it is that to be a success a person must know absolutely nothing about doing the job he is hired to do. De Morgan gave his novel a subtitle, *An Ill-Written Autobiography,* but few of his readers will agree with him.

The Story:

Joseph Vance's father was more often drunk than sober. But he was a good man, never mean when he was drunk. Having lost several positions because of his drinking, he was in no way depressed. He took Joe with him to visit a pub on the night of his discharge from his last position, and while there he quarreled with a chimney sweep and had the poor end of the fight. Forced to spend some time in the hospital after the affair, he decided to give up his excessive drinking.

After his release from the hospital he set himself up as a builder and drain repairman, by virtue of acquiring a signboard advertising the possessor as such a workman. Mr. Vance knew nothing about the building trade, but he believed that it was his ignorance which would cause him to be a success at the business. He appeared to be right. His first job was for Dr. Randall Thorpe, of Poplar Villa, and Dr. Thorpe was so pleased with the work that he recommended Mr. Vance for more jobs until his reputation was such that he was much in demand. Mr. Vance took Joe with him on his first call at Poplar Villa, and there Joe met Miss Lossie Thorpe, the first real young lady he had ever seen. At this time Joe was nine and Lossie fifteen, but he knew from the first meeting that she was to be his lady for the rest of his life.

When Dr. Thorpe learned that Joe was a bright boy, he sent him to school and made him almost one of the family.

Lossie was like a sister to him; in fact, she called him her little brother and encouraged him in his studies. In the Thorpe household were also young Joe Thorpe, called Beppino, a sister Violet, and another brother named Nolly. With these young people Joe Vance grew up, and Dr. Thorpe continued to send him to school, even to Oxford when he was ready. Although Dr. Thorpe had hoped that Joe Vance might excel in the classics, the boy found his interest in engineering. Beppino did grow up to be a poet, but he wrote such drivel that his father was disgusted. Meanwhile a deep friendship had developed between Joe Vance and Lossie, a brother-and-sister love that made each want the other's happiness above all else.

Mr. Vance's business prospered so much that he and his wife took a new house and hired a cook and a maid. After Joe had finished at Oxford, he joined his old school friend, Bony Macallister, and they established an engineering firm. Their offices were in the same building with Mr. Vance. By that time Lossie had married General Desprez, a wealthy army officer, and had moved with him to India. Joe suffered a great deal at the loss of his dear friend, but he knew that General Desprez was a fine man who would care for Lossie and love her tenderly.

Shortly after Lossie sailed for India, Joe's mother died. and his father began to drink once more. Joe tried to think of some way to help his father. Joe thought that if he married his wife might influence his father, and he asked Janey Spencer, a friend of Lossie, to marry him. She accepted, but when she learned that Joe wanted to marry her only for the sake of his father, she broke the engagement and did not relent until two years later. By that time Joe knew he really loved her, and she married him. In the meantime, Joe's father had married Pheener, his housemaid, and for a time she kept him from the bottle.

After Janey and Joe had been married for five years, they took a trip to Italy.

The ship caught on fire and almost all on board were lost. When Janey refused to get into a lifeboat without her husband, they tried to swim to shore. Janey was drowned. Joe's life was empty without her, and only his visits with Dr. Thorpe and his letters from Lossie gave him any comfort.

Joe's business prospered, as did his father's. But one day Mr. Vance, while drunk, caused an explosion and a fire in the building. He was seriously injured, and he seemed to be ruined because he had let his insurance lapse. But before the catastrophe he had given Pheener a tiara worth fifteen thousand pounds, and with the money received from the sale of the jewels he was able to start his business anew.

In the meantime Beppino was grieving his family by an affair with a married woman. For the sake of the Thorpes, Joe took Beppino to Italy. On Joe's return Beppino remained behind. When Beppino returned, he met and married Sibyl Perceval, an heiress, and the family believed he had changed his ways. But Beppino died of typhoid fever shortly after his marriage, and then Joe learned what Beppino had done while in Italy. He had married an Italian girl. using the name of Joe Vance, and she had had a child. The Italian girl had died, too, and her relatives wrote to Joe in the belief that he was the father. Joe told General Desprez of Beppino's duplicity, the General and Lossie having come home for a visit, and the two men agreed that Lossie must never know of her brother's deed. Joe went to Italy and told the girl's relatives that he was a friend of the baby's father. He arranged to send money for the boy's care.

Shortly afterward Joe went to Brazil on an engineering project. While there, he sent for Beppino's boy and adopted him. The next twenty years of his life he spent in Brazil. He heard from Lossie and Dr. Thorpe frequently, but otherwise he had no connection with England. His father died and Pheener remarried. While Joe was in Brazil,

Lossie heard rumors from Italy that he was the baby's real father. She was so disappointed in her foster brother that she never wrote again. Joe returned to England. Living near Lossie, he did not see her or let her know he was back in the country. The boy was attending school in America. Lossie's husband died without telling the real story about the child, and Joe would not tell the truth even to save himself in Lossie's eyes. He wrote the story in his memoirs, but left his papers to be burned after his return to Brazil.

But a maid burned the wrong package, and a publisher's note completed Joe's story. Lossie found a letter from Beppino in some of her husband's papers and surmised the truth. She found Joe Vance before he left for Brazil and made him confess that he had acted only to save her feelings. She begged Joe to forgive her. Reunited, the two friends went to Italy and spent their remaining days together.

Further Critical Evaluation of the Work:

The influences of Sterne and Dickens are very clear in *Joseph Vance*. Sterne especially is evident in the tone of the narration, the descriptions of the characters, and in the philosophizing and digressions, for instance, on Joe's Father's Hat and Human Nature. The author's style is not as smooth and graceful as Sterne's, however, resulting at times in a rather strained and arch humor. The protagonist's father, for example, is too obviously intended to be a grand old "character." The narrative vitality and sense of place, and the minor characters, suggest Dickens. The lower-class dialect is often skilfully utilized, but it is carried to the point of preciousness; mispronunciations and absurd grammar alone do not make a character comic. But the story is crowded with telling and often amusing details, despite the occasionally excessive use of letters to move the story forward, and the minor characters are sketched with precise and vivid portraits.

The development of the protagonist is interesting, for the most part, although the narrative is sometimes confusing. Joseph's bouts with education (especially geometry) and the results when he tries to demonstrate his new learning to his old friends are amusing. De Morgan's power to create character and convey atmosphere provide the principle merits of the novel. Some of the scenes in the house of the Thorpe family, Joseph's adopted relations and protectors, possess a quaint and touching charm.

William De Morgan did not begin his career as a writer until after retiring from his first career as a ceramic artist and inventor. A member of the Pre-Raphaelite circle, he was famous for the quality and beauty of his glazes; much of his work with pottery and tiles is preserved in museums. His second career as a novelist brought him a wide literary reputation and considerable financial success. His last two works were published posthumously. *Joseph Vance,* De Morgan's first novel, is still considered his best fictional effort. The richness of the prose, the humor, and the delightful characterizations should ensure the book a secure, if minor, place in English literature.

JOURNAL OF A TOUR TO THE HEBRIDES

Type of work: Diary
Author: James Boswell (1740-1795)
First published: 1785

Principal personages:
JAMES BOSWELL, the author, a young Scottish lawyer
SAMUEL JOHNSON, his aging friend, the great essayist, biographer, poet, and critic
LORD AUCHINLECK, Boswell's father, a noted Scottish judge

In August, 1773, James Boswell finally succeeded in persuading his distinguished friend Samuel Johnson to accompany him on a tour of his native Scotland, a country for which the learned Dr. Johnson's scorn was legendary. Boswell kept a detailed journal for most of their journey together, and he published it, in a version edited and revised with the help of the Shakespearian scholar, Edmund Malone, in 1785, as a companion volume to Johnson's own account, the *Journey to the Western Islands of Scotland,* that had appeared in 1775. Boswell's original journal was discovered with many of his other private papers in this century, and the modern reader has the opportunity to peruse a considerably franker account than the one that was first issued to the public.

The *Journal of a Tour to the Hebrides* is at once a fascinating travelogue, an unusually full record of life in the Scottish highlands and on the remote islands of the Hebrides, a character sketch of Johnson, and, like Boswell's other diaries, a mirror of his personal idiosyncrasies. Boswell seems especially anxious to show the respect and deference with which his friend was greeted by his countrymen; he wanted to prove to Johnson and to the world that the Scots were indeed capable of being scholars and gentlemen, closely in touch with the world of learning, and, being himself, he naturally felt pride in having the privilege of introducing so great a figure to the professors and noblemen of his homeland.

Perhaps the greatest appeal of Boswell's account lies in the absolute naturalness of both style and content. Discussion of the quality of the food and the beds at every inn along the way is interspersed with Johnson's comments on whatever volumes of prayers, sermons, or poems he was able to procure and with accounts of long conversations between the scholar and many of his hosts on religion, philosophy, politics, and literature. As the trip went on, Boswell tended to fall farther and farther behind in his account, and throughout the journal he casually tossed in collections of Johnsoniana after having forgotten the specific occasions of many of the doctor's comments. He chose, too, to stop his narrative at intervals to give geographical and historical details.

Boswell is brutally frank, in his unpublished account, about the character of some of their hosts. He is relatively sympathetic when treating the weakness of Donald MacLeod, a young kinsman of the chief of the MacLeod clan of Dunvegan, on the isle of Skye, who took their money to town to have it changed and squandered a portion of it on his own refreshment, much to his later chagrin and shame. The arrogance and lack of hospitality of Sir Alexander Macdonald, whose manners seemed to Boswell entirely out of keeping with his station in life, are treated much more harshly. Boswell gives a particularly amusing account of their visit to the Duke and Duchess of Argyll at Inverary. The duchess refused so much as to acknowledge his presence, because he had opposed her in a celebrated law suit, but both she and her husband welcomed Johnson cordially.

Johnson appears throughout the journal as a man remarkably willing to adapt to circumstances, however uncomfortable they might be; it was Boswell, many years his junior, who was most disturbed by the lack of clean bedding and almost overcome by fright when they ran into a storm as they traveled from one island to another in a small boat. Dr. Johnson teased the young daughters of his hosts, flattered and complimented the elderly ladies, and, for the most part, restrained himself from severely attacking those with whose views he differed violently, especially on such questions as the once burning issue of the authenticity of James MacPherson's Ossian poems, published, Johnson thought fraudulently, as translations from the Gaelic.

One of the most delightful episodes in the journal is Boswell's description of Johnson's meeting with his father, Lord Auchinleck, a stanch Whig and Presbyterian. Johnson was an equally dogmatic Tory, whose sympathies with the Jacobite cause led him to inquire with great interest about the activities of "Bonny Prince Charlie" when he escaped to Skye after the disastrous battle of Culloden; he was so loyal a member of the Church of England that he read his own prayers throughout most of his trip rather than participate in Presbyterian services. Boswell cautioned Johnson to avoid the controversial topics of politics and religion whenever possible, and the encounter of the two men the young lawyer revered most was, for a time, smooth. But the "collision," as Boswell calls it, finally came. A medal with Oliver Cromwell's portrait on it was the cause, introducing the subject of Charles I and the Tories, with the inevitable results. Boswell discreetly withholds the details of the argument, but he does mention that afterwards his father dubbed Johnson "Ursa Major," the great bear. In spite of their altercation, however, the two aging gentlemen apparently parted on terms of mutual respect, if not of friendship, and Boswell appears well-satisfied at having brought them together.

Boswell's portrait of himself in this account is less revealing than that in the *London Journal;* age had apparently curtailed some of his frankness and unselfconsciousness, but even here, in the original diary, though not in the published version, he describes in some detail his spiritual experiences in several of the old ruins he visited, and he records with chagrin how quickly his resolutions for increased temperance and self-control were overcome by the offer of a fresh bowl of punch. His concern for his wife, whom he had left at home in Edinburgh, runs throughout his pages, and he had what proved to be false premonitions of disasters befalling her and their children. His uxoriousness did not, however, curtail his critical judgments of the various young ladies he and Johnson met on their travels.

Among the most interesting sections of the book for the modern reader are those that describe in detail the daily life of the heads of the various clans that inhabited the western islands. The civilized manners of the MacLeods of Raasay had made their daughters welcome at fashionable gatherings in Edinburgh and London, yet the lords and their young heirs were acquainted with the most menial tasks involved with the running of their estates. The wide reading of many of the Highlanders, especially of the clergymen, and the education of the young people also surprised the travelers, and Johnson on one occasion presented an arithmetic book to a bright young girl with whose family he had lodged. However, the primitiveness of many of the tenants of the great landholders is presented in sharp contrast to the sophistication of their masters.

The *Journal of a Tour to the Hebrides*, like Boswell's other biographical and autobiographical writings has had and will continue to have great appeal for readers, primarily for the spirit of life that infuses every page. Servants, obscure clergymen, elderly Scotswomen, and youthful lords come to life vividly as do Boswell and Johnson themselves, and the naturalness of Boswell's style makes his work contemporary and fascinating throughout.

A JOURNAL OF THE PLAGUE YEAR

Type of work: Novel
Author: Daniel Defoe (1660?-1731)
Time: 1665
Locale: London, England
First published: 1722

Principal character:
H. F., the narrator, a London saddler

Unlike Defoe's more obviously fictional books and novels, *A Journal of the Plague Year* is rarely read as a whole, though a number of writers, such as Virginia Woolf, testify to its impact. On the other hand, it is more likely than the novels to be anthologized in college compendia of English literature, where its presence is justified not as background material (like Pepys) but either as especially fitted for extraction by its episodic construction or as historically significant. Both grounds are valid and together indicate the nature and worth of the whole work. The book shows on every page more clearly than *Moll Flanders* or the other episodic novels posing as "true accounts," the intricate and slow development of the English novel which attracted writers away from sermons and polemics in the early eighteenth century and established a formal tradition good for some two centuries. Thus when John Drinkwater called Defoe "the founder of the English novel," his justification may be found as much in the *Journal* as in *Robinson Crusoe* or *Roxana.*

The first problem in the development of the novel was to establish a working relationship between fact and fiction; the traditional novel still begins with a factual introduction to assist the "willing suspension of disbelief" so necessary to the novelist's manipulation of material and reader. Defoe's invention was to use a hard core of statistics, tabulated on the pages of the *Journal,* of the weekly death "bills" or returns from the ninety-seven parishes in the City of London and the sixteen or so in Southwark and outside the city limits; but the tables are disposed artistically throughout the work instead of being appendixed and are surrounded by further particulars which become more hedged with conditions as Defoe elaborates them. In a very short time the reader is in a region of rumor which Defoe first solemnly reports, then rationally dismisses or qualifies. Rumor is the middle ground between statisics and the imagination, and Defoe is careful to allow us to believe it or not as we wish. We accept such folklore at face value, perhaps, because gossip is more entertaining than truth. Thus the first sentence of the *Journal* does not begin "Once upon a time," but specifies September, 1664, as the date the narrator first heard that the plague had come to Holland for the second year running. The first paragraph then expands with rumors about its place of origin: "they say . . . some said . . . others . . . all agreed."

The subtitle of the *Journal*—"Being Observations or Memorials of the Most Remarkable Occurences, as well Publick as Private, which happened in London during the last Great Visitation in 1665. Written by a Citizen who continued all the while in London. Never made publick before"—is a bland lie which indicates the second way Defoe encouraged the reader's imagination to work for him: "Observations or Memorials" sufficiently confuses the distinction between what was recorded at the time and what was remembered later. Defoe's sources, beyond the death bills, were not extensive and his memories second-hand, but his imagination was fertile. He carefully controlled and encouraged it by the threefold organization of his *Journal.* Contrary to its title it is not a daily record, and the time references shift from September to

August and over the whole summer of the plague. Instead of daily entries Defoe used time references, from September 1664 to December 1665, as ways of beginning and conclusion of his narrative, ending with the doggerel quatrain which celebrates the narrator's deliverance. Within the work he preserves a gradual movement of the plague from the west to the east parts of the city, ending with a central holocaust; and scattered throughout the work we find his tables of statistics. Neither the geographical, the chronological, nor the numerical progress of the plague is consistently followed. The jumps in geography and time make one want to restore logical order to the work and thereby turn it into a literal "journal," at the same time risking loss of its imaginative qualities.

Defoe's imagination proceeds mechanically but energetically by considering one general topic and its subheadings at a time. Thus we get several pages of increasingly horrific detail about the practices of nurses or a catalogue of various kinds of quacks, fortunetellers, prophets, and necromancers who flourished during that awful summer; the section on women in childbirth, for instance coolly divides their tragedies into those who died in childbirth with and without the plague, and the former are further subdivided into those who died before giving birth, or in the middle of giving birth, or before the cord was cut. Defoe's narrator could see little of these matters for himself, but "they say" and "I heard" fill up the paragraphs one after another until all possible contingencies have been covered.

Defoe's imagination works with three classes of corroborative detail: the quick summary, the brief anecdote, and the extended story, each of which could have supplied him with many more narratives, and did indeed in his *Due Preparations for the Plague* published about the same time in order to catch the same apprehensive market as his *Journal*. The summary paragraph often introduces a series of brief anecdotes but sometimes stands alone, as in his brief recital of the killing of forty thousand dogs and two hundred thousand housecats as a precaution against the spread of the plague. There are many brief anecdotes, such as the frequently anthologized account of purifying a purse, which exhibit at once the common-sense cautiousness Defoe admires, the honesty of the Londoner, and the current belief that the plague was spread by contaminated air. The longest of the stories, filling about one tenth of the *Journal*, is that of the three men and their company who spent the summer camping in Epping Forest. Defoe tells the story at length to show what happened to Londoners who left the city and retired to places where his narrator could not follow them.

Defoe's subject was epic in scope: a great metropolis in the midst of a boom following the Restoration is slowly strangled by a hidden enemy. The size of his subject gives ample scope for the inclusion of all sorts of material, but his handling of it is typically original. Instead of a heroic poem we get the sober account of an average Londoner, a superior type of the real heroes of his book—those from Lord Mayor to beggar who did not abandon their city. The narrator is simply identified by the subscription of "H. F." to the *Journal* (possibly an allusion to Defoe's uncle, Henry Foe) and is described as a saddler engaged in the American trade. This, like all trade and manufacturing, ended with the onslaught of the plague in June, 1665, and left his narrator free to observe the reactions of his townsfolk.

Defoe's choice of narrator serves to control his material by presenting it soberly and thus to press Defoe's own views on the prevention of the plague, as in his saddler's criticism of shutting up the living with the sick when one plague victim was found in the house. But the opinions of the narrator seem contradictory in two respects. The first is purely technical; the saddler recommends shutting up one's house at the beginning of the plague but acknowledges that supplies have to be brought in by servants and thus the plague spreads. He shuts up his house and servants but wanders through the streets even to the deathpits (he observes that one in his parish of Aldgate holds eleven hundred and fourteen corpses when full); he must wander in order to write his "journal." Except for a period of three weeks when he is conscripted as an "examiner" he remains an observer and thus uncharacteristic of the energetic and resourceful citizens, the details of whose organization seem practical and whose spirit Defoe lauds during the plague and bewails when it passes as the plague diminishes.

In a second respect the ambivalence of the narrator is more striking: he lauds common sense and courage where he finds it but ascribes to providence the salvation of the city in the despair most felt at the end of September, when deaths numbered over ten thousand weekly. Then, suddenly, the weekly bills showed a dramatic decrease. To whom should go the praise? Defoe has it both ways, as he had done when he solemnly introduced the scandalous history of Moll Flanders as a moral tract. It is this ambivalence which is the true foundation of the English novel, a recital of fictions which rings, and is, essentially true.

THE JOURNAL OF THOREAU

Author: Henry David Thoreau (1817-1862)
First published: 1906

About Thoreau's Journal no single statement is more appropriate than Walt Whitman's words about his own *Leaves of Grass:* "This no book,/Who touches this touches a man." Thoreau began his journal on October 22, 1837, soon after he had been graduated from Harvard, apparently at the suggestion of Emerson. On the first leaf, Thoreau wrote: " 'What are you doing now?' he asked. 'Do you keep a journal?' So I make my first entry to-day." Practically every day thereafter, almost to the time of his death, he entered his thoughts, sometimes long, sometimes brief, but all the essence of the man. In 1857, Thoreau entered the thought: "Is not the poet bound to write his own biography? Is there any other work for him but a good journal? We do not wish to know how his imaginary hero, but how he, the actual hero, lived from day to day." Thoreau's actual hero recorded in his journal "all his joy, his ecstasy." But he tried to keep his perspective and not misdirect his effort. In February 8, 1841, when he was twenty-three years old, he recorded: "My Journal is that of me which would else spill over and run to waste, gleanings from the field which in action I reap. I must not live for it, but in it for the gods."

Because the Journal was so completely the full life of the man, when he came to write his other works he naturally mined his daily recordings for ideas and recollections, which he then amplified and modified to fit his more immediate purpose. Apparently Thoreau never intended to publish his journal as such, for it was a secret and private depository of his thoughts: " 'Says I to myself' should be the motto of my journal," he recorded in 1851. Thoreau's family after his death also felt that the Journal was too private to be of public interest. Finally, however, the work was issued in 1906 in fourteen volumes. Though called complete, this version was in fact far short of the total work, which in Thoreau's private recording had reached nearly two million words. At least two other volumes of his early journal were omitted. One has subsequently been published, as *Consciousness in Concord,* edited by Perry Miller. And another volume of Thoreau's early journal, consisting of some 42,000 words, is now in the keeping of the New York Public Library.

Because his journal was a private depository of Thoreau's observations and reactions daily replenished, it ranges through the full breadth and depth of its author's experience. During the earlier years it quite naturally was filled with Thoreau's naïve reactions to life, to the books he was reading, and to his exuberant reactions to the philosophy of Transcendentalism espoused by his mentor Emerson and adopted by himself. Thus we find such entries as the following: "All this worldly wisdom was once the unamiable heresy of some wise man" (July 6, 1840). "We should strengthen, and beautify, and industriously mould our bodies to be fit companions of the soul,—assist them to grow up like trees, and be agreeable and wholesome objects in nature. I think if I had had the disposal of this soul of man, I should have bestowed it sooner on some antelope of the plains than upon this sickly and sluggish body" (January 25, 1841).

Occasionally, the plain good sense and restraint of the young man is overwhelmed by his uncontrolled poetic impulses and he shapes a line or figure more florid than effective: "Nature refuses to sympathize with our sorrow. She seems not to have provided for, but by a thousand contrivances against, it. She has bevelled the margins of the eyelids that the tears may not overflow on the cheek"

(July 27, 1841).

Beginning on July 4, 1845, and continuing for two years and two months, Thoreau lived in a hut at Walden Pond. After his return he lived for a year in the Emerson home. After these years Thoreau's mood was one of expansiveness and universalism, stimulated by the air of freedom he breathed in the open country around his native village. The Journal entries reveal his spirit: "I do not prefer one religion or philosophy to another. I have no sympathy with the bigotry and ignorance which make transient and partial and puerile distinctions between one man's faith or form of faith and another's,—as Christian and heathen. I pray to be delivered from narrowness, partiality, exaggeration, bigotry. To the philosopher all sects, all nations, are alike. I like Brahma, Hari, Buddha, the Great Spirit, as well as God" (1850).

The practical Yankee nature never did understand Thoreau. After his death, Thoreau's best friend, Emerson, even deprecated his lack of accomplishment in worldly affairs, lamenting that "instead of engineering for all America, he was the captain of a huckleberry-party. Pounding beans is good to the end of pounding empires one of these days; but if, at the end of years, it is still only beans!" In Thoreau, however, there ran a wide and strong stream of humor which allowed him to accept without irritation the misunderstanding of his neighbors as long as it allowed him to go his individual way. Often in the Journal, as in the famous chapter on "Economy" in *Walden,* he entered his humorous observations in aphoristic understatement, as in "Some circumstantial evidence is very strong, as when you find a trout in the milk" (November 11, 1850).

During the early 1850's Thoreau was reaching the full maturity of his powers. As he more and more balanced his inner strifes and conflicts, he increasingly turned his rapier observations and wit on the disharmonies of the exterior world. He still felt himself undeveloped but his potential great: "Here I am thirty-four years old, and yet my life is almost wholly unexpanded. How much is the germ! There is such an interval between my ideal and the actual in many instances that I may say I am unborn" (July 19, 1851). On another occasion, soon afterwards, he again cautioned himself to exploit himself: "Drain the cup of inspiration to its last dregs. . . . The spring will not last forever" (January 24, 1852). On numerous occasions he lashes out at the injustices of the world, as when he sees a small child, on a cold day, dressed in only one layer of clothes and holey shoes, trudging to school. Thoreau's whole nature is revulsed: "This little mass of humanity, this tender gobbet for the fates, cast into a cold world with a torn lichen leaf wrapped about him,—oh, I should rather hear that America's firstborn were all slain than that his little fingers and toes should feel cold while I am warm" (January 28, 1852).

One of the great ironies in the history of the appreciation of literary works concerns Thoreau's first book, *A Week on the Concord and Merrimack Rivers,* the outcome of which is wryly entered in his journal. This book had been published in an edition of one thousand copies. On October 28, 1853, Thoreau recorded that 706 copies had been returned to him in a wagon. Of the 294 disposed of by the publisher, some seventy-five had been given away. Of the fate of this literary adventure, Thoreau remarked with great irony: "I have now a library of nearly nine hundred volumes, over seven hundred of which I wrote myself. Is it not well that the author should behold the fruits of his labor?"

Up to the very last days of his life, Thoreau's attitude continued to clarify and solidify. Though his attitudes became less and less flexible, he never became a hardened cynic. Always he maintained his faith in himself, not with a blind egotism, but with the feeling that he was representative man. As he said in *Walden,* "If I seem to boast more than is becoming, my excuse is that I brag for humanity rather than for myself." As typical man he felt that his story was worth telling, though confided privately in his journal. One of his late entries states: "Wherever men have lived there is a story to be told, and it depends chiefly on the story-teller or historian whether that is interesting or not" (March 18, 1861).

The story Thoreau told in the Journal is one of the most intimate and revealing ever recounted in American literature.

JOURNAL TO ELIZA

Type of work: Sentimental diary
Author: Laurence Sterne (1713-1768)
First published: 1904

Principal personages:
YORICK, Sterne's *alter ego*, the writer of the journal
ELIZA DRAPER, the object of his sentimental passion

Laurence Sterne's *Journal to Eliza* has been considered by unsuspecting readers as conclusive evidence that its author was a lachrymose sentimentalist. Yet anyone familiar with *Tristram Shandy* and *A Sentimental Journey* will recognize touches of that humorous view of eighteenth century sentimentalism that makes Sterne's novels so appealing.

Sterne was neither a parodist nor a satirist in the usual sense. He seems, in fact, to have enjoyed dramatizing his emotions on numerous occasions, and he could not have created some of his finest fictional scenes without real sensitivity to nuances of feeling. Nevertheless, an ironic humorist always occupied one corner of his mind, ready to appear at any moment to undercut the effect of a particularly touching episode. He was always aware of the ridiculous aspects of human behavior, and he appropriately adopted the name of one of literature's most famous jesters for his *alter ego*. It is as Parson Yorick that he sheds copious tears over the departure of his beloved Eliza and, in *A Sentimental Journey*, invokes her name to protect him from the amorous intrigues that awaited him at every coach station.

The *Journal to Eliza* is not an easy work to analyze; numerous readers have puzzled over its tone. Is it to be considered as an autobiographical document, as a purely literary creation, or as something between the two? Sterne met Eliza Draper, the wife of an employee of the East India Company, in 1767, the year before his death. Extant letters suggest that he fancied himself in love with her, while she regarded him as a friend, but no more. It was not out of character for Sterne to indulge himself in a literary romance that existed primarily in his imagination. Some of the letters he wrote his wife before their marriage are almost identical to the effusions of his journal, and he later addressed other ladies who struck his fancy in similar terms. Whatever his feelings may have been, Sterne was the same man who was composing the brilliantly witty *A Sentimental Journey* during the last months of his life, and it is difficult to believe that he did not perceive the essential absurdity of some of his outpourings of emotion in the *Journal to Eliza*.

Yorick's diary, which is really an extended letter, begins just after Eliza has left for India with her husband. He has promised his "Bramine" that he will record his activities and his feelings every day, and he begins with extravagant protestation of grief at her departure. Few external events find a place in the journal; Yorick visits friends, travels from London to his country home, and, in the latter part of the book, anticipates a visit from his estranged wife and their daughter, but most of the pages are filled with accounts of the parson's illness and the torments of his sorrowing soul.

His laments over his solitary dinner are typical of the ludicrous sentimentality of the work: "I have just been eating my Chicking, sitting over my repast upon it with Tears—a bitter Sause—Eliza! but I could eat it with no other—when Molly spread the Table Cloath, my heart fainted within me—one solitary plate—one knife—one Glass! O Eliza; 'twas painfully distressing. . . ."

The disjointed phrases, the apostrophes to the absent lady, the potent emotional effects of everyday objects characterize the style of the entire journal. The work abounds in tears from start to finish.

Yorick weeps over his dinner, over Eliza's picture, over dreams of her; he joins their friend Mrs. James in lamenting his pale, wan countenance, and he sobs with his maid, Molly, who feelingly comments on how much Mrs. Draper is missed. Sterne is a master of the language of overwrought emotions, and it is not surprising that some readers have taken him completely seriously.

There are, however, clues along the way which suggest that Yorick's laments are not quite what they seem. It is typical that the writer who filled *Tristram Shandy* with bawdy *double entendres* should make much of the fact that Yorick's illness, brought on by grief at Eliza's leaving, has been diagnosed as venereal disease. He protests vehemently " 'tis impossible, at least to be that, replied I—for I have had no commerce whatever with the Sex—not even with my wife, added I, these 15 years." This is not the kind of comment one expects to find in a truly "sentimental" work. Yorick's apology for bringing up the subject simply enhances the humor of the situation: "Tis needless to tell Eliza, that nothing but the purest consciousness of Virtue, could have tempted Eliza's friend to have told her this Story—Thou are too good my Eliza to love aught but Virtue—and too discerning not to distinguish the open character, which bears it, from the artful and double one which affects it."

Immediately after this statement Sterne the novelist comes to the fore: "This, by the way, would make no bad anecdote in T. Shandy's Life." Other references to his writing later in the journal provide reassuring intervals of everyday life in the morass of sentiment.

Yorick began his journal in April, and the entries for that month are long and impassioned. Sterne evidently became less interested in his romance in May; the daily comments are briefer and more perfunctory, although there is an occasional burst of emotion: "Laid sleepless all the night, with thinking of the many dangers and sufferings, my dear Girl! that thou art exposed to—" At the end of the month Yorick records his journey from London to his country cottage, where he nurses himself, fancies Eliza beside him in every picturesque spot in his garden, and daydreams of a sequence of events that would allow them to marry.

The entries for early June initiate a new autobiographical episode that is the chief focus of the rest of the journal. Yorick receives a letter from his daughter announcing that she and her mother, who is throughout the book referred to as Mrs. Sterne, will visit him to discuss financial arrangements to enable them to retire to France permanently. The monetary details, discussed at length, are probably fairly accurate, as is the resentment with which Yorick predicts that the ladies will carry off all his household possessions: "In short I shall be pluck'd bare—all but of your Portrait and Snuff Box and your other dear Presents."

It is, perhaps, significant of Sterne's state of mind that the entries for the month after the receipt of Lydia's letter are much longer and more emotional than those which preceded it. There is considerable discussion of all the happy expression of concern about the forthcoming visit, and one is tempted to speculate that Sterne is using the journal less as a literary game and more as a means of putting his mind at ease. In any case, he seems finally to have grown tired of the project toward the end of the summer. The July entries are fond, but increasingly less frequent, and on August 4 Yorick writes that his family is soon to arrive and that their presence will put an end to his diary. A single paragraph, dated November 1, concludes the work. Mrs. Sterne is to retire to France with an annuity of 300 guineas a year, and Yorick is free to think again of Eliza: "But What can I say,— What can I write—But the Yearnings of heart wasted with looking and wishing for thy Return—Return—Return! my dear Eliza! May heaven smooth the Way for thee to send thee safely to us, and joy for Ever."

The *Journal to Eliza* has attracted considerable attention as a biographical document, though it is one of somewhat dubious value, and as a work illustrating eighteenth century sentimental writing. Unfortunately, it falls far below *Tristram Shandy* and *A Sentimental Journey* in literary interest; the unceasing protestation of love, grief, and despair must inevitably become monotonous, as Sterne himself seems to have discovered. Readers will continue to turn to the journal for the insights it gives into the author's peculiar genius, but his reputation rests not upon it but on the two novels.

JOURNAL TO STELLA

Type of work: Letters
Author: Jonathan Swift (1667-1745)
First published: 1766

The *Journal to Stella* consists of the letters of Jonathan Swift to Esther Johnson. Begun in 1710 and ending in 1713, they mark the long period of separation when Swift was deeply involved in the literary and political affairs of London. Esther Johnson was the woman whom Swift first knew as a child, whom he educated, whom he befriended, and with whom he fell in love. The journal is not, however, in any sense of the word a collection of love letters. The relationship of Swift and Stella was an intellectual one, and the journal is about the ideas and experiences which linked them. It is a great document of life in Augustan London, and of the early life of its author.

The letters are first of all a very detailed picture of Swift's fortunes in the capital. He wrote of his friendships with men such as Harley and St. John, who controlled, for a brief time, the government of the nation. Swift was an adviser and friend to these men, and the journal reveals to what extent he was in their company, how deeply he enjoyed their confidence, and how much they relied on his judgment. It indicates too the exact nature of the day-to-day issues about which they consulted. The central matter was the establishment of a Tory system of government, and of this Swift has a good deal to say. Some of the events mentioned in the letters, in fact, come up in disguised form in the later *Gulliver's Travels.*

Swift was one of the champions of the Tory party, and his considerable powers of satire were often called on for its support. The journal reveals that he was animated by belief in the meaning of Tory principles of government—and by the conviction that he had a good deal to gain personally from his association with that party. Swift devotes a good deal of time to explaining the extent to which he

believed he deserved rewards, and he is particular in recording the degree to which his claims were honored. The journal explains to Stella the reasons for the many affairs of state he attended and the conviction, spoken and unspoken, that he ought to have a voice in matters of policy.

The tone of the letters is noticeably ironic. Swift writes of a great many persons and events, but he does not grant them the heavy seriousness and meaningfulness that other men might too easily have given. Consistently throughout these letters is a tone which sets the great and near great in their places. Over and over again Swift describes people and their varied affairs, but he rarely descends to find in either the people or the events anything of particular consequence. One of the refreshing things about the letters is the fact that people with very little other than their aristocratic positions to recommend them are seen through the prismatic insight of a very liberated intelligence. Swift notes that a servant seems to be drunk and that a lord seems to be stupid. In both cases Swift is habitually insulting, but in both he is also objective. As a memoir this work has distinct advantages over history, for it gives the domestic and mundane side of events that, after all, existed in more than the public dimension.

There is an extraordinary amount of what must be admitted is pure gossip in the journal. This material is present, evidently, for several reasons: it must have pleased the reader; it evidently pleased Swift; and it functions to give a thick social context to the judgments Swift frequently passes on mankind. Swift includes an enormous amount of detail on the private lives of the people among whom he lives and on the methods by which he came by his knowledge of them. Much of it was by word of mouth, although some of it came from the ferociously revelatory newspapers and pamphlets of the time. Swift reveals why certain officers were dismissed from the service (they had dressed a skeleton as the Prime Minister and shot pistols at it); where Richard Steele spent some time unwillingly (in jail for debt); what he thought of certain people attached to the court (they were for the most part idiots). In short, the journal allows the writer to express himself with a good deal of honesty and a certain amount of useful prejudice about the life he is engaged in. To the author of *Gulliver's Travels* such an exposure to the life of the ruling classes was bound to be useful.

One of the greatest themes of this collection of letters is the personal life of the author. He writes often of the hopes he has for his future and of his own estimation of himself. Both were high. The note generally sounded is that of distress as Swift writes of the failure of people and institutions to live up to his conception of their function. He writes of the labyrinthine politics and intrigues of those years and, quite honestly, of his part in some of them.

The journal has a strong element of tenderness towards its object, Stella. Swift continually reveals the strength of his respect for her and the quality of the emotions she causes in him. The personal note, even in a narrative of affairs of state, is never dropped. Swift uses what he called the "little language" of affection between himself and Stella, the language he first used to her when she was a child. In this language both she and he have nicknames, and he refers to these continually rather than to more formal address. Swift makes plain the depth of his feeling for Esther Johnson in his many allusions to the state of her health (she was not entirely well, and died early) and to the frequency of his thoughts about her. In strong contrast to the coldness with which he treats the characters of the journal is the emotion with which he addresses the recipient. He makes plain the loneliness of separation in his frequent admissions that he prefers her company to all of the power and politics of the capital.

The journal is a kind of testing-ground of Swift's humor, and one of its most consistent characteristics is the satirical attitude it displays towards human pretentions. His account of Addison and Steele in a letter of December, 1710, describes their responses to a favor and ironically points out the pride and sullenness which prevents them from benefiting from a kindness. Like the characters of *Gulliver's Travels*, Book I, they are the victims of "rancour of party." In other letters of the same month he reflects with detached amusement on the changes in position of the social puppet-show. He describes a steward who has become a millionaire, a shopkeeper who has become a soldier, and other changes that have resulted from the caprices of the human will. Even Swift's own party is not spared from the objectivity of his wit. In one letter he reflects coolly on the many promises made to him and on the likelihood of these promises ever being honored. Here, as in his literary works, he makes a strong distinction between "promise" and "pretence." The constant attitude is that of skepticism.

As a historical document the journal has provided a fund of information on early eighteenth century events. The attempted assasination of Harley in 1711 is one of the most interesting and detailed of Swift's descriptions and is often referred to by historians. Swift begins by noting that he has written a full account of this matter to his superiors in Dublin and that he is trying to establish a true account of an event that would otherwise be distorted by rumor. He gives the particulars of the stabbing of Harley by Antoine de Guiscard, a man apprehended in the act of treason. In a tense, reportorial manner Swift outlines the event, its aftermath, and the probable consequences for national policy—a later essay in the

Examiner (number 33) goes into the matter in greater detail, and reveals that the first entry in the *Journal,* hasty but objective, is the basis for the longer study. Other entries in the *Journal* clarify the uneasy relationship between Harley and St. John, the two leaders of the Tory party. These men were both partners and rivals; the letters to Stella have many remarks on the nature of their private and public differences. Swift outlines the many difficulties of their relationship with Queen Anne, as well as other matters having to do with the Whig minority and the very combustible elements of the Tory party itself. In short, the journal accomplishes two major objectives: it gives some idea of the depth and quality of feeling that the famous satirist had for the woman he admired, and it establishes a social context for some of the most important political events of its writer's time.